Theorizing Feminism

Theorizing
Feminism

Parallel Trends in the Humanities and Social Sciences

SECOND EDITION

edited by

Anne C. Herrmann
University of Michigan

Abigail J. Stewart
University of Michigan

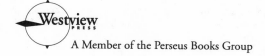
Westview PRESS

A Member of the Perseus Books Group

Copyright © 2001 by Westview Press, A Member of the Perseus Books Group

Published in 2001 in the United States of America by Westview Press, 5500 Central Avenue, Boulder, Colorado 80301-2877, and in the United Kingdom by Westview Press, 12 Hid's Copse Road, Cumnor Hill, Oxford OX2 9JJ

Visit us on the World Wide Web at www.westviewpress.com

Library of Congress Cataloging-in-Publication Data

Theorizing feminism : parallel trends in the humanities and social sciences / edited by Anne C. Herrmann and Abigail J. Stewart.—2nd ed.
  p.   cm.
Includes bibliographical references.
ISBN 0-8133-6788-3
1. Feminist theory.   I. Herrmann, Anne.   II. Stewart, Abigail J.
HQ1190 .T473   2000
305.42'01—dc21   00-043572

The paper used in this publication meets the requirements of the American National Standard for Permanence of Paper for Printed Library Materials Z39.48-1984.

10   9   8   7   6   5   4   3   2   1

Contents

Part Two: Sex, Sexuality, and Gender 131

From Sex to Sexuality

Constructing Gender

Conceptualizing Difference

Part Three: Gender, Race, and Class 271

Race and Gender

Postcolonialism

Credits

Chapter 1   Rosalind Delmar, "What Is Feminism?" reprinted from J. Mitchell and A. Oakley, eds., *What Is Feminism?* (pp. 8–33). New York: Pantheon, 1986.

Chapter 2   "The Combahee River Collective Statement," reprinted from Barbara Smith, ed., *Home Girls: A Black Feminist Anthology* (pp. 272–282). Copyright© 1983 by Rutgers University Press. Used with permission of the author and Kitchen Table: Women of Color Press, P.O. Box 908, Latham, NY 12110.

Chapter 3   Cherríe Moraga, "From a Long Line of Vendidas: Chicanas and Feminism," excerpts reprinted by permission from *Loving in the War Years* (pp. 90–144). © 1986, South End Press, Boston.

Chapter 4   Susan Bickford, "Anti-Anti-Identity Politics: Feminism, Democracy, and the Complexities of Citizenship," from *Hypatia,* vol. 12, no. 4 (Fall 1997): 111–131. Copyright© by Indiana University Press.

Chapter 5   Rachel T. Hare-Mustin and Jeanne Marecek, "Gender and the Meaning of Difference: Postmodernism and Psychology," reprinted from Rachel T. Hare-Mustin and Jeanne Marecek, eds., *Making a Difference: Psychology and the Construction of Gender* (pp. 22–64). New Haven CT: Yale University Press. Copyright© 1990 by Yale University Press.

Chapter 6   Leslie W. Rabine, "Romance in the Age of Electronics: Harlequin Enterprises," originally published in *Feminist Studies,* vol. 11, no. 1 (Spring 1985): 39–60, reprinted by permission of the publisher, Feminist Studies, Inc.

Chapter 7   Suzanne J. Kessler, "The Medical Construction of Gender: Case Management of Intersexed Infants," reprinted from *Signs* 16, no. 1 (1990): 3–26, by permission of The University of Chicago Press and the author. Copyright© 1990 by The University of Chicago Press.

Chapter 8   Jennifer Robertson, "The Politics of Androgyny in Japan: Sexuality and Subversion in the Theater and Beyond," from *American Ethnologist,* vol. 19, no. 3 (August 1992): 419–442, reproduced by permission of the American Anthropological Association. Not for further reproduction.

Chapter 9   Sara Ruddick, "Notes Toward a Feminist Peace Politics," reprinted from Miriam Cooke and Angela Woollacott, eds., *Gendering War Talk* (pp. 109–127). Princeton: Princeton University Press. Copyright© 1993 by Princeton University Press.

Chapter 10   Lisa Duggan, "Making It Perfectly Queer," from *Socialist Review* 92 (January–March 1992), published by Duke University Press. Reprinted by permission of the editor.

Chapter 11   Catharine A. MacKinnon, "Sex Equality: On Difference and Dominance," reprinted by permission from Catharine A. MacKinnon, *Toward a Feminist Theory of the State* (pp. 215–234). Cambridge: Harvard University Press. Copyright© 1989 by Catharine A. MacKinnon.

Chapter 12   Joan W. Scott, "Deconstructing Equality-Versus-Difference: or, The Uses of Poststructuralist Theory for Feminism," originally published in *Feminist Studies,* vol. 14, no. 1 (Spring 1988): 33–50, reprinted by permission of the publisher, Feminist Studies, Inc., c/o Women's Studies Program, University of Maryland, College Park, MD 20742.

Chapter 13   Patricia J. Williams, "On Being the Object of Property," reprinted from *Signs,* vol. 14, no. 1 (1988): 5–24, by permission of The University of Chicago Press and the author. Copyright© 1988 by The University of Chicago Press.

Chapter 14   Amy Kaminsky, "Gender, Race, *Raza,*" originally published in *Feminist Studies,* vol. 20, no. 1 (Spring 1994): 7–31, reprinted by permission of the publisher, Feminist Studies, Inc.

Chapter 15   Marnia Lazreg, "Feminism and Difference: The Perils of Writing as a Woman on Women in Algeria," originally published in *Feminist Studies,* vol. 14, no. 1 (Spring 1988): 81–107, reprinted by permission of the publisher, Feminist Studies, Inc.

Chapter 16   Rey Chow, "Violence in the Other Country: China as Crisis, Spectacle, and Woman," reprinted from Chandra Mohanty, Ann Russo, and Lourdes Torres, eds., *Third World Women and the Politics of Feminism* (pp. 81–100). © 1991, Indiana University Press, Bloomington.

Chapter 17   Leslie Salzinger, "From High Heels to Swathed Bodies: Gendered Meanings Under Production in Mexico's Export-Processing Industry," originally published in *Feminist Studies,* vol. 23, no. 3 (Fall 1997): 33–50, reprinted by permission of the publisher, Feminist Studies, Inc.

Chapter 18   Arlene Elowe MacLeod, "Hegemonic Relations and Gender Resistance: The New Veiling as Accommodating Protest in Cairo," reprinted from *Signs: Journal of Women in Culture and Society,* vol. 17, no. 3 (Spring 1992): 533–557, by permission of The University of Chicago Press and the author. Copyright© 1992 by The University of Chicago Press.

Chapter 19   Rosalind Pollack Petchesky, "Fetal Images: The Power of Visual Culture in the Politics of Reproduction," reprinted from *Feminist Studies,* vol. 13, no. 2 (1987): 263–292, by permission of the author.

Chapter 20   Holloway Sparks, "Dissident Citizenship: Democratic Theory, Political Courage, and Activist Women," reprinted from *Hypatia,* vol. 12, no. 4 (Fall 1997): 74–110. Copyright© by Indiana University Press.

Chapter 21   Judith Halberstam, "Automating Gender: Postmodern Feminism in the Age of the Intelligent Machine," originally published in *Feminist Studies,* vol. 17, no. 3 (Fall 1991): 439–460, reprinted by permission of the publisher, Feminist Studies, Inc.

Chapter 22   Christine Sylvester, "African and Western Feminisms: World-Traveling the Tendencies and Possibilities," reprinted from *Signs: Journal of Women in Culture and Society,* vol. 20, no. 4 (1995): 941–969, by permission of The University of Chicago Press and the author. Copyright© 1995 by The University of Chicago Press.

Reading Feminist Theories
Collaborating Across Disciplines

ANNE C. HERRMANN

ABIGAIL J. STEWART

This is a revised edition of a reader that originally offered a historical overview of twenty years of feminist scholarship from a contemporary perspective. We selected topics because of their centrality to feminist theory in both the humanities and social sciences, highlighting parallels in order to facilitate conversations across disciplines. Although we continue to emphasize issues in terms of their relevance to current controversies and attention to differences among women, we also acknowledge certain changes. Two seem the most salient: (1) Feminist theory is now less directed toward the traditional disciplines from which it emerged, less focused on what we once called the critique of "masculine bias," and (2) feminist theorists increasingly engage each other in debates about issues relevant to feminist scholarship. The first change suggests that feminist theory has shifted from being primarily a critical practice to becoming more of a constructive one, creating new conceptual tools in dialogue with the disciplines that themselves have changed in response to feminist critiques. The second change leads to the conclusion that feminist theory now also exists as a semiautonomous field, wherein feminist theorists less rooted in disciplinary paradigms have conversations with each other.

We once again begin our story with a model of mutual influence. After the first section, we pair essays that offer two different perspectives on a single theoretical issue. The two perspectives may no longer be as clearly situated within the humanities or the social sciences, but we nevertheless remain committed to the construction of what we believe holds potential for generative dialogue. We imagine these dialogues taking the form of conversations within women's studies, across the disciplines, and centered on theoretical points of contact.

This volume no longer is grounded in a particular pedagogical context (a summer seminar on feminist theory we team-taught to faculty members from the College of Literature, Science, and the Arts at the University of Michigan and then expanded into an interdisciplinary graduate course in feminist theory we team-taught in the Women's Studies Program), but we rely on the built-in unpredictability characteristic of pedagogy. Like us, other teachers used the first edition in the classroom and found it useful. We see our renewed collaboration on this second edition as the product of an "imagined pedagogy" that takes the form of a continuing private conversation between us, and thus hopefully among others who come together with different assumptions, different terminology, and different ideas about how knowledge is constructed. In other words, we remain committed not so much to sharing with others our experiences but to the expectation that something productive will happen for others because these essays appear in planned conjunction, not in isolation. They are not a collection of the most famous essays in feminist theory, nor are all essays by the most noted feminist theorists. Rather, we had varied reasons for our essay choices: A particular author's essay was the only one on the topic to reach a larger public; it served a specific purpose through its disciplinary representation; it was accessible to nonspecialists; or it provided a cross-disciplinary parallel.

We encourage readers of this volume to be aware of the challenges and pleasures of cross-disciplinary reading and thinking. The book is intended for both advanced undergraduate and graduate courses in feminist theory; we hope that instructors trained in a single discipline will use it to teach such courses from an interdisciplinary perspective. Advanced undergraduate students, advanced graduate students, and faculty in midcareer may find interdisciplinary reading refreshing and provocative; new graduate students and untenured faculty not already familiar with such an enterprise may find it more troubling. Because we have encountered this reaction, we suggest that careful consideration be given to the implications of the timing of interdisciplinary courses in the graduate curriculum and the timing of faculty members' involvement in teaching such courses.

We hope this reader will also continue to serve as a useful tool for scholars who seek to familiarize themselves with a body of interdisciplinary knowledge that seems either too specialized or too daunting in scope. For this particular audience, we do not assume acquaintance with the past twenty years of academic feminist debate, but rather we recapitulate initial controversies, in some cases in their original historical context, in most cases in their most updated form.

The introductions we have written to the four major sections are meant to demonstrate by example rather than exhaust through incorporation the ways in which one might conduct the kind of cross-disciplinary thinking and discussion we hope to facilitate. The introductions are not meant to provide a lexicon of unfamiliar terms, philosophical schools, or disciplinary histories. Instead they offer a conceptual framework. In that sense we have tried to provoke and inspire rather than expound and edify, and thus we assume some prior familiarity with theoretical inquiry as well as feminist politics.

The book is a product of our collaboration as professors of English and psychology. Our association has continued to be enormously enriching and rewarding, leading us in different directions, even as our respective enterprises rely on the continuation of cross-disciplinary dialogue: At our institution, the University of Michigan, Abby is the first director of the Institute for Research on Women and Gender, and Anne is the first senior faculty member to teach the introductory Women's Studies course. We both continue to participate in the expanding joint Ph.D. programs in Women's Studies and English, Women's Studies and Psychology, and most recently, Women's Studies and History.

The anthology begins with Part One, "Inventing Gender," which introduces the reader to feminism and feminist theory through essays that fall outside of disciplinary paradigms or borrow theoretical frameworks from other disciplines. The chapters in "Defining Feminism and Feminist Theory" attempt to achieve an inclusive understanding of the term "feminism" by distinguishing it from "women's movement" and by juxtaposing points of view from various positions defined by race, class, and sexuality as part of the project of "identity politics." The section "Mutual Influence: Humanities and Social Science" offers examples of essays that emerge from a particular discipline but borrow paradigms from another discipline in order to address disciplinary practices that have been marginalized.

Part Two, "Sex, Sexuality, and Gender," moves from the biological subject as sexed to the social construction of gender, and from gender as woman's biological difference from man to gender difference as the unequal power relations between women and men. "From Sex to Sexuality" considers the question of sexed bodies and socially constructed genders by examining the impact of surgical technologies on intersexed infants in the contemporary United States, and of theatrical practices that involve cross-dressing in female same-sex relationships in twentieth-century Japan. "Constructing Gender" gives meaning to woman's biological difference from man by continuing to gender war as masculine and peace as feminine, while questioning the revalorization of the feminine in feminist peace politics. In contrast, "queer" political practices seek to transcend gender differences by interrogating the stability of gay and lesbian identities. Finally, "Conceptualizing Difference" examines how gender constructed as difference masks male dominance inasmuch as the opposite of (mere) difference is not sameness but inequality.

Part Three, "Gender, Race, and Class," focuses on how these categories, once considered parallel or "hierarchized" forms of oppression, are now grounded in place and time. The section "Race and Gender" examines the specific constructions of race-ethnicity and gender that emerge for particular groups as a function of their history and the history of their relationships with other groups. "Postcolonialism" considers the construction of the "Third World" woman by Western scholars in general, and feminist scholars in particular, as not yet modern and therefore objectifiable. Finally, "Work, Class, and Gender" examines specific locales to show how gender is constructed in workplaces, and how at the same time work shapes gender.

Part Four, "Questioning Feminisms," readdresses gender in relationship to the theoretical discourses of citizenship, postcolonialism, and postmodernism. "Women, Citizenship, and Activism" shows how crucially the conversation about citizenship and politics is changed when women are taken seriously as actors in the public sphere. "Feminism/ Postfeminism" demonstrates the extent to which feminist theory has outgrown the divisions between the humanities and the social sciences. Current theoretical issues—the challenge "intelligent machines" pose to our understanding of gender or "the human," or the psychological and political difference between globalization and "world-traveling"—can no longer be contained within disciplinary boundaries.

Anne C. Herrmann
Abigail J. Stewart

PART ONE
Inventing Gender

We begin our discussion of feminist theory by offering four approaches to some of feminism's central questions: What does it mean to be a woman, how is that meaning created, and what difference do these meanings make to feminist analysis? Rosalind Delmar (Chapter 1) differentiates between "woman" and "feminist" by situating her discussion historically, examining the narrative we have inherited from the nineteenth-century women's movement. The Combahee River Collective (Chapter 2) relies on a notion of "identity politics" to issue a statement in the form of a political manifesto about the struggle of the group's members to end their oppression as black feminists. Cherríe Moraga (Chapter 3) exposes the system of interlocking oppressions she faces as a Chicana lesbian in an autobiographical essay that attempts to understand the mother-daughter relationship within the context of Mexican history. Finally, Susan Bickford addresses recent feminist critiques of identity politics and rethinks the notion of a "politicized identity" by examining the subject of feminism as "suffering self" within the language of citizenship and democratic political action. In each case there is an emphasis not just on "feminist" as political subject but also on how the meaning of that subject is produced.

Delmar begins by insisting on the distinction between feminism and the women's movement, a history of ideas and the history of a social movement. Women organizing based on their shared identity as biological women is not the same as making a political choice to advocate feminism based on a shared set of ideas about the meaning of womanhood. Women may share a description of women's oppression and the ideal of emancipation, but they do not necessarily agree on how to analyze that oppression or how to resist it. Whereas the nineteenth-century women's movement sought to reconceive women as a social group rather than as a sex, culminating in female suffrage, a central concern of the women's movement since the 1970s has been to liberate woman as autonomous female subject. The historical shift from human rights to women's rights has meant an increased focus on the female body and its incumbent sexual needs, such as reproductive rights, freedom from sexual harassment and assault, and surrogate motherhood. At the same time, a consideration of female subjectivity has come to include differences among women based on race, class, ethnicity, sexuality, physical disability, religion, and so on. On the one hand, there is confusion between feminism and the women's movement as a diffuse set of activities based on a consensus about the category "woman." On the other hand, feminism is a form of consciousness about women's oppression that eventually forces the issue of multiple identifications.

The emergence in the 1970s of "woman" as a unified category producing a group identity characterized by "sisterhood" relied on an understanding of politics as grounded in identity rather than in conscious choice or political coalition. Identity politics begins with an understanding of personal experience to produce a political consciousness; political action involves organizing with like identities to end one's own oppression. The critique in the 1980s from women of color of a monolithic construction of "woman" as white, middle class, and straight produced efforts to create new understandings of "woman" by articulating, for instance, the position of the "black feminist" or the "Chicana lesbian feminist." At the same time, women of color described their position as providing no access to race or gender privilege. Thus, no single identity can define the category "woman," nor can the abolition of a single system of oppression liberate all women. This formulation of "simultaneous oppressions" is one of the most lasting contributions of the Combahee River Collective's Statement.

Moraga reveals her indebtedness to the collective, but she nevertheless singles out compulsory heterosexuality as the system of oppression most responsible for maintaining gender inequality within racial and ethnic groups. Through a recuperation of the figure of Malinche, who betrayed the Aztecs to the Spanish colonizers, Moraga portrays herself as a biracial lesbian potentially disloyal to both family and nation. As the daughter of an Anglo father and a Chicana mother, Moraga questions the one category the Combahee River Collective leaves unquestioned—namely race, by "passing" as white. As a lesbian, she puts at issue the unquestioned solidarity women have with men of their own race by invoking the desire she feels for other women, including white women. Her autobiographical discourse allows for an understanding of identity not only in terms of simultaneous oppressions but also in terms of the divisions within oppressed groups. These internal divisions must be contained in order to maintain the unity of the collective, divisions that in the case of both the Combahee River Collective and Moraga can be resolved only through writing in the first person. The role of same-sex desire in a single-sex setting such as the women's movement is most often raised in relationship to "lesbian separatism." "Separatism" invokes as specter the return of a unified notion of woman. As a fear that is rarely if ever based in reality, it could be said to exist as part of feminism's "unconscious."

The notion of identity politics has recently come under attack by feminist theorists who see it as producing a "suffering self" invested in its own subjection and in speaking about this subjection publicly. These suffering selves not only resist forms of collectivity but actually reinforce normalizing forms of power by demanding state protection. Bickford intervenes in this discussion by suggesting that "who I am" and "what I want for us" are not mutually exclusive questions. Without requiring a recommitment to a common political purpose, political identities form coalitions with other identities by means of speaking and listening. She insists on the importance of recognizing "suffering" as one of the languages of citizenship. This language requires in turn "political listening," practitioners of which could hear the claim of victimhood not as an expression of individual suffering but as a response to an exercise of unjust power. The question then becomes what conception of citizenship is being invoked.

The next two essays emerge from the disciplines of psychology and literary criticism even as they borrow from each other's theoretical paradigms and use examples not central to their disciplinary discourses—therapeutic practices and Harlequin novels, respectively. Rachel T. Hare-Mustin and Jeanne Marecek (Chapter 5) use literary theory in the form of Derridean deconstruction to consider the meanings marginalized by psychotherapy; Leslie W. Rabine (Chapter 6) borrows from Nancy Chodorow's theory of psychological development to understand the romantic heroine. In both cases an epistemological framework from one discipline enables a radical rethinking of notions of sexual difference in the other discipline by focusing on how gender is theorized rather than on what gender means within a particular disciplinary context. For the psychologist, the deconstruction of a notion of "family harmony" enables psychological facts to be read as representations, produced by clients through reconstructed memories told by means of narrative conventions interpreted by the therapist. The literary critic places the formulaic narratives of romance fictions within the context of social facts about the entrance of women into the workplace and the profit margins of Harlequin Romances as publishing conglomerate. By relying on a feminine character structure distinguished from a masculine one by its investment in connectedness, Harlequins provide both a fantasy escape from and an eroticized compliance to low-paid clerical work. In the first case, deconstruction mediates between two ways of conceptualizing sexual difference in psychological research—alpha bias (exaggerating sexual difference) and beta bias (ignoring sexual differences)—by focusing on how relations to language and power construct our understanding of men and women. In the second case, psychological theory enables an understanding of how the marketable formula of Harlequins creates a heroine who seeks to have her feminine self recognized by the hero and to make a home for that self in the work world, even as it neutralizes these aspirations by providing only fictional solutions.

What difference does it make that a paradigm has been borrowed from another discipline? In each case it reveals the limitations of a feminist practice that already knows what gender means, in contrast to understanding how gender is produced. In both of these essays, Chodorow's theory of a feminine self as embedded in connectedness is put into question by refocusing on its historical origins in Western industrial capitalism. On the one hand, this reminds psychologists of the dangers of universalizing a particular structure of the feminine self; on the other hand, it enables literary critics to understand the wide appeal of romance novels as both individually consoling and socially productive. The fact that Hare-Mustin and Marecek accept an assumption of postmodernism and say that truth is what we agree on, and that Rabine recognizes forms of intense identification with static literary structures, suggests that the mutual influence of the humanities and social sciences is not only possible but also critical for feminist theorizing.

1   What Is Feminism?

ROSALIND DELMAR

There are many, feminist and non-feminist alike, for whom the question 'what *is* feminism?' has little meaning. The content of terms like 'feminism' and 'feminist' seems self-evident, something that can be taken for granted. By now, it seems to me, the assumption that the meaning of feminism is 'obvious' needs to be challenged. It has become an obstacle to understanding feminism, in its diversity and in its differences, and in its specificity as well.[1]

It is certainly possible to construct a base-line definition of feminism and the feminist which can be shared by feminists and non-feminists. Many would agree that at the very least a feminist is someone who holds that women suffer discrimination because of their sex, that they have specific needs which remain negated and unsatisfied, and that the satisfaction of these needs would require a radical change (some would say a revolution even) in the social, economic and political order. But beyond that, things immediately become more complicated.

For example, popular approaches to feminism often contain references to a style of dress, to looks, to ways of behaving to men and women, to what used to be called 'manners'. It is, in practice, impossible to discuss feminism without discussing the image of feminism and the feminists. Feminists play and have played with a range of choices in the process of self-presentation, registering a relation both to the body and to the social meaning of womanhood. Various, sometimes competing, images of the feminist are thus produced, and these acquire their own social meanings. This is important to stress now because in contemporary feminism the construction of new images is a conscious process. There is a strand whose central concern is to investigate culture (in its widest sense) and to experiment with the means of representation. But feminism's wish that women behave differently is also an historic element: Mary Wollstonecraft at the end of the eighteenth century called for 'a revolution in female manners'.

The diversity of representations of the feminist has undoubtedly grown since then. How difficult it would be to choose between them, to find the 'true' feminist image, the 'proper way' to be a feminist. And yet many books on feminism are written, and feminism is often spoken about, as if there were a 'true' and authentic feminism, unified and consistent over time and in any one place, even if fragmented in its origins and at specific historical moments.

Most people have heard a sentence which begins: 'As a feminist I think. . . .' It is a sentence which speaks of a wish that an agreed way of being a feminist should exist, but is not the product of any genuine agreement among feminists about what they think or how they should live their lives. In the women's movement, there is a strong desire to pin feminism down (whether as support for a series of agreed demands or as preoccupation with central concerns like sexual division or male domination) but this impulse has invariably encountered obstacles. General agreement about the situation in which women find themselves has not been accompanied by any shared understanding of why this state of affairs should exist or what could be done about it. Indeed, the history of the women's movement in the 1970s, a time of apparent unity, was marked by bitter, at times virulent, internal disputes over what it was possible or permissible for a feminist to do, say, think, or feel.

The fragmentation of contemporary feminism bears ample witness to the impossibility of constructing modern feminism as a simple unity in the present or of arriving at a shared feminist definition of feminism. Such differing explanations, such a variety of emphases in practical campaigns, such widely varying interpretations of their results have emerged, that it now makes more sense to speak of a plurality of feminisms than of one.

Recently the different meanings of feminism for different feminists have manifested themselves as a sort of sclerosis of the movement, segments of which have become separated from and hardened against each other. Instead of internal dialogue there is a naming of the parts: there are radical feminists, socialist feminists, marxist feminists, lesbian separatists, women of colour, and so on, each group with its own carefully preserved sense of identity. Each for itself is the only worthwhile feminism; others are ignored except to be criticized.

How much does this matter? Is it not the case that even extreme differences in politics can often mask underlying agreement? Could it not still be that what unites feminists is greater than what divides? Might not current fragmentation be merely an episode in an overriding history of unity?

At times it is rather attractive to think so and to let the matter rest at that. All cats look grey in the dark, and the exclusivism of feminist groups can be reminiscent of what Freud called 'the narcissism of minor differences'.[2] Even so, at a theoretical level, agreements are uncovered only by the exploration of differences—they cannot be assumed. And there is no overwhelming reason to assume an underlying feminist unity. Indeed, one unlooked-for effect of an assumed coherence of feminism can be its marginalization, as discourse or as practice.[3] In many ways it makes more sense to invert the question 'Why is there so much division between feminists?' and ask instead 'Does feminism have any necessary unity, politically, socially, or culturally?'

What is the background to current fragmentation? At the start of the contemporary women's movement in Britain it was often assumed that there was a potentially unificatory point of view on women's issues which would be able to accommodate divergencies and not be submerged by them. From the start the modern women's movement pitched its appeal at a very high level of generality, to all women, and thought of its aims and objectives in very general terms.

The unity of the movement was assumed to derive from a potential identity between women. This concept of identity rested on the idea that women share the same experiences: an external situation in which they find themselves—economic oppression, commercial exploitation, legal discrimination are examples; and an internal response—the feeling of inadequacy, a sense of narrow horizons. A shared response to shared experience was put forward as the basis for a communality of feeling between women, a shared psychology even. Women's politics and women's organizing were then seen as an expression of this community of feeling and experience.[4]

So unproblematically was potential identity between women assumed that the plural form 'we' was adopted, and it is still much used: 'we', women, can speak on behalf of all of us 'women'.[5] (In some of the first women's groups of the late sixties and early seventies every effort was made to encourage women to use this form and speak in terms of 'we' instead of what was heard as the more divisive grammar of 'you' and 'I'. It should be noted, though, that this plural form lends itself to a differently divisive grammar, that of 'us' and 'them'.)

In fact, common ground within women's politics was based on an agreed description rather than an analysis, and the absence of analysis probably enabled such a stress to be laid on what women in general could share. No one predicted (or could predict) that uncontainable divisions would arise between and within women's groups.[6] Early optimism went together with a huge effort to create a solidarity between women (one of the meanings of 'sisterhood') which, it was thought, would arise out of shared perceptions. But in spite of the success of women's liberation in bringing to the fore and reinforcing feelings of sympathy and identity between women, political unity (another of the meanings of 'sisterhood') cannot be said to have been achieved. Analytic differences and the political differences which spring from them have regularly been causes of division in the women's movement.[7] Unity based on identity has turned out to be a very fragile thing. What has been most difficult for the women's movement to cope with has been the plethora of differences between women which have emerged in the context of feminism.

Over the past twenty years a paradox has developed at the heart of the modern women's movement: on the one hand there is the generality of its categorical appeal to all women, as potential participants in a movement; on the other hand there is the exclusivism of its current internal practice, with its emphasis on difference and division. Recognition of and commitment to heterogeneity appear to have been lost, and with those a source of fruitful tension. A further aspect of the same paradox is that the different forms of women's politics, fragmented as they are, have been increasingly called by the same name: *feminism.* Even the term that signifies its rejection—'post-feminism'—incorporates it.

Women's organizing was not, in general, in the late sixties and early seventies, called feminism. Feminism was a position adopted by or ascribed to particular groups. These were the groups which called themselves 'radical feminist' and those groups and individuals who represented the earlier emancipatory struggle. Both often came under fierce attack. The equation between women organizing and feminism has been implicitly adopted since then, and its usage as a blanket term to cover all women's activities urgently needs to be questioned.

Are all actions and campaigns prompted or led by women, feminist? The encampment at Greenham Common is a powerful example of a community of women in its nucleus, support groups, and the character of its demonstrations. The symbolism deployed at Greenham calls up images of the female and the feminine: the spider's web of the support network, the nurturing maternity which leaves its marks of family photographs and knitted bootees on the boundary fence in a battle for space with the symbols of male defence and attack: barbed wire, the nuclear missile. It is its projection of women as those who care which allows the Greenham camp to be represented as useful not just to women, and through them to the species, but to the species first and foremost. Yet is this entirely feminist? Support for Greenham does not rely in the main on feminist groups (although it does rely on women). Greenham actions have been *polyvalent*, capable of attracting multiple meanings and mobilizing various ideological stances in their support: this is part of its strength. Without a women's movement a women's peace camp would probably not have had so much resonance; this is part of the success of the women's movement, but does not make Greenham necessarily feminist.

The politics of Greenham has been keenly debated among feminists. For some, the mobilization of femininity and nurturance is expressive of feminism, for others it represents a deference to that social construction of woman as maternal principle which through their feminism they attempt to challenge.[8] Not only does Greenham represent different things to different feminists, summoning up different meanings of feminism, it is by no means certain that those who participate in Greenham politics, or support the camp, would describe themselves as feminist.

Can an action be 'feminist' even if those who perform it are not? Within contemporary feminism much emphasis has been laid on feminism as *consciousness*. One of the most distinctive practices of modern feminism has been the 'consciousness-raising group'. If feminism is the result of reflection and conscious choice, how does one place those individuals and women's groups who would, for a variety of reasons, reject the description 'feminist' if it were applied to them? Does it make sense to ascribe to them a feminism of which they are unaware? What, in the framework provided by 'feminist consciousness', is then the status of this 'unconscious' feminism?

The various ways in which such questions can be answered connect back to the central question 'what is feminism?' If feminism is a concern with issues affecting women, a concern to advance women's interests, so that therefore anyone who shares this concern is a feminist, whether they acknowledge it or not, then the range of feminism is general and its meaning is equally diffuse. Feminism becomes defined by its object of concern—women—in much the same way as socialism has sometimes been defined by an object—the poor or the working class. Social reformers can then be classified as feminists because of the consequences of their activities, and not because they share any particular social analysis or critical spirit. This way of looking at feminism, as diffuse activity, makes feminism understandably hard to pin down. Feminists, being involved in so many activities, from so many different perspectives, would almost inevitably find it hard to unite, except in specific campaigns.

On the other hand there are those who claim that feminism does have a complex of ideas about women, specific to or emanating from feminists. This means that it should be possible to separate out feminism and feminists from the multiplicity of those concerned with women's issues. It is by no means absurd to suggest that you don't have to be a feminist to support women's rights to equal treatment, and that not all those supportive of women's demands are feminists. In this light feminism can claim its own history, its own practices, its own ideas, but feminists can make no claim to an exclusive interest in or copyright over problems affecting women. Feminism can thus be established as a field (and this even if scepticism is still needed in the face of claims or demands for a unified feminism), but cannot claim women as its domain.

These considerations both have political implications in the present and also underlie the way feminism's past is understood. If a history of feminism, separable from although connected with the history of changes in women's position, is to be constructed, a precondition of such a history is that feminism must be able to be specified.

In the writing of feminist history it is the broad view which predominates: feminism is usually defined as an active desire to change women's position in society.[9] Linked to this is the view that feminism is *par excellence* a social movement for change in the position of women. Its privileged form is taken to be the political movement, the self-organization of a women's politics. So unquestioningly are feminism and a women's movement assumed to be co-terminous that histories of feminism are often written as histories of the women's movement, and times of apparent quiescence of the movement are taken as symptomatic of a quiescence of feminism. This identity between feminism and a women's movement is, moreover, part of the self-image of contemporary feminism. The idea that the new movement of the 1960s was a 'second wave,' a continuation of a struggle started just over a century before and interrupted for forty years (after the hiatus of the vote), pervaded the early years of the contemporary women's movement and still informs many of its debates.[10] The way feminism's past is understood and interpreted thus informs and is informed by the ways in which feminism is understood and interpreted in the present.

The problems involved in writing feminist history throw into relief some of the problems involved in specifying feminism more closely in the present. Feminist historiography highlights different versions of feminism, since it often has overt political motivations which then produce different versions of the same history. Present approaches to feminist history can themselves be historicized by comparison with the ways in which past feminists have read their own history. Even the frustrating assumption of identity between feminism and the women's movement has its advantages: it focuses attention on the area where feminism is most intimately intertwined with a generality of concern with women's issues: women's politics. The problems of separation present themselves acutely here, and this makes it a productive point of entry.

Some of the major conventions of the writing of feminist history, which are only in recent years being questioned and overturned, can be found in the classic history of the nineteenth-century movement: Ray Strachey's *The Cause*.[11] It is an important book in several ways. Not only is it still the best introduction to the subject, but it is the product of the mainstream feminism of the turn of the century. Its author was an active feminist, secretary to Mrs Fawcett and involved in the NUWSS. Her main concern was to chart the period between 1860 and 1920 during which the term feminism took on its dictionary definition, 'advocacy of the claims of women'.[12] It is also the product of a feminism which did not (unlike much contemporary feminism) define itself as 'woman-made' (it would be difficult to write a history of nineteenth-century feminism which did not include at least J. S. Mill and Richard Pankhurst). A detailed look at this work will help clarify how some of the questions raised so far relate to the writing of feminist history.

History Conventions

When Ray Strachey wrote her history the close connection between feminism and the social movement for change in women's position was redolent with meaning: the term 'feminism' was itself coined in the course of the development of the social movement. All the same, within *The Cause* distinctions are made between feminism and the social movement for change in women's position.

She starts her history by proposing two forerunners of the nineteenth-century movement. One is Mary Wollstonecraft, feminist theorist and author of *A Vindication of the Rights of Woman*. The other is Hannah More, Evangelical philanthropist and educationalist. Of the first, Ray Strachey writes that she set out in her great book 'the whole extent of the feminist ideal . . . the whole claim of equal human rights'.[13] Of the other she remarks that 'It may seem strange to maintain that Miss Hannah More and Mrs. Trimmer and the other good ladies who started the Sunday-school and cottage-visiting fashions were the founders of a movement which would have shocked them profoundly; but it is clearly true.'[14]

If the nineteenth-century women's movement is looked at as a movement for increased participation by women in social and political life or as a movement which negotiated the relative and shared positions men and women were to occupy in the social, political, and economic order, it makes sense to invoke each woman as a symbolic figure. Hannah More had a part to play in the general redefinition of women's sphere; Mary Wollstonecraft articulated women's claims, needs and desires at a deeper level. By harnessing the two a neat schema can be constructed. There is theory (Mary Wollstonecraft) and practice (Hannah More), consciousness of the rights of women and lack of consciousness, Mary and Martha coinciding. One is radical, the other conservative; they responded differently to the same social phenomena, yet both had contributions to make. (This schema only works, however, because it ignores Hannah More's intellectual work.)

On the other hand, to combine the two, as Ray Strachey points out, seems 'strange' because if the purpose was to construct a history of feminism, even in Mrs Fawcett's definition of it as 'a movement for the redressal of women's grievances,' it would make little sense to include Hannah More and Mary Wollstonecraft as equal partners. Hannah More was not just not a feminist, she was a rabid anti-feminist: it was she who described Mary Wollstonecraft (whose book she had not read) as 'a hyena in petticoats'. Her practice was part of overall change, but allowed women the public sphere only when domestic duties had been fulfilled. Such a position was far removed from Mary Wollstonecraft's vision, which questioned the value of women's confinement to the domestic sphere and saw increased public participation by women, up to and including political citizenship, as a good in itself.

How does Ray Strachey make her distinctions between feminism and the women's movement? Her discussion of the rise of the women's movement stresses a coincidence of factors which helped bring it into being. These include: women's shared exclusion from political, social and economic life, with a rebellion against this; middle-class women's sense of uselessness; and the formulation of common objectives, culminating in the demand for political citizenship through the vote.

But whilst the sense of uselessness or awareness of grievance might be sufficient to bring someone into the ambit of women's politics or to a lasting achievement which could benefit women in general, this in itself, in Ray Strachey's eyes, did not make someone a feminist. She does not include, for example, Caroline Norton as a feminist, nor Florence Nightingale, even though she includes Florence Nightingale's *Cassandra* as prototypical of feeling amongst middle-class women. She writes of her that 'though she was a feminist of sorts . . . Florence Nightingale had only an incomplete and easily exhausted sympathy with the organised women's movement. In her absorption in her own work she judged the men and women she lived among almost wholly by their usefulness or their uselessness to it.'[15] The inference is clear: Florence Nightingale put her own work first, women's rights were a side issue: a feminist would have put women's rights in the centre of her work. As far as Caroline Norton is concerned, Ray Strachey takes her at her own word and accepts her disavowal of feminism. This definition of a feminist as someone whose *central* concern and preoccupation lies with the position of women and their struggle for emancipation is constant throughout *The Cause;* so is feminism as conscious political choice. Together they allow a relatively objective differentiation between feminists and non-feminists. Feminists are not represented as more 'moral' than non-feminists.[16]

To define a feminist in this way still implies an intimate connection between feminism and the women's movement. The feminists are the leaders, organizers, publicists, lobbyists, of the women's movement; they come into their own and into existence on a relatively large scale in the course of development of a women's movement. The social movement, particularly in its political dimension, provides the context for feminism; feminists are its animating spirits.

This definition is valuable as one dimension of an eventually more complex definition, but cannot stand on its own. It has very little to tell, for example, of the intellectual and cultural life of feminism, of the ideas which might unite or divide feminists in their commitment to a movement or to its different aspects. In Ray Strachey's definition feminists share the same aims and the same general ideas, the same broad commitment to the great cause of female emancipation, and a capacity to put this cause in the centre of their lives. The content of their ideas merits only the briefest of sketches.

Histories of feminism which treat feminism as social movement tend to concentrate on chronicling the vicissitudes of that movement and subordinate any exploration of the intellectual content of feminism to that main purpose. *The Cause* is no exception to this rule. Divergent feminist ideas are charted according to differences in tactics and strategy, or the various issues seized upon and the consequent articulation of aims and objectives. Yet underlying unity is assumed.

Ray Strachey's account of feminism's development in *The Cause* is by now a standard one. First there is the appearance of *A Vindication of the Rights of Woman*, described as 'the text' of the later movement. Then there is a forty-year silence, preceding the emergence of the first women's organizations—the practical movement. Theory precedes practice in this narrative, and Mary Wollstonecraft is, as it were, the harbinger of the movement, a female John the Baptist, heralding what was to follow. True to the correlation between feminism and social movement, it is a narrative according to which feminism finally 'starts' and achieves itself within the form of a social movement of women for their emancipation.

What happens if this story is unpicked, if the history of ideas is allowed parity with the history of a movement?

The idea of a silent period can be compared with the results of the work done by Barbara Taylor and published in *Eve and the New Jerusalem*.[17] This shows how Mary Wollstonecraft's ideas were taken up within the Owenite socialist movement in the years which preceded the appearance of the Langham Place group.[18] The gap proposed by Ray Strachey's account is at least partially filled; rather than silence, broken only by occasional isolated utterances, there is the intermingling of feminism and socialism within utopian politics. This 'discovery' of an active feminism where none had been seen before derives from an approach which takes intellectual history seriously. It also depends on an implicit separation of the terms of the equation feminism = the social movement of women. In terms of that equation the period in question reveals nothing. A shift in emphasis unveils a hidden link in feminism's fortunes.

The exploration of feminist history is severely limited if the appearance of the social movement is assumed to be feminism's apotheosis and privileged form. For one thing, any feminism preceding the Seneca Falls Conference of 1848 in the United States or the Langham Place circle in England in the 1850s is necessarily seen as prototypic, an early example of a later-flowering plant, a phenomenon to be understood in terms of what comes later rather than in its own terms and context.[19]

To accept, with all its implications, that feminism has not only existed in movements of and for women, but has also been able to exist as an intellectual tendency without a movement, or as a strand within very different movements, is to accept the existence of various forms of feminism. The ebb and flow of feminism's intellectual history is important here, since it enables a different perspective to be placed on the movement itself. It also points up feminists' and feminism's ability to use and to combine with diverse ways of thinking politically. A study of these various combinational forms of feminism can illuminate both the means of diffusion of feminist ideas and the different tendencies within feminism when it does exist in conjunction with a social movement of women.

In Ray Strachey's account Mary Wollstonecraft's work gains meaning by becoming 'the text' of the later movement. But is the impression of theoretical continuity this conveys a valid one? Is Mary Wollstonecraft's philosophical radicalism shared by later feminists? The claim is made by Ray Strachey in the absence of any sustained discussion of feminism's intellectual content. Any substantiation depends on an analysis of Mary Wollstonecraft's thought and that of later feminists.

A Vindication of the Rights of Woman combines an appeal on behalf of women with a general social critique which employs key themes from the Enlightenment and uses them to illuminate women's position and needs. The demand for free individual development in a society open to talent, for example, is a demand of the French Revolution. Mary Wollstonecraft extends this idea to women, widening out criticism of hereditary rights, duties and exclusions, to include those which derive from sexual difference.

This drive to extend the field of social criticism in order to encompass women is carried forward in the name of women's basic humanity. The claim is first and foremost that women are members of the human species and therefore have the rights due to all humans. In making this claim several elements are combined. There is a Lockeian Christian argument that God has constructed the world according to the laws of reason, and that humans can reach an understanding of the laws of God by use of that reason. If women are human they have reason and have the right to develop their reason in pursuit, not least, of religious knowledge.[20] There is an argument against women's confinement to the world of artifice and their consequent exclusion from the world of natural rights. Rousseau's *Emile* is specifically pinpointed because within it women are deliberately constructed as objects of sexual desire, and by that confined to a lifetime's subordination within limits defined by male needs.[21] The main thrust of this aspect of the *Vindication* is that as members of the human species, and in the interests of their own development, women should have the same considerations applied to them as are applied to men. This is, importantly, a natural rights argument: it rests its case on the rights due to all humans as species members. Ray Strachey accurately calls it a plea for equal human rights.

This notion of *human* rights, of the Rights of Man, is not held in common between Mary Wollstonecraft and later, nineteenth-century feminists. Their debates took place in the aftermath of a major political defeat of 'natural rights' arguments, which had found their most forceful expression in the slogans of the French Revolution and which stayed alive by entering the political language of socialism.

Some did hold on to a concept of natural rights. For example, Dr. Richard Pankhurst, husband of Emmeline and father of Sylvia and Christabel, pursued the following line of argument in 1867:

> The basis of political freedom is expressed in the great maxim of the equality of all men, of humanity, of all human beings, before the law. The unit of modern society is not the family but the individual. Therefore every individual is *prima facie* entitled to all the franchises and freedoms of the constitution. The political position of women ought, and finally, must be, determined by reference to that large principle . . . Any individual who enjoys the electoral right is not, in the eye of the constitution, invested with it in virtue of being of a certain rank, station or sex. Each individual receives the right to vote *in the character of human being, possessing intelligence and adequate reasoning power. To be human and to be sane are the essential conditions* . . . it is not on the grounds of any difference of sex that the electoral right is in principle either granted or denied.[22] [My emphasis]

By contrast, Helen Taylor, daughter of Harriet Taylor and stepdaughter of J. S. Mill, recommended the Ladies Petition presented by Mill to the Commons in 1866, in the following terms:

> This claim, that since women are permitted to hold property they should also be permitted to exercise all the rights which, by our laws, the posses-

sion of property brings with it, is put forward in this petition on such strictly constitutional grounds, and is advanced so entirely without reference to any abstract rights, or fundamental changes in the institutions of English society, that it is impossible not to feel that the ladies who make it have done so with a practical purpose in view, and that they conceive themselves to be asking only for the recognition of rights which flow naturally from the existing laws and institutions of the country.[23]

She invokes support for female suffrage and the suffragists on the grounds that the suffragists eschew natural rights and support the rights of property. To consider 'a *birthright* as not of *natural* but of *legal* origin is', she writes, 'in conformity with modern habits of thought in regard to civilized men, the natives of civilized societies; but *exactly as it is opposed to any a priori theories of the rights of man,* [my emphasis] it is also opposed to any attempt to give or withhold privileges for merely *natural* reasons, such as differences of sex.'[24] 'Property represented by an individual is the true political unit among us', she claims.

By holding property women take on the rights and the duties of property. If they are not interested in politics their property is. Poor-laws and game-laws, corn-laws and malt-tax, cattle-plague-compensation bills, the manning of the navy, and the conversion of Enfield rifles into breech-loaders—all these things will make the property held by English women more or less valuable to the country at large . . . [and] it is on the supposition that property requires representation that a property qualification is fixed by the law.[25]

Richard Pankhurst and Helen Taylor were expressing an important and deep difference, between the rights of persons and the rights of property, which was at the centre of political and ideological debate in the nineteenth century and is still alive today. The affirmation of property rights over human rights and *vice versa* is sufficiently incompatible for it to be hard to see much meaning in talk of shared ideas. Mary Wollstonecraft and Richard Pankhurst share a philosophic radicalism from which Helen Taylor and others were keen to distance themselves.

It can be objected that as far as Ray Strachey is concerned, this criticism is unjust. Her claim is not, it could be said, that feminists shared a *theory* but that they shared an *ideal*. Is even this true? To the extent to which all the variety of objectives subscribed to by nineteenth-century feminists could be described as tending to produce equality for men and women alike, then it can be said that the ideal of equality was generally shared, but it is difficult to go further than this. The ideal of equal *human* rights did not stay in the centre of feminist preoccupations. The dynamics of feminist activity in the late nineteenth and early twentieth centuries moved away from it, even whilst feminists insisted on equal treatment, by developing much more than previously the concept of inescapable differences between the sexes. The term 'equal rights' became filled with different contents.

The more work that emerges on the history of the nineteenth-century movement the more difficult it is to see any one theme, campaign, or ideal as pivotal. The picture which emerges is of a fragmented movement, its aims like pebbles, thrown into the stream of social, political, economic and cultural life, producing rippling circles which touch and overlap, but of which no *one* could be with any certainty called the focal point. At the turn of the century the vote took on the weight of a symbolic function, uniting the personnel of many different campaigns; and, reciprocally, support for female suffrage became the touchstone of feminism. But the vote was never in any simple way the objective of feminist aspirations.

For Ray Strachey and others like her, however, suffragism was the litmus test of feminism and this is reflected in the narrative of *The Cause:* its climax is the triumph of the vote. Such an emphasis in itself marked a shift. Enfranchisement of women was not a central concern for Mary Wollstonecraft. She introduces the subject with a certain diffidence:

> I really think that women ought to have representatives, instead of being arbitrarily governed without having any direct share allowed them in the deliberations of government. But, as the whole system of representation in this country is only a convenient handle for despotism, they need not complain, for they are as well represented as a numerous class of hard working mechanics.[26]

From the 1850s onwards feminists (in Ray Strachey's definition of the animating spirits of the movement) agreed that women 'ought to have representatives', more forcefully than the idea was ever held by Mary Wollstonecraft. Not all maintained her link between women and 'mechanics': this was often jettisoned together with the concept of natural human rights which informs it. Hence the fierce debate between feminists, as well as between some feminists and non-feminists, about the relationship of women's suffrage to universal adult suffrage. What replaced the notion of 'human' rights was one of 'women's' rights which depended not so much on a concept of woman as species member, but on woman as member of a specific social group composed of herself and other women. Suffragist and suffragette alike, whatever their differences over tactics, usually agreed in constructing 'woman' as a unified category, a specifiable constituency, sufficiently different from any class of

men to need their own representatives, and sufficiently similar for an enfranchised section to represent the disfranchised.

As the campaign developed and resistance to it became more articulated suffragists and suffragettes had to answer a set of questions which
registered various difficulties in relation to womanhood, to the nature of
representation, and to citizenship. Who could best represent women?
Women or selected men? Could women's interests be distinguished from
men's? If so, how and by what? What was a woman? Could women represent men? Could they represent the interests of the state? Could they
take on the duties as well as the rights of the citizen?[27]

The position of married women in particular created a difficulty since
in law married women were entirely represented by their husbands.[28] In
the main suffragettes and suffragists alike were prepared to compromise
with this state of affairs. They demanded equality on the same terms as
men, even though marriage created differences between women and
women as well as between women and men, and they supported bills
which would exclude married women from the vote.

In the name of egalitarianism, therefore, they were prepared to accept
the exclusion of a large number of women from citizenship, for a time at
least. Amongst the arguments used to justify this apparent paradox was
an appeal to an underlying unity between women. Mrs. Fawcett for example reasoned that, because of their shared womanhood, widows and
spinsters would be able to represent their married sisters. Christabel
Pankhurst stressed that women were being excluded on principle, because of their sex: winning the vote for some would break the principle
of exclusion for all. From this point of view it didn't matter which
women were first enfranchised. Both leaders mobilized the concept of a
unity of interest between women to prove that women are the best people to represent other women and that some women could wait: it is constitutive of both their feminisms and shared by them despite their differences. At the level of the concept of woman being deployed, agreement
exists where it may not have been expected, and where at another level
(ideas about how the British Constitution worked, for example) profound disagreement does exist.

An analysis of the shifts and changes which have taken place in the
meaning and content of 'womanhood' for feminists is intrinsic to any
study of feminism as a specific body of thought or practice. The study of
combinational forms of feminism is also important and here the terms of
general social analysis can be crucial. But overall it is even more pertinent
to ask what concept of woman is being mobilized, or indeed, as far as
contemporary feminism is concerned, whether a concept of woman is being employed at all.

Feminists have not always had the same concept of woman, either at any one time or over time, and those moments at which changes have taken place in dominant feminist thinking about women can be pinpointed. Taken together with an appreciation of the different alliances feminists have entered into, the concept of woman can become a means through which the influence feminists have had at a more general political, social and cultural level can be gauged. But these things can only happen if attention is shifted from continuities of feminism to the discontinuities, the breaks, in feminist discourse and practice.

One of the attractions of the history of the nineteenth-century movement for feminists is that it provides a certain reassurance in the example of women acting together in a united way. It is also possible to mould its material into a satisfying narrative. In *The Cause,* the story is one of trials, vicissitudes, but eventual success. Fifty years later, the development of a new movement led to a questioning of the terms of this 'success' and the story has been amended so that it now more often finishes in anti-climax and defeat or else in the creation of the new movement to carry the struggle further. But the underlying structure of the narrative is maintained.

Both this structure and the emotional purposes of feminist history writing relate to its political function. Combined, they can give feminist historiography an evolutionist and progressivist flavour. The present is treated as the culmination of the past and as relatively 'advanced' compared to that past. Characteristics of the modern movement (like the commitment to autonomy, separatism, or whatever) are taken as definitional of feminism and looked for in past experiences. Disjunctures and dead ends tend to be ignored. The past is thus used to authenticate the present when there is no guarantee that past feminisms have anything more in common with contemporary feminism than a name: links between them need to be established and cannot be assumed from the outset.

In my view these problems derived from an overstrict identification of feminism with a women's movement, and of the history of feminism with the history of the achievement of the aims of that movement. Such an identification depends on a definition of feminism as *activity,* whether diffuse or directed to a given end. As a perspective it generates further problems, too.

The focus on feminism as activity, as campaigns around issues, tends to underplay the nature of the general debate about women and the extent to which feminists were involved in setting its terms. Claims are often made, for example, about women's 'silence' or exclusion from public speech in the nineteenth century. It is hard to find much evidence to support this in the journals of the period.[29] A rhetoric of exclusion is taken as factual description. Although there was a good deal of thinking and writing in the politics of nineteenth-century feminism, this is rarely fore-grounded. Pride of place is given to feminism's dramas.

And there is sometimes something rather suspect in this emphasis on feminism as activity, as locus of a particular campaigning spirit. In *The Tamarisk Tree* Dora Russell recalls that after the Labour Party Conference of 1926, at which her group won an endorsement of their birth control campaign, H. G. Wells sent her a postcard, part of which read 'Bertie thinks, I write, but you DO'.[30] On the face of it a compliment. Yet is it? Does it not sum up a certain position in regard to women's politics, to feminism, to its history, to women in general? Men think and write, women do; men thought and wrote, women did (the most famous novel about the New Women was called *The Woman Who Did*). Men reflect; women act out. But in their acting, what ideas were feminist women drawing on, using, transforming, creating? The answers to these questions are often occluded by the presentation of feminism as spectacle.

Present and Past

Instead of a progressive and cumulative history of feminism, it is an historical examination of the dynamics of persistence and change within feminism which is needed. Alongside those narratives which stress the success or failure of particular campaigns, some appraisal of the complicated inheritance of feminist thought and practice is required. This inheritance is not simply a part of the past but lives in the present, both as a part of the conditions of existence of contemporary feminism and as a part of that very feminism.

When the women's liberation movement came into existence in the late 1960s, it emerged into a social order already marked by an assimilation of other feminisms. Feminism was already a part of the political and social fabric. It was not present as a dominant force: feminists were after all the representatives of a subordinate group.[31] But the logic of mainstream feminism—that there could be a politics directed towards women—had been assimilated, even if women have not normally acted as a unified political constituency, and if 'women's politics' had, by the 1960s, become stereotyped.

It had become acceptable, before the emergence of the women's liberation movement, to think about women as a separate social group with needs and interests of their own, even if this way of thinking has been unstable and not always in evidence. This does not mean that only feminists treated 'woman' as a unified category, or that anyone who does so is a feminist. Nor is it to say that all feminists share or have shared the same concept of womanhood. Although the suffrage movement effected a political shift away from exclusive considerations of women as sex to emphasize women as social group, the post-suffrage movement (after much conflict) adopted a concept of woman based on the needs of reproduction and the social value of maternity.[32]

An autonomous female subject, woman speaking in her own right, with her own voice, had also emerged. It has been part of the project of feminism in general to attempt to transform women from an object of knowledge into a subject capable of appropriating knowledge, to effect a passage from the state of subjection to subjecthood.[33] In great measure this project was realized within the feminism of the 1860s to the 1930s, albeit in literary form.[34]

Women's liberation groups formed within a context which already included a programme for women's legal and political emancipation—the unfinished business of 1928—and pressure groups and lobbyists working for it.[35] This simultaneity of what might be called an 'old' feminism and a 'new' is perhaps one reason why broad and loose definitions of feminism have such an appeal, and why such broad definitions can be shared by feminists and non-feminists. The content of the term has not been determined by the women's liberation movement. A preexisting content was already part of culture, and could not be negotiated or wished away.

Modern feminism is an admixture, and the boundaries between its components, between its 'past' and its 'present', are not necessarily that clear. At the start of the contemporary women's liberation movement it was common for women's liberationists to distance themselves from emancipationism, the campaign for equality between the sexes. Despite this, women's liberation has spawned campaigns for legal and financial equality, equal opportunity at work, and other demands which have an emancipationist object. 'Women's right to enter a man's world' is both demanded and criticized. The ambivalence which the issue arouses is important because it indicates areas of uncertainty and confusion about feminist aims, a confusion which might be more productive than a premature clarity.

Nor has the *image* of the feminist been the creation of women's liberation. Traces of the feminist past and its often unsolved problems persist in collective social memories and the various social meanings of feminism. What captures the public imagination about feminism is often indicative of what is both new and a survival, and a good guide to feminism's impact. It is more difficult than might at first be thought to distinguish between a feminist and a non-feminist image of feminism; often only the interpretations differ.

Feminists were, and still are, imagined as confined to the narrow world of women, the marginal world of women's issues, cut off from the general field of human endeavour (which in some vocabularies is called class politics). Fear of separation and marginalization still has a strong inhibitory power. The issue of separatism, the creation of a female culture and community, is at the heart of an unfinished debate within feminism and between feminisms.

Feminists are also imagined as the bearers of female anger, as female incendiaries. The bra-burner of 1968 merges with the *petroleuse* of the Paris Commune; the sex shop arsonist of 1978 with the pillar box arsonist of 1913. The explosive quality of feminism, its fieriness, its anger, is contained within the image of the bra-burner, as is the protest against sexual constraint.[36]

There were in effect various concepts from feminist discourses (and various responses to them) already in circulation when the first new women's groups began to meet in the 1960s. It is possible to look at the three already mentioned (the idea of women as a social group with an underlying unity of interest, the realization of a feminine subject distinguishable from the male, the possibility of a politics which could focus exclusively on women) and mark, after twenty years, the changes each has gone through, if only in a schematic way.

One of the most striking features of women's liberation and radical feminism was their recourse to a new language—the language of liberation rather than emancipation, of collectivism rather than individualism. Radical sociology and marxism were placed in the foreground of attempts to analyse women's position. There were new forms of practice too—the consciousness-raising group, the refusal of formal, delegated structures of political organization, a stress on participation rather than representation—and a new concept: that of 'sexual politics'.

'Sexual politics' held together the idea of women as social group dominated by men as social group (male domination/female oppression), at the same time as turning back to the issue of women as sex *outside* of the bounds of reproduction. It threw political focus onto the most intimate transactions of the bedroom: this became one of the meanings of 'the personal is political'. These two aspects have not always stayed held together: some feminists have attached most value to the study of 'women' as social group and object of political concern. It is, however, the pursuit of questions about the female body and its sexual needs which has become distinctive of contemporary feminism.

For past feminisms it was male sexuality that was at issue: the need was as much to constrain male sexuality as to liberate women from the work of paying the costs of male desire. There are feminists today for whom women's problem is still male desire. But alongside the challenge to male sexuality there goes a curiosity about female desire, female sexuality, and the problems of relations between women.

At the same time the autonomous female subject has become, in a much more pronounced way, the subject of feminism. In 1866, J. S. Mill could be welcomed as an adequate representative of women's aspirations by the first women's suffrage societies. As recently as 1972 Simone de Beauvoir could refer to feminists as 'those women or even men who fight to change the position of women, in liaison with and yet outside the class struggle, without totally subordinating that change to a change in society.'[37] Now, in the mid-eighties, it is practically impossible to speak of 'male feminism'. Feminism is increasingly understood by feminists as a way of thinking created by, for, and on behalf of women, as 'gender-specific'. Women are its subjects, its enunciators, the creators of its theory, of its practice and of its language.[38]

When this intensification of emphasis on women as the subject of feminism coincides with an emphasis on women as feminism's object and focus of attention (women's experience, literature, history, psyche, and so on) certain risks are run. The doubling-up of women, as subject and object, can produce a circular, self-confirming rhetoric and a hermetic closure of thought. The feminine subject becomes trapped by the dynamics of self-reflectivity within the narcissism of the mirror-image.[39]

Feminism's fascination with women is also the condition of the easy slippage from 'feminist' to 'woman' and back: the feminist becomes the representative of 'woman', just as 'feminist history' becomes the same as 'women's history' and so on.

This intensification of the use of concepts already in circulation has produced not so much a continuity of feminisms as a set of crises. It is, for example, one of women's liberation's paradoxes that although it started on the terrain of sexual antagonism between men and women, it moved quickly to a state in which relations between women caused the most internal stress. Women, in a sense, are feminism's greatest problem. The assumption of a potential identity between women, rather than solving the problem, became a condition of increasing tensions.

Of these tensions, not the least important is the intellectual tension generated by a crisis of the concept 'woman' within feminist thought. As a concept, 'woman' is too fragile to bear the weight of all the contents and meanings now ascribed to it. The end of much research by feminists has been to show the tremendous diversity of the meaning of womanhood, across cultures and over time. This result serves feminist purposes by providing evidence that change is possible because the social meaning of womanhood is malleable. But to demonstrate the elusiveness of 'woman' as a category can also subvert feminists' assumption that women can be approached as a unity. It points up the extent to which the concept of womanhood employed by feminists is always partial.

One indication of this crisis is the way in which 'sexual division' and 'sexual difference' are named with increasing frequency as the objects of feminist enquiry. Where this happens there is a shift away from the treatment of 'men' and 'women' as discrete groups and a stress on the relationships between the two. Of particular significance here have been the uses of psychoanalytic and critical theory in the attempt to understand the 'sexed subject', with a consequent movement from the unsatisfactory terms 'man' and 'woman' to the differently unsatisfactory terms 'masculinity' and 'femininity'.

This work is often criticized as 'non-political', but in my view its political implications are what raise alarm. The employment of psychoanalysis and critical theory to question the unity of the subject, to emphasize the fragmented subject, is potentially subversive of any view which asserts a 'central' organizing principle of social conflict. Radical feminism, for example, has depended as much as some marxist political theories on such an assertion: sex war replaces class war as the 'truth' of history, and in its enactment the sexes are given a coherent identity. To deconstruct the subject 'woman', to question whether 'woman' is a coherent identity, is also to imply the question of whether 'woman' is a coherent political identity, and therefore whether women can unite politically, culturally, and socially as 'women' for other than very specific reasons. It raises questions about the feminist project at a very fundamental level.

Such questions are open ones and need to remain so. How far the practico-theoretical fragmentation of what calls itself the women's movement can be related to the lack of cohesiveness of the concept 'woman' is a matter of speculation. The nineteenth-century social movement was also fragmented, and spoke, as do feminisms today, to a general political crisis of representation. This crisis is not restricted to feminists, nor to the political institutions and political languages which they have had a part in making. In what form, forms or combinations feminism will survive is not a question which can yet be answered.

Notes

1. Parts of this article were included in a paper given to the London History Workshop Seminar in April 1983. I would like to thank all those who participated in the discussion which followed and all those friends and colleagues who have discussed the various themes of this article with me. Special thanks are due to Beatrix Campbell, Catherine Hall, Juliet Mitchell, Mike and Ines Newman, Geoffrey Nowell-Smith and Brenda Storey.

2. 'Of two neighbouring towns each is the other's most jealous rival; every little canton looks down on the others with contempt. Closely related races keep one another at arm's length; the South German cannot endure the North German, the Englishman casts every kind of aspersion upon the Scot, the Spaniard despises the Portuguese.' Sigmund Freud, *Group Psychology and the Analysis of the Ego* (Standard Edition, Vol 18, Hogarth, London, 1958), 101. See also *Civilisation and its Discontents*, ch. V (Vol 21 of the same edition).

3. This can happen in both politics and culture. One example is the creation of 'feminist art' as a category within art criticism into which the work of many women artists is conveniently slotted. Far from focusing attention on the work of those artists who are feminists, such a label removes their art practice to the margins, and forecloses the question of whether such a thing as 'feminist art' exists. For a discussion of feminist art practice see Mary Kelly, 'Designing Images/Imaging Desire' in *Wedge*, 6 (New York, 1984).

4. This point of view was expressed, for example, in the London Women's Liberation Workshop Manifesto, drafted in 1970 by a group of London women as the basis of their work together. Part of it read: 'Women's Liberation Workshop believes that women in our society are oppressed. We are economically oppressed; in jobs we do full work for half pay, at home we do unpaid work full time. We are commercially exploited by advertisements, television and the press. Legally women are discriminated against. We are brought up to feel inadequate, educated to narrower horizons than men. It is as women therefore that we are organizing.' The manifesto was circulated as a cyclostyled sheet to all those interested in the Workshop and was published monthly in its magazine *Shrew*. All those who shared its perception of what it meant to be a woman could take part in workshop activities and thus become participants in the women's movement.

5. This 'we' is reminiscent of what Benveniste calls the 'dilated I', a 'we' which 'annexes to the "I" an indistinct globality of other persons', Emile Benveniste, *Problèmes de Linguistique Générale* (Gallimard, Paris, 1966), 235.

6. Indeed, the Workshop manifesto stressed heterogeneity: 'Women's Liberation Workshop is essentially heterogeneous, incorporating within it a wide range of opinions and plans for action.' The assumption was that these opinions and plans could harmonize because in the context of a movement women could find a new way of working together.

7. For example, the statement that women in the home 'do unpaid work full time' is one that could be agreed to by all supporters of the Manifesto. Their analysis that this hidden labour (hidden from the point of view of capital) is the secret of capital's exploitation of women and that therefore there should be a campaign for wages for housework in order to reclaim its value was highly contentious and never gained more than minority backing.

8. For discussions of Greenham Common see Caroline Blackwood, *On the Perimeter* (Heinemann, London/Viking, NY, 1984; Alice Cook and Gwyn Kirk, *Greenham Women Everywhere* (Pluto Press, London/The South End Press, Boston, 1983); Lynne Jones (ed.), *Keeping the Peace* (The Women's Press, London, 1983); and *Breaching the Peace* conference papers by a group of radical feminists (Onlywomen Press, London, 1983).

9. Professor Olive Banks, for example, employs this broad definition: 'Any groups that have tried to *change* the position of women, or ideas about women, have been granted the title feminist' in her *Faces of Feminism* (Martin Robertson, Oxford, 1981), 3.

10. 'In the radical feminist view, the new feminism is not just the revival of a serious political movement for social equality. It is the second wave of the most popular revolution in history', Shulamith Firestone, *The Dialectic of Sex* (Cape,

London, 1971), 16. *The Second Wave* was also the name of a U.S. radical feminist journal. It is a phrase which is still used.

11. Ray Strachey, *The Cause* (Bell, London, 1928; reprinted Virago, London, 1978).

12. *Shorter Oxford English Dictionary*, 1933.

13. Strachey, *The Cause*, 12.

14. Ibid., 13.

15. Ibid., 24.

16. At least, so it seems to me. Margaret Forster writes that feminists like Harriet Martineau regarded Caroline Norton with 'contempt' for her disavowal of feminism, and claims that Caroline Norton's insights were 'more truly feminist than any of the openly feminist tracts of her day', *Significant Sisters* (Secker & Warburg, London, 1984), 50. This argument begs the question of the content of feminist ideas.

17. Barbara Taylor, *Eve and the New Jerusalem* (Virago, London, 1984).

18. For a further account of this period, see Jane Rendall, *The Origins of Modern Feminism* (Macmillan, London, 1985).

19. Cf. Joan Kelly, 'Early Feminist Theory and the *Querelle des Femmes*' in *Signs*, 11, Vol 8, 1982: 'Most histories of the Anglo-American women's movement acknowledge feminist "forerunners" in individual figures such as Anne Hutchinson, and in women inspired by the English and French revolutions, but only with the women's rights conference at Seneca Falls in 1848 do they recognise the beginnings of a continuously developing body of feminist thought.'

20. In *The Reasonableness of Christianity* Locke includes women amongst those 'who cannot know and therefore must believe'; as such they could be excluded from considerations of equality. In his own lifetime Mary Astell and the unknown author of *An Essay in Defence of the Female Sex* used his work on human understanding to stake the claim that 'mind has no sex' and that women, as members of the human species, had rights to equal mental development with men.

21. Both Locke and Rousseau are used against themselves. Their categories of the individual as property owner and *paterfamilias* are subverted by the claim that women have the right to be considered thinking and reasoning subjects (after Locke) and feeling subjects (after Rousseau). This is not a rejection of their arguments, but an incorporation of them. In particular, Rousseau is not, as is sometimes claimed, rejected by Mary Wollstonecraft but is used and assimilated within her work.

22. Dr. Richard Pankhurst, 'The Right of Women to Vote Under the Reform Act, 1867' in *Fortnightly Review*, Vol 10 (September 1868), 250–4.

23. Helen Taylor, 'The Ladies Petition' in *Westminster Review* (January 1867), 63–79.

24. Ibid., 63–4.

25. Ibid., 70.

26. Mary Wollstonecraft, *A Vindication of the Rights of Woman* (Norton, NY, 1967), 220.

27. There was much discussion, for example, of whether women could take on the duties of the armed citizen. It was several years before suffragists began to say that women in childbirth risked their lives as much as did the soldier. The

Conservative politician, Goldwyn Smith, expostulated, 'we have only to imagine the foreign policy of England determined by women, while that of other countries is determined by the men; and this in the age of Bismarck'. ('Female Suffrage', *Macmillan's Magazine*, Vol 30 (June 1874), 139–50.) The concept of woman implicit in this vision was shared by many feminists who asserted that women's gentler nature would attenuate the violence of male politics.

28. The most famous definition of this principle came from Blackwood's *Commentaries:* 'By marriage the very being or legal existence of a woman is suspended, or at least it is incorporated or consolidated into that of the husband, under whose wing, protection, and cover she performs everything and she is therefore called in our law a feme covert' (*femme couverte*). The principle of *coverture* meant that generally speaking the married woman did not exist as legal subject or as property owner.

29. Apart from a stream of articles from various hands published in the *Fortnightly Review* and the *Westminster Review,* the *Edinburgh Review, Contemporary Review, Fraser's Magazine, Macmillan's Magazine,* the *Nineteenth Century,* the *New Review,* the *National Review,* and the *Theological Review,* all carried a range of articles written by women who would have described themselves as feminists.

30. Dora Russell, *The Tamarisk Tree* (Virago, London, 1977), Vol 1, 189.

31. Participants in nineteenth-century campaigns included the daughters of British radicalism, of fathers active in the Anti-Corn Law League, the movement to abolish slavery, the agitation for the 1832 Reform Bill. Their aim was to be incorporated into the ruling group, to have their rights recognized and their ideas re-represented within a liberal consensus. *The Cause* gives a good portrait of this aspect of the suffrage movement. Paul McHugh, in *Prostitution and Victorian Social Reform* (Croom Helm, London, 1980), includes an account of the personnel involved in the Ladies National Association for the Abolition of the Contagious Diseases Act.

32. The years following the suffrage witnessed fierce debates between 'old' feminists and 'new'. The platform of the 'new' feminists, adopted by the National Union of Societies for Equal Citizenship (the new name of the National Union of Women's Suffrage Societies) in 1925, was that feminists should turn away from demands for equality with men, and concentrate on those issues specific to women as women. They linked women's special needs to those concerned with maternity and reproduction, and feminism to issues like birth control and family allowances. See Mary Stocks, *Eleanor Rathbone* (Gollancz, London, 1949) and Rosalind Delmar, 'Afterword' to Vera Brittain, *Testament of Friendship* (Virago and Fontana, London, 1980).

33. One can trace elements of this project in the combination of Mary Wollstonecraft's political and fictional writings. Alexandra Kollontai picks out the theme in the conclusion to her essay 'The New Woman', when she writes that 'Woman, by degrees, is being transformed from an object of tragedy of the male soul into the subject of an independent tragedy', *Autobiography of a Sexually Emancipated Woman* (Orbach and Chambers, London, 1972), 103.

34. This is not so true of cinema and television and is perhaps why feminists have made such a distinctive contribution to the analysis of cinematic representation. See Constance Penley (ed.), *Feminism and Film Theory* (BFI Publishing, London, forthcoming).

35. The Sex Discrimination Act went through Parliament in 1975 after a campaign in which the new women's groups took very little interest; there were other women's organizations carrying that particular torch. May Stott evokes the encounter between these 'old' and 'new' feminists in *Before I Go* (Virago, London, 1985).

36. Although the 'real event' of bra burning is often fiercely denied, and Edith Thomas has questioned the existence of the *petroleuses*, it is interesting that Josephine Butler believed in their existence and justified their actions, assuming them to be women forced into prostitution and released from brothels by the Commune. See her *Some Lessons from Contemporary History* (The Friends Association for the Abolition of State Regulation of Vice, London, 1898). Martha Vicinus explores the recurrent imagery of fire in suffragette writing in her *Independent Women* (Virago, London and University of Chicago Press, 1985).

37. Simone de Beauvoir, interview with Alice Schwartzer; translation published in *7 Days*, London, 8 March 1972.

38. I am grateful to Stephen Heath, whose unpublished paper, 'Male Feminism' helped clarify this point for me. The changes indicated here are expressive of a general shift in relations between men and women *within* feminism.

39. This dimension of feminism is absorbingly represented in the film *Riddles of the Sphinx* by Laura Mulvey and Peter Wollen (BFI, London, 1977). See especially episode 12, 'Maxine's room', described in the script as 'space fragmented by reflections and reflections within reflections' (*Screen*, Vol 18, Summer 1977, 2).

2   The Combahee River Collective Statement

COMBAHEE RIVER COLLECTIVE

We are a collective of Black feminists who have been meeting together since 1974.[1] During that time we have been involved in the process of defining and clarifying our politics, while at the same time doing political work within our own group and in coalition with other progressive organizations and movements. The most general statement of our politics at the present time would be that we are actively committed to struggling against racial, sexual, heterosexual, and class oppression, and see as our particular task the development of integrated analysis and practice based upon the fact that the major systems of oppression are interlocking. The synthesis of these oppressions creates the conditions of our lives. As Black women we see Black feminism as the logical political movement to combat the manifold and simultaneous oppressions that all women of color face.

We will discuss four major topics in the paper that follows: (1) the genesis of contemporary Black feminism; (2) what we believe, i.e., the specific province of our politics; (3) the problems in organizing Black feminists, including a brief herstory of our collective; and (4) Black feminist issues and practice.

The Combahee River Collective was a Black feminist group in Boston whose name came from the guerrilla action conceptualized and led by Harriet Tubman on June 2, 1863, in the Port Royal region of South Carolina. This action freed more than 750 slaves and is the only military campaign in American history planned and led by a woman.

1. The Genesis of Contemporary Black Feminism

Before looking at the recent development of Black feminism we would like to affirm that we find our origins in the historical reality of Afro-American women's continuous life-and-death struggle for survival and liberation. Black women's extremely negative relationship to the American political system (a system of white male rule) has always been determined by our membership in two oppressed racial and sexual castes. As Angela Davis points out in "Reflections on the Black Woman's Role in the Community of Slaves," Black women have always embodied, if only in their physical manifestation, an adversary stance to white male rule and have actively resisted its inroads upon them and their communities in both dramatic and subtle ways. There have always been Black women activists—some known, like Sojourner Truth, Harriet Tubman, Frances E. W. Harper, Ida B. Wells Barnett, and Mary Church Terrell, and thousands upon thousands unknown—who have had a shared awareness of how their sexual identity combined with their racial identity to make their whole life situation and the focus of their political struggles unique. Contemporary Black feminism is the outgrowth of countless generations of personal sacrifice, militancy, and work by our mothers and sisters.

A Black feminist presence has evolved most obviously in connection with the second wave of the American women's movement beginning in the late 1960s. Black, other Third World, and working women have been involved in the feminist movement from its start, but both outside reactionary forces and racism and elitism within the movement itself have served to obscure our participation. In 1973, Black feminists, primarily located in New York, felt the necessity of forming a separate Black feminist group. This became the National Black Feminist Organization (NBFO).

Black feminist politics also have an obvious connection to movements for Black liberation, particularly those of the 1960s and 1970s. Many of us were active in those movements (Civil Rights, Black nationalism, the Black Panthers), and all of our lives were greatly affected and changed by their ideologies, their goals, and the tactics used to achieve their goals. It was our experience and disillusionment within these liberation movements as well as experience on the periphery of the white male left that led to the need to develop a politics that was anti-racist, unlike those of white women, and anti-sexist, unlike those of Black and white men.

There is also undeniably a personal genesis for Black feminism, that is, the political realization that comes from the seemingly personal experiences of individual Black women's lives. Black feminists and many more Black women who do not define themselves as feminists have all experienced sexual oppression as a constant factor in our day-to-day existence. As children we realized that we were different from boys and that we were treated differently. For example, we were told in the same breath to be quiet both for the sake of being "ladylike" and to make us less objectionable in the eyes of white people. As we grew older we became aware of the threat of physical and sexual abuse by men. However, we had no way of conceptualizing what was so apparent to us, what we *knew* was really happening.

Black feminists often talk about their feelings of craziness before becoming conscious of the concepts of sexual politics, patriarchal rule, and most importantly, feminism, the political analysis and practice that we women use to struggle against our oppression. The fact that racial politics and indeed racism are pervasive factors in our lives did not allow us, and still does not allow most Black women, to look more deeply into our own experiences and, from the sharing and growing consciousness, to build a politics that will change our lives and inevitably end our oppression. Our development must also be tied to the contemporary economic and political position of Black people. The post World War II generation of Black youth was the first to be able to minimally partake of certain educational and employment options, previously closed completely to Black people. Although our economic position is still at the very bottom of the American capitalistic economy, a handful of us have been able to gain certain tools as a result of tokenism in education and employment which potentially enable us to more effectively fight our oppression.

A combined anti-racist and anti-sexist position drew us together initially, and as we developed politically we addressed ourselves to heterosexism and economic oppression under capitalism.

2. What We Believe

Above all else, our politics initially sprang from the shared belief that Black women are inherently valuable, that our liberation is a necessity not as an adjunct to somebody else's but because of our need as human persons for autonomy. This may seem so obvious as to sound simplistic, but it is apparent that no other ostensibly progressive movement has ever considered our specific oppression as a priority or worked seriously for the ending of that oppression. Merely naming the pejorative stereotypes attributed to Black women (e.g., mammy, matriarch, Sapphire, whore, bulldagger), let alone cataloguing the cruel, often murderous, treatment we receive, indicates how little value has been placed upon our lives during four centuries of bondage in the Western Hemisphere. We realize that the only people who care enough about us to work consistently for our liberation are us. Our politics evolve from a healthy love for ourselves, our sisters and our community which allows us to continue our struggle and work.

This focusing upon our own oppression is embodied in the concept of identity politics. We believe that the most profound and potentially most radical politics come directly out of our own identity, as opposed to working to end somebody else's oppression. In the case of Black women this is a particularly repugnant, dangerous, threatening, and therefore revolutionary concept because it is obvious from looking at all the political movements that have preceded us that anyone is more worthy of liberation than ourselves. We reject pedestals, queenhood, and walking ten paces behind. To be recognized as human, levelly human, is enough.

We believe that sexual politics under patriarchy is as pervasive in Black women's lives as are the politics of class and race. We also often find it difficult to separate race from class from sex oppression because in our lives they are most often experienced simultaneously. We know that there is such a thing as racial-sexual oppression which is neither solely racial nor solely sexual, e.g., the history of rape of Black women by white men as a weapon of political repression.

Although we are feminists and Lesbians, we feel solidarity with progressive Black men and do not advocate the fractionalization that white women who are separatists demand. Our situation as Black people necessitates that we have solidarity around the fact of race, which white women of course do not need to have with white men, unless it is their negative solidarity as racial oppressors. We struggle together with Black men against racism, while we also struggle with Black men about sexism.

We realize that the liberation of all oppressed peoples necessitates the destruction of the political-economic systems of capitalism and imperialism as well as patriarchy. We are socialists because we believe that work must be organized for the collective benefit of those who do the work and create the products, and not for the profit of the bosses. Material resources must be equally distributed among those who create these resources. We are not convinced, however, that a socialist revolution that is not also a feminist and anti-racist revolution will guarantee our liberation. We have arrived at the necessity for developing an understanding of class relationships that takes into account the specific class position of Black women who are generally marginal in the labor force, while at this particular time some of us are temporarily viewed as doubly desirable tokens at white-collar and professional levels. We need to articulate the real class situation of persons who are not merely raceless, sexless workers, but for whom racial and sexual oppression are significant determinants in their working/economic lives. Although we are in essential agreement with Marx's theory as it applied to the very specific economic relationships he analyzed, we know that his analysis must be extended further in order for us to understand our specific economic situation as Black women.

A political contribution which we feel we have already made is the expansion of the feminist principle that the personal is political. In our consciousness-raising sessions, for example, we have in many ways gone beyond white women's revelations because we are dealing with the implications of race and class as well as sex. Even our Black women's style of talking/testifying in Black language about what we have experienced has a resonance that is both cultural and political. We have spent a great deal of energy delving into the cultural and experiential nature of our oppression out of necessity because none of these matters has ever been looked at before. No one before has ever examined the multilayered texture of Black women's lives. An example of this kind of revelation/conceptualization occurred at a meeting as we discussed the ways in which our early intellectual interests had been attacked by our peers, particularly Black males. We discovered that all of us, because we were "smart," had also been considered "ugly," i.e., "smart-ugly." "Smart-ugly" crystallized the way in which most of us had been forced to develop our intellects at great cost to our "social" lives. The sanctions in the Black and white communities against Black women thinkers are comparatively much higher than for white women, particularly ones from the educated middle and upper classes.

As we have already stated, we reject the stance of Lesbian separatism because it is not a viable political analysis or strategy for us. It leaves out far too much and far too many people, particularly Black men, women, and children. We have a great deal of criticism and loathing for what men have been socialized to be in this society: what they support, how they act, and how they oppress. But we do not have the misguided notion that it is their maleness, per se—i.e., their biological maleness—that makes them what they are. As Black women we find any type of biological determinism a particularly dangerous and reactionary basis upon which to build a politic. We must also question whether Lesbian separatism is an adequate and progressive political analysis and strategy, even for those who practice it, since it so completely denies any but the sexual sources of women's oppression, negating the facts of class and race.

3. Problems in Organizing Black Feminists

During our years together as a Black feminist collective we have experienced success and defeat, joy and pain, victory and failure. We have found that it is very difficult to organize around Black feminist issues, difficult even to announce in certain contexts that we *are* Black feminists. We have tried to think about the reasons for our difficulties, particularly since the white women's movement continues to be strong and to grow in many directions. In this section we will discuss some of the general reasons for the organizing problems we face and also talk specifically about the stages in organizing our own collective.

The major source of difficulty in our political work is that we are not just trying to fight oppression on one front or even two, but instead to address a whole range of oppressions. We do not have racial, sexual, heterosexual, or class privilege to rely upon, nor do we have even the minimal access to resources and power that groups who possess any one of these types of privilege have.

The psychological toll of being a Black woman and the difficulties this presents in reaching political consciousness and doing political work can never be underestimated. There is a very low value placed upon Black women's psyches in this society, which is both racist and sexist. As an early group member once said, "We are all damaged people merely by virtue of being Black women." We are dispossessed psychologically and on every other level, and yet we feel the necessity to struggle to change the condition of all Black women. In "A Black Feminist's Search for Sisterhood," Michele Wallace arrives at this conclusion:

> We exist as women who are Black who are feminists, each stranded for the moment, working independently because there is not yet an environment in this society remotely congenial to our struggle—because, being on the bottom, we would have to do what no one else has done: we would have to fight the world.[2]

Wallace is pessimistic but realistic in her assessment of Black feminists' position, particularly in her allusion to the nearly classic isolation most of us face. We might use our position at the bottom, however, to make a clear leap into revolutionary action. If Black women were free, it would mean that everyone else would have to be free since our freedom would necessitate the destruction of all the systems of oppression.

Feminism is, nevertheless, very threatening to the majority of Black people because it calls into question some of the most basic assumptions about our existence, i.e., that sex should be a determinant of power relationships. Here is the way male and female roles were defined in a Black nationalist pamphlet from the early 1970s:

> We understand that it is and has been traditional that the man is the head of the house. He is the leader of the house/nation because his knowledge of the world is broader, his awareness is greater, his understanding is fuller and his application of this information is wiser . . . After all, it is only reasonable that the man be the head of the house because he is able to defend and protect the development of his home . . . Women cannot do the same things as men— they are made by nature to function differently. Equality of men and women

is something that cannot happen even in the abstract world. Men are not equal to other men, i.e. ability, experience or even understanding. The value of men and women can be seen as in the value of gold and silver—they are not equal but both have great value. We must realize that men and women are a complement to each other because there is no house/family without a man and his wife. Both are essential to the development of any life.[3]

The material conditions of most Black women would hardly lead them to upset both economic and sexual arrangements that seem to represent some stability in their lives. Many Black women have a good understanding of both sexism and racism, but because of the everyday constrictions of their lives, cannot risk struggling against them both.

The reaction of Black men to feminism has been notoriously negative. They are, of course, even more threatened than Black women by the possibility that Black feminists might organize around our own needs. They realize that they might not only lose valuable and hardworking allies in their struggles but that they might also be forced to change their habitually sexist ways of interacting with and oppressing Black women. Accusations that Black feminism divides the Black struggle are powerful deterrents to the growth of an autonomous Black women's movement.

Still, hundreds of women have been active at different times during the three-year existence of our group. And every Black woman who came, came out of a strongly felt need for some level of possibility that did not previously exist in her life.

When we first started meeting early in 1974 after the NBFO first eastern regional conference, we did not have a strategy for organizing, or even a focus. We just wanted to see what we had. After a period of months of not meeting, we began to meet again late in the year and started doing an intense variety of consciousness-raising. The overwhelming feeling that we had is that after years and years we had finally found each other. Although we were not doing political work as a group, individuals continued their involvement in Lesbian politics, sterilization abuse and abortion rights work, Third World Women's International Women's Day activities, and support activity for the trials of Dr. Kenneth Edelin, Joan Little, and Inéz García. During our first summer, when membership had dropped off considerably, those of us remaining devoted serious discussion to the possibility of opening a refuge for battered women in a Black community. (There was no refuge in Boston at that time.) We also decided around that time to become an independent collective since we had serious disagreements with NBFO's bourgeois-feminist stance and their lack of a clear political focus.

We also were contacted at that time by socialist feminists, with whom we had worked on abortion rights activities, who wanted to encourage us to attend the National Socialist Feminist Conference in Yellow Springs. One of our members did attend and despite the narrowness of the ideology that was promoted at that particular conference, we became more aware of the need for us to understand our own economic situation and to make our own economic analysis.

In the fall, when some members returned, we experienced several months of comparative inactivity and internal disagreements which were first conceptualized as a Lesbian-straight split but which were also the result of class and political differences. During the summer those of us who were still meeting had determined the need to do political work and to move beyond consciousness-raising and serving exclusively as an emotional support group. At the beginning of 1976, when some of the women who had not wanted to do political work and who also had voiced disagreements stopped attending of their own accord, we again looked for a focus. We decided at that time, with the addition of new members, to become a study group. We had always shared our reading with each other, and some of us had written papers on Black feminism for group discussion a few months before this decision was made. We began functioning as a study group and also began discussing the possibility of starting a Black feminist publication. We had a retreat in the late spring which provided a time for both political discussion and working out interpersonal issues. Currently we are planning to gather together a collection of Black feminist writing. We feel that it is absolutely essential to demonstrate the reality of our politics to other Black women and believe that we can do this through writing and distributing our work. The fact that individual Black feminists are living in isolation all over the country, that our own numbers are small, and that we have some skills in writing, printing, and publishing makes us want to carry out these kinds of projects as a means of organizing Black feminists as we continue to do political work in coalition with other groups.

4. Black Feminist Issues and Practice

During our time together we have identified and worked on many issues of particular relevance to Black women. The inclusiveness of our politics makes us concerned with any situation that impinges upon the lives of women, Third World and working people. We are of course particularly committed to working on those struggles in which race, sex and class are simultaneous factors in oppression. We might, for example, become involved in workplace organizing at a factory that employs Third World women or picket a hospital that is cutting back on already inadequate health care to a Third World community, or set up a rape crisis center in a Black neighborhood. Organizing around welfare and daycare concerns might also be a focus. The work to be done and the countless issues that this work represents merely reflect the pervasiveness of our oppression.

Issues and projects that collective members have actually worked on are sterilization abuse, abortion rights, battered women, rape and health care. We have also done many workshops and educationals on Black feminism on college campuses, at women's conferences, and most recently for high school women.

One issue that is of major concern to us and that we have begun to publicly address is racism in the white women's movement. As Black feminists we are made constantly and painfully aware of how little effort white women have made to understand and combat their racism, which requires among other things that they have a more than superficial comprehension of race, color, and Black history and culture. Eliminating racism in the white women's movement is by definition work for white women to do, but we will continue to speak to and demand accountability on this issue.

In the practice of our politics we do not believe that the end always justifies the means. Many reactionary and destructive acts have been done in the name of achieving "correct" political goals. As feminists we do not want to mess over people in the name of politics. We believe in collective process and a nonhierarchical distribution of power within our own group and in our vision of a revolutionary society. We are committed to a continual examination of our politics as they develop through criticism and self-criticism as an essential aspect of our practice. In her introduction to *Sisterhood is Powerful* Robin Morgan writes:

> I haven't the faintest notion what possible revolutionary role white heterosexual men could fulfill, since they are the very embodiment of reactionary-vested-interest-power.

As Black feminists and Lesbians we know that we have a very definite revolutionary task to perform and we are ready for the lifetime of work and struggle before us.

Notes

1. This statement is dated April 1977.
2. Wallace, Michele. "A Black Feminist's Search for Sisterhood," *The Village Voice,* 28 July 1975, pp. 6–7.
3. Mumininas of Committee for Unified Newark, Mwanamke Mwananchi (The Nationalist Woman), Newark, N.J., ©1971, pp. 4–5.

3 From a Long Line of Vendidas
Chicanas and Feminism

CHERRÍE MORAGA

If somebody would have asked me when I was a teenager what it means to be Chicana, I would probably have listed the grievances done me. When my sister and I were fifteen and fourteen, respectively, and my brother a few years older, we were still waiting on him. I write "were" as if now, nearly two decades later, it were over. But that would be a lie. To this day in my mother's home, my brother and father are waited on, including by me. I do this out of respect for my mother and her wishes. In those early years, however, it was mainly in relation to my brother that I resented providing such service. For unlike my father, who sometimes worked as much as seventy hours a week to feed my face every day, the only thing that earned my brother my servitude was his maleness.

• • •

What looks like betrayal between women on the basis of race originates, I believe, in sexism/heterosexism. Chicanas begin to turn our backs on each other either to gain male approval or to avoid being sexually stigmatized by them under the name of puta, vendida, jota. This phenomenon is as old as the day is long, and first learned in the school yard, long before it is played out with a vengeance within political communities.

In the seventh grade, I fell in love with Manuel Poblano. A small-boned boy. Hair always perfectly combed and oiled. Uniform shirt pressed neatly over shoulder blades, jutting out. At twelve, Manuel was growing in his identity—sexually, racially—and Patsy Juárez, my one-time fifth-grade friend, wanted him too. Manuel was pals with Leticia and Connie. I remember how they flaunted a school picture of his in front of my face, proving how *they* could get one from him, although I had asked first. The two girls were conspiring to get him to "go" with Patsy, which in the end, he finally did. I, knowing all along I didn't have a chance. Not brown enough. And the wrong last name.

At puberty, it seemed identity alliances were beginning to be made along rigid and immovable lines of race, as it combined with sex. And everyone—boy, girl, anglo, and Chicano—fell into place. Where did *I* stand?

I did not move away from other Chicanos because I did not love my people. I gradually became anglocized because I thought it was the only option available to me toward gaining autonomy as a person without being sexually stigmatized. I can't say that I was conscious of all this at the time, only that at each juncture in my development, I instinctively made choices which I thought would allow me greater freedom of movement in the future. This primarily meant resisting sex roles as much as I could safely manage and this was far easier in an anglo context than in a Chicano one. That is not to say that anglo culture does not stigmatize its women for "gender-transgressions"—only that its stigmatizing did not hold the personal power over me which Chicano culture did.   *important*

Chicanas' negative perceptions of ourselves as sexual persons and our consequential betrayal of each other find their roots in a four-hundred-year-long Mexican history and mythology. They are further entrenched by a system of anglo imperialism which long ago put Mexicanos and Chicanos in a defensive posture against the dominant culture.

The sexual legacy passed down to the Mexicana/Chicana is the legacy of betrayal, pivoting around the historical/mythical female figure of Malintzin Tenepal. As translator and strategic advisor and mistress to the Spanish conqueror of México, Hernan Cortez, Malintzin is considered the mother of the mestizo people. But unlike La Virgen de Guadalupe, she is not revered as the Virgin Mother, but rather slandered as La Chingada, meaning the "fucked one," or La Vendida, sellout to the white race.[1]

Upon her shoulders rests the full blame for the "bastardization" of the indigenous people of México. To put it in its most base terms: Malintzin, also called Malinche, fucked the white man who conquered the Indian peoples of México and destroyed their culture. Ever since, brown men have been accusing her of betraying her race, and over the centuries continue to blame her entire sex for this "transgression."

As a Chicana and a feminist, I must, like other Chicanas before me, examine the effects this myth has on my/our racial/sexual identity and my relationship with other Chicanas. There is hardly a Chicana growing up today who does not suffer under her name even if she never hears directly of the one-time Aztec princess.

The Aztecs had recorded that Quetzalcoatl, the feathered serpent god, would return from the east to redeem his people in the year One Reed according to the Aztec calendar. Destiny would have it that on this very day, April 21, 1519 (as translated to the Western calendar), Cortez and his men, fitting the description of Quetzalcoatl, light-haired and bearded, landed in Vera Cruz.[2]

At the time of Cortez's arrival in México, the Aztecs had subjugated much of the rest of the Indian population, including the Mayans and Tabascans, who were much less powerful militarily. War was a necessity for the Aztecs in order to take prisoners to be used for sacrificial offerings to the warrior-god, Huitzilopochtli. As slaves and potential sacrificial victims to the Aztecs, then, these other Indian nations, after their own negotiations and sometimes bloody exchanges with the Spanish, were eager to join forces with the Spanish to overthrow the Aztec empire. The Aztecs, through their systematic subjugation of much of the Mexican Indian population, decreed their own self-destruction.[3]

Aleida Del Castillo, Chicana feminist theorist, contends that as a woman of deep spiritual commitment, Malinche aided Cortez because she understood him to be Quetzalcoatl returned in a different form to save the peoples of México from total extinction. She writes, "The destruction of the Aztec empire, the conquest of México, and as such, the termination of her indigenous world," were, in Malinche's eyes, "inevitable" in order to make way for the new spiritual age that was imminent.[4]

Del Castillo and other Chicana feminists who are researching and reinterpreting Malinche's role in the conquest of México are not trying to justify the imperialism of the Spanish. Rather, they are attempting to create a more realistic context for, and therefore a more sympathetic view of, Malinche's actions.

The root of the fear of betrayal by a woman is not at all specific to the Mexican or Chicano. The resemblance between Malinche and the Eve image is all too obvious. In chronicling the conquest of México and founding the Catholic Church there, the Spanish passed on to the mestizo people as legacy their own European-Catholic interpretation of Mexican events. Much of this early interpretation originated from Bernal del Castillo's eye-witness account of the conquest. As the primary source of much contemporary analysis as well, the picture we have of Mexican Indian civilization during that period often contains a strong Catholic and Spanish bias.

In his writings, Bernal Diaz del Castillo notes that upon the death of Malinche's father, the young Aztec princess was in line to inherit his estate. Malinche's mother wanted her son from her second marriage to inherit the wealth instead. She therefore sold her own daughter into slavery. According to Gloria Anzaldúa, there are writings in México to refute this account.[5] But it was nevertheless recorded—or commonly believed—that Malinche was betrayed by her own mother. It is this myth of the inherent unreliability of women, our natural propensity for treachery, which has been carved into the very bone of Mexican/Chicano collective psychology.

Traitor begets traitor.

Little is made of this early betrayal, whether or not it actually occurred, probably because no man was immediately affected. In a way, Malinche's mother would only have been doing her Mexican wifely duty: *putting the male first.*

There is none so beautiful as the Latino male. I have never met any kind of Latino who, although he may have claimed his family was very woman-dominated ("mi mamá made all the real decisions"), did not subscribe to the basic belief that men are better. It is so ordinary a statement as to sound simplistic and I am nearly embarrassed to write it, but that's the truth in its kernel.

Ask, for example, any Chicana mother about her children and she is quick to tell you she loves them all the same, but she doesn't. *The boys are different.* Sometimes I sense that she feels this way because she wants to believe that through her mothering, she can develop the kind of man she would have liked to have married, or even have been. That through her son she can get a small taste of male privilege, since without race or class privilege that's all there is to be had. The daughter can never offer the mother such hope, straddled by the same forces that confine the mother. As a result, the daughter must constantly earn the mother's love, prove her fidelity to her. The son—he gets her love for free.

After ten years of feminist consciousness and activism, why does this seem so significant to me—to write of the Mexican mother favoring the son? I think because I had never quite gone back to the source. Never said in my own tongue, *the boys, they are men, they can do what they want . . . after all, he's a man.*

Journal Entry: April 1980

Three days ago, my mother called me long distance full of tears, loving me, wanting me back in her life after such a long period of separation. My mother's tears succeed in getting me to break down the edge in my voice, the protective distance. My mother's pleading "mi'jita, I love you, I hate to feel so far away from you," succeeds in opening my heart again to her.

I don't remember exactly why my heart had been shut, only that it had been very necessary to keep my distance, that in a way we had agreed to that. But, it only took her crying to pry my heart open again.

I feel myself unriveting. The feelings begin to flood my chest. Yes, this is why I love women. This woman is my mother. There is no love as strong as this, refusing my separation, never settling for a secret that would split us off, always at the last minute, like now, pushing me to the brink of revelation, speaking the truth.

I am as big as a mountain! I want to say, "Watch out, Mamá! I love you and I am as big as a mountain!" And it is on the brink of this precipice where I feel my body descending into the places where we have not spoken, the times I did not fight back. I am descending, ready to speak the truth, finally.

And then suddenly, over the phone, I hear another ring. My mother tells me to wait. There is a call on my father's work phone. Moments later, "It is your brother," she says. My knees lock under me, bracing myself for the fall . . . Her voice lightens up. "Okay, mi'jita. I love you. I'll talk to you later," cutting off the line in the middle of the connection.

I am relieved when I hang up that I did not have the chance to say more. The graceful reminder. This man doesn't have to earn her love. My brother has always come first.

Seduction and betrayal. Since I've grown up, no woman cares for me for free. There is always a price. My love.

What I wanted from my mother was impossible. It would have meant her going against Mexican/Chicano tradition in a very fundamental way. You are a traitor to your race if you do not put the man first. The potential accusation of "traitor" or "vendida" is what hangs above the heads and beats in the hearts of most Chicanas seeking to develop our own autonomous sense of ourselves, particularly through sexuality.

• • •

Because heterosexism—the Chicana's sexual commitment to the Chicano male—is proof of her fidelity to her people, the Chicana feminist attempting to critique the sexism in the Chicano community is certainly between a personal rock and a political hard place.

Although not called "the sexism debate," as it has been in the literary sectors of the Black movement, the Chicano discussion of sexism within our community has like that movement been largely limited to heterosexual assumption: "How can we get our men right?" The feminist-oriented material which appeared in the late 70s and early 80s for the most part strains in its attempt to stay safely within the boundaries of Chicano—male-defined and often anti-feminist—values.

Over and over again, Chicanas trivialize the women's movement as being merely a white middle-class thing, having little to offer women of color. They cite only the most superficial aspects of the movement. For example, in "From a Woman to a Woman," Silvia S. Lizarraga writes:

> class distinction is a major determinant of attitudes toward other subordinated groups. In the U.S. we see this phenomenon operating in the goals expressed in the Women's Liberation Movement. . . . The needs represent a large span of interests—from those of *capitalist women,* women in business and professional careers, to *witches* and *lesbians.* However, the needs of the unemployed and working class women of different ethnic minorities are generally overlooked by this movement.[6] (my emphasis)

This statement typifies the kind of one-sided perspective many Chicanas have given of the women's movement in the name of Chicana liberation. My question is *who* are they trying to serve? Certainly not the Chicana who is deprived of some very critical information about a ten-year grassroots feminist movement where women of color, including lesbians of color (certainly in the minority and most assuredly encountering "feminist" racism), have been actively involved in reproductive rights, especially sterilization abuse, battered women's shelters, rape crisis centers, welfare advocacy, Third World women's conferences, cultural events, health and self-help clinics and more.

Interestingly, it is perfectly acceptable among Chicano males to use white theoreticians, e.g. Marx and Engels, to develop a theory of Chicano oppression. It is unacceptable, however, for the Chicana to use white sources by women to develop a theory of Chicana oppression. Even if one subscribes to a solely economic theory of oppression, how can she ignore that over half of the world's workers are females who suffer discrimination not only in the workplace, but also at home and in all the areas of sex-related abuse I just cited? How can she afford not to recognize that the wars against imperialism occurring both domestically and internationally are always accompanied by the rape of women of color by both white and Third World men? Without a feminist analysis what name do we put to these facts? Are these not deterrents to the Chicana developing a sense of "species being"? Are these "women's issues" not also "people's issues"? It is far easier for the Chicana to criticize white women who on the face of things could never be *familia* than to take issue with or complain, as it were, to a brother, uncle, father.

The most valuable aspect of Chicana theory thus far has been its reevaluation of our history from a woman's perspective through unearthing the stories of Mexican/Chicana female figures that early on exhibited a feminist sensibility. The weakness of these works is that much of it is undermined by what I call the "alongside-our-man-knee-jerk-phenomenon." In speaking of Maria Hernández, Alfredo Mirandé and Evangelina Enríquez offer a typical disclaimer in *La Chicana:*

Although a feminist and leader in her own right, she is always quick to
point to the importance of the family unity in the movement and to acknowledge the help of her husband . . . [7]

And yet we would think nothing of the Chicano activist never mentioning the many "behind-the-scenes" Chicanas who helped him!

In the same text, the authors fall into the too-common trap of coddling
the Chicano male ego (which should be, in and of itself, an insult to Chicano men) in the name of cultural loyalty. Like the Black Superwoman,
the Chicana is forced to take on extra-human proportions. She must keep
the cultural home-fires burning while going out and making a living.
She must fight racism alongside her man, but challenge sexism single-
handedly, all the while retaining her "femininity" so as not to offend or
threaten *her man*. This is what being a Chicana feminist means.

In recent years, however, truly feminist Chicanas are beginning to
make the pages of Chicano, feminist, and literary publications. This, of
course, is only a reflection of a fast-growing Chicana/Third World feminist movement. I am in debt to the research and writings of Norma Alarcón, Martha Cotera, Gloria Anzaldúa, and Aleida Del Castillo, to name a
few. Their work reflects a relentless commitment to putting the female
first, even when it means criticizing el hombre.[8]

To be critical of one's culture is not to betray that culture. We tend to be
very righteous in our criticism and indictment of the dominant culture
and we so often suffer from the delusion that, since Chicanos are so ma-
ligned from the outside, there is little room to criticize those aspects from
within our oppressed culture which oppress us.

I am not particularly interested in whether or not Third World people
learned sexism from the white man. There have been great cases made to
prove how happy men and women were together before the white man
made tracks in indigenous soil. This reflects the same mentality of white
feminists who claim that all races were in harmony when the "Great
Mother" ruled us all. In both cases, history tends to prove different. In either case, the strategy for the elimination of racism and sexism cannot occur through the exclusion of one problem or the other. As the Combahee
River Collective, a Black feminist organization, states, women of color experience these oppressions "simultaneously."[9] The only people who can
afford not to recognize this are those who do not suffer this multiple oppression.

I remain amazed at how often so-called "Tercermundistas" in the U.S.
work to annihilate the concept and existence of white supremacy, but
turn their faces away from male supremacy. Perhaps this is because when
you start to talk about sexism, the world becomes increasingly complex.
The power no longer breaks down into neat little hierarchical categories,

Very powerful statement

but becomes a series of starts and detours. Since the categories are not easy to arrive at, the enemy is not easy to name. It is all so difficult to unravel. It *is* true that some men hate women even in their desire for them. And some men oppress the very women they love. But unlike the racist, they allow the object of their contempt to share the table with them. The hatred they feel for women does not translate into separatism. It is more insidiously intra-cultural, like class antagonism, but different, because it lives and breathes in the flesh and blood of our families, even in the name of love.

In Toni Cade Bambara's novel, *The Salt Eaters,* the curandera asks the question, *Can you afford to be whole?*[10] This line represents the question that has burned within me for years and years through my growing politicization. *What would a movement bent on the freedom of women of color look like?* In other words, what are the implications of not only looking outside of our culture, but into our culture and ourselves and from that place beginning to develop a strategy for a movement that could challenge the bedrock of oppressive systems of belief globally?

The one aspect of our identity which has been uniformly ignored by every existing political movement in this country is sexuality, both as a source of oppression and a means of liberation. Although other movements have dealt with this issue, sexual oppression and desire have never been considered specifically in relation to the lives of women of color. Sexuality, race, and sex have usually been presented in contradiction to each other, rather than as part and parcel of a complex web of personal and political identity and oppression.

·   ·   ·

Unlike most white people, with the exception of the Jews, Third World people have suffered the threat of genocide to our races since the coming of the first European expansionists. The family, then, becomes all the more ardently protected by oppressed peoples, and the sanctity of this institution is infused like blood into the veins of the Chicano. At all costs, la familia must be preserved: for when they kill our boys in their own imperialist wars to gain greater profits for American corporations; when they keep us in ghettos, reservations, and barrios which ensure that our own people will be the recipients of our frustrated acts of violence; when they sterilize our women without our consent because we are unable to read the document we sign; when they prevent our families from getting decent housing, adequate child care, sufficient fuel, regular medical care; then we have reason to believe—although they may no longer technically be lynching us in Texas or our sisters and brothers in Georgia, Alabama, Mississippi—they intend to see us dead.

So we fight back, we think, with our families—with our women pregnant, and our men, the indisputable heads. We believe the more severely we protect the sex roles within the family, the stronger we will be as a unit in opposition to the anglo threat. And yet, our refusal to examine *all* the roots of the lovelessness in our families is our weakest link and softest spot.

Our resistance as a people to looking at the relationships within our families—between husband and wife, lovers, sister and brother, father, son, and daughter, etc.—leads me to believe that the Chicano male does not hold fast to the family unit merely to safeguard it from the death-dealings of the anglo. Living under Capitalist Patriarchy, what is true for "the man" in terms of misogyny is, to a great extent, true for the Chicano. He, too, like any other man, wants to be able to determine how, when, and with whom his women—mother, wife, and daughter—are sexual. For without male imposed social and legal control of our reproductive function, reinforced by the Catholic Church, and the social institutionalization of our roles as sexual and domestic servants to men, Chicanas might very freely "choose" to do otherwise, including being sexually independent *from* and/or *with* men. In fact, the forced "choice" of the gender of our sexual/love partner seems to precede the forced "choice" of the form (marriage and family) that partnership might take. The control of women begins through the institution of heterosexuality.

Homosexuality does not, in and of itself, pose a great threat to society. Male homosexuality has always been a "tolerated" aspect of Mexican/Chicano society, as long as it remains "fringe." A case can even be made that male homosexuality stems from our indigenous Aztec roots.[11] But lesbianism, in any form, and male homosexuality which openly avows both the sexual and emotional elements of the bond, challenges the very foundation of la familia. The "faggot" is the object of the Chicano/Mexicano's contempt because he is consciously choosing a role his culture tells him to despise. That of a woman.

The question remains. Is the foundation as it stands now sturdy enough to meet the face of the oppressor? I think not. There is a deeper love between and amongst our people that lies buried between the lines of the roles we play with each other. It is the earth beneath the floor boards of our homes. We must split wood, dig bare-fisted into the packed ground to find out what we really have to hold in our hands as muscle.

Family is *not* by definition the man in a dominant position over women and children. Familia is cross-generational bonding, deep emotional ties between opposite sexes, and within our sex. It is sexuality, which involves, but is not limited to, intercourse or orgasm. It springs forth from touch, constant and daily. The ritual of kissing and the sign of the cross with every coming and going from the home. It is finding familia among friends where blood ties are formed through suffering and celebration shared.

The strength of our families never came from domination. It has only endured in spite of it—like our women.

•   •   •

Chicanos' refusal to look at our weaknesses as a people and a movement is, in the most profound sense, an act of self-betrayal. The Chicana lesbian bears the brunt of this betrayal, for it is she, the most visible manifestation of a woman taking control of her own sexual identity and destiny, who so severely challenges the anti-feminist Chicano/a. What other reason is there than that for the virtual dead silence among Chicanos about lesbianism? When the subject is raised, the word is used pejoratively.

For example, Sonia A. López writes about the anti-feminism in El Movimiento of the late 1960s.

> The Chicanas who voiced their discontent with the organizations and with male leadership were often labeled "women's libbers," and "lesbians." This served to isolate and discredit them, a method practiced both covertly and overtly.[12]

This statement appears without qualification. López makes no value judgment on the inherent homophobia in such a divisive tactic. Without comment, her statement reinforces the idea that lesbianism is not only a white thing, but an insult to be avoided at all costs.

Such attempts by Chicana feminists to bend over backwards to prove criticism of their people is love (which, in fact, it is) severely undermines the potential radicalism of the ideology they are trying to create. Not quite believing in their love, suspecting their own anger, and fearing ostracism from Chicano males (being symbolically "kicked out of bed" with the bait of "lesbian" hanging over their work), the Chicana's imagination often stops before it has a chance to consider some of the most difficult, and therefore, some of the most important, questions.

It is no wonder that the Chicanas I know who *are* asking "taboo" questions are often forced into outsiderhood long before they began to question el carnal in print. Maybe like me they now feel they have little to lose.

It is important to say that fearing recriminations from my father never functioned for me as an obstacle in my political work. Had I been born of a Chicano father, I sometimes think I never would have been able to write a line or participate in a demonstration, having to repress all questioning in order that the ultimate question of my sexuality would never emerge. Possibly, even some of the compañeras whose fathers died or left in their early years would never have had the courage to speak out as Third World lesbians the way they do now, had their fathers been a living part of their daily lives. The Chicana lesbians I know whose fathers are very much a part of their lives are seldom "out" to their families.

During the late 60s and early 70s, I was not an active part of la causa. I never managed to get myself to walk in the marches in East Los Angeles (I merely watched from the sidelines); I never went to one meeting of MECHA on campus. No soy tonta. I would have been murdered in El Movimiento—light-skinned, unable to speak Spanish well enough to hang; miserably attracted to women and fighting it; and constantly questioning all authority, including men's. I felt I did not belong there. Maybe I had really come to believe that "Chicanos" were "different," not "like us," as my mother would say. But I fully knew that there was a part of me that was a part of that movement, but it seemed that part would have to go unexpressed until the time I could be a Chicano and the woman I had to be, too.

The woman who defies her role as subservient to her husband, father, brother, or son by taking control of her own sexual destiny is purported to be a "traitor to her race" by contributing to the "genocide" of her people—whether or not she has children. In short, even if the defiant woman is *not* a lesbian, she is purported to be one; for, like the lesbian in the Chicano imagination, she is una *Malinchista*. Like the Malinche of Mexican history, she is corrupted by foreign influences which threaten to destroy her people. Norma Alarcón elaborates on this theme of sex as a determinant of loyalty when she states:

> The myth of Malinche contains the following sexual possibilities: woman is sexually passive, and hence at all times open to potential use by men whether it be seduction or rape. The possible use is double-edged: that is, the use of her as pawn may be intracultural—"amongst us guys"—or intercultural, which means if we are not using her then "they" must be using her. Since woman is highly pawnable, nothing she does is perceived as choice.[13]

Lesbianism can be construed by the race then as the Chicana being used by the white man, even if the man never lays a hand on her. *The choice is never seen as her own.* Homosexuality is *his* disease with which he sinisterly infects Third World people, men and women alike. (Because Malinche is female, Chicano gay men rebelling against their prescribed sex roles, although still considered diseased, do not suffer the same stigma of traitor.) Further, the Chicana lesbian who has relationships with white women may feel especially susceptible to such accusations, since the white lesbian is seen as the white man's agent. The fact that the white woman may be challenging the authority of her white father, and thereby could be looked upon as a potential ally, has no bearing on a case closed before it was ever opened.

Her . . . Story

The line of reasoning goes:

Malinche sold out her indio people by acting as courtesan and translator for Cortez, whose offspring symbolically represent the birth of the bastardized mestizo/Mexicano people. My mother then is the modern-day Chicana, Malinche marrying a white man, my father, to produce the bastards my sister, my brother, and I are. Finally, I—a half-breed Chicana—further betray my race by *choosing* my sexuality which excludes all men, and therefore most dangerously, Chicano men.

I come from a long line of Vendidas.

I am a Chicana lesbian. My own particular relationship to being a sexual person; and a radical stand in direct contradiction to, and in violation of, the woman I was raised to be.

• • •

Coming from such a complex and contradictory history of sexual exploitation by white men and from within our own race, it is nearly earthshaking to begin to try and separate the myths told about us from the truths; and to examine to what extent we have internalized what, in fact, is not true.

Although intellectually I knew different, early on I learned that women were the willing cooperators in rape. So over and over again in pictures, books, movies, I experienced rape and pseudo-rape as titillating, sexy, as what sex was all about. Women want it. Real rape was dark, greasy-looking bad men jumping out of alleys and attacking innocent blonde women. Everything short of that was just sex; the way it is: dirty and duty. We spread our legs and bear the brunt of penetration, but we do spread our legs. In my mind, inocencia meant dying rather than being fucked.

I learned these notions about sexuality not only from the society at large, but more specifically and potently from Chicano/Mexicano culture, originating from the myth of La Chingada, Malinche. In the very act of intercourse with Cortez, Malinche is seen as having been violated. She is not, however, an innocent victim, but the guilty party—ultimately responsible for her own sexual victimization. Slavery and slander is the price she must pay for the pleasure our culture imagined she enjoyed. In *The Labyrinth of Solitude,* Octavio Paz gives an explanation of the term "chingar," which provides valuable insights into how Malinche, as symbolized by La Chingada, is perceived. He writes:

> The idea of breaking, of ripping open. When alluding to a sexual act, violation or deception gives it a particular shading. The man who commits it never does so with the consent of the chingada.
> Chingar then is to do violence to another, i.e., rape. The verb is masculine, active, cruel: it stings, wounds, gashes, stains. And it provokes a bitter, resentful satisfaction. The person who suffers this action is passive, inert, and open, in contrast to the active, aggressive, and closed person who inflicts it. The chingón is the macho, the male; he rips open the chingada, the female, who is pure passivity, defenseless against the exterior world.[14]

If the simple act of sex then—the penetration itself—implies the female's filthiness, non-humanness, it is no wonder Chicanas often divorce ourselves from the conscious recognition of our own sexuality. Even if we enjoy having sex, draw pleasure from feeling fingers, tongue, penis inside us, there is a part of us that must disappear in the act, separate ourselves from realizing what it is we are actually doing. Sit, as it were, on the corner bedpost, watching the degradation and violence some "other" woman is willing to subject herself to, not us. And if we have lesbian feelings—want not only to be penetrated, but to penetrate—what perverse kind of monstrosities we must indeed be! It is through our spirits that we escape the painful recognition of our "base" sexual selves.

●   ●   ●

What the white women's movement tried to convince me of is that lesbian sexuality was *naturally* different than heterosexual sexuality. That the desire to penetrate and be penetrated, to fill and be filled, would vanish. That retaining such desires was "reactionary," not "politically correct," "male-identified." And somehow reaching sexual ecstasy with a woman lover would never involve any kind of power struggle. Women were different. We could simply magically "transcend" these "old notions," just by seeking spiritual transcendence in bed.

The fact of the matter was that all these power struggles of "having" and "being had" were being played out in my own bedroom. And in my psyche, they held a particular Mexican twist. White women's feminism did little to answer my questions. As a Chicana feminist my concerns were different. As I wrote in 1982:

> What I need to explore will not be found in the feminist lesbian bedroom, but more likely in the mostly heterosexual bedrooms of South Texas, L.A., or

even Sonora, México. Further, I have come to realize that the boundaries white feminists confine themselves to in describing sexuality are based in white-rooted interpretations of dominance, submission, power-exchange, etc. Although they are certainly *part* of the psychosexual lives of women of color, these boundaries would have to be expanded and translated to fit my people, in particular, the women in my family. And I am tired, always, of these acts of translation.[15]

Mirtha Quintanales corroborates this position and exposes the necessity for a Third World feminist dialogue on sexuality when she states:

The critical issue for me regarding the politics of sexuality is that as a Latina Lesbian living in the U.S., I do not really have much of an opportunity to examine what constitutes sexual conformity and sexual defiance in my own culture, in my own ethnic community, and how that may affect my own values, attitudes, sexual life *and* politics. There is virtually no dialogue on the subject anywhere and I, like other Latinas and Third World women, especially Lesbians, am quite in the dark about what we're up against besides negative feminist sexual politics.[16]

During the late 70s, the concept of "women's culture" among white lesbians and "cultural feminists" was in full swing; it is still very popular today. "Womon's history," "wommin's music," "womyn's spirituality," "wymyn's language," abounded—all with the "white" modifier implied and unstated. In truth, there was/is a huge amount of denial going on in the name of female separatism. Women do not usually grow up in women-only environments. Culture is sexually mixed. As Bernice Reagon puts it:

. . . we have been organized to have our primary cultural signals come from factors other than that we are women. We are not from our base, acculturated to be women people, capable of crossing our first people boundaries: Black, White, Indian, etc.[17]

Unlike Reagon, I believe that there are certain ways we *have* been acculturated to be "women people," and there is therefore such a thing as "women's culture." This occurs, however, as Reagon points out, within a context formed by race, class, geography, religion, ethnicity, and language.

I don't mean to imply that women need to have men around to feel at home in our culture, but that the way one understands culture is influenced by men. The fact that some aspects of that culture are indeed oppressive does not imply, as a solution, throwing out the entire business of racial/ethnic culture. To do so would mean risking the loss of some very essential aspects of identity, especially for Third World women.

. . .

In failing to approach feminism from any kind of materialist base, failing to take race, ethnicity, class into account in determining where women are at sexually, many feminists have created an analysis of sexual oppression (often confused with sexuality itself) which is a political dead-end. "Radical Feminism," the ideology which sees men's oppression of women as the root of and paradigm for all other oppressions, allows women to view ourselves as a class and to claim our sexual identity as the *source* of our oppression and men's sexual identity as the *source* of the world's evil. But this ideology can never then fully integrate the concept of the "simultaneity of oppression" as Third World feminism is attempting to do. For, if race and class suffer the woman of color as much as her sexual identity, then the Radical Feminist must extend her own "identity" politics to include her "identity" as oppressor as well. (To say nothing of having to acknowledge the fact that there are men who may suffer more than she.) This is something that, for the most part, Radical Feminism as a movement has refused to do.

Radical Feminist theorists have failed to acknowledge how their position in the dominant culture—white, middle-class, often Christian—has influenced every approach they have taken to implement feminist political change—to "give women back their bodies." It follows then that the anti-pornography movement is the largest organized branch of Radical Feminism. For unlike battered women's, anti-rape, and reproductive rights workers, the anti-porn "activist" never has to deal with any live woman outside of her own race and class. The tactics of the anti-pornography movement are largely symbolic and theoretical in nature. And, on paper, the needs of the woman of color are a lot easier to represent than in the flesh. Therefore, her single-issued approach to feminism remains intact.

It is not that pornography is not a concern to many women of color. But the anti-materialist approach of this movement makes little sense in the lives of poor and Third World women. Plainly put, it is our sisters working in the sex industry.

Many women involved in the anti-porn movement are lesbian separatists. Because the Radical Feminist critique is there to justify it, lesbianism can be viewed as the logical personal response to a misogynist political system. Through this perspective, lesbianism has become an "idea"—a political response to male sexual aggression, rather than a sexual response to a woman's desire for another woman. In this way, many

[margin, handwritten: Failing to consider all aspects]

ostensibly heterosexual women who are not active sexually can call themselves lesbians. Lesbians "from the neck up." This faction of the movement has grown into a kind of cult. They have taken whiteness, class privilege, and an anglo-american brand of "return-to-the-mother" which leaps back over a millennium of patriarchal domination, attempted to throw out the man, and call what is left female. While still retaining their own racial and class-biased cultural superiority.

The lesbian separatist retreats from the specific cultural contexts that have shaped her and attempts to build a cultural-political movement based on an imagined oppression-free past. It is understandable that many feminists opt for this kind of asexual separatist/spiritualist solution rather than boldly grappling with the challenge of wresting sexual autonomy from such a sexually exploitative system. Every oppressed group needs to imagine through the help of history and mythology a world where our oppression did not seem the pre-ordained order. Aztlán for Chicanos is another example. The mistake lies in believing in this ideal past or imagined future so thoroughly and single-mindedly that finding solutions to present-day inequities loses priority, or we attempt to create too-easy solutions for the pain we feel today.

As culture—our race, class, ethnicity, etc.—influences our sexuality, so too does heterosexism, marriage, and men as the primary agents of those institutions. We can work to tumble those institutions so that when the rubble is finally cleared away we can see what we have left to build on sexually. But we can't ask a woman to forget everything she understands about sex in a heterosexual and culturally specific context or tell her what she is allowed to think about it. Should she forget and not use what she knows sexually to untie the knot of her own desire, she may lose any chance of ever discovering her own sexual potential.

• • •

Among Chicanas, it is our tradition to conceive of the bond between mother and daughter as paramount and essential in our lives. It is the daughters that can be relied upon. Las hijas who remain faithful a la madre, a la madre de la madre.

When we name this bond between the women of our race, from this Chicana feminism emerges. For too many years, we have acted as if we held a secret pact with one another never to acknowledge directly our commitment to one another. Never to admit the fact that we count on one another *first*. We were never to recognize this in the face of el hombre. But this is what being a Chicana feminist means—making bold and political the love of the women of our race.

•   •   •

A political commitment to women does not equate with lesbianism. As a Chicana lesbian, I write of the connection my own feminism has had with my sexual desire for women. This is my story. I can tell no other one than the one I understand. I eagerly await the writings by heterosexual Chicana feminists that can speak of their sexual desire for men and the ways in which their feminism informs that desire. What is true, however, is that a political commitment to women must involve, by definition, a political commitment to lesbians as well. To refuse to allow the Chicana lesbian the right to the free expression of her own sexuality, and her politicization of it, is in the deepest sense to deny one's self the right to the same. I guarantee you, there will be no change among heterosexual men, there will be no change in heterosexual relations, as long as the Chicano community keeps us lesbians and gay men political prisoners among our own people. Any movement built on the fear and loathing of anyone is a failed movement. The Chicano movement is no different.

Notes

1. Norma Alarcón examines this theme in her article "Chicana's Feminist Literature: A Re-Vision Through Malintzin/or Malintzin: Putting Flesh Back on the Object," in *This Bridge Called My Back: Writings by Radical Women of Color,* ed. Cherríe Moraga and Gloria Anzaldúa (Watertown, Mass.: Persephone Press, 1981).

2. Aleida R. Del Castillo, "Malintzin Tenepal: A Preliminary Look into a New Perspective," in *Essays on La Mujer,* ed. Rosaura Sánchez and Rosa Martínez Cruz (University of California at Los Angeles: Chicano Studies Center Publications, 1977), p. 133.

3. Ibid., p. 131.

4. Ibid., p. 141.

5. Gloria Anzaldúa, unpublished work in progress. Write: The Third World Women's Archives, Box 159, Bush Terminal Station, Brooklyn, NY 11232.

6. Silvia S. Lizarraga, "From a Woman to a Woman," in *Essays on La Mujer,* p. 91.

7. Alfredo Mirandé and Evangelina Enríquez, *La Chicana; The Mexican-American Woman* (Chicago: University of Chicago Press, 1979), p. 225.

8. Some future writings by Latina feminists include: Gloria Anzaldúa's *La Serpiente Que Se Come Su Cola: The Autobiography of a Chicana Lesbian* (Write: The Third World Women's Archives, see address above); *Cuentos: Stories by Latinas,* ed. Alma Gómez, Cherríe Moraga, and Mariana Romo-Carmona (Kitchen Table: Women of Color Press, Box 2753 Rockefeller Center Station, New York, NY 10185, 1983); and *Compañeras: Antologia Lesbiana Latina,* ed. Juanita Ramos and Mirtha Quintanales (Write: The Third World Women's Archives, see address above).

9. The Combahee River Collective, "A Black Feminist Statement," in *But Some of Us Are Brave: Black Women's Studies,* ed. Gloria T. Hull, Patricia Bell Scott, and Barbara Smith (Old Westbury, N.Y.: The Feminist Press, 1982), p. 16.

10. Toni Cade Bambara, *The Salt Eaters* (New York: Random House, 1980), pp. 3 and 10.

11. Bernal Díaz del Castillo, *The Bernal Diaz Chronicles,* trans. and ed. Albert Idell (New York: Doubleday, 1956), pp. 86–87.

12. Sonia A. López, in *Essays on La Mujer,* p. 26.

13. Norma Alarcón, in *This Bridge Called My Back,* p. 184.

14. Octavio Paz, *The Labyrinth of Solitude: Life and Thought in Mexico* (N.Y.: Grove Press, 1961), p. 77.

15. Cherríe Moraga, "Played Between White Hands," in *Off Our Backs,* July 1982, Washington, D.C.

16. Mirtha Quintanales with Barbara Kerr, "The Complexity of Desire: Conversations on Sexuality and Difference," in *Conditions: Eight,* Box 56 Van Brunt Station, Brooklyn, N.Y., p. 60.

17. Bernice Reagon, "Turning the Century Around" in *Home Girls: A Black Feminist Anthology,* ed. Barbara Smith (Brooklyn, N.Y.: Kitchen Table: Women of Color Press, 1983).

4 Anti-Anti-Identity Politics

Feminism, Democracy, and the Complexities of Citizenship

SUSAN BICKFORD

In this essay, I argue that recent leftist criticisms of "identity politics" do not address problems of inequality and interaction that are central in thinking about contemporary democratic politics. I turn instead to a set of feminist thinkers who share these critics' vision of politics, but who critically mobilize identity in a way that provides a conception of democratic citizenship for our inegalitarian and diverse polity.

• • •

Radical democratic political action attempts to perform the paradoxical task of achieving egalitarian goals in egalitarian ways in an inegalitarian context. The danger is that bracketing social and economic inequality "as though" we were all equal risks reproducing inequity under the guise of neutrality, yet taking those inequalities into account in some systematic way risks reentrenching them.[1] In this essay, I will argue that this central challenge of contemporary democratic theory and practice requires an expansive conception of the languages of citizenship. Specifically, I contend that the language of "identity" need not be regarded as inimical to democratic politics, as it is by many contemporary critics of identity politics. My ungainly title, then, is meant to invoke Clifford Geertz's article "Anti-Anti-Relativism," because I have much the same purpose with respect to identity politics that he had with respect to relativism. That is, my purpose is not to defend something called "identity politics"—nor to dismiss it. I aim instead to contest the particular versions of identity politics that some critics construct and the consequent dangers they envision.

"Identity" itself is obviously a term thick with meanings. It can indicate my sense of self, who I think I am; this is often bound up with group membership, those people with whom I identify or am identified. There is, further, the linguistic or conceptual sense of identity as a category that designates the "self-same entity," defined by unity, fixity, and the expulsion of difference (Young 1990, 98–99). The diverse meanings of identity are pursued in a variety of academic discourses, from the most abstract philosophical investigations of "the identities of persons" to the most richly empirical developmental psychological work on the formation of identity.

There are also a variety of meanings of "identity politics" circulating, although it is striking that in most commentaries (including some of those discussed here) the precise meaning is left implicit. Among other uses, "identity politics" can refer to articulating a claim in the name of a particular group; being concerned with cultural specificity, particularly in an ethnic-nationalist sense; acting as though group membership necessitates a certain political stance; focusing to an excessive degree on the psychological; and various combinations of these.

Thus identity politics has become, as Geertz said about relativism, "the anti-hero with a thousand faces" (Geertz 1984, 273). Appropriately, then, its opponents also take a variety of forms. Although much public discourse has centered on the disagreements between those who take group identity seriously and their conservative critics, recently a chorus of voices from the left has stressed the dangers of identity politics. In this essay, I address these leftist arguments, which have been made from a variety of theoretical perspectives (feminist, communitarian, poststructuralist, democratic, old New Left) and in a variety of venues (books from academic as well as popular presses, journals from *Dissent* and *Tikkun* to *Political Theory*). I use the designation "left" broadly to indicate that these criticisms stem from a concern with the prospects of democratic politics; these writers share with those they criticize a commitment to transfiguring an oppressive and inegalitarian social order. Let me also stress that these leftist writers differ profoundly from one another in terms of their overall intellectual and political projects, as well as in the terms of their critique of identity politics.

What is noteworthy, however, is that criticisms of identity politics play a role in so many different contemporary "leftish" enterprises. I discern three primary themes in leftist critiques, three interrelated dangers allegedly embedded in identity politics that hamper political action oriented toward radical social change. The first danger has to do with subjectivity, with the kind of self that identity politics produces. The second has to do with community, or the kind of collectivity that identity politics precludes. And finally, these constructions of self and community are regarded as dangerous because they encourage and prevent certain kinds of political action.

It is precisely the interaction of these two phenomena—self and community, subjectivity and intersubjectivity—that is the focus of some feminist rethinking of politics and identity. As a counter to the leftist critiques I will discuss, I want to offer a reading of feminist theorists of inequality and identity whose work has been influential in feminist contexts both academic and nonacademic. These writers, I will argue, help us think through the complex relations between identity and politics in an inegalitarian and diverse polity; they suggest a different understanding of the political and rhetorical uses of identity.[2] By examining the works of these writers, I hope to counter the political and theoretical moves made by leftist critics who "read" identity claims in a particular way. But I also intend to address their concerns by showing how feminist writers have begun to construct a conception of citizenship and identity that is adequate to this social and political context and to the aims of emancipation.

My goal, again, is not to defend some activity or orientation called identity politics. Rather, my intent is to show that feminist work on reconceptualizing the link between identity and politics is central to thinking about democratic citizenship. My concern is that the value of this work gets obscured or blocked out in a public discourse characterized by the increasingly common invocation of identity politics as an all-purpose anti-hero. That practice of dismissal sets up a frame in which linking identity with politics is automatically suspect, regardless of how we characterize that link. So my argument against that phenomenon—against anti-identity politics—proceeds by analyzing the politically and theoretically vital way that some feminist writers have conceptualized the connection.

First, however, we need to sort through the significance of the claims that leftist critics are making against something they call identity politics.

The Failings of "Identity Politics": Ressentiment, Balkanization, and Regulation

Identity politics, some critics argue, creates and perpetuates an understanding of public identity composed in terms of the suffering self: the oppressed are innocent selves defined by the wrongs done them. The concept of "ressentiment" is often used in making this argument, to indicate a corrosive resentfulness on the part of those political actors motivated by or engaging in "identity politics."[3] Ressentiment prompts a focus on victimhood and powerlessness, and an obsessive demand for recognition (Brown 1995, Elshtain 1995, Tapper 1993; see also Patai and Koertge 1994, Patai 1992, Gitlin 1993). The political pursuits of this suffering self are directed toward securing rights from a strong State "protector" (Brown 1995; Wolin 1993).

Consider an example from the work of Wendy Brown, who has provided the fullest and most complex version of these arguments by analyzing the historical, cultural, and political-economic conditions in which contemporary identity politics has emerged. Brown cites as indicative of identity politics a Santa Cruz, California, city ordinance forbidding discrimination on a variety of grounds ranging from race to weight to personal appearance. She argues that attempts to establish such a wide variety of components as relevant to *public* identity end up reinforcing the disciplinary, normalizing power of the regulatory apparatus of the state. When such definitions of identity become part of "liberal administrative discourse," it ensures that "persons describable according to them will now become regulated through them" (1995, 65–66).

Why would political actors pursue social change in such a counterproductive, self-destructive (or self-disciplinary) way? Brown locates the answer in "the complex logics of *ressentiment*"—ressentiment inherent in liberal culture, but amplified considerably by contemporary political, economic, and cultural conditions (1995, 66–69). These conditions produce or provoke identity politics—or, in her words, "politicized identity"—which is rooted in an "acquisition of recognition through its history of subjection (a recognition predicated on injury, now righteously revalued)." The coherence of the group identity itself, according to Brown, rests on its marginalization. In other words, politicized identity has an ontological investment in its own subjection—its very existence is constituted by its oppression—thus it must continually concentrate on its own wounds of marginalization, exclusion, subjugation (Brown 1995, 70–74; see also Patai and Koertge 1994, chap. 3). The logic of ressentiment (the "moralizing revenge of the powerless") is such that politicized identity has to maintain and reiterate its suffering publicly, in order to maintain its existence.

> Politicized identity thus enunciates itself, makes claims for itself, only by entrenching, restating, dramatizing, and inscribing its pain in politics; it can hold out no future—for itself or others—that triumphs over this pain. (Brown 1995, 74)

The very gestures made to combat this pain compulsively reopen or reinfect the wound (Brown 1995, 73). Brown's analysis almost irresistibly conjures up an image of identity politics as a kind of obsessive scratching at scabs; "politicized identity" is politically neurotic.

Other political projects have been identified as neurotic in this way, and as having the same sort of political results. Marion Tapper argues that some feminist-inspired practices in academic institutions employ, perhaps unwittingly, modern forms of disciplinary power. She cites, for example, the establishment of policies that course content and teaching materials be nonsexist, that women be included in candidate pools and on selection committees, that research activities incorporate gender issues (Tapper 1993, 136–38). To address injustices in academic institutions in this way, Tapper argues, is to end up creating within universities "docile" subjects amenable to a variety of forms of surveillance of their teaching and research. The impulse toward "intellectual authoritarianism" that underlies these politics springs from ressentiment, which is "both a backward-looking spirit—it needs to keep on remembering past injustices—and an expansive spirit—it needs to find new injustices everywhere." As both Tapper and Brown note, this spirit is particularly invested not just in its own pain, but in its purity and powerlessness. Ressentiment involves "the need to see the other as powerful and responsible for my powerlessness, and then the transformation of this thought into the thought that my powerlessness is a proof of my goodness and the other's evil" (Tapper 1993, 134–35; see also Brown 1995, chap. 2).

The implications of ressentiment for politics, then, are twofold. It is not just that bureaucratic, regulatory practices are enhanced and expanded through the pursuit of this kind of "strikingly unemancipatory political project" (Brown 1995, 66).[4] The further problem is that the assumption of morally pure and powerless victims eliminates the possibilities for democratic disagreement. Rather than articulating political claims in contestable ways, victims wield "moral reproach" against power. The myth of moral truth serves as a weapon in the "complaint against strength"; its own power rests in its being differentiated from power (Brown 1995, 42–46). As Brown describes this view, "Truth is always on the side of the damned or the excluded; hence Truth is always clean of power, but therefore always positioned to reproach power" (1995, 46). The problem then is that these bifurcations—into good-evil, powerless-powerful, true-oppressive—evade the necessity for political argument about uncertain things, obscure the reality that all are implicated in power, and truncate both the capacity for political judgment and the practice of public debate (Brown 1995, chap. 2; Elshtain 1995, xvi–xvii, 44–45, 58–59).

Other leftist critics claim that identity politics visits another kind of harm on democratic politics. Their concern is not so much the logic of ressentiment and the kinds of selves it necessitates, but rather the "assertion of group difference" and the kind of community such assertions preclude. The criticism here is one of balkanization. For example, Todd Gitlin argues that radical politics, in academic and other forms, is no longer grounded in an interest in "universal human emancipation."[5] The left no longer relies on (indeed, it abjures) the "potentially inclusive language" at the heart of "two hundred years of revolutionary tradition, whether liberal or radical" (1993, 174). The resulting identity politics (particularly in its academic manifestations) is a politics of "dispersion and separateness," of distinct and embattled groupings. Identity politics is simply old-style pluralism in revolutionary guise, a politics that prevents us from imagining "a common enterprise."[6] The "academic left," Gitlin concludes, "has lost interest in the commonalities that undergird its obsession with difference" (1993, 177). This is not just a problem in the academy, of course. A similar point is made in Wolin's grim assessment of our current political conditions, to which "the politics of difference and the ideology of multiculturalism have contributed by rendering suspect the language and possibilities of collectivity, common action, and shared purposes" (Wolin 1993, 481; see also Hitchens 1993). As Jean Bethke Elshtain puts it:

> To the extent that citizens begin to retribalize into ethnic or other "fixed-identity" groups, democracy falters. Any possibility for human dialogue, for democratic communication and commonality, vanishes. . . . Difference becomes more and more exclusivist. . . . Mired in the cement of our own identities, we need never deal with one another. (1995, 74)

This kind of identity politics entrenches boundaries between groups at the expense of commonality; our attachment to the *res publica* is attenuated, and the identity that suffers is that of "citizen" (Wolin 1993, 477–81).

Ironically, Wolin notes, the focus on difference instead of commonality provokes an attachment to sameness, to "the illusion of internal unity within each difference" (1993, 477). The notion of identity as exclusive, seamless, stable, and not open to critique has been challenged by others as well, in a different theoretical vein. To make identity the source of our commonality not only precludes a broader kind of public togetherness, it prevents "a radical inquiry into the political construction and regulation of identity itself" (Butler 1990, ix). Some feminist theorists question the idea that feminists need a stable notion of gender identity, of the category "women." They argue against the idea that identity—as both a particular sense of subjectivity and a concomitant sense of collectivity—can be a foundation for politics. Identification with a collectivity is itself an achievement of power; this is to say that we are constructed through the workings of power to be certain kinds of subjects, members of certain groups. Claims that this membership can be a source for collective political action distract us from investigating the ways membership (identity) is produced, and obscure the workings of power that produce it. As Butler contends, "the identity of the feminist subject ought not to be the foundation of feminist politics, if the formation of the subject takes place within a field of power regularly buried through the assertion of that foundation" (1990, 6).

The "regulatory practice of identity" (Butler 1990, 32) implants a desire for a stable oneness, an unproblematic "I" or "we." The pursuit of unity inevitably generates exclusions, because who "we" are can be defined only by the presence of the not-we, the abnormal. Identity politics is charged with ignoring how norms of identity always produce exclusion (Brown 1995), how the effort to secure identity prevents us from contesting its production (Butler 1990, 1992), and how that production is temporally specific and politically variable, not fixed (Riley 1988).

In sum, these diverse leftist critics provide overlapping, although not identical, indictments of identity politics. Some criticize the production of a resentful self focused on redress of its (incurable) injuries and desirous of unity, stability, and the (unachievable) exclusion of difference. Others are critical of the construction of political collectivities that "nurture an irreducible core of exclusivity" (Wolin 1993, 479) and thus thwart the commitment to commonality and shared purposes. And they all question the kinds of politics that such groups pursue (an enhancement of the regulatory state, or separatist enclaves) and the kind that they preclude (communicative democratic interaction).

The Failings of Anti-Identity Politics

Leftist critics of identity politics are not unaware that the very arguments for the political relevance of identity arose as a response to certain conceptions of the political self and the political community. Feminists have long argued that men are the implicit norm of "universal" conceptions of the individual or the citizen (Okin 1979, 1989; Lloyd 1984; Young 1990; Pateman 1988). And feminism as a radical political movement arose in part from women's experience of oppression in the radical "political community" (Evans 1980). As some theorists have concluded, appeals to the "shared purposes" or "common interests" of a community are not neutral; they often serve to falsely universalize the perspectives of the powerful, while the concerns of those not part of the dominant culture are marked out as particular, partial, and selfish (perhaps also whiny, backward-looking, self-absorbed?). The language of commonality itself can perpetuate inequality, particularly when invoked by those who command political, communicative, or economic resources (Mansbridge 1983; Young 1990; Fraser 1992).

One central problem, then, with some leftist critiques of identity politics is that they do not address the insights of the last few decades of radical (particularly feminist) political thought. Simply to re-invoke "shared purposes" seems to me to ignore what we have learned about how the language of commonality can actively exclude. Simply to reassert "citizenship" as a public identity that transcends or integrates other commitments is to evade the question of what conception of citizenship would not automatically privilege certain commitments. And to see identity claims as obsessed with suffering is to overlook the fact that it is the perspective of the dominant culture that marks them out that way.[7]

Thus part of what makes identity relevant to politics is precisely the context of inequality in which even radical democratic political (inter)action takes place.[8] In such a context, the central democratic point cannot be simply that group identities get in the way of strong commitment to the *res publica,* the broader political community (as I think Gitlin and even Wolin would have it). Rather, the question is more like: in a context of inequality and oppression, *how* are multiple "we's" to be democratically part of the same public thing? What can make possible democratic communication with differentially placed others?

The *ressentiment* argument suggests that pursuing this question through regulatory means is likely to be self-subversive. Certainly, any effective approach to political change must examine the possibility that particular strategies for emancipatory political action may end up undermining the freedom of those for whom emancipation is intended. Tapper and Brown make a distinctive contribution to this analysis with their argument that certain forms of political action run the risk of further entrenching normalizing conceptions of identity and the power of regulatory apparatuses to enforce and police them. Investigations of these sorts of risks have been part of feminist discussions for many years, particularly with respect to the dangers and necessity of working for emancipatory change through the state, and Brown's nuanced analysis of the masculinist dimensions of state power will undoubtedly be central to future discussions (1995, chap. 7).[9]

However, to root feminist practices or other kinds of identity politics primarily in ressentiment is a much less justifiable move. I do not necessarily want to argue that the logic of ressentiment is not evident in contemporary sociopolitical life; it is one contestable interpretation of the desires at work in particular identity-based claims. I do contest it as a *primary* characterization of the political uses of identity, which is to say that I reject it as a wholesale description of contemporary social movements concerned with identity. (Brown does say that the story of identity politics could be told in other ways, but implies that such alternatives miss the critical dynamics of identity-based claims [1995, 61–62].) I think what is necessary is a more variegated political analysis, one that takes seriously the multiple sources of the discursive production of identity. The kinds of sources not evident in an analysis like Brown's are the ones that I discuss below, that involve the conscious articulation by political actors of the uses and complications of "politicized identity." I point to these articulations not to suggest that they are epistemologically privileged or that they somehow trump other explanations, but rather that they play a role in the discursive production of identity—they are (widely read) attempts to materialize in the world positive accounts of identity, ones that do not ignore its location in and production by broader social forces. They are articulations of the links between identity and politics that do not preclude discussions of the claims made in identity's name.

The feminist theorists of race, class, gender, and sexuality whom I analyze below have been centrally concerned with the relationship between identity, community, and emancipatory politics. Rather than rejecting identity, they delve into its complicated political meanings. They provide a way of understanding the political dimensions and consequences of group identity, one that moves beyond thinking of political identity as an expression of ressentiment, or group self-assertion, at the expense of democratic politics. They articulate a more complex account of group membership and its political significance, and a contrasting phenomenology of the passionate citizen's capacities and desires. Yet these feminist theorists pursue a conception of politics—active, agonistic, communicative—that is very similar to the one desired by leftist critics of identity politics. By critically theorizing political identity and interaction, these feminists offer a conception of democratic citizenship for our inegalitarian and diverse polity.

Refusing the Split: Materializing
Feminist Democratic Citizenship

> One woman wrote, "Because you are Black and Lesbian, you seem to speak with the moral authority of suffering." Yes, I am Black and Lesbian, and what you hear in my voice is fury, not suffering. Anger, not moral authority. There is a difference. (Audre Lorde 1984, 132)

In works such as *This Bridge Called My Back, Borderlands/La Frontera, Sister Outsider,* and *Making Face, Making Soul/Haciendo Caras,* the political character of identity is analyzed in terms of its multidimensionality. I use the word "multidimensional" to indicate more than that identity is multiple, although multiplicity is part of it. The further point is that identity plays different kinds of political roles, is related to power in different ways. "Identity" thus has multidimensional *effects* in the world. And the primary phenomena that identity (the assumption, assignment, and experience of identity) brings about are relations and separations. I put the point this way in order to distinguish it from the claim that identity as a concept means categorical sameness, and thus inevitably produces its

Other as the difference that makes the category possible. That logic of identity is certainly one of the forces shaping contemporary social orders. But identity also produces other kinds of effects, ones that (I will argue) enable democratic political action.

Mobilizing a group identity as politically relevant is an attempt to respond to power in its constraining and oppressive form. Prevailing relations of power allow institutions and individuals to define less powerful groups—through cultural images, bureaucratic practices, economic arrangements—in order to control, constrain, condemn, or isolate them (see esp. Moraga and Anzaldúa 1983, Anzaldúa 1990d, Collins 1991). To say that a group of people is oppressed is to say that they are marked out *as* members of particular groups in ways that prevent them from exercising (in Iris Young's terms) self-determination and self-development. In such a political context, it is hard to imagine how one could articulate a political claim against oppression without naming group identities. But, *pace* Brown, the existence of the group does not depend solely on the public reiteration of its injuries. For identity has another relationship to politics, one that manifests a different kind of power: power as an enabling, empowering force or capacity. Far from being constituted solely by their oppression and exclusion, group identities may be cherished as a source of strength and purpose. Our race, ethnic heritage, gender identity, or religion can be a vital motivation in our political lives, one that sustains us in struggle and makes political action possible (Morales 1983a, b; Quintales 1983; Moschkovich 1983; Moraga 1983; also Anzaldúa 1987). Reclaiming these identities as expressly political identities often involves insisting on the recognition of oppression, but it also means reclaiming (in bell hooks's words) a "legacy of defiance, of will, of courage" (hooks 1989, 9).

This reclamation, however, is complicated by identity's multiple worldly manifestations and effects, which are often discrepant—some rooted in imposed definitions, in how others see us, some in how we see ourselves. The identities that are imposed on us do not necessarily neatly mesh with what we want to reclaim; other individuals or institutions may define us differently than we would define ourselves, or take as defining characteristics ones that we do not. Controlling definitions of group identity that are imposed from the outside establish particular lines of sameness (of those within the group) and difference (from those not in the group). This premise of homogeneity within groups is often repeated and enforced by the groups themselves (Anzaldúa 1990b; Zook 1990; Lorde 1990, 1988).

The premise of homogeneity and boundedness is questioned in two related ways by the theorists I am citing: first, by insisting on the multiplicity of group memberships, and second, by highlighting the necessity of actively interpreting what an identity means. Adrienne Rich's conceptual language is useful here. Near the beginning of the long poem *Sources*, Rich asks:

> *With whom do you believe your lot is cast?*
> *From where does your strength come?*
>
> I think somehow, somewhere
> every poem of mine must repeat those questions
>
> which are not the same. (1986, 6)

Our strength may come from those around whom we grew up, those who taught us our racial heritage, incited our religious passions, constituted our ethnic or economic or sexed milieu. As we live on, our strength may come from others discovered or created as an "us," those with whom we come to share an ethics, a politics, a set of practices—a movement of feminists, say, or of radical artists. At the same time, we may reject, sustain, or revise the meanings of our earlier identifications, and we may confront conflicts between those identifications.

Politically speaking, Rich's poem reminds us, there is a further question: *with whom do you believe your lot is cast?* If this is not the same question as *from where does your strength come?* it must be because our lot is cast beyond the groups that give us strength, beyond those with whom we share an intense history or passionate commitment. Indeed, the feminist writers I am discussing consistently emphasize that the achievement of freedom for oppressed groups depends on freedom for all. Their analyses invoke and explore group specificity *at the same time* that they insist that freedom requires combating all systems of oppression; they argue that we cannot ignore group difference, despite its constructed nature, nor can we ignore how the fates of different groups are intertwined.[10]

The difficulty of making this political analytic point stems, on the one hand, from the cultural legacy of liberal humanism, which assumes that individual freedom can be achieved by ignoring group difference. On the other hand, its difficulty stems from this particular political context, in which casting one's lot widely with others can be seen as disloyalty to a particular group.

> "Your allegiance is to La Raza, the Chicano movement," say the members of my race. "Your allegiance is to the Third World," say my Black and Asian friends. "Your allegiance is to your gender, to women," say the feminists. Then there's my allegiance to the Gay movement, to the socialist revolution, to the New Age, to magic and the occult. . . . They would chop me up into little fragments and tag each piece with a label. (Anzaldúa 1983a, 205)

Such calls to singular allegiance overlook the possibilities inherent in the experience of identity as noncategorical, as multiple. Anzaldúa's response to this fragmenting competition is not to accept the implied contradictions, but rather to assert the connections: "only your labels split me." "Refusing the split" is another recurring theme in these works, as an alternative to the proliferation of ever more narrowly defined social locations or hyphenated identities.[11] These writers insist that political identity cannot be captured simply by a would-be comprehensive listing of our group affiliations, *and* they maintain that our group identities are central to our political identity.

The language of "refusing the split" may seem to indicate the kind of desire for wholeness that our postmodern eyes are trained to treat suspiciously. But this desire to "bring together" parts of the self is a response to a political landscape that tries to impose a single piece as the whole. This response, this desire, involves not the achievement of solidity, but "allowing power from particular sources of my living to flow back and forth freely through all my different selves, without the restriction of externally imposed definition" (Lorde 1984, 121; see also Moraga 1983, xvii–xix, and 1993, 146–47). Refusing the split does not involve achieving a neatly unified sense of self. It means refusing the closure of fragmentation, and recognizing the specific but related "sources of living" that can be brought to bear on political action. This insistence on the multiplicity and the incompleteness of identity, with its concomitant refusal of fragmentation, provides an important alternative for thinking about the self-as-citizen. This conception challenges neat "categories of marginality" (Anzaldúa 1990c) and thus suggests a new model for political togetherness as well.[12]

Central to this alternative is the treatment of identity as something *created*, constructed in this specific world, in the presence of complex others—and largely through words (speech and writing). "Making faces" is Anzaldúa's "metaphor for constructing one's identity." These faces are different from the masks "others have imposed on us," for such masks keep us fragmented: "After years of wearing masks we may become just a series of roles, the constellated self limping along with its broken limbs." Breaking through these masks is not, for Anzaldúa, a matter of revealing one's true inner nature, or essential self; rather we "*remake* anew both inner and outer faces" (Anzaldúa 1990c, xv–xvi, my emphasis). Identity is then a matter of active re-creation, which happens through speech and action.

According to the ancient *nahuas*, one was put on earth to create one's "face" (body) and "heart" (soul). To them, the soul was a speaker of words and the body a doer of deeds. Soul and body, words and actions are embodied in

Moyocoyani, one of the names of the Creator in the Aztec framework. (Anzaldúa 1990c, xvi)

Speech and action here are entwined with embodiedness and embeddedness, not simply as constraints or necessary conditions, but as the
materials with which we create, and out of which we are created. "We
have 'recovered' our ancient identity, digging it out like dark clay, pressing it to our current identity, molding past and present, inner and outer"
(Anzaldúa 1990b, 147). Anzaldúa stresses the conscious making of identity, but such consciousness is not separate from the physical and social
materiality of our lives. Our group identities provide fuel for the creative
motion and cause us to think about the materials, locations, and activities, the desires and demands, out of which identity is created. In this understanding, we have the capacity to create a public identity that is more
than just a string of labels, without ignoring the relevance to our lives of
the groups those labels name. As Lugones says, "one cannot disown
one's culture. One can reconstruct it in struggle" (1990, 53).[13]

This depiction of identity is suggestive not simply because of its stress
on active construction, but also because of what is being constructed. A
face is an outward appearance—"the world knows us by our faces" (Anzaldúa 1990c, xvi)—we cannot see our own face, except in a mirror. A
face is oriented toward others. Identity is not, then, a merely internal affair; it takes shape partly in appearing to others. The "face" metaphor is
instructive because it both admits of a conscious expressiveness (I can to
some extent compose my face to reflect or conceal what I want) but also
an inescapable concreteness (my face is physically my face, its color,
shape, its moles and markings and features undeniably mine.)[14] "Face" is
a particularly apt metaphor for political identity, for it stresses intersubjectivity and brings together—rather than regards as contradictory—our
embeddedness in the socially constructed givens of our existence, and
our capacity to present ourselves self-consciously in a way that engages
but does not simply reflect those givens.

The stress on intersubjectivity involved in the metaphor of making
faces points toward the implications of this creative understanding for
groups (and not simply individuals). Groups based on identity have in
recent decades been building a place in the world by creating bookstores,
presses, coffee houses, record labels, cultural centers, shelters, newspapers, and cooperative businesses and residences. These places, and the
political groups rooted in them, can provide a community context where
some people feel they can appear as most themselves; these groups are a
political "home," to use Bernice Johnson Reagon's terminology. Thus
these autonomous institutions have important empowering roles. However, as Reagon points out in her much-cited article on coalition politics,

the hominess of such groups often turns out to be based on exclusion, or a false sense of sameness. Our multiplicity and distinctiveness as individuals makes for differences even within groups that are seen (from within or without) as homogeneous (Reagon 1983, 357–60; Anzaldúa 1990a, b).

This recognition of multiplicity within groups as well as within individuals has pointed feminists to the need for a second model of political togetherness, beyond the model of "home." The understanding here is that established or enforced social groups do not exhaust the possibilities of human togetherness; it is not simply individual identities that are recreated rather than unyieldingly given, but those of political groups as well. Our politics need not be constrained and delimited by lines that we had no hand in drawing. Moraga says, "I would grow despairing if I believed ... we were unilaterally defined by color and class" (Moraga 1983, xiv). Anzaldúa agrees: we cannot let "color, class and gender separate us from those who would be kindred spirits" (Anzaldúa 1983a, 205–6; see also Pérez 1993, 65; Morales 1983b). Political collectivities can be created, and created in ways that do not necessarily accord with already existing groups or with fully shared experiences. This insight has led to criticisms of "sisterhood" as a model for feminist solidarity and to an increasing emphasis, in feminist theory and practice, on alliances and coalitions.[15] These specifically political groups are created through a conscious decision to ally with others, perhaps because we share political commitments or interests, but also simply because by working together we can change the meanings and merits of this common material world in which we coexist.

Thus group identities are politically relevant not only by virtue of their imposition and reclamation, but through the possibility of creation as well. The creation of these alliances contests the lines of difference and sameness that would sort us only in established ways. This conception of action allows us both to claim and to transfigure given identities—to challenge the terms on which identity is given by creating new political confederations. Coalitions enact a particular kind of political togetherness, one that is not restricted by established group identity but not dismissive of it either. Coalitions, then, are an example of a specifically democratic intersubjectivity; that is, of political relations between partially constituted and partially constituting subjects in a context of variegated power.

This notion of coalition might not satisfy Gitlin, for it does not require the presupposition of deep or universal commonalities underlying our differences. But this conception of identities and politics seems to me to offer an extraordinary amount of promise. Such a conception underscores the point that the achievement of democratic politics does not rest on placing commitment to "common purposes" above commitment to one's group(s), but rather on acting together in ways that could *create* a democratic commons—one that is plural, egalitarian, and communicative.

The further point is that this move against closure in intersubjective relations is prompted by, and utilizes the material of, subjective identity. Theorizing the lived experience of noncategorical identity here informs a politics of freedom, gives shape to a genuinely democratic public. Brown contrasts arguing from identity with arguing from a desire for a collective good (Brown 1995, 51); yet there is no reason why an argument about "what I want for us" is incompatible with articulating "who I am." Indeed, the works of these theorists show that getting my opinions about "what I want for us" heard may require a prior or ongoing argument about "who I am"—who I am to you, to us, to "the sheer possibility *de un 'nosotras'*" (Lugones 1990, 50). This thinking about identity does not really fit Butler's vision of "identities that are alternately instituted and relinquished according to the purposes at hand" (1990, 16). But it chimes in some ways with her analysis of the centrality of performance to identity, and it ends up at a vision of democratic politics that is not unlike Brown's: active, argumentative, and oriented toward change (Butler 1990, 1993; Brown 1995, esp. 47–51, 74–76).

This understanding of identity and politics starts from the recognition that group identity is implicated in power in multiple ways—ways that both perpetuate inequality and provide means to resist—and therefore that group identity is politically relevant to who we are as citizens. But that identity does not fix us and segregate us; identity is a personal and political force open to active re-creation through our words and actions. Such recreation is not an exercise clean of power, nor is it an exercise of sovereignty; it obviously has uncertain effects, located as it is in the context of the bureaucratic state, global capitalism, and other forms of dominating and productive power. Yet politicizing identity in this way opens the possibility of collective intervention in those other forms of power, through participation in an alternative performance of democratic identity.

In this forging of identity, we connect with others and engage in collective work. I contend that this is an understanding of what democratic citizenship is, and needs to be, in an inegalitarian or egalitarian context. These kinds of actors—conditioned *and* creative, situated but not static— are citizens. And these activities should be understood not simply as "feminist work" or "coalition politics" but as the practice, the performance, of citizenship. It is through such practices that we might create a common world that wants, among other things, "an end to suffering" (Rich 1986, 25).

The Passions of Citizenship

In conclusion, however, let me stress that this understanding of identity and politics is not one that concentrates primarily on suffering or on the moral purity of powerlessness. This way of politicizing identity and intersubjectivity foregrounds certain sensibilities and capacities that enable democratic political action. The authors discussed above argue for a political ethic that focuses not on suffering, innocence, or compassion—but on anger, responsibility, and courage.

Anger, as Lorde theorizes it, is very different from Nietzschean ressentiment. Anger is indeed reactive; it is a response to injustices, like racism. It is a specific kind of reaction, though; Lorde distinguishes anger from hatred, the latter being marked by a craving for the destruction and elimination of others. By contrast, "anger is a grief of distortions between peers, and its object is change" (1984, 129). Unlike ressentiment, then, anger's reactive character does not "reiterate impotence" or constrain the ability to act.[16] Anger is energy directed toward another in an attempt to create a relationship between subjects that is not "distorted" (made unjust) by hierarchies of power and the way subjects work within those hierarchies. If those hierarchies are to be changed through political interaction, then recreating the relationship between subjects is a central step. To recognize anger as a possible force in that reconstruction is to recognize the specificity of the creatures who engage with one another; it neither requires us to deny ourselves nor prevents our connecting with others.

But materializing the possibility of relation and change that anger carries with it depends both on our own actions and on the responses of others. The uses of anger require creativity, as Lorde makes clear in characterizing the "symphony of anger": "And I say *symphony* rather than *cacophony* because we have had to learn to orchestrate those furies so that they do not tear us apart. We have had to learn to move through them and use them for strength and force and insight within our daily lives" (1984, 129). But we also have to learn how to *hear* anger, how not to treat it as destructive, offputting, guilt-inducing. As Lorde points out, it is not the anger of Black women that is corroding the world we live in (1984, 133).

> It is not the anger of other women that will destroy us but our refusals to stand still, to listen to its rhythms, to learn within it. . . . The angers between women will not kill us if we can articulate them with precision, if we listen to the content of what is said with at least as much intensity as we defend ourselves against the manner of saying. (1984, 130–31)

The political uses of anger require creative action on both sides: articulating with precision, listening with intensity. We are responsible, then, for how we speak *and* how we hear each other.

Lorde's analysis of anger provides a possible way of rethinking "resentment." But it is important to recognize that the public passion of anger is not always or automatically used in the service of democratic or progressive aims. The anger and hatred behind "ethnic cleansing" or militant militias reveals in the most disturbing way how this all-too-human emotion can lead to the deepest inhumanity. Anger can indeed tear citizens apart, and lead them to tear others apart. There is no one meaning inherent in the political expression of feeling, whether anger or suffering. The question would seem to be not how to rid politics of anger, but whether and how we can create conditions in which anger is put to the service of a just world.

This is relevant to the contemporary leftist abhorrence of claims of "victimhood" and suffering. As long as some people are oppressed, claims about suffering are relevant in public discourse. Let me suggest an alternative way of hearing these claims. A claim of victimhood is not automatically an assertion of powerlessness or innocence; it is an assertion about the exercise of unjust power. It is a protest against certain relations of power *and* an assertion of alternative ones, for to speak against the exercise of unjust power—to speak against being victimized—is to say that I am a peer, a rightful participant in the argument about the just and the unjust, in the collective exercise of power. Claims about suffering, as well as claims made in anger, can be attempts to enact democratic political relationships. Both are part of the languages of citizenship. What I am suggesting is that this conception of democratic citizenship requires, as part of its conditions for realization, a practice of political listening. Such listening is best understood not as an attempt to get at an "authentic" meaning, but as participation in the construction of meaning. And I think we democratic theorists need to begin to imagine supple institutional spaces that might support such interaction and foster and sustain coalition politics.[17]

Enacting these relationships, speaking and listening to these languages of citizenship, is not particularly easy. If anger is "loaded with information and energy" (Lorde 1984, 127), we may justifiably fear its intensity and the intensity of our own response. Hence the necessity for courage, which has been connected to citizenship for centuries of political thought, although usually in ways that emphasized virility and battle strength. I have argued elsewhere (Bickford 1996) that Anzaldúa, Lorde, and others point to the necessity for a feminist reworking of courage and give us the resources to begin that transfiguration.[18] Fearlessness, as Lorde says, is a luxury we do not have, and need not wait for.

> We can learn to work and speak when we are afraid in the same way we have learned to work and speak when we are tired. For we have been socialized to respect fear more than our own needs for language and definition, and while we wait in silence for the final luxury of fearlessness, the weight of that silence will choke us. (1984, 44)

An ethic of courage is thus an ethic oriented toward political action, not psychological pain. Yet it takes seriously the psychological state, for that is what necessitates the exercise of courage. Implicit in this understanding of courage is the recognition that we "can sit down and weep, and still be counted as warriors" (Rich 1986, 25); the articulation of suffering is not incompatible with the daring exercise of citizenship. Such courage—the courage to act, to take responsibility for the world and ourselves, despite risk—is a necessary quality for radical democratic politics and theory in a context of difference and inequality.[19]

As citizens, we need to foster the courage necessary to take the risks of political action. But we also need to learn to recognize its exercise. This involves reconceptualizing political identity as active, and thus reinterpreting identity claims. Suffering and citizenship are not antithetical; they are only made so in a context in which others hear claims of oppression solely as assertions of powerlessness. A conception of citizenship adequate to the world in which we live must recognize both the infuriating reality of oppression and the continual exercise of courage with which citizens meet that oppression. It must recognize, in other words, that claims of inequality and oppression are articulated by political actors. As Lorde says—and I end, in tribute, with her words—"I am not only a casualty, I am also a warrior" (1984, 41).

Notes

For their kind and critical attention to earlier versions of this essay, I am grateful to Kimberley Curtis, Lisa Disch, Michael Lienesch, Gregory E. McAvoy, John McGowan, Siobhan Moroney, Stephen G. Salkever, and Holloway Sparks.

1. Martha Minow (1987) calls this "the dilemma of difference." An example of the argument against bracketing is Fraser (1992).

2. The primary texts I will draw from are *Sister Outsider* (Lorde 1984); *Borderlands/La Frontera* (Anzaldúa 1987); *The Last Generation* (Moraga 1993); and the edited collections *This Bridge Called My Back* (Moraga and Anzaldúa 1983), *Making Face, Making Soul/Haciendo Caras* (Anzaldúa 1990d), and *Frontline Feminism* (Kahn 1995). Specific essays in edited volumes will be cited by the individual author's name.

3. Accounts that focus on the resentment of those with officially privileged group identities can be found in Connolly (1987, 1991).

4. What is sometimes attached to the argument that identity politics enhances bureaucratic state power is the criticism of rights as an emancipatory vehicle. I do not address this issue here, but see Brown (1995, chap. 4); Elshtain (1995) and the sources cited therein.

5. Gitlin does join forces with the ressentiment folks in claiming that the "hardening" of group boundaries and the "thickening" of identity politics results in "a

grim and hermetic bravado celebrating victimization and stylized marginality" (1993, 172–73).

6. See also Patai and Koertge's critique of women's studies programs, in which they refer to identity politics as "the ugly spawn of old-fashioned special-interest jockeying and ethnic politics" (1994, 51, 72–77).

7. Brown almost makes this point with her brief suggestion that we learn to "read" identity claims differently (1995, 75).

8. As the analysis in the next section should make clear, I agree with Fraser's argument that even in an egalitarian setting, multiple group identities would be central to public identity (Fraser 1992, esp. 125–28).

9. The works I discuss in the next section do not for the most part address this question about relationships with the state, since they are primarily focused on relations between citizens. Some recent feminist discussions of the state (in addition to Brown, 1995) include Cooper (1995) and Pringle and Watson (1992). See Wolin (1981, 1989, 1992) for particularly insightful analyses of the impact of the contemporary state on democratic citizenship.

10. Examples include Collins (1991, 37–39); hooks (1989, esp. chap. 4); Lorde (1984, 133); Moraga and Anzaldúa (1983, esp. the section titled "El Mundo Zurdo/The Vision"); Pharr (1995); Segrest (1994, esp. Part 3) and Smith (1995).

11. See esp. Anzaldúa (1983a, 205); Moraga (1983, 34); Lugones (1990, 47); also Lorde (1984); Morales (1983a, b); Moraga (1993). Alarcón, in her analysis of *This Bridge Called My Back*, notes as a common theme this recognition that the subjectivity of women of color is a "multiple-voiced" one, its very multiplicity "lived in resistance to competing notions for one's allegiance or self-identification" (Alarcón 1990, 365–66; see also Sandoval 1991).

12. This point, and the next several paragraphs, draw directly from my analysis in Bickford (1996).

13. Thus Moraga's (1993) imagining of Queer Aztlan; thus Anzaldúa's (1987) persistent theorization of creative mestiza consciousness.

14. Unless I undergo plastic surgery, of course. For an interesting set of reflections on the connection between identity and face from the perspective of one undergoing reconstructive surgery, see Grealy (1993). For a fascinating, provocative account from a feminist analyzing cosmetic surgery, see Davis (1993).

15. For the critique of "sisterhood," see Dill (1983, 131–50); hooks (1984, chap. 4); Ackelsberg (1983). On coalition/alliances, see Reagon (1983) and the following collections: Albrecht and Brewer (1990); Moraga and Anzaldúa (1983); Anzaldúa (1990d).

16. The analysis of ressentiment as impotent reaction, as "a substitute for action, for power," is in Brown (1995, 69–73).

17. Although such institutions should not only be electoral ones, an example that comes immediately to mind is Lani Guinier's work on alternative voting schemes (1994). See also Lisa Disch's argument (1997) that ballot reform for third parties could encourage meaningful (although still party-based) coalition building.

18. For a more detailed account of courage, and of the social and institutional conditions which support it, see Holloway Sparks's essay in this volume. Interestingly, as Sparks points out, Wendy Brown has also urged a reclamation of courage; see Brown (1988, 206–7).

19. On responsibility, see especially Lorde (1995); Anzaldúa (1983b) and Segrest (1994).

References

Ackelsberg, Martha A. 1983. Sisters or comrades? The politics of friends and families. In *Families, politics, and public policy,* ed. Irene Diamond. London: Longman.

Alarcón, Norma. 1990. The theoretical subject(s) of *This bridge called my back* and Anglo-American feminism. In *Making face, making soul/Haciendo caras.* See Anzaldúa 1990d.

Albrecht, Lisa, and Rose M. Brewer, eds. 1990. *Bridges of power: Women's multicultural alliances.* Philadelphia: New Society Publishers.

Anzaldúa, Gloria. 1983a. La prieta. In *This bridge called my back.* See Moraga and Anzaldúa 1983.

_____. 1983b. Speaking in tongues: A letter to third world women writers. In *This bridge called my back.* See Moraga and Anzaldúa 1983.

_____. 1987. *Borderlands/La frontera.* San Francisco: Spinsters/Aunt Lute Foundation.

_____. 1990a. Bridge, drawbridge, sandbar, or island: Lesbians-of-color hacienda alianzas. In *Bridges of power: Women's multicultural alliances,* ed. Lisa Albrecht and Rose M. Brewer. Philadelphia: New Society Publishers.

_____. 1990b. En rapport, in opposition: Cobrando cuentas a las nuestras. In *Making face, making soul/Haciendo caras.* See Anzaldúa 1990d.

_____. 1990c. Haciendo caras, una entrada/An introduction. In *Making face, making soul/Haciendo caras.* See Anzaldúa 1990d.

_____, ed. 1990d. *Making face, making soul/Haciendo caras.* San Francisco: Aunt Lute Foundation.

Bickford, Susan. 1996. *The dissonance of democracy: Listening, conflict, and citizenship.* Ithaca: Cornell University Press.

Brown, Wendy. 1988. *Manhood and politics.* Totowa, NJ: Rowman and Littlefield.

_____. 1995. *States of injury: Power and freedom in late modernity.* Princeton: Princeton University Press.

Butler, Judith. 1990. *Gender trouble.* New York: Routledge.

_____. 1992. Contingent foundations: Feminism and the question of "postmodernism." In *Feminists theorize the political,* ed. Judith Butler and Joan W. Scott. New York: Routledge.

_____. 1993. *Bodies that matter.* New York: Routledge.

Collins, Patricia Hill. 1991. *Black feminist thought.* New York: Routledge.

Connolly, William E. 1987. *Politics and ambiguity.* Madison: University of Wisconsin Press.

_____. 1991. *Identity/difference: Democratic negotiations of political paradox.* Ithaca: Cornell University Press.

Cooper, Davina. 1995. *Power in struggle: Feminism, sexuality, and the state.* New York: New York University Press.

Davis, Kathy. 1993. Cultural dopes and she-devils: Cosmetic surgery as ideological dilemma. In *Negotiating at the margins,* ed. Sue Fisher and Kathy Davis. New Brunswick, N.J.: Rutgers University Press.

Dill, Bonnie Thornton. 1983. Race, class, and gender: Prospects for an all-inclusive sisterhood. *Feminist Studies* 9(1): 131–50.

Disch, Lisa. 1997. Fusion politics in the 1990s: Beyond wishful democracy. Paper presented at the Western Political Science Association Meeting, Tucson, Arizona, March 13–15.

Elshtain, Jean Bethke. 1995. *Democracy on trial.* New York: Basic Books.

Evans, Sara M. 1980. *Personal politics.* New York: Vintage Books.

Fraser, Nancy. 1992. Rethinking the public sphere. In *Habermas and the public sphere,* ed. Craig Calhoun. Cambridge, Mass.: MIT Press.

Geertz, Clifford. 1984. Anti-anti-relativism. *American Anthropologist* 86(2): 263–78.

Gitlin, Todd. 1993. The rise of "identity politics": An examination and critique. *Dissent* 40(2): 172–77.

Grealy, Lucy. 1993. Mirrorings: To gaze upon my reconstructed face. *Harper's* 286(1713): 66–74.

Guinier, Lani. 1994. *The tyranny of the majority.* New York: Free Press.

Hitchens, Christopher. 1993. The new complainers. *Dissent* 40(4): 560–64.

hooks, bell. 1984. *Feminist theory: From margin to center.* Boston: South End Press.

———. 1989. *Talking back.* Boston: South End Press.

Kahn, Karen. 1995. *Frontline feminism, 1975–1995: Essays from Sojourner's first twenty years.* San Francisco: Aunt Lute Books.

Lloyd, Genevieve. 1984. *The man of reason.* Minneapolis: University of Minnesota Press.

Lorde, Audre. 1984. *Sister outsider.* New York: Crossing Press.

———. 1988. *A burst of light.* Ithaca: Firebrand Books.

———. 1990. Between ourselves. In *Making face, making soul/Haciendo caras.* See Anzaldúa 1990d.

———. 1995. A new spelling of our name. In *Frontline feminism, 1975–1995: Essays from Sojourner's first twenty years.* See Kahn 1995.

Lugones, María. 1990. Hablando cara a cara/Speaking face to face. In *Making face, making soul/Haciendo caras.* See Anzaldúa 1990d.

Mansbridge, Jane J. 1983. *Beyond adversary democracy.* Chicago: University of Chicago Press.

Minow, Martha. 1987. Justice engendered. *Harvard Law Review* 101: 10–95.

Moraga, Cherríe. 1983. Preface. In *This bridge called my back.* See Moraga and Anzaldúa 1983.

———. 1993. *The last generation.* Boston: South End Press.

Moraga, Cherríe, and Gloria Anzaldúa, eds. 1983. *This bridge called my back.* New York: Kitchen Table: Women of Color Press.

Morales, Rosario. 1983a. I am what I am. In *This bridge called my back.* See Moraga and Anzaldúa 1983.

———. 1983b. We're all in the same boat. In *This bridge called my back.* See Moraga and Anzaldúa 1983.

Moschkovich, Judit. 1983. "—But I know you, American woman." In *This bridge called my back.* See Moraga and Anzaldúa 1983.

Okin, Susan Moller. 1979. *Women in western political thought*. Princeton: Princeton University Press.

———. 1989. *Justice, gender, and the family*. New York: Basic Books.

Patai, Daphne. 1992. The search for feminist purity threatens the goals of feminism. *Education Digest* 57(9): 27–31.

Patai, Daphne, and Noretta Koertge. 1994. *Professing feminism: Cautionary tales from the strange world of women's studies*. New York: Basic Books.

Pateman, Carole. 1988. *The sexual contract*. Stanford: Stanford University Press.

Pérez, Emma. 1993. Sexuality and discourse: Notes from a Chicana survivor. In *Chicana critical issues*, ed. Norma Alarcón et al. Berkeley: Third Woman Press.

Pharr, Suzanne. 1995. Rural organizing: Building community across difference. In *Frontline feminism, 1975–1995: Essays from Sojourner's first twenty years*. See Kahn 1995.

Pringle, Rosemary, and Sophie Watson. 1992. "Women's interests" and the post-structuralist state. In *Destabilizing theory*, ed. Michèle Barrett and Anne Phillips. Stanford: Stanford University Press.

Quintales, Mirtha. 1983. I paid very hard for my immigrant ignorance. In *This bridge called my back*. See Moraga and Anzaldúa 1983.

Reagon, Bernice Johnson. 1983. Coalition politics: Turning the century. In *Home girls: A Black feminist anthology*, ed. Barbara Smith. New York: Kitchen Table: Women of Color Press.

Rich, Adrienne. 1986. *Your native land, your life*. New York: W. W. Norton.

Riley, Denise. 1988. *"Am I that name?" Feminism and the category of "women" in history*. Minneapolis: University of Minnesota Press.

Sandoval, Chela. 1991. U.S. third world feminism: The theory and method of oppositional consciousness in the postmodern world. *Genders* 10: 1–24.

Segrest, Mab. 1994. *Memoir of a race traitor*. Boston: South End Press.

Smith, Barbara. 1995. Black feminism: A movement of our own. In *Frontline feminism, 1975–1995: Essays from Sojourner's first twenty years*. See Kahn 1995.

Tapper, Marion. 1993. *Ressentiment* and power. In *Nietzsche, feminism, and political theory*, ed. Paul Patton. New York: Routledge.

Wolin, Sheldon. 1981. The people's two bodies. *Democracy* 1: 9–24.

———. 1989. *The presence of the past: Essays on the state and constitution*. Baltimore: Johns Hopkins Press.

———. 1992. What revolutionary action means today. In *Dimensions of radical democracy*, ed. Chantal Mouffe. London: Verso.

———. 1993. Democracy, difference, and re-cognition. *Political Theory* 21(3): 464–83.

Young, Iris Marion. 1990. *Justice and the politics of difference*. Princeton: Princeton University Press.

Zook, Kristal Brent. 1990. Light skinned-ded naps. In *Making face, making soul/Haciendo caras*. See Anzaldúa 1990d.

5 Gender and the Meaning of Difference

Postmodernism and Psychology

RACHEL T. HARE-MUSTIN

JEANNE MARECEK

Conventional meanings of gender typically focus on difference, emphasizing how women differ from men. These differences have furnished support for the norm of male superiority. Until recently, psychological inquiry into gender has held to the construction of gender as difference. Thus, psychologists have focused on documenting differences between men and women, and their findings have served as scientific justification for male-female inequality (Lott, 1985; Morawski, 1985; Shields, 1975; Weisstein, 1971). When we examine theories of psychotherapy, we find that they, too, have supported the cultural meanings of gender (Hare-Mustin, 1983).

One recent line of inquiry by feminist psychologists has involved reexamining gender with the goal of de-emphasizing difference by sorting out genuine male-female differences from stereotypes. Some examples include Janet Hyde's (1981) meta-analyses of cognitive differences, Eleanor Maccoby and Carolyn Jacklin's (1975) review of sex differences, and Jacquelynne Eccles's work on math achievement (Eccles, 1989; Eccles & Jacobs, 1986). The results of this work dispute the contention that many male-female differences are universal, dramatic, or enduring (Deaux, 1984; Unger, 1979; Wallston, 1981). Moreover, this line of inquiry sees the origins of difference as largely social and cultural rather than biological. Thus, most differences between males and females are seen as culturally specific and historically fluid.

Another line of inquiry, exemplified in recent feminist psychodynamic theories (e.g., Chodorow, 1978; Eichenbaum & Orbach, 1983; Miller,

1986), takes as its goal the reaffirmation of gender differences. Although these theories provide varying accounts of the origins of difference, they all emphasize deep-seated and enduring differences between women and men in what is referred to as core self-structure, identity, and relational capacities. Other theorists have extended this work to suggest that these gender differences in psychic structure give rise to cognitive differences, such as differences in moral reasoning and in acquiring and organizing knowledge (cf. Belenky, Clinchy, Goldberger & Tarule, 1986; Gilligan, 1982; Keller, 1985). These theories represent differences between men and women as essential, universal (at least within contemporary Western culture), highly dichotomized, and enduring.

These two lines of inquiry have led to two widely held but incompatible representations of gender: one that sees considerable similarity between males and females, and another that sees profound differences. Both groups of theorists have offered empirical evidence, primarily quantitative in the first case and qualitative in the second. We believe that it is unlikely that further empirical evidence will resolve the question of whether men and women are similar or different. The two lines of inquiry described here emerge from different intellectual traditions, construe their domains of study differently, and rely on such different methods that consensus on a given set of conclusions seems unlikely. Moreover, even if consensus were possible, the question of what constitutes differentness would remain.

What constitutes differentness is a vexing question for psychologists who study sex and gender. Research that focuses on average differences between men and women may produce one conclusion while research that focuses on the full range of variations and the overlap (or lack of overlap) at the extremes of the range may produce another (Luria, 1986). An illustration can make this clearer: Although on average, American men are several inches taller than American women, we can readily think of some men who are shorter than many or even most women. The size and direction of gender differences in social behaviors, such as aggression or helping, often vary according to the norms and expectations for men and women that are made salient by the setting in which the behavior takes place (Eagly & Crowley, 1986; Eagly & Steffen, 1986). Studies in experimental laboratories can produce different results from field observations in real settings. Even more troubling, the very criteria for deciding what should constitute a difference as opposed to a similarity are disputed. How much difference makes a difference? Even the anatomical differences between men and women seem trivial when humans are compared to daffodils or ducks.

What are we to make of the difference versus no difference debate? Rather than debating which of these representations of gender is "true," we shift to the metaperspective provided by postmodernism. From this perspective, we can entertain new and possibly more fruitful questions about representations of gender, including the political and social functions that the difference and no difference positions serve. This perspective opens the way to alternative representations of gender that would raise new questions or recast old ones for psychologists.

Postmodernism and Meaning

Two recent intellectual movements, constructivism and deconstruction, challenge the idea of a single meaning of reality and a single truth. Rather than concerning themselves with a search for "the truth," they inquire instead about the way meanings are negotiated, the control over meanings by those in authority, and how meanings are represented in language. The current interest in constructivism and deconstruction reflects the growing skepticism about the positivist tradition in science and essentialist theories of truth and meaning (Rorty, 1979). Both constructivism and deconstruction challenge these positions, asserting that the social context shapes knowledge, and that meanings are historically situated and constructed and reconstructed through the medium of language.

The connection between meaning and power has been a focus of postmodernist thinkers (Foucault, 1973; Jameson, 1981). Their inquiry into meaning focuses especially on language as the medium of cognitive life and communication. Language is seen not simply as a mirror of reality or a neutral tool (Taggart, 1985; Wittgenstein, 1960; 1967). As Bruner (1986) points out, language "imposes a point of view not only about the world to which it refers but toward the use of the mind in respect to this world" (121). Language highlights certain features of the objects it represents, certain meanings of the situations it describes. "The word—no matter how experimental or tentative or metaphoric—tends to replace the things being described" (Spence, 1987, 3). Once designations in language become accepted, one is constrained by them not only in communicating ideas to others, but in the generation of ideas as well (Bloom, 1981). Language inevitably structures one's own experience of reality as well as the experience of those to whom one communicates. Just as in any interaction we cannot "not communicate," so at some level we are always influencing one another and ourselves through language.

Meaning-making and control over language are important resources held by those in power. Like other valuable resources, they are not distributed equitably across the social hierarchy. Indeed, Barthes (1972) has called language a sign system used by the powerful to label, define, and rank. Language is never innocent. Throughout history, dominant groups have asserted their authority over language. Our purpose here is to draw attention to the fact that men's influence over language is greater than that of women; we do not argue that women have had no influence over language. Within most social groups, males have had privileged access to education and thus have had higher rates of literacy than females; this remains true in many developing countries today (Newland, 1979). Men's dominance in academic institutions influences the social production of knowledge, including the concepts and terms in which people think about the world (Andersen, 1983). In addition, more men are published and men control the print and electronic media (Strainchamps, 1974). The arbiters of language usage are primarily men, from Samuel Johnson and Noah Webster to H. L. Mencken and Strunk and White.

When meaning-making through language is concentrated among certain groups in society, the meanings put forth can only be partial, because they exclude the experiences of other social groups. Yet the dominant group's influence over meaning-making is such that partial meanings are represented as if they were complete. In the instance of male control over language, the use of the generic masculine is a ready example of representing a partial object, the masculine, as complete, that is, as encompassing both male and female. Although not all men have influence over language, for those who do, such authority confers the power to create the world from their point of view, in the image of their desires.

In this chapter, we try to rethink the psychology of gender from the vantage point of constructivism and deconstruction. We first take up constructivism. We examine various constructions of gender and identify the problems associated with the predominant meaning of gender, that of male-female difference. We then turn to deconstruction. We show how a deconstructive approach can reveal alternative meanings associated with gender. In therapy, deconstruction can be a means of disrupting clients' understanding of reality by revealing alternative meanings. New meanings offer new possibilities for action and thus can foster change. We do not provide an exhaustive review of sex differences in psychology or propose a new theory of gender. Rather, we shift the discussion to a metatheoretical level in order to consider gender theorizing. Our purpose is not to answer the question of what is the meaning of gender but to examine where the question has taken us thus far and then to move on to new areas of inquiry.

The Construction of Reality

Constructivism asserts that we do not discover reality, we invent it (Watzlawick, 1984). Our experience does not directly reflect what is out there but is a selecting, ordering, and organizing of it. Knowing is a search for "fitting" ways of behaving and thinking (Von Glaserfeld, 1984). Rather than passively observing reality, we actively construct the meanings that frame and organize our perceptions and experience. Thus, our understanding of reality is a representation, not an exact replica, of what is out there. Representations of reality are shared meanings that derive from shared language, history, and culture. Rorty (1979) suggests that the notion of accurate representation is a compliment we pay to those beliefs that are successful in helping us do what we want to do. The "realities" of social life are products of language and agreed-on meanings.

Constructivism challenges the scientific tradition of positivism, which holds that reality is fixed and can be observed directly, uninfluenced by the observer (Gergen, 1985; Sampson, 1985; Segal, 1986). As Heisenberg (1952) has pointed out, a truly objective world, devoid of all subjectivity, would have no one to observe it. Constructivism also challenges the presumption of positivist science that it is possible to distinguish facts from values. For constructivists, values and attitudes determine what are taken to be facts (Howard, 1985). It is not that formal laws and theories in psychology are wrong or useless; rather, as Kuhn (1962) asserted, they are explanations based on a set of agreed-on social conventions. Whereas positivism asks what are the facts, constructivism asks what are the assumptions; whereas positivism asks what are the answers, constructivism asks what are the questions.

The positivist tradition holds that science is the exemplar of the right use of reason, neutral in its methods, socially beneficial in its results (Flax, 1987). Historically, the scientific movement challenged the canons of traditional belief and the authority of church and state. Science was a reform movement that struggled to supplant faith as the sole source of knowledge by insisting on the unity of experience and knowing. For Western society today, science has largely displaced church and state authority so that *scientific* has itself become a euphemism for *proper*.

Constructivism holds that scientific knowledge, like all other knowledge, cannot be disinterested or politically neutral. In psychology, constructivism, drawing on the ideas of Bateson and Maturana, has influenced epistemological developments in systems theories of the family (Dell, 1985). Constructivist views have also been put forth in developmental psychology (Bronfenbrenner, Kessel, Kessen & White, 1986; Scarr, 1985), in the psychology of women (Unger, 1983, and this book), and in the study of human sexuality (Tiefer, 1987). Constructivist views also form the basis of the social constructionism movement in social psychology, which draws inspiration from symbolic anthropology, ethnomethodology, and related movements in sociology and anthropology (Gergen, 1985; Kessler & McKenna, 1978).

From a constructivist perspective, theories of gender, like all scientific theories, are representations of reality that are organized within particular assumptive frameworks and that reflect certain interests. Below, we examine gender theorizing in psychology and indicate some of the assumptions and issues that a constructivist approach makes apparent.

The Construction of Gender as Difference

From a constructivist standpoint, the real nature of male and female cannot be determined. Constructivism focuses our attention on representations of gender rather than on gender itself. We note first that most languages, including our own, are elaborately gendered. Gender differentiation is a preeminent phenomenon of symbolic life and communication in our society, although this is not the case in all languages and cultures. Nonetheless, the English language still lacks adequate terms for speaking of each gender. *Male-female* has the advantage of referring to individuals across the entire life span, but the terms imply biological characteristics and fail to distinguish humans from other species. *Men-women* is more restrictive, referring specifically to humans, but it has the disadvantage of omitting childhood and adolescence. In this chapter, we use *men* and *women* for the most part, but we use *male* and *female* when we wish to include individuals at any point in the life span.

The very term *gender* illustrates the power of linguistic categories to determine what we know of the world. The use of *gender* in contexts other than discussions of grammar is quite recent. *Gender* was appropriated by contemporary American feminists to refer to the social quality of distinctions between the sexes (Scott, 1985). *Gender* is used in contrast to terms like *sex* and *sexual difference* for the explicit purpose of creating a space in which socially mediated differences between men and women can be explored apart from biological differences (Unger, 1979). The germinal insight of feminist thought was the discovery that *woman* is a social category. So although sexual differences can be reduced to the reproductive system in males (sperm production) and females (ovulation, pregnancy, childbirth, and lactation), sex differences do not account for gender, for women's social, political, and economic subordination or women's child care responsibilities.

From the vantage point of constructivism, theories of gender are representations based on conventional distinctions. In our view, such theories embody one of two contrasting biases, alpha bias and beta bias (Hare-Mustin, 1987). Alpha bias is the tendency to exaggerate differences; beta bias is the tendency to minimize or ignore differences.

The alpha-beta schema is in some ways analogous to that in scientific hypothesis testing in experimental psychology and thus is a schema familiar to psychologists. In hypothesis testing, alpha or Type 1 error involves reporting a significant difference when one does not exist; beta or

Type 2 error involves overlooking a significant difference when one does exist. In our formulation, the term *bias* refers not to the probability of error (which would imply that there is a correct position), but to a systematic slant or inclination to emphasize certain aspects of experience and overlook other aspects. This inclination or tendency is presumably related to the standpoint of the knower, that is, the position where he or she is located within and as part of the context. Thus, the standpoint of the knower necessarily shapes her or his view of reality. Far from deterring the knower from gaining knowledge, taking a standpoint can be a positive strategy for generating new knowledge (Hartsock, 1985). Our use of the term *bias* underscores our contention that all ideas about difference are social constructs; none can be mirrors of reality. Alpha and beta bias can be seen in representations of gender, race, class, age, and the like that either emphasize or overlook difference. Here we use the alpha-beta schema to examine recent efforts to theorize gender.

Alpha Bias

Alpha bias is the exaggeration of differences. The view of male and female as different and opposite and thus as having mutually exclusive qualities transcends Western culture and has deep historical roots. Ideas of male-female opposition are present in Eastern thought and throughout Western philosophy, including the writings of Aristotle, Aquinas, Bacon, and Descartes, as well as the writings of liberal theorists such as Locke and romanticists such as Rousseau (Grimshaw, 1986). Throughout Western history, woman has been regarded as the repository of nonmasculine traits, an "otherness" men assign to women.

The scientific model developed by Francis Bacon was based on the distinction between "male" reason and its "female" opposites—passion, lust, and emotion (Keller, 1985). Because women were restricted to the private sphere, they did not have access to the knowledge available in the public realm. The knowledge women did have, such as witchcraft, was disparaged or repudiated. As Evelyn Fox Keller points out, women's knowledge was associated with insatiable lust; men's knowledge was assumed to be chaste. In Bacon's model of science, nature was cast in the image of the female, to be subdued, subjected to the penetrating male gaze, and forced to yield up her secrets (cf. Keller, 1985; Merchant, 1980). Bacon's views are but one manifestation of the long-standing association of women with nature and emotion and men with reason, technology, and civilization (Ortner, 1974). The material body has been a symbol of human limitation and decay since at least early Christian times. Hence, men sought to be other than their bodies, to transcend their bodies. They dissociated themselves from their bodies and associated women with materiality, the sphere of nature, and the body (Butler, 1987). The opposition of reason and emotion, as well as the opposition of civilization and nature, emphasized in the Enlightenment, served in later times to reinforce liberalism's emphasis on rationality as the capacity that distinguishes humans from animals (Grimshaw, 1986).

In psychology, alpha bias can be readily seen in most psychodynamic theories. Freudian theory is not neutral about sexual differences but imposes meanings. It takes masculinity and male anatomy as the human standard; femininity and female anatomy are deviations from that standard. Thus, Freud characterized women's bodies as *not having* a penis rather than as *having* the female external genitalia. Similarly, he portrayed feminine character in terms of its deficiencies relative to masculine character. The Jungian idea of the animus and the anima also places the masculine and the feminine in opposition.

More recent psychodynamic theories also depict women as sharply divergent from men. For example, Erikson (1964) wrote that female identity is predicated on "inner space," a somatic design that "harbors . . . a biological, psychological, and ethical commitment to take care of human infancy . . . " (586), and a sensitive indwelling. Male identity is associated with "outer space," which involves intrusiveness, excitement, and mobility, leading to achievement, political domination, and adventure seeking. In Lacan's (1985) poststructuralist view, women are "outside" language, public discourse, culture, and the law. For Lacan, the female is defined not by what is, but by the absence or lack of the phallus as the prime signifier. In these ways psychodynamic theories overlook similarities between males and females and instead emphasize differences.

Parsons's sex-role theory, which dominated the social theories of the 1950s and 1960s, also emphasizes male-female differences (Parsons & Bales, 1955). The very language of sex-role theory powerfully conveys the sense that men's and women's roles are fixed and dichotomous, as well as separate and reciprocal (Thorne, 1982). Parsons asserted that men were instrumental and women were expressive, that is, men were task-oriented and women were oriented toward feelings and relationships. Parsons's sex-role theory was hailed as providing a scientific basis for relegating men and women to separate spheres. Men's nature suited them for paid work and public life; women's nature suited them for family work and home life. Thus women became first in "goodness" by putting their own needs secondary to those of their families and altruistically donating their services to others (Lipman-Blumen, 1984). Parsons believed that separate spheres for men and women were functional in reducing competition and conflict in the family and thus preserving harmony. The role definitions that Parsons put forward came to serve as criteria for distinguishing normal individuals and families from those who were pathological or even pathogenic (cf. Broverman, Broverman, Clarkson, Rosenkrantz & Vogel, 1970). The criteria associated with sex-role differentiation continue to be applied to family structure and functioning in such theories as contemporary exchange theory (Nye, 1982) and structural family therapy (Minuchin, 1974).

Alpha bias, or the inclination to emphasize differences, can also be seen in feminist psychodynamic theories (cf. Chodorow, 1978; Eichenbaum & Orbach, 1983; Gilligan, 1982; Miller, 1986). According to Nancy Chodorow (1978), boys and girls undergo contrasting experiences of identity formation during their early years under the social arrangement in which the care of infants is provided exclusively by women. Her influential work, which is based on object-relations theory, argues that girls' early experiences involve similarity and attachment to their mothers while boys' early experiences emphasize difference, separateness, and independence. These experiences are thought to result in broad-ranging gender differences in identity, personality structure, and psychic needs in adulthood. Women develop a deep-seated motivation to have children, whereas men develop the capacity to participate in the alienating work structures of advanced capitalism. Thus, according to Chodorow, the social structure produces gendered personalities that reproduce the social structure. Although Chodorow locates the psychodynamics of personality development temporally and situationally in Western industrial capitalism, psychologists who draw on her work often overlook this point concerning the social context. Her work is used to assert that there are essential differences between women and men and to view these, rather than the social structure, as the basis for gender roles (cf. Chernin, 1986; Eichenbaum & Orbach, 1983; Schlachet, 1984; Jordan & Surrey, 1986). In any case, both Chodorow's theory and the work of her followers emphasize gender difference and thus exemplify alpha bias.

In her approach to women's development, Carol Gilligan (1982) harks back to Parsons's duality, viewing women as relational and men as instrumental and rational. Her theory of women's moral development echoes some of the gender differences asserted by Freud (1964) and Erikson (1964). She describes female identity as rooted in connections to others and relationships. She views female morality as based on an ethic of care and responsibility rather than fairness and rights. Unlike Freud, however, she views women's differences from men in a positive light.

Both traditional psychodynamic theories and the recently developed feminist psychodynamic theories emphasize differences between men and women while overlooking the similarities between them. Whereas the emphasis on difference in traditional theories went hand in hand with a devaluation of what was seen as female, feminists' emphasis on difference is coupled with a positive evaluation of women's attributes.

Their emphasis on women's unique capacities for relationships and on the richness of women's inner experience has been an important resource for the movement within feminism known as cultural feminism. Cultural feminism encourages the development and expression of a women's culture, celebrates the special qualities of women, and values relationships among women.

Beta Bias

The inclination to ignore or minimize differences, *beta bias,* has been less prominent in psychological theory than alpha bias, and thus our treatment of it is necessarily briefer. One example of beta bias in theory development is the practice, common until recent decades, of drawing generalizations about human behavior, adult development, and personality from observations limited to males (Wallston, 1981). Male experience was assumed to represent all experience. This is an instance of beta bias insofar as generalizations about human experience based only on the male life course assume that women's experiences are no different than men's. Such generalizations offer only a partial view of humanity.

Another common instance of beta bias is the tendency to overlook both the differences in the social and economic resources that men and women typically have at their disposal as well as the differences in the social meanings and consequences of their actions. Thus, beta bias can be seen in social policies that provide equivalent benefits for men and women but overlook their disparate needs (Weitzman, 1985). Two examples, which we take up later, are comparable parental leave and no-fault divorce. Beta bias can also be seen in educational and therapeutic programs that focus on transforming the individual while leaving the social context unchanged. For example, some programs purport to groom women for personal or professional success by providing training in what are deemed male behaviors or skills, such as assertiveness, authoritative speech patterns, or certain managerial styles. Thus, if a woman wants to succeed as a manager, she is instructed to copy the demeanor and actions of successful men. Such programs presume that a certain manner of speaking or acting will elicit the same reaction from others regardless of the sex of the actor. This can be questioned (Gervasio & Crawford, 1989; Marecek & Hare-Mustin, 1987); for example, asking for a date, a classic task in assertiveness training, is judged differently for a woman than a man (Muehlenhard, 1983).

Beta bias can also be seen in theories of gender that represent masculine and feminine roles of traits as counterparts, as the construct of psychological androgyny does. The idea of masculinity and femininity as counterparts implies their symmetry and equivalence and thus obscures gender differences in power and social value. Sandra Bem's (1976) theory of psychological androgyny, which called for the creation of more balanced and healthy individuals by integrating positive masculine and feminine qualities, implies the equivalence of such qualities (Morawski, 1985; Worell, 1978).

Bem's original hypotheses suggested that individuals who identified themselves as highly feminine and those who identified themselves as highly masculine would be equally handicapped in performing "cross-sex" tasks and equally disadvantaged in terms of psychological well-being. But attempts to demonstrate this empirically did not yield such symmetrical effects (Morawski, 1987); rather, a masculine sex-role orientation tended to be associated with greater adaptiveness, as well as higher scores on indices of self-esteem and other aspects of psychological well-being. This is perhaps not surprising: If society values masculine qualities more highly than feminine qualities, individuals who have (or perceive themselves to have) those qualities should feel better about themselves. This is not to say that every quality associated with masculinity is regarded as positive. Aggression, for instance, is deplored outside of combat situations and competitive sports.

Beta bias can also be seen in theories of family functioning that ignore gender. In all societies, four primary axes along which hierarchies are established are class, race, gender, and age. Within families, class and race usually are constant, but gender and age vary. Family systems theories, however, disregard gender and view generation (that is, age) as the central organizing principle in the family (Hare-Mustin, 1987). Such theories emphasize the importance of the boundaries that define the differences in power and responsibility between the parental generation and the children. In so doing, they deflect attention from questions about the distribution of power and resources *within* generations of a family. Are mothers as powerful as fathers? Are daughters afforded the same resources and degree of autonomy as sons? By regarding all members of a generation as equal interacting participants in the family system, systems theories put forward a neutered representation of family life (Libow, 1985).

The Question of Utility

Rather than debate the correctness of various representations of gender, the "true" nature of which cannot be known, constructivism turns to the utility or consequences of these representations. How, we ask, do representations of gender provide the meanings and symbols that organize scientific and therapeutic practice in psychology? What are the consequences of representing gender in ways that either emphasize or minimize male-female differences? We use the alpha-beta schema as a framework for discussing the utility of gender theories.

The Utility of Alpha Bias

Because alpha bias has been the prevailing representation of gender we take up the question of its utility first. Alpha bias has had a number of effects on our understanding of gender. An important positive consequence of alpha bias, or focusing on differences between women and men, is that it has allowed some theorists to assert the worth of certain so-called feminine qualities. This assertion has the positive effect of countering the cultural devaluation of women and encouraging greater self-acceptance among women (Echols, 1983). Further, the focus on women's special qualities by some feminists has also prompted a critique of those cultural values that excuse or even encourage aggression, extol the pursuit of self-interest, and foster narrow individualism. It has furnished an impetus for the development of a feminist social ethics and for a variety of related philosophical endeavors (Eisenstein, 1983). The emphasis on women's differences from men fosters a corresponding appreciation of the commonalities women share, an appreciation that can help to generate positive emotional bonds among women. Sisterhood and solidarity have spurred collective action by women to gain recognition and power.

Unfortunately, exaggerating gender difference does not always support the aims of feminism. By construing women as different and devaluing them, alpha bias fosters solidarity between men by construing women as a deviant out-group, which can then be devalued. In Durkheim's terms, deviance supports in-group solidarity. Defining a sharp boundary between male and female supports the status quo by exacerbating male fears of being viewed as feminine. This serves to enforce conformity by males to masculine stereotypes. Moreover, exaggerating women's difference from men fosters the view of woman as the Other (Beauvoir, 1953). Further, this distancing and alienating view of women by the dominant male culture opens the way to treating women as objects, as is apparent in certain pornographic images and in much of the physical and sexual abuse of females.

Alpha bias also supports the status quo by denying that change is needed in the structure of work and family life (Gilder, 1987; Marshner, 1982). So, for example, traditionalists assert that women are not as intellectually capable as men, women are temperamentally better suited for care-taking roles and, as was argued in the Sears sex discrimination case, women prefer not to undertake stereotyped male roles (Erikson, 1964; Rosenberg, 1986; Rossi, 1984). Women's presumed differences from men are used to justify unequal treatment. Yet, as Patricia Mills (1987) suggests, it is women's confinement to the family that secures her difference. The possibility that it is the unequal treatment that might lead to the apparent differences between men and women is hidden from view.

The idea that male and female are opposites masks inequality between men and women as well as conflict between them. By construing rationality as an essential male quality and relatedness as an essential female quality, for example, such theories as those of Gilligan and Parsons conceal the possibility that those qualities result from social inequities and power differences. Men's propensity to reason from principles might stem from the fact that the principles were formulated to promote their interests; women's concern with relationships can be understood as a need to please others that arises from lack of power (Hare-Mustin & Marecek, 1986). Typically, those in power advocate rules, discipline, control, and rationality, while those without power espouse relatedness and compassion. Thus, in husband-wife conflicts, husbands call on rules and logic, whereas wives call on caring. But, when women are in the dominant position, as in parent-child conflicts, they emphasize rules while their children appeal for sympathy and understanding or for exceptions based on special circumstances. This suggests that rationality and relatedness are not gender-linked traits, but rather stances evoked by one's position in a social hierarchy.

Others have offered related accounts of how women's greater concern with relationships might be a consequence of women's position in the social hierarchy rather than an essential female attribute. Wilden (1972), for example, proposes that low social status imparts a need to monitor where one stands in a relationship: "Anyone in a social relationship which defines him or her as inferior must necessarily be much more concerned to discover what the relationship is about than to communicate or receive any particular message within it" (297).

Women's caring is but one example of a behavior that has been represented as a gender difference but can be more adequately represented as a way of negotiating from a position of low power. As Bernice Lott discusses below, many other differences between men and women are best construed as stances associated with their relative positions in the social hierarchy rather than as differences of gender per se. These alternative accounts open the way for psychologists to consider why every woman is not concerned with caring and relationships and why some men are.

Feminist psychodynamic theories make assertions of extensive male-female personality differences throughout life. Even when these theories applaud the personality attributes of women, they can serve as justification for restricting individuals to a particular social place. Further, critics have challenged the idea that a brief period in infancy could be responsible for creating the broad-ranging differences that psychodynamic theo-

rists assert and overriding subsequent experiences in human development. Critics similarly challenge whether personality differences alone
could be responsible for the gendering of all social institutions throughout history (cf. Kagan, 1984; Lott, 1987; Scott, 1985); that is, feminist psychodynamic theories have been criticized for overplaying the influence
of early experience and individual personality to the neglect of economic
conditions, social role conditioning, and historical change.

A further question has been raised as to whether changes in patterns of
infant care-giving such as Nancy Chodorow (1978) and Dorothy Dinnerstein (1976) propose are sufficient to undermine gender difference and
thereby to effect social transformation. There is an uncomfortable literal-
ism in imputing such power to such a small segment of experience. Joan
Scott (1985) has drawn attention to this problem in terms of representing
the well-ordered family as the foundation of a well-ordered society.

In focusing on the question of why *differences* exist, feminist psychodynamic theories disregard the question of why *domination* exists. Iris
Young (1983) points out that psychodynamic theories posit a masculine
desire for power but fail to account for how men achieve power. The
identification of a problem does not constitute an explanation.

Alpha bias, the exaggerating of differences between groups, has the
additional consequence of ignoring or minimizing the extent of differences (or variability) among members of each group. The focus on
Woman obliterates the sight of women. Further, such out-groups as
women are viewed as more homogeneous than dominant groups (Park &
Rothbart, 1982). Differences among men are readily identified, but all
women are regarded as pretty much the same. Thus, men are viewed as
individuals, but women are viewed as women. As a result, most psychological theories of gender have been slow to concern themselves with differences among women that are due to race, ethnicity, class, age, marital
status, and a variety of social circumstances.

Another consequence of alpha bias is the tendency to view men and
women not only as different but as opposite. The conception of masculine and feminine as embodying opposite and mutually exclusive traits is
not only prevalent in the culture at large, but it has been embedded in
certain well-established psychological tests. These include the Terman-
Miles (1936) Masculinity-Femininity Personality Scale (M-F), the California Personality Inventory (Gough, 1964), and the Minnesota Multiphasic
Personality Inventory (Hathaway & McKinley, 1943). The existence of
these scales testifies to fifty years of psychological effort to evaluate the
constructs of masculinity and femininity, an unrelenting search for the
presumed core of what defines masculine and feminine (Morawski,
1987). Anne Constantinople (1973) has questioned the usefulness of the
M-F construct, pointing out the vague definitions used in test construc-

tion: M-F is defined as whatever masculinity-femininity tests measure. She concluded that such tests merely measured the differences in the responses of men and women.

These tests are constructed so that a respondent must disavow feminine qualities in order to be categorized as masculine and vice versa. Thus, masculinity-femininity is represented as a single bipolar dimension, a unitary continuum. Masculinity and femininity are defined in terms of one another; what one is, the other is not.

Such dichotomies caricature human experience; for example, to maintain the illusion of male autonomy, the contribution of women's work at home and in the workplace must be overlooked. Feminist social scientists have observed that women and the family have been asked to compensate for the indifference and hostility of the outer world. Thus, the home is viewed as a haven (Lasch, 1977), but it is actually that *women* are the haven for men. The home is a metaphor that serves to obscure men's dependence on women and thus perpetuates the illusion of male autonomy. Similarly, the corporate world is seen as the locus of men's achievement and independence, but this overlooks the contribution of women. The extent to which female support personnel, such as secretaries and receptionists, cover up their bosses' absences and shortcomings, administer their work day, and provide personal service is obscured. In both cases, women are expected to provide for men's physical needs and mediate their social relations.

The portrayal of women as relational also ignores the complexity of their experiences. Rearing children involves achievement, and nurturing others involves power over those in one's care (Hare-Mustin & Marecek, 1986). When gender is represented as dichotomized traits, the extent to which presumed opposites include aspects of each other is overlooked. It is of interest to note that when women enter the "man's world" of business, they often flounder at first because they assume it operates according to formal rules and principles; they underestimate the importance of informal relationships, reciprocal favors, and personal influence.

Gender dichotomies regarding work and housework also caricature the actual experiences of both housewives and working women. In industrialized societies one's value is associated with the money one earns. Those who do not earn money—housewives, children, and old people— have an ambiguous status (Hare-Mustin, 1978). The contemporary focus on industrial production has led to the belief that households no longer produce anything important, and consequently that housewives no longer have much to do. But what exists is better represented as a two-tiered production system in which work for money is carried on outside the home while a familial production system continues within. As Ruth Schwartz Cowan (1983) has pointed out, women produce without payment meals, clean laundry, healthy children, well-fed adults, and transportation for goods and people at a level unknown in past times. Yet paid workers are seen as productive and housewives are not.

The view of male and female as opposite also supports the idea of separate spheres. The idea of separate spheres lives on, even though the majority of women are now in the paid labor force and operate in both spheres. A false symmetry embodied in the notion of separate spheres obscures women's dual roles and work overload (Hare-Mustin, 1988).

The representation of gender as dichotomies or opposites has had a long history in human thought. Even the autonomy-relatedness dichotomy was foreshadowed by earlier dichotomies such as agentic-communal (Bakan, 1966) and instrumental expressive (Parsons & Bales, 1955). Indeed, man-woman may serve as a universal binary opposition. If so, this is not the result simply of a faulty definition, but as Wilden (1972) says, of prevailing ideology. The representation of gender as opposition has its source not in some accidental confusion of logical typing, but in the dominant group's interest in preserving the status quo. Calling the psychosocial and economic relations of men and women *opposition* imputes symmetry to a relationship that is unequal. As Dorothy Dinnerstein (1976) pointed out, women have been discontent with the double standard, but men on the whole are satisfied with it. Further, denying the interrelationships between male and female serves to maintain inequality.

Alpha bias, or exaggerating differences, thus plays an important role in preserving the status quo. Perhaps for this reason, the mass media often promulgate representations of gender that emphasize difference and underplay those that minimize difference. As Martha Mednick (1989) documents, the media have given extensive coverage to women's difference, such as their "fear of success," their lack of a "math gene," and their "different voice." Similarly, popular self-help books appeal to women's supposedly greater expressiveness, empathy, and sensitivity, while holding women responsible for all that goes wrong in intimate relationships (Worrell, 1988). Points of similarity between women and men do not make news, nor are refutations of exaggerated claims of male-female difference considered newsworthy.

The Utility of Beta Bias

Beta bias, or minimizing differences, also has consequences for understanding gender, but its consequences have received less attention. On the positive side, equal treatment under the law has enabled women to gain greater access to educational and occupational opportunities, as well as equal pay for equal work. This is largely responsible for the improvement in the status of some women over the last two decades (Dionne, 1989).

Arguing for no differences between women and men, however, draws attention away from women's special needs and from differences in power and resources between women and men. A ready example is seen in the statutes legislating equal pay for equal work, which have had relatively little effect on equalizing incomes across gender. This is because most women work in female-identified sectors of the economy in which wages are low. In a society in which one group holds most of the power, ostensibly neutral actions usually benefit members of that group. In Lenore Weitzman's (1985) research, for example, no-fault divorce settlements were found to have raised men's standard of living 42 percent while lowering that of women and children 73 percent. Another example is the effort to promote public policies granting comparable parental leave for mothers and fathers of newborns. Such policies overlook the physical effects of giving birth from which women need to recuperate and the demands of breastfeeding that are met uniquely by women who nurse their infants.

Giving birth is, paradoxically, both an ordinary event and an extraordinary one, as well as the only visible biological link in the kinship system. The failure of the workplace to accommodate women's special needs associated with childbirth represents beta bias, in which male needs and behaviors set the norm, and women's unique experiences are overlooked.

In therapy, treating men and women as if they were equal is not always equitable (Gilbert, 1980; Margolin, Talovic, Fernandez & Onorato, 1983). In marital and family therapy, treating partners as equals can overlook structural inequalities within the relationship. Some family systems theorists have tried to dismiss the concept of power as an epistemological error, arguing that both partners in a relationship contribute to the maintenance of the relationship. The notion of reciprocity, however, implies that the participants are not only mutually involved but equally involved in maintaining the interaction, and that they can equally influence its outcome (MacKinnon & Miller, 1987). As Virginia Goldner points out, this is not unlike the "kind of moral relativism in which the elegant truth that master and slave are psychologically interdependent drifts into the morally repugnant and absurd notion that the two are therefore equals" (1987, 111). As long as the social status and economic resources of the husband exceed those of the wife, marital contracts and quid pro quo bargaining strategies for resolving conflicts between partners will not lead to equitable results. *Sex-fair* or *gender-neutral* therapies that advocate nonpreferential and nondifferential treatment of women and men to achieve formal equality can inadvertently foster inequality (Bernal & Ysern, 1986; Jacobson, 1983; Marecek & Kravetz, 1977).

Our purpose in examining representations of gender has not been to catalogue every possible consequence of alpha and beta bias but to demonstrate that representation is never neutral. From the vantage point of constructivism, theories of gender can be seen as representations that construct our knowledge of men and women and inform social and scientific practice. Gender selects and gives meaning to sexual differences. Deconstruction provides another approach for examining representation and meaning in language. We now turn to the ways in which deconstruction can be used to examine the meanings of gender in the practice of therapy.

Deconstruction

Just as constructivism denies that there is a single fixed reality, the approach to literary interpretation known as deconstruction denies that texts have a single fixed meaning. Deconstruction offers a means of examining the way language operates outside our everyday awareness to create meaning (Culler, 1982). Deconstruction is generally applied to literary texts, but it can be applied equally to scientific texts, or, as we suggest below, to therapeutic discourse.

A primary tenet of deconstruction is that texts can generate a variety of meanings in excess of what is intended. In this view, language is not a stable system of correspondences of words to objects but "a sprawling limitless web where there is constant circulation of elements" (Eagleton, 1983, 129). The meaning of a word depends on its relation to other words, specifically, its difference from other words.

Deconstruction is based on the philosophy of Derrida, who moves beyond the structuralist thesis that posits closed language systems. Derrida has pointed out that Western thought is built on a series of interrelated hierarchical oppositions, such as reason-emotion, presence-absence, fact-value, good-evil, male-female (Culler, 1982). In each pair, the terms take their meaning from their opposition to (or difference from) each other; each is defined in terms of what the other is not. The first member of each pair is considered "more valuable and a better guide to the truth" (Nehamas, 1987, 32). But Derrida challenges both the opposition and the hierarchy, drawing attention to how each term contains elements of the other and depends for its meaning on the other. It is only by marginalizing their similarities that their meaning as opposites is stabilized and the value of one over the other is sustained.

Just as the meaning of a word partly depends on what the word is not, the meaning of a text partly depends on what the text does not say. Deconstructive readings thus rely on gaps, inconsistencies, and contradictions in the text, and even on metaphorical associations. Deconstruction

can serve as a tool for probing what psychology has represented as oppositions, such as autonomy-nurturance, instrumentality-expressiveness,
mental health-mental illness. Our intention here is not to provide a detailed explication of deconstruction but to suggest some ways that it can
be used to understand meaning and gender. Our focus here is on psychotherapy.

Therapy, Meaning, and Change

Therapy centers on meaning, and language is its medium. Therapy is an
oral mode, and narratives, proverbs, metaphors, and interpretations are
its substance. The metaphorical language used in therapy to represent
the world is a way to try to comprehend partially what cannot be com-
prehended totally (Spence, 1987). A deconstructivist view of the process
of therapy draws attention to the play of meanings in the therapist-client
dialogue and the way a therapist poses alternative meanings to create
possibilities for change. This renegotiation of the client's meanings can
take place explicitly, as in psychodynamic therapies, cognitive therapy, or
rational-emotive therapy. Or it can take place implicitly, as when a behavior therapist instructs a client on how to bring anxiety symptoms under
voluntary control, or a pharmacotherapist reattributes symptoms of depression to disturbances in body chemistry. The therapeutic process can
be seen as one in which the client asks the therapist to reveal something
about the client beyond the client's awareness, something that the client
does not know.

Clients in therapy talk not about actual experiences but about reconstructed memories that resemble the original experiences only in certain
ways. The client's story conforms to prevailing narrative conventions
(Spence, 1982). This means that the client's representation of events
moves further and further away from the experience and into a descriptive mode. The client as narrator is a creator of his or her world, not a disinterested observer.

The therapist's task of listening and responding to the client's narratives is akin to a deconstructive reading of a text. Both seek subtexts and
multiple levels of meaning. Just as deconstructive readings disrupt the
frame of reference that organizes conventional meanings of a text, so a
therapist's interventions disrupt the frame of reference within which the
client customarily sees the world. Such disruptions enable new meanings
to emerge (Watzlawick, Weakland & Fisch, 1974). As a multiplicity of
meanings becomes apparent through such therapist actions as questioning, explaining, interpreting, and disregarding, more possibilities for
change emerge. The deconstructive process is most apparent in psychoanalysis, but, indeed, all therapy involves changing meaning as part of

changing behavior. The metaphor of therapy as healing is an idealization that obscures another metaphor, that therapists manipulate meanings. These metaphors are not contrary to each other; rather, as part of helping clients change, therapists change clients' meanings (Frank, 1987; Haley, 1976).

Gender and Meaning in Therapy

Just as a poem can have many readings, a client's experience can have many meanings. Certain meanings are privileged, however, because they conform to the explanatory systems of the dominant culture. As a cultural institution whose purpose is to help individuals adapt to their social condition, therapy usually reflects and promulgates such privileged meanings. But some therapists, such as radical therapists and feminist therapists, bring a social critique to their work. Such therapists, rather than attempting to bring clients' meanings in line with those of the culture, disrupt the meanings privileged by the culture. Below, we examine certain privileged and marginalized meanings in relation to gender issues, issues that have been at the center of considerable debate among therapists and in society at large (Brodsky & Hare-Mustin, 1980).

We begin with Freud's classic case of Dora (1963). When we look at Dora's case from a deconstructive perspective, we can see it as a therapist's attempt to adjust the meaning a client attached to her experience to match the prevailing meanings of the patriarchal society in which she lived. A "landmark of persuasion unsurpassed in clinical literature" is the way Spence described Dora's case (1987, 122). Dora viewed the sexual attentions of her father's associate, Herr K, as unwanted and uninvited. She responded to them with revulsion. Freud insistently reframed the sexual encounters with Herr K as desired and desirable for a fourteen-year-old girl and interpreted Dora's revulsion as a disguise for her true state of sexual arousal. When Dora refused to accept Freud's construction, he labeled her as vengeful and declared therapy a failure.

From our vantage point ninety years after Dora's encounter with Freud, the case shows how meanings embedded in the dominant culture often go unrecognized or unacknowledged. Freud evidently viewed Herr K's lecherous advances as acceptable behavior, although Herr K was married and Dora was only fourteen and the daughter of a close family friend. We can surmise that the cultural belief in the primacy of men's sexual needs prevented Freud from seeing Dora's revulsion as genuine.

Freud's analysis of Dora provides an example of how a therapist attempts to reaffirm privileged meanings and marginalize and discourage other meanings, to fill in the gaps and make intelligible a narrative.

Where does Dora leave off and Freud begin? The many meanings of Dora's behavior—and Freud's as well—are evident in the numerous reanalyses, filmic representations, and critical literary readings of the case, which continue to be produced up to the present day.

Conventional meanings of gender are embedded in the language of therapy. Like all language, the language used in therapy can be thought of as metaphoric: it selects, emphasizes, suppresses, and organizes certain features of experience, and thus it imparts meaning to experience; for example, *Oedipus complex* imposes the complexity of adult erotic feelings onto the experiences of small children and emphasizes the male and the primacy of the phallus. The metaphor of the family ledger in family therapy implies that family relations are (or should be) organized as mercantile exchanges and centered on male achievements (Boszormenyi-Nagy & Sparks, 1973).

Dominant meanings are often embedded in everyday language and commonplace metaphors. By challenging linguistic conventions and unpacking metaphors, therapists can disrupt these meanings. With respect to gender, for example, a therapist can unpack the metaphor of family harmony and expose the gender hierarchy by pointing out that accord within the family often is maintained by women's acquiescence and accommodation (Haavind, 1984; Hare-Mustin, 1978; 1987). Moreover, the stress generated by women's prescribed family roles is often marginalized or overlooked (Baruch, Biener & Barnett, 1987). Psychologists studying stress have focused largely on men with men's workplace identified as a stressor. The home, in contrast, has been viewed as a benign environment in which one recuperates from work. This picture is drawn from a male perspective. For most women, the home *is* the workplace or at least one of their workplaces. Further, women's roles associated with the home are not free of undue stress. Family harmony involves a woman's pleasing a husband and keeping a home attractive, activities that are frequently incompatible with meeting children's needs (Piotrkowski & Repetti, 1984).

In unpacking the metaphor of family loyalty, the therapist can draw attention to the way the needs of some family members are subordinated to those of dominant members in the name of loyalty. In maintaining the ties in the family network, women provide for others while their own needs go unmet (Belle, 1982).

The metaphor of women's dependency can also serve to conceal the extent to which women as wives and mothers provide for the needs of men and boys. Women have traditionally been characterized as dependent, but Harriet Lerner (1983) raises the provocative questions: Have women been dependent enough? Have they been able to call on others to meet their needs? As Westkott (1986) observes, the assumption of male entitlement to unconditional nurturance from females is rarely questioned; nor is it labeled as dependency and regarded as a psychological problem.

Finally, both private concerns with preserving the family and public rhetoric about the decline of the family can be challenged by drawing attention to the use of "the family" as a metaphor for male dominance (Pogrebin, 1983). Is it the family that is threatened or just a form of the family that supports men's greater power and status? Judith Stacey (1983) also draws attention to the way feminist theory has deconstructed the family as a natural unit and reconstructed it as a social unit.

As we have shown, the resemblance of therapeutic discourse to narrative offers the possibility of using deconstruction as a resource for understanding meaning and the process of therapy. Therapy typically confirms privileged meanings, but deconstruction directs attention to marginalized meanings. Doing therapy from a feminist standpoint is like the deconstructionist's "reading as a woman" (Culler, 1982). The therapist exposes gender-related meanings that reside in such culturally embedded metaphors as family harmony but go unacknowledged in the conventional understanding of those metaphors. These new meanings can change the ways that clients understand their own behaviors and the behaviors of others—the *click* experience that women in the consciousness-raising groups of the 1960s and 1970s so often reported. New meanings allow and often impel clients to make changes in their lives.

Paradoxes in Gender Theorizing

The issue of gender differences has been a divisive one for feminist scholars. Some believe that affirming difference affirms women's value and special nature. Others believe that insisting on equality (that is, no difference) is necessary for social change and the redistribution of power and privilege. But both ways of representing gender involve paradoxes. Like every representation, both conceal as they reveal. A paradox is contrary (*para*) to received opinion (*doxa*), a logical impossibility or a result contrary to what is desired.

One such paradox is that efforts to affirm the special value of women's experience and to valorize women's inner life turn attention away from efforts to change the material conditions of women's lives (Fine, 1985; Russ, 1986; Tobias, 1986). Feelings of emotional intensity may not lead to an understanding of oneself or of society. A change in consciousness and symbolic life alone does not necessarily produce a change in the social conditions of individuals' lives and institutional structures.

Another paradox arises from the assertion of a female way of knowing, involving intuition and experiential understanding rather than logical abstraction. This assertion implies that all other ways of knowing are male. If taken to an extreme, the privileging of emotion and bodily knowledge over reason can lead to the rejection of rational thought. It can also be taken to imply that women are incapable of rational thought and of acquiring the knowledge of the dominant culture.

There is yet another paradox. Qualities such as caring, expressiveness, and concern for relationships are extolled as women's superior virtues and the wellspring of public regeneration and morality. But they are also seen as arising from women's subordination (Miller, 1986) and from women's being outsiders and oppressed. Thus has Bertrand Russell spoken of the superior virtue of the oppressed. When we extol such qualities as women's caring, do we necessarily also extol women's subordination (Echols, 1983)? Joan Ringleheim (1985) has suggested that the idealization of women's experience serves as a palliative for oppression. If subordination makes women better people, then the perpetuation of women's so-called goodness would seem to require continued subordination.

It is not only alpha bias that leads to paradoxes and logical confusion. Beta bias also can. Saying that women are as good as men is a statement of self-acceptance and pride for some women. But asserting that women are equal to men is not the same as asserting that women and men are equal; it reveals that *man* is the hidden referent in our language and culture. As Dale Spender (1984) points out, "women can only aspire to be as good as a man, there is no point in trying to be as good as a woman" (201). Paradoxically, this attempt at denying differences reaffirms male behavior as the standard against which all behavior is judged.

There is a paradox faced by any social change movement, including feminism: its critique is necessarily determined by the nature of the prevailing social system, and its meanings are embedded in that system. Sennett (1980) has observed a further paradox, that even when one's response to authority is defiance, that stance serves to confirm authority just as compliance does. Thus, the feminist critique simultaneously protests and protects the status quo. In this regard, Dorothy Dinnerstein (1976) has suggested that woman is not really the enemy of the system but its loyal opposition.

Moreover, feminist separatism, the attempt to avoid male influence by separating from men, leaves intact the larger system of male control in the society. Separatism can provide space for self-affection and woman-to-woman bonding, but as an ultimate goal it is caught as a mirror image of the masculine reality it is trying to escape (Cornell & Thurschwell, 1987).

The meaning of gender as male-female difference presents us with paradoxes. Whether such representations of gender emphasize difference or minimize it, they are fraught with logical contradictions and hidden meanings. The representation of gender as male-female difference obscures and marginalizes the interrelatedness and commonalities of women and men. It also obscures institutional sexism and the extent of male authority. Just as our examination of the utility of alpha bias and beta bias revealed no clear answer for those who ask the question of which is better, so too the paradoxes that arise reveal further complexities and contradictions. Can we look beyond these representations to new ways of understanding gender?

Conclusion

Male-female difference is a problematic and paradoxical way to construe gender. What we see is that alpha and beta bias have similar assumptive frameworks despite their diverse emphases. Both take the male as the standard of comparison. Both construct gender as attributes of individuals, not as the ongoing relations of men and women. Neither effectively challenges the gender hierarchy, and ultimately neither transcends the status quo. They are changes within the larger system of assumptions, but they leave the system itself unchanged. The multiple representations all frame the problem of what gender is in such a way that the solution is "more of the same" (Watzlawick, Weakland & Fisch, 1974).

Gender is not a property of individuals but a socially prescribed relationship, a process, and a social construction. Like race and class, however, gender cannot be renounced voluntarily. Representing gender as a continuum of psychological difference serves to simplify and purify the concept of gender. The riddle of gender is presumed to be solved when heterogeneous material is reduced to the homogeneity of logical thought (Gallop, 1982). To establish a dichotomy is to avoid complexity. The idea of gender as opposites obscures the complexity of human action and shields both men and women from the discomforting recognition of inequality.

The issue of difference is salient for men in a way that it is not for women. Those who are dominant have an interest in emphasizing those differences that reaffirm their superiority and in denying their similarity to subordinate groups. By representing nonsymmetrical relationships as symmetrical, those who are dominant obscure the unequal social arrangements that perpetuate male dominance. Thus, notions of gender that are part of our cultural heritage rely on defensive masculine models of gender (Chodorow, 1979). In accepting male-female difference as the meaning of gender, feminists have acceded to the construction of reality of the dominant group, "a gentle slide into the prevailing hegemony" (Bouchier, 1979, 397).

Even when differences are minimized and gender is represented as male-female similarity, equality remains elusive. Male themes and male views are presented as human experience. As Sandra Harding (1986) has observed, women are asked to degender themselves for a masculine version of experience without asking for a similar degendering of men. Even women's need to define themselves derives from and is perpetuated by their being the nondominant group. The dominant group does not define itself with respect to its group or order. Thus men do not refer to their masculine status, they do not add "as a man." But women speak "as a woman." Specifying "as a woman" reserves generality for men.

Deconstruction focuses attention on oppositions and hidden meanings in language. Language mirrors social relations, but it is also recursive on the social experiences that generate it. Thus, from a postmodernist perspective, there is no one right view of gender. Each view is partial and will present certain paradoxes. Feminist psychology has concentrated on male-female difference. Though the remapping of difference could go further, such a map of difference, even if perfected, will never reveal the entire terrain of gender. A map is not the terrain. Rather a map offers a construction of the terrain. With regard to gender, there are other maps to be drawn. For instance, some would map gender in terms of the principles that organize male-female relations in particular cultures (Stacey & Thorne, 1985). Some would map gender in terms of the discourses through which men and women position one another and define themselves (Hollway, 1984). Other maps, charting gender in yet other terms, are still [to] be invented.

Postmodernism accepts multiplicity, randomness, incoherence, indeterminacy, and paradox, which positivist paradigms are designed to exclude. Postmodernism creates distance from the seemingly fixed language of established meanings and fosters skepticism about the fixed nature of reality. Recognizing that meaning is what we agree on, postmodernism describes a system of possibilities. Constructing gender is a process, not an answer. In using a postmodernist approach, we open the possibility of theorizing gender in heretofore unimagined ways. Postmodernism allows us to see that as observers of gender we are also its creators.

References

Andersen, M. L. (1983). *Thinking about women: Sociological and feminist perspectives.* New York: Macmillan.

Bakan, D. (1966). *The duality of human existence.* Chicago: Rand McNally.

Barthes, R. (1972). *Mythologies* (A. Lavers, Trans.). New York: Hill & Wang. (Original work published 1957.)

Baruch, G. K., Biener, L., & Barnett, R. C. (1987). Woman and gender in research on work and family stress. *American Psychologist, 42,* 130–36.

Beauvoir, S. de. (1953). *The second sex* (H. M. Parshley, Trans. & Ed.). New York: Knopf.

Belenky, M. F., Clinchy, B. M., Goldberger, N. R. & Tarule, J. M. (1986). *Women's ways of knowing: Development of self, voice, and mind.* New York: Basic Books.

Belle, D. (1982). Social ties and social support. In D. Belle (Ed.), *Lives in stress: Women and depression* (133–44). Beverly Hills, CA: Sage.

Bem, S. L. (1976). Probing the promise of androgyny. In A. G. Kaplan & J. P. Bean (Eds.), *Beyond sex-role stereotypes: Reading toward a psychology of androgyny* (48–62). Boston: Little, Brown.

Bernal, G. & Ysern, E. (1986). Family therapy and ideology. *Journal of Marital and Family Therapy, 12,* 129–35.

Bloom, A. H. (1981). *The linguistic shaping of thought.* Hillsdale, NJ: Erlbaum.

Boszormenyi-Nagy, I. & Sparks, G. M. (1973). *Invisible loyalties.* New York: Harper & Row.

Bouchier, D. (1979). The deradicalisation of feminism: Ideology and utopia. *Sociology, 13,* 387–402.

Brodsky, A. M., & Hare-Mustin, R. T. (1980). *Women and psychotherapy: An assessment of research and practice.* New York: Guilford.

Bronfenbrenner, U., Kessel, F., Kessen, W. & White, S. (1986). Toward a critical social history of developmental psychology: A propaedeutic discussion. *American Psychologist, 41,* 1218–30.

Broverman, I. K., Broverman, D. M., Clarkson, F. E., Rosenkrantz, P. & Vogel, S. R. (1970). Sex role stereotypes and clinical judgments of mental health. *Journal of Consulting Psychology, 34,* 1–7.

Bruner, J. (1986). *Actual minds, possible worlds.* Cambridge, MA: Harvard University Press.

Butler, J. (1987). Variations on sex and gender. In S. Benhabib & D. Cornell (Eds.), *Feminism as critique: On the politics of gender* (128–42). Minneapolis: University of Minnesota Press.

Chernin, K. (1986). *The hungry self: Women, eating, and identity.* New York: Perennial Library.

Chodorow, N. (1978). *The reproduction of mothering.* Berkeley: University of California Press.

Chodorow, N. (1979). Feminism and difference: Gender, relation, and difference in psychoanalytic perspective. *Socialist Review, 9* (4), 51–70.

Constantinople, A. (1973). Masculinity-femininity: An exception to a famous dictum? *Psychological Bulletin, 80,* 389–407.

Cornell, D. & Thurschwell, A. (1987). Feminism, negativity, intersubjectivity. In S. Benhabib & D. Cornell (Eds.), *Feminism as critique: On the politics of gender* (143–62). Minneapolis: University of Minnesota Press.

Cowan, R. S. (1983). *More work for mother: The ironies of household technology from open hearth to microwave.* New York: Basic Books.

Culler, J. (1982). *On deconstruction: Theory and criticism after structuralism.* Ithaca, NY: Cornell University Press.

Deaux, K. (1984). From individual differences to social categories: Analysis of a decade's research on gender. *American Psychologist, 39,* 105–16.

Dell, P. F. (1985). Understanding Bateson and Maturana: Toward a biological foundation for the social sciences. *Journal of Marital and Family Therapy, 11,* 1–20.

Dinnerstein, D. (1976). *The mermaid and the minotaur.* New York: Harper & Row.

Dionne, E. J. (1989, August 22). Struggle for work and family fueling women's movement. *New York Times,* A1, A18.

Eagleton, T. (1983). *Literary theory: An introduction.* Minneapolis: University of Minnesota Press.

Eagly, A. H. & Crowley, M. (1986). Gender and helping behavior: A meta-analytic review of the social psychological literature. *Psychological Bulletin, 100,* 283–308.

Eagly, A. H. & Steffen, V. J. (1986). Gender and aggressive behavior: A meta-analytic review of the social psychological literature. *Psychological Bulletin, 100,* 309–30.

Eccles, J. S. (1989). Bringing young women to math and science. In M. Crawford & M. Gentry (Eds.), *Gender and thought* (36–58). New York: Springer-Verlag.

Eccles, J. & Jacobs, J. (1986). Social forces shape math participation. *Signs, 11,* 368–80.

Echols, A. (1983). The new feminism of yin and yang. In A. Snitow, C. Stansell & S. Thompson (Eds.), *Powers of desire: The politics of sexuality* (440–59). New York: Monthly Review Press.

Eichenbaum, L. & Orbach, S. (1983). *Understanding women: A feminist psychoanalytic approach.* New York: Basic Books.

Eisenstein, H. (1983). *Contemporary feminist thought.* Boston: G. K. Hall.

Erikson, E. H. (1964). Inner and outer space: Reflections on womanhood. *Daedelus, 93,* 582–606.

Fine, M. (1985). Reflections on a feminist psychology of women. *Psychology of Women Quarterly, 9,* 167–83.

Flax, J. (1987). Postmodernism and gender relations in feminist theory. *Signs, 12,* 621–43.

Foucault, M. (1973). *The order of things.* New York: Vintage.

Frank, J. D. (1987). Psychotherapy, rhetoric, and hermeneutics: Implications for practice and research. *Psychotherapy, 24,* 293–302.

Freud, S. (1963). *Dora: An analysis of a case of hysteria.* New York: Collier Books. (Original work published 1905.)

Freud, S. (1964). Some psychical consequences of the anatomical distinction between the sexes. In J. Strachey (Ed. and Trans.), *Standard edition of the complete psychological works of Sigmund Freud* (Vol. 19, 243–58). London: Hogarth Press. (Original work published 1925.)

Gallop, J. (1982). *The daughter's seduction: Feminism and psychoanalysis.* Ithaca, NY: Cornell University Press.

Gergen, K. J. (1985). The social constructionist movement in modern psychology. *American Psychologist, 40,* 266–75.

Gervasio, A. H. & Crawford, M. (1989). The social evaluation of assertion: A critique and speech act reformulation. *Psychology of Women Quarterly, 13,* 1–25.

Gilbert, L. A. (1980). Feminist therapy. In A. M. Brodsky & R. T. Hare-Mustin (Eds.), *Women and psychotherapy: An assessment of research and practice* (245–65). New York: Guilford.

Gilder, G. (1987). *Men and marriage.* Los Angeles: Pelican.

Gilligan, C. (1982). *In a different voice: Psychological theory and women's development.* Cambridge, MA: Harvard University Press.

Goldner, V. (1987). Instrumentalism, feminism, and the limit of family therapy. *Journal of Family Psychology, 1,* 109–16.

Gough, H. G. (1964). *California psychological inventory: Manual.* Palo Alt, CA: Consulting Psychologists Press.

Grimshaw, J. (1986). *Philosophy and feminist thinking.* Minneapolis: University of Minnesota Press.

Haavind, H. (1984). Love and power in marriage. In H. Holter (Ed.), *Patriarchy in a welfare society* (136–67). Oslo: Universitets Forlaget. Distribution in U.S.: New York: Columbia University Press.

Haley, J. (1976). *Problem-solving therapy.* San Francisco: Jossey-Bass.

Harding, S. (1986). *The science question in feminism.* Ithaca, NY: Cornell University Press.

Hare-Mustin, R. T. (1978). A feminist approach to family therapy. *Family Process, 17,* 181–94.

Hare-Mustin, R. T. (1983). An appraisal of the relationship of women and psychotherapy: 80 years after the case of Dora. *American Psychologist, 1983, 38,* 593–601.

Hare-Mustin, R. T. (1987). The problem of gender in family therapy theory. *Family Process, 26,* 15–27.

Hare-Mustin, R. T. (1988). Family change and gender differences: Implications for theory and practice. *Family Relations, 37,* 36–41.

Hare-Mustin, R. T. & Marecek, J. (1986). Autonomy and gender: Some questions for therapists. *Psychotherapy, 23,* 205–12.

Hartsock, N. C. M. (1985). *Money, sex, and power: Toward a feminist historical materialism.* Boston: Northeastern University Press.

Hathaway, S. R. & McKinley, J. C. (1943). *The Minnesota Multiphasic Personality Test.* New York: Psychological Corporation.

Heisenberg, W. (1952). *Philosophical problems of nuclear science* (F. C. Hayes, Trans.). New York: Pantheon.

Hollway, W. (1984). Gender difference and the production of subjectivity. In J. Henriques, W. Hollway, C. Urwin, C. Venn & V. Walkerdine (Eds.), *Changing the subject* (26–59). London: Methuen.

Howard, G. (1985). The role of values in the science of psychology. *American Psychologist, 40,* 255–65.

Hyde, J. S. (1981). How large are cognitive gender differences? *American Psychologist, 36,* 892–901.

Jacobson, N. S. (1983). Beyond empiricism: The politics of marital therapy. *American Journal of Family Therapy, 11* (2), 11–24.

Jameson, F. (1981). *The political unconscious: Narrative as a socially symbolic act.* Ithaca, NY: Cornell University Press.

Jordan, J. V. & Surrey, J. L. (1986). The self-in-relation: Empathy and the mother-daughter relationship. In T. Bernay & D. W. Cantor (Eds.), *The psychology of today's woman: New psychoanalytic visions* (81–104). New York: The Analytic Press.

Kagan, J. (1984). *The nature of the child.* New York: Basic Books.

Keller, E. F. (1985). *Reflections on gender and science*. New Haven: Yale University Press.

Kessler, S. J. & McKenna, W. (1978). *Gender: An ethnomethodological approach*. Chicago: University of Chicago Press.

Kuhn, T. S. (1962). *The structure of scientific revolutions*. Chicago, IL: University of Chicago Press.

Lacan, J. (1985). *Feminine sexuality* (J. Mitchell & J. Rose, Eds.; J. Rose, Trans.). New York: Norton.

Lasch, C. (1977). *Haven in a heartless world*. New York: Basic Books.

Lerner, H. G. (1983). Female dependency in context: Some theoretical and technical considerations. *American Journal of Orthopsychiatry, 53*, 697–705.

Libow, J. (1985). Gender and sex role issues as family secrets. *Journal of Strategic and Systemic Therapies, 4*, (2), 32–41.

Lipman-Blumen, J. (1984). *Gender roles and power*. Englewood Cliffs, NJ: Prentice-Hall.

Lott, B. (1985). The potential enrichment of social/personality psychology through feminist research and vice versa. *American Psychologist, 40*, 155–64.

Lott, B. (1987). *Women's lives: Themes and variations*. Belmont, CA: Brooks/Cole.

Luria, Z. (1986). A methodological critique: On "In a different voice." *Signs, 11*, 316–21.

Maccoby, E. E. & Jacklin, C. N. (1975). *The psychology of sex differences*. Stanford, CA: Stanford University Press.

MacKinnon, L. K. & Miller, D. (1987). The new epistemology and the Milan approach: Feminist and sociopolitical considerations. *Journal of Marital and Family Therapy, 13*, 139–55.

Marecek, J. & Hare-Mustin, R. T. (1987, March). *Cultural and radical feminism in therapy Divergent views of change*. Paper presented at the meeting of the American Orthopsychiatric Association, Washington, DC.

Marecek, J. & Kravetz, D. (1977). Women and mental health: A review of feminist change efforts. *Psychiatry, 40*, 323–29.

Margolin, G., Talovic, S., Fernandez, V. & Onorato, R. (1983). Sex role considerations and behavioral marital therapy: Equal does not mean identical. *Journal of Marital and Family Therapy, 9*, 131–45.

Marshner, C. (1982). *The new traditional woman*. Washington, DC: Fress Congress Education and Research Foundation.

Mednick, M. T. (1989). On the politics of psychological constructs: Stop the bandwagon, I want to get off. *American Psychologist, 44*, 1118–23.

Merchant, C. (1980). *The death of nature: Women, ecology, and the scientific revolution*. San Francisco: Harper & Row.

Miller, J. B. (1986). *Toward a new psychology of women* (2d ed.). Boston: Beacon Press.

Mills, P. J. (1987). *Woman, nature, and psyche*. New Haven: Yale University Press.

Minuchin, S. (1974). *Families and family therapy*. Cambridge, MA: Harvard University Press.

Morawski, J. G. (1985). The measurement of masculinity and femininity: Engendering categorical realities. *Journal of Personality, 53*, 196–223.

Morawski, J. G. (1987). The troubled quest for masculinity, femininity, and androgyny. In P. Shaver & C. Hendrick (Eds.), *Review of Social and Personality Psychology: Vol. 7. Sex and gender* (44–69). Beverly Hills, CA: Sage.

Muehlenhard, C. L. (1983). Women's assertion and the feminine sex-role stereotype. In V. Frank & E. D. Rothblum (Eds.), *The stereotyping of women: Its effects on mental health* (153–71). New York: Springer.

Nehamas, A. (1987, 5 October). Truth and consequences: How to understand Jacques Derrida. *The New Republic*, pp. 31–36.

Newland, K. (1979). *The sisterhood of man*. New York: Norton.

Nye, F. I. (1982). *Family relationships: Rewards and costs*. Beverly Hills, CA: Sage.

Ortner, S. B. (1974). Is female to male as nature is to culture? In M. Z. Rosaldo & L. Lamphere (Eds.), *Women, culture, and society* (67–87). Stanford: Stanford University Press.

Park, B., & Rothbart, M. (1982). Perception of out-group homogeneity and levels of social categorization: Memory for the subordinate attributes of in-group and out-group members. *Journal of Personality and Social Psychology, 42,* 1051–68.

Parsons, T. & Bales, R. F. (1955). *Family, socialization, and interaction process*. Glencoe, IL: Free Press.

Piotrkowski, C. S. & Repetti, R. L. (1984). Dual-earner families. In B. B. Hess & M. B. Sussman (Eds.), *Women and the family: Two decades of change* (99–124). New York: Haworth Press.

Pogrebin, L. C. (1983). *Family politics: Love and power on an intimate frontier*. New York: McGraw-Hill.

Ringleheim, J. (1985). Women and the Holocaust: A reconsideration of research. *Signs, 10,* 741–61.

Rorty, R. (1979). *Philosophy and the mirror of nature*. Princeton: Princeton University Press.

Rosenberg, R. (1986). Offer of proof concerning the testimony of Dr. Rosalind Rosenberg (EEOC v. Sears, Roebuck, and Company), *Signs, 11,* 757–66.

Rossi, A. (1984). Gender and parenthood. *American Sociological Review, 49,* 1–19.

Russ, J. (1986). Letter to the editor. *Women's Review of Books, 3* (12), 7.

Sampson, E. E. (1985). The decentralization of identity: Toward a revised concept of personal and social order. *American Psychologist, 40,* 1203–11.

Scarr, S. (1985). Constructing psychology: Making facts and fables for our times. *American Psychologist, 40,* 499–512.

Schlachet, B. C. (1984). Female role socialization: The analyst and the analysis. In C. M. Brody (Ed.), *Women therapists for working with women* (55–65). New York: Springer.

Scott, J. W. (1985, December). *Is gender a useful category of historical analysis?* Paper presented at the meeting of the American Historical Association, New York.

Segal, L. (1986). *The dream of reality: Heinz von Foerster's constructivism*. New York: Norton.

Sennett, R. (1980). *Authority*. New York: Knopf.

Shields, S. A. (1975). Functionalism, Darwinism, and the psychology of women. A study in social myth. *American Psychologist, 30,* 739–54.

Spence, D. P. (1982). *Narrative truth and historical truth*. New York: Norton.

Spence, D. P. (1987). *The Freudian metaphor: Toward a paradigm change in psycho-analysis.* New York: Norton.

Spender, D. (1984). Defining reality: A powerful tool. In C. Kramarae, M. Schulz & W. M. O'Barr (Eds.), *Language and power* (194–205). Beverly Hills, CA: Sage.

Stacey, J. (1983). The new conservative feminism. *Feminist Studies, 9,* 559–83.

Stacey, J. & Thorne, B. (1985). The missing feminist revolution in sociology. *Social Problems, 32,* 301–16.

Strainchamps, E. (Ed.). (1974). *Rooms with no view: A woman's guide to the man's world of the media.* New York: Harper & Row.

Taggart, M. (1985). The feminist critique in epistemological perspective: Questions of context in family therapy. *Journal of Marital and Family Therapy, 11,* 113–26.

Terman, L. & Miles, C. C. (1936). *Sex and personality.* New York: McGraw-Hill.

Thorne, B. (1982). Feminist rethinking of the family: An overview. In B. Thorne & M. Yalom (Eds.), *Rethinking the family: Some feminist questions* (1–24). New York: Longmans.

Tiefer, L. (1987). Social constructionism and the study of human sexuality. In P. Shaver & C. Hendrick (Eds.), *Review of Social and Personality Psychology: Vol. 7. Sex and gender* (70–94). Beverly Hills, CA: Sage.

Tobias, S. (1986). "In a different voice" and its implications for feminism. *Women's Studies in Indiana, 12,* (2), 1–2, 4.

Unger, R. K. (1979). Toward a redefinition of sex and gender. *American Psychologist, 34,* 1085–94.

Unger, R. K. (1983). Through the looking glass: No wonderland yet! (The reciprocal relationship between methodology and models of reality). *Psychology of Women Quarterly, 8,* 9–32.

Von Glaserfeld, E. (1984). An introduction to radical constructivism. In P. Watzlawick (Ed.), *The invented reality: Contributions to constructivism* (17–40). New York: Norton.

Wallston, B. S. (1981). What are the questions in psychology of women? A feminist approach to research. *Psychology of Women Quarterly, 5,* 597–617.

Watzlawick, P. (Ed.) (1984). *The invented reality: Contributions to constructivism.* New York: Norton.

Watzlawick, P., Weakland, J. H. & Fisch, R. (1974). *Change: Principles of problem formation and problem resolution.* New York: Norton.

Weisstein, N. (1971). Psychology constructs the female. In V. Gornick & B. K. Moran (Eds.), *Woman in sexist society* (133–46). New York: Basic Books.

Weitzman, L. J. (1985). *The divorce revolution: The unexpected social and economic consequences for women and children in America.* New York: Free Press.

Westkott, M. (1986). Historical and developmental roots of female dependency. *Psychotherapy, 23,* 213–20.

Wilden, A. (1972). *System and structure: Essays in communication and exchange.* London: Tavistock Publications.

Wittgenstein, L. (1960). *Preliminary studies for the "Philosophical Investigations": The blue and brown books.* Oxford: Blackwell.

Wittgenstein, L. (1967). *Philosophical investigations.* Oxford: Blackwell. (Original work published 1953.)

Worell, J. (1978). Sex roles and psychological well-being: Perspectives on methodology. *Journal of Consulting and Clinical Psychology, 46,* 777–91.

Worell, J. (1988). Women's satisfaction in close relationships. *Clinical Psychology Review, 8,* 477–98.

Young, I. M. (1983). Is male gender identity the cause of male domination? In J. Trebilcot (Ed.), *Mothering: Essays in feminist theory* (129–46). Totowa, NJ: Rowman & Allenheld.

6 Romance in the Age of Electronics

Harlequin Enterprises

LESLIE W. RABINE

Harlequin, as it advertises itself, is the 'world's no. 1 publisher of romance fiction'. Like its imitators and rivals, Dell's Candlelight Romances, Bantam's Loveswept, and Simon & Schuster's Silhouette Romances, Harlequin turns out on its giant, computerized printing presses an ever-increasing number of uniformly jacketed and uniformly written romantic narratives per month.[1] Formerly a moderately successful Canadian publishing house, in 1971 it hired Lawrence Heisley, a Proctor & Gamble marketing man, as its new president. He turned feminine romantic love into superprofits for his then all-male board of directors by transferring to the sale of books the techniques used to sell detergent to housewives. By turning love into a consumer product, Harlequin increased its net earnings from $110,000 in 1970 to over $21 million by 1980.

But packaging alone cannot account for the loyalty of 14 million readers. The novels' flyleaf assures readers that 'no one touches the heart of a woman quite like Harlequin', and marketing statistics—188 million books sold in 1980, sales accounting for 30 per cent of all mass market paperbacks in a major bookstore chain—support this claim.[2] What exactly is the secret to a woman's heart that Harlequin and its rivals have learned, and how have they turned this knowledge into profits for themselves?

Secrets of a Woman's Heart

Harlequin may owe its dramatic growth in popularity to the fact that the romances now respond to specific needs of working women. Focusing on the juncture between their sexual, emotional needs on the one hand and their needs concerning work relations on the other, it involves both their deepest, most private, most intimate feelings, and at the same time their very broad relations to the process of social history. Impressive analyses by Tania Modleski, Ann Barr Snitow and Janice A. Radway[3] have explained the popularity of mass market romances by examining how they respond to women's deep yearnings, but have not talked about why these romances have gained their phenomenal popularity just in the past 10 to 15 years. Moreover, in the past couple of years, since Snitow and Modleski wrote their studies, the romance industry has been undergoing an accelerated process of change. Given the fact that their heroines' stories increasingly join the personal, sexual relations of private life to the work relations of the marketplace, we might ask what in the Harlequin formula responds to new needs of women as a result of recent profound changes in both their domestic and paid labor situations, and how that formula might change in the future.

As Harlequin Romances have become more popular, more and more of their heroines have jobs. Yet these working heroines have more subversive desires than simply to join the labor force: they are reacting to the limits of a sterile, harsh, alienating fragmented work world itself. In spite of some fairly glamorous jobs, the working Harlequin heroines, melodramatically engaged in defiant struggles with their heroes, who are usually their bosses, demand from them and their world two additional changes in their situation. First, as the heroine struggles against the irresistible power of her hero, she also struggles *for* something, which she calls 'love', but beyond that does not define any further. What she wants from the hero is recognition of herself as a unique, exceptional individual. In addition to acknowledging her sexual attraction and her professional competence, he must also recognize her as a subject, or recognize her from her own point of view.

Second, the heroines seek more than simply to succeed in the man's world. An analysis of the romances will show that on an implicit level they seek not so much an improved life within the possibilities of the existing social structure, but a different social structure. The very facts that the hero is both boss and lover, that the world of work and business is romanticized and eroticized, and that in it love flourishes suggest that the Harlequin heroines seek an end to the division between the domestic world of love and sentiment and the public world of work and business.

Since in Harlequin the struggle to gain recognition for a deep feminine self merges with the struggle—however implicit or utopian—to create a new, more integrated world, a reading of these romances uncovers a certain power possessed by even formulaic narratives. Because they cannot help but recount a woman's life all of a piece, they may be able to reveal certain insights about women's lives and women's desires that escape empirical science. These romance narratives show us that an individual woman's need to be recognized in her own sense of self and the need to change a more global social structure are interdependent.

In *Loving with a Vengeance: Mass-produced fantasies for women*, Tania Modleski says that 'in Harlequin Romances, the need of women to find meaning and pleasure in activities which are not wholly male-centered such as work or artistic creation is generally scoffed at'.[4] But in the past few years that has changed. Although in the mid-1970s, the average Harlequin heroine was either just emerging from home, or was a secretary or nurse who quit her unrewarding job at marriage, by the late 1970s, many Harlequin heroines had unusual and interesting, if not bizarre careers. More and more frequently both hero and heroine started taking the heroine's job or creative activity seriously.

Almost never images of passive femininity, their heroines of the late 1970s are active, intelligent and capable of at least economic independence. Nicole, in *Across the Great Divide*, is a dedicated and competent swimming coach; Anna in *Battle with Desire* is an internationally known violinist at the age of 22; Kerry in *The Dividing Line*, also 22, is on the board of directors of a prestigious department store. Furthermore, the hero often gives moral support to the heroine in her career, and intends to continue supporting her career aspirations after their marriage.[5]

By the early 1980s, the heroines' careers go beyond the wildest dreams of the most ardent member of the National Organization for Women and often become the selling point that distinguishes one romance from another. As one example, Danni in *Race for Revenge* is about to 'succeed triumphantly in the male dominated world of motor racing',[6] and Karla Mortley in Candlelight Romance's *Game Plan* 'joins the rugged New York flyers as a ballet trainer', only to find that 'the womanizing quarterback MacGregor proves hard to tackle'.[7] In 1984 Harlequin added to its line a new, more sophisticated series, Harlequin Temptations, where the hero worries that the heroine will place her career before him. In the romances of the mid-1980s the careers range from the banal, like movie actresses and famous pop singers, to the unique, like engineering PhD Frankie Warburton in *Love Circuits*, who falls in love with the electronics heir that contracts for her services as a computer consultant. More than one heroine is an advertising executive who falls in love with her client. University editorial assistant Liza Manchester in *Public Affair* is an 'outspoken member of Graham University's feminist community' who falls in love with Professor Scott Harburton. And—inevitably—Garbriella Constant in *By Any Other Name* is a best-selling romance writer who falls in love with her publisher.[8]

Although the hero of these romances is not always the heroine's boss, he most often either is the boss or holds a position of economic or professional power over the heroine. More important, as the advertising brochure for the new Harlequin Temptations series demonstrates, the boss figure remains the prototype for the Harlequin hero. Promising to let us experience 'The passionate torment of a woman torn between two loves . . . the siren call of a career . . . the magnetic advances of an impetuous employer', it advertises its flagship novel of the new series, *First Impressions*, by saying: 'Tracy Dexter couldn't deny her attraction to her new boss.'[9]

Because in Harlequin Romances, plot, characters, style and erotic scenes have been set by formula, freedom to vary the heroine's job gives an author one of the few avenues for bringing originality, individuality and creative freedom into a romance. An unusual job offers compositional opportunities for an unusual setting and unusual conflicts between the hero and heroine. But the job situation also serves a deeper purpose. Beyond showing the uncanny ability of mass culture to ingest any kind of social, economic, or cultural historic change in women's lives, these heroines with their fabulous jobs might help to explain why women respond to romance so much more massively than to other mass market reading. New Right how-to books exhort their readers to be 'real' women by staying home to protect the family; liberal how-to books, such as *The Cinderella Complex,* urge women to cease wanting to 'be *part* of somebody else' and 'to get into the driver's seat' of 'the man's world'[10]; and women's magazines claim to show readers how to excel in each separate segment—sex, work, family, emotion—of their madly disarticulated, schizophrenic lives. Supermarket romances, alone among mass market literature, focus on the conflictive relations among these segments.

Women's Work/Women's Culture

The same socioeconomic changes of the 1960s and 1970s, which created a new kind of working woman, also created the conditions for Harlequin's commercial success. These are, according to Harry Braverman in *Labor and Monopoly Capital,* the restructuring of business into huge international conglomerates; the 'extraordinary growth of commercial concerns' (like Harlequin) in comparison with production; and along with this the extraordinary explosion of bureaucracy and office work with its systems management, computerization and assembly-line processing of paper.[11] These conditions include new categories of work, and, occurring around 1960, 'the creation of a new class of workers', low-paid clerical workers, overwhelmingly female. According to Roslyn L. Feldberg and Evelyn Nakano Glenn, between 1960 and 1980 employment in clerical and kindred occupations doubled. They cite dramatic growth in work categories created by the new technology, and also by the business expansion that Braverman describes.[12]

The women who work for these huge conglomerates and bureaucracies, in clerical positions, in service positions and as assemblers of the new electronic machinery, as well as the women whose shopping, banking, education, medical care and welfare payments have been changed by these new developments, constitute a large part of the readership of Harlequin Romances. And the musicians, painters, poets, coaches, car racers, Olympic athletes, photographers and female executives of the romances, with their glamorous jobs, are these readers' idealized alter egos. Although readers are well aware that the romances are unreal fantasies, their passionate attachment to the genre could not be explained without an intense identification with the heroine on the level of ego ideal.

Between 40 and 60 per cent of the mass market romance readership works outside the home.[13] The assumption has been that these romances contain housewifely fantasies, but if that is so then why do so many of them revolve around work situations, however glamorized? Among the many possible reasons for this, the most obvious is that as countless statistics show, almost all these readers can expect to work sometime in their lives, moving in and out of the labor market. Moreover, a good number of them can expect to be single mothers, for at least part of their lives. But these fantasies involving work situations suggest that feminists, and especially feminist organizers, might do away with this categorization of women into working women on the one hand and housewives on the other. The content of Harlequins suggest that the readers, like the heroines, do not compartmentalize their lives in this way, becoming different people when they go to work. Although the immediate concerns caused by workplace or home may be different, our deeper abiding concerns remain the same, whether at home or on the job. To draw a strong division between working women and housewives comes perhaps from applying to women a male model. For the average man, work and home really are very different. At work the man must accept the power of his employer, while at home he is master of his family and finds relaxation. The average woman, on the other hand, finds herself contending with a masculine power both at home and at work. By combining the sexual domination of a lover and the economic domination of an employer in the same masculine figure, Harlequins draw attention to the specificity of the contemporary feminine situation.

In a sensitive study that explains the popularity of mass market romances by interviewing a group of readers from one bookstore, Janice Radway says that women report they read the romances for relaxation and escape. 'When asked to specify what they are fleeing from,' she says, 'they invariably mention the "pressures" and "tensions" they experience as wives and mothers.'[14] A group of working women I spoke to also said they read the romances to escape. But the escape portrayed in the working heroine's romances is somewhat more precise about the pressures and tensions it aims to soothe.

The heroines' fantasy dilemmas compensate exactly for those elements of women's work in the clerical factories—and for that matter in any factories—that critics of job automation find most oppressive. A reading of Harlequin Romances in the context of these critiques yields insight into the heroines' (and perhaps the authors' and readers') conflicts; their grievances against their living, working and sexual situations; and the intensity with which they feel these grievances, but also into the extent to which the romances and their authors have adopted the basic corporate structure of present work relations as the invisible and unchallenged framework of their romantic visions.

Two themes of revolt and fantasy escape that run most strongly through the romances concern the depersonalization of the cybernetic world and the powerlessness of the feminine individual within it. Surprisingly enough, the heroine's lack of power and freedom corresponds rather closely to what sociologists have found out about the worker's lack of power and freedom in the computerized and bureaucratized workplace. According to Braverman, contemporary clerical workers and low-paid factory workers suffer from a lack of control over the work process, over the social use to which products will be put, over their own mental processes, and even over their own bodies. The assembly line structuring of clerical work, says Braverman, results from applying to office work the techniques of Taylorism, which factory owners began using in the 1920s and 1930s to gain maximum efficiency by breaking down the unity of the labor process into its smallest discrete elements. While Taylorization yields greater productivity, its effects on the worker, whose tasks and bodily movements are also broken down to their smallest elements, are devastating.

With every movement of the office worker or lower-paid assembler controlled for maximum efficiency, and every moment of her day accounted for, she has lost all decision-making power not only over the products she is making, but also over her own bodily movements and minutest scheduling of her own time. Braverman talks about clerical workers feeling 'shackled' and quotes a vice-president of an insurance company as saying of a room full of key punchers: 'All they lack is a chain!'[15] Ida Russakoff Hoos, in *Automation in the Office,* reports interviewing a supervisor who described key punchers keeping supplies of tranquilizers in their desks and feeling 'frozen'.[16] And Ellen Cantarow cites findings of 'appalling rates of coronary heart disease in women clerical workers'[17] as a result of lack of control.

The force of Harlequin comes from its ability to combine, often in the same image, the heroine's fantasy escape from these restraints and her idealized, romanticized and eroticized compliance with them. It does this through diverse types of story elements, which are remarkably consistent from romance to romance. A first and most simple compensation of the readers' situation is that, by contrast to the jobs most working readers have, the jobs of Harlequin heroines, while greatly varied, almost always have in common that the work is meaningful in itself, challenging, has a direct effect on the well-being of other people, is a craft that requires skill or talent and is one that gains recognition for a job well done. A second, slightly more complex compensatory fantasy is that Harlequin heroines do fight for, and win, control over their jobs and a great deal of freedom.

A central, and one of the most attractive, compensations offered by Harlequin is that the romances respond to the depersonalization of the Harlequin reader's life, not only in her workplace, but also in her shopping, her banking, in her relations to government, to school and to all the services she now obtains from giant, faceless bureaucracies, which make her feel, as Tessa in *The Enchanted Island* thinks, 'like a small, impersonal cog in a machine'.[18] The relations between the heroines and their bosses may be love/hate relations, but they are intensely intimate. Although decisions about how the reader spends her time in the corporate workplace are made by real men, she never sees them. In the conglomerate, the real decision-makers may be in another state or another country, and in terms of the corporate hierarchy, they are in another universe. They are so removed from the secretary or assembler as to seem disembodied gods. In the world of Harlequin, the god descends from the executive suite and comes to her.

But in addition to this direct compensation for the depersonalized relations of the corporate world, the working heroines also idealize the reader's sense that she herself has been reduced to one more interchangeable part of the office's 'integrated systems'. In *Battle with Desire* Gareth the hero, who is also violinist Anna's conductor, tells her: 'You and I together, Anna, will give them a performance they'll never forget. . . . The music will be a prelude to our love' (157). Yet Anna is hurt and asks herself: 'But was it love for herself, or because she had been the instrument of such superb music?' Although Anna's position is a highly idealized fantasy, it raises the same conflict experienced by those women in Hoos's study who feel their bosses regard them (if at all) as an instrument or as part of the machinery.

A fourth and still more complex compensation concerns directly the theme of power. In the romances, the heroine fights ardently against the power the hero has over her. Because the power figure represents both her lover and her boss, this relation between one man and one woman reverberates on a larger network of social relations, all structured according to inequality of power. Thus the boss-lover can become an analogy for other men in the reader's life, such as her husband. The heroines reject the dependence or submissiveness that is most often forced upon their resisting spirit: Nicole in *Across the Great Divide* finds in her new boss Lang 'something too suggestive of a rugged relentlessness . . . that she just couldn't bring herself to suffer meekly and which set her on the offensive'. In her own mind, she rejects arrogant hierarchies, and when the board of the swim club threatens to fire her 'she was determined not to submit tamely. If she was going down, she would be going down fighting!' (30, 165).

In the most complex and contradictory of story elements, the romances combine in one image and escape from the 'frozen' feeling of working readers and an eroticized acquiescence to it. The heroine's struggle-filled, stormy relationship with the hero involves a strange combination of tempestuous physical movement and physical restraint by the hero. In one of dozens of examples, Nicole, in *Across the Great Divide*, struggles with Lang.

> 'I hate the lot of you!' she sobbed brokenly. 'And don't touch me!' trying to jerk out of his hold. 'You're all a load of two faced liars, only interested in your own egotistical aims.' Then, when he didn't release her, 'I said don't *touch* me!' as she began pummelling violently at his broad chest.
>
> 'For God's sake, Nicky!' Lang gripped her wrists grimly in one hand and wrenched open the car door with the other. 'Get in,' he muttered, and bundled her flailing figure on to the back seat. Slamming the door behind them, he pinned her helplessly to his muscular form until she had exhausted her struggles and consented to stay there, crying quietly. (140)

The 'shackles' of the office or factory job are on the one hand compensated for by vigorous movement; on the other hand they are romanticized and eroticized. The hero restrains the heroine not out of an impersonal desire for efficiency, but out of a very personal desire to have her respond to him. He restrains her in an attempt to control her anger, to arouse her sexually, to fulfill his burning desire to have her confess her feelings for him, or all three. The heroine's anxiety no longer has its source in the cold, nagging unpleasant fear that her boss will fire her if she rebels (or that her husband will reject her or worse) but in the warm, seductive, obsessive fear that she will not be able to resist his potent sexual magnetism, especially since he goes to considerable effort to create intimate situations where he can exert it. Transformed by the romances, the heroine's restraint becomes on the one hand intermittent, and on the other hand emotionally and sexually gratifying. Instead of having to take tranquilizers to repress her internalized rage, like the office workers in Hoos's study and Cantarow's article, the Harlequin heroine is privileged to vent it violently and directly against her restrainer, even while this restraint takes an idealized form.

This strange mingling of protest and acquiescence to the situation of many contemporary women makes the Harlequin Romances so seductive and contradictory. On the one hand, the heroine is empowered to revolt without risking masculine rejection because the hero desires her more the angrier she becomes, but on the other hand, the romances also sexualize her impotence. This particular combination of elements intensifies our emotional involvement with a story that both arouses and nullifies the very subversive impulses that attracted us to it in the first place.

Changing Times, Changing Conflict

Harlequin's double message is all the more potent in that the heroine's conflict is also double. At stake for her in the romances that put the work situation at the center of the plot is both her social identity and the deepest core of her feminine self. A surprising number of Harlequins employ the same vocabulary to describe the inner conflict of the heroine as she struggles against the hero on his own grounds where he has all the weapons. His main weapon in this idealized world is his powerful sexual attraction; her main weakness is her susceptibility to that attraction, which quickly becomes total love. Her struggle aims to prevent the hero from exploiting her love for his own sexual desires, and the conflict this struggle awakens in her is described by the key words 'humiliation' and 'pride'. Nicole finds that

> the most galling part of the whole episode had been her unqualified surrender to Lang's lovemaking. That she should have so readily submitted—no, welcomed it was far more honest, she confessed painfully—was something she found impossible to accept. The only thought left to salvage at least some of her *pride* being the knowledge that Lang wasn't aware how deeply her feelings were involved. Her *humiliation* was bad enough now, but it would have known no bounds if she had inadvertently revealed how she really felt about him. (144, my italics)

In *Stormy Affair* Amber faces the same problem: 'She could not say: "I would love to live here and marry you but only if you say you love me. . . ." At least she still had sufficient *pride* to avoid the *humiliation* such a statement would cause.'[19]

Through the heroine's impossible choice between two painful and destructive alternatives, summed up by the terms 'humiliation' and

'pride', Harlequin Romances call attention to a feminine character structure that differs from the masculine one. Both Radway and Snitow have
discussed this feminine character structure in the Harlequin heroine,
and both have relied on Nancy Chodorow's theory to analyze it.[20] According to Chodorow, capitalist-patriarchal family structure and child-
rearing practices produce in boys more strongly defined and closed-off
ego boundaries, and in girls more fluid ego boundaries, so that men
tend to define themselves as a separate, self-sufficient entity, while
women tend to define themselves in terms of their relation to other people. Unable to adopt a rocklike, closed, thinglike self, such as the one the
hero seems to possess, the Harlequin heroine's self alternates until the
end of the romance between two forms of destruction: 'humiliation',
which signals a dissolution of her self into the masculine self, and
'pride', a self-control that shrivels up her self by denying its needs and
desires. Solution: the hero must recognize and adopt the relational, feminine form of the self.

This difference in character structure between women and men, which
Harlequins emphasize as the cause of the heroine's problems, is inherited
from the industrial revolution. With the separation of work from home,
women were socialized to immerse themselves in the intense emotional
world of the domestic sphere. Self-perpetuating family practices made
that socialization seem like a 'natural' feminine character. Now with the
cybernetic revolution, women must also, like men, make their way in the
rationalistic world of business, but they take with them the emotional
makeup they have inherited from the past. They do not have, and in
many cases do not want to have, the harder, more competitive, success-
oriented emotional equipment with which men have been socialized in
order to succeed, or even simply to survive.

If Harlequin heroines' character structure is inherited from the industrial revolution, their narrative structure is also inherited from one of the
most prominent literary genres of the industrial revolution, the romantic
novel. Although Sally Mitchell and Tania Modleski have traced the genealogy of Harlequin Romances back to forms of nineteenth-century
popular fiction, such as seduction novels, historical romances, penny
magazine, aristocratic romances, and gothic novels,[21] the quest for self-
fulfillment carried out by the heroes and heroines of nineteenth-century
high romanticism has also found a twentieth-century refuge in contemporary mass market romances. As writer Louella Nelson told me of her
romance *Freedom's Fortune:* 'This book is about a woman's quest for
courage and self-worth.'[22]

The inner conflict of the Harlequin heroines is a more explicitly sexualized version of feminine conflicts analyzed by authors writing during the
industrial revolution, such as the Brontë sisters. Problems of sexual dif-

ference that beset the Harlequin heroines also confront the heroines of
Brontë's *Shirley*, where Caroline Helstone says:

> 'Shirley, men and women are so different: they are in such a different posi-
> tion. Women have so few things to think about—men so many: you may
> have a friendship with a man while he is almost indifferent to you. Much of
> what cheers your life may be dependent on him, while not a feeling or inter-
> est of moment in his eyes may have reference to you.'

Shirley answers:

> 'Caroline,' demanded Miss Keeldar abruptly, 'don't you wish you had a pro-
> fession—a trade?'[23]

The Harlequin heroines do have a trade—and a lot of things to think
about—but they still resemble the Brontëan heroines in that for them sexual sensation, feelings of love and rational thought are all intimately connected. They cannot be compartmentalized and sealed off from each
other. When these heroines fall in love, they think about love and their
lover all the time. The heroes of Harlequin Romances, like the heroes of
Jane Eyre and *Shirley*, are emotionally divided between the world of love
and the world of business and public affairs, and therefore fragmented in
their psychic structure. For them, or so it seems to the heroine, sex is divorced from other feelings, and love from other areas of their life. It
seems that whenever he wills it, the hero can simply shut her image off
and think about other things.

From this fragmentation, the Harlequin heroes, like their nineteenth-
century brothers M. Emanuel in *Villette* or Robert Moore in *Shirley*, draw
their strength for success in the world. But since the Harlequin heroines
must now also survive alone in that world, they can only, as Nicole says,
attempt to conceal their feelings, try to pretend to be like the hero. But the
heroine's wholeness, which is also her weakness, means that her outer
appearance and actions cannot but reflect her inner emotions. The heroines are transparent where the heroes are opaque.

In fact the heroine frequently suspects until the end of the novel that
the hero has no tender feelings under his harsh surface, and that therefore he does not have to exhaust all his energy in the fight for self-control
the way she does. In *Stormy Affair*, for instance, Amber thinks that 'she
must pull herself together and not let Hamed Ben Slouma see that he in
any way affected her' (25). But 'Hamed with his keen perception knew
exactly what was going on in her mind. . . . "Perhaps your desires were
greater than mine, or do you think it could be that I have more self-

control? You're very *transparent,* my charming one"' (100, my italics). The effect of all these differences between the hero and heroine is to increase the hero's power over this outsider in his world. But even this conflict contains within it wish-fulfilling compensations. If Ben Slouma finds Amber transparent, at least he cares enough to observe her transparency and is interested enough in her to notice what goes on inside her. If the heroine's anger is impotent, at least she has the chance to vent it with great rage at its rightful target, and at least he stays around to listen to it, even, as in the case of Tessa's boss Andrew, 'with interest' (*The Enchanted Island,* 157).

Utopian and formulaic as they are, in Harlequin Romances the heroine's struggle and conflict serve to overcome something more than a merely psychological passivity or a role that a woman could simply choose to play or not to play. Although its roots in a total social situation are not so clearly shown as in the novels of the Brontës, the Harlequin heroine's conflict is shown to be a very real lack of power to be herself in relations controlled by others. Her very activity and anger are signs of her impotence in the face of the more powerful male. Thus Nicole 'seethed impotently' (*Across the Great Divide,* 99), and Debra 'tried to control the rage and humiliation she was feeling', while Jordan's 'composure wasn't disturbed by [Kathleen's] burst of anger'.[24]

Like their nineteenth-century predecessors Jane Eyre, Caroline Helstone and Lucy Snowe, the Harlequin heroines seek recognition as a subject in their own right from their own point of view. And also like these earlier heroines, Harlequin heroines find that this recognition must take a different form from that sought by romantic heroes. A hero like St. John Rivers in *Jane Eyre* becomes closed in on himself, static and self-sufficient as an absolute totality when he achieves this recognition. Brontë rejects this form of the self and the narcissistic form of love it demands, and seeks fulfillment for a form of the self which is essentially fluid, essentially changing, and essentially involved in a dynamic, living network of intimate relations with others.

Like the Brontë heroines, although in a less reflective and more narcissistic way,[25] the Harlequin heroines find that women in our society are already endowed with this relational form of the self, but that it never achieves recognition or fulfillment. The cause of pain and obscurity rather than success, it in fact tends to get lost altogether in a relation with the hero's harder, closed self, and to merge into his. This is what Anna finds in *Battle with Desire:* 'Anna knew she mustn't give in. . . . And it wasn't getting any easier to resist, the urge to fight was melting away, so she made one final attempt at self-respect' (19). What really melts here are the boundaries of the heroine's personhood and her sense of individuality as she loses herself in the other. Harlequins, unlike 'real life', provide a solution: the hero adopts the feminine form of the self, recognizes it as valid, and gives the heroine the same tender devotion she gives him.

The genius of the Harlequin Romances is to combine the struggle for the recognition of feminine selfhood and the struggle to make the work world a home for that self. As the cover blurb of *The Dividing Line* tells us of Kerry and Ross who have inherited interests in a department store: 'She liked old-fashioned friendliness and service. He was all for modern impersonal efficiency. Between them, Sinclairs was becoming a battle ground.' Even the idealized form of Kerry's angry struggle against Ross, and violinist Anna's questioning resentment against Gareth, suggest a need to go beyond an analysis like that in *Hearth and Home: Images of women in the mass media,* edited by Gaye Tuchman, Arlene Kaplan Daniels and James Benet. The book criticizes the mass media image of women for implying that 'her fate and her happiness rest with a man, not with participation in the labor force',[26] but it would be impoverishing even the impoverished romances to say that their heroines really want both. They want so much more besides. Not content with Helen Gurley Brown's rationalistic advice to 'have it all', they don't want it the way it is now; they want the world of labor to change so that women can find happiness there, and they want men to change so that men will just as much find *their* happiness with women.

Hearth and Home sees hope for equality in 'economically productive women who insist on the abandonment of old prejudices and discriminatory behaviors'.[27] But Harlequin Romances suggest women abandon the present structures of economic production because those structures force women to give up their values, their ethos, and even their particular sense of self for success, or, more likely, for mere survival. The vastly popular Harlequin Romances implicitly and potentially pose a demand for profound structural transformations of the total social world we inhabit. And like their romantic forebears, the heroines desire that this new world be not just our same old world improved, but a different, better world. The problem is that Harlequin Enterprises, having learned these secrets to a woman's heart, exploited them by turning them into marketable formulae which divorced the conflicts from their causes and cut off the path towards reflecting upon any realistic solutions.

Romantic Aspirations—Rationalized Form

In her analysis of women readers, Radway has pointed out that

> we would do well not to condescend to romance readers as hopeless traditionalists who are recalcitrant in their refusal to acknowledge the emotional

costs of patriarchy. We must begin to recognize that romance reading is fueled by dissatisfaction and disaffection.[28]

Yet there is a crucial distinction to be made between dismissing the very justifiable fantasies and desires of Harlequin readers or the undoubted achievements of romance writers, and criticizing a multinational publishing corporation that exploits those fantasies and achievements. Modleski is probably closer to the mark when she says of Harlequin that 'their enormous and continuing popularity . . . suggests that they speak to very real problems and tensions in women's lives', but that the texts arouse subversive anxieties and desires, and then 'work to neutralize them'.[29]

The methods of editing, producing, marketing and distributing Harlequin Romances are part and parcel of the depersonalized, standardized, mechanistic conglomerate system that the Harlequin heroines oppose. Harlequin heroines seek interconnectedness in the social, sexual and economic world as a whole. Yet their very search is contained in a static, thinglike, literary structure, which denies their quest and turns it into its opposite.

Radway reports that the readers she interviewed understand very well that 'the characters and events . . . of the typical romance do not resemble the people and occurrences they must deal with in their daily lives'.[30] At issue in the case of Harlequin, however, is not the illusion that the events in the romances are real, but the illusion that reading a romance constitutes only a relation to a text and to an author. To see the act of reading a romance as simply a relation between the reader and the printed page is to isolate this act from its larger context.

We are used to thinking of a publisher as a mediator between the readers and a book written by an individual author, but Harlequin changed this. Although Harlequin is studied in few university literature classes, it is referred to in management classes as a sterling example of successful business practices that students should learn to emulate. According to business professor Peter Killing, Harlequin's success is due precisely to its doing away with the reader–text and reader–author relation:

Harlequin's formula was fundamentally different from that of traditional publishers: content, length, artwork, size, basic formats, and print, were all standardized. Each book was not a new product, but rather an addition to a clearly defined product line. The consequences of this uniformity were significant. The reader was buying a *Harlequin novel*, rather than a book of a certain title by a particular author. . . . There was no need to make decisions about layouts, artwork, or cover design. The standardized size made warehousing and distribution more efficient. Employees hired from mass-marketing companies such as Proctor and Gamble had skills and aptitudes which led them to do well at Harlequin.[31]

Harlequin thought of everything—except the readers, the authors and the creative freedom which has traditionally been the cornerstone of literature in western culture. This publishing giant molded romantic aspirations into superrationalist forms of communication, the very antithesis of the readers' desires.

It is not the idealization of marriage in the romances, nor any specific content, that neutralizes their challenges to patriarchal ideology, but rather the form of the romances, and the form of communication Harlequin sets up between the corporate giant and the readers. Like the Brontëan heroes and heroines, whose desires for sublime sexual communion were a protest against the rationalizing forces of the industrial revolution, the Harlequin romances both protest against and compensate for their readers' dissatisfaction with the Taylorization of their lives as workers and consumers of goods and services. But when Harlequin instituted its new methods, the romantic quest and the sublime sexual communion were themselves Taylorized, so that the apparent escape from a depersonalized, coldly compartmentalized world led the reader right back into it.

Harlequin reduced romantic aspirations to the rational distillation of a formula. The General Editorial Guidelines of 1982 for *Worldwide Library Superromances,* in its directions to writers, broke down the fluid process of the romantic quest into its component set of static categories—structure, characters, plot, subplots, romance, sex, viewpoint and writing style— and in the past even set forth each step in the plot.

- Introduction of hero and heroine, their meeting.
- Initial attraction or conflict between them.
- Romantic conflicts or heroine's qualms about hero.
- Counterbalance to developing romance (i.e., sensual scenes, getting to know each other, growth of love vs. conflicts).
- Hero's role in creating conflict.
- Resolution of conflicts and happy ending, leading to marriage.
- The development of the romance should be the primary concern of the author, with other story elements integrated into the romance.[32]

Sex (always of course coupled with 'shared feeling rather than pure male domination'—General Editorial Guidelines) is meted out in measured amounts and in measured doses of 'sensuality' at measured intervals of the plot. As a further rationalization, the romantic quest can even be broken down numerically and quantified, so that, as the 1982 Guidelines for Writing Harlequin's *New* American Romances tell us, 'parts of the plot can take place anywhere in the world provided that at least 80% of the novel takes place in the United States'.[33]

But in 1984, with changes in readers' tastes and the growth of the authors' professional association Romance Writers of America, the Editorial Guidelines deny there is a formula: 'Every aspiring Harlequin writer has a very clear picture of what makes these lines so successful, to the extent that some people have even tried to reduce it to a formula'.[34]

A Changing Genre: The Author as Heroine

Yet so much has changed and continues to change since 1980, when growth in the industry led authors to organize Romance Writers of America as a support group, that it is impossible to tell what will happen in the future. Present developments could lead not only to changes in the texts of the romances, but also to changes in the romance industry. Harlequin's very success could open up the potential contradictions inherent in the corporation's methods. The same kinds of struggle against rationalizing power its themes portray could be turned against it. When Romance Writers of America held its first national convention in 1981, the organization saw as its main opponent a literary establishment and vaguely defined public that did not recognize the value of romance as 'women's literature'.[35] But as conditions governing author–corporate relations change, the industry itself might become another opponent.

Harlequin has responded to declining sales in face of competition by the classic strategy of buying out its major competitor (Silhouette Romances). But authors have had a quite different response to growth in the romance industry. Although Harlequin's monopolizing strategy should work to make even more impersonal the author-publisher relation, authors have been seeking (as if in imitation of their own heroines) more affirming relations with the publisher and greater job satisfaction.

In her study of Harlequin Romances, Margaret Ann Jensen reports that the experience of becoming writers has caused many romance authors to 'identify themselves as feminists', to become self-assertive, and to become more aware of themselves as working women who have succeeded in a profession quite difficult to break into. In addition to combatting 'the negative image of romance in the literary world', romance writers, she says, have two new concerns. They 'are attempting to organize to improve the standards within their field'; they are also engaging in 'an increasing outspokenness about the romantic fiction industry' and making 'critical responses to it'.[36] At a Romance Writers of America meeting in Southern California, one candidate for office in the organization raised these same two issues. She spoke first of the need to 'raise the standards of writing' and prevent 'mediocre' writing. Then, after mentioning other writers' organizations that are more 'militant', she spoke of the need to 'increase our clout with publishers' and 'improve the deal we're getting on contracts'.[37]

Although authors still speak with indignation of the scorn that they face, saying that romances deserve the same respect as mysteries and science fiction, they also raise the above-mentioned other issues concerning the romance industry itself. Authors find themselves disadvantaged by the very marketing practice of Harlequin to which Peter Killing attributes Harlequin's economic success: Harlequin promotes its lines but rarely its authors. And Silhouette has followed suit. In a 1980 interview, Silhouette president P.J. Fennel said: 'We're out to get brand name loyalty, so we're not selling individual titles.'[38] Because of this practice, and because a romance is on the market for only a month, romance authors have to hustle their own books and find their own markets. They can also, they report, have a difficult time getting royalties from the publisher, with waits of up to two years.[39]

Although this kind of issue is just beginning to be addressed, the issues concerning quality of writing and personal creativity have already begun to be acted upon. Each product line in the romance industry has its own formula, and as the formulae have multiplied, they have also loosened. As a result, an author can pick the line that gives her the most freedom. More important, through Romance Writers of America, authors have formed their own critique groups, so that influences on their writing now also come from their peers and not only from the publishing institutions. Romances are beginning to be better and more carefully written, with more variety in the formulae and with more attention to detail. Although some romances repeat a mechanical version of the formula, other romances like Leigh Roberts's *Love Circuits* are different. Roberts's work, where the hero, tender and loving from the beginning, wears a Charlotte Brontë T-shirt, and where the heroine has a witty sense of humour, brings some surprising transformations to the formula. Like any kind of formula writing—or any kind of writing—romance writing requires skill and talent.

As the corporation follows its destiny of expansion, conglomeration and product diversification, differences between the mass production needs of the corporation and authors' needs may prove to be potential cracks in the Harlequin machine. The authors' own quest for creative individuality, for economic independence and for recognition may make them the heroines of their own real life romance, with conflicts and adventures outside the text just as gripping as those inside.

Notes

1. Catering to an exclusively feminine audience, mass market romances are an international phenomenon, with single romances or whole romance series being translated into as many as fourteen languages. Harlequin Enterprises, the best-selling and most successful publisher of this genre, has been imitated by many competitors both in America and in Europe. Harlequin publishes a set number of romances per month, categorized into different series according to a carefully measured degree of explicit sex, known as 'sensuality' in the trade. Harlequin publishes Harlequin Romances, Harlequin Presents and Harlequin Temptations, as well as a mystery-romance series, a gothic romance series, a longer series called Superromances, and an American romance series. Like any corporate consumer product, Harlequin and its competitors are constantly 'diversifying' their line, proliferating into a dizzying array of series.

Other publishers now have romance series for more mature and/or divorced women, like Berkeley-Jove's Second Chance at Love, or for adolescent girls, like Simon & Schuster's First Love. This series shares the teen-romance shelves with the Sweet Dream series from Bantam; Young Love from Dell; Caprice from Grosset & Dunlap; and two series from Scolastic, whose Wishing Star and Wild Fire sold 2.25 million copies in 1982.

Information taken from Brett Harvey, 'Boy crazy', *Village Voice* 27 (10–16 February 1982), pp. 48–9; Stanley Meisler, 'Harlequins: the romance of escapism', *Los Angeles Times*, 15 November 1980. pt 1, pp. 7–8; Rosemary Nightingale, 'True romances', *Miami Herald*, 5 January 1983; J. D. Reed, 'From bedroom to boardroom: romance novels court changing fancies and adorable profits', *Time,* 13 April 1981, pp. 101–4; interview with Jany Saint-Marcoux, editor of Collections sentimentales, Editions Tallandier; 'Romantic novels find receptive market', *Santa Ana Register,* 26 July 1979, section E, p. 1; *Standard and Poor's Corporation Records* 43 (New York, May 1982), p. 8475.

2. See Reed, 'From bedroom to boardroom'. According to Margaret Ann Jensen, the very success of Harlequin has caused these figures to decline drastically. Because so many publishers are now imitating Harlequin and competing with it, Harlequin's 'share of the market has dropped to 45 per cent. . . . All signs indicate that Harlequin is a financially distressed corporation.' See Jensen, *Love's $weet Return: The Harlequin story* (Toronto: Women's Educational Press, 1984). In order to offset this decline, Harlequin is purchasing Silhouette Romances.

3. Tania Modleski, *Loving with a Vengeance: Mass-produced fantasies for women* (Hamden: Archon Books, 1982); Ann Barr Snitow, 'Mass Market Romance: pornography for women is different', *Radical History Review* 20 (Spring–Summer 1979), pp. 141–61, reprinted in *Powers of Desire: The politics of sexuality,* ed. Ann Snitow, Christine Stansell and Sharon Thomas (New York: Monthly Review Press, 1983); Janice A. Radway, 'Women read the romance: the interaction of text and context', *Feminist Studies* 9 (Spring 1983), pp. 53–78.

4. Modleski, *Loving with a Vengeance,* p. 113.

5. Kerry Allyne, *Across the Great Divide* (1980); Ann Cooper, *Battle with Desire* (1980); Kay Thorpe *The Dividing Line* (1980). All books published by Harlequin

Books, Toronto, London, New York, Amsterdam, Sydney, Hamburg, Paris, Stockholm. Page numbers appear in parentheses in the text.

6. Lynsey Stevens, *Race for Revenge* (Toronto: Harlequin, 1981), back cover.

7. Advertisement for Sara Jennings, *Game Plan* (Garden City, NY: Candlelight Ecstasy Romances, 1984), back cover.

8. Leigh Roberts, *Love Circuits* (Harlequin Temptations, 1984); Sarah James, *Public Affair* (Harlequin American Romance, 1984); Marion Smith Collins, *By Any Other Name* (Harlequin Temptations, 1984). All books published by Harlequin Enterprises, Toronto. Page numbers appear in parentheses in the text.

9. Advertisement for Harlequin Temptations, found in Harlequin books of July 1984 (Toronto: Harlequin Enterprises, 1984).

10. Colette Dowling, *The Cinderella Complex: Women's hidden fear of independence* (New York: Simon & Schuster Pocket Books, 1981), pp. 2, 54.

11. Harry Braverman, *Labor and Monopoly Capital: The degradation of work in the twentieth century*, Special Abridged Ed. (Special Issue of *Monthly Review* 26 (July–August 1974)), p. 50.

According to Braverman, by 1970 in the United States, clerical work was one of the fastest-growing occupations and had become one of the lowest paid, its pay 'lower than that of every type of so-called blue collar work' (p. 51). Of its 10 million members, by 1978, 79.6 per cent were women. In 1970, clerical work included 18 per cent of all gainfully employed persons in the United States, a percentage equal to that of production work of all sorts.

12. Roslyn L. Feldberg and Evelyn Nakano Glenn, 'Technology and work degradation: effects of office automation on women clerical workers', in *Machina ex Dea*, ed. Joan Rothschild (New York: Pergamon Press, 1983), p. 62.

13. Radway, 'Women read the romance', p. 57, reports that 42 per cent of the women in her study work outside the home, and says that Harlequin claims that 49 per cent of its audience works outside the home. A 1984 Waldenbooks survey found that 63 per cent of its romance readers held jobs outside the home (Doug Brown, 'Research dissects the romantic novel', *Los Angeles Times*, 19 September 1984, V. 8).

14. Ibid., p. 60.

15. Braverman, *Labor and Monopoly Capital*, p. 61.

16. Ida Russakoff Hoos, *Automation in the Office* (Washington, 1961), p. 53, cited in Braverman, op. cit.

17. Ellen Cantarow, 'Working can be dangerous to your health', *Mademoiselle*, August 1982, pp. 114–16.

18. Eleanor Farnes, *The Enchanted Island* (Toronto: Harlequin Enterprises, 1971). Page numbers appear in parentheses in the text.

19. Margaret Mayo, *Stormy Affair* (Toronto: Harlequin Enterprises, 1980). Page numbers appear in parentheses in the text.

20. Radway, 'Women read the romance'; Snitow, 'Mass market romance'; and Nancy Chodorow, *The Reproduction of Mothering: Psychoanalysis and the sociology of gender* (Berkeley: University of California Press, 1978).

21. Sally Mitchell, *The Fallen Angel: Chastity, class, and women's reading, 1835–1880* (Bowling Green, Ohio: Bowling Green University Press, 1981); and Modleski, *Loving with a Vengeance*.

22. Personal communication from Louella Nelson, author of *Freedom's Fortune*, Harlequin Superromance (Toronto: Harlequin Books, 1984).

23. Charlotte Brontë, *Shirley* (Baltimore: Penguin, 1974), pp. 234–5.

24. Janet Dailey, *The Matchmakers* (Toronto: Harlequin Enterprises, 1978); Elizabeth Graham, *Come Next Spring* (Toronto: Harlequin Enterprises, 1980).

25. For the role of narcissism in the Harlequin Romances, see Modleski, *Loving with a Vengeance.*

26. Gaye Tuchman, Arlene Kaplan Daniels, and James Benet, eds, *Hearth and Home: Images of women in the mass media* (New York: Oxford University Press, 1978), p. 18.

27. Ibid., p. 4.

28. Radway, 'Women read the romance', p. 68.

29. Modleski, *Loving with a Vengeance,* pp. 14, 30.

30. Radway, 'Women read the romance', p. 59.

31. Peter Killing, *Harlequin Enterprises Limited: Case material of the western school of business administration* (London, Ontario: University of Western Ontario, 1978), p. 3.

32. General Editorial Guidelines, *Worldwide Library Superromances* (Toronto: Harlequin Enterprises, 1982), p. 2.

33. Guidelines for Writing Harlequin's *New* American Romances (Toronto: Harlequin Enterprises, 1982), p. 3.

34. Harlequin Romance and Harlequin Presents Editorial Guidelines (Ontario: Harlequin Books, 1984), p. 1.

35. George Christian, 'Romance writers, going to the heart of the matter (and the market) call for recognition', *Publishers Weekly,* 24 July 1980. The first national conference of Romance Writers of America was held in Houston, in June 1981, with 800 participants, mostly women.

36. Jensen, *Love's $weet Return,* pp. 73–4.

37. Speech given at a meeting of Romance Writers of America, Orange County Chapter.

38. Vivien Lee Jennings, 'The romance wars', *Publisher's Weekly,* 24 August 1984, p. 53.

39. Information gathered from conversations with authors at meeting. See note 37.

PART TWO
Sex, Sexuality, and Gender

The section "From Sex to Sexuality" reopens the question of the relationship between biology and the social construction of gender by considering the impact on the sex-gender system of surgical technologies in the United States and theatrical practices in Japan. Suzanne J. Kessler, an ethnomethodologist (Chapter 7), and Jennifer Robertson, a cultural anthropologist (Chapter 8), consider the constructedness of sex through medical intervention and the naturalness of playing male gender in Japan's all-female Takarazuka Revue. The first essay is about gender assignment when sex (i.e., the genitals) appears ambiguous at birth; the second is about the implications of "putting on" the other gender for the state regulation of female sexuality through theater for a mass audience. Kessler examines the case management of intersexed infants based on interviews with physicians; Robertson analyzes articles in the Japanese mass print media between 1900 and 1945 and from the 1960s onward.

As an ethnomethodologist, Kessler is interested in how physicians make the decisions that transform ambiguous genitals into irrevocable gender assignments and discovers that although medical specialists are claiming to discover an infant's "real" gender, they in fact are artificially producing it based on sex, specifically the size of the micropenis and its future potential to satisfy a (heterosexual) partner. Thus, instead of reducing the complexity of gender to two biological sexes, a two-gender culture is maintained by denying the complexity of biology.

Robertson, as historical anthropologist, is interested in the history of Japanese theater that in its incarnation as Kabuki and as the Takarazuka Revue beginning in 1913, makes no claims for masculinity and femininity as the province of male and female bodies. "Takarasiennes" are assigned "secondary genders" based on physical and sociopsychological characteristics (not genitals) in order to perform as men. The performance of masculinity is justified as a way to understand men in order to produce "good wives, wise mothers" on the part of both actors and audience members. Here the nation regulates gender roles via the theater, even as it promotes cross-dressing, as opposed to medical science that converts the non-normative into the normative, even when not mandated by biology. Postwar Japanese fans nevertheless see not an ideal man but an exemplary woman who transgresses gender boundaries, thereby appropriating these dramatic representations for a lesbian subculture.

Robertson invokes the concept of "androgyny" as a way to think about the relationship among sex, gender, and sexuality by using the term to refer to the "surface politics of the body," the very surface that medical science refuses to politicize. Doctors who specialize in intersexuality resist seeing physical deformities as "natural" and gender as artificial, governed by the aesthetics of genital appearance. Gender as performance makes use of the manipulation of appearance by historical women for alternative sexual meanings, including both homo- and heterogendered representations of homosexual desire.

The section "Constructing Gender" attempts to address the question of gender as woman's biological "difference" from man. Sara Ruddick, a philosopher (Chapter 9), and Lisa Duggan, a political theorist (Chapter 10), consider the double bind of woman as the same as and different from man by, on the one hand, revalorizing the feminine and, on the other hand, transcending the sexed body, both in the name of political action. Ruddick focuses on feminist peace politics as a way of differentiating caring labor from war making. Duggan promotes "queer" politics as a way to overcome the limitations of the essentializing identities that inform gay and lesbian politics. In both cases the point is how to understand the theories of gender that underlie particular political practices.

Ruddick argues that the difference between caregivers and "just-war" theorists is not that caregivers are better people or even that they are less armed, but that they are ready to disobey. Whereas war making is predicated on the willingness to injure, engaging in caring means a willingness to refrain from assaulting bodies. Militarists react violently to the "embodied willfulness" of enemy soldiers; caretakers foster that willfulness in children and the infirm. These two activities do not involve conflicting norms of rationality. Rather, they rely on contrasting attitudes to the manipulation of sexual desire and affectionate attachment. Nearly everyone agrees that "war is in some sense 'masculine'"; equally, caregiving relies on "feminine" maternal practices, understood as caring for those one is unwilling to dominate. The question then becomes how to translate private caregiving into a public action that fosters peace.

Duggan "makes it perfectly clear" that the label "queer" functions as a critique of gay and lesbian politics. The terms "gay and lesbian" rely on a notion of fixed identities borne by a social minority; "queer" offers a critical relation to gender that recognizes the mobility of desire. Thus, "queer politics" refers to a conscious coalition—similar to "women of color"—an "oxymoronic community of difference" in which what is shared is dissent from the dominant organization of sex and gender rather than a unitary, unchanging sexual identity based on same-sex object choice. "Queerness," confrontational in its revalorizing of an epithet and contradictory in its lack of definition, theorizes not only the destabilizing of identity but also the opposition between theory and practice. At the same time, it positions the construction of sexualities at the center of any thinking about culture.

Ruddick begins with the gendering of war and peace while insisting that they do not rely on persons; Duggan tries to imagine a politics that relies not on persons but on coalitions. In the first case, it is never clear how and to what extent men have access to "maternal practices." In the second, it is not clear what the referent of "queer" is, and whether that matters in terms of politics.

In the section "Conceptualizing Difference," the focus is on the construction of gendered meanings not in relationship to sexed bodies but in relationships of power. Both Catharine A. MacKinnon (Chapter 11) and Joan W. Scott (Chapter 12) address an understanding of gender as "difference," as opposed to sameness, by asking how this understanding constrains meaning. In both cases, gender as difference masks male dominance inasmuch as the choice between equality and difference obscures the fact that the opposite of equality is not difference but inequality. For MacKinnon, the meaning of this choice is constrained because it assumes social equality already exists; for Scott, presenting women with this impossible choice makes it difficult for them to recognize how it has been falsely constructed.

MacKinnon as legal theorist examines sex equality within the context of sex discrimination law. In this setting, a woman must be found to be the same as a man before she can file for sex discrimination; any distinction between men and women that is traceable to biology is not discrimination but difference. To claim that they are the same—that is, similarly situated—women must be close to the male standard. For instance, women must be lawyers rather than clerical workers, for whom there is no male standard and therefore no sex discrimination, only difference. In other words, women must be equal to men before they can protest inequality. The question of whether the sexes are ever similarly situated is never asked. Thus, to presume equality already exists, other than in exceptional cases, makes it almost impossible to produce it in law.

Scott, a historian, focuses not on bringing equality to the law but on deconstructing a famous sex discrimination case, *EEOC v. Sears*. Difference is not the distinction that prevents one from recognizing discrimination, but a fixed set of oppositions that produce meaning through metaphors that need to be deconstructed as not natural. It is the "indifference to difference"—the inability to see the opposition of two terms structured as hierarchical and interdependent—that makes it impossible to understand how meaning is produced. But more important, the obscuring of differences within each category of the pair makes it difficult to see that not only are men and women not the same, but women are different from each other. Just as only the female lawyer can suffer sex discrimination because she comes closest to a male standard of "lawyer," historians cannot adequately interpret the history of women's work without understanding the gendered meanings of "worker." Whereas MacKinnon argues that difference is "the velvet glove on the iron fist of domination," Scott insists on the importance of feminism as a series of double moves: Expose the operations of difference; insist that equality rests on difference, not sameness. Gender as difference obscures inequalities between men and women; differences within gender (among women and among men) reveal how sexualities differ. Differences within gender, based on desire, also show how sexual identity is less stable than other categories of analysis.

7 The Medical Construction of Gender

Case Management of Intersexed Infants

SUZANNE J. KESSLER

The birth of intersexed infants, babies born with genitals that are neither clearly male nor clearly female, has been documented throughout recorded time.[1] In the late twentieth century, medical technology has advanced to allow scientists to determine chromosomal and hormonal gender, which is typically taken to be the real, natural, biological gender, usually referred to as "sex."[2] Nevertheless, physicians who handle the cases of intersexed infants consider several factors beside biological ones in determining, assigning, and announcing the gender of a particular infant. Indeed, biological factors are often preempted in their deliberations by such cultural factors as the "correct" length of the penis and capacity of the vagina.

In the literature of intersexuality, issues such as announcing a baby's gender at the time of delivery, postdelivery discussions with the parents, and consultations with patients in adolescence are considered only peripherally to the central medical issues—etiology, diagnosis, and surgical procedures.[3] Yet members of medical teams have standard practices for managing intersexuality that rely ultimately on cultural understandings of gender. The process and guidelines by which decisions about gender (re)construction are made reveal the model for the social construction of gender generally. Moreover, in the face of apparently incontrovertible evidence—infants born with some combination of "female" and "male" reproductive and sexual features—physicians hold an incorrigible belief in and insistence upon female and male as the only "natural" options. This paradox highlights and calls into question the idea that female and male are biological givens compelling a culture of two genders.

Ideally, to undertake an extensive study of intersexed infant case management, I would like to have had direct access to particular events, for example, the deliveries of intersexed infants and the initial discussions among physicians, between physicians and parents, between parents, and among parents and family and friends of intersexed infants. The rarity with which intersexuality occurs, however, made this unfeasible.[4] Alternatively, physicians who have had considerable experience in dealing with this condition were interviewed. I do not assume that their "talk" about how they manage such cases mirrors their "talk" in the situation, but their words do reveal that they have certain assumptions about gender and that they impose those assumptions via their medical decisions on the patients they treat.

Interviews were conducted with six medical experts (three women and three men) in the field of pediatric intersexuality: one clinical geneticist, three endocrinologists (two of them pediatric specialists), one psychoendocrinologist, and one urologist. All of them have had extensive clinical experience with various intersexed syndromes, and some are internationally known researchers in the field of intersexuality. They were selected on the basis of their prominence in the field and their representation of four different medical centers in New York City. Although they know one another, they do not collaborate on research and are not part of the same management team. All were interviewed in the spring of 1985, in their offices, and interviews lasted between forty-five minutes and one hour. Unless further referenced, all quotations in this article are from these interviews.

The Theory of Intersexuality Management

The sophistication of today's medical technology has led to an extensive compilation of various intersex categories based on the various causes of malformed genitals. The "true intersexed" condition, where both ovarian and testicular tissue are present in either the same gonad or in opposite gonads, accounts for fewer than 5 percent of all cases of ambiguous genitals.[5] More commonly, the infant has either ovaries or testes, but the genitals are ambiguous. If the infant has two ovaries, the condition is referred to as female pseudohermaphroditism. If the infant has two testes, the condition is referred to as male pseudohermaphroditism. There are numerous causes of both forms of pseudohermaphroditism, and although there are life-threatening aspects to some of these conditions, having ambiguous genitals per se is not harmful to the infant's health.[6] Although most cases of ambiguous genitals do not represent true intersex, in keeping with the contemporary literature, I will refer to all such cases as intersexed.

Current attitudes toward the intersex condition are primarily influenced by three factors. First are the extraordinary advancements in surgical techniques and endocrinology in the last decade. For example, female genitals can now be constructed to be indistinguishable in appearance from normal natural ones. Some abnormally small penises can be enlarged with the exogenous application of hormones, although surgical skills are not sufficiently advanced to construct a normal-looking and functioning penis out of other tissue.[7] Second, in the contemporary United States the influence of the feminist movement has called into question the valuation of women according to strictly reproductive functions, and the presence or absence of functional gonads is no longer the only or the definitive criterion for gender assignment. Third, contemporary psychological theorists have begun to focus on "gender identity" (one's sense of oneself as belonging to the female or male category) as distinct from "gender role" (cultural expectations of one's behavior as "appropriate" for a female or male).[8] The relevance of this new gender identity theory for rethinking cases of ambiguous genitals is that gender must be assigned as early as possible in order for gender identity to develop successfully. As a result of these three factors, intersexuality is now considered a treatable condition of the genitals, one that needs to be resolved expeditiously.

According to all of the specialists interviewed, management of intersexed cases is based upon the theory of gender proposed first by John Money, J. G. Hampson, and J. L. Hampson in 1955 and developed in 1972 by Money and Anke A. Ehrhardt, which argues that gender identity is changeable until approximately eighteen months of age.[9] "To use the Pygmalion allegory, one may begin with the same clay and fashion a god or a goddess."[10] The theory rests on satisfying several conditions: the experts must insure that the parents have no doubt about whether their child is male or female; the genitals must be made to match the assigned gender as soon as possible; gender-appropriate hormones must be administered at puberty; and intersexed children must be kept informed about their situation with age-appropriate explanations. If these conditions are met, the theory proposes, the intersexed child will develop a gender identity in accordance with the gender assignment (regardless of the chromosomal gender) and will not question her or his assignment and request reassignment at a later age.

Supportive evidence for Money and Ehrhardt's theory is based on only a handful of repeatedly cited cases, but it has been accepted because of the prestige of the theoreticians and its resonance with contemporary ideas about gender, children, psychology, and medicine. Gender and children are malleable; psychology and medicine are the tools used to transform them. This theory is so strongly endorsed that it has taken on the character of gospel. "I think we [physicians] have been raised in the Money theory," one endocrinologist said. Another claimed, "We always approach the problem in a similar way and it's been dictated, to a large extent, by the work of John Money and Anke Ehrhardt because they are the only people who have published, at least in medical literature, any data, any guidelines." It is provocative that this physician immediately followed this assertion with: "And I don't know how effective it really is." Contradictory data are rarely cited in reviews of the literature, were not mentioned by any of the physicians interviewed, and have not diminished these physicians' belief in the theory's validity.[11]

The doctors interviewed concur with the argument that gender be assigned immediately, decisively, and irreversibly, and that professional opinions be presented in a clear and unambiguous way. The psychoendocrinologist said that when doctors make a statement about the infant, they should "stick to it." The urologist said, "If you make a statement that later has to be disclaimed or discredited, you've weakened your credibility." A gender assignment made decisively, unambiguously, and irrevocably contributes, I believe, to the general impression that the infant's true, natural "sex" has been discovered, and that something that was there all along has been found. It also serves to maintain the credibility of the medical profession, reassure the parents, and reflexively substantiate Money and Ehrhardt's theory.

Also according to the theory, if operative correction is necessary, it should take place as soon as possible. If the infant is assigned the male gender, the initial stage of penis repair is usually undertaken in the first year, and further surgery is completed before the child enters school. If the infant is assigned the female gender, vulva repair (including clitoral reduction) is usually begun by three months of age. Money suggests that if reduction of phallic tissue were delayed beyond the neonatal period, the infant would have traumatic memories of having been castrated.[12] Vaginoplasty, in those females having an adequate internal structure (e.g., the vaginal canal is near its expected location), is done between the ages of one and four years. Girls who require more complicated surgical procedures might not be surgically corrected until preadolescence.[13] The complete vaginal canal is typically constructed only when the body is fully grown, following pubertal feminization with estrogen, although more recently some specialists have claimed surgical success with vaginal construction in the early childhood years.[14] Although physicians speculate about the possible trauma of an early childhood "castration" memory, there is no corresponding concern that vaginal reconstructive surgery delayed beyond the neonatal period is traumatic.

Even though gender identity theory places the critical age limit for gender reassignment between eighteen months and two years, the physicians acknowledge that diagnosis, gender assignment, and genital reconstruction cannot be delayed for as long as two years, since a clear gender assignment and correctly formed genitals will determine the kind of interactions parents will have with the child.[15] The geneticist argued that when parents "change a diaper and see genitalia that don't mean much in terms of gender assignment, I think it prolongs the negative response to the baby. . . . If you have clitoral enlargement that is so extraordinary that the parents can't distinguish between male and female, it is sometimes helpful to reduce that somewhat so that the parent views the child as female." Another physician concurred: parents "need to go home and do their job as child rearers with it very clear whether it's a boy or a girl."

Diagnosis

A premature gender announcement by an obstetrician, prior to a close examination of an infant's genitals, can be problematic. Money and his colleagues claim that the primary complications in case management of intersexed infants can be traced to mishandling by medical personnel untrained in sexology.[16] According to one of the pediatric endocrinologists interviewed, obstetricians improperly educated about intersexed conditions "don't examine the babies closely enough at birth and say things just by looking, before separating legs and looking at everything, and jump to conclusions, because 99 percent of the time it's correct. . . . People get upset, physicians I mean. And they say things that are inappropriate." For example, he said that an inexperienced obstetrician might blurt out, "I think you have a boy, or no, maybe you have a girl." Other inappropriate remarks a doctor might make in postdelivery consultation with the parents include, "You have a little boy, but he'll never function as a little boy, so you better raise him as a little girl." As a result, said the pediatric endocrinologist, "the family comes away with the idea that they have a little boy, and that's what they wanted, and that's what they're going to get." In such cases parents sometimes insist that the child be raised male despite the physician's instructions to the contrary. "People have in mind certain things they've heard, that this is a boy, and they're not likely to forget that, or they're not likely to let it go easily." The urologist agreed that the first gender attribution is critical: "Once it's been announced, you've got a big problem on your hands." "One of the worst things is to allow [the parents] to go ahead and give a name and tell everyone, and it turns out the child has to be raised in the opposite sex."[17]

Physicians feel that the mismanagement of such cases requires careful remedying. The psychoendocrinologist asserted, "When I'm involved, I spend hours with the parents to explain to them what has happened and how a mistake like that could be made, *or not really a mistake but a different decision*" (my emphasis). One pediatric endocrinologist said, "[I] try to dissuade them from previous misconceptions, and say, 'Well, I know what they meant, but the way they said it confused you. This is, I think, a better way to think about it.'" These statements reveal physicians' efforts not only to protect parents from concluding that their child is neither male nor female but also to protect other physicians' decision-making processes. Case management involves perpetuating the notion that good medical decisions are based on interpretations of the infant's real "sex" rather than on cultural understandings of gender.

"Mismanagements" are less likely to occur in communities with major medical centers, where specialists are prepared to deal with intersexuality and a medical team (perhaps drawing physicians from more than one teaching hospital) is quickly assembled. The team typically consists of the original referring doctor (obstetrician or pediatrician), a pediatric endocrinologist, a pediatric surgeon (urologist or gynecologist), and a geneticist. In addition, a psychologist, psychiatrist, or psychoendocrinologist might play a role. If an infant is born with ambiguous genitals in a small community hospital, without the relevant specialists on staff, she or he is likely to be transferred to a hospital where diagnosis and treatment are available. Intersexed infants born in poor rural areas where there is less medical intervention might never be referred for genital reconstruction. Many of these children, like those born in earlier historical periods, will grow up and live through adulthood with the condition of genital ambiguity—somehow managing.

The diagnosis of intersexed conditions includes assessing the chromosomal sex and the syndrome that produced the genital ambiguity, and may include medical procedures such as cytologic screening; chromosomal analysis; assessing serum electrolytes; hormone, gonadotropin, and steroids evaluation; digital examination; and radiographic genitography.[18] In any intersexed condition, if the infant is determined to be a genetic female (having an XX chromosome makeup), then the treatment—genital surgery to reduce the phallus size—can proceed relatively quickly, satisfying what the doctors believe are psychological and cultural demands. For example, 21-hydroxylase deficiency, a form of female pseudohermaphroditism and one of the most common conditions, can be determined by a blood test within the first few days.

If, on the other hand, the infant is determined to have at least one Y chromosome, then surgery may be considerably delayed. A decision must be made whether to test the ability of the phallic tissue to respond to (HCG) androgen treatment, which is intended to enlarge the microphallus enough to be a penis. The endocrinologist explained, "You do

HCG testing and you find out if the male can make testosterone. . . . You can get those results back probably within three weeks. . . . You're sure the male is making testosterone—but can he respond to it? It can take three months of waiting to see whether the phallus responds." If the Y-chromosome infant cannot make testosterone or cannot respond to the testosterone it makes, the phallus will not develop, and the Y-chromosome infant is not considered to be a male after all.

Should the infant's phallus respond to the local application of testosterone or a brief course of intramuscular injections of low-potency androgen, the gender assignment problem is resolved, but possibly at some later cost, since the penis will not grow again at puberty when the rest of the body develops.[19] Money's case management philosophy assumes that while it may be difficult for an adult male to have a much smaller than average penis, it is very detrimental to the morale of the young boy to have a micropenis.[20] In the former case the male's manliness might be at stake, but in the latter case his essential maleness might be. Although the psychological consequences of these experiences have not been empirically documented, Money and his colleagues suggest that it is wise to avoid the problems of both the micropenis in childhood and the still undersized penis postpuberty by reassigning many of these infants to the female gender.[21] This approach suggests that for Money and his colleagues, chromosomes are less relevant in determining gender than penis size, and that, by implication, "male" is defined not by the genetic condition of having one Y and one X chromosome or by the production of sperm but by the aesthetic condition of having an appropriately sized penis.

The tests and procedures required for diagnosis (and, consequently, for gender assignment) can take several months.[22] Although physicians are anxious not to make a premature gender assignment, their language suggests that it is difficult for them to take a completely neutral position and think and speak only of phallic tissue that belongs to an infant whose gender has not yet been determined or decided. Comments such as "seeing whether the male can respond to testosterone" imply at least a tentative male gender assignment of an XY infant. The psychoendocrinologist's explanation to parents of their infant's treatment program also illustrates this implicit male gender assignment. "Clearly this baby has an underdeveloped phallus. But if the phallus responds to this treatment, we are fairly confident that surgical techniques and hormonal techniques will help this child to look like a boy. But we want to make absolutely sure and use some hormone treatments and see whether the tissue reacts." The mere fact that this doctor refers to the genitals as an "underdeveloped" phallus rather than an overdeveloped clitoris suggests that the infant has been judged to be, at least provisionally, a male. In the case of the undersized phallus, what is ambiguous is not whether this is a penis but whether it is "good enough" to remain one. If at the end of the treatment period the phallic tissue has not responded, what had been a potential penis (referred to in the medical literature as a "clitoropenis") is now considered an enlarged clitoris (or "penoclitoris"), and reconstructive surgery is planned as for the genetic female.

The time-consuming nature of intersex diagnosis and the assumption, based on gender identity theory, that gender should be assigned as soon as possible thus present physicians with difficult dilemmas. Medical personnel are committed to discovering the etiology of the condition in order to determine the best course of treatment, which takes time. Yet they feel an urgent need to provide an immediate assignment and genitals that look and function appropriately. An immediate assignment that will need to be retracted is more problematic than a delayed assignment, since reassignment carries with it an additional set of social complications. The endocrinologist interviewed commented: "We've come very far in that we can diagnose eventually, many of the conditions. But we haven't come far enough. . . . We can't do it early enough. . . . Very frequently a decision is made before all this information is available, simply because it takes so long to make the correct diagnosis. And you cannot let a child go indefinitely, not in this society you can't. . . . There's pressure on parents [for a decision] and the parents transmit that pressure onto physicians." A pediatric endocrinologist agreed: "At times you may need to operate before a diagnosis can be made. . . . In one case parents were told to wait on the announcement while the infant was treated to see if the phallus would grow when treated with androgens. After the first month passed and there was some growth, the parents said they gave it a boy's name. They could only wait a month."

Deliberating out loud on the judiciousness of making parents wait for assignment decisions, the endocrinologist asked rhetorically, "Why do we do all these tests if in the end we're going to make the decision simply on the basis of the appearance of the genitalia?" This question suggests that the principles underlying physicians' decisions are cultural rather than biological, based on parental reaction and the medical team's perception of the infant's societal adjustment prospects given the way her/his genitals look or could be made to look. Moreover, as long as the decision rests largely on the criterion of genital appearance, and male is defined as having a "good-sized" penis, more infants will be assigned to the female gender than to the male.

The Waiting Period: Dealing with Ambiguity

During the period of ambiguity between birth and assignment, physicians not only must evaluate the infant's prospects to be a good male but also must manage parents' uncertainty about a genderless child. Physicians advise that parents postpone announcing the gender of the infant until a gender has been explicitly assigned. They believe that parents should not feel compelled to tell other people. The clinical geneticist interviewed said that physicians "basically encourage [parents] to treat [the infant] as neuter." One of the pediatric endocrinologists reported that in France parents confronted with this dilemma sometimes give the infant a neuter name, such as Claude or Jean. The psychoendocrinologist concurred: "If you have a truly borderline situation, and you want to make it dependent on the hormone treatment . . . then the parents are . . . told, 'Try not to make a decision. Refer to the baby as "baby." Don't think in terms of boy or girl.'" Yet, when asked whether this is a reasonable request to make of parents in our society, the physician answered: "I don't think so. I think parents can't do it."

New York State requires that a birth certificate be filled out within forty-eight hours of delivery, but the certificate need not be filed with the state for thirty days. The geneticist tells parents to insert "child of" instead of a name. In one case, parents filled out two birth registration forms, one for each gender, and they refused to sign either until a final gender assignment had been made.[23] One of the pediatric endocrinologists claimed, "I heard a story; I don't know if it's true or not. There were parents of a hermaphroditic infant who told everyone they had twins, one of each gender. When the gender was determined, they said the other had died."

The geneticist explained that when directly asked by parents what to tell others about the gender of the infant, she says, "Why don't you just tell them that the baby is having problems and as soon as the problems are resolved we'll get back to you." A pediatric endocrinologist echoes this suggestion in advising parents to say, "Until the problem is solved [we] would really prefer not to discuss any of the details." According to the urologist, "If [the gender] isn't announced people may mutter about it and may grumble about it, but they haven't got anything to get their teeth into and make trouble over for the child, or the parents, or whatever." In short, parents are asked to sidestep the infant's gender rather than admit that the gender is unknown, thereby collaborating in a web of white lies, ellipses, and mystifications.[24]

Even while physicians teach the parents how to deal with others who will not find the infant's condition comprehensible or acceptable, physicians must also make the condition comprehensible and acceptable to the parents, normalizing the intersexed condition for them. In doing so they help the parents consider the infant's condition in the most positive way. There are four key aspects to this "normalizing" process.

First, physicians teach parents normal fetal development and explain that all fetuses have the potential to be male or female. One of the endocrinologists explains, "In the absence of maleness you have female-

ness. . . . It's really the basic design. The other [intersex] is really a variation on a theme." This explanation presents the intersex condition as a
natural phase of every fetal development. Another endocrinologist
"like[s] to show picture[s] to them and explain that at a certain point in
development males and females look alike and then diverge for such and
such reason." The professional literature suggests that doctors use dia-
grams that illustrate "nature's principle of using the same anlagen to produce the external genital parts of the male and female."[25]

Second, physicians stress the normalcy of the infant in other aspects.
For example, the geneticist tells parents, "The baby is healthy, but there
was a problem in the way the baby was developing." The endocrinologist says the infant has "a mild defect, just like anything could be considered a birth defect, a mole or a hemangioma." This language not only
eases the blow to the parents but also redirects their attention. Terms like
"hermaphrodite" or "abnormal" are not used. The urologist said that he
advised parents "about the generalization of sticking to the good things
and not confusing people with something that is unnecessary."

Third, physicians (at least initially) imply that it is not the gender of the
child that is ambiguous but the genitals. They talk about "undeveloped,"
"maldeveloped," or "unfinished" organs. From a number of the physicians interviewed came the following explanations: "At a point in time
the development proceeded in a different way, and sometimes the development isn't complete and we may have some trouble . . . in determining
what the *actual* sex is. And so we have to do a blood test to help us" (my
emphasis); "The baby may be a female, which you would know after the
buccal smear, but you can't prove it yet. If so, then it's a normal female
with a different appearance. This can be surgically corrected"; "The gender of your child isn't apparent to us at the moment"; "While this looks
like a small penis, it's actually a large clitoris. And what we're going to
do is put it back in its proper position and reduce the size of the tip of it
enough so it doesn't look funny, so it looks right." Money and his colleagues report a case in which parents were advised to tell their friends
that the reason their infant's gender was reannounced from male to female is that "the baby was . . . 'closed up down there' . . . when the
closed skin was divided, the female organs were revealed, and the baby
discovered to be, *in fact*, a girl" (emphasis mine). It was mistakenly assumed to be a male at first because "there was an excess of skin on the
clitoris."[26]

The message in these examples is that the trouble lies in the doctor's
ability to determine the gender, not in the baby's gender per se. The real
gender will presumably be determined/proven by testing, and the "bad"
genitals (which are confusing the situation for everyone) will be "re-
paired." The emphasis is not on the doctors creating gender but in their

completing the genitals. Physicians say that they "reconstruct" the genitals rather than "construct" them. The surgeons reconstitute from remaining parts what should have been there all along. The fact that gender in an infant is "reannounced" rather than "reassigned" suggests that the first announcement was a mistake because the announcer was confused by the genitals. The gender always was what it is now seen to be.[27]

Finally, physicians tell parents that social factors are more important in gender development than biological ones, even though they are searching for biological causes. In essence, the physicians teach the parents Money and Ehrhardt's theory of gender development.[28] In doing so, they shift the emphasis from the discovery of biological factors that are a sign of the "real" gender to providing the appropriate social conditions to produce the "real" gender. What remains unsaid is the apparent contradiction in the notion that a "real" or "natural" gender can be, or needs to be, produced artificially. The physician/parent discussions make it clear to family members that gender is not a biological given (even though, of course, their own procedures for diagnosis assume that it is), and that gender is fluid. The psychoendocrinologist paraphrased an explanation to parents thus: "It will depend, ultimately, on how everybody treats your child and how your child is looking as a person. . . . I can with confidence tell them that generally gender [identity] clearly agrees with the assignment." Similarly, a pediatric endocrinologist explained: "[I] try to impress upon them that there's an enormous amount of clinical data to support the fact that if you sex-reverse an infant . . . the majority of the time the alternative gender identity is commensurate with the socialization, the way that they're raised, and how people view them, and that seems to be the most critical."

The implication of these comments is that gender identity (of all children, not just those born with ambiguous genitals) is determined primarily by social factors, that the parents and community always construct the child's gender. In the case of intersexed infants, the physicians merely provide the right genitals to go along with the socialization. Of course, at normal births, when the infant's genitals are unambiguous, the parents are not told that the child's gender is ultimately up to socialization. In those cases, doctors do treat gender as a biological given.

Social Factors in Decision Making

Most of the physicians interviewed claimed that personal convictions of doctors ought to play no role in the decision-making process. The psychoendocrinologist explained: "I think the most critical factors [are] what is the possibility that this child will grow up with genitals which look like that of the assigned gender and which will ultimately function according to gender . . . That's why it's so important that it's a well-established team, because [personal convictions] can't really enter into it. It has to be what is surgically and endocrinologically possible for that baby to be able to make it . . . It's really much more within medical criteria. I don't think many social factors enter into it." While this doctor eschews the importance of social factors in gender assignment, she argues forcefully that social factors are extremely important in the development of gender identity. Indeed, she implies that social factors primarily enter the picture once the infant leaves the hospital.

In fact, doctors make decisions about gender on the basis of shared cultural values that are unstated, perhaps even unconscious, and therefore considered objective rather than subjective. Money states the fundamental rule for gender assignment: "never assign a baby to be reared, and to surgical and hormonal therapy, as a boy, unless the phallic structure, hypospadiac or otherwise, is neonatally of at least the same caliber as that of same-aged males with small-average penises."[29] Elsewhere, he and his colleagues provide specific measurements for what qualifies as a micropenis: "A penis is, by convention, designated as a micropenis when at birth its dimensions are three or more standard deviations below the mean. . . . When it is correspondingly reduced in diameter with corpora that are vestigial . . . it unquestionably qualifies as a micropenis."[30] A pediatric endocrinologist claimed that although "the [size of the] phallus is not the deciding factor . . . if the phallus is less than 2 centimeters long at birth and won't respond to androgen treatments, then it's made into a female."

These guidelines are clear, but they focus on only one physical feature, one that is distinctly imbued with cultural meaning. This becomes especially apparent in the case of an XX infant with normal female reproductive gonads and a perfect penis. Would the size and shape of the penis, in this case, be the deciding factor in assigning the infant "male," or would the perfect penis be surgically destroyed and female genitals created? Money notes that this dilemma would be complicated by the anticipated reaction of the parents to seeing "their apparent son lose his penis."[31] Other researchers concur that parents are likely to want to raise a child with a normal-shaped penis (regardless of size) as "male," particularly if the scrotal area looks normal and if the parents have had no experience with intersexuality.[32] Elsewhere Money argues in favor of not neonatally amputating the penis of XX infants, since fetal masculinization of brain structures would predispose them "almost invariably [to] develop behaviorally as tomboys, even when reared as girls."[33] This reasoning implies, first, that tomboyish behavior in girls is bad and should be avoided; and, second, that it is preferable to remove the internal female organs, implant prosthetic testes, and regulate the "boy's" hormones for his entire life than to overlook or disregard the perfection of the penis.[34]

The ultimate proof to these physicians that they intervened appropriately and gave the intersexed infant the correct gender assignment is that the reconstructed genitals look normal and function normally once the patient reaches adulthood. The vulva, labia, and clitoris should appear ordinary to the woman and her partner(s), and the vagina should be able to receive a normal-sized penis. Similarly, the man and his partner(s) should feel that his penis (even if somewhat smaller than the norm) looks and functions in an unremarkable way. Although there is no reported data on how much emphasis the intersexed person, him- or herself, places upon genital appearance and functioning, the physicians are absolutely clear about what they believe is important. The clinical geneticist said, "If you have . . . a seventeen-year-old young lady who has gotten hormone therapy and has breast development and pubic hair and no vaginal opening, I can't even entertain the notion that this young lady wouldn't want to have corrective surgery." The urologist summarized his criteria: "Happiness is the biggest factor. Anatomy is part of happiness." Money states, "The primary deficit [of not having a sufficient penis]—and destroyer of morale—lies in being unable to satisfy the partner."[35] Another team of clinicians reveals their phallocentrism, arguing that the most serious mistake in gender assignment is to create "an individual unable to engage in genital [heterosexual] sex."[36]

The equation of gender with genitals could only have emerged in an age when medical science can create credible-appearing and functioning genitals, and an emphasis on the good phallus above all else could only have emerged in a culture that has rigid aesthetic and performance criteria for what constitutes maleness. The formulation "good penis equals male; absence of good penis equals female" is treated in the literature and by the physicians interviewed as an objective criterion, operative in all cases. There is a striking lack of attention to the size and shape requirements of the female genitals, other than that the vagina be able to receive a penis.[37]

In the late nineteenth century when women's reproductive function was culturally designated as their essential characteristic, the presence or absence of ovaries (whether or not they were fertile) was held to be the ultimate criterion of gender assignment for hermaphrodites. The urologist interviewed recalled a case as late as the 1950s of a male child reassigned to "female" at the age of four or five because ovaries had been discovered. Nevertheless, doctors today, schooled in the etiology and treatment of the various intersex syndromes, view decisions based primarily on gonads as wrong, although, they complain, the conviction that the gonads are the ultimate criterion "still dictates the decisions of the uneducated and uninformed."[38] Presumably, the educated and informed now know that decisions based primarily on phallic size, shape, and sexual capacity are right.

While the prospect of constructing good genitals is the primary consideration in physicians' gender assignments, another extramedical factor was repeatedly cited by the six physicians interviewed—the specialty of the attending physician. Although generally intersexed infants are treated by teams of specialists, only the person who coordinates the team is actually responsible for the case. This person, acknowledged by the other physicians as having chief responsibility, acts as spokesperson to the parents. Although all of the physicians claimed that these medical teams work smoothly with few discrepancies of opinion, several of them mentioned decision-making orientations that are grounded in particular medical specializations. One endocrinologist stated, "The easiest route to take, where there is ever any question . . . is to raise the child as female. . . . In this country that is usual if the infant falls into the hands of a pediatric endocrinologist. . . . If the decision is made by the urologists, who are mostly males, . . . they're always opting, because they do the surgery, they're always feeling they can correct anything." Another endocrinologist concurred: "[Most urologists] don't think in terms of dynamic processes. They're interested in fixing pipes and lengthening pipes, and not dealing with hormonal, and certainly not psychological issues. . . . 'What can I do with what I've got.'" Urologists were defended by the clinical geneticist: "Surgeons here, now I can't speak for elsewhere, they don't get into a situation where the child is a year old and they can't make anything." Whether or not urologists "like to make boys," as one endocrinologist claimed, the following example from a urologist who was interviewed explicitly links a cultural interpretation of masculinity to the medical treatment plan. The case involved an adolescent who had been assigned the female gender at birth but was developing some male pubertal signs and wanted to be a boy. "He was ill-equipped," said the urologist, "yet we made a very respectable male out of him. He now owns a huge construction business—those big cranes that put stuff up on the building."

Postinfancy Case Management

After the infant's gender has been assigned, parents generally latch onto the assignment as the solution to the problem—and it is. The physician as detective has collected the evidence, as lawyer has presented the case, and as judge has rendered a verdict. Although most of the interviewees claimed that the parents are equal participants in the whole process, they gave no instances of parental participation prior to the gender assignment.[39] After the physicians assign the infant's gender, the parents are encouraged to established the credibility of that gender publicly by, for example, giving a detailed medical explanation to a leader in their community, such as a physician or pastor, who will explain the situation to curious casual acquaintances. Money argues that "medical terminology has a special layman's magic in such a context; it is final and authoritative and closes the issue." He also recommends that eventually the mother "settle [the] argument once and for all among her women friends by allowing some of them to see the baby's reconstructed genitalia."[40] Apparently, the powerful influence of normal-looking genitals helps overcome a history of ambiguous gender.

Some of the same issues that arise in assigning gender recur some years later when, at adolescence, the child may be referred to a physician for counseling.[41] The physician then tells the adolescent many of the same things his or her parents had been told years before, with the same language. Terms like "abnormal," "disorder," "disease," and "hermaphroditism" are avoided; the condition is normalized, and the child's gender is treated as unproblematic. One clinician explains to his patients that sex organs are different in appearance for each person, not just those who are intersexed. Furthermore, he tells the girls "that while most women menstruate, not all do . . . that conception is only one of a number of ways to become a parent; [and] that today some individuals are choosing not to become parents."[42] The clinical geneticist tells a typical female patient: "You are female. Female is not determined by your genes. Lots of other things determine being a woman. And you are a woman but you won't be able to have babies."

A case reported by one of the pediatric endocrinologists involving an adolescent female with androgen insensitivity provides an intriguing insight into the postinfancy gender-management process. She was told at the age of fourteen "that her ovaries weren't normal and had been removed. That's why she needed pills to look normal. . . . I wanted to convince her of her femininity. Then I told her she could marry and have normal sexual relations . . . [her] uterus won't develop but [she] could adopt children." The urologist interviewed was asked to comment on this handling of the counseling. "It sounds like a very good solution to it. He's stating the truth, and if you don't state the truth . . . then you're in trouble later." This is a strange version of "the truth," however, since the adolescent was chromosomally XY and was born with normal testes that produced normal quantities of androgen. There were no existing ovaries or uterus to be abnormal. Another pediatric endocrinologist, in commenting on the management of this case, hedged the issue by saying that he would have used a generic term like "the gonads." A third endocrinologist said she would say that the uterus had never formed.

Technically these physicians are lying when, for example, they explain to an adolescent XY female with an intersexed history that her "ovaries . . . had to be removed because they were unhealthy or were producing 'the wrong balance of hormones.'"[43] We can presume that these lies are told in the service of what the physicians consider a greater good—keeping individual/concrete genders as clear and uncontaminated as the notions of female and male are in the abstract. The clinician suggests that with some female patients it eventually may be possible to talk to them "about their gonads having some structures and features that are testicular-like."[44] This call for honesty might be based at least partly on the possibility of the child's discovering his or her chromosomal sex inadvertently from a buccal smear taken in a high school biology class. Today's litigious climate is possibly another encouragement.

In sum, the adolescent is typically told that certain internal organs did not form because of an endocrinological defect, not because those organs could never have developed in someone with her or his sex chromosomes. The topic of chromosomes is skirted. There are no published studies on how these adolescents experience their condition and their treatment by doctors. An endocrinologist interviewed mentioned that her adolescent patients rarely ask specifically what is wrong with them, suggesting that they are accomplices in this evasion. In spite of the "truth" having been evaded, the clinician's impression is that "their gender identities and general senses of well-being and self-esteem appear not to have suffered."[45]

Conclusion

Physicians conduct careful examinations of intersexed infants' genitals and perform intricate laboratory procedures. They are interpreters of the body, trained and committed to uncovering the "actual" gender obscured by ambiguous genitals. Yet they also have considerable leeway in assigning gender, and their decisions are influenced by cultural as well as medical factors. What is the relationship between the physician as discoverer and the physician as determiner of gender? Where is the relative emphasis placed in discussions with parents and adolescents and in the consciousness of physicians? It is misleading to characterize the doctors whose words are provided here as presenting themselves publicly to the parents as discoverers of the infant's real gender but privately acknowledging that the infant has no real gender other than the one being determined or constructed by the medical professionals. They are not hypocritical. It is also misleading to claim that physicians' focus shifts from discovery to determination over the course of treatment: first the doctors regard the infant's gender as an unknown but discoverable reality; then the doctors relinquish their attempts to find the real gender and treat the infant's gender as something they must construct. They are not medically incompetent or deficient. Instead, I am arguing that the peculiar balance of discovery and determination throughout treatment permits physicians to handle very problematic cases of gender in the most unproblematic of ways.

This balance relies fundamentally on a particular conception of the "natural."[46] Although the deformity of intersexed genitals would be immutable were it not for medical interference, physicians do not consider it natural. Instead they think of, and speak of, the surgical/hormonal alternation of such deformities as natural because such intervention returns the body to what it "ought to have been" if events had taken their typical course. The nonnormative is converted into the normative, and the normative state is considered natural.[47] The genital ambiguity is remedied to conform to a "natural," that is, culturally indisputable, gender dichotomy. Sherry Ortner's claim that the culture/nature distinction is itself a construction—a product of culture—is relevant here. Language and imagery help create and maintain a specific view of what is natural about the two genders and, I would argue, about the very idea of gender—that it consists of two exclusive types: female and male.[48] The belief that gender consists of two exclusive types is maintained and perpetuated by the medical community in the face of incontrovertible physical evidence that this is not mandated by biology.

The lay conception of human anatomy and physiology assumes a concordance among clearly dimorphic gender markers—chromosomes, genitals, gonads, hormones—but physicians understand that concordance and dimorphism do not always exist. Their understanding of biology's complexity, however, does not inform their understanding of gender's complexity. In order for intersexuality to be managed differently than it currently is, physicians would have to take seriously Money's assertion that it is a misrepresentation of epistemology to consider any cell in the body authentically male or female.[49] If authenticity for gender resides not in a discoverable nature but in someone's proclamation, then the power to proclaim something else is available. If physicians recognized that implicit in their management of gender is the notion that finally, and always, people construct gender as well as the social systems that are grounded in gender-based concepts, the possibilities for real societal transformations would be unlimited. Unfortunately, neither in their representations to the families of the intersexed nor among themselves do the physicians interviewed for this study draw such far-reaching implications from their work. Their "understanding" that particular genders are medically (re)constructed in these cases does not lead them to see that gender is always constructed. Accepting genital ambiguity as a natural option would require that physicians also acknowledge that genital ambiguity is "corrected" not because it is threatening to the infant's life but because it is threatening to the infant's culture.

Rather than admit to their role in perpetuating gender, physicians "psychologize" the issue by talking about the parents' anxiety and humiliation in being confronted with an anomalous infant. The physicians talk as though they have no choice but to respond to the parents' pressure for a resolution of psychological discomfort, and as though they have no choice but to use medical technology in the service of a two-gender culture. Neither the psychology nor the technology is doubted, since both shield physicians from responsibility. Indeed, for the most part, neither physicians nor parents emerge from the experience of intersex case management with a greater understanding of the social construction of gender. Society's accountability, like their own, is masked by the assumption that gender is a given. Thus, cases of intersexuality, instead of illustrating nature's failure to ordain gender in these isolated "unfortunate" instances, illustrate physicians' and Western society's failure of imagination—the failure to imagine that each of these management decisions is a moment when a specific instance of biological "sex" is transformed into a culturally constructed gender.

Notes

I want to thank my student Jane Weider for skillfully conducting and transcribing the interviews for this article.

1. For historical reviews of the intersexed person in ancient Greek and Roman periods, see Leslie Fielder, *Freaks: Myths and Images of the Second Self* (New York: Simon & Schuster, 1978); Vern Bullough, *Sexual Variance in Society and History* (New York: Wiley, 1976). For the Middle Ages and Renaissance, see Michel Foucault, *History of Sexuality* (New York: Pantheon, 1980). For the eighteenth and nineteenth centuries, see Michel Foucault, *Herculine Barbin* (New York: Pantheon, 1978); and for the early twentieth century, see Havelock Ellis, *Studies in the Psychology of Sex* (New York: Random House, 1942).

2. Suzanne J. Kessler and Wendy McKenna, *Gender: An Ethnomethodological Approach* (1978; reprint, Chicago: University of Chicago Press, 1985).

3. See, e.g., M. Bolkenius, R. Daum, and E. Heinrich, "Pediatric Surgical Principles in the Management of Children with Intersex," *Progressive Pediatric Surgery* 17 (1984): 33–38; Kenneth I. Glassberg, "Gender Assignment in Newborn Male Pseudohermaphrodites," *Urologic Clinics of North America* 7 (June 1980): 409–21; and Peter A. Lee et al., "Micropenis. I. Criteria, Etiologies and Classification," *Johns Hopkins Medical Journal* 146 (1980): 156–63.

4. It is impossible to get accurate statistics on the frequency of intersexuality. Chromosomal abnormalities (like XOXX or XXXY) are registered, but those conditions do not always imply ambiguous genitals, and most cases of ambiguous genitals do not involve chromosomal abnormalities. None of the physicians inter-

viewed for this study would venture a guess on frequency rates, but all agreed that intersexuality is rare. One physician suggested that the average obstetrician may see only two cases in twenty years. Another estimated that a specialist may see only one a year, or possibly as many as five a year.

5. Mariano Castro-Magana, Moris Angulo, and Platon J. Collipp, "Management of the Child with Ambiguous Genitalia," *Medical Aspects of Human Sexuality* 18 (April 1984): 172–88.

6. For example, infants whose intersexuality is caused by congenital adrenal hyperplasia can develop severe electrolyte disturbances unless the condition is controlled by cortisone treatments. Intersexed infants whose condition is caused by androgen insensitivity are in danger of malignant degeneration of the testes unless they are removed. For a complete catalog of clinical syndromes related to the intersexed condition, see Arye Lev-Ran, "Sex Reversal as Related to Clinical Syndromes in Human Beings," in *Handbook of Sexology II: Genetics, Hormones and Behavior*, ed. John Money and H. Musaph (New York: Elsevier, 1978), 157–73.

7. Much of the surgical experimentation in this area has been accomplished by urologists who are trying to create penises for female-to-male transsexuals. Although there have been some advancements in recent years in the ability to create a "reasonable-looking" penis from tissue taken elsewhere on the body, the complicated requirements of the organ (both urinary and sexual functioning) have posed surgical problems. It may be, however, that the concerns of the urologists are not identical to the concerns of the patients. While data are not yet available from the intersexed, we know that female-to-male transsexuals place greater emphasis on the "public" requirements of the penis (e.g., being able to look normal while standing at the urinal or wearing a bathing suit) than on its functional requirements (e.g., being able to carry urine or achieve an erection) (Kessler and McKenna, 128–32). As surgical techniques improve, female-to-male transsexuals (and intersexed males) might increase their demands for organs that look and function better.

8. Historically, psychology has tended to blur the distinction between the two by equating a person's acceptance of her or his genitals with gender role and ignoring gender identity. For example, Freudian theory posited that if one had a penis and accepted its reality, then masculine gender role behavior would naturally follow (Sigmund Freud, "Some Psychical Consequences of the Anatomical Distinctions Between the Sexes" [1925], vol. 18 of *The Complete Psychological Works*, ed. and trans. J. Strachey [New York: Norton, 1976]).

9. Almost all of the published literature on intersexed infant case management has been written or cowritten by one researcher, John Money, professor of medical psychology and professor of pediatrics, emeritus, at the Johns Hopkins University and Hospital, where he is director of the Psychohormonal Research Unit. Even the publications that are produced independently of Money reference him and reiterate his management philosophy. Although only one of the physicians interviewed publishes with Money, all of them essentially concur with his views and give the impression of a consensus that is rarely encountered in science. The one physician who raised some questions about Money's philosophy and the gender theory on which it is based has extensive experience with intersexuality in a nonindustrialized culture where the infant is managed differently with no

apparent harm to gender development. Even though psychologists fiercely argue issues of gender identity and gender role development, doctors who treat intersexed infants seem untouched by these debates. There are no renegade voices either from within the medical establishment or, thus far, from outside. Why Money has been so single-handedly influential in promoting his ideas about gender is a question worthy of a separate substantial analysis. His management philosophy is conveyed in the following sources: John Money, J. G. Hampson, and J. L. Hampson, "Hermaphroditism: Recommendations Concerning Assignment of Sex, Change of Sex, and Psychologic Management," *Bulletin of the Johns Hopkins Hospital* 97 (1955): 284–300; John Money, Reynolds Potter, and Clarice S. Stoll, "Sex Reannouncement in Hereditary Sex Deformity: Psychology and Sociology of Habilitation," *Social Science and Medicine* 3 (1969): 207–16; John Money and Anke A. Ehrhardt, *Man and Woman, Boy and Girl* (Baltimore: Johns Hopkins University Press, 1972); John Money, "Psychologic Consideration of Sex Assignment in Intersexuality," *Clinics in Plastic Surgery* 1 (April 1974): 215–22, "Psychological Counseling: Hermaphroditism," in *Endocrine and Genetic Diseases of Childhood and Adolescence,* ed. L. I. Gardner (Philadelphia: Saunders, 1975): 609–18, and "Birth Defect of the Sex Organs: Telling the Parents and the Patient," *British Journal of Sexual Medicine* 10 (March 1983): 14; John Money et al., "Micropenis, Family Mental Health, and Neonatal Management: A Report on Fourteen Patients Reared as Girls," *Journal of Preventive Psychiatry* 1, no. 1 (1981): 17–27.

10. Money and Ehrhardt, 152.

11. Contradictory data are presented in Milton Diamond, "Sexual Identity, Monozygotic Twins Reared in Discordant Sex Roles and a BBC Follow-up," *Archives of Sexual Behavior* 11, no. 2 (1982): 181–86.

12. Money, "Psychologic Consideration of Sex Assignment in Intersexuality."

13. Castro-Magana, Angulo, and Collipp (n. 5 above).

14. Victor Braren et al., "True Hermaphroditism: A Rational Approach to Diagnosis and Treatment," *Urology* 15 (June 1980): 569–74.

15. Studies of normal newborns have shown that from the moment of birth the parent responds to the infant based on the infant's gender. Jeffrey Rubin, F. J. Provenzano, and Z. Luria, "The Eye of the Beholder: Parents' Views on Sex of Newborns," *American Journal of Orthopsychiatry* 44, no. 4 (1974): 512–19.

16. Money et al. (n. 9 above).

17. There is evidence from other kinds of sources that once a gender attribution is made, all further information buttresses that attribution, and only the most contradictory new information will cause the original gender attribution to be questioned. See, e.g., Kessler and McKenna (n. 2 above).

18. Castro-Magana, Angulo, and Collipp (n. 5 above).

19. Money, "Psychological Consideration of Sex Assignment in Intersexuality" (n. 9 above).

20. Technically, the term "micropenis" should be reserved for an exceptionally small but well-formed structure. A small, malformed "penis" should be referred to as a "microphallus" (Lee et al. [n. 3 above]).

21. Money et al., 26. A different view is argued by another leading gender identity theorist: "When a little boy (with an imperfect penis) knows he is a male, he

creates a penis that functions symbolically the same as those of boys with normal penises" (Robert J. Stoller, *Sex and Gender* [New York: Aronson, 1968], 1:49).

22. W. Ch. Hecker, "Operative Correction of Intersexual Genitals in Children," *Pediatric Surgery* 17 (1984): 21–31.

23. Elizabeth Bing and Esselyn Rudikoff, "Divergent Ways of Parental Coping with Hermaphrodite Children," *Medical Aspects of Human Sexuality* (December 1970), 73–88.

24. These evasions must have many ramifications in everyday social interactions between parents and family and friends. How people "fill in" the uncertainty so that interactions remain relatively normal is an interesting issue that warrants further study. Indeed, the whole issue of parental reaction is worthy of analysis. One of the pediatric endocrinologists interviewed acknowledged that the published literature discusses intersex management only from the physicians' point of view. He asks, "How [do parents] experience what they're told, and what [do] they remember . . . and carry with them?" One published exception to this neglect of the parents' perspective is a case study comparing two couples' different coping strategies. The first couple, although initially distressed, handled the traumatic event by regarding the abnormality as an act of God. The second couple, more educated and less religious, put their faith in medical science and expressed a need to fully understand the biochemistry of the defect (ibid.).

25. Tom Mazur, "Ambiguous Genitalia: Detection and Counseling," *Pediatric Nursing* 9 (November/December 1983): 417–31; Money, "Psychologic Consideration of Sex Assignment in Intersexuality" (n. 9 above), 218.

26. Money, Potter, and Stoll (n. 9 above), 211.

27. The term "reassignment" is more commonly used to describe the gender changes of those who are cognizant of their earlier gender, e.g., transsexuals— people whose gender itself was a mistake.

28. Although Money and Ehrhardt's socialization theory is uncontested by the physicians who treat intersexuality and is presented to parents as a matter of fact, there is actually much debate among psychologists about the effect of prenatal hormones on brain structure and ultimately on gender role behavior and even on gender identity. The physicians interviewed agreed that the animal evidence for prenatal brain organization is compelling but that there is no evidence in humans that prenatal hormones have an inviolate or unilateral effect. If there is any effect of prenatal exposure to androgen, they believe it can easily be overcome and modified by psychosocial factors. It is this latter position that is communicated to the parents, not the controversy in the field. For an argument favoring prenatally organized gender differences in the brain, see Milton Diamond, "Human Sexual Development: Biological Foundations for Social Development," in *Human Sexuality in Four Perspectives,* ed. Frank A. Beach (Baltimore: Johns Hopkins University Press, 1976), 22–61; for a critique of that position, see Ruth Bleier, *Science and Gender: A Critique of Biology and Its Theories on Women* (New York: Pergamon, 1984).

29. Money, "Psychological Counseling: Hermaphroditism" (n. 9 above), 610.

30. Money et al. (n. 9 above), 18.

31. John Money, "Hermaphroditism and Pseudohermaphroditism," in *Gynecologic Endocrinology,* ed. Jay J. Gold (New York: Hoeber, 1968), 449–64, esp. 460.

32. Mojtaba Besheshti et al., "Gender Assignment in Male Pseudohermaphrodite Children," *Urology* (December 1983): 604–7. Of course, if the penis looked normal and the empty scrotum were overlooked, it might not be discovered until puberty that the male child was XX, with a female internal structure.

33. John Money, "Psychologic Consideration of Sex Assignment in Intersexuality" (n. 9 above), 216.

34. Weighing the probability of achieving a perfect penis against the probable trauma such procedures might involve is another social factor in decision making. According to an endocrinologist interviewed, if it seemed that an XY infant with an inadequate penis would require as many as ten genital operations over a six-year period in order to have an adequate penis, the infant would be assigned the female gender. In this case, the endocrinologist's practical and compassionate concern would override purely genital criteria.

35. Money, "Psychologic Consideration of Sex Assignment in Intersexuality," 217.

36. Castro-Magana, Angulo, and Collipp (n. 5 above), 180.

37. It is unclear how much of this bias is the result of a general, cultural devaluation of the female and how much the result of physicians' greater facility in constructing aesthetically correct and sexually functional female genitals.

38. Money, "Psychologic Consideration of Sex Assignment in Intersexuality," 215. Remnants of this anachronistic view can still be found, however, when doctors justify the removal of contradictory gonads on the grounds that they are typically sterile or at risk for malignancy (J. Dewhurst and D. B. Grant, "Intersex Problems," *Archives of Disease in Childhood* 59 [July–December 1984]: 1191–94). Presumably, if the gonads were functional and healthy their removal would provide an ethical dilemma for at least some medical professionals.

39. Although one set of authors argued that the views of the parents on the most appropriate gender for their child must be taken into account (Dewhurst and Grant, 1192), the physicians interviewed denied direct knowledge of this kind of participation. They claimed that they personally had encountered few, if any, cases of parents who insisted on their child's being assigned a particular gender. Yet each had heard about cases where a family's ethnicity or religious background biased them toward males. None of the physicians recalled whether this preference for male offspring meant the parents wanted a male regardless of the "inadequacy" of the penis, or whether it meant that the parents would have greater difficulty adjusting to a less-than-perfect male than with a "normal" female.

40. Money, "Psychological Counseling: Hermaphroditism" (n. 9 above), 613.

41. As with the literature on infancy, most of the published material on adolescents is on surgical and hormonal management rather than on social management. See, e.g., Joel J. Roslyn, Eric W. Fonkalsrud, and Barbara Lippe, "Intersex Disorders in Adolescents and Adults," *American Journal of Surgery* 146 (July 1983): 138–44.

42. Mazur (n. 25 above), 421.

43. Dewhurst and Grant, 1193.

44. Mazur, 422.

45. Ibid.

46. For an extended discussion of different ways of conceptualizing "natural," see Richard W. Smith, "What Kind of Sex Is Natural?" in *The Frontiers of Sex Research,* ed. Vern Bullough (Buffalo, N.Y.: Prometheus, 1979), 103–11.

47. This supports sociologist Harold Garfinkel's argument that we treat routine events as our due as social members and that we treat gender, like all normal forms, as a moral imperative. It is no wonder, then, that physicians conceptualize what they are doing as natural and unquestionably "right" (Harold Garfinkel, *Studies in Ethnomethodology* [Englewood Cliffs, N.J.: Prentice-Hall, 1967]).

48. Sherry B. Ortner, "Is Female to Male as Nature Is to Culture?" in *Woman, Culture, and Society,* ed. Michelle Zimbalist Rosaldo and Louise Lamphere (Stanford, Calif.: Stanford University Press, 1974), 67–87.

49. Money, "Psychological Counseling: Hermaphroditism" (n. 9 above), 618.

8 The Politics of Androgyny in Japan

Sexuality and Subversion in the Theater and Beyond

JENNIFER ROBERTSON

Androgyny," as I employ the term here, refers not to a physiological condition (that is, an intersexed body) but to a "surface politics of the body" (Butler 1990:136). Androgyny involves the scrambling of gender markers—clothes, gestures, speech patterns, and so on—in a way that both undermines the stability of a sex-gender system premised on a male-female dichotomy and retains that dichotomy by either juxtaposing or blending its elements. My emphasis on the constructed and performative aspects of gender, and on its distinction from sex, is more than just a theoretical premise or literary exercise; these aspects are outstandingly evident in the two theaters—Kabuki, an all-male theater, and the Takarazuka Revue, an all-female theater—which are the main sites of my investigation into the politics of androgyny in Japan. Because so much has been written on the Kabuki theater and so little on the Takarazuka

The gendered body is constructed and performative. Androgyny involves the scrambling of gender markers (clothes, gestures, speech patterns) in a "surface politics of the body." I explore the politics of androgyny in Japan as they have been embodied and enacted by same-sex theater actors and expressed in Japanese society at large. The referent of androgyny, or the body of the androgyne, has changed over the past 300 years from male to female. Since the early 20th century, androgyny has been deployed in both dominant and marginal discourses to camouflage "unconventional" female sexual choices and practices by creating the illusion of an asexual identity. It has also been evoked in reference to females who "do" both "female" and "male" gender without being constrained by either. [androgyny, gender, sexuality, theater, girls and women, Japan]

Revue, and because I am interested here in a female-embodied androgyny, I will devote most of my attention to the Revue—its actors, audience, and critics—and particularly to its early history.

I begin by summarizing the spectrum of English and Japanese terms for and usages of androgyny and, in this connection, review the differences between sex, gender, and sexuality. I then move on to my main project, which, after an introduction to the Takarazuka Revue, is to explore some of the ways in which androgyny has been deployed to both support and subvert dominant representations of women and men in Japan. Over the past three centuries the referent of androgyny has changed from male to female. Androgyny has been evoked in variously cited discourses to camouflage "unconventional" sexual practices, creating the illusion of an asexual—in effect, a disembodied—identity. Androgyny has also been used to describe Takarazuka actors who perform both "female" and "male" gender roles without being constrained by either.

How is a dominant gender ideology constructed, reproduced, resisted, and even subverted, sometimes simultaneously, by females and males whose private and professional lives confound tidy, universalistic schemata, whether of literary or of theoretical origin? Real people tend to be messy, inconsistent, hypocritical, and mostly opaque when the relations between sex, gender, and sexuality are at issue. Thus, I examine debates and differences among the Revue's directors, performers, and fans, the mass media, and the state[1] about the significance and symbolism of the Takarazuka Revue. Moreover, the stereotype of the Japanese as a homogeneous people has had the extended effect of whitewashing a colorful variety of gender identities and sexual practices. It is my general impression that more often than not the differing experiences of female and male members of Japanese society have been insufficiently problematized and have been confused with dominant, naturalized gender ideals (for example, housewife and workaholic) and the behavior of fictive characters. This article should help to dismantle some of the more tenacious stereotypes of Japanese women and men and to provoke discussion on the complicated relations between sex, gender, and sexuality in Japan and elsewhere.

Words and Usages

Since the mid-1980s the English loanword *andorojenii* (androgyny) has appeared frequently in the Japanese mass media and elsewhere in reference to clothing fashions, including "cross-dressing," an expression most often used in reference to men's clothing adapted by and for women (Asahi Shinbun, 3 December 1984; Asano 1989; Yagi 1989). Since *andorojenii* is a transliteration, the term is often simultaneously defined in

Japanese as either *ryōsei* (both sexes/genders) or *chūsei* (between sexes/genders).[2] In English, following ancient Greek usage, "androgyny" literally means "male-female," although what the word signifies and represents is far from literal. Heilbrun, for example, presents androgyny—which she defines as the realization of man in woman and woman in man—as an ideal, nonpolarized way of being necessary for the survival of human society (1982 [1964]:xx). Rich, on the other hand, argues that the very structure of the word androgyny "replicates the sexual dichotomy and the priority of *andros* (male) over *gyne* (female)" (1976:76–77).

Japanese scholars have taken similar theoretical and political positions. Asano, for example, adopts Jung's quasi-biological theory of androgyny[3] in exploring the idea of androgyny as it has been expressed in Japanese popular religious texts (1989). She bemoans the progressive loss of "traditional" androgyny (qua "the harmony of 'male' and 'female' qualities") over the course of Japan's modernization but observes a revival of androgyny (qua "cross-dressing") in the present (1989:201–202). Similarly, Akiyama evokes Jung's theory of the "inherent androgyny" of all people to debunk the notion of "sexual perversion" *(seitōsaku)*, insisting that the sexual choices available to women and men are as varied as the combinations of feminine and masculine tendencies they embody (Akiyama 1990; see also Ifukube 1932). And Kurahashi Yukiko suggests the corporeality of Jung's "animus," or "male archetypical essence," in her neologism for "a female who wants to be a man": *penisuto*, or "penist" (cited in Hyūga 1971:26). Yagi, on the other hand, like Rich, dismisses androgyny as an idea (and ideal) that suppresses women's sexual difference in the name of equality (1989).

Medical—anatomical and psychological—descriptions and interpretations of androgyny were especially plentiful in early 20th-century Japan. The works of Euro-American sexologists—Freud, Jung, Krafft-Ebing, Ellis, Carpenter, Hirschfeld—were exported directly to Japan, where they were studied, translated, adapted, and augmented by Japanese sexologists (Hanafusa 1930; Ifukube 1932; Ōsaka Mainichi, 31 January 1935; - Ōsumi 1931; Yasuda 1935). Physiological androgyny, or an intersexed body, was of special interest at that time to scholars of forensic medicine, who addressed the phenomenon in terms of conscription, patrilineality (specifically family name and inheritance), political service, and civil rights, all of which were contingent upon the establishment of a person's body as male-sexed (for example, Takada 1926 [1917]:285–291).

A brief discussion of the relationship between sex, gender, and sexuality is called for at this juncture. Regardless of their popular conflation, the three are different. "Sex," as I use it here, refers to the physical body distinguished by either female or male genitalia—or, in the case of intersexed persons, both, to varying degrees—and their usual capabilities, such as menstruation, seminal ejaculation, and orgasm. (Thus, when I use the term "female body," I am referring to a female-sexed body.) "Gender" refers to sociocultural and historical conventions of deportment, costume, gesture, and so on, attributed and ascribed to female- and male-sexed bodies. "Sexuality" may overlap with sex and gender, but refers to a domain of desire and erotic pleasure more complex and varied than the hegemonic construction of reproductive heterosexuality would have it (see Kessler and McKenna 1985 [1978]:1–12; Vance 1985:9).

Sex, gender, and sexuality may be related, but they are not the same thing; the pattern of their articulation is negotiable and negotiated constantly. Although the three may be popularly perceived as irreducibly joined, their alignment remains a situational and not a permanently fixed condition. In the words of Butler—whose recent book problematizes the "Western" belief in the vertical alignment of sex, gender, and sexuality (namely, female-feminine-heterosexual)—"*man* and *masculine* might just as easily signify a female body as a male one, and *woman* and *feminine* a male body as easily as a female one" (Butler 1990:6).

Among Japanese feminists and scholars influenced by feminist theory, sex and gender and sexuality have been distinguished in principle since about 1970 (Yuri 1985). In Japanese, linguistic distinctions between sex and gender are created by suffixes. Generally speaking, *sei* is used to denote sex—and *seisei* to denote sexuality (literally, the sex of sex)—as in *josei* for female and *dansei* for male. Since the *dan* in *dansei* can refer both to male sex and to "male" gender, the suffix *sei*, with its allusions to fundamental parts (for example, genitalia), is necessary in order to specifically denote sex. Gender is denoted by the suffix *rashii*, with its allusion to appearance or likeness (Fukutomi 1985; Kōjien 1978a, 1978b). A "female"-gendered person is *onnarashii*, a "male"-gendered person, *otokorashii*.[4] The emphasis here is on a person's proximity to a gender stereotype. When attention is to be drawn to an individual's resemblance to a particular female or male, the term often used is *joseiteki* (like a/that female) or *danseiteki* (like a/that male). That an individual resembles a particular female or male in the first place is precisely because both parties approximate a more generic gender stereotype. The difference between *onnarashii* or *otokorashii* and *joseiteki* or *danseiteki* is significant, although the two terms are often used interchangeably in popular parlance. Further complicating matters is the use of the terms *onna* and *otoko* to refer to both sex and gender, the distinction being evident only in the context used.

Two of the most frequently encountered Japanese terms referring to androgyny are *ryōsei* and *chūsei*, which were coined in the early 20th century when they first appeared in journal and newspaper articles on homosexuality and "abnormal sexual desire" (Kabeshima, Hida, and Yonekawa 1984:185). *Ryōsei* was and is most generally used to refer either to someone with both female and male genitalia or to someone with both feminine and masculine characteristics. Consequently, *ryōsei* has been used to refer to intersexed bodies (see Hyūga 1971; Komine and Minami 1985:57, 296–301) as well as to persons who behave as if they were at once masculine and feminine. The latter combine and embody the stereotyped and otherwise polarized and mutually exclusive characteristics attributed to females and males (see Akiyama 1990; Asano 1989; Ifukube 1932; Komine and Minami 1985:57).

Chūsei, on the other hand, has been used to mean "neutral" or "in between," and thus neither woman nor man. Whereas *ryōsei* emphasizes the juxtaposition or blending of either sex or gender differences, *chūsei* emphasizes erasure or nullification of differences. A person whose body is intersexed usually is raised or passes as one or the other sex/gender (see Sawada 1921; Komine and Minami 1985:296–301). A "neutral" body, on the other hand, is one whose surface appearance (costume, hairstyle, intonations, speech patterns, gestures, movements, deportment, and so on) confounds the conventional alignment of sex with gender and scrambles received gender markers. The normalizing principle at work here posits that, say, masculinity is a "natural" attribute of male-sexed bodies. However, "masculinity" is not a product of nature—that is, some sort of agentless creation—but a sociohistorical representation of male-sexed bodies, a representation that is subject to manipulation and change. Gender, in other words, names an unstable "amalgam of signifiers" (Pacteau 1986:80). Despite the workings of this normalizing principle, it remains the case that in Japan, as attested in part by Kabuki and Takarazuka, neither femininity nor masculinity has been deemed the exclusive province of either female or male bodies.

During the early Edo (or Tokugawa) period (1603–1868), androgyny was embodied by the *onnagata*, the Kabuki theater actor specializing in girls' and women's roles. From the 1910s to the present, generally speaking, androgyny has been embodied by the *otokoyaku*, the Takarazuka Revue actor specializing in boys' and men's roles. Watanabe attributes the disappearance of male-embodied androgyny to the "de-eroticisation of the male body" resulting from the modernization of political and social institutions toward the end of the 19th century, when the xenophobic Tokugawa Shogunate was overthrown by imperialists and a new civil code was drawn up on the Prussian model (Watanabe and Iwata 1989 [1987]:130). Further contextualizing Watanabe's hypothesis, I propose that the "de-eroticisation of the male body" paralleled the emergence at this time of a "woman problem," part of which involved contradictory and contested images of and roles for Japanese women. Significantly, the

Takarazuka Revue, founded in 1913, was among the modern theaters marking the return of females to a major public stage after they were banned from the Kabuki theater by the Shogunate in 1629.[5] Moreover, in the early 20th century—as to a significant extent today—the Takarazuka Revue was the focus of heated debates about the construction and performance of gender. A brief introduction to the Takarazuka Revue and its actors follows.

The Takarazuka Revue

The all-female Takarazuka Revue (Takarazuka Kagekidan) was founded in the hot springs resort of Takarazuka by Kobayashi Ichizō (1873–1957), the Hankyū railroad-and-department store tycoon.[6] Today, with two huge theaters in Takarazuka and Tokyo and regularly scheduled regional and international tours, not to mention television and radio broadcasts, the Revue remains one of the most widely recognized and watched of the so-called theaters for the masses (taishū engeki) that were created in the early 20th century (see Robertson 1991b). Takarazuka productions range from Japanese historical dramas, such as the Tale of Genji, to Western musicals, such as Oklahoma. The widespread popularity and social impact of the Revue are evident in the literally hundreds of articles that have been published in a wide range of print media since its founding. In fact, this article was inspired in part by the many early articles linking the establishment of the Takarazuka Revue to the problematic emergence of "androgynous" females and the diagnosis in women of a newly coined affliction, "abnormal sexual desire" (hentai seiyoku).

The Revue's actors are called "Takarasiennes" (takarajiennu), after Parisiennes, in recognition of the original influence of the French revue. They include otokoyaku, the "male" gender specialists, and musumeyaku, the "female" gender specialists. Upon their successful application to the Takarazuka Music Academy, founded in 1919 as a part of the Revue complex, the student actors are assigned (what I call) their "secondary" genders. Unlike "primary" gender, which is assigned at birth on the basis of an infant's genitalia, secondary gender is based on both physical (but not genital) and sociopsychological criteria: height, physique, facial shape, voice, personality, and, to a certain extent, personal preference. Secondary gender attributes or markers are premised on contrastive gender stereotypes themselves; for example, men are supposed to be taller than women; to have a more rectangular face, thicker eyebrows, a higher-bridged nose, darker skin, straighter shoulders, narrower hips, and a lower voice than women; and to exude charisma (kosei), which is disparaged in women. The assignment of gender involves the selection and cosmetic exaggeration of purported (nongenital) physical differences between females and males, and it reinforces socially prescribed behavioral differences between women and men. Ironically, in the Takarazuka Revue, gender(ed) differences that are popularly perceived as inherent in female and male bodies are embodied by females alone.

The femininity embodied and enacted by the *musumeyaku* serves as a foil for the masculinity of the *otokoyaku*.[7] Much of the training of the Revue actors involves learning a vocabulary of gendered gestures, movements, intonations, speech patterns, and the like. An *otokoyaku*, for example, must stride forthrightly across the stage, her arms held stiffly away from her body, her fingers curled around her thumbs. In contrast, a *musumeyaku* pivots her forearms from the elbows, which are kept pinned against her side, constraining her freedom of movement and consequently making her appear more "feminine." In keeping with the patriarchal values informing the Takarazuka Revue, *musumeyaku* have represented the fictional Woman with little if any connection to the actual experiences of females. The *otokoyaku*, however, have been actively encouraged to study the behavior and actions of men offstage (as well as in films) in order to more effectively idealize men on stage, be they samurai or cowboys. Personal or contrary motivations and desires aside, both *musumeyaku* and *otokoyaku* are the products of a masculinist imagination in their official stage roles.

Conceptualizing Androgyny

There seems to have been no formal concept of androgyny prior to Yoshizawa Ayame's development of a theory and method for the Kabuki *onnagata*, or "female" gender specialist, in the early Edo period. Ayame himself (historical figures are often referred to by the given name) was a Kabuki *onnagata*, and his theory was a twist on the Buddhist concept of *henshin*, bodily transformation or metamorphosis. *Hen* is the term for change, in both a transitive and an intransitive sense. *Shin* (also pronounced *mi*) is the term for body in the most comprehensive sense: that is, a physical, mental, social, historical, and spiritual entity (Gunji 1988; Hattori 1975:31–35; Ichikawa 1985:38–47; Imao 1982:29). The term *henshin* originally referred to the process whereby deities assumed a human form in order to better promulgate Buddhist teachings among the masses of sentient beings.

Related to *henshin* is the process of *henjo nanshi* (also *tennyo jōnan*), whereby a female body is transformed, or metamorphoses, into a male body. Since female bodies are regarded in orthodox Buddhist doctrine as not only polluted but also marks of a lower form of existence, enlightenment is not possible for them unless they manage to metamorphose into male bodies. The effect is not the creation of an androgyne, but a female's total transformation into "the opposite" sex—in short, rebirth as a male over the course of several generations. It is clear that the orthodox Buddhist concept of *henshin* refers to physical bodies (including genitalia) and not only to embodied markers of gender.[8] However, the term *henjo nanshi* was also used popularly during the Edo period in reference to intersexed bodies. For example, a peasant woman was deemed to be suffering from *henjo nanshi sho* (the *henjo nanshi* syndrome) when, at the age of 27, she developed "male genitalia" (Tomioka 1938:104).

Henshin is also central to the Kabuki theater and refers specifically to the received process by which an *onnagata* becomes Woman, as opposed to impersonating a given woman. Ayame's theory resembles the Buddhist concept of *henshin* with the exception that gender (and not sex) is involved in an *onnagata*'s transformation from a man to Woman. Ayame conceived of the *onnagata* not as "a male acting in a role in which he becomes a 'woman',"[9] but rather as "a male who is a 'woman' acting a role."[10] In other words, the transformation is not part of a particular role but precedes it.

Ayame insisted that an *onnagata* embody femininity in his daily life.[11] Simply impersonating a given woman was neither adequate nor appropriate. To clinch his point, Ayame insisted that the construction of Woman not be left up to the idiosyncratic notions of a particular actor. Instead, he introduced categories of Woman, each with predetermined characteristics. The role of a "chaste woman" *(teijo)*, for example, was to be based on *Onna Daigaku* (*Greater Learning for Females* [1672]), an influential primer on femininity written by a leading (male) Confucian scholar (cf. Imao 1982:147–153). Given the Kabuki theater's ambivalent reception by the Tokugawa Shogunate, coupled with the low, outsider status of actors during the Edo period, the construction and performance of femininity on the basis of *Onna Daigaku* quite likely added a modicum of legitimacy to the urban theater.[12]

Ayame eschewed what he called the prevailing "androgynous" figure of the *onnagata*, describing it as *futanarihira*—literally, "double-bodied" (Imao 1982:145–146; Maeda 1973:750, 867, 884; Takada 1926 [1917]:287).[13] An androgynous *onnagata* blurred the boundaries between sex and gender, male and female, femininity and masculinity (Imao 1982:145–147). Ayame's apparent objective in formulating a theory and method for the *onnagata* was to make distinct both those boundaries and the bounded, all the while recognizing that sex and gender were not "naturally" aligned in any one body.

An *onnagata*, then, according to Ayame, was not an androgyne but an embodiment of patriarchally inscribed, state-regulated "female" gender. He/she was unequivocally Woman, a model for females offstage to emulate and for males offstage to proposition. Apparently, during Ayame's time there was even "tacit approval" for the *onnagata* "to bathe at the public baths reserved for women" (Watanabe and Iwata 1989 [1987]:86). From Ayame's point of view, the process of *henshin*, or transformation, precluded a blending of the two genders. However, because an *onnagata* was a male-sexed body enacting a type of femininity and thus disturbing the conventional alignment of sex, gender, and sexuality, Watanabe regards the Kabuki actor as an androgyne (Watanabe and Iwata 1989 [1987]:74–135). For Ayame, "female" gender superseded and even negated a male body, and thus the *onnagata*, having become Woman, could bathe with females at public bathhouses; in Watanabe's view, the "female" gender and male body of the Kabuki actor formed a dialectic. According to Watanabe, the androgyny of the *onnagata* was achieved by style (coiffure and clothing) in addition to (homo)sexual practices, specifically the taking of a "passive" feminine role.

With the Meiji Restoration of 1868[14] and the modernizing (or westernizing) state's insistence on short hair and Western clothing for men, the "feminine beauty" hitherto ascribed to and achieved by male bodies was transferred to female bodies (Watanabe and Iwata 1989 [1987]:130–133). Watanabe describes the effect of the Meiji state's gender regulations in terms of an "anti-androgyne complex," according to which males were prevented from having any qualities in common with females (Watanabe and Iwata 1989 [1987]:127); that is, they were prevented, by convention, from embodying and performing femininity outside the Kabuki theater. The establishment of the Takarazuka Revue, in contrast, sanctioned the embodiment and performance of masculinity by females. However, *henshin* was not a process officially prescribed for Takarazuka *otokoyaku*. Kobayashi, the Revue's founder, was no Ayame, and he was keen on limiting an *otokoyaku*'s appropriation of "male" gender to the Takarazuka stage. Along with many early 20th-century sexologists, he believed that a masculine female outside the context of the Revue was something abnormal and perverted.

Kobayashi proclaimed that "the [Takarazuka] *otokoyaku* is not male but is more suave, more affectionate, more courageous, more charming, more handsome, and more fascinating than a real male" (Kobayashi 1960:38). But, although her body served as the main vehicle for the representation and enactment of masculinity, an *otokoyaku*, according to Kobayashi, was not to become unequivocally Man, much less a model for males offstage to emulate. Whereas the *g[k]ata* in *onnagata* means model or archetype, the *yaku* in *otokoyaku* connotes the serviceability and dutifulness of a role-player: "The Takarazuka *otokoyaku* affects a 'male' guise, while the [Kabuki] *onnagata* . . . is completely transformed into a 'female.' As the term *otokoyaku* attests, the female who plays a man is but performing a duty" (Nozaka Akiyuki, cited in Tanabe and Sasaki 1983:130). Thus, Revue directors refer to the actor's achievement of "male" gender not in terms of transformation or metamorphosis *(henshin)* but in terms of "putting something on the body" *(mi ni tsukeru)*—in this case, markers of masculinity.

Kobayashi viewed the theater as one of the most powerful means of influence. He envisioned the Takarazuka Revue as the cornerstone of the "state theater" movement in the 1930s and 1940s, a movement whose agenda included the portrayal of state-regulated gender roles—particularly that of the "good wife, wise mother"—and an emphasis on the patriarchal, conjugal household (Robertson 1991b). Therefore, it would not do to enhance the exemplariness and semiotic authority of the *otokoyaku* by stipulating that she also be a man in her daily life.

Female Sexualities

I now turn to a review of the discourses of gender and sexuality that informed the social climate in which the Takarazuka Revue was established and received. Any interpretation of the Revue's popularity today must take into account its historical beginnings and unprecedented impact on the status quo. Therefore, as I noted earlier, a substantial part of my description and analysis focuses on developments in the early history of the Revue and in the society at large. Where pertinent, and especially in the last section of this article, I discuss gender and androgyny as performed and constructed in the Revue from the 1960s onward.

It was in the context of state formation and nationalism that the *ryōsai kenbo,* or "good wife, wise mother," was codified as the model of "female" gender in the patriarchal Meiji Civil Code.[15] The end of the Tokugawa Shogunate and its 250-year seclusion policy was marked by the restoration of the emperor to a ruling position, by the promulgation of a European-inspired constitution, and by the international emergence of Japan as a new nation-state. The discourse of sexualities is closely linked to nationalism and state formation (see Corrigan and Sayer 1985; Mosse 1985; Watson 1990). At the same time, the printed word is a key factor in the conceiving of the nation and the promoting of nationalism (Anderson 1983). Many of the dozens of articles on femininity, marriage, sex, gender, sexuality, androgyny, and the revue genre published in the many news and literary journals founded at this time were written from a nativist and nationalist angle. Some of the authors even elaborated on the links between all of these issues (for example, Sugita 1935; Takada 1934). In fact, only decades after the Meiji Restoration, social commentators began to react negatively to what they interpreted as the "masculinizing" effect of westernization on Japanese women (for example, Tachibana 1890). And in 1935 one Japanese sexologist claimed in a newspaper interview that women's interest in adopting men's dress was fostered by the revue theater and foreign films (Hori Kentarō, cited in Osaka Mainichi, 31 January 1935). As I have discussed elsewhere, Kobayashi himself recognized the potential of theater, as an agent of the state, to orchestrate the construction and regulation of gender and to stage the enactment of gender roles in society (Robertson 1991b).

Newspaper, magazine, and journal articles published between 1900 and 1945 make it clear that female sexualities, and particularly certain homosexual practices, provoked the most perplexity and made the biggest headlines. The "woman problem" *(fujin mondai)*—the term for issues related to females' civil rights that were made problematic by Meiji feminists—appeared to be accompanied by problem women.[16] Before and even after the Meiji period, published writers and critics—the vast majority of whom were male—relegated sexual desire in females to courtesans and prostitutes (see Robertson 1991a). "Ordinary" women were defined by the gender roles of "daughter," "wife," and "daughter-in-law." Motherhood and mothering emerged as additional components of state-regulated sex and gender in the Meiji period (Koyama 1982, 1986; Mitsuda 1985; Nolte and Hastings 1991). Nearly all of the women's journals founded in the first two decades of the 20th century were devoted to promoting, among their hundreds of thousands of readers, the socialization of women as "good wives, wise mothers" (Watashitachi no rekishi o tsuzuru kai 1987). One exception was *Seitō (Bluestocking)*, a feminist journal founded by Hiratsuka Raichō in 1911 and under surveillance by the government shortly afterward for publishing articles critical of the patriarchal household and family system (Hara 1987:16, 22). The "Taishō Democracy," as the Taishō period (1912–25) is popularly called, was hardly democratic with respect to the condition of women. Not only was the Seitōsha (Bluestocking Society) banned, but under the auspices of the Public Peace Law of 1925, women were banned from congregating in public and from participating in political activity in general.

In the spring of 1938, the now explicitly militarist Shōwa (1926–89) government banned from women's journals any articles related to sex and sexuality that did not trumpet the state's patriarchal values and pronatal policies (Hara 1987:16–21). Not surprisingly, in August 1939 the Osaka prefectural government outlawed *otokoyaku*—"the acme of offensiveness"—from public performances in that prefecture (Ōsaka Nichinichi, 20 August 1939). Kobayashi, who from July 1940 to April 1941 served (in the second Konoe cabinet) as Minister of Commerce and Industry, colluded with government censors to produce musicals that exalted the image of the "good wife, wise mother," an image further reified at that time as *Nippon fujin,* or the "Japanese Woman" (Ōsaka Chōhō, 7 September 1940). Typical of the musicals staged during this period of militarization and state censorship was *Illustrious Women of Japan (Nippon meifu den,* 1941), a nationalistic extravaganza dedicated to heroines, mothers of heroes, and "women of chastity" (English Mainichi, 22 February 1941). Takarasiennes were also recruited into patriotic women's associations and charged with entertaining farm workers, troops in the field, and the war wounded.

Since becoming a fully adult female involved marriage and motherhood, unmarried girls and women were referred to (during and after the Meiji period) by the term *shōjo,* which means, literally, a "not-quite-female" female. (Over the past several years, "gal" [*gyaru*] has emerged as the term for an older, more "female" *shōjo. Shōjo* now tends to be used in reference to teenage girls, and *gyaru* to unmarried women in their early twenties.)[17] *Shōjo* denotes both females between puberty and marriage and that period of time itself in a female's life *(shōjoki)* (Kawahara 1921:112; Tamura 1913). *Shōjo* also implies heterosexual inexperience and homosexual experience, a point to which I will return. (*Gyaru,* on the other hand, does not imply homosexual experience, but rather conjures up the figure of a self-assertive, self-sufficient woman who cultivates boyfriends.)

The state emphasized universal—if segregated and sexist—education, together with the notion that a brief stint in the burgeoning urban industrial and commercial workforce was a desirable thing for females. This emphasis had the effect of increasing the number of years between puberty and marriage (see Murakami 1983). Kobayashi was among the many influential persons who published articles in women's journals reminding their female readers that working outside the home for wages should be construed not as a career in itself but rather as preparation for marriage (Shida and Yuda 1987:115).

The *shōjo* category included the "new working woman" *(shinshokugyō fujin)* and her jaunty counterpart, the "modern girl" *(modan gāru,* or *moga),* herself the antithesis of the "good wife, wise mother." The flapper-like *mga* fancied themselves actors whose stage was the Ginza, at that time Tokyo's premier boulevard. Along with the "new working women," they were Takarazuka fans. Many of the urban-based "new working women" aspired to the Revue stage, and, by the same token, Takarazuka *otokoyaku* were often referred to in the press as "modern girls," especially after 1932, when the "male" gender specialists began sporting short haircuts (Osaka Mainichi, 29 May 1923).

Generally speaking, not only sexism but also ageism was the rule in the workplace. Male employers preferred women up to 24 years of age, and there were few employment opportunities for women over the age of 30. In fact, not many women could afford the financial strain of remaining single; those who did manage to support themselves included doctors, teachers, midwives, nurses, and, to a certain extent, actors

(Shida and Yuda 1987:114). Some women, in the first half of the 20th century at least, "passed" as men in order to secure employment as rickshaw drivers, construction supervisors and laborers, fishers, department store managers, grocers, and so on (Tomioka 1938:103).[18] "Passing" was associated with sexual deviancy only in the case of urban upper-middle-class girls and women who, it was argued, wore masculine attire not to secure a livelihood but to flaunt their "moral depravity." As privileged and educated—in short, bourgeois—girls and women, they were supposed to fulfill the state-sanctioned "good wife, wise mother" gender role. Consequently, those who resisted were vilified in journal and newspaper articles on "masculinized" (danseika) females and were roundly criticized in texts and treatises on "female" psychology (Sakabe 1934; Sugita 1929, 1935; Ushijima 1943; Yasuda 1935).

Ironically, given Kobayashi's views on work and marriage, tenure in the Takarazuka Revue further lengthened the shōjo period, and many of the actors continued to perform into their thirties before retiring well beyond the average age of marriage.[19] Perhaps in response to criticism, the Revue management in 1936 revealed an informal "retirement policy" (teinensei), the first of several, whereby Takarasiennes whose tenure in the Revue exceeded 20 years would be encouraged to retire (Shin Nippō, 17 June 1936). For the most part, however, it continues to be the case that, provided an actor does not marry or leave to pursue other avenues of show business, she can spend her life as a Takarasienne, if not always on stage, then as an instructor or supervisor.

Apart from conceiving of an all-female revue as a commercially viable complement of the all-male Kabuki theater, Kobayashi was interested in producing (through resocialization and retraining) "good wives, wise mothers." In his autobiographical Takarazuka manpitsu (Takarazuka Jottings) and earlier essays, he made clear his antagonism toward the "modern girl" (moga) and masculinized females. Kobayashi theorized that by performing as men, females learned to understand and appreciate males and the masculine psyche. Consequently, when they eventually retired from the stage and married, which Kobayashi urged them to do, they would be better able to perform as "good wives, wise mothers," knowing exactly what their husbands expected of them (Kobayashi 1960:38, 91; Ueda 1974:139). Elsewhere, I have shown how a number of Takarasiennes appropriated their secondary gender in such a way as to resist and subvert Kobayashi's designs: some used their tenure in the Revue as a springboard into the wider world of show business; some sought to present the otokoyaku as an alternative "female" gender role; some did both (Robertson 1989).

Girls' schools, including the Takarazuka Music Academy, and the Revue, along with their (unmarried) female instructors and students, were singled out by sexologists and social critics as the sites and agents of homosexuality among females (see Sugita 1929, 1935; Tamura 1913; Ushijima 1943).[20] In 1910, one of the first articles on this subject was published in a leading women's newspaper, the *Fujo Shinbun* (Fukushima 1984 [1935]:561–563). Distinctions were drawn between two types of homosexual relationships between females: *dōseiai* (same-sex love) and *ome no kankei* (male-female relations).[21] It is clear from the article that what the editorial staff meant by "same *sex*" was actually "same *gender*" and that *ome* referred to a "butch-femme"-like couple (that is, same sex, different genders). Characterized as a passionate but supposedly platonic friendship, the *dōseiai* relationship was regarded as typical among girls and women from all walks of life, but especially among girls' school students and graduates, female educators, female civil servants, and thespians (Fukushima 1984 [1935]:561; see also Tamura 1913; Yasuda 1935). Such relationships were also referred to as "S" or "Class S" *(kurasu esu)*, with the "S" standing for sister, *shōjo*, sex, or all three combined. Class S continues to conjure up the image of two schoolgirls, often a junior-senior pair, with a crush on each other (Miyasako 1986:61).

Ome relationships, on the other hand, were described as

> a strange phenomenon difficult to diagnose on the basis of modern psychology and physiology.[22] . . . One of the couple has malelike [*danseiteki*] characteristics and dominates the [femalelike] other. . . . Unlike the [*dōseiai* couple], friends whose spiritual bond has taken a passionate turn, the latter have developed a strange, carnal relationship [*niku no sesshoku*] . . . stemming from their carnal depravity [*nikuteki daraku*]. . . . The malelike female is technically proficient at manipulating women. . . . Doctors have yet to put their hoes to this uncultivated land [*mikaikonchi*]. [Fukushima 1984 (1935):562]

This article and others like it (for example, Tamura 1913; Yasuda 1935) make it clear that even an overheated *dōseiai* (that is, homogender) relationship was not pathological in the way that an *ome* (that is, heterogender) relationship was, the latter being not only explicitly sexual but also a heretical refraction of the heterosexual norm codified in the Meiji Civil Code. The most objective writers, not surprisingly, referred to an *ome* couple as *fūfu* (husband and wife), a marital metaphor that safely contained (and in effect neutralized) the sexual difference represented and practiced by the two females.

The *Fujo Shinbun* article introduced recent "medical" findings in surmising that females were more prone than males to homosexuality. It was postulated that the "natural" passivity *(muteikōshugi)* of females made them susceptible to neurasthenia *(shinkeishitsu)*, which in turn occasioned a pessimism expressed in the form of homosexuality.[23] *Ome* ("butch-femme") relationships, however, seemed to stymie the sexologists and worry the social critics of the day, since unmarried women (that is, *shōjo*) in particular were stereotypically regarded as blissfully unaware of sexual desire and since females in general were certainly not supposed to play an active role in sex. "Moral depravity" fostered by modernization (westernization) seemed to be the only viable "explanation" for *ome* relationships among urban women, at least until the appearance of Takarazuka *otokoyaku* prompted critics to come up with new ideas to account for the increasingly visible masculinized female.

Overall, it seems that the majority of print space was devoted to defending the typicality and relative "normality" of *dōseiai* (homogender) relationships among *shōjo* and to insisting on their—ideally, at least—platonic character. Apart from eyecatching headlines and titles, proportionately little attention was paid to the *ome* relationship itself, although the "origins" of the "abnormal and anomalous" *(hentaiteki)* masculine partner generated several speculations. The author of a 1930 newspaper article on the Takarazuka Revue, for example, went so far as to assert that the emergence of *ome*-type relationships was the "direct result of females' playing men's roles," and suggested that the Revue was the medium through which Class S couples were transformed into *ome* couples, an evolutionary thesis absent from the *Fujo Shinbun* article published 20 years earlier (Osaka Nichinichi, 21 July 1930; see also Yoshiwara 1935:187, for essentially the same argument). The headline summed up the author's argument: "From Class S to Feverish Yearning for *Otokoyaku*."[24]

Androgyny as Erasure

The "psychiatric style of reasoning" imported from Europe and the United States late in the 19th century—and alluded to in the 1910 *Fujo Shinbun* article and others—provided a whole new set of concepts that made it possible to separate questions of sexual and gender identity from facts about anatomy (Davidson 1987:22; see also Hanafusa 1930; Izawa 1931; Kure 1920; Yasuda 1935). Female sexualities, now problematic, were linked to experiences, to environment, and to "impulses, tastes, aptitudes, satisfactions, and psychic traits" (Davidson 1987:22). For example, in the *Fujo Shinbun* article, "abusive stepmothers, exploitative employers, constant hardship, others' callousness, false accusations, and unrequited love" were blamed for causing girls and women to adopt *dōseiai* practices. Certain sexologists and social critics regarded the so-called masculinized female in particular as a prime example of a newly defined disorder, "abnormal psychology" *(hentai seiri* or *hentai shinri)*. After establishing cross-dressing *(hensō)* itself as "abnormal" *(fuseijō)*, one sexology writer went on to distinguish between "natural," or congenital, cross-dressing and "unnatural," or acquired, cross-dressing among females and males.[25] According to this writer, the former involved an intersexed person attempting to pass as either a woman or a man, while the latter involved a person motivated by curiosity, criminal intentions, or the desire to secure a livelihood. Masculinized females associated with the theater, the author claimed, cross-dressed out of curiosity (Tomioka 1938:98–103).

Beginning in the 1920s, so far as I can assess from the print media, Takarazuka *otokoyaku* as well as the girls and women who were attracted to them (and sent "love letters") were referred to by unsympathetic critics as "abnormal" and "anomalous" (Kawahara 1921:13; Osaka Nichinichi, 21 July 1930; Sugita 1935). Their desire was interpreted as being out of alignment with their female bodies. The sympathetic use of the term *chūsei* ("neutral," or "in between" woman and man) to describe the Takarazuka *otokoyaku*, and masculinized females in general, conveniently circumvented the issue of erotic desire and parried allegations of "abnormal" sexuality. *Chūsei* was used defensively to deflect negative attention from both the sexual difference represented by the Takarazuka *otokoyaku* and the social ramifications of that difference. Describing someone as *chūsei* suggested that she had a childlike naiveté about anything beyond a passionate friendship between *shōjo* sisters. A group interview with ten Takarasiennes on their thoughts about a Hungarian movie star known in Japan for her "*otokoyaku*-like" appearance illustrates the deflective, defensive use of *chūsei*. Active in the 1930s, she is described in the interview as not only neutral *(chūseiteki)* but also childish *(kodomoppoi)*, mischievous *(itazurakko)*, and "not coquettish, but rather romantic in a childish sense" *(kodomoppoi romanchikusa)*. The reporter notes that she is *chūsei*, "in the sense of childlike" *(chairudo to iu imi)*, the implication being that despite her provocative wink, she is asexual (Yomiuri Shinbun, 23 May 1935).

Some of the more "progressive" writers and critics sympathetic to the Revue, such as the novelist Yoshiya Nobuko (1896–1973), a lesbian,[26] preferred the safe ambiguity of *chūsei*, with its allusions—like Yoshiya's fiction—to a "dream world" *(yume no sekai)* free from the constraints of fixed, dichotomous, and hierarchical gender roles. Takarazuka itself was conceived of as a dream world—"a place where dreams are made and sold," according to the Revue's advertisements—and the early theater complex was named, appropriately, "Paradise" *(Paradaisu)*. Kobayashi collaborated with Yoshiya and shared her romantic vision, but colored it heterosexual: his dream world was one in which gallant men were sustained by adoring women.

Detractors, on the other hand, referred to the *otokoyaku* and other "modern girls" as abnormal, masculinized females, who sported short hair *(danpatsu)* and wore pants (Maruki 1929; Sugita 1929:80, 1935). Such females were also called *"garçons,"*[27] since they had "forgotten what it means to be feminine," one of the accusations leveled at Yoshiya Nobuko herself (Osaka Mainichi, 10 February 1932). If the "good wife, wise mother" was praised as the embodiment of social stability, the masculinized female was criticized as a disturbing sign of the disorder accompanying the growth of the modern, westernized city (Sugita 1929, 1935; Yoshida 1935).

From the mid-1930s onward the expression *dansō no reijin*, meaning literally "a beautiful person [that is, a female] in masculine attire," was used sympathetically in reference to both Takarazuka *otokoyaku* and masculinized females.[28] This expression, a euphemism for *chūsei*, was apparently coined in 1932 by the novelist Muramatsu Shōfu. His serialized short story "Dansō no reijin" was inspired by Kawashima Yoshiko (1906–48), who had donned a military uniform and passed as a man during the early stages of Japanese imperialism in China and Manchuria.[29] Several years later, in 1935, the affluent *moga* Masuda Yasumare (née Fumiko) made headlines as a *dansō no reijin* when she attempted suicide after her ("butch-femme") love affair with Saijō Eriko of the Shōchiku Revue became public knowledge (Nakano 1935; Saijō 1935; Tani 1935).[30] From a patriarchal perspective, the expression *dansō no reijin* subordinates the female body to the masculine clothes *(dansō)* covering it. At the same time, a priori knowledge of the underlying female body neutralizes both the masculinity of the costume and, by extension, the "male" gender identity of the female in question. The *dansō no reijin* is reduced to a caricature of a man, and her sexuality read as ambiguous, unresolved, or un(der)developed—and unthreatening.[31] Ideologically speaking, when people lack a priori knowledge of the sex of a body, gender must be overdetermined in order to facilitate their perception of that body as either female or male.

Kobayashi's response to the Masuda-Saijō affair in an official Takarazuka fan magazine made problematic the sexual ambiguity of the *dansō no reijin* figure. In an editorial titled "What is the *'dansō no reijin'*?" Kobayashi expressed his concern that the current spate of scandalmongering press reports on all-female revues was bound to create public misunderstandings about Takarazuka, the "'main household' [*honke*] of the *shōjo* revue":

> The *dansō no reijin*, ... a symbol of abnormal love, ... is becoming a social problem.... Good [that is, upper-class] households especially are affected.... Nothing must compromise [Takarazuka's] reputation or worry the parents of [Takarazuka Music Academy] students. [Kobayashi 1935:10–12][32]

In the editorial, Kobayashi included part of a letter to Ashihara Ku-niko, a leading *otokoyaku*, asking her to make sure that new students understood they were not to use masculine words or to behave in a masculine fashion in their daily lives.[33] Ashihara's fans called her *aniki* (elder brother), a matter which distressed Kobayashi greatly and for which he had chastised her two years earlier (Ashihara 1979:157). Her reply—which, in keeping with precedent, may actually have been written by him—was included in the editorial.[34] In that ostensible reply, the senior *otokoyaku* reassured Kobayashi that she and "the others are all just 'ordinary girls' . . . who practice the tea ceremony and flower arrangement when not performing." Masculine words, she added, "are not used by any of the students or actors even though their use is popular among girls' school students and [Takarazuka] fans" (cited in Kobayashi 1935:11–12). But even sympathetic contemporary accounts of the Revue contradicted this "ordinary girl" image of the Takarasiennes: Hirai, for example, profiled one *otokoyaku* who was "malelike in her everyday life" (Hirai 1933:168). It appears, rather, that Kobayashi's editorial was a timely and opportunistic measure undertaken not only to deflect any negative repercussions on the Revue from the highly publicized Masuda-Saijō affair but also to reinforce his patriarchal agenda for the Takarasiennes.

Conclusion: Postwar Androgyny

Here, I will shift from a discussion of largely historical (prewar and interwar) references to androgyny to a consideration of several more recent (postwar) constructions of androgyny in the context of the Takarazuka Revue. Knowledge of precedents and of the early, varied reception of the Revue is essential to an understanding of contemporary experiments with androgyny. The Revue continues both to uphold the dominant ideal of heterosexuality and to inform a lesbian subcultural style. In this connection, the allegorical tension that has marked Takarazuka from the beginning still frustrates the patriarchal management. With respect to state formation (that is, the production and reproduction of the status quo), the Revue continues to attract the attention of the mass media, although the charges of "moral depravity" and "abnormal sexual desire" are rarely leveled, as openly at least, at the Takarasiennes. Suffice it to say for the time being that the waning of overt criticism is due less to a greater tolerance for diverse sexualities than to an avoidance of sexual practices and expressions other than the heterosexual and/or (androcentrically) pornographic.

One of the reasons why the newly revived musical *The Rose of Versailles*, first staged in the mid-1970s, has been such a success among female fans of all ages is that it dwells on the adventures of Oscar, a female raised as a boy in order to insure the continuity of a patriline of generals.[35] The Oscar character represents a slippage between sex and gender and is referred to in the literature as a "classic" *dansō no reijin* (Tsuji 1976:97, 107–108; Yabushita 1990:108). (See Figure 1.) Significantly, Oscar has been acted exclusively by *otokoyaku*, whose own acting careers in the Revue have followed a similar trajectory. Clothing is the means to, and even the substance of, the character's commutable gender, as the expression *dansō no reijin* suggests; accordingly, Oscar switches at one point from masculine to feminine attire. The alternative subtextual meaning of this play is that gender as performance undercuts the ideological fixity of received gender differences (Kuhn 1985:53; see also Komashaku 1989; Tsuji 1976:107–130).

The Rose of Versailles is one of the Revue's most reflexive productions in that the relationship between Oscar and her/his father is analogous to that between the *otokoyaku* and the Revue's patriarchal directorship. When reading the following dialogue between Oscar and the General, bear in mind that Kobayashi had insisted that Takarasiennes call him "Father":

Oscar: Father, please answer me!

General: Oscar?!

Oscar: If . . . if I had been raised as an ordinary female, would I have been forced to marry at age 15 like my sisters? I could be playing the clavichord, singing arias, dressing up every night in fine clothes and laughing away the time in high society. . . .

General: Oscar!!

Oscar: Please answer me! I could be wearing velvet beauty marks and rose perfume; I could fill my arabesque compact with cosmetics; I could bear children—and raise them.

General: Oscar!!

Oscar: Answer me, please!

General: (Pensively.) Yes, it's as you say—had you been raised as an ordinary female.

Oscar: Father, thank you.

General: (Is taken aback.)

Oscar: Thank you for giving me a chance to live the kind of life I have, in as broad a world as I have, even though I am a female. Even while struggling to deal with the stupidity of pathetic people. . . .

General: Oscar.

Oscar: I am no longer remorseful. I . . . I'll live as the child of Mars, god of war. I'll devote this body of mine to the sword; I'll devote it to the can-

Figure 1. Oscar, acted by otokoyaku Shion Yū in the 1990 production of The Rose of Versailles. *Photograph from the program (Takarazuka Kagekidan 1990).*

non. My livelihood is the military and I'll serve as the child of Mars,
god of war. [Ikeda Riyoko, cited in Tsuji 1976:165–166]

Oscar (and by the same token, the Takarazuka *otokoyaku*) is able to
transcend the fixed, narrow life course of "ordinary females" because of
Father's pragmatic decision to name her "son." Recognizing that "male"
gender affords access to a wider world, Oscar is effusively grateful for
the opportunity to be the household's *otokoyaku*. Oscar's military uniform not only accentuates the difference between masculinity and femininity—the former identified with swords and cannons, the latter with
flowers and children—but magnifies the tension between "male" gender
and the female body it camouflages. The overall effect at once exagger-
ates and masks the slippage between sex and gender. Both the General
and the audience know that Oscar, like the Takarasienne, is a masculinized female. That gender is a property of attribution and convention, and
not anatomy, is made doubly obvious by the synonymy between Oscar
and the *otokoyaku* performing Oscar. At the same time, both demonstrate
the irony that access to a supposedly more "liberating" gender identity is
granted by privileged father figures.[36]

In the fall of 1985, the Takarazuka Revue staged a show called *Androgyny (Andorojenii)*, which the (male) playwright/director felt captured the
"bewitching charm" of the androgyne. The show called for *otokoyaku* to
appear alternately as "neutral boys" *(nyutoraru boi)*, resplendent in
gaudy, glittery jumpsuits and equally colorful wigs, and as well-known
(non-Japanese) masculinized females, such as George Sand. Fan magazines described it as a show "ahead of its time" and "unprecedented"
(Mure 1985:38).

Although the 1985 revue may have been the first show titled *Androgyny*, the theme and phenomenon themselves have constituted an essential part not only of the Takarazuka Revue's repertoire but also of its public image, as I have discussed. Moreover, in the late 1960s *otokoyaku* were
encouraged to impart an "androgynous charm" by blending markers of
"female" and "male" gender. They did so mainly by ratting their often
peroxided hair to create puffy pompadours and by using pastel makeup
to soften the darker, sharper, deeply chiseled features of the "classic"
otokoyaku (see Figures 2 and 3). These 1960s *otokoyaku* foreshadowed the
interstitial Oscar character: Kō Nishiki described herself as "an *otokoyaku*
who was close to being feminine," although she also threatened to resign
if forced to appear as a woman on stage (Okazaki 1971:49; Yoshizawa
1966:52); Anna Jun claimed to have been a "womanish" *(onnappoi) otokoyaku* (Anna 1979:197); Dai Takiko declared that even though she was a
"leading man," she took care not to forfeit her femininity (Yamada
1968:70).

Figure 2. Anna Jun as a 1960s "androgynous" otokoyaku. Photograph from the cover of
Takarazuka Gurafu *(Fujii 1968).*

Figure 3. Kasugano Yachiyo as a "classic" otokoyaku. Photograph from the cover of
Takarazuka Fuan *(Kishi 1954).*

By allowing "the woman" to permeate "the man," these *otokoyaku* in
effect drew attention to the facticity of their female bodies and, *from the
standpoint of convention,* to the primacy of their femininity, thus ensuring
that their secondary, "male" gender was kept in check by their primary,
"female" gender. The directors did not want the *otokoyaku* to be too successful in her appropriation and performance of masculinity. Similarly, as
a way of clarifying the limits of the actors' "honorary" masculinity, the
directors staged shows in which *otokoyaku* were to appear as women,
much to the consternation of the actors and their fans. Allowing "the
woman" to permeate "the man" was one thing, but being assigned to
women's roles was quite another. Many *otokoyaku* protested the directors'
gender-switching antics and claimed to have experienced a sense of conflict or resistance *(teikō)*, along with a loss of confidence (Misato 1974:68;
Okazaki 1971:49; Takarazuka Gurafu 1977:38; Yamada 1968:70–71;
Yoshizawa 1967:71). Gō Chigusa, an *otokoyaku* who retired in 1972, remarked that on the rare occasion she was assigned to perform as a

woman, her fans complained bitterly of their resultant dis-ease *(kimochi warui),* that eerie feeling when the familiar is suddenly defamiliarized (Yoshizawa 1967:71). The androgynous charm of the *otokoyaku* was compromised by the compulsory femininity of "the woman."

Otokoyaku have been characterized as "sexy but sexless," the argument being that ambiguous gender translates as an asexual identity (Asahi Shinbun, Osaka ed., 21 December 1977). An *otokoyaku* performing on stage as a man may be the object of desire, but she herself is purportedly without sexuality. Partly to rationalize and sustain the perception of asexuality, all Takarasiennes must remain unmarried, and ostensibly heterosexually inexperienced, throughout their tenure in the Revue—a policy implemented by Kobayashi at the founding of the Revue. Implicitly acknowledging that a theatrical vocation virtually precludes distinctions between on- and offstage experiences, several *otokoyaku* have noted that "it would be ridiculous to be married *and* perform as a man on stage," but their explanation contradicts the management's rationale: "Female fans probably will not be charmed by a married *otokoyaku*" (Kageki 1962:41). From the beginning, the Revue management has sought to limit the female fans' infatuation to the ideal man performed by an *otokoyaku.* My archival research and interviews suggest that, on the contrary, female fans of all ages, classes, and educational levels do not *see* a man on stage, but rather *acknowledge* a female body performing in a capacity that transgresses the boundaries of received femininity (Hoshi 1987; Maruo 1950:252–278; Osaka Jiji, 12 December 1934; Fujin Kōron 1935; Tanabe and Sasaki 1983:135–136).[37] The *otokoyaku,* in short, is appreciated as an exemplary female who can successfully negotiate both genders, and their attendant roles, without being constrained by either.

Much of the Euro-American literature on androgyny deals with nonethnographic theoretical issues, with film and literary characters (for example, Bell-Metereau 1985; Bergstrom 1991; Butler 1990; Heilbrun 1982 [1964]; Pacteau 1986; Stimpson 1989 [1974]), or with intersexed and transsexed bodies (for example, Foucault 1980 [1978]; Millot 1990 [1983]). I have benefited from this insightful literature in devising strategies for making visible the construction and uses of androgyny in Japan as a "surface politics of the body." However, I have tried to avoid the tendency to force Japanese cultural practices into Western analytical categories. Of course, moments and sites of historical conjunction must be acknowledged, and cultural practices should be distinguished from the dominant gender ideology operating in Japan.

My work also differs from the Euro-American literature in that I have aimed to show how androgyny has been constructed, performed, practiced, and deployed by real females and males, who include the Takarazuka actors, their fans, and their critics. Bergstrom's discussion of the dual iconicity of androgyny, for example, closely resembles my dis-

cussion of the terms *ryōsei* and *chūsei:* "Where androgyny, as a fashionable, contemporary look, can indicate 'more' sexuality, meaning *both* feminine *and* masculine appeal, virtually the same image can be used to signal the eradication of sexuality" (1991:36). But whereas her cogent
analysis is based on Calvin Klein underwear advertisements and select
science fiction films, I have shown how the different semantic and semiotic values of androgyny were actually (re)produced and deployed by
Japanese females and males on and off the Revue stage.

In Japan the term *chūsei* has been used since the turn of this century to
name three basic, but overlapping, types of females: those whose bodies
approximate the masculine stereotype; those who are charismatic, unconventional, and therefore not feminine females; and those who have
been assigned to do "male" gender or who have appropriated it on their
own initiative. The characterization of their appearance as "androgynous" is necessarily premised on a priori knowledge of the underlying *female* body—knowledge that nullifies or compromises the "male" gender
of the surface. It goes without saying that a female who passes successfully as a man does not appear androgynous.[38] The androgynous appearance of masculinized females has been read by some as not only "abnormal" but a sign of their asexuality. The expression *dansō no reijin* directed
attention away from the body and toward the masculine clothing of a female who made unconventional choices, sexual and otherwise.

I have shown that the appeal to and experiments with androgyny in
the Takarazuka Revue served the interests of the patriarchal management and the female actors and fans alike by deflecting negative attention from the sexual difference posed by the *otokoyaku.* By allowing "the
woman" to permeate "the man," the experiments with androgyny in the
late 1960s and early 1980s in effect emphasized the facticity of the female
body doing "male" gender. The directors used these experiments to ensure that an *otokoyaku*'s secondary, "male" gender would be kept in check
by her primary, "natural" femininity. Female fans, on the other hand, saw
the *otokoyaku* as a female unconstrained by a sexual and gendered division of labor. Androgyny, as a "surface politics of the body," has been
used historically to interrogate the naturalized dualities of male and female, masculine and feminine. By the same token, androgyny has also
been used—in various ways by various agents—to exaggerate, essentialize, and mystify those dualities.

Notes

Acknowledgments. My fieldwork and archival research in Japan (Tokyo, Kyoto,
and Takarazuka) were funded by the following fellowships and grants: Japan
Foundation Professional Fellowship (June–September 1987); Northeast Asia

Council of the Association for Asian Studies Grant (June–September 1987); Social Science Research Council Research Grant (June–September 1987); University of California, San Diego, Japanese Studies Program Travel Grant (summer 1987); University of California, San Diego, Affirmative Action Faculty Career Development Grant (July–September and November–June 1989–90); Fulbright Research Grant (January–August 1990). Abridged versions of this article were presented as "The Androgynous Body in Japan," at the American Ethnological Society Annual Meeting, Atlanta, 19–22 April 1990; as "The Image of the Androgyne: Female Sexualities in Modern Japan," at the E. O. Reischauer Institute of Japanese Studies, Harvard University, 12 October 1990; and as "The Politics of Androgyny in Japan," at the Japan Colloquium, University of California, Los Angeles, 31 May 1991. Thanks are due to the four anonymous reviewers for their informative critiques, to Don Brenneis and Kris Fossum for their editorial expertise, and to Maria Teresa Koreck for her insightful reading.

All translations from Japanese to English are my own unless otherwise indicated. For Japanese individuals, the family name precedes the given name.

1. By "the state," I mean not simply an "organ of coercion" or a "bureaucratic lineage" but a "repertoire of activities and institutions" that shape and are shaped by sociohistorical circumstances and experiences (Corrigan and Sayer 1985:2–3). Although for the sake of convenience I refer to the state as a thing in itself, namely, "the state," I regard the state as an "ideological project," an "exercise in legitimation" (Phillip Abrams, cited in Corrigan and Sayer 1985:8).

2. Yasui (1953) notes that a vernacular expression for androgyny is *otoko-onna*—literally, "man-woman"—although references to androgyny in social scientific, literary, and scientific writings tend to be limited to the terms *ryōsei* and *chūsei*.

3. Jung proposed that all people were androgynous; any person, whether female or male, had both a feminine side and a masculine side. "Anima" was his term for the feminine archetype in males, "animus" for the masculine archetype in females. The sexist essentialism of Jung's proposal is evident in his description of these terms. The anima included irrationality, spirituality, and emotionalism, and the animus rationality, courage, and strong convictions (Hyde and Rosenberg 1980 [1976]:19).

4. The *jo* in *josei* may also be read as *onna*, and the *dan* in *dansei* as *otoko*.

5. Although a female, the legendary dancer Okuni from Izumo, is credited with having initiated Kabuki at the start of the 17th century, females have been banned from that stage since 1629. Apparently, the newly installed Shogunate was disturbed by the general disorder, including unlicensed prostitution, following the performances, when patrons quarreled with one another for access to their favorite dancers. Replacing the females with boys did not solve the problem, for the male patrons were equally attracted to the boys. Eventually, the prohibition of females and later of boys prompted the sanctioned emergence of the *onnagata*, adult males who specialized in femininity.

6. For a more detailed discussion of the Revue's early history, see Robertson 1989 and 1991b.

7. The Takarasiennes, in short, specialize in performing "male" and "female" gender. However, the Revue has never staged a play featuring contemporary Japanese characters (other than patriotic youths in wartime productions). Plays

with Japanese characters are limited to stories set in the Heian through Edo periods, roughly the 9th through the mid-19th century. Plays set in the 20th century present non-Japanese "male" and "female" characters exclusively. Thus, the repertoire of an *otokoyaku* does not include contemporary Japanese men, although the Takarasienne learns about masculinity by watching, among others, Japanese males. The representation of contemporary Japanese "male" gender appears to be off-limits to Takarazuka *otokoyaku*.

8. Asano (1989) notes that there are several sutras written to facilitate the *henjo nanshi* process and that certain unorthodox sects, such as the Fujikō (late 16th century), Nyoraikyō (late 19th century), and Ōmotokyō (early 20th century), incorporated the concept of androgyny qua "cross-dressing" into their doctrines and ritual practices.

9. *Otoko ga onna ni nari yaku o enjiru.*

10. *Onna de aru otoko ga yaku o enjiru.*

11. *Onnagata wa nichijōteki ni onna de aru koto.* An Ayamian *onnagata* is more specifically referred to as a *ma no onnagata*, or "true" *onnagata*, in contradistinction to some present-day Kabuki actors who perform as *onnagata* in addition to taking on a plethora of "male" roles.

12. The primer was written by Kaibara Ekken, a leading representative of the "practical school" of Confucianism and a self-appointed critic of females. Ekken proclaimed that while necessary for the reproduction of male heirs, female genitalia promoted dull wittedness, laziness, lasciviousness, a hot temper, and a tremendous capacity to bear grudges. He was not alone in suggesting that a female-sexed body was contrary to and even precluded "female" gender (see Robertson 1991a).

Political leadership during the Edo period was monopolized by the Tokugawa clan under the leadership of the shogun, who ruled from the capital city of Edo. The Confucian orientation of the Shogunate was reflected in the four-part social status hierarchy, in which samurai occupied the top rank, followed by farmers, artisans, and merchants. Actors, along with outcastes and criminals, were lumped into a fifth, "nonpeople" category below the merchants. Although individuals of higher status could fall, those of the lowest status could not rise. Kabuki was among the literary, fine, and performing arts whose development accompanied the consolidation of a mercantilistic urban culture during this period.

13. The term *futanarihira* is also a play on the name of Arihara no Narihira, a 9th-century bisexual courtier eulogized in Edo-period fiction as "the god of *yin* and *yang*" (Schalow 1990:10). The *futa* (double) preceding *narihira* would seem to imply an "overdetermined" Narihira, or perhaps a "body-double" Narihira.

14. In 1868 the Shogunate was defeated by anti-Tokugawa court nobles, and the emperor (who adopted the reign name of Meiji) was restored to power.

15. The civil code promulgated during the Meiji period (1868–1912) was operative from 1898 to 1947.

16. For more information in English on the "woman problem," see Nolte and Hastings (1991), Sievers (1983), and Silverberg (1991).

17. In 1990, the expression *ojin gyaru* (older man-gal) was coined to refer to "gals" who enjoy drinking, gambling, and singing (*karaoke*-style) after work, presumably just like their fathers and other older men. There is even an *ojin gyaru*

anthem, "Senchimentaru gyaru" ("Sentimental Gal"), which was broadcast regularly in the spring of 1990 on the government television station's (NHK) weekly hit parade. The phrase *ojin gyaru* suggests androgyny inasmuch as it refers to a female who has appropriated masculine pastimes.

18. Tomioka refers to such women as examples of "acquired 'male' impersonation" *(kotenteki dansō),* although he notes that these "working women are not mentally disturbed, but rather passing as men in order to earn a livelihood" (1938:103). It is clear from his article, especially the section on "inherent [*sententeki*] 'male'/'female' impersonation," that he uses "cross-dressing" to mean androgyny. Generally speaking, his "inherent" androgyny corresponds to *ryōsei,* and his "acquired" androgyny to *chūsei.*

19. On 2 April 1940, a *Shin Nippō* newspaper article on a leading Takarasienne appeared under the headline "Still a *Shōjo* at 36!" Takarasiennes were by definition unmarried, but the reporter was drawing attention to the disturbing lack of correspondence between chronological age and *shōjo* status. The same point had been made 15 years earlier in a newspaper series on *shōjo* theater groups (Osakato, 15, 17–20, and 22 July 1925).

20. The Meiji government ruled in 1872 that primary education, if sex segregated, was compulsory for girls and boys alike, although home economics constituted the bulk of education for girls. Public and private secondary schools for girls and young women, called "higher schools," were established countrywide in the early 1900s, and by 1907, 40,273 female students were enrolled in 133 higher schools (Pflugfelder 1989:7). For a comparative perspective, see Vicinus' work on English boarding school friendships (1989).

21. Early-20th-century sexologists used the term *dōseiai* (literally, "same-sex love") for homosexuality and the term *iseiai* (literally, "different-sex love") for heterosexuality (see, for example, Kure 1920). These and other terms appeared not only in specialized medical journals but also in a wide range of print media, including novels and women's newspapers and journals; they were thus familiar to a broad spectrum of literate people.

Although *dōseiai* is a generic term, it is defined more specifically in this particular article as an essentially platonic if passionate relationship. *Ome* is an abbreviation of *osu* (male) and *mesu* (female), terms reserved for plants and animals and applied pejoratively to humans. An 1818 reference to *ome* refers not to a same-sex couple but to an androgyne, in this case a female who passed as a man (Tomioka 1938:102).

22. The author was alluding to the fact that the "male" partner was not intersexed but had a "normal" female body.

23. *Shinkeishitsu* originated around the turn of the century as a category of sociosexual disease, diagnosed most often in urban middle-class women (who represented about 30 percent of the female population at that time).

24. In a 1934 newspaper interview, a Japanese sexologist drew distinctions between what he called "pseudo-homosexuality" *(gisei dōseiai)* and "true homosexuality" *(shinsei dōseiai),* the former consisting of a "transitory love relationship" *(awai ren'ai kankei)* and the latter of "actual sexual practices" *(honkakuteki na seikoi).* According to his criteria, Class S relations would fall into the category of pseudo-homosexuality and *ome* relations into that of true homosexuality (Hori Kentarō,

cited in Osaka Mainichi, 31 January 1935). See Robertson (1989) for expressions used by Takarasiennes for female-female couples.

25. The writer used "cross-dressing" where others used "androgyny," and he tucked information about contemporary practices between long accounts of Edo-period cross-dressers, possibly as a way to avoid the wartime censors.

26. Yoshiya, an openly recognized lesbian, wrote popular, widely disseminated articles and short stories on such topics as "same-sex love," the superfluousness of husbands, and patriotism. The mass media referred to Yoshiya and her life-partner, Monma Chiyo, as a *dōseiai fūfu* (same-sex love husband and wife) (Usumi 1935:43).

27. The use of *garçons* probably reflects the French influence on the development of the all-female revue and the role of the "male" gender specialist.

28. A variant of this expression appears in a 1935 newspaper (Osaka Mainichi, 15 January) article as *dansō no reijō*, literally, a "beautiful [unmarried] female in masculine attire."

29. Kawashima, born into the Chinese royal family but raised by her adopted family in Japan, began to wear men's clothes at the age of 16 (Kamisaka 1984:87). She was eventually executed in Japan on charges of treason. Muramatsu's short story was serialized in a leading women's journal, *Fujin Kōron*.

30. Founded in Tokyo (Asakusa) in 1928, the all-female Shōchiku Revue later established an Osaka branch (near Takarazuka) and quickly became Takarazuka's main rival in every respect. From the start, the Shōchiku Revue, which was formally disbanded in early 1990 (although special performances are to be scheduled annually), was cast as the opposite of Takarazuka. For example, where Takarazuka productions were stereotyped as naive and romantic, the Shōchiku actors performed allegedly more mature and erotic revues. Fans partial to one revue rarely attended performances staged by the rival troupe. Moreover, following the establishment of the Tokyo Takarazuka theater in the Ginza area in 1934, an areal distinction was drawn between the two revues. Takarazuka was cast as an "uptown" theater attractive to girls and women from wealthy households, and Shōchiku as a "lowtown" theater appealing to a blue-collar clientele.

Mizunoe Takiko (Tākii), Shōchiku's leading *otokoyaku* for decades, was the first revue actor to cut her hair short and is the subject of many books and articles. Generally speaking, articles, books, and, in recent decades, television programs on Takarazuka far outnumber those on the Shōchiku Revue. See Robertson (1989) for an account of same-sex ("butch-femme") affairs in the Takarazuka Revue.

31. Although it would seem that the reasoning behind the concept of *dansō no reijin* fits the experience of the Kabuki *onnagata*, the two are not symmetrical. Whereas the former is reduced to a caricature of a man, the latter is promoted as a paragon of femininity. The asymmetry reflects the arbitrary operations of a dominant ideology premised on male dominance and agency.

32. Kobayashi's concern about upper-class households reflects the fact that Masuda was from a wealthy family, as was (and is) the typical Takarazuka student.

33. For Kobayashi, the most problematic "male" words were *aniki* (elder brother), *boku* (a self-referent denoting "male" gender), and *kimi* (a masculine form of "you") (Kobayashi 1935).

34. Ashihara suspected Kobayashi of forging a letter detailing a fan's negative reaction to her nickname, *aniki* (Ashihara 1979:157).

35. In 1989, the play was revived—to satisfy nostalgic "old fans" and attract new fans. A two-year run was planned. *The Rose of Versailles,* by Ikeda Riyoko, was serialized from 1972 to 1974 in the weekly *Margaret* and published in several volumes in 1983 (Ikeda 1983).

36. Kuhn observes that if "clothing can be costume, capable of being modified at the wearer's will, it follows that the gender identity conventionally signified by dress may be just as easily changeable" (1985:53). What is most problematic about this theoretical statement with respect to the Takarazuka *otokoyaku* is the matter of the "wearer's will." "Will" does not figure in one's initial gender assignment (based on genitalia), nor is a Takarasienne's secondary gender assignment necessarily congruent in every respect with her will.

Interestingly, in recent decades Takarasiennes and their fans have sometimes referred to the *otokoyaku* as a female who has metamorphosed *(henshin shita)* (Takarazuka Gurafu 1986), indicating a recontextualization of this hitherto androcentric term to fit their stage experience. Their use of the term outside the Buddhist and Kabuki *(onnagata)* contexts may have been prompted by the tremendous continuing popularity of the *"henshin* dramas" *(dorama)* that were first aired in the late 1960s. These television dramas, some of them animated, feature mostly "ordinary" boys and young men who have the ability to change *(henshin)* suddenly into other, more powerful forms. In another incarnation the brainy Pa-man, for example, is Mitsuo-*kun*, an average elementary school student. His inventors suggest that what audiences find intriguing is the possibility of "one person living in two worlds" (Asahi Shinbun, Osaka ed., 13 January 1968). Many comic book characters and toy robots (such as Transformers) are also based on the idea of *henshin.*

37. Since the postwar period (roughly the 1950s onward), females of all ages have constituted the overwhelming majority of the Takarazuka audience and fan population. Throughout the prewar and interwar years, about half of the audience was made up of males, although the most zealous (and problematic) fans were female. The unabated postwar popularity of Takarazuka among females probably has much to do with the dominant gender ideology. Voting rights (1947) and nominal equal employment opportunity laws (1986) notwithstanding, sexist discrimination—from the boys-first order of school roll calls to short-term "mommy track" jobs—is the prevailing state of affairs. The gender "norm" of "women inside, men outside" is reinforced by "public opinion" polls commissioned by the Prime Minister's Office and others, despite the fact that over 60 percent of all adult females—80 percent of them married and mothers—work for wages outside the home (see Asahi Shinbun, Osaka ed., 29 March 1990; Atsumi 1988; Japan Times, 10 April 1990).

38. In *Gender Blending,* Devor's use of the term "androgyny" is different from mine here. She presents the life histories of females who do not consciously attempt to pass as men but who, because of their appearance, are perceived as such (1989).

References Cited

Akiyama Satoko
1990   Ryōseiguyūsei to seitōsaku. Imago 1(2):57–61.

Anderson, Benedict
1983   Imagined Communities: Reflections on the Origin and Spread of Capitalism. New York: Schocken Books.

Anna Jun
1979   "Berubara" de taitō shita iroke no enshutsu. Fujin Kōron, August: 196–201.

Asano Miwako
1989   Minshu shūkyō ni okeru ryōseiguyūkan. *In* Shiriizu: Josei to bukkyō. Vol. 2: Sukui to oshie. Nishiguchi J. and Osumi K., eds. pp. 200–229. Tokyo: Heibonsha.

Ashihara Kuniko
1979   Waga seishun no Takarazuka. Tokyo: Zenbonsha.

Atsumi, Reiko
1988   Dilemmas and Accommodations of Married Japanese Women in White-Collar Employment. Bulletin of Concerned Asian Scholars 20(3):54–62.

Bell-Metereau, Rebecca
1985   Hollywood Androgyny. New York: Columbia University Press.

Bergstrom, Janet
1991   Androids and Androgyny. *In* Close Encounters: Film, Feminism, and Science Fiction. C. Penley, E. Lyon, L. Spigel, and J. Bergstrom, eds. pp. 33–60. Minneapolis: University of Minnesota Press.

Butler, Judith
1990   Gender Trouble: Feminism and the Subversion of Identity. New York: Routledge.

Corrigan, Philip, and Derek Sayer
1985   The Great Arch: English State Formation as Cultural Revolution. London: Basil Blackwell.

Davidson, Arnold
1987   Sex and the Emergence of Sexuality. Critical Inquiry 14:16–48.

Devor, Holly
1989   Gender Blending: Confronting the Limits of Duality. Bloomington: University of Indiana Press.

Foucault, Michel, ed.
1980[1978]   Being the Recently Discovered Memoirs of a Nineteenth-Century French Hermaphrodite. R. McDougall, trans. New York: Pantheon Books.

Fujii Kenzō, ed.
1968 [Cover photograph.] Takarazuka Gurafu 248.

Fujin Kōron
1935 Shōjo kageki o kataru—musume to haha no kai. Fujin Kōron, April:288–297.

Fukushima Shirō, ed.
1984[1935] Fujinkai sanjūgonen. Tokyo: Fuji Shuppansha.

Fukutomi Mamoru
1985 "Rashisa" no shinrigaku. Kōdansha gendai shinsho 797. Tokyo: Kōdansha.

Gunji Masakatsu
1988 Kabuki to nō no henshin, henge. Shizen to Bunka 19:4–9.

Hanafusa Shirō
1930 Petchi, ruiza, sono hoka. Hanzai Kagaku, December:75–79.

Hara Kie
1987 Fujin Kōron. *In* Fujin zasshi kara mita 1930 nendai. Watashitachi no rekishi o tsuzuru kai, ed. pp. 16–46. Tokyo: Dōjidaisha.

Hattori Yukio
1975 Hengeron: Kabuki no seishinshi. Tokyo: Heibonsha.

Heilbrun, Carolyn
1982[1964] Toward a Recognition of Androgyny. New York: Norton.

Hirai Fusato
1933 Takarazuka monogatari. Tokyo: Shōjo Gahō.

Hoshi Sumire
1987 Ano onna (hito) e no rabu reta. Bessatsu Takarjima 64:54–55.

Hyde, Janet, and B. G. Rosenberg
1980[1976] Half the Human Experience: The Psychology of Women. Lexington, MA: D. C. Heath.

Hyūga Akiko
1971 Sei no henshin ganbō. Dentō to Gendai 2(6):26–37.

Ichikawa Hiroshi
1985 "Mi" no kozo: Shintairon o koete. Tokyo: Aonisha.

Ifukube Takateru
1932 Dōseiai e no ikkōsatsu. Hanzai Kagaku, January:290–293.

Ikeda Riyoko
1983 Beusaiyu no bara (The Rose of Versailles). Tokyo: San'yūsha.

Imao Tetsuya
1982   Henshin no shisō. Tokyo: Hōsei Daigaku.

Izawa Mitsuki
1931   Dōseiaikō. Hanzai Kagaku, September:224–228.

Kabeshima Tadao, Hida Yoshifumi, and Yonekawa Akihiko
1984   Meiji Taishō shingo jiten. Tokyo: Tōkyodo.

Kageki
1962   Jidai ni kakaru hashi: San'nin musume no merodorama hōdan. Kageki
       444:38–44.

Kamisaka Fuyuko
1984   Dansōno reijin: Kawashima Yoshiko den. Tokyo: Bungei Shunjū.

Kawahara Yomogi
1921   Takarazuka kageki shōjo no seikatsu. Osaka: Ikubunkan.

Kessler, Suzanne, and Wendy McKenna
1985[1978]   Gender: An Ethnomethodological Approach. Chicago: University of
       Chicago Press.

Kishi Sumie, ed.
1954   [Cover photograph.] Takarazuka Fuan 93.

Kobayashi Ichizō
1935   "Dansō no reijin" to wa? Kageki 169:10–12.
1960   Takarazuka manpitsu. Tokyo: Jitsugyō no Nihonsha.

Kōjien
1978a   S.v. *rashii. In* Kōjien. Tokyo: Iwanami Shoten.
1978b   S.v. *sei. In* Kōjien. Tokyo: Iwanami Shoten.

Komashaku Kimi, ed.
1989   Onna o yosou. Tokyo: Keiso Shobo.

Komine Shigeyuki and Minami Takao
1985   Dōseiai to dōsei shinjū no kenkyū. Tokyo: Komine Kenkyūjo.

Koyama Shizuko
1982   Kindaiteki joseikan to shite no ryōsaikenbo shisō. Joseigaku Nenpō 3:1–8.
1986   Ryōsaikenboshugi no reime. Joseigaku Nenpō 7:11–20.

Kuhn, Annette
1985   The Power of the Image: Essays on Representation and Sexuality. London:
       Routledge and Kegan Paul.

Kure Shōzō
1920   Dōsei no ai. Fujin Gahō, October:24–27.

Maeda Isamu
1973   Edogo daijiten. Tokyo: Kōdansha.

Maruki Sado
1929   Modan kigo. Kaizō, June:29–32.

Maruo Chōken
1950   Takarazuka sutā monogatari. Tokyo: Jitsugyō no Nihonsha.

Millot, Catherine
1990[1983]   Horsexe: Essay on Transsexuality. K. Hylton, trans. New York: Autonomedia.

Misato Kei
1974   Sutā no tankyū. Takarazuka Gurafu 326:68–69.

Mitsuda Kyōko
1985   Kindaiteki boseikan no juyō to henkei. *In* Bosei o tou. Wakita H., ed. pp. 100–129. Tokyo: Jinbun Shoin.

Miyasako Chizuru
1986   Nakahara Atsukazu no hikari to kage. Shōjoza 2:58–61.

Mosse, George
1985   Nationalism and Sexuality: Middle-Class Morality and Sexual Norms in Modern Europe. Madison: University of Wisconsin Press.

Murakami Nobuhiko
1983   Taishōki no shokugyōfujin. Tokyo: Dōmesu Shuppan.

Mure Isao
1985   '85nen kōenhyō: Tendā Guriin, Andorojenii. Takarazuka Gurafu 462:38–39.

Nakano Eitarō
1935   Dansō no reijin to Saijō Eriko. Fujin Kōron, March:161–167.

Nolte, Sharon, and Sally Hastings
1991   The Meiji State's Policy Towards Women, 1890–1910. *In* Recreating Japanese Women, 1600–1945. G. Bernstein, ed. pp. 151–174. Berkeley: University of California Press.

Okazaki Fumi
1971   Miwaku no sutā, Kō Nishiki. Takarazuka Gurafu 287:48–51.

Ōsumi Tanezo
1931   Hentai seiyoku. Hanzai Kagaku, April:75–83.

Pacteau, Francette
1986   The Impossible Referent: Representations of the Androgyne. *In* Formations of Fantasy. V. Burgin, J. Donald, and C. Kaplan, eds. pp. 62–84. New York: Methuen.

Pflugfelder, Gregory
1989   "Smashing" in Cross-Cultural Perspective: Japan and the United States. MS, files of the author.

Rich, Adrienne
1976   Of Woman Born: Motherhood as Experience and Institution. New York: Norton.

Robertson, Jennifer
1989   Gender-Bending in Paradise: Doing "Male" and "Female" in Japan. Genders 5:50–69.
1991a   The Shingaku Woman: Straight from the Heart. *In* Recreating Japanese Women, 1600–1945. G. Bernstein, ed. pp. 88–107. Berkeley: University of California Press.
1991b   Theatrical Resistance, Theatres of Restraint: The Takarazuka Revue and the "State Theatre" Movement. Anthropological Quarterly 64(4):165–177.

Saijō Eriko
1935   Dansō no reijin, Masuda Fumiko no shi o erabu made. Fujin Kōron, March:168–178.

Sakabe Kengi
1934   Fujin no shinri to futoku no kisō. Tokyo: Hokubunkan.

Sawada Bushō
1921   Onna ga shujutsu o ukete otoko ni natta hanashi. Fujin Kōron, August:59–70.

Schalow, Paul
1990   Introduction. *In* The Great Mirror of Male Love. Ihara Saikaku. P. Schalow, trans. pp. 1–46. Stanford, CA: Stanford University Press.

Shida Aiko and Yuda Yoriko
1987   Shufu no Tomo. *In* Fujin zasshi kara mita 1930 nendai. Watashitachi no rekishi o tsuzuru kai, ed. pp. 48–121. Tokyo: Dōjidaisha.

Sievers, Sharon
1983   Flowers in Salt: The Beginnings of Feminist Consciousness in Modern Japan. Stanford, CA: Stanford University Press.

Silverberg, Miriam
1991   The Modern Girl as Militant. *In* Recreating Japanese Women, 1600–1945. G. Bernstein, ed. pp. 239–266. Berkeley: University of California Press.

Stimpson, Catharine
1989[1974]   The Androgyne and the Homosexual. *In* Where the Meanings Are: Feminism and Cultural Spaces. pp. 54–61. New York: Routledge.

Sugita Naoki
1929   Seihonnō ni hisomu sangyakusei. Kaizō, April:70–80.
1935   Shōjo kageki netsu no shinden. Fujin Kōron, April:274–278.

Tachibana Kaoru
1890   Fūzoku hōtan. Fūzoku Gahō 14:15–16.

Takada Gi'ichirō
1926[1917]   Hōigaku. Tokyo: Kasseido.

Takada Tamotsu
1934   Rebyū jidai kōsatsuki. Shinchō, March:57–64.

Takarazuka Guraf
1977   Sensei to kataru. Takarazuka Gurafu 362:36–38.
1986   People: Oura Mizuki. Takarazuka Gurafu 470:48–49.

Takarazuka Kagekidan
1990   Berusaiyu no bara. Takarazuka, Japan: Takarazuka Kagekidan.

Tamura Toshiko
1913   Dōsei no koi. Chūō Kōron, January:165–168.

Tanabe Seiko and Sasaki Keiko
1983   Yume no kashi o tabete: Waga itoshi no Takarazuka. Tokyo: Kōdansha.

Tani Kazue
1935   "Dansō no reijin" no jogakusei jidai o kataru. Hanashi, April:250–256.

Tomioka Naomichi
1938   Dansei josō to josei dansō. Kaizō, October:98–105.

Tsuji Misako
1976   Niji no fuantajia. Tokyo: Shinromansha.

Ueda Yoshitsugu
1974   Takarazuka ongaku gakkō. Tokyo: Yomiuri Raifu.

Ushijima Yoshitomo
1943   Joshi no shinri. Tokyo: Ganshodo.

Usumi Saijin
1935   Joryū sakka seikatsu ura omote. Hanashi, April:42–43.

Vance, Carole, ed.
1985   Pleasure and Danger: Exploring Female Sexuality. Boston: Routledge and
        Kegan Paul.

Vicinus, Martha
1989 Distance and Desire: English Boarding School Friendships, 1870–1920. *In*
Hidden from History: Reclaiming the Gay and Lesbian Past. M. Duberman,
M. Vicinus, and G. Chauncey, eds. pp. 212–229. New York: New American Library.

Watanabe, Tetsuo, and Jun'ichi Iwata
1989[1987] The Love of the Samurai: A Thousand Years of Japanese Homosexuality. D. R. Roberts, trans. London: GMP.

Watashitachi no rekishi o tsuzuru kai, ed.
1987 Fujin zasshi kara mita 1930 nendai. Tokyo: Dōjidaisha.

Watson, Sophie, ed.
1990 Playing the State: Australian Feminist Interventions. New York: Verso.

Yabushita Tetsuji
1990 Yume o ikiru hitobito. Shingeki 442:106–113.

Yagi Kimiko
1989 Onna no fukusō. *In* Onna o yosou. Komashaku K., ed. pp. 80–115. Tokyo:
Keiso Shobo.

Yamada Kōshi
1968 Rittaiteki ni miryoku o saguru. Takarazuka Gurafu 252:70–72.

Yasuda Tokutarō
1935 Dōseiai no rekishikan. Chūō Kōron, March:146–152.

Yasui Shūhei
1953 Otoko ga onna ni, onna ga otoko ni dōshite nareta ka. Fujin Asahi,
March:84–85.

Yoshida Genjirō
1935 Musume no ren'ai, dōseiai to haha. Fujin Kōron, March:156–160.

Yoshiwara Ryūko
1935 Gekkei shōchōki ni aru musume o motsu okasama e. Fujin Kōron,
March:184–187.

Yoshizawa Jin
1966 Kō Nishiki no kako, genzai, mirai. Takarazuka Gurafu 229:51–53.
1967 Gō Chigusa no kako, genzai, mirai. Takarazuka Gurafu 236:69–71.

Yuri Sachi
1985 Jendā. Asahi Shinbun (Tokyo evening ed.), 2 July.

Newspapers

Asahi Shinbun. 13 January 1968, 21 December 1977, 3 December 1984, 29 March 1990.

English Mainichi. 22 February 1941.

Japan Times. 10 April 1990.

Ōsaka Chōhō. 7 September 1940.

Ōsaka Jiji. 12 December 1934.

Ōsaka Mainichi. 29 May 1923, 10 February 1932, 15 January 1935, 31 January 1935.

Ōsaka Nichinichi. 21 July 1930, 20 August 1939.

Ōsakato. 15 July 1925, 17–20 July 1925, 22 July 1925.

Shin Nippō. 17 June 1936, 2 April 1940.

Yomiuri Shinbun. 23 May 1935.

9 Notes Toward a Feminist Peace Politics

SARA RUDDICK

In this paper, I outline one version of a feminist peace politics. The peace politics I imagine is not preoccupied with the question, When, if ever, is it right to kill? Nor is it committed to the absolute renunciation of violence often associated with pacifism. Rather, this politics expresses a sturdy suspicion of organized violence even in the best of causes. Accordingly, it seeks to expose the multiple costs of violence and to disrupt the plans of those who organize it. This politics also ferrets out hidden or less organized violence wherever it appears—in boardroom or bedroom, government council or factory. Finally, this politics is committed to inventing myriad forms of nonviolent disruption, cooperation, respect, restraint, and resistance that would replace violence and would constitute "peace." Speaking generally, a feminist peace politics contributes in distinctively feminist ways to the threefold aim of fomenting sturdy suspicion of organized violence, disclosing hidden violences, and inventing the strategies and ideals of nonviolence.

Both within the United States and throughout the world there are many feminisms, some explicitly militarist, some suspicious of any "larger" cause that might dilute feminist energies. In these remarks I develop one variant of antimilitarist feminism in which feminist and antimilitarist commitments are interwoven from the start.[1] Someone—a woman or man—becomes, simultaneously, feminist and antimilitarist at least partly because she or he sees war making as an extension of "masculine" domination and "masculine" domination as a reflection of and preparation for war. In a letter she wrote during the First World War, Virginia Woolf expressed colloquially one version of this feminist/antimilitarist weave.

I become steadily more feminist, owing to the Times, which I read at break-
fast and wonder how this preposterous masculine fiction [the war] keeps
going a day longer—without some vigorous woman pulling us together and
marching through it.[2]

In order to outline three aspects of an emerging feminist peace politics,
I will take far more seriously than she could have intended the rhetoric of
Virginia Woolf's letter: War is masculine, war is a fiction, and a vigorous
woman—or womanliness—might march us through it.

War's Masculinity

Nearly everyone agrees that war is in some sense "masculine." Throughout history and across the globe, whatever the "race" or history of particular cultures, men have greatly predominated among the generals, chiefs
of staff, and heads of cadre, tribe, nation, or state who direct wars. In
technologically developed states, men predominate among the business
entrepreneurs who fund wars and among the defense intellectuals and
philosophers who justify them. Still today, men predominate among the
soldiers who execute war strategies. But there is no ready conclusion to
draw from war's masculinity. Many militarists celebrate and many civilians accept the conjunction of war and manliness as a "natural" or necessary component of war. By contrast, many feminists who clearly perceive
and heartily resent war's masculinity challenge military practices in the
hope of securing for women a citizen's right to fight and to command
fighters.

Antimilitarist feminists address war's masculinity in a double voice.
They aim to *challenge* the connection between war and masculinity
which, along with the belief that masculinity is biologically determined,
renders men "naturally" warlike and war a "natural" male and, therefore, legitimate human activity. Therefore, speaking in one register, they
recognize many "masculinities," all of which, whatever their connection
to biology, are socially constructed and subject to change. Yet despite
their skeptical and pluralistic stance toward gender categories, antimilitarist feminists also underscore the masculinity of war. Their aim is to
make a familiar masculinity freshly evident and also evidently objectionable in ways that demean both war and one norm of warlike masculinity.

To this end, antimilitarist feminists attend relentlessly to a "male"-
defining, women-excluding misogyny and homophobia[3] that threads
through military speech and practice. The "monstrous male, loud of
voice, hard of fist," who goes off to war singing of the "Persian pukes" he
is ready to "nape," the faggot assholes he is ready to sodomize, the dead
and diseased whore he is ready to rape, expresses even as he caricatures

this common military attitude.[4] This conception of masculinity is expressed in a lower register in boot camp training rituals, soldiers' chants and songs, graffiti on bombs and guns, tough talk by generals, metaphors of strategists, and the gestures, bonding, and "boyish" boasts of soldiers returning from battles and bombing raids. Criminally, this "masculinity" is expressed in actual acts of rape, sexual assault, and torture.

Certain feminists go beyond merely reporting on soldiers' attitudes and offer a psychoanalytic account of the acquisition of a "normal" masculinity which is expressed under pressure in defensive, aggressive misogyny. According to these psychoanalytic feminists, in social groups where men hold the principal governing posts and are responsible for hunting, war, or other "legitimate" forms of aggression, and where women are responsible for child tending, masculinity is highly valued, potentially aggressive, and fragile.[5] Men must ward off their envy of female birth giving and their longing to be cared for by mothering women, and at the same time affirm their male privilege and assuage their misgivings (if any) about male dominance and aggression. To this end they learn, as boys becoming "men," to define themselves as not-female and better than female. Accordingly, they tend to devalue bodilyness and emotionality, both of which are evoked by physical vulnerability and associated with the bodies and emotions of females, whose care they need, fear, and long for.

If this story is to be believed, men's culturally prized masculinity may never be so vaunted, fragile, and incipiently misogynist as in war. Women are metaphorically and psychologically "behind the lines," resented for their safety, scorned for their ignorance of the "real" and really masculine experience.[6] Yet images of women—one's own at home, the enemy's at hand—are ever present, representing, as they often do in civilian life, vulnerability and emotionality. In extraordinary circumstances, soldiers must control ordinary emotions of fear, rage, and desire. Understandably, many rage against absent women and the emotionality they represent. They may also blame women for their own longings for women that allegedly divert them from soldierly duty, thereby endangering them and their comrades.[7] In this strained emotional ambience of danger and separation, commanders often encourage "masculine" aggressive impulses. Given this encouragement and the pressures to which their "normal masculine" defenses are subject, it is not surprising if many soldiers imaginatively elaborate or actually engage in rapes and assaults on women.

Assaultive misogynist masculinity is not even the only model of military masculinity. The just warrior, restrained and self-sacrificing, protective of women and vulnerable people, is also marked as masculine. So too is the conquering hero, dashing and well mounted (previously on horseback, now in tank or plane), who enacts the national interest/glory. The models of swaggering assaultiveness, restrained warrior, and conquering hero combine with other conceptions of masculinity ranging from the eternal boyishness of competitive jousters to the comradely victory lust of team players. Together they create an ideal of soldierly brotherhood that unites men against women, who cannot share the bond of battle, and often, also, against civilian/government/fathers who "slay their sons."[8]

Different militaries, different wars invoke for their soldiers and project onto the enemy models of masculinity that spur fighting. Especially among racially assimilable enemies, both sides have heroes, while a too easy surrender is contemptible and feminine, and spoils a good fight. Typically, masculinities are also divided between the enemy and "our troops." "We" are the just warrior-protectors. By contrast, a particularly malignant form of swaggering masculinity—a criminal, sexualized aggression—is attributed to the enemy. When enemy males are racialized as predators from whom innocent countries or women-and-children need protection, they become killable killers ready to be burned and buried in their trenches.

In highlighting swaggering, assaultive masculinity, feminists do not simplify the motives of individual soldiers. In war, as in civilian life, the ideal of assaultive masculinity is oppressive to many men who struggle with and against a gender identity that would immerse them by "nature" in violence. It does seem that in the best of causes, there are men who love war and take excited, sometimes explicitly sexual pleasure in assaulting bodies. Yet many of the soldiers who are excited by, and act upon, the sexual and aggressive lusts of battle are also often ashamed of their emotions and deeds later in the day, or in later years. Whatever the cause, war stories reveal men on all sides of battle lines who are running, surrendering, or hiding. There are also courageous but constrained and reluctant fighters as well as men with equal courage who refuse to kill. And in the worst of causes, there are soldiers who believe that they are fighting justly and protecting others.[9] By highlighting—and deploring—soldiers' arrogant, homophobic, assaultive misogyny, antimilitarist feminists have at least three aims. First, they want to make one variant of masculinity evident and repellent whenever it appears, whether in political, domestic, or military battle. Second, they want to block the split between our masculinity and theirs, revealing instead *war's* ugliness. And, finally, by stressing the social construction of assaultive masculinity while also revealing its repellent character, they want to make it easier for men to reject this particular gender norm.

In highlighting assaultive, misogynist masculinity, antimilitarist feminists also address themselves to women. In most cultures, war's masculinity is constructed in tandem with a distinctly military femininity. As Virginia Woolf lamented in the midst of the Second World War, "No, I don't see what's [to] be done about war. Its manliness; and manliness breeds womanliness—both so hateful."[10] "Womanly" militarists acknowledge the exclusionary male bonding of battle. They take up *distinctive* war work that is either feminine, such as nursing the wounded, or is seen as only a temporary substitute for the work that men will return to when they come home from war. Less prosaically, they express, within the confines of loyalty, the losses and sexual dangers of war. Bereaved women weep for war's victims; endangered women cry out for protection from the enemy's rapacious, cruel marauders.

The loyal military female, in contrast to misogynist soldier, is androphiliac. In the midst of battle excitement, she eroticizes "our" heroes, memorializes "our" just warriors, and matronizingly cheers "our" boyish adventurers. Masking or denying the sexual assaultiveness of "our troops," she ascribes to enemy men "the naked, hideous male gratification" of assaultive masculinity.[11] After battle, she can repair military enmity by mourning *all* casualties and, if the war has not been too bitter or self-righteous, she can honor all heroic fighters.

In highlighting assaultive masculinity, antimilitarist feminists aim to destabilize military femininity. Their hope is that a woman who sees *wars* as eliciting assaultive masculinity will be disarmed of the racist and military split between "their" marauding males and "our troops." Then her military hero may look like an abuser, not an unfamiliar figure in civilian life; conversely, the civilian abuser will be deprived of any militarist glamour. While the military woman's generalized, romantic androphilia is disrupted, she will still love particular men; only now war's mores of abusiveness threaten to transform the beloved lover/mate/brother/son/father into "a boisterous male . . . hard of fist."[12] Fearing the effect of war's manliness on men she loves as well as the effect in her own life of abusive, war-made men, the loyal lady of sorrows may well begin to weep disloyally, to politicize her fears.

The misogynist domination that pervades military life and lore fosters brutality and domination both on and off official battlefields. While an ethos of assaultive masculinity legitimates abusive war and warlike abuse, a myth of manly protection, sustained by military androphilia, prevents men and women from seeing what they already know: wars almost always leave everyone in their vicinity radically *un*protected. By looking through myths of manliness, women and men should be better able to see the cruel realities of war engraved on bodies of all ages and both sexes.

Preposterous Fiction

Many women and men would continue to support war for moral reasons even if they deplored its psychosexual character. "Warism," "the belief that war is morally justified in principle and often justified in fact,"[13] is a dominant and a majority ideology in most past and present societies and states. To arouse sturdy suspicion of war, it is necessary to undermine the kinds of *thinking* that legitimate war making as an institution and, within that institution, sanction particular wars.

In many wars, and notably in the recent Persian Gulf War, warism is influentially and attractively expressed in just-war theory. Just-war theorists are cognizant of war's horrors and begin by condemning war in general, though allowing it in principle. Their task, then, is to judge particular causes and particular ways of fighting according to standards of "justice." Briefly, one can go to war only as a last resort, only if the fight is justly conducted, and only if the cause is just: one's own or another state is attacked; innocent people are being slaughtered; or, more controversially, the balance of peacekeeping power is threatened.

In judging wars, just-war theorists take seriously several realities. Men are transformed by uniform and recruitment procedures into "soldiers," who are legitimate killers and targets of killers. Boundaries, often initially established by military conquest or imperial negotiation, become the real, legitimate markers of states. Wars are spatially and temporally bounded events. They are fought on or above "battlefields,"[14] begin with the detonation of weapons or the "exchange of fire," and end with victory or surrender. These and other realities—for example, innocent civilians, military targets, clean, smart weapons selectively aimed—are the primitive terms, the basic referents, for the abstract language through which wars are judged to be just or unjust.

In late-twentieth-century high-technology wars, it becomes increasingly difficult for anyone to believe in the bounded realities to which just-war theorists refer.[15] By way of contributing to an increasing skepticism of the realities just-war theory assumes, antimilitarists can bring into play recent feminist critiques of prevailing ideals of rationality. According to these feminist critiques, prevailing ideals of reason reflect compulsive tendencies to defend, dissociate, and abstract.[16] To the extent that "men of reason" are governed by these dominant Western ideals, they thrive on boundaries and definition, eschew ambiguity, suspect particular attachments, and separate thought from feeling, mind from body. On the other hand, men of reason seem almost compulsively attached to detachment. To adapt a phrase from Klaus Theweleit, they thrive on a fantasy of transcendence based on a "tradition of freeing the thinking brain from the depths of the most pressing situations and sending it off to some (fictive) summit for a panoramic overview."[17] Yet the discourses of reason barely conceal the emotions that permeate them—anxiety, defensiveness, addictive sexual assertion or fear of sexuality, distaste for and envy of female sexual and birth-giving bodies, and competitive aggression.

These ideals, I suggest, are exemplified in just-war languages and the "realities" to which they refer. In Western philosophy, ideals of reason have sometimes been created in explicit connection with the ideals of war. As Plato put the point boldly, an education in reason "must not be useless to warlike men [or women]"; rulers must prove themselves "best in philosophy and with respect to war."[18] Whatever the historical connections between reason and war, contemporary war theorists, like other men of reason, resort to abstraction, binary oppositions, and sharply bounded concepts. Most notably, "defense intellectuals," who "create the theory that informs and legitimates American nuclear [and high-technology] strategic practices" conceal, even from themselves, the bodily mutilation their policies require.[19] Also, like their philosophical counterparts, these defense intellectuals reveal the anxieties, aggression, and even the sexual and procreative envies and desires, that are familiar from soldiers' stories.

Superficially, the languages of justice and strategy seem quite unlike. Just-war theorists do not deny war's sufferings; if war weren't so damaging, one would not require a *moral* theory first to justify and then to control the damage. Unlike technostrategists who explicitly eschew moral questions, just-war theorists insist upon the interdependence of ethics and politics, thereby providing the moral (soft and feminine) counterpart to realistic (hard and masculine) instrumentality.

Yet despite these differences, the justificatory languages of morality and strategy are intertwined. The success of just warriors is dependent on the strategies that defense intellectuals legitimate. Just conduct of a war (*jus in bello*) depends upon the "smartness" and "cleanliness" of weapons, who acquire these virtues within the strategic discourse that brackets pain and suffering as "collateral damage." To be sure, there is a frightening disconnection between morality and strategy: might does not make right, but it does make victories. The capacity to defeat and demoralize depends far more upon economic and technological than on moral resources. But the high moral tone and abstract moral puzzles of just-war theory tend to divert attention from this fundamental, often heartbreaking indifference of war to virtue.

Taken on its own terms, just-war theory is far more like its technostrategic counterpart than its moral concern would suggest. Like their strategist counterparts, just-war theorists resort to abstraction, dichotomy, and bounded definition. Like their counterparts, just-war theorists employ abstraction to take a distance from unreasoned emotionality. Partly because the language of just-war theory is less evidently sexual/aggressive itself, it is even more able than strategic discourse to occlude the sexual aggressivity of war. The moral emotions just-war theorists do invoke—righteousness, indignation, and (perhaps) shame and guilt[20]—conceal as well as license the cruelty and delight in destruction that war provides. Most seriously, like its technostrategic counterpart, the language of morality too easily obscures the realities of terrorizing and injuring, the defining activities of war. To repeat: Just-war theory does *not* deny, and indeed insists on, the pain of victims. But as one learns to speak within the theory, to unravel the puzzles the theory sets for itself, to assess "causes" and strategies by criteria the theory establishes, it becomes increasingly difficult to give *weight* to the varieties of loss and pain suffered by individual victims and conquerors, their communities, and their lands.[21]

Confronted with the apparent irrationality, the "craziness," of war, many people are compelled to be, to feel, and to appear "reasonable"— deliberative, coherent, and controlled. Although, and partly because, they obscure war's messy realities, both technostrategic and just-war discourse provide the illusion of rationality. In order to combat just-war thinking, it is necessary to offer alternative modes of reasoning that can provide the comforts of reason but that do not obscure emotion and pain. To this end, I would invoke ideals of reason that are central to the "different voices" of a feminist "ethics of care."[22] Very briefly, these alternative modes of reasoning arise out of attention to concrete particulars, develop insights within ongoing, changing relationships, test these insights in the context of collective and often passionate and conflictual enterprises, and convey them in open-ended narration.[23]

It seems likely that women or men who reason predominantly in these alternative modes will be less apt to accept the realities of just-war theory. Although as aware as any just-war theorist of the blessings of nonviolent stability, they might not take so seriously extant boundaries established by diplomacy and war. They might be less apt to appreciate the moral significance of burning soldiers up as opposed to burying them in their trenches or of bombing a water supply rather than a market. Indeed, because they are generally skeptical of moral discourse governed by abstract distinctions and procedural rules, they might reject the fundamental premise of just-war theory: young men (and women) can be transformed by policy, weapon, and uniform into legitimate killers and targets.

As I have learned from the frustrations of teaching just-war theory, people who reason in these "different voices" can appear disturbingly uninterested in just causes and rules of war that are meant to constrain battle and whose violation is often an anguished focus of war memoirs. It is not that these skeptics are unable to distinguish between the pain and destructiveness of rifle shot and napalm, smart bomb and random missile. Nor do they confuse killing armed, fighting soldiers with bombing those same soldiers in retreat or dealing with them cruelly when they have surrendered. They appreciate the particularity of horrors—rape or torture of individuals, undiscriminating slaughter of people, burning of whole villages or cities. But they see all the horror—the lesser and greater—as predictable ingredients of high-technology wars. Hence they refuse to believe in the categories and conventions through which just wars are presented, refuse to be drawn into a fiction of good-enough combat that is used to sanitize and legitimate violence.

Those who reason in a concrete, contextual, narrative mode would also be slow to accept the fundamental fiction that war is a discrete phenomenon that is arranged by diplomats and takes place on battlefields. There is, of course, a sense in which wars are temporally bounded events whose beginnings and endings have clear consequences. Few see so differently that they deny the terror of a bombing raid or the relief of "peace." But wars rarely have the neat endings their planners envision. Moreover, the rewards even of neat victory are often compromised or reversed in decades, if not in months. In women's "postwar" stories, there is a thematic, recurrent underlining of the unboundedness of war.[24] Physical disabilities, psychic injuries, social disruptions, and socioecological destructions of battle last long after surrender.

Nor does war begin only on the day of invasion. As the (then) East German writer Christa Wolf enjoined: "You can tell when a war starts, but when does the pre-war start? If there are rules about that we should hand them on. Hand them down inscribed in clay, in stone. Do not let your own people deceive you."[25] Discrete episodes of legitimate violence are predictable consequences of daily warlike ways of living. Speaking in a voice she explicitly attributes to her experience as a woman, Virginia Woolf envisioned a system of violences in which "the public and private worlds are inseparably connected; the tyrannies and servilities of the one are the tyrannies and servilities of the other."[26] Looking at the patriarchal (her word) family, and particularly at education and professional life in England, Woolf saw an ethos of male dominion and military domination in the making. People are taught "not to hate force but to use it" in order to keep their possessions, defend their grandeur and power, through varieties of economic, racial, and sexual violences.[27]

A contemporary feminist, Cynthia Enloe, has looked with equal suspicion at the connection, particularly as wrought by the United States, of militarism, international corporate capitalism, racism, sexism, and assaults against the poor. In *Bananas, Beaches and Bases,* Enloe reveals an economic and military war *system* that allows the United States to initiate, fund, fight, or avoid discrete "wars." In this system a military ethos, sustained by military spending, prepares for and exploits racial and masculine domination despite, and partly because of, the fact that armed service appears to provide minority and female citizens, especially those who are poor, material advantages and symbolic status otherwise unavailable to them. To further the system, war planners manipulate allegedly private and sharply genderized relationships, playing upon class interests, racial fears, and sexual norms in order to recruit women's bodies, services, and labor for military affairs.[28]

In rejecting the realities of just-war theory, feminist antimilitarists do not deny the existence of conquest, massacre, tyranny, enslavement, exploitation, and economic injustice. The issue is *how*, not whether, to resist these evils. A feminist peace politics, like peace politics generally, searches for alternatives to exploding, cutting, bombing, and starving. The abstract, bounded, justificatory concepts of just-war theory short circuit this search by allowing the morally troubled to accept good-enough wars in place of the many kinds of cooperation, compromise, and resistance required for peace.

A "Vigorous Womanliness": Toward a Politics of Care

The most thorough unraveling of the concepts and fantasies that legitimate violence will only lead to despair without viable conceptions of peace making, or new ways of cooperating and fighting. Conversely, if people cannot imagine peace, they will be unable to see war wholly or to reject it steadily, especially when war's cause is dear to them.

As there is no sharp division between the violences of domestic, civic, and military life, there is also no sharp division between the practices and thinking of private and public peace. Even in the midst of war, people cooperate, and care for each other. In their ordinary lives, most women and men, including many who are frequently violent, sometimes express anger and resolve conflict without injuring. One of the tasks of peace making is to transform this ordinary peacefulness that surrounds us into a public commitment to, and capacity for, making peace.

As war is associated with men, peace is associated with women and the "womanly." These dual associations are expressed most succinctly in the clichéd opposition of mother and soldier, and, more generally and prosaically, of caregiving and war. Although most mothers and the majority of caregivers may be women, neither mothering nor caregiving generally are intrinsically female or feminine. Some men fully engage in mothering and most are, at some time in their lives, active caregivers. Many women are uninterested in mothering and reject the caregiving that is expected of them. Yet, historically, the obligations of care thread through women's lives, creating, in specific social conditions, distinctively feminine patterns, as well as burdens, of knowledge and of love. It is understandable, then, that some feminists, already partisans of women, would look to "womanly" practices of caregiving for intimations of ordinary peacefulness.

Caregiving *appears* to depend upon peace and to be peacelike. War, like other less attractive violences, always disrupts and often ruins the caring labors of feeding, clothing, sheltering, nursing, tending children and the elderly, maintaining kind and neighborhood ties. The contradiction between caregiving and organized violence may be most poignantly expressed in the laments of mothers who are unable to protect their children amid war, who may even kill their children rather than let them continue to suffer violence.[29] Yet despite the opposition between war making and caregiving, most caregivers have complied with, and often enough have devoted their energies to, war. To set militarism and care at political odds, to give their opposition emotional and political weight, it will be necessary to contrast in detail caregiving and military enterprises.

In the spirit of detailed comparison, I have contrasted maternal with military battle. Mothers fight with children and on their behalf. They "make peace" between children in their household, neighborhood, and extended family. Often, they also fight in the same household, family, or neighborhood in which they make peace. The mothers I have known are often overcome with a sense of failure—with memories of their abuse or neglect of their children or of their collusion with those who hurt them. Nonetheless, I have come to believe that there are enough maternal practices that are sufficiently governed by nonviolent principles to provide one model of nonviolent action. These maternal principles of reconciliation, resistance, and refusal to injure are analogous to, although also different from, principles developed by Gandhi and King.[30]

In a similar spirit, I would like to contrast military and caregiving concepts of control. Like militarists, caregivers often set out to control the wills of others—to get children to stop fighting, turn out their lights, go to school; to get patients to cooperate with painful testing; to get an elderly person to eat. Like militarists, caregivers control within a particular conjunction of power and powerlessness.

Typically, militarists strive for a position of superior strength from which they can dominate people and resources by threatened or actual assault. Only an enemy's efforts to achieve "equal strength" lead militarists to settle for a "balance" of power or terror. By contrast, caregivers are already powerful; they attempt to control people who are, by dint of the caregiving relationship, vulnerable to threats of damage or neglect. For many years, mothers can injure, terrify, or humiliate their children. In other caring relations such as nursing, aiding the disabled, or tending the frail elderly, caregivers often seem able to neglect at will, or to subtly threaten or hurt the bodies and psyches of people dependent upon them. Unlike militarists, caregivers are unable to rely upon balances of power or equal strength to control their own or others' aggression. Unequal strength is a structural feature of caring labor. Vulnerability, as we like to remember, often elicits protection. But vulnerability also allows for, and sometimes excites, domination, abuse, or neglect. Powerful caregivers may be more than usually tempted by sadism, self-indulgent aggression, self-interested exploitation, and self-protective indifference to the real needs of people whose demands seem overwhelming.

Both militarists and caregivers often feel and are powerless. Militarists who feel powerless attempt to arm themselves. Initially their efforts may be defensive, but strategies, weapons, social policies and group motivation conspire to turn defense into offensive threat and action. Militarists then can display the power that caregivers take for granted. Despite undeniable power, caregivers also often feel powerless in the face of the willful, resentful impatience of those they care for. But powerless caregivers cannot arm themselves; they are already armed. The simplest implements at hand—a toy block, a kitchen knife—can be put to deadly use; bribes and punishments can be backed up by threatened or real physical force. Armed yet powerless caregivers can, and sometimes do, resort to violence. But violent display of power only increases powerlessness. A beaten child beats her brother, a patient whose arm is twisted behind her back still spits her medicine in her nurse's face. Some strong and armed caregivers nonetheless become entrapped in patterns of escalating violence that excite and relieve even as they fail in their purpose. But often enough, and ideally, caregivers, despite their strength and the "arms" at their disposal, see through the promise of violence and discipline themselves to nonviolent strategies.

The resulting contrast between powerful/powerless nonviolent caregivers' and violent militarists' control reflects fundamentally contrasting attitudes toward embodied willfulness. By "embodied willfulness" I refer to two facts. For humans the capacity to will is rooted and expressed in bodily life; and human bodies are subject to pain, fear, and memory. It follows from these facts that people are able, in general, though certainly not in every case, to dominate the will of others if they can credibly threaten to injure or can actually damage their bodies.

Militarism and militarized diplomacy involve, by definition, a readiness to exploit embodied willfulness, that is, to impose one's will upon others by threatening or actually injuring them. That militarists often injure for the sake of causes that are, or appear to be, just does not alter their *willingness* to injure. Probably most militarists would prefer to threaten rather than injure, bomb empty factories rather than air-raid shelters, destroy launchers rather than water supplies, provoke blood[l]ess surrender rather than burn men up or bury them in the sand. Nonetheless, the willingness to burn, bury, cut, blow apart, and starve bodies is essential to militarist enterprises; forms of coercion that rule out in advance deliberate damage to bodies are not militarist.

By contrast, caregiving involves a *commitment* to refrain from neglecting or assaulting bodies. Someone who claims to be caring but who, over time, willingly abuses the bodies in her charge and is neither remorseful nor ready to change is not engaged in caring labor. Ordinary "good enough" caregivers often fail to fulfill their commitments, and their failure often is no fault of their own but rather of policies and communities that have denied them the resources of care. But to be committed to caregiving work, to be engaged in caregiving labor, means, among other things, to count assault or neglect as "failure." However often a caregiver fails, her refusal to exploit embodied willfulness through injury and threat of injury is a requirement of "success."

This nonviolent stance to bodily life is not simply given to caregivers. A violent stance toward embodied willfulness also arises plausibly from daily work under pressure amid disturbingly willful, uncontrollable, vulnerable bodies. In the most malignant form of caregiving, resentful or cruel mothers exploit their children's bodies as the site and opportunity of sadism, sexual exploitation, and domination. Less dramatically, many ordinary "good enough" caregivers struggle against a compulsion for order and effectiveness that could lead them to dominate their "unruly" subjects through bodily shame, neglect, or threat. Even the most benign caregivers are sometimes likely to take their child's "nature," or their elderly parent's or patient's willful embodied being, as an enemy to be conquered. Caregivers are not, predictably, better people than are militarists. Rather, they are engaged in a different project. Militarists aim to dominate by creating the structural vulnerabilities that caregivers take for granted. They arm and train so that they can, if other means of domination fail, terrify and injure their opponents. By contrast, in situations where domination through bodily pain, and the fear of pain, is a structural possibility, caregivers try to resist temptations to assault and neglect, even though they work among smaller, frailer, vulnerable people who may excite domination.

Positively, caregivers, at their best, foster the embodied willfulness and desires of those they care for. Mothers learn to accept, even treasure, the messy, unpredictable, willful bodies of children. Those who work with failing, faltering, soiling bodies resist their own impatience, fear, and disgust in order to foster, against the odds, a sense of effective willfulness amid bodily disarray. Even the smallest infant, the sickest patients, and the feeblest elderly thrive upon a caregiver's ability to identify and respond to their self-generated, willful acts. Recognizing, as militarists do, that for anyone, at any age, in any stage of health, the capacity to will is enacted in a bodily subject vulnerable to intrusion and pain, caregivers set themselves to respect bodily integrity. They thereby protect the willfulness of a person they are *unwilling* to dominate, a person lively with her or his own desires and projects.

There are many ways of contrasting caring labor with war making. As I mentioned earlier, some people are looking at conflicting norms of rationality in the two enterprises. My remarks about war's masculinity begin to contrast two attitudes toward the manipulation of sexual desire and affectionate attachment. I would like to see studies of the two practices that compared for each of them the place of passion and the meaning of particular emotions such as bitterness and anger or the weight of attitudes such as trust and forgiveness. I would like to explore self-realization and self-loss in the two practices, and the stances of each toward change, or their respective identifications of evil. To reveal the peacefulness of care it will be necessary to compare, in detail, and over a wide range of characteristics, militarist and caregiving enterprises. In the act of comparing, it is crucial to highlight militaristic or, more generally, domineering and oppressive aspects or liabilities of caregiving. It is certain *struggles within* the caregiving enterprise that will illuminate struggles for peace.

Even when all the comparisons are in, it will not be easy, conceptually or politically, to extend the values of domestic battle to public wars. One cannot simply *apply* rationalities and moral orientations that arise in particular relationships between a few people to more public, impersonal domains. Caregiving depends upon caregivers—upon people with real power who are committed to self-restraint. Most evidently, maternal nonviolence depends upon a mother whose power is limited but real and upon children who are subject to that mother's power. State governments and their leaders are not bad mothers—they are not mothers at all. Adult citizens are not "children," nor can adult citizenship be described in terms of the illness or frailty of citizens, though some citizens are of course ill and frail. Most adult citizens may retain fantasies of politicized parental or healing power; leaders may imagine themselves as good parents or as physicians to a sick populace. But social democracy depends upon renouncing, or at least checking, familial or medical fantasies and creating in their stead robust images of responsible participation in states and communities. Social democrats can draw upon *ideals* of mutuality and reciprocity that govern the actions of many caregivers. But social democrats would have to express these borrowed ideals in a language that did not presume anything like maternal will or childlike compliance.

People can learn from the moral orientations of care whether or not they are caregivers. It is more ambitious to imagine caregivers themselves creating a new, antimilitarist political identity. Of the many difficulties attending this creation, two seem preeminent.

Given the pervasiveness of militarism, obedience is the handmaid of war, resistance the prerequisite of peace. Socially, caregivers tend to be powerless; often they expect, and expect themselves, to delegate "political" decisions to others. Even in a just world where caregivers were empowered, caregivers—mothers in particular—are responsible for insuring their charges' respect for authorities, including for the caregivers themselves. Minimal obedience is a requirement of safety and, for children especially, of education and moral development.

Many caretakers do "resist," even within the context of obedience, simply by continuing to care under appalling conditions of tyranny, poverty, and neglect. There are also many examples of mothers and other caregivers—especially physicians and nurses—who resist collectively and *politically*, in the name of care. These women and men bequeath a history of resistance for feminist peacemakers and caregivers to extend and transform. Without denying the proper place of obedience within the work of care, feminist antimilitarists can strive to represent, in speech and act, a political identity that includes within the requirements of care a reflective readiness to disobey.

Caregivers' disobedience is far more likely when authorities threaten their "own" work, their "own" people. Caregivers are notoriously "partial." Mothering especially is rightly seen to be embedded in passionate loyalty to one's own children and the people they live among. Ordinary partiality of good-enough mothers is magnified by warlike circumstances in which violence is legitimated and fueled by racism and one people's children are set against another's.

Despite maternal partiality, there is a literary and historical record of maternal identification with "other" mothers and their children—including those of the enemy. To cite only one example, many mothers (Madres) in Argentina who suffered quite particular and brutal assault against their own children came in the course of protest to identify with anyone who had disappeared in their country, and then with children across the globe who had suffered direct violent or abuses of neglect.[31] This is not transcendent impartiality but a sympathetic apprehension of another grounded in one's own particular suffering.

Such a groundedness may prove sturdier than transcendence. The partiality of caregiving, most often seen as a liability, is also a strength. *People are partial, passionate, local.* What looks like the ability to transcend particular attachment is often defensive, self-deceived, or a luxury of the strong and safe. Political relationships of mutuality and respect will have to be created in the midst of passionate particularity, not outside of it.

But I do not want to deny the real and inevitable tension between caring for one's own and caring for others. Those of us who are trying to translate caregiving commitment into public action begin with different metaphysical orientations. Many of us are able to draw upon and modify religious accounts of each person's inclusion in divine care. Others of us require a secular and agnostic grounding for a translation from one's own to the world's (as to God's) children.

The work of extending care is in its beginnings; it is a work worth doing. Nonviolent caregiving offers one construction of power which refuses domination, respects embodied willfulness, but does not let abuse go unchallenged. The morality of care originates in everyday life amid fantasies and experiences of violence and love. Most men and women are caregivers, to varying degrees, at different times in their lives. Everyone is sometimes subject to practices of care whose mix of violence and nonviolence is enacted on their bodily spirit at its most vulnerable. Anyone who is willing to remember honestly and listen attentively can learn care's lessons. Caregiving is only one of many ordinary practices that offers hints of peace and of the price of its violation. Given the pervasiveness of warism and the multiple costs of war, peacemakers can ill afford a competition among themselves to decide who is the best peacemaker. It is enough to identify a practice whose ubiquity and emotional potency makes it one distinctly valuable resource for peace.

Notes

I have delivered versions of this paper to various feminist and peace studies audiences. I am grateful to the many people who listened and offered correction, insight, and amplification and would like to mention especially Berenice Fisher and E. Ann Kaplan. A different version of this paper was published under the title "A Fierce and Human Peace" in a volume produced by Concerned Philosophers for Peace entitled *Just War, Non-violence and Nuclear Deterrence*, edited by Duane Cady and Richard Werner. I am grateful to Duane Cady for a careful, useful reading of that earlier version. Throughout the preparation of this final version, I have profited from informative, entertaining, and critical conversations with Miriam Cooke about this paper and, more generally, about issues of war and peace.

1. I develop one version (my own) of one variant of feminist peace politics. I draw upon a larger literature in ways its authors might not have intended. For brevity, I speak generally of feminist peace politics—e.g., "feminist antimilitarists hope, believe . . ." I hope to represent fairly widely held tendencies in some versions of feminist peace politics but I am finally imagining a prospectus that I invent.

2. Virginia Woolf, *Collected Letters*, vol. 2. ed. Nigel Nicolson and Joanne Trautman (New York: Harcourt Brace and Jovanovich, 1976), letter 748, p. 76. Woolf remained suspicious of violence even in the best of causes. In her life, these best causes were armed resistance to Franco's forces in the Spanish Civil War and the war against Nazi Germany. Currently, many critics are assessing the origins, strengths, and limitations of Woolf's feminist antimilitarism. For an overview

with references, see Mark Hussey, ed., *Virginia Woolf and War* (Syracuse, N.Y.: Syracuse University Press, 1991).

3. While militarist misogyny seems culturally pervasive, it is not always intertwined with homophobia, as it is in the United States. Plato, for example, imagined an army of gay men.

4. For methodologically and politically distinct accounts of assaultive masculinity, see Klaus Theweleit, *Male Fantasies*, vols. 1 and 2 (Minneapolis: University of Minnesota Press, 1987, 1990); Robin Morgan, *Demon Lover* (New York: Random House, 1988); Christa Wolf, *Cassandra* (New York: Farrar, Straus and Giroux, 1984). In this passage I am drawing especially upon Joan Smith, "Crawling from the Wreckage," in her *Misogynies* (New York: Ballantine Books, 1990), and Virginia Woolf, *Three Guineas* (New York: Harcourt Brace/HBJ, 1966). The literature is vast and, I assume, familiar. I do not mean to be reporting on this literature; rather I am reflecting upon its feminist or antimilitarist purposes.

5. Both Klaus Theweleit and Joan Smith explicitly invoke an object relations variant of psychoanalytic theory. See also Nancy Hartsock, "The Feminist Standpoint," concluding chapter of *Money, Sex and Power* (New York: Longman, 1983). For a more generally Freudian and influential account, see Dorothy Dinnerstein, *The Mermaid and the Minotaur* (New York: Harper and Row, 1976).

6. In addition to the writers cited in note 4, see William Broyles, "Why Men Love War," in Walter Capps, ed., *The Vietnam Reader* (New York: Routledge, 1991); Tania Modelski, "A Father Is Being Beaten: Male Feminism and the War Film," in *Feminism Without Women* (New York: Routledge, 1991); and Susan Jeffords, *The Remasculinization of America* (Bloomington: Indiana University Press, 1988).

7. For an example of "good" war stories by a "good" soldier who nonetheless uses women in this way, see Tim O'Brien, *The Things They Carried* (Boston: Houghton Mifflin, 1990). In O'Brien's stories death is embodied in the death of a nine-year-old girl; thoughts of a sweetheart lead a man (as he sees it) to neglect his men; women won't answer letters or respond to men's wars; a dumb Cooze (middle-aged woman of liberal sentiments) does not understand O'Brien's stories.

8. Wilfred Owen, "The Parable of the Old Man and the Young," *Collected Poems* (London: Chatto and Windus, 1963). On the genderization of war experience, including governments, see especially Jeffords, *Remasculinization of America.*

9. Indeed, if the *New York Times* of May 1, 1991, reporting on the military's aid to Kurdish refugees is to be believed, soldiers would rather comfort than create the victims of war.

10. Virginia Woolf to Shena, Lady Simon, January 1941, in *Collected Letters* 6:464.

11. Wolf, *Cassandra*, p. 74.

12. Woolf, *Three Guineas*, p. 105.

13. I take this definition from Duane Cady, *From Warism to Pacifism* (Philadelphia: Temple University Press, 1989).

14. Any city, village, or "territory" can, of course, be marked as a battlefield.

15. See, for example, Miriam Cooke, "Postmodern Wars: Phallomilitary Spectacles in the DTO," *Journal of Urban and Cultural Studies* 2, no. 1:27–40.

16. Many feminists have contributed to these critiques. In addition to Theweleit see, especially, Evelyn Fox Keller, *Reflections on Gender and Science* (New Haven: Yale University Press, 1985), and Carol Cohn "Sex and Death in the Rational World of Defense Intellectuals," *Signs* 12, no. 4 (Summer 1987): 687–718.

17. Theweleit, *Male Fantasies* 1:364.

18. Plato, *Republic*, 543a, 521d. See also Genevieve Lloyd, "Selfhood, War and Masculinity," in Carole Pateman and Elisabeth Grosz, eds., *Feminist Challenges* (Boston: Northeastern University Press, 1987).

19. Cohn, "Sex and Death," p. 688. Cohn coined the term *technostrategic rationality.*

20. Michael Walzer in *Just and Unjust Wars* (New York: Harper Collins, 1992) is somewhat sardonic about J. Glenn Gray's discussion of guilt in *The Warriors* (New York: Harper and Row, 1970). For the connection between abstract thought and abstract emotions see, Gray, *Warriors,* and Hannah Arendt's foreword to the 1970 edition.

21. Many feminists have argued that dominant ideals of reason, in both their civilian philosophical and military forms, reflect a subjectivity that is both "masculine" and reflective of social privilege. They point out that these ideals have been articulated mostly by economically advantaged men of dominant "races" or ethnicities (though similarly advantaged men have also articulated alternative ideals); that many male philosophers explicitly have stated that ideals of rationality were inaccessible to women of any social group, to men of laboring classes, and to anyone of "inferior" "race" or ethnicity; and that these ideals legitimate and serve male-dominated and culturally dominating institutions such as war, academia, or the law. In diagnosing "masculinity" within a system of privilege, some feminists refer only to texts, while others explain the acquisition of philosophical masculinity by the same social constellation of female caregiving, "legitimate" male aggression, and masculine privilege that allegedly gives rise to military misogyny. This literature and comment upon it is vast. For sample specimens of feminist critique see Keller, *Reflections on Gender and Science;* and Christina Di Stefano, *Configurations of Masculinity* (Ithaca: Cornell University Press, 1991).

22. It has been claimed, notoriously, that this "different" voice is heard more frequently in women than in men, that it pervades African and African-American women's thinking, and that its values arise from a strong identification and engagement with mothering and other forms of caregiving and with community survival and resistance to oppression. (As Margaret Urban Walker pointed out, many people have been so preoccupied with deciding who speaks in a different voice and why that they have barely attended to what the different voice is saying.) I claim here that whoever speaks in the "different voice" will find it difficult to speak just-war theory.

23. I am drawing here, especially, on Margaret Urban Walker, "Alternative Epistemologies for Feminist Ethics," in Eve Browning Cole and Susan Coltrap McQuinn, eds., *Explorations in Feminist Ethics* (Bloomington: Indiana University Press, 1992). Walker gives a perspicuous overview of various feminist writers, including Carol Gilligan and Nel Noddings. Walker's account seems to me sub-

stantiated in Patricia Hill Collins, *Black Feminist Thought: Knowledge, Consciousness and the Politics of Empowerment* (Boston: Unwin Hyman, 1990).

24. Many men's war stories also talk about the postwar fate of the soldier—giving special prominence to his fate, and his transformation as an individual. Ron Kovic's story as told in the movie *Born on the Fourth of July* offers a splendid and moving example. The women's stories I think of first highlight the effect of the soldier's return or loss on his family and community. Rebecca West's post–First World War novel *Return of the Soldier* (reprint, New York: Dial Press, 1982) names and typifies the genre. Two classics that also recall the First World War, Toni Morrison's *Sula* (New York: Knopf, 1973) and Virginia Woolf's *Mrs. Dalloway* (London: Hogarth Press, 1925), inextricably entwine the violences of war and postwar as they are played out in family, community, and—behind the scene—official policies of state.

25. Wolf, *Cassandra*, p. 66.

26. Woolf, *Three Guineas*, p. 18.

27. Ibid., p. 142. "Do they [the facts of history] not prove that education . . . does not teach people to hate force but to use it? Do they not prove that education makes [the educated] . . . so anxious to keep their possessions, that 'grandeur and power' of which the poet speaks, that they will use not force but much subtler methods than force when they are asked to share them? And are not force and possessiveness very closely connected with war?" (p. 29). "The Facts . . . seem to prove that the professions have an undeniable effect upon the professors. They make the people who practice them possessive, jealous of any infringements of their rights, and highly combative if anyone dares dispute them. . . . And do not such qualities lead to war?" (p. 66).

28. Cynthia Enloe, *Bananas, Beaches and Bases* (Berkeley: University of California Press, 1990). In this connection, Duane Cady called to my attention George Bush's celebration, during black history month, of the military as an equal opportunity employer.

29. See, for example, Linda Johnson, "No Words Can Describe: Japanese Women's World War II Narratives" (unpublished manuscript) on Japanese mothers who killed their children rather than let them starve or—in one case—insisted on saving them only to watch them die painfully. In Toni Morrison's *Beloved*, the heroine, Sethe, attempts to kill her children to prevent them from returning to slavery and succeeds in killing one.

30. *Maternal Thinking*, (Boston: Beacon Press, 1989) chap. 7.

31. I wrote about the Madres in *Maternal Thinking*, chap. 8.

10 Making It Perfectly Queer

LISA DUGGAN

During the past few years, the new designation "queer" has emerged from within lesbian, gay and bisexual politics and theory. "Queer Nation" and "Queer Theory," now widely familiar locations for activists and academics, are more than just new labels for old boxes. They carry with them the promise of new meanings, new ways of thinking and acting politically—a promise sometimes realized, sometimes not. In this essay I want to elucidate and advocate this new potential within politics and theory.

Because I am a Southern girl, I want to arrive at my discussion of these new meanings through a process of storytelling. From an account of concrete events—recent events that gripped and provoked me personally—I will construct a certain political history, and from that history raise certain theoretical questions. Because the position "queer" has arisen most proximately from developments in lesbian and gay politics, the trajectory I follow here reflects my own passage through those politics. Were I to follow another trajectory—through feminist or socialist politics, for example—I

This essay was first presented at the University of Illinois at Champaign–Urbana's Unit for Criticism and Interpretive Theory Colloquium in April 1991, then at the 5th Annual Lesbian and Gay Studies Conference at Rutgers University in November 1991. I would like to thank Alan Hance and Lee Furey for their comments in Urbana, and Kathleen McHugh, Carole Vance, Cindy Patton, Jeff Escoffier, Jonathan Ned Katz, and especially Nan D. Hunter, for their invaluable contributions to my thinking. I would also like to thank Gayle Rubin and Larry Gross for providing me with copies of important but obscure articles from their voluminous files, and the SR Bay Area collective for their helpful editorial suggestions.

215

would arrive at a similar position, with many of the same questions and suggestions. But the stories would be different, and the "work" of those stories would be differently constructed. Here, I want to take up the position of "queer" largely in order to criticize (but not completely displace) the liberal and nationalist strategies in gay politics and to advocate the constructionist turn in lesbian and gay theories and practices.

Scene #1: New York City, March 1991.
The St. Patrick's Day Parade.

The Irish Lesbian and Gay Organization (ILGO) has been denied permission to march. After much public protest of this exclusion, a deal has been struck with the march organizers. ILGO members will be permitted to march as the guests of a contingent of the Ancient Order of Hibernians, but they have had to agree not to carry any identifying banners or signs. Mayor David Dinkins, who helped to broker the deal, has decided to walk with the lesbian and gay group. On the day of the parade, this group, marked out for the curious by the presence of Dinkins, becomes the target of repeated outbursts of intense hostility on the part of spectators, parade organizers, and officials of the Catholic Church.

These events received extensive nationwide news coverage, which focused largely on the spectacle of the mayor under attack. Dinkins himself used this spectacle to frame an analogy between the treatment of the lesbian and gay marchers in the St. Patrick's Day parade and the hostile treatment of civil rights marchers in the South decades earlier. In an op-ed published in *The New York Times* several days after the parade, he extended and elaborated on this analogy:

On Saturday, despite our taking great care to see that the parade rules were observed, a fearful rage erupted—a rage of intolerance. The anger hurled at the gay and lesbian Irish Americans and me was so fierce that one man threw a filled beer can at us. Perhaps the anger from those watching the parade stemmed from a fear of a lifestyle unlike their own; perhaps it was the violent call of people frightened by a future that seems unlike the past.

It is strange that what is now my most vivid experience of mob hatred came not in the South but in New York—and was directed against me, not because I was defending the rights of African Americans but of gay and lesbian Americans.

Yet, the hostility I saw was not unfamiliar. It was the same anger that led a bus driver to tell me back in 1945, when I was en route to North Carolina in Marine uniform, that there was no place for me: "Two more white seats," he said. It was the same anger that I am sure Montgomery marchers and Birmingham demonstrators experienced when they fought for racial tolerance. It is the fury of people who want the right to deny another's identity.

We cannot flinch from our responsibility to widen the circle of tolerance. For the true evil of discrimination is not in the choice of groups to hate but in the fact that a group is chosen at all. Not only does our Bill of Rights protect us all equally, but every religious tradition I know affirms that, in the words of Dr. Martin Luther King, Jr., "Every man is somebody because he is a child of God."[1]

I quote the Dinkins op-ed extensively here even though it is in most respects formulaic and unsurprising, an invocation of the themes and images of a familiar brand of liberal politics, with its limited call for "tolerance" and an end to "discrimination." I quote it because even my most radical and cynical lesbian and gay friends found it deeply moving, because it was in one important respect quite rare. Dinkins' analogy to the civil rights movement, an analogy liberal gay organizations have outlined and pursued for decades, is still seldom heard outside lesbian and gay circles. In the hands of David Dinkins, a political figure with national visibility and a well-known record of civil rights activism, this analogy mobilizes images of noble suffering in the face of naked hatred. It invokes the culturally resonant figure of Martin Luther King, Jr. on behalf of lesbians and gay men, thereby endowing our struggle for equality with a precious and, for us, elusive political resource— moral authority.

Appeals to Liberalism

For nearly fifty years now, lesbian and gay organizations have worked to forge a politically active and effective lesbian and gay "minority" group, and to claim the liberal "rights" of privacy and formal equality on its behalf. As a rhetorical strategy, this positioning has aimed to align lesbian and gay populations with racial, ethnic, and religious minority groups and women in a quest for full economic, political and cultural participation in U.S. life. This rhetorical move, when successful, opens up avenues of political and legal recourse forged by the civil rights and feminist movements to lesbian and gay action: support for group-specific antidiscrimination statutes; participation in political coalitions to design, pass, and enforce broad civil rights provisions; application to the courts for equal protection under various constitutional provisions; organization to elect and pressure public officials; lobbying of media organizations for fair and equitable representation, and so on.

But this rhetorical overture to the logic of liberal tolerance has generally met with very limited success. The inclusion of lesbians and gay men in the pantheon of unjustly persecuted groups is everywhere unstable and contested. Political coalitions risk their legitimacy when they include lesbian and gay groups or issues. Group-specific municipal antidiscrimination ordinances are constantly subject to repeal attempts. Cultural groups from the National Endowment for the Arts to the Modern Language Association are attacked or ridiculed for the presence of lesbian and gay topics on their agendas. And the legal climate for lesbian and gay organizations has been poisoned for the rest of this century (at least) by the nasty, brutish and short 1986 decision of the U.S. Supreme Court in *Bowers vs. Hardwick* (upholding the state of Georgia's statute criminalizing consensual sodomy).

The spectacle of the suffering mayor walking with downcast gays and lesbians in the St. Patrick's Day parade brings both these failures and the important achievements of liberal gay politics into vivid relief. The hostility of the spectators, the parade organizers, and the Roman Catholic Cardinal underscored the precarious position of the ILGO and, by extension, of gay communities more generally. Inclusion could be negotiated only on humiliating terms, and even then public civility could not be enforced.

But as the subsequent press coverage and the Dinkins op-ed show, the parade was also a moment of highly visible achievement for the rhetoric of liberal gay politics. The circulation of images from the parade evoked a response supportive of Dinkins and the ILGO from nongay politicians and pundits, a response which frequently framed the issues in language that liberal gay organizations have proposed, appropriating the American Dream for the "minority" that seems to reside permanently at the bottom of the list.

At this historical moment, marked by the precarious and contested achievements illustrated by the example of the St. Patrick's Day parade, the liberal strategy has also come under increasing attack from within lesbian and gay communities. Of course, this strategy has never occupied the field of gay politics unopposed. Challenges to it have appeared from the overlapping yet distinguishable positions of militant nationalism and radical constructionism. In the 1990s, both of these positions appear to be gaining ground.

The Call to Militant Nationalism

Scene #2: New York City, Spring 1991.

> *Posters of celebrities labeled "Absolutely Queer" appear on Manhattan walls. One, featuring an image of actress Jodie Foster, is captioned "Actress, Yalie, Dyke." These posters have not been produced by homophobic conservatives, but by gay militants engaged in the practice of "outing."*

"Outing" is a political tactic inaugurated by New York City's now defunct gay weekly newspaper *Outweek* (though the term for it was coined

by *Time*), and associated most closely with the paper's "lifestyle" colum-
nist, Michelangelo Signorile. As a practice, it is an extension of the early
gay liberationist appeal to lesbians and gay men to "come out of the
closet," reveal their hidden lives, and reject the fear and stigma attached
to their identities. In "outing," this appeal is transformed from an invita-
tion into a command. Journalists and activists expose "closeted" lesbians
or gay men in public life, especially those deemed hypocritical in their
approach to gay issues. Their goal is to end the secrecy and hypocrisy
surrounding homosexuality, to challenge the notion that gay life is somehow shameful, and to show the world that many widely admired and respected men and women are gay.

Both "outing" and *Outweek* sprang from the efflorescence of militance
surrounding the rhetoric and politics of ACT UP and its spinoff, Queer
Nation. Many of these new gay militants reject the liberal value of privacy and the appeal to tolerance which dominate the agendas of more
mainstream gay organizations. Instead, they emphasize publicity and
self-assertion; confrontation and direct action top their list of tactical options; the rhetoric of difference replaces the more assimilationist liberal
emphasis on similarity to other groups.

But the challenge that the new politics poses to the liberal strategy is
not only the challenge of militance—the familiar counterposing of anger
to civility, of flamboyance to respectability, often symbolized through
"style"—but also the challenge of nationalism.[2]

Nationalisms have a long history in gay and lesbian politics and culture. From turn-of-the-century German homosexual emancipationist
Magnus Hirschfeld to contemporary radical-feminist philosopher Mary
Daly, the "nation" and its interests have been defined in varying ways.
With no geographical base or kinship ties to provide boundaries, gay and
lesbian nationalists have offered biological characteristics (as in the
"Third Sex"), or shared experience (whether of sexual desire or gender
solidarity) as common ground. Of these various nationalisms, two
broadly distinguishable competing forms have appeared and reappeared
since the mid-nineteenth century: (1) the ethnic model of a fixed minority
of both sexes defined by biology and/or the experience of desire (most
often estimated at ten percent)[3] and (2) the single-sex union of gender
loyalists, the no-fixed-percentage model associated with lesbian separatism (theoretically, all women could belong to the Lesbian Nation).[4]

The ethnic model also underpins the liberal strategy, of course. The argument for "rights" is made on behalf of a relatively fixed minority constituency. It becomes the basis for a more militant nationalism when the
"ethnic" group is represented as monolithic, its interests primary and utterly clear to a political vanguard. The example of "outing" serves as an
illustration of this brand of gay politics. Outers generally not only believe

in the existence of a gay nation, but are confident of their ability to identify its members and of their authority to do so. They have no doubts
about definitions or boundaries, and do not hesitate to override the welfare and autonomy of individuals "in the national interest."[5]

Outers present their version of gay nationalism as radical but, like
other nationalisms, its political implications are complex, and often actually reactionary. These new nationalists define the nation and its interests
as unitary; they suppress internal difference and political conflict. Self-
appointed ayatollahs explain it all.

This reactionary potential was especially apparent in the pages of
Outweek in 1990, when Malcolm Forbes, then recently deceased, was
"outed" and presented as a role model for gay youth. The same magazine had earlier reviled Tim Sweeney, a longtime gay activist and executive director of Gay Men's Health Crisis in New York City, for compromising the gay national interests by negotiating with African-American
groups over the conditions for appointment of a New York City health
commissioner.[6] *Outweek*'s "nation," it appears, is white, values wealth
and celebrity for their own sake, and pursues self-interest in the narrow-
est possible terms.

This particularly virulent strain of gay nationalism has been criticized
with increasing vehemence by those excluded, misrepresented, or terror-
ized by it. C. Carr, writing in *The Village Voice* under the banner headline,
"Why Outing Must Stop," called it "the most absurd excuse for political
thinking I have ever encountered," and commented:

> Anyone who thinks . . . that a lesbian can proclaim her sexuality in an indus-
> try as male-centered as Hollywood, where even straight women have trou-
> ble getting work . . . has to be out of his fucking mind.

Voicing the sentiments of many, Carr also noted that "I'm still waiting
for the news of Malcolm Forbes' homosexuality to improve my life."[7]

Carr's critique of "outing" takes up the liberal defense of "privacy"—
emphasizing the continuing strategic value of a "right to privacy" for lesbians and gay men threatened with everyday persecution. But her column also echoes the criticisms of gay political discourses that women
and people of color (especially, though not exclusively) have forged and
developed over the past two decades.

Whose Identity?

Both the liberal assimilationist and the militant nationalist strands of gay
politics posit gay identity as a unitary, unproblematic given—the political project revolves around its public articulation. But for people with

multiple "marked" identities, the political project begins at the level of the very problematic construction of identities and their relation to different communities and different political projects. In Audre Lorde's much quoted words: "It was a while before we came to realize that our place was the very house of difference rather than the security of any one particular difference."[8]

Thus Carr hypothesizes that, for Jodie Foster, being a woman defines her relationship to Hollywood in a way that shifts the meaning of being "gay," and the consequences of "coming out." From this perspective, advocacy of "outing" is colonizing. Foster's situation is appropriated by a single-issue politics that cannot honor the complexity of her differences.

The charge I want to make here against both the liberal and nationalist strategies, but especially against the latter, is this: *any* gay politics based on the primacy of sexual identity defined as unitary and "essential," residing clearly, intelligibly and unalterably in the body or psyche, and fixing desire in a gendered direction, ultimately represents the view from the subject position "twentieth-century, Western, white, gay male."

Scene #3: San Francisco, February 1991.
The Second Annual Lesbian and Gay Writers' Conference.

The designation of this conference as simply "lesbian and gay" is contested everywhere I look. An organized bisexual lobby is highly visible and voluble. The designation "Queer" is ubiquitous, sometimes used in the "in-your-face" manner of the many "Faggot" and "Dyke" buttons that I see, but also used to designate a more broadly inclusive "community."

Louise Sloan, reporting on this conference in the *San Francisco Bay Guardian*, wrote that it constructed a "community":

of men, women, transsexuals, gay males, lesbians, bisexuals, straight men and women, African Americans, Chicanos, Asian Americans, Native Americans, people who can see and/or walk and people who cannot, welfare recipients, trust fund recipients, wage earners, Democrats, Republicans, and anarchists—to name a few. . . . Indeed, since difference from the "norm" is about all that many people in the "gay community" have in common with each other, these sorts of "gay and lesbian" gatherings, at their best and worst and most radical, seem to be spaces where cross-sections of the human multiverse can gather to thrash out differences and perhaps to lay the groundwork for peaceful and productive futures. . . . In my most naively hopeful moments, I often imagine it will be the "queer community"—the oxymoronic community of difference—that might be able to teach the world how to get along.[9]

Sloan's description of the "oxymoronic community of difference" at the writers' conference challenges the oversimplified notion that the essentialist-versus-social-constructionist debate, now saturating the gay press, is a controversy of activist politics versus academic theory.

In its most clichéd formulations, this controversy is presented in one of two ways: valiant and dedicated activists working to get civil rights for gay and lesbian people are being undermined by a bunch of obscure, arcane, jargon-ridden academics bent on "deconstructing" the gay community before it even comes into full visibility; or theoretically informed writers at the cutting edge of the political horizon are being bashed by anti-intellectual activists who cling naively to the discursive categories of their oppressors.[10] Both these formulations fail to acknowledge the vigor and longevity of the constructionist strand in lesbian and gay politics, a strand which theorists have taken up, not produced.

From the first appearance of the homosexual/heterosexual polarity just over a hundred years ago, "essentialist" theories, both homophile and homophobic, have had to account for the observed malleability of sexual desire. Each theoretical assertion of the fixity of desire has had attached to it a residual category—a catchall explanation for those formations of pleasure that defy the proffered etiologies. In Havelock Ellis' scheme, flexible, "acquired" sexual inversion accompanied the more permanent, "congenital" type. In the lexicon of contemporary sociology, "situational" homosexuality occurs among "heterosexual" persons under special circumstances—in prisons or other single-sex institutions, for example. ("Situational" heterosexuality is seldom discussed.)[11] In each theoretical paradigm, the "essential" nature and truth of the homo/hetero dyad is shored up with a rhetoric of authenticity. The "real" is distinguished from the "copy," the "true inverts" from those merely susceptible to seduction.

Such constructionist branches on the tree of essentialism grew up on their own during the heady days of early gay liberation. Drawing on the more constructionist versions of psychoanalytic theories of sexuality, visionaries painted a utopia in which everyone was potentially polymorphously sexual with everyone else.[12] During the 1970s, lesbian-feminists outlined a somewhat more ambivalent position, with a sharper political edge. They aggressively denaturalized heterosexuality and presented it as a central apparatus in the perpetuation of patriarchy. But these same women often presented lesbianism as the naturalized alternative. When Alix Dobkin sang that "Any Woman Can Be a Lesbian," the implication was that any woman not suffering from false consciousness *would* be.[13]

The current revival of constructionist rhetoric in activist discourses is, like its constructionist predecessors, also partial and ambivalent—but in a very different sense. The new political currency of the term "bisexual," for instance, which has been added to the titles of lesbian/gay organizations from coast to coast in the United States, has had contradictory effects. Activists have used the term "bisexual" to disrupt the natural status of the dualism heterosexual/homosexual. But they have then paradoxically reinstated sexual polarity through the addition of a third naturalized term, as rigidly gendered as the original two, only doubled. The tendency of bisexual writers and organizations to appropriate wholesale the rhetoric of the lesbian and gay rights movement reinforces the latter effect.[14]

Defining a Queer Community

The notion of a "queer community" can work somewhat differently. It is often used to construct a collectivity no longer defined solely by the gender of its members' sexual partners. This new community is unified only by a shared dissent from the dominant organization of sex and gender. But not every individual or group that adopts the name "queer" means to invoke these altered boundaries. Many members of Queer Nation, a highly decentralized militant organization, use the term "queer" only as a synonym for lesbian or gay. Queer Nation, for some, is quite simply a gay nationalist organization. For others, the "queer" nation is a newly defined political entity, better able to cross boundaries and construct more fluid identities. In many other instances, various contradictory definitions coexist—in a single group, or in an individual's mind. This ambivalent mixture is illustrated in a series of interviews with Queer Nation activists published in *Out/Look*:

> *Miguel Gutierrez:* Queerness means nonassimilationist to me.
>
> *Rebecca Hensler:* A lot of what the "queer generation" is arguing for is the same stuff that was being fought for by gay liberation.
>
> *Alexander Chee:* The operant dream is of a community united in diversity, queerly ourselves. . . . [The facilitators] took great care to explain that everyone was welcome under the word *queer.*
>
> *Laura Thomas:* I don't see the queer movement as being organized to do anything beyond issues of antiassimilation and being who we want to be.
>
> *Adele Morrison:* Queer is not an "instead of," it's an "inclusive of." . . . It's like the whole issue of "people of color."
>
> *Gerard Koskovich:* I think *queer* has been adopted here in San Francisco by people who are using their experience of marginalization to produce an aggressive critique of the prevailing social system. . . . I think we're seeing in its early stages a reorganization of some of those forces into a new community of people where the range of defining factors is rather

fluid. People's limits have shifted significantly from the traditional urban gay community of the 1970s.[15]

Or, as former *Outweek* editor Gabriel Rotello explained to a *New York Times* reporter,

When you're trying to describe the community, and you have to list gays, lesbians, bisexuals, drag queens, transsexuals (post-op and pre-), it gets unwieldy. Queer says it all.[16]

In addition to the appearance of organizations for "bisexuals" and "queers," the boundaries of community have also been altered by a new elasticity in the meanings of "lesbian" and "gay." When Pat Califia announced that sex between lesbians and gay men is "gay sex," and *Outweek* published a cover story on "Lesbians Who Sleep With Men," the notion of a fixed sexual identity determined by a firmly gendered desire began to slip quietly away.[17]

Queer Theory on the Move

The constructionist perspective began to generate theoretical writing beginning in the 1970s. British historical sociologist Jeffrey Weeks, influenced by the earlier work of Mary McIntosh, appropriated and reworked the sociological theories known as "symbolic interactionism" or "labeling theory" to underpin his account of the emergence of a homosexual identity in Western societies during the nineteenth century. Other British writers associated with the Gay Left Collective produced work from within this same field of influence. U.S. historians Jonathan Ned Katz and John D'Emilio, influenced primarily by feminist theory and the work of Marxists such as E.P. Thompson, began to produce "social construction" theories of homosexuality by the early 1980s.[18]

This theory, though rich with implications for theoretical investigations of identity and subjectivity generally, remained severely ghettoized until relatively recently. Gay authors and gay topics, stigmatized and tabooed in the academy, have found audiences and sources of support elsewhere. But lesbian and gay history and theory have suffered from this ghettoization, as have history and theory more broadly.[19]

The figure who most clearly marks the recent movement of this theory out of the ghetto is Michel Foucault. His reputation and influence placed his investigations of the emergence of homosexual identity within a theoretical context, embedded in a body of work, that legitimated it—and ultimately served to legitimate the work of other, more stigmatized and marginalized theorists. The history of sexuality ultimately became a subject, a disciplinary location, largely as an effect of the circulation of Foucault's work through the work of (predominantly) lesbian and gay authors.[20]

Since the publication of Foucault's *History of Sexuality,* the cultural work of lesbian and gay theory has shifted. After a couple of decades of staking out a position, a territory, a locale, our theories are now preparing to travel. After defining a viewpoint, articulating a set of questions, and producing a body of knowledges, we are determined now to transport these resources across cultural boundaries. Theory is now working—finally—to get us out of the academic ghetto.

"Constructionist" theories accomplish this in a way "essentialist" theories never could. Lesbian and gay identities, theorized as fixed and borne by a minority, place certain limits on the horizon of theory as well as politics. They contain desire and naturalize gender through the operations of their very definitions. Constructionist theories, on the other hand, recognize the (constrained) mobility of desire and support a critical relation to gender. They stake out a new stance of opposition, which many theorists now call "queer." This stance is constituted through its dissent from the hegemonic, structured relations and meanings of sexuality and gender, but its actual historical forms and positions are open, constantly subject to negotiation and renegotiation.

Queer theories do their ghetto-busting work by placing the production and circulation of sexualities at the core of Western cultures, defining the emergence of the homosexual/heterosexual dyad as an issue that *no* cultural theory can afford to ignore. As Eve Sedgwick put it in the first paragraph of her book *Epistemology of the Closet:*

> This book will argue that an understanding of virtually any aspect of modern Western culture must be, not merely incomplete, but damaged in its central substance to the degree that it does not incorporate a critical analysis of modern homo/heterosexual definition.[21]

This project works in at least two directions—taking queer questions and knowledges into the domain of mainstream theoretical paradigms, and bringing the formulations of feminist, Marxist, postmodernist and poststructuralist theories to bear on issues of queer culture and politics.

In the case of a major figure such as Foucault, the project involved the smuggling of queer questions into the very foundations of contemporary theory. Without being *completely* crude and reductive, it is possible to ask: From what subject position do prisons, mental asylums, confessionals and sexuality seem connected and central to the operations of power? Foucault's own queerness, seldom stated but widely known, may have shaped his questions and his work in ways that endowed it with its current legitimating power.[22]

In the area of literary studies, Eve Sedgwick's work is now performing the work of legitimation and de-ghettoization. She is importing "queer readings" into the house of critical theory. She is able to accomplish this effectively in part because, as the "Judy Garland" of gay studies, she does not bear the stigma of homosexuality herself. She can be perceived (however wrongly) as in some sense "disinterested," and therefore as a more "credible" standard bearer for theoretical queerness. (This is not a criticism of Sedgwick, but of the conditions of reception for her work.)

Sedgwick's work performs its magic primarily for the benefit of gay male readers and readings, and on the texts of the traditional, white, male "canon."[23] Within the field defined by queer literary theory, lesbian visions remain profoundly ghettoized, though they are gaining ground from within feminist theory (which is itself only newly emerging from its own ghetto). Only a few literary theorists have embarked on queer readings of the texts of lesbians, especially those from less privileged class backgrounds or from communities of color.[24]

It is precisely from within feminist theory, however, that a "queer" critique of the dominant categories of sexuality and gender is emerging most imaginatively and persuasively. The work of film theorist Teresa de Lauretis, especially, has effected the de-ghettoization of a queer perspective in feminist theory. As she wrote in *Technologies of Gender* in 1987:

> The problem, which is a problem for all feminist scholars and teachers, is one we face almost daily in our work, namely, that most of the available theories of reading, writing, sexuality, ideology, or any other cultural production are built on male narratives of gender, whether oedipal or anti-oedipal, bound by the heterosexual contract; narratives which persistently tend to reproduce themselves in feminist theories. They *tend* to, and will do so unless one constantly resists, suspicious of their drift.[25]

We can surmise who is the "one" who is most likely to become and remain so relentlessly suspicious.

Following on the work of de Lauretis, feminist philosopher Judith Butler has hacked away at the heterosexual assumptions built into the foundations of theories of gender, whether feminist, nonfeminist, or antifeminist. Her *Gender Trouble: Feminism and the Subversion of Identity*, draws upon the queer practices of drag and cross-dressing (treated in the earlier work of anthropologist Esther Newton) and the queer "styles" of lesbian butch-fem to build her own conception of gender as performance, and of gender parodies as subversive bodily acts.[26]

Though neither de Lauretis nor Butler has staked out a position named specifically as "queer," the elaboration of such a locale within feminist theory could work a radical magic similar to that of the category "women of color." As many feminists have argued, the category "women of color," as proposed in such groundbreaking anthologies as *This Bridge Called My Back,* is a significant conceptual and political innovation.[27] As Donna Haraway wrote in 1985:

> This identity marks out a self-consciously constructed space that cannot affirm the capacity to act on the basis of natural identification, but only on the basis of conscious coalition, of affinity, of political kinship. Unlike the "woman" of some streams of the white women's movement in the United States, there is no naturalization of the matrix, or at least this is what [Chela] Sandoval argues is uniquely available through the power of oppositional consciousness.[28]

This description (I would argue) applies equally well to the political community and theoretical standpoint constructed by the designation "queer."

Activism Versus Academia?

The challenge for queer theory as it emerges from the academic ghetto is to engage intellectually with the political project in the best sense of "theory," while avoiding jargon and obscurantism in the worst sense of "academic." The record to date is at best uneven. On the downside, there is a tendency among some queer theorists to engage in academic debates at a high level of intellectual sophistication, while erasing the political and activist roots of their theoretical insights and concerns. Such theorists cite, modify, or dispute Foucault, Lacan, and Derrida, while feminist, lesbian, and gay innovations and political figures disappear from sight. They use formal languages to exclude all but the most specialized from the audience for theory.

On the upside, some queer theorists work in a way that disrupts the activist/theorist opposition, combining sophisticated thinking, accessible language, and an address to a broadly imagined audience. Writer/activists such as Gloria Anzaldúa, Kobena Mercer, Douglas Crimp and Gayle Rubin offer us the possibility of escape from the twin pitfalls of anti-intellectual posturing among some activists *and* the functional elitism of some would-be radical theorists.[29]

The continuing work of queer politics and theory is to open up possibilities for coalition across barriers of class, race, and gender, and to somehow satisfy the paradoxical necessity of recognizing differences, while producing (provisional) unity. Can we avoid the dead end of various nationalisms and separatisms, without producing a bankrupt universalism?

I think queer politics and theory offer us promising new directions for intervention in U.S. life—though in different ways in differing arenas. In the arena of academic cultural theory, queer theory is breaking into the mainstream, making a difference and providing (some, limited) material support in the form of careers. This is possible because queer theory shares with much academic cultural theory a critique of U.S. liberalism and a focus on the process of political marginalization. But in the arena of political activism—the kind that takes place in mass institutions from mainstream media to Congress—queer politics occupies the critical margins. This is because the language and logic of liberalism still occupy the progressive edge of the possible in mainstream U.S. politics. Lesbian and gay liberal politics offer us the best opportunities we have to make gains in courtrooms, legislatures, and TV sitcoms. Queer politics, with its critique of the categories and strategies of liberal gay politics, keeps the possibility of radical change alive at the margins. It also infuses a remarkable efflorescence of off-center cultural production—art, music, dance, theater, film and video, and more.

Jeffrey Escoffier and Allan Bérubé describe this paradoxical reality in the special *Out/Look* section on Queer Nation:

> The new generation calls itself *queer,* not *lesbian, gay, and bisexual*—awkward, narrow, and perhaps compromised words. *Queer* is meant to be confrontational—opposed to gay assimilationists and straight oppressors while inclusive of people who have been marginalized by anyone in power. Queer Nationals are undertaking an awesome task. They are trying to combine contradictory impulses: to bring together people who have been made to feel perverse, queer, odd, outcast, different, and deviant, and to affirm sameness by defining a common identity on the fringes.
>
> Queer Nationals are torn between affirming a new identity—"I am queer"—and rejecting restrictive identities—"I reject your categories," between rejecting assimilation—"I don't need your approval, just get out of my face"—and wanting to be recognized by mainstream society—"We queers are gonna get in your face."
>
> These queers are constructing a new culture by combining elements that usually don't go together. They may be the first wave of activists to embrace the retrofuture/classic contemporary styles of postmodernism. They are building their own identity from old and new elements—borrowing styles and tactics from popular culture, communities of color, hippies, AIDS activists, the antinuclear movement, MTV, feminists, and early gay liberationists. Their new culture is slick, quick, anarchic, transgressive, ironic. They are dead serious, but they also just wanna have fun. If they manage not to blow up in contradiction or get bogged down in process, they may lead the way into new forms of activism for the 1990s.[30]

For the foreseeable future, we need both our liberal and radical fronts. But queer politics and theory, in their best guises and combinations, offer us a possible future full of provocations and possibilities.

Notes

1. David N. Dinkins, "Keep Marching for Equality," the *New York Times*, March 21, 1991.

2. The ideas in this discussion of gay nationalism were generated in conversations with Jenny Terry, Jackie Urla, and Jeff Escoffier. It was Urla who first suggested to me that certain strains in gay politics could be considered nationalist discourses.

3. For a description and defense of the "ethnic model," see Steven Epstein, "Gay Politics, Ethnic Identity: The Limits of Social Constructionism," *Socialist Review*, vol. 17, no. 3/4 (May–August 1987).

4. For an account of a 1970s incarnation of this form of nationalism—based on gender rather than sexuality *per se*—see Charlotte Bunch, "Learning from Lesbian Separatism," in her *Passionate Politics: Feminist Theory in Action* (New York: St. Martin's Press, 1987).

5. See, for example, Michelangelo Signorile, "Gossip Watch," *Outweek*, April 18, 1990, pp. 55–57. For an extended discussion of these issues, see Steve Beery *et al.*, "Smashing the Closet: The Pros and Cons of Outing," *Outweek*, May 16, 1990, pp. 40–53. The many opinions expressed in this issue indicate that not all editors of *Outweek* agreed with Signorile—though the editor-in-chief, Gabriel Rotello, was in complete agreement.

6. See Michelangelo Signorile, "The Other Side of Malcolm," *Outweek*, March 18, 1990, pp. 40–45. The Tim Sweeney controversy continued in the pages of the magazine for several months.

7. C. Carr, "Why Outing Must Stop," *The Village Voice*, March 19, 1991, p. 37. She was later joined in the letters column of the *Voice* by B. Ruby Rich, who announced the formation of DAO—Dykes Against Outing.

8. Audre Lorde, *Zami: A New Spelling of My Name* (Watertown, MA: Persephone Press, 1982), p. 226.

9. Louise Sloan, "Beyond Dialogue," *San Francisco Bay Guardian Literary Supplement*, March 1991, p. 3.

10. For an excellent account of the political ramifications of this debate, see Jeffrey Escoffier, "Inside the Ivory Closet: The Challenges Facing Lesbian and Gay Studies," *Out/Look: National Lesbian and Gay Quarterly*, no. 10 (Fall 1990), pp. 40–48. For a theoretical discussion, see Diana Fuss, "Lesbian and Gay Theory: The Question of Identity Politics," in her *Essentially Speaking: Feminism, Nature and Difference* (New York: Routledge, 1989), pp. 97–112. (Neither of these writers offers the clichéd version of the debate that I have caricatured.)

11. For discussions of the emergence of the homosexual/heterosexual dyad and its representations in various medical-scientific discourses, see Jeffrey Weeks, *Coming Out: Homosexual Politics in Britain from the Nineteenth Century to the Present* (London: Quartet Books, 1977) and his *Sex, Politics and Society: The Regulation of*

Sexuality Since 1800 (London: Longman, 1981). See also Jonathan Katz, "The Invention of the Homosexual, 1880–1950," in his *Gay/Lesbian Almanac* (New York: Harper & Row, 1983), pp. 137–174.

12. See Dennis Altman, *Homosexual Oppression and Liberation* (New York: Avon Books, 1971), especially Chapter 3, "Liberation: Toward the Polymorphous Whole."

13. Alix Dobkin, "Any Woman Can Be a Lesbian," from the album *Lavender Jane Loves Women.* The best known example of this move—the denaturalization of heterosexuality, and the naturalization of lesbianism—is Adrienne Rich, "Compulsory Heterosexuality and Lesbian Existence," reprinted in *Powers of Desire: The Politics of Sexuality,* ed. A. Snitow, C. Stansell and S. Thompson (New York: Monthly Review Press, 1983), pp. 177–205. It is important to note that male-dominated gay politics has seldom supported a critique of the convention of heterosexuality for most people (the 90% or so seen as "naturally" heterosexual). Lesbian-feminists *always* regarded heterosexuality as an oppressive institution, which any woman (potentially all women) might escape through lesbianism.

14. See for example the anthology edited by Loraine Hutchins and Lani Kaahumani, *Bi Any Other Name: Bisexual People Speak Out* (Boston: Alyson Publications, 1991).

15. "Birth of a Queer Nation," *Out/Look: National Lesbian and Gay Quarterly,* no. 11 (Winter 1991), pp. 14–23. The interviews and articles in this special section were collected from New York and San Francisco, though there are other groups all over the country. My account of Queer Nation is drawn from my own (limited) knowledge of the New York and Chicago groups, and from articles and interviews in the gay and lesbian press. Because Queer Nation has no central "organization," I'm not attempting to describe it exhaustively; I am pointing to several tendencies and possibilities within it.

16. "'Gay' Fades as Militants Pick 'Queer'," the *New York Times,* April 6, 1991.

17. Pat Califia, "Gay Men, Lesbians and Sex: Doing It Together," *The Advocate,* July 7, 1983, pp. 24–27; Jorjet Harper, "Lesbians Who Sleep With Men," *Outweek,* February 11, 1990, pp. 46–52.

18. These developments are summarized by Jeffrey Escoffier in "Inside the Ivory Closet." See note 10.

19. See Lisa Duggan, "History's Gay Ghetto: The Contradictions of Growth in Lesbian and Gay History," in this volume [L. Duggan and N. D. Hunter, eds., *Sex Wars: Sexual Dissent and Political Culture* (New York, Routledge, 1995), pp. 155–172—Eds.]; and John D'Emilio, "Not a Simple Matter: Gay History and Gay Historians," *Journal of American History,* vol. 76, no. 2 (September 1989), pp. 435–442.

20. The most influential single text in the United States was the English translation of *The History of Sexuality: Volume 1* (New York: Pantheon, 1978). My point about the ubiquity of lesbian and gay authors in the field of "history of sexuality" can be confirmed with a glance at the list of editors for the new journal, *Journal of the History of Sexuality.* All but a few are known to be lesbian or gay.

21. Eve Kosofsky Sedgwick, *Epistemology of the Closet* (Berkeley: University of California Press, 1990), p. 1.

22. In a fascinating interview with Foucault, published in the gay periodical *The Advocate* just after his death from AIDS in 1984, he comments: "Sexuality is

something that we ourselves create. . . . We have to understand that with our desires, through our desires, go new forms of relationships, new forms of love, new forms of creation." Bob Gallagher and Alexander Wilson, "Foucault and the Politics of Identity," *The Advocate,* August 7, 1984, pp. 27–30, 58.

23. See Julie Abraham's review of Sedgwick's *Epistemology of the Closet* in *The Women's Review of Books,* vol. 8, no. 7 (April 1991), pp. 17–18. Abraham concludes provocatively that *"Epistemology of the Closet* is an extraordinary book. The questions Sedgwick addresses, and those her work provokes, together create a great deal of theoretical space. But all the women are straight, all the gays are male (and all the males are, potentially, gay). The sisters are still doing it for themselves."

24. See especially Biddy Martin, "Lesbian Identity and Autobiographical Difference(s)," in *Life/lines: Theorizing Women's Autobiography,* Bella Brodzky and Celeste Schenck, eds. (Ithaca, NY: Cornell University Press, 1988), pp. 77–103. The texts of privileged lesbians such as Gertrude Stein, Radclyffe Hall and Willa Cather have received relatively more attention, of course.

25. Teresa de Lauretis, *Technologies of Gender* (Bloomington: Indiana University Press, 1987), p. 25.

26. Judith Butler, *Gender Trouble: Feminism and the Subversion of Identity* (New York: Routledge, 1990). See especially pp. 136–139.

27. Cherríe Moraga and Gloria Anzaldúa, *This Bridge Called My Back: Writings by Radical Women of Color* (Watertown, MA: Persephone Press, 1981).

28. Donna Haraway, "A Manifesto for Cyborgs: Science, Technology, and Socialist Feminism in the 1980s," *Socialist Review,* vol. 15, no. 2 (March–April 1985), pp. 73–74. Haraway is citing Chela Sandoval, "Dis-Illusionment and the Poetry of the Future: The Making of Oppositional Consciousness," Ph.D. qualifying essay, University of California, Santa Cruz, 1984.

29. Gloria Anzaldúa, *Borderlands/La Frontera: The New Mestiza* (San Francisco: Spinsters/Aunt Lute, 1987); Kobena Mercer, "Skin Head Sex Thing: Racial Difference and the Homoerotic Imaginary," in *How Do I Look? Queer Film and Video,* ed. Bad Objects Collective (Seattle: Bay Press, 1991), pp. 169–210; Douglas Crimp with Adam Rolston, *AIDS DemoGraphics* (Seattle: Bay Press, 1990); Gayle Rubin, "Thinking Sex: Notes for a Radical Theory of the Politics of Sexuality," in *Pleasure and Danger: Explorations in Female Sexuality,* ed. Carole S. Vance (New York: Routledge, 1984), pp. 267–319.

30. Jeffrey Escoffier and Allan Bérubé, "Queer/Nation," *Out/Look: National Lesbian and Gay Quarterly,* no. 11 (Winter 1991), pp. 14–16.

11 Sex Equality

On Difference and Dominance

CATHARINE A. MACKINNON

There is one thing of which one can say neither that it is one meter long nor that it is not one meter long, and that is the standard meter in Paris.

—**Ludwig Wittgenstein**

The measure of man is man.

—**Pythagoras**

[Men] think themselves superior to women, but they mingle that with the notion of equality between men and women. It's very odd.

—**Jean-Paul Sartre**

Inequality because of sex defines and situates women as women. If the sexes were equal, women would not be sexually subjected. Sexual force would be exceptional, consent to sex could be commonly real, and sexually violated women would be believed. If the sexes were equal, women would not be economically subjected, their desperation and marginality cultivated, their enforced dependency exploited sexually or economically. Women would have speech, privacy, authority, respect, and more resources than they have now. Rape and pornography would be recognized as violations, and abortion would be both rare and actually guaranteed.

In the United States, it is acknowledged that the state is capitalist; it is not acknowledged that it is male. The law of sex equality, constitutional by interpretation and statutory by joke, erupts through this fissure, exposing the sex equality that the state purports to guarantee.[1] If gender hierarchy and sexuality are reciprocally constituting—gender hierarchy providing the eroticism of sexuality and sexuality providing an enforcement mechanism for male dominance over women—a male state would predictably not make acts of sexual dominance actionable as gender inequality. Equality would be kept as far away from sexuality as possible. In fact, sexual force is not conventionally recognized to raise issues of sex inequality, either against those who commit the acts or against the state that condones them. Sexuality is regulated largely by criminal law, occasionally by tort law, neither on grounds of equality.[2] Reproductive control, similarly, has been adjudicated primarily as an issue of privacy. It is as if a vacuum boundary demarcates sexual issues on the one hand from the law of equality on the other. Law, structurally, adopts the male point of view: sexuality concerns nature not social arbitrariness, interpersonal relations not social distributions of power, the sex difference not sex discrimination.

Sex discrimination law, with mainstream moral theory, sees equality and gender as issues of sameness and difference. According to this approach, which has dominated politics, law, and social perception, equality is an equivalence not a distinction, and gender is a distinction not an equivalence. The legal mandate of equal treatment—both a systemic norm and a specific legal doctrine—becomes a matter of treating likes alike and unlikes unlike, while the sexes are socially defined as such by their mutual unlikeness. That is, gender is socially constructed as difference epistemologically, and sex discrimination law bounds gender equality by difference doctrinally. Socially, one tells a woman from a man by their difference from each other, but a woman is legally recognized to be discriminated against on the basis of sex only when she can first be said to be the same as a man. A built-in tension thus exists between this concept of equality, which presupposes sameness, and this concept of sex, which presupposes difference. Difference defines the state's approach to sex equality epistemologically and doctrinally. Sex equality becomes a contradiction in terms, something of an oxymoron. The deepest issues of sex inequality, in which the sexes are most constructed as socially different, are either excluded at the threshold or precluded from coverage once in. In this way, difference is inscribed on society as the meaning of gender and written into law as the limit on sex discrimination.

In sex discrimination law, sex inequality in life becomes "sex classification" in law, each category defined by its difference from the other. A classification in law or in fact is or is not a sex-based discrimination depending upon the accuracy of its "fit"[3] with gender and upon the validity of its purpose for government or business. A classification, in the classic formulation of the "rational relation" test "must be reasonable, not arbitrary, and must rest upon some ground of difference having a fair and substantial relation to the object of the legislation, so that all persons similarly circumstanced shall be treated alike."[4] Under the equal protection clause of the Fourteenth Amendment, the line drawn by a rule or practice being challenged as discriminatory is required to track the gender line more closely than this. To be nondiscriminatory, the relation between gender and the line's proper objectives must be more than rational but need not be perfect. In what has been termed "intermediate scrutiny"—a judicial standard of care for women only—gender lines are scrutinized more carefully than most, but not as strictly as some.[5] They are not prohibited absolutely, as they would have been under the dominant interpretation of the Equal Rights Amendment (ERA).[6] Seen on this doctrinal continuum, which scrutinizes the correlation between gender lines and the purposes of drawing them, the ERA was not a new departure but a proposal to take the standard equal protection approach to its conclusion.

Equality is comparative in sex discrimination law. Sex in law is compared with sex in life, and women are compared with men. Relevant empirical similarity to men is the basis for the claim to equal treatment for women. For differential treatment to be discriminatory the sexes must first be "similarly situated" by legislation, qualifications, circumstance, or physical endowment.[7] This standard applies to sex the broader legal norm of neutrality, the law's version of objectivity. To test for gender neutrality, reverse the sexes and compare. To see if a woman was discriminated against on the basis of sex, ask whether a similarly situated man would be or was so treated. Relevant difference supports different treatment, no matter how categorical, disadvantageous, or cumulative. Accurate reflections of situated disparities are thus rendered either noncomparable or rational, therefore differences not inequalities for legal purposes. In this view normative equality derives from and refers to empirical equivalence. Situated differences produce differentiated outcomes without necessarily involving discrimination.

In this mainstream epistemologically liberal approach,[8] the sexes are by nature biologically different, therefore socially properly differentiated for some purposes. Upon this natural, immutable, inherent, essential, just, and wonderful differentiation, society and law are thought to have erected some arbitrary, irrational, confining, and distorting distinctions. These are the inequalities the law against sex discrimination targets. As one scholar has put it, "any prohibition against sexual classifications must be flexible enough to accommodate two legitimate sources of distinctions on the basis of sex: biological differences between the sexes and the prevailing heterosexual ethic of American society."[9] The proposed federal ERA's otherwise uncompromising prohibition on sex-based distinctions provides parallel exceptions for "unique physical characteristics" and "personal privacy."[10] Laws or practices that express or reflect sex "stereotypes," understood as inaccurate overgeneralized attitudes often termed archaic" or "outmoded," are at the core of this definition of discrimination.[11] Mistaken illusions about real differences are actionable, but any distinction that can be accurately traced to biology or heterosexuality is not a discrimination but a difference.

From women's point of view, gender is more an inequality of power than a differentiation that is accurate or inaccurate. To women, sex is a social status based on who is permitted to do what to whom; only derivatively is it a difference. For example, one woman reflected on her gender: "I wish I had been born a doormat, or a man."[12] Being a doormat is definitely different from being a man. Differences between the sexes do descriptively exist. But the fact that these are a woman's realistic options, and that they are so limiting, calls into question the perspective that considers this distinction a "difference." Men are not called different because they are neither doormats nor women, but a woman is not socially permitted to be a woman and neither doormat nor man.

From this perspective, considering gender a matter of sameness and difference covers up the reality of gender as a system of social hierarchy, as an inequality. The differences attributed to sex become lines that inequality draws, not any kind of basis for it. Social and political inequality begins indifferent to sameness and difference. Differences are inequality's post hoc excuse, its conclusory artifact, its outcome presented as its origin, its sentimentalization, its damage that is pointed to as the justification for doing the damage after the damage has been done, the distinctions that perception is socially organized to notice because inequality gives them consequences for social power. Gender might not even code as difference, might not mean distinction epistemologically, were it not for its consequences for social power. Distinctions of body or mind or behavior are pointed to as cause rather than effect, with no realization that they are so deeply effect rather than cause that pointing to them at all is an effect. Inequality comes first; difference comes after. Inequality is material and substantive and identifies a disparity; difference is ideational and abstract and falsely symmetrical. If this is so, a discourse and a law of gender that center on difference serve as ideology to neutralize, rationalize, and cover disparities of power, even as they appear to criticize or problematize them. Difference is the velvet glove on the iron fist of domination. The problem then is not that differences are not valued; the problem is that they are defined by power. This is as true when difference is affirmed as when it is denied, when its substance is applauded or disparaged, when women are punished or protected in its name.

Doctrinally speaking, two alternative paths to sex equality for women exist within the mainstream approach to sex discrimination, paths that follow the lines of the sameness/difference tension. The leading one is: be the same as men. This path is termed "gender neutrality" doctrinally and the single standard philosophically. It is testimony to how substance becomes form in law that this rule is considered formal equality. Because it mirrors the values of the social world, it is considered abstract, meaning transparent to the world and lacking in substance. Also for this reason it is considered to be not only *the* standard, but *a* standard at all. Legally articulated as conforming normative standards to existing reality, as law reflecting life, the strongest doctrinal expression of sameness would prohibit taking gender into account in any way, with exceptions for "real differences." This is so far the leading rule that the words "equal to" are code for, or/and equivalent to, the words "the same as"—with the referent for both unspecified.

To women who want equality yet find themselves "different," the doctrine provides an alternative route: be different from men. This equal recognition of difference is termed the special benefit rule or special protection rule legally, the double standard philosophically. It is in rather bad odor, reminiscent of women's exclusion from the public sphere and of protective labor laws.[13] Like pregnancy, which always brings it up, it is something of a doctrinal embarrassment. Considered an exception to true equality and not really a rule of law at all, it is the one place where the law of sex discrimination admits it is recognizing something substantive. Together with the Bona Fide Occupational Qualification (BFOQ) and the exception for unique physical characteristics under ERA policy, compensatory legislation, and sex-conscious relief in particular litigation, affirmative action is thought to live here.[14] Situated differences can produce different treatment—indulgences *or* deprivations. This equality law is agnostic as to which.

The philosophy underlying the sameness/difference approach applies liberalism to women. Sex is a natural difference, a division, a distinction, beneath which lies a stratum of human commonality, sameness.[15] The moral thrust of the sameness branch of the doctrine conforms normative rules to empirical reality by granting women access to what men have: to the extent women are no different from men, women deserve what men have. The differences branch, which is generally regarded as patronizing and unprincipled but necessary to avoid absurdity, exists to value or compensate women for what they are or have become distinctively as women—by which is meant, unlike men, or to leave women as "different" as equality law finds them.

Most scholarship on sex discrimination law concerns which of these paths to sex equality is preferable in the long run or more appropriate to any particular issue, as if they were all there is.[16] As a prior matter, however, treating issues of sex equality as issues of sameness and difference is to take a particular approach. This approach is here termed the sameness/difference approach because it is obsessed with the sex difference. Its main theme is: "we're the same, we're the same, we're the same." Its counterpoint theme (in a higher register) goes: "but we're different, but we're different, but we're different." Its story is: on the first day, difference was; on the second day, a division was created upon it; on the third day, occasional dominance arose. Division may be rational or irrational. Dominance either seems or is justified or unjustified. Difference *is*.

Concealed is the substantive way in which man has become the measure of all things. Under the sameness rubric, women are measured according to correspondence with man, their equality judged by proximity to his measure. Under the difference rubric, women are measured according to their lack of correspondence from man, their womanhood judged by their distance from his measure. Gender neutrality is the male standard. The special protection rule is the female standard. Masculinity or maleness is the referent for both. Approaching sex discrimination in this way, as if sex questions were difference questions and equality questions were sameness questions, merely provides two ways for the law to hold women to a male standard and to call that sex equality.

Sameness/difference doctrine has mediated what women have gotten as women from this state under the rubric of sex discrimination. It does address a very important problem: how to get women access to everything women have been excluded from, while also valuing everything that women are or have been allowed to become or have developed as a consequence of their struggle either not to be excluded from most of life's pursuits or to be taken seriously under the terms that have been permitted to be women's terms. It negotiates what women have managed in relation to men. Its guiding impulse is: we are as good as you. Anything you can do, we can do. Just get out of the way. It has improved elite access to employment and education—the public pursuits, including academic and professional and blue-collar work—to the military, and more than nominal access to athletics.[17] It has moved to alter the dead ends that were all women were seen as good for, and what passed for lack of physical training, which was serious training in passivity and enforced weakness. The military draft has presented the sameness route to equality in all its simple dignity and complex equivocality: as citizens, women should have to risk being killed just like men.[18] Citizenship is whole. The consequences of women's resistance to its risks should count as men's count.[19]

The sameness standard has mostly gotten men the benefit of those few things women have historically had—for all the good they did. Under gender neutrality, the law of custody and divorce has shifted once again, giving men what is termed an equal chance at custody of children and at alimony.[20] Men often look like better parents under gender-neutral rules like level of income and presence of nuclear family, because men make more money and (as it is termed) initiate the building of family units.

They also have greater credibility and authority in court. Under gender neutrality, men are in effect granted a preference as parents because society advantages them before they get to court. But law is prohibited from taking that preference into account because that would mean taking gender into account, which would be sex discrimination. Nor are the group realities that make women more in need of alimony permitted to matter, because only individual factors, gender-neutrally considered, may matter. So the fact that women will live their lives, as individuals, as members of the group women, with women's chances in a sex-discriminatory society, may not count or it is sex discrimination. The equality principle in this form mobilizes the idea that the way to get things for women is to get them for men. Men have gotten them. Women have lost their children and financial security and still have not gained equal pay or equal work, far less equal pay for equal work, and are close to losing separate enclaves like women's schools through this approach.[21]

What this doctrine apparently means by sex inequality is not what happens to women, and what it means by sex equality is only getting things for women that can also be gotten for men. The law of sex discrimination seems to be looking only for those ways women are kept down which have *not* wrapped themselves up as a difference, whether original, imposed, or imagined. As to original differences: what to do about the fact that women have an ability men still lack, gestating children in utero? Pregnancy is therefore a difference, yet it does not define a perfect gender line because not all women become pregnant.[22] Gender here is first defined biologically—to encompass that which affects all women and only women—and then the most biological of differences, pregnancy, is excluded because it is not biological (that is, 100 percent) enough. Besides, pregnancy is a difference, on the basis of which differentiations can be made without being discriminatory. Pregnancy is both too gendered and not gendered enough, so women can safely not be compensated for job absences, guaranteed jobs on return, and so on. Gender neutrality suggests, indeed, that it may be sex discrimination to give women what they need because only women need it. It would certainly be considered special protection. But it is not, in this approach, sex discrimination *not* to give only women what they need, because then only women will not get what they need.[23] On this logic, sex discrimination law prohibits virtually nothing that socially disadvantages women and only women. Other than *de jure*, sex discrimination is a null set.

Consider imposed differences: what to do about the fact that most women are segregated into low-paying jobs where there are no men? Arguing that the structure of the marketplace will be subverted if comparable worth is put into effect (an interesting comment on the radical potential of a reform with much in common with "wages for housework" proposals),[24] difference doctrine says that because there is no man to set a standard from which women's treatment is a deviation, there is no sex discrimination, only a sex difference. Never mind that there is no man to compare with because no man would do that job if he had a choice, and because he is a man, he does, so he does not. Straightforward cases of sex discrimination run aground on the same rock. For example, in *Sears v. EEOC*, the Equal Employment Opportunities Commission argued that massive statistical disparities between women and men in some categories of better-paying jobs showed sex discrimination by Sears. One expert, Alice Kessler Harris, assuming women's sameness with men in the name of feminism, supported them, saying that whenever women were permitted to be exceptions, they were. Defendant Sears argued that women were different from men, did not necessarily want the same things men want, such as better-paying jobs. Another expert, Rosalind Rosenberg, arguing women's differences from men in the name of feminism, supported them. Given that the women in the data overwhelmingly divided on gender lines, and that neither the doctrinal assumptions nor the sex inequality of the job definitions was challenged, not to mention the social sexism that constructs what people "want," the argument on women's differences won, and women lost.[25]

Now consider de facto discrimination, the so-called subtle reaches of the imposed category. Most jobs require that a qualified gender-neutral person not be the primary caretaker of the worker's preschool child.[26] Pointing out that this fact raises a concern of gender in a society in which women are expected to care for young children is taken as day one of taking gender into account in the structuring of jobs. To do that would violate the rule against not noticing situated differences based on gender. So it is never clear that day one of taking gender into account in job structuring was the day the job was structured with the expectation that its occupant would not have primary childcare responsibilities.

Imaginary sex differences, such as those between equally qualified male and female applicants for estate administration,[27] sex discrimination doctrine can handle. But if women were not taught to read and write (as was once the case, the women are still a majority of the world's illiterates), the gender difference between women and men in estate administration would not be imaginary. Such a society would be in even greater need of a law against sex inequality, yet this doctrine would be incapable of addressing it as an inequality problem. Illusions and mistakes sex discrimination law can deal with. Realities are another thing entirely. The result is, due to sex inequality, even when women are "similarly situated" to men they are often not seen as such. The deeper problem is, due to sex inequality, they are seldom permitted to become "similarly situated" to men.

This law takes the same approach to the social reality of sex inequality that the ideology of sex inequality takes to social life, and considers itself legitimate because the two correspond. For this reason, sex equality law is always being undermined by the problem it is trying to solve. It cannot recognize, for instance, that men do not have to be the same as anyone to be entitled to most benefits. It cannot recognize that every quality that distinguishes men from women is already affirmatively compensated in society's organization and values, so that it implicitly defines the standards it neutrally applies. Men's physiology defines most sports, their health needs largely define insurance coverage, their socially designed biographies defined work-place expectations and successful career patterns, their perspectives and concerns define quality in scholarship, their experiences and obsessions define merit, their military service defines citizenship, their presence defines family, their inability to get along with each other—their wars and rulerships—defines history, their image defines god, and their genitals define sex. These are the standards that are presented as gender neutral. For each of men's differences from women, what amounts to an affirmative action plan is in effect, otherwise known as the male-dominant structure and values of American society. But whenever women are found different from men and insist on not having it held against them, every time a difference is used to keep women second class and equality law is brought in as redress, the doctrine has a paradigm trauma.

Clearly, there are many differences between women and men. Systematically elevating one-half of a population and denigrating the other half would not likely produce a population in which everyone is the same. What sex equality law fails to notice is that men's differences from women are equal to women's differences from men. Yet the sexes are not equally situated in society with respect to their relative differences. Hierarchy of power produces real as well as fantasied differences, differences that are also inequalities. The differences are equal. The inequalities, rather obviously, are not.

Missing in sex equality law is what Aristotle missed in his empiricist notion that equality means treating likes alike and unlikes unlike.[28] No one has seriously questioned it since. Why should one have to be the same as a man to get what a man gets simply because he is one? Why does maleness provide an original entitlement, unquestioned on the basis of its gender, while women who want to make a case of unequal treatment in a world men have made in their image (this is really the part Aristotle missed)[29] have to show in effect that they are men in every relevant respect, unfortunately mistaken for women on the basis of an accident of birth?

The women that gender neutrality benefits, and there are some, expose this method in highest relief. They are mostly women who have achieved a biography that somewhat approximates the male norm, at least on paper. They are the qualified, the least of sex discrimination's victims. When they are denied a man's chance, it looks the most like sex bias. The more unequal society gets, the fewer such women are permitted to exist. The more unequal society gets, the less likely this sex equality doctrine is to be able to do anything about it, because unequal power creates both the appearance and the reality of sex differences along the same lines as it creates sex inequalities.

The special benefits side of the sameness/difference approach has not compensated women for being second class. Its double standard does not give women the dignity of the single standard, nor does it suppress the gender of its referent: female. The special benefits rule is the only place in mainstream sex equality doctrine where one can identify as a woman and not have that mean giving up all claim to equal treatment. But it comes close. Originally, women were permitted to be protected in the workforce, with dubious benefit.[30] Then, under its double standard, women who stood to inherit something when their husbands died were allowed to exclude a small percentage of inheritance tax, Justice Douglas waxing eloquent about the difficulties of all women's economic situation.[31] If women are going to be stigmatized as different, the compensation should at least fit the disparity. Women have also gotten three more years than men get before being advanced or kicked out of the military hierarchy. This is to compensate them for being precluded from combat, the usual way to advance.[32] Making exceptions for women, as if they are a special case, often seems preferable to correcting the rule itself, even when women's "specialness" is dubious or shared or statutorily created.

Excluding women is always an option if sex equality feels in tension with the pursuit itself. For example, women have been excluded from contact jobs in male-only prisons in the name of "their very womanhood" because they might get raped, the Court taking the viewpoint of the reasonable rapist on women's employment opportunities.[33] The conditions that create women's rapability are not seen as susceptible to legal change, nor is predicating women's employment upon their inevitability seen as discriminatory. Apparently, rapability is a difference. Women have also been protected out of hazardous jobs because they did not wish to be sterilized, or the employer did not want to run that risk. The job has health hazards, and somebody who might be a real person some day and therefore could sue—a fetus—might be hurt if potentially fertile women were given jobs that would subject their bodies to possible harm.[34] Fertile women are apparently not real persons and therefore cannot sue either for the hazard to their health or for the lost employment opportunity—although only women are treated in this way. Men, it seems, are never excludable as such, even when their fertility (as with health hazards) or their lives (as with combat) are threatened, even though only men are being harmed.

These two routes to sex equality, the sameness route and the difference route, divide women according to their relations with men and according to their proximity to a male standard. Women who step out of women's traditional relations with men and become abstract persons—exceptional to women's condition rather than receiving the protections of it—are seen as seeking to be like men. They are served equality with a vengeance. If they win, they receive as relief the privilege of meeting the male standard, of paying the price of admission which men are trained for as men and are supposed to pay, even if regularly they do not. Women who assert claims under the difference route, claims in traditional role terms, may, if they win, be protected, or they may be left in sex-specific disadvantage. Different situations may justify different treatment—better or worse.

The result of gender neutrality is that at the same time that very few women gain access to the preconditions effectively to assert equality on male terms, women created in society's traditional mold lose the guarantees of those roles to men asserting sex equality. Women asking courts to enforce the guarantees that have been part of the bargain of women's roles receive less and less, while also not receiving the benefits of the social changes that would qualify them for rights on the same terms as men. This is not a transitional problem. Abstract equality necessarily reinforces the inequalities of the status quo to the extent that it evenly reflects an unequal social arrangement. The law of sex discrimination has largely refused to recognize that it is women who are unequal to men, and has called this refusal the equality principle.

Because, in this doctrine, equality of rights rests upon a claim to similarity, and gender is actually a hierarchy, men who fail as men readily qualify for women's special treatment, while few women attain the prerequisites to claim equality with men. Many of the doctrinally definitive sex discrimination cases that have reached the Supreme Court since 1971 have been brought by men seeking access to the few benefits women had.[35] Many have won, while women plaintiffs seeking opportunities previously reserved for men lose and lose and lose, and usually do not even get to the Supreme Court.[36] As a result of men's easier downward mobility combined with men's comparatively greater access to resources and credibility, access men almost never lose; sex discrimination law's compensatory, preferential, or protective rationales on women's behalf have most often been articulated in the context of challenges by men to sex-specific provisions that cushion or qualify but do not change women's status. As often they reinforce it in backhanded ways. One such case upheld a male-only statutory rape law against a sex equality challenge on the grounds that only women get pregnant, ignoring that young men also get raped, that the youngest raped women do not get pregnant, and that women over the age of majority get raped as well as pregnant. Because rape was not recognized as an act of sex inequality, the Court preserved young men as sexual actors, even with adult women, and divided the female population into categories of accessibility to forced sex. The age line kept little girls sexually taboo and thus sexually targeted, by definition unable to consent. Girls one day older and women were left effectively consenting, presumed equals unless proved otherwise.[37] Another case preserved the male-only draft, forcing only men to risk their lives in combat, and, with it, men as society's primary combatants, its legitimate violence in their hands.[38]

Granted, some widowers are like most widows: poor because their spouse has died. Some husbands are like most wives: dependent on their spouse. A few fathers, like most mothers, are primary caretakers. But to occupy these positions is consistent with female gender norms; most women share them. The gender-neutral approach to sex discrimination law obscures, and the protectionist rationale declines to change, the fact that women's poverty and consequent financial dependence on men (whether in marriage, welfare, the workplace, or prostitution), forced motherhood, and sexual vulnerability substantively constitute their social status *as women*, as members of their gender. That some men at times find themselves in similar situations does not mean that they occupy that status as men, as members of their gender. They do so as exceptions, both in norms and in numbers. Unlike women, men are not poor or primary caretakers of children on the basis of sex.

The standards of sex discrimination law are for society's exceptions. To claim that they are situated similarly to men, women must be exceptions. They must be able to claim all that sex inequality has, in general, systematically taken from women: financial independence, job qualifications, business experience, leadership qualities, assertiveness and confidence, a sense of self, peer esteem, physical stature, strength or prowess, combat skills, sexual impregnability, and, at all stages of legal proceedings, credibility. Taking the sexes "as individuals," meaning one at a time, as if they do not belong to genders, perfectly obscures these collective realities and substantive correlates of gender group status behind the mask of recognition of individual rights. It is the woman who has largely escaped gender inequality who is best able to claim she has been injured by it. It seems a woman must already be equal before she can complain of inequality.

Sex discrimination law requires that women either be gender objects or emulate maleness to qualify as subject. These criteria interestingly parallel the two-pronged "passionlessness" that Nancy Cott identifies as women's side of the bargain under which women were historically allowed access to this form of institutional equality at all. "Passionlessness"—sexual acted-uponness as female gender definition—was the price of women's admission to Victorian moral equality.[39] Passionless women merit equal protection (equal treatment, separate version female) or qualified permission to be second-class men (equal treatment, version male). Passionateness would merely break the rule, disentitling the women to moral equality but leaving passionlessness standing as the rule for women. Nonpassionless women—perhaps self-acting, self-defined, self-respecting, not sexually defined, and resisting sex inequality from that position—simply do not exist in these terms. If gender status is sexually based, sexual equality would be real equality. In this light, this form of sexual objectification as the price for equality looks like inequality as the price for equality, and the bourgeois bargain—the terms on which women as a gender were admitted to abstract personhood and individuality in the first place—is revealed to have had a sexual price.

Under sex equality law, to be human, in substance, means to be a man. To be a person, an abstract individual with abstract rights, may be a bourgeois concept, but its content is male. The only way to assert a claim *as* a member of the socially unequal group women, as opposed to seeking to assert a claim as *against* membership in the group women, is to seek treatment on a sexually denigrated basis. Human rights, including "women's rights," have implicitly been limited to those rights that men have to lose. This may be in part why men persistently confuse procedural and abstract equality with substantive equality: for them, they are the same. Abstract equality has never included those rights that women as women most need and never have had. All this appears rational and neutral in law because social reality is constructed from the same point of view.

Stereotyping—inaccurate or exaggerated misreflections—is the archetypal liberal injury. It happens in the head or in symbolic social space. It freezes the process of objectification (of which it is a bona fide part) at its moment of inaccuracy, failing to grasp, thus being always potentially defeated by, images that become behaviorally and emotionally real. Most do. Taking, for example, job applicants on an individual basis obscures rather than relieves this fact, although it surely helps some individuals. That women and girls may not be physically strong, or do not appear physically intimidating compared with men and boys, may be consequences as much as causes of the social image of proper womanhood as weak and of manhood as strong. The issue is not simply one of rigid assumption of biological causality in the face of social variation to the contrary. It is a question of one's account of the reality of gender at the point of dismantling it. Power in society includes both legitimate force and the power to determine decisive socialization processes and therefore the power to produce reality. The distinction between women and men is not simply etched onto perceived reality, but superimposed on a picture that already exists in the mind because it exists in the social world. If a stereotype has a factual basis, if it is not merely a lie or a distortion but has become empirically real, it is not considered sex discriminatory. It is a difference. To criticize sexual objectification as a process of sex inequality, by contrast, is to see actual disparity as part of the injury of inequality through which stereotypes are made most deeply injurious at the point at which they become empirically real.

In cases in which sex-differential treatment is not facial, discrimination law is increasingly requiring a showing that discriminatory "motive" or "intent"[40] animated the challenged behavior. Much like the mental element in rape, this requirement defines the injury of sex discrimination from the standpoint of the perpetrator. If he did not mean harm, no harm was done. If the perpetrator did not intend his acts to be based on sex, they were not based on sex.[41] Discrimination is a moral lapse. Women know that much if not most sexism is unconscious, heedless, patronizing, well-meant, or profit-motivated. It is no less denigrating, damaging, or sex-specific for not being "on purpose."[42] Intent requires proof that defendants first know women's value but then choose to disregard it. But the point at which bigotry is most determinative is the point at which women are not seen as full human beings at all. Often members of both sexes value women's work less highly, on the basis only of their knowledge that a woman did the work. Yet, not knowing that one has sexist attitudes, or not knowing that they are influencing one's judgments, is legally taken as a reason that sex discrimination did not occur.

Similarly, burdens of proof effectively presume a non-sex-discriminatory universe, the one men largely occupy, to which plaintiffs are required to prove themselves and their situation exceptions. As a context within which to evaluate claims and weigh evidence, the doctrine permits women bringing cases to receive no benefit of a recognition that discrimination against women occurs. Defendants need only "articulate a legitimate and nondiscriminatory reason" for their actions[43] to recover the benefit of the assumption that the merit system generally works. This in spite of the evidence that women overwhelmingly are not advanced according to ability. This allocation of burden of proof is presented as neutral and unbiased and merely technical. Presuming that equality in general exists militates against finding inequality in particular cases as surely as presuming that inequality in general exists militates in favor of finding inequality in particular cases. Social inequality makes neutral ground unavailable: the law against it must assume that either equality or inequality is the social norm.

Assuming that equality generally exists, and that each challenged instance is an exception, makes it almost impossible to produce equality by law.

Sex discrimination law is fundamentally undercut by its concepts of sex, of inequality, and of law. The underlying strategy is to conceive sex as a difference; to diagnose the evil of sex inequality as mistaken differences; to imagine that sex equality—the elimination of unreal differences—has been achieved; and to generate rules from this projected point as a strategy for reaching it. Its reflective method—law mirrors the reality of sex, the reality of sex inequality—embodies this strategy. To suppose that legally assuming the situation really *is* equal in order to make it so is the sentimentality of liberalism. The distanced aperspectivity that achieves the sought-after blindness to sex differences also achieves blindness to sex inequality. Such an approach cannot distinguish separatism from segregation, nondiscrimination from forced integration, or diversity from assimilation. It also misdiagnoses the stake the dominant have in maintaining the situation, because neither it nor they know they are dominant. Ronald Dworkin, for example, defines the equality standard of liberalism as one that "imposes no sacrifice or constraint on any citizen in virtue of an argument that the citizen could not accept without abandoning his sense of equal worth."[44] He seems not to recognize that the inferiority of women is necessary, substantively, to masculine self-worth in unequal societies, indeed that this is part of the reason sex inequality persists.

All these doctrines—the intent requirement, the allocations of burden of proof, but most fundamentally the requirement of similar situation across the gender line—authoritatively deny that social reality is split by sex inequality. This denial, which makes sense from the male point of view, merges the legal standard for a cognizable inequality with objectivity as an epistemological stance. Objectivity assumes that equally competent observers similarly situated see, or at least report seeing, the same thing. Feminism radically questions whether the sexes are ever, under current conditions, similarly situated even when they inhabit the same conditions. (It questions some standards for competence as well.) The line between subjective and objective perception which is supposed to divide the idiosyncratic, nonreplicable, religious, partial, and unverifiable—the unscientific—from the real presumes the existence of a single object reality and its noncontingence upon angle of perception. But if women's condition exists, there are (at least) two *object* realms of social meaning. Women's point of view is no more subjective than men's if women inhabit a sex-discriminatory object reality.

In this analysis, social circumstances, to which gender is central, produce distinctive interests, hence perceptions, hence meanings, hence definitions of rationality. This observation neither reduces gender to thinking differently, rightness to relative subjectivity, nor principle to whose ox is gored. It does challenge the view that neutrality, specifically gender neutrality as an expression of objectivity, is adequate to the nonneutral objectified social reality women experience. If differentiation were the problem, gender neutrality would make sense as an approach to it. Since hierarchy is the problem, it is not only inadequate, it is perverse. In questioning the principledness of neutral principles,[45] this analysis suggests that current law to rectify sex inequality is premised upon, and promotes, its continued existence.

The analytical point of departure and return of sex discrimination law is thus the liberal one of gender differences, understood rationally or irrationally to create gender inequalities. The feminist issue, by contrast, is gender hierarchy, which not only produces inequalities but shapes the social meaning, hence legal relevance, of the sex difference. To the extent that the biology of one sex is a social disadvantage, while the biology of the other is not, or is a social advantage, the sexes are equally different but not equally powerful. The issue becomes the social meaning of biology, not any facticity or object quality of biology itself. Similarly, both sexes possess a sexuality that occupies a place in "the heterosexual ethic." To the extent that the sexuality of one sex is a social stigma, target, and provocation to violation, while the sexuality of the other is socially a source of pleasure, adventure, power (indeed, the social definition of potency), and a focus for deification, entertainment, nurturance, and derepression, the sexuality of each is equally different, equally heterosexual or not, but not equally socially powerful. The relevant issue is the social meaning of the sexuality and gender of women and men, not their sexuality or gender "itself"—if such a distinction can be made. To limit efforts to end gender inequality at the point where biology or sexuality is encountered, termed differences, without realizing that these exist in law or society only in terms of their specifically sexist social meanings, amounts to conceding that gender inequality may be challenged so long as the central epistemological pillars of gender as a system of power are permitted to remain standing.

So long as this is the way these issues are framed, women's demands for sex equality will appear to be demands to have it both ways: the same when women are the same as men, different when different. But this is the way men have it: equal and different too. The same as women when they are the same and want to be, and different from women when they are different or want to be, which usually they do. Equal and different too would be parity. But under male supremacy, while being told women get it both ways—the specialness of the pedestal and an even chance at the race, the ability to be a woman and a person, too—few women get much benefit of either. The sameness route ignores the fact that the indices or injuries of sex or sexism often ensure that simply being a woman may mean seldom being in a position sufficiently similar to a man's to have unequal treatment attributed to sex bias. The difference route incorporates and reflects rather than alters the substance of women's inferior status, presenting a protection racket as equal protection of the laws. In this way, the legal forms available for arguing the injuries of sex inequality obscure the gender of this equality's reference point while effectively precluding complaint for women's sex-specific grievances.

When sameness is the standard for equality, a critique of gender hierarchy looks like a request for special protection in disguise. In fact, it envisions a change that would make a simple equal chance possible for the first time. To define the reality of gender as difference and the warrant of equality as sameness not only guarantees that sex equality will never be achieved; it is wrong on both counts. Sex in nature is not a bipolarity, it is a continuum; society makes it into a bipolarity. Once this is done, to require that one be the same as those who set the standard—those from whom one is already socially defined as different—simply means that sex equality is conceptually designed in law never to be achieved. Those who most need equal treatment will be the *least* similar, socially, to those whose situation sets the standard against which their entitlement to equal treatment is measured. The deepest problems of sex inequality do not find women "similarly situated" to men. Practices of inequality need not be intentionally discriminatory. The status quo need only be reflected unchanged. As a strategy for maintaining social power, descriptively speaking, first structure social reality unequally, and then require that entitlement to alter it be grounded on a lack of distinction in situation; first structure perception so that different equals inferior, and then require that discrimination be activated by evil minds who *know* that they are treating equals as less, in a society in which, epistemologically speaking, most bigots will be sincere.

The mainstream law of equality assumes that society is already fundamentally equal. It gives women legally no more than they already have socially, and little it cannot also give men. Actually doing anything for women under sex equality law is thus stigmatized as special protection or affirmative action rather than simply recognized as nondiscrimination or equality for the first time. So long as sex equality is limited by sex difference—whether valued or negated, staked out as a ground for feminism or occupied as the terrain of misogyny—women will be born, degraded, and die. Protection will be a dirty word and equality will be a special privilege.

Notes

1. Sex inequality was first found unconstitutional by interpretation of the equal protection clause of the Fourteenth Amendment in 1971. Reed v. Reed, 404 U.S. 71

(1971). When Title VII of the Civil Rights Act of 1964 was debated, racist southern congressmen attempted to defeat the provisions on racial discrimination by adding "sex" to the prohibited bases. Their *reductio ad absurdum* failed when it passed; *Congressional Record,* February 8, 1964, p. 2577. See also Willingham v. Macon Telegraph Publishing Co., 507 F.2d 1084, 1090 (5th Cir. 1975).

2. The law of sexual harassment, recognized only recently under sex equality law, is an exception, achieved by putting into practice the analysis argued in this book. See Catharine A. MacKinnon, *Sexual Harassment of Working Women: A Case of Sex Discrimination* (New Haven: Yale University Press, 1979). Sex equality cases that address sexual issues such as rape (Michael M. v. Superior Court of Sonoma County, 450 U.S. 464 [1981]; Dothard v. Rawlinson, 433 U.S. 321 [1977]) do so in a context of the drawing of gender lines.

3. J. Tussman and J. tenBroek, "The Equal Protection of the Laws," 37 *California Law Review* 341 (1949), were the first to use the term *fit* to characterize the necessary relation between a valid equality rule and the world to which it refers.

4. Royster Guano Co. v. Virginia, 253 U.S. 412, 415 (1920).

5. Craig v. Boren, 429 U.S. 190 (1976).

6. Barbara Brown, Thomas I. Emerson, Gail Falk, and Ann E. Freedman, "The Equal Rights Amendment: A Constitutional Basis for Equal Rights for Women," 80 *Yale Law Journal* 871 (1971).

7. "Regardless of their sex, persons within any one of the enumerated classes . . . are similarly situated . . . By providing dissimilar treatment for men and women who are thus similarly situated, the challenged section violates the Equal Protection Clause." Reed v. Reed, 404 U.S. 71, 77 (1971); Rostker v. Goldberg, 453 U.S. 57 (1981) (because women are differently situated for combat by legislation, male-only registration for draft does not violate equal protection). See also Califano v. Webster, 430 U.S. 313 (1977); Parham v. Hughes, 441 U.S. 347, 355 (1979) (mothers not similarly situated to fathers for purposes of legitimizing children because only fathers have legal power to do so); Schlesinger v. Ballard, 419 U.S. 498 (1975); Michael M. v. Superior Court of Sonoma County, 450 U.S. 464, 471 (1981) (women are dissimilarly situated from men "with respect to the problems and risks of sexual intercourse," meaning pregnancy).

8. There is another approach, gaining ascendancy, discussed in Chapter 13.

9. G. Rutherglen, "Sexual Equality in Fringe-Benefit Plans," 65 *Virginia Law Review* 199, 206 (1979).

10. Brown, Emerson, Falk, and Freedman, "The Equal Rights Amendment."

11. Nadine Taub, "Keeping Women in Their Place: Stereotyping Per Se as a Form of Employment Discrimination," 21 *Boston College Law Review* 345 (1980); see also Barbara Kirk Cavanaugh, "'A Little Dearer than His Horse': Legal Stereotypes and the Feminine Personality," 6 *Harvard Civil Rights–Civil Liberties Law Review* 260 (1971).

12. Jean Harris, quoted by Shana Alexander in *Very Much a Lady,* in a review by Anne Bernays, *New York Times Book Review,* March 27, 1983, p. 13.

13. See B. Babcock, A. Freedman, E. Norton, and S. Ross, *Sex Discrimination and the Law* (Boston: Little, Brown, 1975), pp. 23–53.

14. The Bona Fide Occupational Qualification exception to Title VII of the Civil Rights Act of 1964, 42 U.S.C. Section 2000e-2(e), permits sex to be a job qualifica-

tion when it is a valid one. For ERA theory, see Brown, Emerson, Falk, and Freedman, "The Equal Rights Amendment."

15. This observation applies even to enlightened liberals like John Rawls, who rejects the naturalism of social orderings as prescriptive but accepts them as descriptive of unjust societies. Inequality exists in nature; society can accept or reject it. It is not in itself a social construct, nor are differences a function of it; John Rawls, *A Theory of Justice* (Cambridge, Mass.: The Belknap Press of Harvard University Press, 1971), p. 102.

16. For examples, see Wendy Williams, "The Equality Crisis: Some Reflections on Culture, Courts, and Feminism," 7 *Women's Rights Law Reporter* 175 (1982); Herma Kay, "Models of Equality," 1985 *University of Illinois Law Review* 39; Fran Olsen, "Statutory Rape: A Feminist Critique of Rights Analysis," 63 *Texas Law Review* 387 (1984); Wendy Williams, "Equality's Riddle: Pregnancy and the Equal Treatment/Special Treatment Debate," 13 *New York University Review of Law and Social Change* 325 (1985); Sylvia Law, "Rethinking Sex and the Constitution," 132 *University of Pennsylvania Law Review* 955 (1984); Stephanie Wildman, "The Legitimation of Sex Discrimination: A Critical Response to Supreme Court Jurisprudence," 63 *Oregon Law Review* 265 (1984); Herma Kay, "Equality and Difference: The Case of Pregnancy," 1 *Berkeley Women's Law Journal* 1 (1985); Dowd, "Maternity Leave: Taking Sex Differences into Account," 54 *Fordham Law Review* 699 (1986). Frances Olsen, "From False Paternalism to False Equality: Judicial Assaults on Feminist Community, Illinois 1869–1895," 84 *Michigan Law Review* 1518 (1986), sees the definition of the issues as limiting.

17. Examples in employment: Title VII of the Civil Rights Act of 1964, 42 U.S.C. 2000e; Phillips v. Martin-Marietta, 400 U.S. 542 (1971). Education: Title IX of the Civil Rights Act of 1964, 20 U.S.C. 1681; Cannon v. University of Chicago, 441 U.S. 677 (1979); Delacruz v. Tormey, 582 F.2d 45 (9th Cir. 1978). Academic employment: women appear to lose most of the cases that go to trial, but cf. Sweeney v. Board of Trustees of Keene State College, 604 F.2d 106 (1st Cir. 1979). Professional employment: Hishon v. King & Spalding, 467 U.S. 69 (1984). Blue-collar employment: Vanguard Justice v. Hughes, 471 F. Supp. 670 (D. Md. 1979); Meyer v. Missouri State Highway Commission, 567 F. 2d 804 (8th Cir. 1977); Payne v. Travenol Laboratories Inc., 416 F. Supp. 248 (N.D. Miss. 1976). See also Dothard v. Rawlinson, 433 U.S. 321 (1977) (height and weight requirements invalidated for prison guard positions because of disparate impact on the basis of sex). Military: Frontiero v. Richardson, 411 U.S. 677 (1973); Schlesinger v. Ballard, 419 U.S. 498 (1975). Athletics: This situation is relatively complex. See Gomes v. R.I. Interscholastic League, 469 F. Supp. 659 (D.R.I. 1979); Brenden v. Independent School District, 477 F.2d 1292 (8th Cir. 1973); O'Connor v. Board of Education of School District No. 23, 645 F.2d 578 (7th Cir. 1981); Cape v. Tennessee Secondary School Athletic Association, 424 F. Supp. 732 (E.D. Tenn. 1976), rev'd, 563 F.2d 793 (6th Cir. 1977); Yellow Springs Exempted Village School District Board of Education v. Ohio High School Athletic Association, 443 F. Supp. 753 (S.D. Ohio 1978); Aiken v. Lieuallen, 593 P.2d 1243 (Or. App. 1979).

18. See Rostker v. Goldberg, 453 U.S. 57 (1981) (upholding male-only draft registration). See also Lori S. Kornblum, "Women Warriors in a Men's World: The Combat Exclusion," 2 *Law & Inequality: A Journal of Theory and Practice* 351 (1984).

19. The undercurrent is: what's the matter, don't you want me to learn to kill . . . just like you? This conflict might be expressed as a dialogue between women in the afterlife. The feminist says to the soldier: we fought for your equality. The soldier says to the feminist: oh, no, *we* fought for *your* equality.

20. On alimony and other economic factors, see L. Wietzman, "The Economics of Divorce: Social and Economic Consequences of Property, Alimony, and Child Support Awards," 28 *UCLA Law Review* 1181, 1251 (1981), which documents a decline in women's standard of living of 73 percent and an increase in men's of 42 percent within a year after no-fault divorce in California. Weitzman attributes to no-fault what, in my view, should be attributed to gender neutrality. On custody, see Phyllis Chesler, *Mothers on Trial* (New York: McGraw-Hill, 1986).

21. For data and analysis see Barbara F. Reskin and Heidi Hartmann, eds., *Women's Work, Men's Work: Sex Segregation on the Job* (Washington, D.C.: National Academy Press, 1986). Comparing the median income of the sexes from ages twenty-five to fifty for 1975–1983, the U.S. Department of Labor Women's Bureau reports that women in 1975 made about $8,000 to men's $14,000, and in 1983 $15,000 to men's $24,000; U.S. Department of Labor, Women's Bureau, *Time of Change: 1983 Handbook of Women Workers*, Bulletin 298 (Washington, D.C., 1983), p. 456. The Equal Pay Act was passed in 1963. On equal pay for equal work, see Christensen v. State of Iowa, 563 F.2d 353 (8th Cir. 1977); Gerlach v. Michigan Bell Tel. Co., 501 F. Supp. 1300 (E.D. Mich. 1980); Odomes v. Nucare, Inc., 653 F.2d 246 (6th Cir. 1981); Power v. Barry County, Michigan, 539 F. Supp. 721 (W.D. Mich. 1982); Lemons v. City and County of Denver, 17 FEP Cases 906 (D. Colo. 1978), *aff'd*, 620 F.2d 228 (10th Cir. 1980), *cert. denied*, 449 U.S. 888 (1980). See also Carol Jean Pint, "Value, Work and Women," 1 *Law & Inequality: A Journal of Theory and Practice* 159 (1983). To see the demise of women's schools on the horizon, combine the result of Bob Jones University v. United States, 461 U.S. 574 (1983) (private university loses tax exemption because internal racial segregation violates public policy) with Mississippi University of Women v. Hogan, 458 U.S. 718 (1982) (all-women public nursing school is sex discrimination).

22. General Electric v. Gilbert, 429 U.S. 125 (1976); Geduldig v. Aiello, 417 U.S. 484 (1974).

23. A recent example of the Supreme Court's understanding this better than the women's movement is California Federal Savings and Loan Assn. v. Guerra, 479 U.S. 272 (1987), concerning statutory maternity leave. No feminist group supported the position the Supreme Court ultimately adopted: that it was not sex discrimination for a state legislature to require maternity leaves and job security for pregnant women. All but one feminist group (which argued that reproduction is a fundamental right) argued that it was.

24. Lemons v. City and County of Denver, 17 FEP Cases 906 (D. Colo. 1978); AFSCME v. Washington, 770 F.2d 1401 (9th Cir. 1985).

25. EEOC v. Sears, Roebuck and Co., Civil Action # 79-C-4373 (N.D. Ill. 1987), "Offer of Proof Concerning the Testimony of Dr. Rosalind Rosenberg," "Written Testimony of Alice Kessler Harris," "Written Rebuttal Testimony of Dr. Rosalind Rosenberg," Rosalind Rosenberg, "The Sears Case: An Historical Overview" (Mimeograph, November 25, 1985); Rosalind Rosenberg, "Women and Society Seminar: The Sears Case" (Paper, December 16, 1985); Jon Weiner, "The Sears

Case: Women's History on Trial," *The Nation*, September 7, 1985, pp. 1, 176–180; Alice Kessler-Harris, "Equal Employment Opportunity Commission v. Sears, Roebuck and Company: A Personal Account," *Radical History Review* 35 (1986): 57–79. EEOC v. Sears, 628 F. Supp. 1264 (N.D. Ill., 1986) (Sears did not discriminate), *aff'd*, 839 F.2d 302 (7th Cir. 1988).

26. Phillips v. Martin-Marietta, 400 U.S. 542 (1971).

27. Reed v. Reed, 404 U.S. 71 (1971).

28. Aristotle, *Politics: A Treatise on Government*, trans. A. D. Lindsay (New York: E. P. Dutton, 1912), bk. 3, chap. 16: "Nature requires that the same right and the same rank should necessarily take place amongst all those who are equal by nature" (p. 101); idem, *Ethica Nicomachea*, trans. W. Ross (London: Oxford University Press, 1972), bk. 13, 1131a–b: "Things that are alike should be treated alike, while things that are unalike should be treated unalike in proportion to their unalikeness."

29. On women's nature: "Although moral virtue is common to all . . . yet the temperance of a man and a woman are not the same, nor their courage, nor their justice . . . for the courage of the man consists in commanding, the woman's in obeying"; Aristotle, *Politics*, p. 24.

30. J. Landes, "The Effect of State Maximum-Hours Laws on the Employment of Women in 1920," *Journal of Political Economy* 88 (1980): 476.

31. Kahn v. Shevin, 416 U.S. 351, 353 (1974).

32. Schlesinger v. Ballard, 419 U.S. 498 (1975).

33. Dothard v. Rawlinson, 433 U.S. 321 (1977). If courts learned that sexual harassment is as vicious and pervasive and damaging to women in workplaces everywhere as rape is to women guards in men's prisons, one wonders if women could be excluded from the workplace altogether. Meritor Savings Bank, FSB v. Vinson, 477 U.S. 57 (1986), includes a complaint for sexual harassment based on two and a half years of rape by a bank supervisor.

34. Doerr v. B.F. Goodrich, 484 F. Supp. 320 (N.D. Ohio 1979); Hayes v. Shelby Memorial Hospital, 546 F. Supp. 259 (N.D. Ala. 1982); Wright v. Olin Corp., 697 F.2d 1172 (4th Cir. 1982).

35. David Cole, "Strategies of Difference: Litigating for Women's Rights in a Man's World, 2 *Law & Inequality: A Journal of Theory and Practice* 34 n.4 (1984) (collecting cases).

36. It is difficult to document what does not happen. One example is American Booksellers Assn., Inc. v. Hudnut, 771 F.2d 323 (7th Cir. 1985), summarily affirmed by the Supreme Court without argument. 475 U.S. 1001 (1986), reh. denied 475 U.S. 1132 (1986).

37. Michael M. v. Superior Court of Sonoma County, 450 U.S. 464 (1981).

38. Rostker v. Goldberg, 453 U.S. 57 (1981).

39. Nancy Cott, "Passionlessness: An Interpretation of Victorian Sexual Ideology, 1790–1950," *Signs: A Journal of Women in Culture and Society* 4 (1978): 219–236.

40. Personnel Administrator of Massachusetts v. Feeney, 442 U.S. 256 (1979). See also Washington v. Davis, 426 U.S. 229 (1976); U.S. Postal Service v. Aikens, 460 U.S. 711 (1983).

41. Sexual harassment law has mostly avoided requiring women to prove that the man who made sexual advances toward them did so intending to discrimi-

nate against women. Katz v. Dole, 709 F. 2d 251, 255–256, esp. 256 n.7 (4th Cir. 1983); but cf. Norton v. Vartanian, 31 FEP Cases 1259, 1260 (D. Mass. 1983). Judges have, for the most part, been brought to comprehend that women who are targets of unwanted heterosexual advances would not be in that position if they were not women. Barnes v. Costle, 561 F.2d 983 (D.C. Cir. 1977).

42. Consider this discussion of the connection between gender issues and motive: "It is clear to me that I was denied tenure because I was a lesbian. It is also clear to me that no one who voted to deny me tenure thought s/he was 'discriminating' against me as a lesbian, but that each thought s/he was making 'a difficult decision about the quality and direction of my work'"; Judith McDaniel, "We Were Fired: Lesbian Experiences in Academe," *Sinister Wisdom* 20 (Spring 1982): 30–43.

43. Furnco Construction Corp. v. Walters, 438 U.S. 567 (1978). Cases on Title VII burden of proof that treat race, as this one does, also apply to sex.

44. Ronald Dworkin, *A Matter of Principle* (Cambridge, Mass.: Harvard University Press, 1985), p. 205.

45. The classic articulation of "neutral principles in constitutional adjudication" is by Herbert Wechsler, in his attack on the Supreme Court for deinstitutionalizing racial segregation by law in *Brown v. Board of Education*. Herbert Wechsler, "Toward Neutral Principles of Constitutional Law," 73 *Harvard Law Review* 1 (1959).

12 Deconstructing Equality-Versus-Difference

or, The Uses of Poststructuralist Theory for Feminism

JOAN W. SCOTT / *1988*

That feminism needs theory goes without saying (perhaps because it has been said so often). What is not always clear is what that theory will do, although there are certain common assumptions I think we can find in a wide range of feminist writings. We need theory that can analyze the workings of patriarchy in all its manifestations—ideological, institutional, organizational, subjective—accounting not only for continuities but also for change over time. We need theory that will let us think in terms of pluralities and diversities rather than of unities and universals. We need theory that will break the conceptual hold, at least, of those long traditions of (Western) philosophy that have systematically and repeatedly construed the world hierarchically in terms of masculine universals and feminine specificities. We need theory that will enable us to articulate alternative ways of thinking about (and thus acting upon) gender without either simply reversing the old hierarchies or confirming them. And we need theory that will be useful and relevant for political practice.

It seems to me that the body of theory referred to as poststructuralism best meets all these requirements. It is not by any means the only theory nor are its positions and formulations unique. In my own case, however, it was reading poststructuralist theory and arguing with literary scholars that provided the elements of clarification for which I was looking. I found a new way of analyzing constructions of meaning and relationships of power that called unitary, universal categories into question and historicized concepts otherwise treated as natural (such as man/woman) or absolute (such as equality or justice). In addition, what attracted me was the historical connection between the two movements. Poststructuralism and contemporary feminism are late-twentieth-century movements that share a certain self-conscious critical relationship to established philosophical and political traditions. It thus seemed worthwhile for feminist scholars to exploit that relationship for their own ends.[1]

This article will not discuss the history of these various "exploitations" or elaborate on all the reasons a historian might look to this theory to organize her inquiry.[2] What seems most useful here is to give a short list of some major theoretical points and then devote most of my effort to a specific illustration. The first part of this article is a brief discussion of concepts used by poststructuralists that are also useful for feminists. The second part applies some of these concepts to one of the hotly contested issues among contemporary (U.S.) feminists—the "equality-versus-difference" debate.

· · ·

Among the useful terms feminists have appropriated from poststructuralism are language, discourse, difference, and deconstruction.

Language. Following the work of structuralist linguistics and anthropology, the term is used to mean not simply words or even a vocabulary and set of grammatical rules but, rather, a meaning-constituting system: that is, any system—strictly verbal or other—through which meaning is constructed and cultural practices organized and by which, accordingly, people represent and understand their world, including who they are and how they relate to others. "Language," so conceived, is a central focus of poststructuralist analysis.

Language is not assumed to be a representation of ideas that either cause material relations or from which such relations follow; indeed, the idealist/materialist opposition is a false one to impose on this approach. Rather, the analysis of language provides a crucial point of entry, a starting point for understanding how social relations are conceived, and therefore—because understanding how they are conceived means understanding how they work—how institutions are organized, how relations of production are experienced, and how collective identity is established. Without attention to language and the processes by which meanings and categories are constituted, one only imposes oversimplified models on the world, models that perpetuate conventional understandings rather than open up new interpretive possibilities.

The point is to find ways to analyze specific "texts"—not only books and documents but also utterances of any kind and in any medium in-

cluding cultural practices—in terms of specific historical and contextual meanings. Poststructuralists insist that words and texts have no fixed or intrinsic meanings, that there is no transparent or self-evident relationship between them and either ideas or things, no basic or ultimate correspondence between language and the world. The questions that must be answered in such an analysis, then, are how, in what specific contexts, among which specific communities of people, and by what textual and social processes has meaning been acquired? More generally, the questions are: How do meanings change? How have some meanings emerged as normative and others have been eclipsed or disappeared? What do these processes reveal about how power is constituted and operates?

Discourse. Some of the answers to these questions are offered in the concept of discourse, especially as it has been developed in the work of Michel Foucault. A discourse is not a language or a text but a historically, socially, and institutionally specific structure of statements, terms, categories, and beliefs. Foucault suggests that the elaboration of meaning involves conflict and power, that meanings are locally contested within discursive "fields of force," that (at least since the Enlightenment) the power to control a particular field resides in claims to (scientific) knowledge embodied not only in writing but also in disciplinary and professional organizations, in institutions (hospitals, prisons, schools, factories), and in social relationships (doctor/patient, teacher/student, employer/worker, parent/child, husband/wife). Discourse is thus contained or expressed in organizations and institutions as well as in words; all of these constitute texts or documents to be read.[3]

Discursive fields overlap, influence, and compete with one another; they appeal to one another's "truths" for authority and legitimation. These truths are assumed to be outside human invention, either already known and self-evident or discoverable through scientific inquiry. Precisely because they are assigned the status of objective knowledge, they seem to be beyond dispute and thus serve a powerful legitimating function. Darwinian theories of natural selection are one example of such legitimating truths; biological theories about sexual difference are another. The power of these "truths" comes from the way they function as givens or first premises for both sides in an argument, so that conflicts within discursive fields are framed to follow from rather than question them. The brilliance of so much of Foucault's work has been to illuminate the shared assumptions of what seemed to be sharply different arguments, thus exposing the limits of radical criticism and the extent of the power of dominant ideologies or epistemologies.

In addition, Foucault has shown how badly even challenges to fundamental assumptions often fared. They have been marginalized or silenced, forced to underplay their most radical claims in order to win a short-term goal, or completely absorbed into an existing framework. Yet the fact of change is crucial to Foucault's notion of "archaeology," to the way in which he uses contrasts from different historical periods to present his arguments. Exactly how the process happens is not spelled out to the satisfaction of many historians, some of whom want a more explicit causal model. But when causal theories are highly general, we are often drawn into the assumptions of the very discourse we ought to question. (If we are to question those assumptions, it may be necessary to forgo existing standards of historical inquiry.) Although some have read Foucault as an argument about the futility of human agency in the struggle for social change, I think that he is more appropriately taken as warning against simple solutions to difficult problems, as advising human actors to think strategically and more self-consciously about the philosophical and political implications and meanings of the programs they endorse. From this perspective, Foucault's work provides an important way of thinking differently (and perhaps more creatively) about the politics of the contextual construction of social meanings, about such organizing principles for political action as "equality" and "difference."

Difference. An important dimension of poststructuralist analyses of language has to do with the concept of difference, the notion (following Ferdinand de Saussure's structuralist linguistics) that meaning is made through implicit or explicit contrast, that a positive definition rests on the negation or repression of something represented as antithetical to it. Thus, any unitary concept in fact contains repressed or negated material; it is established in explicit opposition to another term. Any analysis of meaning involves teasing out these negations and oppositions, figuring out how (and whether) they are operating in specific contexts. Oppositions rest on metaphors and cross-references, and often in patriarchal discourse, sexual difference (the contrast masculine/feminine) serves to encode or establish meanings that are literally unrelated to gender or the body. In that way, the meanings of gender become tied to many kinds of cultural representations, and these in turn establish terms by which relations between women and men are organized and understood. The possibilities of this kind of analysis have, for obvious reasons, drawn the interest and attention of feminist scholars.

Fixed oppositions conceal the extent to which things presented as oppositional are, in fact, interdependent—that is, they derive their meaning from a particularly established contrast rather than from some inherent or pure antithesis. Furthermore, according to Jacques Derrida, the interdependence is hierarchical with one term dominant or prior, the opposite term subordinate and secondary. The Western philosophical tradition, he argues, rests on binary oppositions: unity/diversity, identity/difference, presence/absence, and universality/specificity. The leading terms are accorded primacy; their partners are represented as weaker or derivative. Yet the first terms depend on and derive their meaning from the second to such an extent that the secondary terms can be seen as generative of the definition of the first terms.[4] If binary oppositions provide insight into the way meaning is constructed, and if they operate as Derrida suggests, then analyses of meaning cannot take binary oppositions at face value but rather must "deconstruct" them for the processes they embody.

Deconstruction. Although this term is used loosely among scholars— often to refer to a dismantling or destructive enterprise—it also has a precise definition in the work of Derrida and his followers. Deconstruction involves analyzing the operations of difference in texts, the ways in which meanings are made to work. The method consists of two related steps: the reversal and displacement of binary oppositions. This double process reveals the interdependence of seemingly dichotomous terms and their meaning relative to a particular history. It shows them to be not natural but constructed oppositions, constructed for particular purposes in particular contexts.[5] The literary critic Barbara Johnson describes deconstruction as crucially dependent on difference.

> The starting point is often a binary difference that is subsequently shown to be an illusion created by the working of differences much harder to pin down. The differences *between* entities . . . are shown to be based on a repression of differences *within* entities, ways in which an entity differs from itself. . . . The "deconstruction" of a binary opposition is thus not an annihilation of all values or differences; it is an attempt to follow the subtle, powerful effects of differences already at work within the illusion of a binary opposition.[6]

Deconstruction is, then, an important exercise, for it allows us to be critical of the way in which ideas we want to use are ordinarily expressed, exhibited in patterns of meaning that may undercut the ends we seek to attain. A case in point—of meaning expressed in a politically self-defeating way—is the "equality-versus-difference" debate among feminists. Here a binary opposition has been created to offer a choice to feminists, of either endorsing "equality" or its presumed antithesis "difference." In fact, the antithesis itself hides the interdependence of the two terms, for equality is not the elimination of difference, and difference does not preclude equality.

•   •   •

In the past few years, "equality-versus-difference" has been used as a shorthand to characterize conflicting feminist positions and political

EQUALITY Vs — difference.

strategies.[7] Those who argue that sexual difference ought to be an irrelevant consideration in schools, employment, the courts, and the legislature are put in the equality category. Those who insist that appeals on behalf of women ought to be made in terms of the needs, interests, and characteristics common to women as a group are placed in the difference category. In the clashes over the superiority of one or another of these strategies, feminists have invoked history, philosophy, and morality and have devised new classificatory labels: cultural feminism, liberal feminism, feminist separatism, and so on.[8] Most recently, the debate about equality and difference has been used to analyze the Sears case, the sex discrimination suit brought against the retailing giant by the Equal Employment Opportunities Commission (EEOC) in 1974, in which historians Alice Kessler-Harris and Rosalind Rosenberg testified on opposite sides.

There have been many articles written on the Sears case, among them one by Ruth Milkman. Milkman insists that we attend to the political context of seemingly timeless principles: "We ignore the political dimensions of the equality-versus-difference debate at our peril, especially in a period of conservative resurgence like the present." She concludes:

> As long as this is the political context in which we find ourselves, feminist scholars must be aware of the real danger that arguments about "difference" or "women's culture" will be put to uses other than those for which they were originally developed. That does not mean we must abandon these arguments or the intellectual terrain they have opened up; it does mean that we must be self-conscious in our formulations, keeping firmly in view the ways in which our work can be exploited politically.[9]

Milkman's carefully nuanced formulation implies that equality is our safest course, but she is also reluctant to reject difference entirely. She feels a need to choose a side, but which side is the problem. Milkman's ambivalence is an example of what the legal theorist Martha Minow has labeled in another context "the difference dilemma." Ignoring difference in the case of subordinated groups, Minow points out, "leaves in place a faulty neutrality," but focusing on difference can underscore the stigma of deviance. "Both focusing on and ignoring difference risk recreating it. This is the dilemma of difference."[10] What is required, Minow suggests, is a new way of thinking about difference, and this involves rejecting the idea that equality-versus-difference constitutes an opposition. Instead of framing analyses and strategies as if such binary pairs were timeless and true, we need to ask how the dichotomous pairing of equality and difference itself works. Instead of remaining with the terms of existing political discourse, we need to subject those terms to critical examination. Until

ignoring diff risk recreating it.

we understand how the concepts work to constrain and construct specific meanings, we cannot make them work for us.

A close look at the evidence in the Sears case suggests that equality-versus-difference may not accurately depict the opposing sides in the Sears case. During testimony, most of the arguments against equality and for difference were, in fact, made by the Sears lawyers or by Rosalind Rosenberg. They constructed an opponent against whom they asserted that women and men differed, that "fundamental differences"—the result of culture on long-standing patterns of socialization—led to women's presumed lack of interest in commission sales jobs. In order to make their own claim that sexual difference and not discrimination could explain the hiring patterns of Sears, the Sears defense attributed to EEOC an assumption that no one had made in those terms—that women and men had identical interests.[11] Alice Kessler-Harris did not argue that women were the same as men; instead, she used a variety of strategies to challenge Rosenberg's assertions. First, she argued that historical evidence suggested far more variety in the jobs women actually took than Rosenberg assumed. Second, she maintained that economic considerations usually offset the effects of socialization in women's attitudes to employment. And, third, she pointed out that, historically, job segregation by sex was the consequence of employer preferences, not employee choices. The question of women's choices could not be resolved, Kessler-Harris maintained, when the hiring process itself predetermined the outcome, imposing generalized gendered criteria that were not necessarily relevant to the work at hand. The debate joined then not around equality-versus-difference but around the relevance of general ideas of sexual difference in a specific context.[12]

To make the case for employer discrimination, EEOC lawyers cited obviously biased job applicant questionnaires and statements by personnel officers, but they had no individuals to testify that they had experienced discrimination. Kessler-Harris referred to past patterns of sexual segregation in the job market as the product of employer choices, but mostly she invoked history to break down Rosenberg's contention that women as a group differed consistently in the details of their behavior from men, instead insisting that variety characterized female job choices (as it did male job choices), that it made no sense in this case to talk about women as a uniform group. She defined equality to mean a presumption that women and men might have an equal interest in sales commission jobs. She did not claim that women and men, by definition, had such an equal interest. Rather, Kessler-Harris and the EEOC called into question the relevance for hiring decisions of generalizations about the necessarily antithetical behaviors of women and men. EEOC argued that Sears's hiring practices reflected inaccurate and inapplicable notions of sexual difference; Sears argued that "fundamental" differences between the sexes (and not its own actions) explained the gender imbalances in its labor force.

The Sears case was complicated by the fact that almost all the evidence offered was statistical. The testimony of the historians, therefore, could only be inferential at best. Each of them sought to explain small statistical disparities by reference to gross generalizations about the entire history of working women; furthermore, neither historian had much information about what had actually happened at Sears. They were forced, instead, to swear to the truth or falsehood of interpretive generalizations developed for purposes other than legal contestation, and they were forced to treat their interpretive premises as matters of fact. Reading the cross-examination of Kessler-Harris is revealing in this respect. Each of her carefully nuanced explanations of women's work history was forced into a reductive assertion by the Sears lawyers' insistence that she answer questions only by saying yes or no. Similarly, Rosalind Rosenberg's rebuttal to Alice Kessler-Harris eschewed the historian's subtle contextual reading of evidence and sought instead to impose a test of absolute consistency. She juxtaposed Kessler-Harris's testimony in the trial to her earlier published work (in which Kessler-Harris stressed differences between female and male workers in their approaches to work, arguing that women were more domestically oriented and less individualistic than men) in an effort to show that Kessler-Harris had misled the court.[13] Outside the courtroom, however, the disparities of the Kessler-Harris argument could also be explained in other ways. In relationship to a labor history that had typically excluded women, it might make sense to overgeneralize about women's experience, emphasizing difference in order to demonstrate that the universal term "worker" was really a male reference that could not account for all aspects of women's job experiences. In relationship to an employer who sought to justify discrimination by reference to sexual difference, it made more sense to deny the totalizing effects of difference by stressing instead the diversity and complexity of women's behavior and motivation. In the first case, difference served a positive function, unveiling the inequity hidden in a presumably neutral term; in the second case, difference served a negative purpose, justifying what Kessler-Harris believed to be unequal treatment. Although the inconsistency might have been avoided with a more self-conscious analysis of the "difference dilemma," Kessler-Harris's different positions were quite legitimately different emphases for different contexts; only in a courtroom could they be taken as proof of bad faith.[14]

The exacting demands of the courtroom for consistency and "truth" also point out the profound difficulties of arguing about difference. Although the testimony of the historians had to explain only a relatively small statistical disparity in the numbers of women and men hired for full-time commission sales jobs, the explanations that were preferred were totalizing and categorical.[15] In cross-examination, Kessler-Harris's multiple interpretations were found to be contradictory and confusing, although the judge praised Rosenberg for her coherence and lucidity.[16] In part, that was because Rosenberg held to a tight model that unproblematically linked socialization to individual choice; in part it was because her descriptions of gender differences accorded with prevailing normative views. In contrast, Kessler-Harris had trouble finding a simple model that would at once acknowledge difference *and* refuse it as an acceptable explanation for the employment pattern of Sears. So she fell into great difficulty maintaining her case in the face of hostile questioning. On the one hand, she was accused of assuming that economic opportunism equally affected women and men (and thus of believing that women and men were the same). How, then, could she explain the differences her own work had identified? On the other hand, she was tarred (by Rosenberg) with the brush of subversion, for implying that all employers might have some interest in sex typing the labor force, for deducing from her own (presumably Marxist) theory, a "conspiratorial" conclusion about the behavior of Sears.[17] If the patterns of discrimination that Kessler-Harris alluded to were real, after all, one of their effects might well be the kind of difference Rosenberg pointed out. Caught within the framework of Rosenberg's use of historical evidence, Kessler-Harris and her lawyers relied on an essentially negative strategy, offering details designed to complicate and undercut Rosenberg's assertions. Kessler-Harris did not directly challenge the theoretical shortcomings of Rosenberg's socialization model, nor did she offer an alternative model of her own. That would have required, I think, either fully developing the case for employer discrimination or insisting more completely on the "differences" line of argument by exposing the "equality-versus-difference" formulation as an illusion.

In the end, the most nuanced arguments of Kessler-Harris were rejected as contradictory or inapplicable, and the judge decided in Sears's favor, repeating the defense argument that an assumption of equal interest was "unfounded" because of the differences between women and men.[18] Not only was EEOC's position rejected, but the hiring policies of Sears were implicitly endorsed. According to the judge, because difference was real and fundamental, it could explain statistical variations in Sears's hiring. Discrimination was redefined as simply the recognition of "natural" difference (however culturally or historically produced), fitting in nicely with the logic of Reagan conservatism. Difference was substituted for inequality, the appropriate antithesis of equality, becoming inequality's explanation and legitimation. The judge's decision illustrates a

Judges Decision

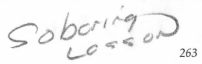

process literary scholar Naomi Schor has described in another context: it "essentializes difference and naturalizes social inequity."[19]

The Sears case offers a sobering lesson in the operation of a discursive, that is, a political field. Analysis of language here provides insight not only into the manipulation of concepts and definitions but also into the implementation and justification of institutional and political power. References to categorical differences between women and men set the terms within which Sears defended its policies *and* EEOC challenged them. Equality-versus-difference was the intellectual trap within which historians argued not about tiny disparities in Sears's employment practices, but about the normative behaviors of women and men. Although we might conclude that the balance of power was against EEOC by the time the case was heard and that, therefore, its outcome was inevitable (part of the Reagan plan to reverse affirmative action programs of the 1970s), we still need to articulate a critique of what happened that can inform the next round of political encounter. How should that position be conceptualized?

When equality and difference are paired dichotomously, they structure an impossible choice. If one opts for equality, one is forced to accept the notion that difference is antithetical to it. If one opts for difference, one admits that equality is unattainable. That, in a sense, is the dilemma apparent in Milkman's conclusion cited above. Feminists cannot give up "difference"; it has been our most creative analytic tool. We cannot give up equality, at least as long as we want to speak to the principles and values of our political system. But it makes no sense for the feminist movement to let its arguments be forced into preexisting categories and its political disputes to be characterized by a dichotomy we did not invent. How then do we recognize and use notions of sexual difference and yet make arguments for equality? The only response is a double one: the unmasking of the power relationship constructed by posing equality as the antithesis of difference and the refusal of its consequent dichotomous construction of political choices.

Equality-versus-difference cannot structure choices for feminist politics; the oppositional pairing misrepresents the relationship of both terms. Equality, in the political theory of rights that lies behind the claims of excluded groups for justice, means the ignoring of differences between individuals for a particular purpose or in a particular context. Michael Walzer puts it this way: "The root meaning of equality is negative; egalitarianism in its origins is an abolitionist politics. It aims at eliminating not all differences, but a particular set of differences, and a different set in different times and places."[20] This presumes a social agreement to consider obviously different people as equivalent (not identical) for a stated purpose. In this usage, the opposite of equality is inequality or inequivalence, the noncommensurability of individuals or groups in certain circumstances, for certain purposes. Thus, for purposes of democratic citizenship, the measure of equivalence has been, at different times, independence or ownership of property or race or sex. The political notion of equality thus includes, indeed depends on, an acknowledgment of the existence of difference. Demands for equality have rested on implicit and usually unrecognized arguments from difference; if individuals or groups were identical or the same there would be no need to ask for equality. Equality might well be defined as deliberate indifference to specified differences.

The antithesis of difference in most usages is sameness or identity. But even here the contrast and the context must be specified. There is nothing self-evident or transcendent about difference, even if the fact of difference—sexual difference, for example—seems apparent to the naked eye. The questions always ought to be, What qualities or aspects are being compared? What is the nature of the comparison? How is the meaning of difference being constructed? Yet in the Sears testimony and in some debates among feminists (sexual) difference is assumed to be an immutable fact, its meaning inherent in the categories female and male. The lawyers for Sears put it this way: "The reasonableness of the EEOC's *a priori* assumptions of male/female sameness with respect to preferences, interests, and qualifications is . . . the crux of the issue."[21] The point of the EEOC challenge, however, was never sameness but the irrelevance of categorical differences.

The opposition men/women, as Rosenberg employed it, asserted the incomparability of the sexes, and although history and socialization were the explanatory factors, these resonated with categorical distinctions inferred from the facts of bodily difference. When the opposition men/women is invoked, as it was in the Sears case, it refers a specific issue (the small statistical discrepancy between women and men hired for commission sales jobs) back to a general principle (the "fundamental" differences between women and men). The differences within each group that might apply to this particular situation—the fact, for example, that some women might choose "aggressive" or "risk-taking" jobs or that some women might prefer high- to low-paying positions—were excluded by definition in the antithesis between the groups. The irony is, of course, that the statistical case required only a small percentage of women's behaviors to be explained. Yet the historical testimony argued categorically about "women." It thus became impossible to argue (as EEOC and Kessler-Harris tried to) that within the female category, women typically exhibit and participate in all sorts of "male" behaviors, that socialization is a complex process that does not yield uniform choices. To make the argument would have required a direct attack on categorical thinking about gender. For the generalized opposition male/female serves to obscure the differences among women in behavior, character, desire, subjectivity, sexuality, gender identification, and historical experience. In the light of Rosenberg's insistence on the primacy of sexual difference, Kessler-Harris's insistence on the specificity (and historically variable aspect) of women's actions could be dismissed as an unreasonable and trivial claim.

The alternative to the binary construction of sexual difference is not sameness, identity, or androgyny. By subsuming women into a general "human" identity, we lose the specificity of female diversity and women's experiences; we are back, in other words, to the days when "Man's" story was supposed to be everyone's story, when women were "hidden from history," when the feminine served as the negative counterpoint, the "Other," for the construction of positive masculine identity. It is not sameness *or* identity between women and men that we want to claim but a more complicated historically variable diversity than is permitted by the opposition male/female, a diversity that is also differently expressed for different purposes in different contexts. In effect, the duality this opposition creates draws one line of difference, invests it with biological explanations, and then treats each side of the opposition as a unitary phenomenon. Everything in each category (male/female) is assumed to be the same; hence, differences within either category are suppressed. In contrast, our goal is to see not only differences between the sexes but also the way these work to repress differences within gender groups. The sameness constructed on each side of the binary opposition hides the multiple play of differences and maintains their irrelevance and invisibility.

Placing equality and difference in antithetical relationship has, then, a double effect. It denies the way in which difference has long figured in political notions of equality and it suggests that sameness is the only ground on which equality can be claimed. It thus puts feminists in an impossible position, for as long as we argue within the terms of a discourse set up by this opposition we grant the current conservative premise that because women cannot be identical to men in all respects, we cannot expect to be equal to them. The only alternative, it seems to me, is to refuse to oppose equality to difference and insist continually on differences—differences as the condition of individual and collective identities, differences as the constant challenge to the fixing of those identities, history as the repeated illustration of the play of differences, differences as the very meaning of equality itself.

Alice Kessler-Harris's experience in the Sears case shows, however, that the assertion of differences in the face of gender categories is not a sufficient strategy. What is required in addition is an analysis of fixed

gender categories as normative statements that organize cultural understandings of sexual difference. This means that we must open to scrutiny
the terms women and men as they are used to define one another in particular contexts—workplaces, for example. The history of women's work
needs to be retold from this perspective as part of the story of the creation
of a gendered workforce. In the nineteenth century, for example, certain
concepts of male skill rested on a contrast with female labor (by definition unskilled). The organization and reorganization of work processes
was accomplished by reference to the gender attributes of workers,
rather than to issues of training, education, or social class. And wage differentials between the sexes were attributed to fundamentally different
family roles that preceded (rather than followed from) employment
arrangements. In all these processes the meaning of "worker" was established through a contrast between the presumably natural qualities of
women and men. If we write the history of women's work by gathering
data that describes the activities, needs, interests, and culture of "women
workers," we leave in place the naturalized contrast and reify a fixed categorical difference between women and men. We start the story, in other
words, too late, by uncritically accepting a gendered category (the
"woman worker") that itself needs investigation because its meaning is
relative to its history.

If in our histories we relativize the categories woman and man, it
means, of course, that we must also recognize the contingent and specific
nature of our political claims. Political strategies then will rest on analyses of the utility of certain arguments in certain discursive contexts, without, however, invoking absolute qualities for women or men. There are
moments when it makes sense for mothers to demand consideration for
their social role, and contexts within which motherhood is irrelevant to
women's behavior; but to maintain that womanhood is motherhood is to
obscure the differences that make choice possible. There are moments
when it makes sense to demand a reevaluation of the status of what has
been socially constructed as women's work ("comparable worth" strategies are the current example) and contexts within which it makes much
more sense to prepare women for entry into "nontraditional" jobs. But to
maintain that femininity predisposes women to certain (nurturing) jobs
or (collaborative) styles of work is to naturalize complex economic and
social processes and, once again, to obscure the differences that have
characterized women's occupational histories. An insistence on differences undercuts the tendency to absolutist, and in the case of sexual difference, essentialist categories. It does not deny the existence of gender
difference, but it does suggest that its meanings are always relative to
particular constructions in specified contexts. In contrast, absolutist categorizations of difference end up always enforcing normative rules.

Equality requires the recognition + inclusion of Differences.

It is surely not easy to formulate a "deconstructive" political strategy in the face of powerful tendencies that construct the world in binary terms. Yet there seems to me no other choice. Perhaps as we learn to think this way solutions will become more readily apparent. Perhaps the theoretical and historical work we do can prepare the ground. Certainly we can take heart from the history of feminism, which is full of illustrations of refusals of simple dichotomies and attempts instead to demonstrate that equality requires the recognition and inclusion of differences. Indeed, one way historians could contribute to a genuine rethinking of these concepts is to stop writing the history of feminisms as a story of oscillations between demands for equality and affirmations of difference. This approach inadvertently strengthens the hold of the binary construction, establishing it as inevitable by giving it a long history. When looked at closely, in fact, the historical arguments of feminists do not usually fall into these neat compartments; they are instead attempts to reconcile theories of equal rights with cultural concepts of sexual difference, to question the validity of normative constructions of gender in the light of the existence of behaviors and qualities that contradict the rules, to point up rather than resolve conditions of contradiction, to articulate a political identity for women without conforming to existing stereotypes about them.

In histories of feminism and in feminist political strategies there needs to be at once attention to the operations of difference and an insistence on differences, but not a simple substitution of multiple for binary difference for it is not a happy pluralism we ought to invoke. The resolution of the "difference dilemma" comes neither from ignoring nor embracing difference as it is normatively constituted. Instead, it seems to me that the critical feminist position must always involve *two* moves. The first is the systematic criticism of the operations of categorical difference, the exposure of the kinds of exclusions and inclusions—the hierarchies—it constructs, and a refusal of their ultimate "truth." A refusal, however, not in the name of an equality that implies sameness or identity, but rather (and this is the second move) in the name of an equality that rests on differences—differences that confound, disrupt, and render ambiguous the meaning of any fixed binary opposition. To do anything else is to buy into the political argument that sameness is a requirement for equality, an untenable position for feminists (and historians) who know that power is constructed on and so must be challenged from the ground of difference.

Notes

I am extremely grateful to William Connolly, Sanford Levinson, Andrew Pickering, Barbara Herrnstein Smith, and Elizabeth Weed for their thoughtful suggestions, which sharpened and improved my argument.

1. On the problem of appropriating poststructuralism for feminism, see Biddy Martin, "Feminism, Criticism, Foucault," *New German Critique* 27 (Fall 1982): 3–30.

2. Joan W. Scott, "Gender: A Useful Category of Historical Analysis," *American Historical Review* 91 (December 1986); 1053–75; Donna Haraway, "A Manifesto for Cyborgs: Science, Technology, and Socialist Feminism in the 1980s," *Socialist Review* 15 (March-April 1985): 65–107.

3. Examples of Michel Foucault's work include *The Archaeology of Knowledge* (New York: Harper & Row, 1976), *The History of Sexuality*, vol. 1, *An Introduction* (New York: Vintage, 1980), and *Power/Knowledge: Selected Interviews and Other Writings, 1972–1977* (New York Pantheon, 1980). See also Hubert L. Dreyfus and Paul Rabinow, *Michel Foucault: Beyond Structuralism and Hermeneutics* (Chicago: University of Chicago Press, 1983).

4. The Australian philosopher Elizabeth Gross puts it this way: "What Derrida attempts to show is that within these binary couples, the primary or dominant term derives its privilege from a curtailment or suppression of its opposite. Sameness or identity, presence, speech, the origin, mind, etc. are all privileged in relation to their opposites, which are regarded as debased, impure variations of the primary term. Difference, for example, is the lack of identity or sameness; absence is the lack of presence; writing is the supplement of speech, and so on." See her "Derrida, Irigaray, and Deconstruction," *Leftwright, Intervention* (Sydney, Australia): 20 (1986): 73. See also Jacques Derrida, *Of Grammatology* (Baltimore: Johns Hopkins University Press, 1976); and Jonathan Culler, *On Deconstruction: Theory and Criticism After Structuralism* (Ithaca: Cornell University Press, 1982).

5. Again, to cite Elizabeth Gross's formulation: "Taken together, reversal and its useful displacement show the necessary but unfounded function of these terms in Western thought. One must both reverse the dichotomy and the values attached to the two terms, as well as displace the excluded term, placing it beyond its oppositional role, as the internal condition of the dominant term. This move makes clear the violence of the hierarchy and the debt the dominant term owes to the subordinate one. It also demonstrates that there are other ways of conceiving these terms than dichotomously. If these terms were only or necessarily dichotomies, the process of displacement would not be possible. Although historically necessary, the terms are not logically necessary." See Gross, 74.

6. Barbara Johnson, *The Critical Difference: Essays in the Contemporary Rhetoric of Reading* (Baltimore: Johns Hopkins University Press, 1980): x–xi.

7. Most recently, attention has been focused on the issue of pregnancy benefits. See, for example, Lucina M. Finley, "Transcending Equality Theory: A Way Out of the Maternity and the Workplace Debate," *Columbia Law Review* 86 (October 1986): 1118–83. See Sylvia A. Law, "Rethinking Sex and the Constitution," *University of Pennsylvania Law Review* 132 (June 1984): 955–1040.

8. Recently, historians have begun to cast feminist history in terms of the equality-versus-difference debate. Rather than accept it as an accurate characterization of antithetical positions, however, I think we need to look more closely at how feminists used these arguments. A close reading of nineteenth-century French feminist texts, for example, leads me to conclude that they are far less easily categorized into difference or equality positions than one would have sup-

posed. I think it is a mistake for feminist historians to write this debate uncritically into history for it reifies an "antithesis" that may not actually have existed. We need instead to "deconstruct" feminist arguments and read them in their discursive contexts, all as explorations of "the difference dilemma."

9. Ruth Milkman, "Women's History and the Sears Case," *Feminist Studies* 12 (Summer 1986): 394–95. In my discussion of the Sears case, I have drawn heavily on this careful and intelligent article, the best so far of the many that have been written on the subject.

10. Martha Minow, "Learning to Live with the Dilemma of Difference: Bilingual and Special Education," *Law and Contemporary Problems* 48, no. 2 (1984): 157–211; quotation is from p. 160; see also pp. 202–6.

11. There is a difference, it seems to me, between arguing that women and men have identical interests and arguing that one should presume such identity in all aspects of the hiring process. The second position is the only strategic way of not building into the hiring process prejudice or the wrong presumptions about differences of interest.

12. Rosenberg's "Offer of Proof" and Kessler-Harris's "Written Testimony" appeared in *Signs* 11 (Summer 1986): 757–79. The "Written Rebuttal Testimony of Dr. Rosalind Rosenberg" is part of the official transcript of the case. U.S. District Court for the Northern District of Illinois, Eastern Division, *EEOC vs Sears*, Civil Action No. 79-C-4373. (I am grateful to Sanford Levinson for sharing the trial documents with me and for our many conversations about them.)

13. Appendix to the "Written Rebuttal Testimony of Dr. Rosalind Rosenberg," 1–12.

14. On the limits imposed by courtrooms and the pitfalls expert witnesses may encounter, see Nadine Taub, "Thinking About Testifying," *Perspectives* (American Historical Association Newsletter) 24 (November 1986): 10–11.

15. On this point, Taub asks a useful question: "Is there a danger in discrimination cases that historical or other expert testimony not grounded in the particular facts of the case will reinforce the idea that it is acceptable to make generalizations about particular groups?" (p. 11).

16. See the cross-examination of Kessler-Harris, *EEOC vs Sears*, 16376–619.

17. The Rosenberg "Rebuttal" is particularly vehement on this question: "This assumption that all employers discriminate is prominent in her (Kessler-Harris's) work. . . . In a 1979 article, she wrote hopefully that women harbor values, attitudes, and behavior patterns potentially subversive to capitalism" (p. 11). "There are, of course, documented instances of employers limiting the opportunities of women. But the fact that some employers have discriminated does not prove that all do" (p. 19). The rebuttal raises another issue about the political and ideological limits of a courtroom or, perhaps it is better to say, about the way the courtroom reproduces dominant ideologies. The general notion that employers discriminate was unacceptable (but the general notion that women prefer certain jobs was not). This unacceptability was underscored by linking it to subversion and Marxism, positions intolerable in U.S. political discourse. Rosenberg's innuendos attempted to discredit Kessler-Harris on two counts—first, by suggesting she was making a ridiculous generalization and, second, by suggesting that only people outside acceptable politics could even entertain that generalization.

18. Milkman, 391.

19. Naomi Schor, "Reading Double: Sand's Difference," in *The Poetics of Gender*, ed. Nancy K. Miller (New York: Columbia University Press, 1986), 256.

20. Michael Walzer, *Spheres of Justice: A Defense of Pluralism and Equality* (New York: Basic Books, 1983), xii. See also Minow, 202–3.

21. Milkman, 384.

PART THREE
Gender, Race, and Class

Articulating the relationships among gender, race, and class has been at the center of a great deal of feminist theorizing. The three sets of paired articles considered here approach these interrelationships from different perspectives. The first pair centers on issues of gender and race, though class surfaces importantly in the analyses; the second pair focuses on the reproduction of colonial relations that often arose in feminist theorizing about "Third World women"; the third pair offers analyses of the different meanings of gender that emerge for particular groups of women in Third World contexts. Taken together, the six articles encompass a critique of some forms of feminist theorizing that treat "women" as a homogeneous category. They demonstrate, in analyses of site-specific and historically situated contexts, how gender, race, and class are neither parallel nor intersecting, but mutually constitutive.

In two essays relatively free from particular disciplinary preoccupations, feminist legal scholar Patricia J. Williams (Chapter 13) and literary critic Amy Kaminsky (Chapter 14) address the construction of racial meanings through social-historical processes. Williams examines the painful legacy of slavery in her own family; Kaminsky traces the meanings of *raza* in three different periods of exchange among Spain, Spanish America, and the United States. Both authors rely on "stories" as their core texts, though Williams uses an evocative, personal voice to offer autobiographical accounts, and Kaminsky writes in a more detached, impersonal voice but draws on personal fictional and theoretical texts. The authors offer alternate accounts of the construction of "race" by pointing to the powerful influences of macrosocial forces and events as well as of family relationships and family lineage in creating social and personal understandings of race. Both contextualize racial meanings in time and space by showing how they differ in particular historical moments and different places. Williams examines the long echoes and reverberations of a particular set of historical events (associated with U.S. slavery as an institution) and emphasizes the impact of economic relations and actions. In contrast, Kaminsky differentiates the history of Spanish, Spanish American, and U.S. relations into periods (imperial, postcolonial, and expatriate) that have different implications for the formation of the meanings of *raza*. Whereas Williams articulates her own challenges to dominant racial and gender categories, Kaminsky analyzes the challenges created by "expatriate" feminist theorists—that is, Latinas creating new understandings of both gender and race.

Both Williams and Kaminsky show how race and gender mutually define each other, since neither has the same meaning when inflected by the other. For example, Williams explores the cold brutality of whiteness through her powerful image of polar bears, but we discover that image is also powerfully masculine in her closing passage. Kaminsky shows that cultural beliefs about gender differences were used in the past to naturalize emergent "racial fictions" and argues that the same function is served today by the government's census categories. These two quite different essays are similar, too, because they not only articulate theoretical meanings of racial categories and their operation in texts but both also recognize the psychological implications of those categories for individuals. Williams writes, "I must assume, not just as history, but as an ongoing psychological force, that, in the eyes of white culture, irrationality, lack of control, and ugliness signify not just the whole slave personality, not just the whole black personality, but *me*" [emphasis added]. Kaminsky cites lesbian Latina feminists who avoid "complicity with any racializing project that demands [their] sexual complicity. . . . [They] resist the smoothing out of difference . . . [because they] find strength in their own multiplicity as they engage in struggle, within and with the culture."

The next two essays address the dilemmas of the Western feminist academic project vis-à-vis non-Western women and the dilemma of the Westernized non-Western feminist academic (as potentially complicit with colonialism). They articulate limitations of feminist theory and feminist scholarship generally in describing or analyzing the situation of women outside "the West." Both essays identify part of the problem in the same homogenizing, universalizing impulses in feminist theory that posed difficulties in articulating differences among U.S. and Western women (e.g., by race, class, and sexuality). But they also locate part of the problem in the association of Western feminism with a liberal and imperialist agenda. They call for changes in feminist theorizing that would make it both less oppressive and more useful, better able to address the situatedness of women in the Third World with attention to historical specificity and to differences among women in those settings.

Marnia Lazreg (Chapter 15) points to the parallels between traditional social science discourse that U.S. or Western feminists have critiqued and feminist discourse about women in the Middle East, showing that "women in Algeria (or in any other part of the Third World) are dealt with precisely in the ways with which academic feminists do not wish to be dealt." Some of the intellectual practices Lazreg points to are quite particular to scholarship on the Middle East (e.g., demonization of Islam, equation of the situation of women with their religion, exclusive focus on veiling), whereas others are more generally applicable (e.g., the tendency to homogenize as "Middle Eastern" women from and within at least twenty separate countries).

Literary critic Rey Chow (Chapter 16) is similarly critical of many uses of feminist theory for understanding women in China. Beginning with the apparent irrelevance of gender to an analysis of the 1989 Tiananmen Square uprising, Chow calls for an approach that recognizes variation in the centrality or salience of gender to a particular situation. She argues that events experienced by the Chinese population as ethnic trauma are mere spectacle for Western observers. At the same time, she views Western feminist theory as too blunt an instrument for the long and varied historical circumstances of women and China, circumstances in which women frequently disappear into a "degendered" traditional China. Finally, by comparing representations of white women in *King Kong* and *Gorillas in the Mist*, she defines an impulse (she associates with the figure of Dian Fossey in the latter film) that requires that the "wild" stay "alive" in its original habitat, rather than permitting it to change, to become "more civilized," or to speak for itself. Both Chow and Lazreg speak from complex personal backgrounds and identities, and both argue for a more truly "postcolonial" feminist theory and for less institutionalized discourse and more talk in different voices.

The last two essays in Part Three represent (indirectly) responses to the arguments made by Lazreg and Chow and take up themes expressed by Williams and Kaminsky. Both essays begin by assuming that gender is defined by power relations and has implications for personal identity. Similarly, both refuse the opposition of active/passive and victim/oppressor, asserting instead the simultaneous operation of both in most actions and most persons. These two essays are different from the other four in this part in that both are empirical studies involving field research and participant observation; they examine theoretical issues not by reference to autobiographical narratives, fiction, or other theoretical texts but through analysis of gendered practices and experiences of contemporary women. Both articles focus on women in Third World countries (Egypt and Mexico), and both focus on the construction of gendered meanings in the context of the work lives of lower-middle- or working-class women. In this way both essays foreground the importance of class structures in shaping women's experiences, without adopting a comparative "class differences" empirical approach. In fact, both essays aim to uncover variations in the meanings of gender within a single class and ethnicity. As sociologist Leslie Salzinger (Chapter 17) spells out, "Poststructuralist feminist theorists have argued that gender is a discursive construction and emphasized its variable content. [This research] seeks to ground and specify these assertions." In this way, these two essays may be seen as seeking to address precisely the criticisms Lazreg and Chow leveled at earlier feminist scholars.

Salzinger uses a participant observer methodology and a comparative strategy to identify differences among women, as a function of the social structures (particular workplaces) they inhabit. She identifies the different degree of centrality of gender in three workplaces, as well as the different valences of gendered meanings (with femininity highly valued in one but much less so in the others) and the different content of gender (for example, with femininity deeply sexualized in one and not in the others). Although Salzinger's strategy is to uncover the particular meanings of gender within particular workplaces, she also recognizes the dominant cultural meanings of gender within which these differences exist. Finally, she sees women as sometimes partly participating in the struggle to define gendered meanings and also as the object of social definitions they do not control.

Political scientist Arlene Elowe MacLeod (Chapter 18) uses a slightly different research strategy. Though she engaged in a participant observation study of women in twenty-eight households in Cairo, the material for this essay is drawn from more focused interviews with twenty-five younger women from those households and emphasizes work and the "new veiling" movement. More than Salzinger, but like Lazreg and Chow, MacLeod foregrounds her own complex ethnic identity as a factor in the research. She analyzes the women's accounts of what the new veiling means to them as expressing contradictory and multiple meanings, which she summarizes with the notion of "accommodating protest." She recognizes that the new veiling means different things to different women and argues against seeing it as either "traditional" or "feminist." Moreover, she situates its different meanings within class, situational (e.g., private versus public, home versus work), and historical context. Finally, MacLeod notes the importance of the different meanings of their veiling actions to the women themselves (e.g., as keeping them safer from sexual harassment) and to observers of the women (as signaling their seriousness).

It is interesting that both essays analyze features of dress as carrying gender meanings. Whereas MacLeod's primary goal is to examine one aspect of dress, Salzinger uncovers the importance of clothing in the three workplaces she studied by noticing the extreme differences both in the actual dress and in the gendered implications of it. Despite the very different cultural locations of the two studies, both find that "swathing" women's bodies (with veils or with smocks and caps) not only keeps the women literally "under wraps" but also is felt to lessen the salience of gender in the workplace. Women and men are cited in both studies as viewing the concealment of women's bodies as facilitating a smoothly operating, nonsexualized workplace. In this way these articles contribute to our understanding of the importance of dress to definitions of gender and of gender to definitions of the workplace.

13 On Being the Object of Property

PATRICIA J. WILLIAMS

On Being Invisible

Reflections

For some time I have been writing about my great-great-grandmother. I have considered the significance of her history and that of slavery from a variety of viewpoints on a variety of occasions: in every speech, in every conversation, even in my commercial transactions class. I have talked so much about her that I finally had to ask myself what it was I was looking for in this dogged pursuit of family history. Was I being merely indulgent, looking for roots in the pursuit of some genetic heraldry, seeking the inheritance of being special, different, unique in all that primogeniture hath wrought?

I decided that my search was based in the utility of such a quest, not mere indulgence, but a recapturing of that which had escaped historical scrutiny, which had been overlooked and underseen. I, like so many blacks, have been trying to pin myself down in history, place myself in the stream of time as significant, evolved, present in the past, continuing into the future. To be without documentation is too unsustaining, too spontaneously ahistorical, too dangerously malleable in the hands of those who would rewrite not merely the past but my future as well. So I have been picking through the ruins for my roots.

What I know of my mother's side of the family begins with my great-great-grandmother. Her name was Sophie and she lived in Tennessee. In 1850, she was about twelve years old. I know that she was purchased when she was eleven by a white lawyer named Austin Miller and was immediately impregnated by him. She gave birth to my great-grandmother Mary, who was taken away from her to be raised as a house servant.[1] I know nothing more of Sophie (she was, after all, a black single mother—in today's terms—suffering the anonymity of yet another statistical teenage pregnancy). While I don't remember what I was told about Austin Miller before I decided to go to law school, I do remember that just before my first day of class, my mother said, in a voice full of secretive re-assurance, "The Millers were lawyers, so you have it in your blood."[2]

When my mother told me that I had nothing to fear in law school, that law was "in my blood," she meant it in a very complex sense. First and foremost, she meant it defiantly; she meant that no one should make me feel inferior because someone else's father was a judge. She wanted me to reclaim that part of my heritage from which I had been disinherited, and she wanted me to use it as a source of strength and self-confidence. At the same time, she was asking me to claim a part of myself that was the dis-possessor of another part of myself; she was asking me to deny that dis-enfranchised little black girl of myself that felt powerless, vulnerable and, moreover, rightly felt so.

In somewhat the same vein, Mother was asking me not to look to her as a role model. She was devaluing that part of herself that was not Harvard and refocusing my vision to that part of herself that was hard-edged, pro-ficient, and Western. She hid the lonely, black, defiled-female part of her-self and pushed me forward as the projection of a competent self, a cool rather than despairing self, a masculine rather than a feminine self.

I took this secret of my blood into the Harvard milieu with both the pride and the shame with which my mother had passed it along to me. I found myself in the situation described by Marguerite Duras, in her novel *The Lover:* "We're united in a fundamental shame at having to live. It's here we are at the heart of our common fate, the fact that [we] are our mother's children, the children of a candid creature murdered by society. We're on the side of society which has reduced her to despair. Because of what's been done to our mother, so amiable, so trusting, we hate life, we hate ourselves."[3]

Reclaiming that from which one has been disinherited is a good thing. Self-possession in the full sense of that expression is the companion to self-knowledge. Yet claiming for myself a heritage the weft of whose gen-esis is my own disinheritance is a profoundly troubling paradox.

Images

A friend of mine practices law in rural Florida. His office is in Belle Glade, an extremely depressed area where the sugar industry reigns supreme, where blacks live pretty much as they did in slavery times, in dormitories called slave ships. They are penniless and illiterate and have both a high birth rate and a high death rate.

My friend told me about a client of his, a fifteen-year-old young woman pregnant with her third child, who came seeking advice because her mother had advised a hysterectomy—not even a tubal ligation—as a means of birth control. The young woman's mother, in turn, had been advised of the propriety of such a course in her own case by a white doctor some years before. Listening to this, I was reminded of a case I worked on when I was working for the Western Center on Law and Poverty about eight years ago. Ten black Hispanic women had been sterilized by the University of Southern California—Los Angeles County General Medical Center, allegedly without proper consent, and in most instances without even their knowledge.[4] Most of them found out what had been done to them upon inquiry, after a much-publicized news story in which an intern charged that the chief of obstetrics at the hospital pursued a policy of recommending Caesarian delivery and simultaneous sterilization for any pregnant woman with three or more children and who was on welfare. In the course of researching the appeal in that case, I remember learning that one-quarter of all Navajo women of childbearing age—literally all those of childbearing age ever admitted to a hospital—had been sterilized.[5]

As I reflected on all this, I realized that one of the things passed on from slavery, which continues in the oppression of people of color, is a belief structure rooted in a concept of black (or brown, or red) anti-will, the antithetical embodiment of pure will. We live in a society in which the closest equivalent of nobility is the display of unremittingly controlled will-fulness. To be perceived as unremittingly will-less is to be imbued with an almost lethal trait.

Many scholars have explained this phenomenon in terms of total and infantilizing interdependency of dominant and oppressed.[6] Consider, for example, Mark Tushnet's distinction between slave law's totalistic view of personality and the bourgeois "pure will" theory of personality: "Social relations in slave society rest upon the interaction of owner with slave; the owner, having total domination over the slave. In contrast, bourgeois social relations rest upon the paradigmatic instance of market relations, the purchase by a capitalist of a worker's labor power; that transaction implicates only a part of the worker's personality. Slave relations are total, engaging the master and slave in exchanges in which each must take account of the entire range of belief, feeling, and interest embodied by the other; bourgeois social relations are partial, requiring only that participants in a market evaluate their general productive characteristics without regard to aspects of personality unrelated to production."[7]

Although such an analysis is not objectionable in some general sense, the description of master-slave relations as "total" is, to me, quite troubling. Such a choice of words reflects and accepts—at a very subtle level, perhaps—a historical rationalization that whites had to, could do, and did do everything for these simple, above-animal subhumans. It is a choice of vocabulary that fails to acknowledge blacks as having needs beyond those that even the most "humane" or "sentimental" white slave-master could provide.[8] In trying to describe the provisional aspect of slave law, I would choose words that revealed its structure as rooted in a concept of, again, black anti-will, the polar opposite of pure will. I would characterize the treatment of blacks by whites in whites' law as defining blacks as those who had no will. I would characterize that treatment not as total interdependency, but as a relation in which partializing judgments, employing partializing standards of humanity, impose generalized inadequacy on a race: if pure will or total control equals the perfect white person, then impure will and total lack of control equals the perfect black man or woman. Therefore, to define slave law as comprehending a "total" view of personality implicitly accepts that the provision of food, shelter, and clothing (again assuming the very best of circumstances) is the whole requirement of humanity. It assumes also either that psychic care was provided by slave owners (as though a slave or an owned psyche could ever be reconciled with mental health) or that psyche is not a significant part of a whole human.

Market theory indeed focuses attention away from the full range of human potential in its pursuit of a divinely willed, invisibly handed economic actor. Master-slave relations, however, focused attention away from the full range of black human potential in a somewhat different way: it pursued a vision of blacks as simple-minded, strong-bodied economic actants.[9] Thus, while blacks had an indisputable generative force in the marketplace, their presence could not be called activity; they had no active role in the market. To say, therefore, that "market relations disregard the peculiarities of individuals, whereas slave relations rest on the mutual recognition of the humanity of master and slave"[10] (no matter how dialectical or abstracted a definition of humanity one adopts) is to posit an inaccurate equation: if "disregard for the peculiarities of individuals" and "mutual recognition of humanity" are polarized by a "whereas," then somehow regard for peculiarities of individuals must equal recognition of humanity. In the context of slavery this equation mistakes whites' overzealous and oppressive obsession with projected specific peculiarities of blacks for actual holistic regard for the individual. It overlooks the fact that most definitions of humanity require something beyond mere biological sustenance, some healthy measure of autonomy beyond that of which slavery could institutionally or otherwise conceive. Furthermore, it overlooks the fact that both slave and bourgeois systems regarded certain attributes as important and disregarded certain others, and that such regard and disregard can occur in the same glance, like the wearing of horseblinders to focus attention simultaneously toward and

away from. The experiential blinders of market actor and slave are focused in different directions, yet the partializing ideologies of each makes
the act of not seeing an unconscious, alienating component of seeing.
Restoring a unified social vision will, I think, require broader and more
scattered resolutions than the simple symmetry of ideological bipolarity.

Thus, it is important to undo whatever words obscure the fact that
slave law was at least as fragmenting and fragmented as the bourgeois
worldview—in a way that has persisted to this day, cutting across all ideological boundaries. As "pure will" signifies the whole bourgeois personality in the bourgeois worldview, so wisdom, control, and aesthetic
beauty signify the whole white personality in slave law. The former and
the latter, the slavemaster and the burgermeister, are not so very different
when expressed in those terms. The reconciling difference is that in slave
law the emphasis is really on the inverse rationale: that irrationality, lack
of control, and ugliness signify the whole slave personality. "Total" interdependence is at best a polite way of rationalizing such personality
splintering; it creates a bizarre sort of yin-yang from the dross of an oppressive schizophrenia of biblical dimension. I would just call it schizophrenic, with all the baggage that that connotes. That is what sounds
right to me. Truly total relationships (as opposed to totalitarianism) call
up images of whole people dependent on whole people; an interdependence that is both providing and laissez-faire at the same time. Neither
the historical inheritance of slave law nor so-called bourgeois law meets
that definition.

None of this, perhaps, is particularly new. Nevertheless, as precedent
to anything I do as a lawyer, the greatest challenge is to allow the full
truth of partializing social constructions to be felt for their overwhelming
reality—reality that otherwise I might rationally try to avoid facing. In
my search for roots, I must assume, not just as history but as an ongoing
psychological force, that, in the eyes of white culture, irrationality, lack of
control, and ugliness signify not just the whole slave personality, not just
the whole black personality, but me.

Vision

Reflecting on my roots makes me think again and again of the young
woman in Belle Glade, Florida. She told the story of her impending sterilization, according to my friend, while keeping her eyes on the ground at
all times. My friend, who is white, asked why she wouldn't look up,
speak with him eye to eye. The young woman answered that she didn't
like white people seeing inside her.

My friend's story made me think of my own childhood and adolescence: my parents were always telling me to look up at the world; to look

straight at people, particularly white people; not to let them stare me down; to hold my ground; to insist on the right to my presence no matter what. They told me that in this culture you have to look people in the eye because that's how you tell them you're their equal. My friend's story also reminded me how very difficult I had found that looking-back to be. What was hardest was not just that white people saw me, as my friend's client put it, but that they looked through me, that they treated me as though I were transparent.

By itself, seeing into me would be to see my substance, my anger, my vulnerability, and my wild raging despair—and that alone is hard enough to show, to share. But to uncover it and have it devalued by ignore-ance, to hold it up bravely in the organ of my eyes and to have it greeted by an impassive stare that passes right through all that which is me, an impassive stare that moves on and attaches itself to my left ear-lobe or to the dust caught in the rusty vertical geysers of my wiry hair or to the breadth of my freckled brown nose—this is deeply humiliating. It re-wounds, relives the early childhood anguish of uncensored seeing, the fullness of vision that is the permanent turning-away point for most blacks.

The cold game of equality-staring makes me feel like a thin sheet of glass: white people see all the worlds beyond me but not me. They come trotting at me with force and speed; they do not see me. I could force my presence, the real me contained in those eyes, upon them, but I would be smashed in the process. If I deflect, if I move out of the way, they will never know I existed.

Marguerite Duras, again in *The Lover*, places the heroine in relation to her family. "Every day we try to kill one another, to kill. Not only do we not talk to one another, we don't even look at one another. When you're being looked at you can't look. To look is to feel curious, to be interested, to lower yourself."[11]

To look is also to make myself vulnerable; yet not to look is to neutralize the part of myself which is vulnerable. I look in order to see, and so I must look. Without that directness of vision, I am afraid I will will my own blindness, disinherit my own creativity, and sterilize my own perspective of its embattled, passionate insight.

On Ardor

The Child

One Saturday afternoon not long ago, I sat among a litter of family photographs telling a South African friend about Marjorie, my godmother and my mother's cousin. She was given away by her light-skinned mother when she was only six. She was given to my grandmother and my great-aunts to be raised among her darker-skinned cousins, for Marjorie was very dark indeed. Her mother left the family to "pass," to marry a white man—Uncle Frederick, we called him with trepidatious presumption yet without his ever knowing of our existence—an heir to a meat-packing fortune. When Uncle Frederick died thirty years later and the fortune was lost, Marjorie's mother rejoined the race, as the royalty of resentful fascination—Lady Bountiful, my sister called her—to regale us with tales of gracious upper-class living.

My friend said that my story reminded him of a case in which a swarthy, crisp-haired child was born, in Durban, to white parents. The Afrikaner government quickly intervened, removed the child from its birth home, and placed it to be raised with a "more suitable," browner family.

When my friend and I had shared these stories, we grew embarrassed somehow, and our conversation trickled away into a discussion of laissez-faire economics and governmental interventionism. Our words became a clear line, a railroad upon which all other ideas and events were tied down and sacrificed.

The Market

As a teacher of commercial transactions, one of the things that has always impressed me most about the law of contract is a certain deadening power it exercises by reducing the parties to the passive. It constrains the lively involvement of its signatories by positioning enforcement in such a way that parties find themselves in a passive relationship to a document: it is the contract that governs, that "does" everything, that absorbs all responsibility and deflects all other recourse.

Contract law reduces life to fairy tale. The four corners of the agreement become parent. Performance is the equivalent of obedience to the parent. Obedience is dutifully passive. Passivity is valued as good contract-socialized behavior; activity is caged in retrospective hypotheses about states of mind at the magic moment of contracting. Individuals are judged by the contract unfolding rather than by the actors acting autonomously. Nonperformance is disobedience; disobedience is active; activity becomes evil in contrast to the childlike passivity of contract conformity.

One of the most powerful examples of all this is the case of Mary Beth Whitehead, mother of Sara—of so-called Baby M. Ms. Whitehead became a vividly original actor *after* the creation of her contract with William Stern; unfortunately for her, there can be no greater civil sin. It was in this upside-down context, in the picaresque unboundedness of breachor, that her energetic grief became hysteria and her passionate creativity was funneled, whorled, and reconstructed as highly impermissible. Mary Beth Whitehead thus emerged as the evil stepsister who deserved nothing.

Some time ago, Charles Reich visited a class of mine.[12] He discussed with my students a proposal for a new form of bargain by which emotional "items"—such as praise, flattery, acting happy or sad—might be contracted for explicitly. One student, not alone in her sentiment, said, "Oh, but then you'll just feel obligated." Only the week before, however (when we were discussing the contract which posited that Ms. Whitehead "will not form or attempt to form a parent-child relationship with any child or children"), this same student had insisted that Ms. Whitehead must give up her child, because she had *said* she would: "She was obligated!" I was confounded by the degree to which what the student took to be self-evident, inalienable gut reactions could be governed by illusions of passive conventionality and form.

It was that incident, moreover, that gave me insight into how Judge Harvey Sorkow, of New Jersey Superior Court, could conclude that the contract that purported to terminate Ms. Whitehead's parental rights was "not illusory."[13]

(As background, I should say that I think that, within the framework of contract law itself, the agreement between Ms. Whitehead and Mr. Stern was clearly illusory.[14] On the one hand, Judge Sorkow's opinion said that Ms. Whitehead was seeking to avoid her *obligations*. In other words, giving up her child became an actual obligation. On the other hand, according to the logic of the judge, this was a service contract, not really a sale of a child; therefore delivering the child to the Sterns was an "obligation" for which there was no consideration, for which Mr. Stern was not paying her.)

Judge Sorkow's finding the contract "not illusory" is suggestive not just of the doctrine by that name, but of illusion in general, and delusion, and the righteousness with which social constructions are conceived, acted on, and delivered up into the realm of the real as "right," while all else is devoured from memory as "wrong." From this perspective, the rhetorical tricks by which Sara Whitehead became Melissa Stern seem very like the heavy-worded legalities by which my great-great-grandmother was pacified and parted from her child. In both situations, the real mother had no say, no power; her powerlessness was imposed by state law that made her and her child helpless in relation to the father. My great-great-grandmother's powerlessness came about as the result of a contract to which she was not a party; Mary Beth Whitehead's powerlessness came about as a result of a contract that she signed at a discrete point of time—yet which, over time, enslaved her. The contract-reality in both instances was no less than magic: it was illusion transformed into not-illusion. Furthermore, it masterfully disguised the brutality of enforced arrangements in which these women's autonomy, their flesh and their blood, were locked away in word vaults, without room to reconsider—*ever*.

In the months since Judge Sorkow's opinion, I have reflected on the similarities of fortune between my own social positioning and that of Sara Melissa Stern Whitehead. I have come to realize that an important part of the complex magic that Judge Sorkow wrote into his opinion was a supposition that it is "natural" for people to want children "like" themselves. What this reasoning raised for me was an issue of what, exactly, constituted this "likeness"? (What would have happened, for example, if Ms. Whitehead had turned out to have been the "passed" descendant of my "failed" godmother Marjorie's mother? What if the child she bore had turned out to be recessively and visibly black? Would the sperm of Mr. Stern have been so powerful as to make this child "his" with the exclusivity that Judge Sorkow originally assigned?) What constitutes, moreover, the collective understanding of "un-likeness"?

These questions turn, perhaps, on not-so-subtle images of which mothers should be bearing which children. Is there not something unseemly, in our society, about the spectacle of a white woman mothering a black child? A white woman giving totally to a black child; a black child totally and demandingly dependent for everything, for sustenance itself, from a white woman. The image of a white woman suckling a black child; the image of a black child sucking for its life from the bosom of a white woman. The utter interdependence of such an image; the selflessness, the merging it implies; the giving up of boundary; the encompassing of other within self; the unbounded generosity, the interconnectedness of such an image. Such a picture says that there is no difference; it places the hope of continuous generation, of immortality of the white self in a little black face.

When Judge Sorkow declared that it was only to be expected that parents would want to breed children "like" themselves, he simultaneously created a legal right to the same. With the creation of such a "right," he encased the children conforming to "likeliness" in protective custody, far from whole ranges of taboo. Taboo about touch and smell and intimacy and boundary. Taboo about ardor, possession, license, equivocation, equanimity, indifference, intolerance, rancor, dispossession, innocence, exile, and candor. Taboo about death. Taboos that amount to death. Death and sacredness, the valuing of body, of self, of other, of remains. The handling lovingly in life, as in life; the question of the intimacy versus the dispassion of death.

In effect, these taboos describe boundaries of valuation. Whether something is inside or outside the marketplace of rights has always been a way of valuing it. When a valued object is located outside the market, it is generally understood to be too "priceless" to be accommodated by ordinary exchange relationships; when, in contrast, the prize is located within the marketplace, all objects outside become "valueless." Traditionally, the Mona Lisa and human life have been the sorts of subjects removed from the fungibility of commodification, as "priceless." Thus when black people were bought and sold as slaves, they were placed beyond the bounds of humanity. And thus, in the twistedness of our brave new world, when blacks have been thrust out of the market and it is white children who are bought and sold, black babies have become "worthless" currency to adoption agents—"surplus" in the salvage heaps of Harlem hospitals.

The Imagination

"Familiar though his name may be to us, the storyteller in his living immediacy is by no means a present force. He has already become something remote from us and something that is getting even more distant. . . . Less and less frequently do we encounter people with the ability to tell a tale properly. . . . It is as if something that seemed inalienable to us, the securest among our possessions, were taken from us: the ability to exchange experiences."[15]

My mother's cousin Marjorie was a storyteller. From time to time I would press her to tell me the details of her youth, and she would tell me instead about a child who wandered into a world of polar bears, who was prayed over by polar bears, and in the end eaten. The child's life was not in vain because the polar bears had been made holy by its suffering. The child had been a test, a message from god for polar bears. In the polar bear universe, she would tell me, the primary object of creation was polar bears, and the rest of the living world was fashioned to serve polar bears. The clouds took their shape from polar bears, trees were designed to give shelter and shade to polar bears, and humans were ideally designed to provide polar bears with meat.[16]

The truth, the truth, I would laughingly insist as we sat in her apartment eating canned fruit and heavy roasts, mashed potatoes, pickles and vanilla pudding, cocoa, Sprite, or tea. What about roots and all that, I coaxed. But the voracity of her amnesia would disclaim and disclaim and disclaim; and she would go on telling me about the polar bears until our plates were full of emptiness and I became large in the space which described her emptiness and I gave in to the emptiness of words.

On Life and Death

Sighing into Space

There are moments in my life when I feel as though a part of me is missing. There are days when I feel so invisible that I can't remember what day of the week it is, when I feel so manipulated that I can't remember my own name, when I feel so lost and angry that I can't speak a civil word to the people who love me best. Those are the times when I catch sight of my reflection in store windows and am surprised to see a whole person looking back. Those are the times when my skin becomes gummy as clay and my nose slides around on my face and my eyes drip down to my chin. I have to close my eyes at such times and remember myself, draw an internal picture that is smooth and whole; when all else fails, I reach for a mirror and stare myself down until the features reassemble themselves like lost sheep.

Two years ago, my godmother Marjorie suffered a massive stroke. As she lay dying, I would come to the hospital to give her her meals. My feeding her who had so often fed me became a complex ritual of mirroring and self-assembly. The physical act of holding the spoon to her lips was not only a rite of nurture and of sacrifice, it was the return of a gift. It was a quiet bowing to the passage of time and the doubling back of all things. The quiet woman who listened to my woes about work and school required now that I bend my head down close to her and listen for mouthed word fragments, sentence crumbs. I bent down to give meaning to her silence, her wandering search for words.

She would eat what I brought to the hospital with relish; she would reject what I brought with a turn of her head. I brought fruit and yogurt, ice cream and vegetable juice. Slowly, over time, she stopped swallowing. The mashed potatoes would sit in her mouth like cotton, the pudding would slip to her chin in slow sad streams. When she lost not only her speech but the power to ingest, they put a tube into her nose and down to her stomach, and I lost even that medium by which to communicate. No longer was there the odd but reassuring communion over taste. No longer was there some echo of comfort in being able to nurture one who nurtured me.

This increment of decay was like a little newborn death. With the tube, she stared up at me with imploring eyes, and I tried to guess what it was that she would like. I read to her aimlessly and in desperation. We entertained each other with the strange embarrassed flickering of our eyes. I told her stories to fill the emptiness, the loneliness, of the white-walled hospital room.

I told her stories about who I had become, about how I had grown up to know all about exchange systems, and theories of contract, and monetary fictions. I spun tales about blue-sky laws and promissory estoppel, the wispy-feathered complexity of undue influence and dark-hearted theories of unconscionability. I told her about market norms and gift economy and the thin razor's edge of the bartering ethic. Once upon a time, I rambled, some neighbors of mine included me in their circle of barter. They were in the habit of exchanging eggs and driving lessons, hand-knit sweaters and computer programming, plumbing and calligraphy. I accepted the generosity of their inclusion with gratitude. At first, I felt that, as a lawyer, I was worthless, that I had no barterable skills and nothing to contribute. What I came to realize with time, however, was that my value to the group was not calculated by the physical items I brought to it. These people included me because they wanted me to be part of their circle, they valued my participation apart from the material things I could offer. So I gave of myself to them, and they gave me fruit cakes and dandelion wine and smoked salmon, and in their giving, their goods became provisions. Cradled in this community whose currency was a relational ethic, my stock in myself soared. My value depended on the glorious intangibility, the eloquent invisibility of my just being *part* of the collective; and in direct response I grew spacious and happy and gentle.

My gentle godmother. The fragility of life; the cold mortuary shelf.

Dispassionate Deaths

The hospital in which my godmother died is now filled to capacity with AIDS patients. One in sixty-one babies born there, as in New York City generally, is infected with AIDS antibodies.[17] Almost all are black or Hispanic. In the Bronx, the rate is one in forty-three.[18] In Central Africa, experts estimate that, of children receiving transfusions for malaria-related anemia, "about 1000 may have been infected with the AIDS virus in each of the last five years."[19] In Congo, 5 percent of the entire population is infected.[20] The *New York Times* reports that "the profile of Congo's population seems to guarantee the continued spread of AIDS."[21]

In the Congolese city of Pointe Noir, "the annual budget of the sole public health hospital is estimated at about $200,000—roughly the amount of money spent in the United States to care for four AIDS patients."[22]

The week in which my godmother died is littered with bad memories. In my journal, I made note of the following:

Good Friday: Phil Donahue has a special program on AIDS. The segues are:

a. from Martha, who weeps at the prospect of not watching her children grow up

b. to Jim, who is not conscious enough to speak just now, who coughs convulsively, who recognizes no one in his family any more

c. to Hugh who, at 85 pounds, thinks he has five years but whose doctor says he has weeks

d. to an advertisement for denture polish ("If you love your Polident Green/then gimmeeya SMILE!")

e. and then one for a plastic surgery salon on Park Avenue ("The only thing that's expensive is our address")

f. and then one for what's coming up on the five o'clock news (Linda Lovelace, of *Deep Throat* fame, "still recovering from a double mastectomy and complications from silicone injections" is being admitted to a New York hospital for a liver transplant)

g. and finally one for the miracle properties of all-purpose house cleaner ("Mr. Cleeean/is the man/behind the shine/is it wet or is it dry?" I note that Mr. Clean, with his gleaming bald head, puffy musculature and fever-bright eyes, looks like he is undergoing radiation therapy). Now back to our show.

h. "We are back now with Martha" (who is crying harder than before, sobbing uncontrollably, each jerking inhalation a deep unearthly groan). Phil says, "Oh honey, I hope we didn't make it worse for you."

Easter Saturday: Over lunch, I watch another funeral. My office windows overlook a graveyard as crowded and still as a rush-hour freeway. As I savor pizza and milk, I notice that one of the mourners is wearing an outfit featured in the window of Bloomingdale's (59th Street store) only since last weekend. This thread of recognition jolts me, and I am drawn to her in sorrow; the details of my own shopping history flash before my eyes as I reflect upon the sober spree that brought her to the rim of this earthly chasm, her slim suede heels sinking into the soft silt of the graveside.

Resurrection Sunday: John D., the bookkeeper where I used to work, died, hit on the head by a stray but forcefully propelled hockey puck. I cried copiously at his memorial service, only to discover, later that afternoon when I saw a black rimmed photograph, that I had been mourning the wrong person. I had cried because the man I *thought* had died is John D. the office messenger, a bitter unfriendly man who treats me with disdain; once I bought an old electric typewriter from him which never worked. Though he promised nothing, I have harbored deep dislike since then; death by hockey puck is only one of the fates I had imagined for him. I washed clean my guilt with buckets of tears at the news of what I thought was his demise.

The man who did die was small, shy, anonymously sweet-featured and innocent. In some odd way I was relieved; no seriously obligatory mourning to be done here. A quiet impassivity settled over me and I forgot my grief.

Holy Communion

A few months after my godmother died, my Great Aunt Jag passed away in Cambridge, at ninety-six the youngest and the last of her siblings, all of whom died at ninety-seven. She collapsed on her way home from the polling place, having gotten in her vote for "yet another Kennedy." Her wake was much like the last family gathering at which I had seen her, two Thanksgivings ago. She was a little hard of hearing then and she stayed on the outer edge of the conversation, brightly, loudly, and randomly asserting enjoyment of her meal. At the wake, cousins, nephews, daughters-in-law, first wives, second husbands, great-grand-nieces gathered round her casket and got acquainted all over again. It was pouring rain outside. The funeral home was dry and warm, faintly spicily cleansmelling; the walls were solid, dark, respectable wood; the floors were cool stone tile. On the door of a room marked "No Admittance" was a sign that reminded workers therein of the reverence with which each body was held by its family and prayed employees handle the remains with similar love and care. Aunt Jag wore yellow chiffon; everyone agreed that laying her out with her glasses on was a nice touch.

Afterward, we all went to Legal Seafoods, her favorite restaurant, and ate many of her favorite foods.

On Candor

Me

I have never been able to determine my horoscope with any degree of accuracy. Born at Boston's now-defunct Lying-In Hospital, I am a Virgo, despite a quite poetic soul. Knowledge of the *hour* of my birth, however, would determine not just my sun sign but my moons and all the more intimate specificities of my destiny. Once upon a time, I sent for my birth certificate, which was retrieved from the oblivion of Massachusetts microfiche. Said document revealed that an infant named Patricia Joyce, born of parents named Williams, was delivered into the world "colored." Since no one thought to put down the hour of my birth, I suppose that I will never know my true fate.

In the meantime, I read what text there is of me.

My name, Patricia, means patrician. Patricias are noble, lofty, elite, exclusively educated, and well mannered despite themselves. I was on the cusp of being Pamela, but my parents knew that such a me would require lawns, estates, and hunting dogs too.

I am also a Williams. Of William, whoever he was: an anonymous white man who owned my father's people and from whom some escaped. That rupture is marked by the dark-mooned mystery of utter silence.

Williams is the second most common surname in the United States; Patricia is *the* most common prename among women born in 1951, the year of my birth.

Them

In the law, rights are islands of empowerment. To be un-righted is to be disempowered, and the line between rights and no rights is most often the line between dominators and oppressors. Rights contain images of power, and manipulating those images, either visually or linguistically, is central in the making and maintenance of rights. In principle, therefore, the more dizzyingly diverse the images that are propagated, the more empowered we will be as a society.

In reality, it was a lovely polar bear afternoon. The gentle force of the earth. A wide wilderness of islands. A conspiracy of polar bears lost in timeless forgetting. A gentleness of polar bears, a fruitfulness of polar bears, a silent black-eyed interest of polar bears, a bristled expectancy of polar bears. With the wisdom of innocence, a child threw stones at the polar bears. Hungry, they rose from their nests, inquisitive, dark-souled, patient with foreboding, fearful in tremendous awakening. The instinctual ferocity of the hunter reflected upon the hunted. Then, proud teeth and warrior claws took innocence for wilderness and raging insubstantiality for tender rabbit breath.

In the newspapers the next day, it was reported that two polar bears in the Brooklyn Zoo mauled to death an eleven-year-old boy who had entered their cage to swim in the moat. The police were called and the bears were killed.[23]

In the public debate that ensued, many levels of meaning emerged. The rhetoric firmly established that the bears were innocent, naturally territorial, unfairly imprisoned, and guilty. The dead child (born into the urban jungle of a black, welfare mother and a Hispanic alcoholic father who had died literally in the gutter only six weeks before) was held to a similarly stern standard. The police were captured, in a widely disseminated photograph,[24] shooting helplessly, desperately, into the cage, through three levels of bars, at a pieta of bears; since this image, conveying much pathos, came nevertheless not in time to save the child, it was generally felt that the bears had died in vain.[25]

In the egalitarianism of exile, pluralists rose up as of one body, with a call to buy more bears, control juvenile delinquency, eliminate all zoos, and confine future police.[26]

In the plenary session of the national meeting of the Law and Society Association, the keynote speaker unpacked the whole incident as a veritable laboratory of emergent rights discourse. Just seeing that these complex levels of meaning exist, she exulted, should advance rights discourse significantly.[27]

At the funeral of the child, the presiding priest pronounced the death of Juan Perez not in vain, since he was saved from growing into "a lifetime of crime." Juan's Hispanic-welfare-black-widow-of-an-alcoholic mother decided then and there to sue.

The Universe Between

How I ended up at Dartmouth College for the summer is too long a story to tell. Anyway, there I was, sharing the town of Hanover, New Hampshire, with about two hundred prepubescent males enrolled in Dartmouth's summer basketball camp, an all-white, very expensive, affirmative action program for the street-deprived.

One fragrant evening, I was walking down East Wheelock Street when I encountered about a hundred of these adolescents, fresh from the courts, wet, lanky, big-footed, with fuzzy yellow crew cuts, loping toward Thayer Hall and food. In platoons of twenty-five or so, they descended upon me, jostling me, smacking me, and pushing me from the sidewalk into the gutter. In a thoughtless instant, I snatched off my brown silk headrag, my flag of African femininity and propriety, my sign of meek and supplicatory place and presentation. I released the armored rage of my short nappy hair (the scalp gleaming bare between the angry wire spikes) and hissed: "Don't I exist for you?! See Me! And deflect, godammit!" (The quaint professionalism of my formal English never allowed the rage in my head to rise so high as to overflow the edges of my text.)

They gave me wide berth. They clearly had no idea, however, that I was talking to them or about them. They skirted me sheepishly, suddenly polite, because they did know, when a crazed black person comes crashing into one's field of vision, that it is impolite to laugh. I stood tall and spoke loudly into their ranks: "I have my rights!" The Dartmouth Summer Basketball Camp raised its collective eyebrows and exhaled, with a certain tested nobility of exhaustion and solidarity.

I pursued my way, manumitted back into silence. I put distance between them and me, gave myself over to polar bear musings. I allowed myself to be watched over by bear spirits. Clean white wind and strong bear smells. The shadowed amnesia; the absence of being; the presence of polar bears. White wilderness of icy meat-eaters heavy with remem-

brance; leaden with undoing; shaggy with the effort of hunting for silence; frozen in a web of intention and intuition. A lunacy of polar bears.
A history of polar bears. A pride of polar bears. A consistency of polar
bears. In those meandering pastel polar bear moments, I found cool fragments of white-fur invisibility. Solid, black-gummed, intent, observant.
Hungry and patient, impassive and exquisitely timed. The brilliant
bursts of exclusive territoriality. A complexity of messages implied in our
being.

Notes

1. For a more detailed account of the family history to this point, see Patricia
Williams, "Grandmother Sophie," *Harvard Blackletter* 3 (1986): 79.

2. Patricia Williams, "Alchemical Notes: Reconstructing Ideals from Deconstructed Rights," *Harvard Civil Rights—Civil Liberties Law Review* 22 (1987): 418.

3. Marguerite Duras, *The Lover* (New York: Harper & Row, 1985), 55.

4. *Madrigal v. Quilligan,* U.S. Court of Appeals, 9th Circuit, Docket no. 78-3187,
October 1979.

5. This was the testimony of one of the witnesses. It is hard to find official con-
firmation for this or any other sterilization statistic involving Native American
women. Official statistics kept by the U.S. Public Health Service, through the
Centers for Disease Control in Atlanta, come from data gathered by the National
Hospital Discharge Survey, which covers neither federal hospitals nor peniten-
tiaries. Services to Native American women living on reservations are provided
almost exclusively by federal hospitals. In addition, the U.S. Public Health Service breaks down its information into only three categories: "White," "Black,"
and "Other." Nevertheless, in 1988, the Women of All Red Nations Collective of
Minneapolis, Minnesota, distributed a fact sheet entitled "Sterilization Studies of
Native American Women," which claimed that as many as 50 percent of all Native American women of childbearing age have been sterilized. According to
"Surgical Sterilization Surveillance, Tubal Sterilization and Hysterectomy in
Women Aged 15–44, 1979–1980," issued by the Centers for Disease Control in
1983, "In 1980, the tubal sterilization rate for black women . . . was 45 percent
greater than that for white women" (7). Furthermore, a study released in 1984 by
the Division of Reproductive Health of the Center for Health Promotion and Education (one of the Centers for Disease Control) found that, as of 1982, 48.8 percent of Puerto Rican women between the ages of 15 and 44 had been sterilized.

6. See, generally, Stanley Elkins, *Slavery* (New York: Grosset & Dunlap, 1963);
Kenneth Stampp, *The Peculiar Institution* (New York: Vintage, 1956); Winthrop
Jordan, *White over Black* (Baltimore: Penguin Books, 1968).

7. Mark Tushnet, *The American Law of Slavery* (Princeton, N.J.: Princeton University Press, 1981), 6. There is danger in the analysis that follows, of appearing to
"pick" on Tushnet. That is not my intention, nor is it to impugn the body of his research, most of which I greatly admire. The choice of this passage for analysis has
more to do with the randomness of my reading habits; the fact that he is one of
the few legal writers to attempt, in the context of slavery, a juxtaposition of politi-

cal theory with psychoanalysis theories of personality; and the fact that he is perceived to be of the political left, which simplifies my analysis in terms of its presumption of sympathy, i.e., that the constructions of thought revealed are socially derived and unconscious rather than idiosyncratic and intentional.

8. In another passage, Tushnet observes: "The court thus demonstrated its appreciation of the ties of sentiment that slavery could generate between master and slave and simultaneously denied that those ties were relevant in the law" (67). What is noteworthy about the reference to "sentiment" is that it assumes that the fact that emotions could grow up between slave and master is itself worth remarking: slightly surprising, slightly commendable for the court to note (i.e., in its "appreciation")—although "simultaneously" with, and presumably in contradistinction to, the court's inability to take official cognizance of the fact. Yet, if one really looks at the ties that bound master and slave, one has to flesh out the description of master-slave with the ties of father-son, father-daughter, half-sister, half-brother, uncle, aunt, cousin, and a variety of de facto foster relationships. And if one starts to see those ties as more often than not intimate family ties, then the terminology "appreciation of . . . sentiment . . . between master and slave" becomes a horrifying mockery of any true sense of family sentiment, which is utterly, utterly lacking. The court's "appreciation," from this enhanced perspective, sounds blindly cruel, sarcastic at best. And to observe that courts suffused in such "appreciation" could simultaneously deny its legal relevance seems not only a truism, it misses the point entirely.

9. "Actants have a kind of phonemic, rather than a phonetic role: they operate on the level of function, rather than content. That is, an actant may embody itself in a particular character (termed an acteur) or it may reside in the function of more than one character in respect of their common role in the story's underlying 'oppositional' structure. In short, the deep structure of the narrative generates and defines its actants at a level beyond that of the story's surface content" (Terence Hawkes, *Structuralism and Semiotics* [Berkeley: University of California Press, 1977], 89).

10. Tushnet, 69.

11. Duras, 54.

12. Charles Reich is author of *The Greening of America* (New York: Random House, 1970) and professor of law at the University of San Francisco Law School.

13. See, generally, In the Matter of Baby "M," A Pseudonym for an Actual Person, Superior Court of New Jersey, Chancery Division, Docket no. FM-25314-86E, March 31, 1987. This decision was appealed, and on February 3, 1988, the New Jersey Supreme Court ruled that surrogate contracts were illegal and against public policy. In addition to the contract issue, however, the appellate court decided the custody issue in favor of the Sterns but granted visitation rights to Mary Beth Whitehead.

14. "An illusory promise is an expression cloaked in promissory terms, but which, upon closer examination, reveals that the promisor has committed himself not at all" (J. Calamari and J. Perillo, *Contracts*, 3d ed. [St. Paul: West Publishing, 1987], 228).

15. Walter Benjamin, "The Storyteller," in *Illuminations*, ed. Hannah Arendt (New York: Schocken, 1969), 83.

16. For an analysis of similar stories, see Richard Levins and Richard Lewontin, *The Dialectical Biologist* (Cambridge, Mass.: Harvard University Press, 1985), 66.

17. B. Lambert, "Study Finds Antibodies for AIDS in 1 in 61 Babies in New York City," *New York Times* (January 13, 1988), sec. A.

18. Ibid.

19. "Study Traces AIDS in African Children," *New York Times* (January 22, 1988), sec. A.

20. J. Brooke, "New Surge of AIDS in Congo May Be an Omen for Africa," *New York Times* (January 22, 1988), sec. A.

21. Ibid.

22. Ibid.

23. J. Barron, "Polar Bears Kill a Child at Prospect Park Zoo," *New York Times* (May 20, 1987), sec. A.

24. *New York Post* (May 22, 1987), p. 1.

25. J. Barron, "Officials Weigh Tighter Security at Zoos in Parks," *New York Times* (May 22, 1987), sec. B.

26. Ibid.

27. Patricia Williams, "The Meaning of Rights" (address to the annual meeting of the Law and Society Association, Washington, D.C., June 6, 1987).

14 Gender, Race, *Raza*

AMY KAMINSKY

Since the publication of *This Bridge Called My Back: Writings of Radical Women of Color* (1981) and *All the Women Are White, All the Blacks Are Men, but Some of Us Are Brave* (1982), scholarship by and about women of color has become increasingly central to the project of academic feminism in the United States.[1] Many white academic feminists have, for their part, made a concerted effort to pay attention to issues of race in their theoretical, critical, and pedagogical work.[2] This important and necessary change is increasingly affecting the way gender itself is understood. Nevertheless, the acknowledgment of racial difference and even the publication of important feminist/womanist work concerning women of color has not meant that race has been sufficiently theorized in the context of feminism. Here I am referring not simply to challenging the homogeneity of a racial community, or to looking simultaneously at race and gender, but, rather, to analyzing the instability of race itself and the part gender plays in naturalizing what gets called "race" in and across cultures.[3] In an attempt to do some of this work here, I use a comparative, gender-conscious approach to examine configurations of race as they occur in and between Spain, Spanish America, and the United States. I name and discuss three discrete but overlapping moments of Hispanic racial formation: the Imperial, the postcolonial, and the expatriate. The Imperial moment occurs between 1492 (when the last Moslem kingdom in Spain was defeated by Ferdinand and Isabella and Columbus landed in America) and the mid- to late-nineteenth century, when Spain lost its American colonies. The postcolonial moment begins with that nineteenth-century independence from Spain and continues through the present. It refers geographically to Spanish America. The expatriate moment is primarily a late-twentieth-century phenomenon marked by the emigration of Spanish Americans to Europe (including Spain) and the United States. My discussion elaborates the notion that as a cultural construction race is unstable and has different meanings and different purposes in different times and places and that gender is fundamental in making those meanings and revealing those purposes.

The ease with which so many North Americans can cross most geographical borders too easily deceives us into thinking that we are able to cross all borders—linguistic, cultural, historical—with similar ease. The average English speaker's faith in literal translation, together with the belief that race is biologically determined, creates the illusion that when we talk about racial difference across cultures and over time we mean the same things. Yet the differing linguistic-geographical axes in English and Spanish have a profound effect on meanings of crucial categories of analysis. Like the Spanish *género,* whose primary meanings of genre and grammatical gender make it a false cognate for "gender" as it is used in English, *raza* does not quite mean "race."[4]

"Race" in English has polished its veneer of scientific objectivity, but *raza* still relies on affective connotations of culture and affinity. In the politicized borderlands of the United States that were formerly northern Mexico, *raza* means "Chicano." For the Chicano movement, which takes language itself as a vehicle for constituting an oppositional culture, the very Spanishness of the word is an irreducible part of its meaning. In this context, *raza,* unlike "race," is not a category that may include many possible variants. Heavy with connotations of Chicano family, history, and politics, *raza* actively resists translation.

In another use of the term, originating in Spain, the Imperial Spanish *Día de la Raza* (Columbus Day, literally "Day of the Race") celebrates an expansionist consolidation of race by means of conquest and colonization, the drive toward a great and inclusive Hispanic race, first under the protection of Empire (as José Piedra argues), and later as an affirmation of independence.[5] Its goal—and enabling belief—has been the assimilation of difference into a homogenizing *Hispanidad,* a term that might provisionally be translated as "Hispanicity." *Hispanidad* wills a whitening first of Spain and then of what Carlos Fuentes has called Afro-Indo-Ibero-America.[6] The purifying noun, *Hispanidad,* suggests the promise of supremacy for all those who submit to inclusion under its rubric. The English word "Hispanic," on the other hand, is an adjective signifying a form of non-whiteness, a marker of difference with implications of inferiority.[7]

As a U.S. racial term, "Hispanic" is a relatively new, vague, and contested category.[8] Its emergence marks the third moment of racial formation I discuss in this article. This expatriate moment is characterized by a shift from a position of dominance and majority status, particular to the Imperial and postcolonial moments, to a position of subordination and minority status. The term "Hispanic" is imposed by a hostile dominant culture in the United States and derives from a history of colonialism, insofar as it refers to people whose ancestors lived in areas of the Americas colonized by Spain, including descendants of the Spaniards themselves. It is largely linguistic, with Spanish a cultural connector, even if—as is often the case among third-generation Chicanos, for example—the language is no longer spoken. It even sometimes includes Asians and Jews, as well as the descendants of those Blacks and Native peoples forcibly melted into the pot of *Hispanidad* under Empire. Not least problematically, it collapses particular national identities and cultural heritages into a single, undifferentiated category.[9]

Feminists in the United States tend to treat race as a stable (if complex) category. Among white feminists, moreover, there is a danger of fetishizing, and thereby immobilizing, race in the desire to engage in responsible feminist practice. One manifestation of this phenomenon can be found in anthologies of feminist literary criticism which consist of large numbers of essays on white writers that pay little attention to race, overshadowing a single article on a racially identified writer or subject.[10] As a fetish, race becomes a receptacle for meaning instead of a locus of the production of signification. At its worst, the reification of race creates the expectation that women of color will write only from a fixed standpoint and a demand that they be spokespeople for a group, writing from an "experience" that is uniform and already known.[11] This sort of essentialism limits agency, negates change, and stunts theoretical growth. As long as race is assumed to be a monolithic category, and as long as only people of color are assumed to "have" race, it will be the lump in the batter of feminist theory; and all our adding and stirring will be futile. Only when we conceptualize race as mutable and multivalenced can we hope to make sense of the ways in which it interacts with the differently nuanced category of gender.

Race, like gender, can be thought of as a cluster of characteristics that are explained in terms of purported biological difference. (And in Spanish America there is far less resistance than in the United States to the notion of biological gender.) Both gender and race, as sets of behavioral expectations rationalized through biology, are hard categories to shake loose from beliefs about the constraints of biology. The inherited traits of race would seem to adhere to one another, as if hair texture, say, were only the visible sign of other, hidden, properties. Moreover, the absence of revealing physical characteristics are understood not to negate the existence of these deeper truths: blood will tell. Racial metaphors range from the invisibly internal (the aforementioned blood, particularly dear to sixteenth- and seventeenth-century Spaniards bent on proving the "purity" of theirs) to the blatantly external (skin "color," the favorite of contemporary North Americans). In all cases the referent is something of which only traces remain in the individual: her or his parentage. Even in English, race is, ultimately, less about science than social organization, more about lineage than gene pool, while hierarchized racial difference is a function of conditions of political and economic dependency. Race is legitimated by something that looks like biology, made scientific in the nineteenth century by the newly developing field of physical anthropology.[12] It is constituted through a cluster of prescribed, proscribed, or permitted behaviors not unlike those associated with a feudal notion of social organization. Unlike laws of nature, however, rules of behavior can be transgressed. When they are, authority takes care that the transgressor is either punished or pardoned, so that through its intervention the fundamental structures of racially or gender-appropriate behavior can be recovered.

For example, in 1797, after his father petitioned the king of Spain to allow him to continue his studies and attain a formal degree, activities prohibited to Blacks in the Spanish colonies, José Ponciano de Ayarza was granted permission to attend the University of Santa Fé in Bogotá (Colombia) and become a lawyer. The king wrote that *"the character of mulatto being held extinguished in him,* he be admitted, *without its serving as precedent,* to the degrees he may seek in the university. . . ."[13] Similarly, when the pope allowed Catalina de Erauso (1585–?), who had lived much of her life as a soldier of the Conquest in the New World, to resume her masculine clothing and way of life, he did not repeal the laws of gender-appropriate behavior of his day but instead reasserted them by the very act of granting Catalina her singular privilege.[14] These exceptions to authorized gender and race behaviors quite explicitly do not unmake the rule.

Unlike gender in Western culture, which breaks down into a pair of bipolar opposites, where male/female is another way of saying male/not male, race cannot be split neatly in two.[15] As defined by the U.S. Bureau of the Census, for example, race is a melange of governmentally determined classifications that follow no particular pattern. The 1990 U.S. Census designates the following racial categories, in the following order: White, Black or Negro, Indian (Amer.), Eskimo, Aleut, Asian or Pacific Islander (with a series of geographical locators).[16] There is a mechanism for refusing any of these classifications: the slot designated "Other race." Even so, these categories are clearly insufficient. Ashkenazi Jews often classify themselves as white in relation to African Americans but as racially different in relation to white gentiles. Arab Americans, like Latinos, are increasingly identified and identifying in ways that are part ethnic and part racial, a phenomenon no doubt intensified by the current political climate in the Middle East. "The Black or Negro category," according to the census material, "also includes persons who identify as

African-American, Afro-American, Haitian, Jamaican, West Indian, Nigerian, and so on."[17] That is, the category contains anybody who has African ancestry, and who, if light skinned, chooses to self-define. American Indian includes anyone of a bureaucratically, designated percentage of Native American ancestry, whose self-identification is ratified by a tribal group.

The racial categories defined by the U.S. Bureau of the Census may be bureaucratically consolidated, but they derive in part from the individual's sense of identity within community and subsequently modify the community's perception of itself. This perception is affected, in turn, by the dominant culture's participation in the naming process. Racial identification, then, rests on multiple factors, including self-definition, external attribution, and political exigency, in different proportions, and resulting in a gaggle of official racial groupings. Despite this pileup of color-coded categories—black, red, brown, white, yellow—there remains a tendency in the United States to think of race in terms of white/not-white, where not-white oscillates between Black and a litany of othernesses.[18]

Although "female" and "not-male" are pretty much coterminous, "Black" is merely one version of "not-white." The tendency in the United States to categorize racial "others" in relation to whiteness, and to elide the differences among these others, serves to maintain the symbiotic fictions of "white" as norm and "Black" as race. The emerging racial category "Hispanic" easily disappears into the realm of "non-white," eliding the multiple differences in U.S. society, all the while burying ever more deeply the differences within "Hispanic." In the Census material, interestingly, "Hispanic" is not classified as a race. It is, instead, a specially designated ethnic classification, unique among all U.S. ethnicities in appearing on the form.[19] "Hispanic" itself is broken down into four categories: Mexican, Mexican-Am, Chicano; Puerto Rican; Cuban; other Spanish/Hispanic (including the rest of Spanish America and Spain). The officially recognized internal differences are geographical and, astonishingly, political (namely, Chicano and Mexican-Am). Despite the fact that the Census does not classify Spanish/Hispanic under "race," but rather gives it its own slot on the form, in the popular imagination "Hispanic" is a racial classification, insofar as it is invoked along with African American, American Indian, and Asian as a designated minority group. Stuart Hall's observation that whereas racial identity was once tied to nationality it is now tied to ethnicity is perfectly congruent with the argument I am making here.[20]

The construction of "Hispanic" as race in the first, Imperial, moment and in the second, postcolonial, moment is nicely illustrated in two unself-consciously gendered tales of racial formation under the sign of *His-*

panidad, one Spanish, the other Mexican. In the third, expatriate, moment, the stories no longer unconsciously reproduce cultural givens concerning gender in their production of racial formations but, rather, interrogate both gender and race. I invoke these stories not as magic mirrors that reflect without distortion the essence of their moment, nor as signposts pointing baldly to turns in the road, but rather as texts in a larger discursive field that serve as catalyst and reference point for my discussion. The Spanish story is from the anonymous picaresque novel, *Lazarillo de Tormes* (c. 1554). What characterizes the picaresque, and its prototype, *Lazarillo de Tormes,* is its caustic and purportedly didactic representation of the underside of society during the time of the consolidation of the Spanish empire. In the following passage the title character recalls his mother, in the first-person narration typical of the Spanish picaresque:

> My widowed mother, finding herself without a husband or anyone to take care of her, decided to [ally herself with good folk in order to] be like them. So she came to the city to live. She rented a little house and began to cook for some students. She washed clothes for some stableboys who served the Commander of La Magdalena, too, so a lot of time she was around the stables. She and a dark man—one of those who took care of the animals—got to know each other. Sometimes he would come to our door and wouldn't leave till the next morning; and other times he would come to our door in the daytime pretending that he wanted to buy eggs, and then he would come inside.
>
> When he first began to come I didn't like him; he scared me because of the color of his skin and his [evil aspect]. But when I saw that with him around the food got better, I began to like him quite a lot. He always brought bread and pieces of meat, and in the winter he brought in firewood so we could keep warm.
>
> So with his visits and the relationship going right along, it happened that my mother gave me a pretty little black baby, and I used to bounce [him] on my knee and help keep [him] warm.
>
> I remember one time when my black stepfather was playing with the little fellow, the child noticed that my mother and I were white but that [he was not, and, frightened, he shrank from him and toward my mother and pointing his finger said, "Mama, bogeyman!"] And my stepfather laughed: "[Son-of-a-bitch]."
>
> Even though I was still a young boy, I thought about the word my little brother had used, and I said to myself: How many people there must be in the world who run away from others [because] they don't see themselves.[21]

In the underclass world of the *Lazarillo,* there is a rough equivalency between the parents: the gender role of one and the race of the other are both markers of subordination. The white mother is a widow who needs to feed her family, the Black father is a slave; gender and race meet on the common ground of poverty. The woman without a husband to provide for her finds her counterpart in the Black who is made to serve a master in a discourse in which his unmarked, dominant, gender meets up with her unmarked, dominant race.[22] The sexual relationship between Zaide and Lazarillo's mother is a matter of mutual agreement.

In the next generation, race as *Hispanidad* emerges from the resolution of the fear of difference. Both Lazarillo and his brother dread what is unfamiliar in the Black father. The baby is afraid only of Zaide's color; Lazarillo, who is old enough to recognize culturally appropriate behavior, is frightened of both his stepfather's color and his unfamiliar countenance, which he calls "evil." But Zaide is a good man who provides for his family, a kind father who plays with his child. Lazarillo's fear disappears when he connects Zaide's presence to food and warmth in the house. When the baby shows fear of his father's color, Zaide responds with good humor. Not incidentally, this baby recognizes racial difference at the point when he enters into language—that is, when language makes it possible for him to articulate difference. At the same time, the sentence that tells of this differentiation is ambiguous and in need of some disentangling to get to which "he" is the stepfather and which is the baby. That is to say, differentiation threatens to collapse back into sameness even as it is being articulated.

Lazarillo would have his audience believe that he is telling this tale for its moral: that many people fear in others what they do not see in themselves. The baby assumes he is white, because white is standard in the household (Lazarillo and his mother stay, Zaide comes and goes), but he cannot see his own dark face. Lazarillo has to overcome a fear of the other, but the baby has to get over what amounts to a fear and ignorance of the self. That Lazarillo then generalizes the baby's response suggests that this racial splitting and lack of self-awareness is a societal problem, not a question of individual childhood development. Although we cannot know whether Lazarillo's mother entered into a relationship with Zaide for reasons of pure survival, Lazarillo tells us that Zaide is motivated by love, and we see that theirs is a stable, long-term relationship.[23] Zaide and Lazarillo's mother part only because the state separates them, denying Lazarillo's mother contact with Zaide after the two are caught and punished for his crime of stealing and hers of possessing stolen goods:

> As luck would have it, talk about Zaide [. . .] reached the ears of the foreman, and when a search was made they found out that he'd been stealing about half of the barley that was supposed to be given to the animals. He'd pretended that the bran, wool, currycombs, aprons, and the horse covers

and blankets had been lost; and when there was nothing else left to steal, he took the shoes right off the horses' hooves. And he was using all this to buy things for my mother so that she could bring up my little brother. [. . .]

And they found him guilty of everything I've said and more. [. . .]

They whipped my poor stepfather and scalded his wounds with boiling fat, and they gave my mother a stiff sentence besides the usual hundred lashes: they said that she couldn't go into the house of the Commander (the one I mentioned) and that she couldn't take poor Zaide into her own house.[24]

Here gender and racial difference are imposed from the outside, by the authorities; for although the crimes the couple commits are not specifically racial or gendered, the penalties are. To suffer whipping and scalding with boiling fat, as Zaide does, is a penalty reserved for slaves. The mother is punished beyond the hundred lashes that any white, male, Christian criminal would get; she is deprived both of her source of income doing domestic work for the commander's stable hands and of the company and support of her child's father.[25] After the forced separation of the parents, the child, who earlier had to learn he was Black, is simply absorbed into the white family. Once the authorities banish Zaide, effectively erasing his (further) presence in the text, the child becomes a Spaniard, like any other. After this incident, Lazarillo refers to the child only once again and with no racial reference whatever. Ironically, it is language, which enabled Lazarillo's baby brother to articulate difference, that also subsumes him into the sameness offered by *Hispanidad*.

"Language has always been the companion of empire."[26] So wrote Antonio de Nebrija in 1492, in dedicating his *Grammar of the Spanish Language* to Queen Isabella. José Piedra recalls Nebrija in his assertion that *Hispanidad* is a linguistic contract, consolidated in and through Empire, at a time of Spanish sovereignty and power:

The unification of all races into the Text [the Castilian of Nebrija's 1492 *Grammar*] was propelled by many social, religious, and historical circumstances, chief among which were Spain's own racially ill-defined origins, its occupation by lighter and darker-skinned conquerors who imported their own black slaves and citizens, and the rest of Europe's prejudices about Spain's imprecise racial heritage. This constellation of circumstances led to a theoretical welcoming, on paper, of black newcomers under the far-reaching umbrella of a "Hispanic" race.[27]

This Imperial incorporation of the racial other, begun in 1492 and continuing until the Spanish empire was dissolved, is the first of three moments of the elaboration of *Hispanidad* I have mentioned. The second moment, which registers the separation of the countries of Spanish America from Spain, is expressed in Octavio Paz's story of Mexican racial formation, "Los hijos de la Malinche" (The sons of Malinche), in his influential 1950 book of essays on the Mexican national character, *The Labyrinth of Solitude.* Here Paz identifies the common epithet with the historical figure of Malinche, the indigenous woman who served as Hernán Cortés's translator and sexual partner during his conquest of Mexico.

This story, unlike the *Lazarillo* episode, is a tale of racial and sexual plunder in which there is no reconciliation.[28] In it power relations are exaggerated, and gender and race are called into play as markers of oppression in an unbalanced equation, where the father is the white European male who rapes the racial and gendered other, the Indian woman. She is shamed, as women often are in rape stories: pitied for the violation of her body, blamed for betraying her people. The child of this union is the *mestizo,* the mixed-race Mexican who still needs to come to terms with his violent beginnings:

> If the *Chingada* is a representation of the raped Mother, it does not seem to me forced to associate her with the Conquest, which was also a rape, not only in the historical sense but in the very flesh of Indian women. The symbol of surrender is doña Malinche, the lover of Cortés. It is true that she gives herself voluntarily to the Conqueror, but he, once she stops being useful to him, forgets her. Doña Marina has become a figure that represents Indian women, fascinated, or violated, or seduced by the Spaniards. And in the same way that the child does not forgive his mother for abandoning him to seek his father, the Mexican people do not forgive Malinche her betrayal. She incarnates what is open, what is fucked, in contrast to our Indian men, stoic, impassive and closed.
>
> When he repudiates Malinche [. . .] the Mexican breaks his ties with the past, renounces his origins, and enters history alone.[29]

In this account the child is not ignorant of his origins (as is Lazarillo's brother), nor is racial identity incorporated into the healthy self. Rather, the racially mixed offspring repudiates—or represses—his parentage, denies his history, and is in need of something like psychoanalysis to come to terms with the lacerating violation that produced him. Racial identity, a matter of self-definition mediated by sociocultural attribution, requires a conscious desire for self-awareness. At the same time, gender oppression is validated and naturalized by Paz's transformation of the rape of the mother into a voluntary act of sexual submission, which he asserts with some vehemence. *"It is true,"* Paz affirms, on no particular evidence, *"that she gives herself voluntarily* to the Conqueror."[30] Unlike Lazarillo's mother, with whom the narrator sympathizes, Paz's Malinche, unceremoniously abandoned by her bored "lover" rouses little compassion. Moreover, it is not only Cortés, but also Paz, who abandons Malinche. Lazarillo's mother is present in the text both before Zaide enters the scene and after he is banished from it; Malinche is invoked only as an effect of Cortés's actions. Her sexuality is no more than a function of his desire—including his desire that she be a willing participant—unlike Lazarillo's mother who is in control of her body, and who, whether for love or more practical motives, enters into a mutually satisfying sexual arrangement with Zaide.

Bringing the Spanish and Mexican stories together, and remembering what José Piedra calls "Spain's own racially ill-defined origins," we are reminded how shaky is the story of a single, monochromatic *Hispanidad*. The child of Zaide and the widow, born in the late fifteenth or early sixteenth century, could easily have grown up to be one of Cortés's soldiers. The pure European conqueror was more than a little African, and racial differentiation in Europe as well as America turns out not to be binary but multiple.

Piedra claims that the consolidating device the empire would impose to mask racial difference was language itself. Equally important in the Hispanicization of the other, however, was the imposition of religious homogeneity. In the *Lazarillo* episode, for example, although no overt mention is made of it, race is closely tied to religion. Like the Jews, the Moors, understood as both Black and Muslim, were considered dangerous to Catholic Spain, and that danger derived equally from religion and race, because the two were constructed as inseparable. The instability of racial incorporation is, in fact, most visible in the Inquisition, which regularly routed out those newly Christianized (read Hispanicized) subjects who were insufficiently incorporated into an *Hispanidad* that Piedra defines as "a grand metaphor for unrealized promises of universal harmony."[31] To this day, Spaniards tie language to religion. As a student, when I rudely spoke English in front of my Spanish friends they would tell me in no uncertain terms, "Habla cristiano"—talk Christian—benignly oblivious to the complexity of such a demand on a Jew.

By the end of the nineteenth century, all that was left of the Spanish empire was language. As Miguel de Unamuno proudly, pathetically, claimed: "To speak of the Spanish race is not to know what one is talking about. . . . The language is the race."[32] As power shifted in Europe, Spain became insignificant, starting in the late seventeenth century and culminating in the nineteenth with the loss of its last American colonies. Until the final quarter of the twentieth century Spain was out of step with the rest of the continent—the Spanish Civil War anticipated the Second World War but also precluded Spain from acting in it, and when the rest of Europe was rebuilding, Spain under Franco stagnated. During the same period, the countries of Spanish America were consolidating their own identity, while becoming increasingly important to, and dominated by, the United States. *Hispanidad* now changed meaning, as it shifted its center from Spain to its former colonies. It took on the theme of a unified Spanish America, with the linguistic and cultural bond of a colonial past against which to define itself. At the same time, it was challenged by racial and national differences within.

This second, postcolonial, moment in the formation of *Hispanidad* consists of the forging of new nationalities within Spanish America in opposition to the European colonizer. This gesture fluctuates between asserting national and pan-American identities, and it relies on the difference from the former colonizer, whether idealized, as in José Vasconcelos's *Cosmic Race* or troubled, as in Paz's *Labyrinth of Solitude*.[33] Ironically, however, the stabilization of race as a function of nationality, which a number of countries have addressed via the ideology of *mestizaje*, results in a mystification of racial hierarchy and difference that mimics the colonial gesture of Imperial incorporation. The principle of *mestizaje*, because it tacitly justifies colonization in the forging of a new race/nation that blends conqueror and conquered, materially threatens indigenous people who resist assimilation in the new nation/race.[34] Furthermore, Paz's *mestizaje* symbolically erases women as products of the new racial blend. In his account, all women are sexually available to men and as such occupy the space of the conquered Indian mother.

Two and a half decades after Paz invoked the rape of Malinche as the engendering moment of a Mexican race, Victoria Ocampo wrote what would be one of many feminist revisions of the Malinche story, echoing the victimization theme but rescuing the Indian woman from what Ocampo believed to be ill-deserved scorn and censure.[35] Unlike Paz, feminist writers do not blame Malinche for her "betrayal" of her people but, rather, sympathize with her position and admire her ability to survive enslavement in two oppressive cultures. A frequent theme in the feminist retellings of the story is Malinche's betrayal *by* her people. Ocampo, writing from an upper-class, but also pan-American, position in Argentina, a country whose national identity is not built on an ideological foundation of *mestizaje*, invokes Malinche as an example of mistreated, misunderstood womanhood. Rosario Castellanos, writing from within Mexico just a few years before Ocampo, not only absolves Malinche of blame but also downplays her victimization and dilutes her symbolic role as the nation's mother. In Castellanos's play, *The Eternal Feminine*, Malinche is one of a group of female figures from Mexico's past for whom the writer is creating a revisionist history.[36]

A significant number of feminist-revisionist Malinche stories are written by Chicanas on the other side of the Mexico/United States divide. As the frontier is crossed, a subtle change takes place in these retellings: the border is a geographical sign separating the postcolonial from the expatriate moment in racial formation. However, the border, as Gloria Anzaldúa has perceptively noted, is not a one-dimensional line but an inhabited space that joins as well as divides. The Chicanas who rewrite Malinche are deeply marked by a U.S.-style racial consciousness, and by their feminism, which is played out in most of their accounts by an exploration of the mother/daughter relationship. They are also marked by Paz's canonical Mexican version of the story.

Historian Cordelia Candelaria considers Malinche a "feminist prototype, a girl-child"

> given away by her mother who sought to gain control of her daughter's inheritance for a son by her second husband. . . . Malinal was given to itinerant traders who eventually sold her to the ruling *cacique* of Tabasco. . . . After his takeover of Tabasco, and in keeping with age-old historic traditions, Cortés received from the *cacique* a gift of twenty maidens to serve as domestic labor for the warrior's adventurers. Malinal was part of the group.[37]

Along the same lines, Adelaida R. Del Castillo frames the story as a New World version of Snow White, with the mother as primary villain.[38] Cherríe Moraga echoes Gloria Anzaldúa's implication that the mother may not have been the one to decide her daughter's fate and that holding her responsible is just another version of woman blaming.[39]

Most of the Chicana writers, like Castellanos, contest the portrayal of Malinche as helpless victim, and the majority reclaim her as a sexual subject. Del Castillo takes Paz to task for equating women's sexuality with passivity and violation and suggests that Malinche was a willing sexual partner. Poet Alma Villanueva's Malinche, in contrast, denounces her rape, and as an angry goddess she demands retribution, while Margarita Cota-Cárdenas writes a Malinche who loves Cortés but defies all attempts to pin her down to a single interpretation.[40]

The Chicanas who write as the spiritual daughters of Malinche as part of a resistance to an oppression in which race and gender are inextricably intertwined displace the paradigmatic male child of the conquest and interpose a female subject. This subject sustains the vision of gender evoked and then suppressed in Paz's version. Nomenclature helps reveal the story's racial subtext: Paz usually calls the woman Malinche, which is how the Spaniards rendered her name; but many Chicana writers, recuperating the story still further as one of racial as well as gender revindication, insist on the indigenous form, Malinal, Malinalli, or Malintzín. Despite the differences between the female- and male-centered versions of these stories, what they all share is the extreme polarization that disallows the nuance of intersecting identities. The result is that the *mestiza* daughter holds fast to her Indian identity, while the father is the irredeemably white oppressor. "My Chicana identity is grounded in the Indian woman's history of resistance," Anzaldúa writes.[41] This declaration of Indian strength is a source of pride, and in Moraga's case it figures a lesbian feminist reading of the contemporary Chicana who claims her heritage through her mother.

Yet this polarization, whereby race is marked by and as gender, cannot be sustained. The figure of Malinche has been injected with multiple and contradictory meanings precisely because the racially marked other she represents has been overly simplified. As Norma Alarcón has perceptively noted, "issues of 'class' and 'color' [. . .] per se have not entered the [Chicana] reappropriation [of history, sexuality, and language] because [. . .] the person and symbol of Malintzin—indigenous female slave in her own society as well as in the one taking shape under the Spaniards—implicitly subsumes those as part of her condition, hence the possibility of her suppression as feminine/maternal speaking subject."[42]

Malinche, as she is written by Paz, oscillates between betraying and founding "the race," or "her people." But there are two different races/peoples here: the betrayed Indian and the founded *mestizo.* The latter contains and transforms the former and can only exist without anguish if the idea of racial purity is discarded as a possibility, or at least as an ideal. Adelaida R. Del Castillo, whose self-described "mystical interpretation" of Malinche is grounded in historical sources, points out that there was no single people for Malinche to betray. To accuse Malinche of betraying her people is to project her into the future, to have her betray the very *mestizo* nation that she begot: the betrayal is in the begetting itself.

Del Castillo's account is compelling for the way it fuses (and refuses) the various Malinche stories. Melodramatically, she repeats the story of Malinche as the mother of a race: "In the midst of the horror of destroyed bodies, of disease and wounds and the stench of decaying corpses of both men and animals, Marina shed her own blood with that of the men. In the midst of all this death, she made love to a decaying Cortés, thus giving birth to a new people." Del Castillo abandons her purple prose to report the death and displacement of Malinche's actual *mestizo* children. The Spaniards killed her son: hers was not to be the first of a new race. The dispossession of Malinche's daughter tragically parodies her own childhood experience. But this time it is the father who is solely to blame for the daughter's fate: "Don Martín Cortés Tenépal, natural son of Hernán Cortés and Doña Marina, was accused of treason and tortured by the Spaniards to obtain a confession, after which he was executed. María Jaramillo, legitimate daughter of Don Juan Jaramillo and Doña Marina, was robbed of her inheritance of land and money by her own father soon after Doña Marina's death."[43]

The tale of Malinche's children anticipates the future. Her son is literally accused of the treason that she has come to stand for, and he is annihilated. Her daughter's fate becomes that of the contemporary *mestiza*, Mexican or Chicana, who, robbed of her patrimony, is denied the full meaning of her *mestizaje*. But this child cannot simply claim her identity as an Indian either. The Chicana is not Malinche's daughter but her daughter's daughter: Moraga writes that she comes from "a *long line* of vendidas."[44]

The third-moment Chicana inclination to identify with the Indian mother (which is not only a feminist gesture but also one that marks the Chicano movement in general) undermines the second-moment Mexican nationalist project of the *mestizo* as alloy, a fully blended and fully stable being. This identification is, I think, both a form of solidarity with the growing international indigenous movements and a testament to the force of racial formation in the United States, which seeks ontological singularity.

Like the Spanish empire, the U.S. empire has its reasons for maintaining the fiction of a Hispanic race. The unified identity of the attributed Hispanic label serves to provide an "other" that consolidates North American (and European) white supremacy. This monolithic Hispanicity obscures racial classifications within Spanish American countries.[45] Alongside the early, careful, measuring-cup terms that denote the amount of one's African ancestry in Spanish America, there are myriad terms, not all of them benign, for various racial ancestries and mixtures, from *criollo* and *mestizo* to *mulato* and *zambo*. (In the United States terms like "half-breed," "octaroon," and "mulatto" are not only racist but antiquated. Moreover, the resolution of the concepts they denote into absolute racial categories testifies to how U.S.-style dominant whiteness demands sharp divisions.) Class differential plays an important role in racial attribution within many Spanish American societies, where such markers of superior economic and social class as the wearing of business attire and the use of standard speech are perceived as markers of whiteness as well. This more fluid approach to race does not mean that differentiation and hierarchy do not exist, only that they are expressed in other ways.

In Puerto Rico, the question of national identity as it is tied to racial difference is a central issue in such major twentieth-century writers as Francisco Arriví, Luis Palés Matos, and René Marqués, who often lodge this theme in stories of sexuality and reproduction. Younger Puerto Rican writers like Rosario Ferré and Ana Lydia Vega explore the same conjunction of elements from a decidedly feminist perspective. But as a person crosses over onto the U.S. mainland, Puerto Rican intracultural differences are supplanted by a unitary racial attribution. Aurora Levins Morales describes the shock of "white" Puerto Ricans from the island who come to the mainland and find they are "brown."[46] In a parodic echo of Nebrija's unifying grammar, the Spanish language, or its residual mark, the accent, is a determinant, now marking the outsider instead of the insider.[47]

Feminists from other parts of Spanish America also note this linguistically charged racialization. María Lugones, for example, is a philosopher and social activist from Argentina, of European background and living in the United States, who tells of experiencing the expatriate moment of Hispanicization when she entered the United States. Lugones's strategy has been to embrace this racial assignment and use it in opposition to the system that imposes it. Identifying politically with Chicanos and other Latinos, Lugones speaks specifically as a Latina in her scholarship.[48] She simultaneously theorizes and enacts this position by writing bilingually, thereby inverting the insider/outsider dichotomy imposed by the dominant culture and empowering the bilingual reader by injecting Spanish into the prestigious venues of what had been English-only academic journals.

Lugones plays successfully with markers of status, but on the whole, class in the United States is masked. For this reason, class differences are suppressed in the transformation of racial classifications in the border crossing. What seems to remain is the differing ability of distinct Latino groups to assimilate or to prosper. Cubans, for example, for reasons of politics and class, have tended to the latter but not the former. Class and race overlap: many of the middle-class Cubans who came to the United States after the revolution were white, and many of the poor, who remained because their lives were improved, were Black. On the other hand, certain words associated with nationality can carry both class and racial meanings in the United States. For some Midwesterners, "Mexican" is marked by class to mean "migrant worker." An upper-class, light-skinned "Mexican" is unthinkable; such a person would be reinvented, not "Mexican," but "from Mexico."[49] The prepositional phrase makes nationality seem contingent, unlike the adjectival noun, which is marked indelibly. To be Mexican is to be "other" in racial and class terms. To be "from Mexico" is to have something interesting to add to a Minnesota evening's conversation. This distinction is a liberal gesture that may begin to de-essentialize racial categories but at the high cost of perpetuating class divisions and toying with national and ethnic identities.

The racial construction characteristic of the expatriate moment—a consolidation of Hispano-American otherness defined not from within but from without—derives in part from a simplified version of postcolonial national/racial identity, which in turn has roots in Imperial *Hispanidad*. It occurs in Europe as well as in the United States. Cristina Peri Rossi's short story, "La influencia de Edgar A. Poe en la poesía de Raimundo Arias" (The influence of Edgar A. Poe on the poetry of Raimundo Arias), serves as an illustration.[50] In Peri Rossi's tale of racial unhinging, Alicia, the child of America, a girl whose particular heritage is apparently Caucasian, takes advantage of the European assumption that all Spanish Americans are the exotic "other." The story takes place in Spain, the site chosen for exile in Alicia's father's mistaken belief that a common language would mean a relatively painless assimilation, and where, since 1972, Peri Rossi has been living out what began as her own exile from Uruguay. In effect, Alicia's father anachronistically pins his faith on the promise of Imperial *Hispanidad*; Alicia quickly learns better. Dressed in what in her own country was a costume for a school play in which the audience would recognize her as a white child disguised as an Indian, she begs for money from a European public that sees her as foreign and exotic. Alicia gets away with this impersonation because, as far as her audience is concerned, it is no impersonation. It is not the outlandish costume, which is blatantly phony (it looks like early Hollywood Indian), that allows the urban Europeans to see Alicia as racially other but her Spanish American-ness that makes the costume credible. Her father, on the other hand, who tries to assert the sameness promised by the Imperial contract, is rendered invisible. He fails at even the deracinated version of modern commerce—selling soap out of a briefcase—that is the parodic sign of participation in First World modernity. It is only as racial (and therefore cultural) other that the child of Spanish America can be seen at all. The act of dressing up may be a falsification of what she knows to be her identity, but it confirms the European version of the racial identity now ascribed to the undifferentiated Spanish American. The European response to the racialized Spanish American other is chronicled by exiles like Peri Rossi, forced to leave their countries during the military dictatorships of the 1970s and early 1980s. Other Peri Rossi stories return to the exile either as invisible or as the exotic other. In "La ciudad" (The city), for example, a European woman figures Spanish America as the other to Europe: dirty, dangerous, exotic.[51] "Las estatuas, o la condición del extranjero" (Statues, or the foreigner's condition) evokes the foreigner whose presence is simply not acknowledged.[52] Peri Rossi's stories return the once-colonized figure to Spain for redefinition. The process of homogenization and racialization of Spanish America that these stories represent highlights the radical failure of the Imperial gesture. This process also occurs in the United States, which similarly creates an undifferentiated Spanish American, whom it calls "Hispanic" once she or he crosses the border into this country. Ironically, although Spain now participates in the othering of Spanish America, Spaniards who come to the United States are not exempt from the racializing Hispanicization that Spanish Americans undergo. In a classic example of chickens coming home to roost, first moment *Hispanidad* (the Spanish empire's colonizing notion of a people) converges with Hispanicization— the desire of dominant U.S. society to racialize this particular other.

The United States is coming to categorize Hispanic as race as a way of invoking a purported biological border at a time when the geographical border between North and South America is more and more permeable, and when there are as many Spanish Americans or their descendants living in the United States as in some Spanish American countries. Like the two earlier moments in Hispanic moments of racial formation discussed in this article, the current one relies on a form of homogenization. Although each of these homogenizing gestures has its own distinguishing features, each is the work of a dominant group representing state power, and each has been resisted by those on whom it has been imposed.

Whereas the Imperial moment is characterized by the incorporation of the racial other into the expansionist Imperial body and the postcolonial moment by assimilation into the new national body, the expatriate moment is characterized by the crossing—or shifting—of boundaries so that "Hispanic" becomes the name of the alien, menacing the body. The term "expatriate," when applied to Puerto Ricans, whose nation remains a virtual colony, is almost wishful. When applied to Chicanos, it is grimly ironic. It is not they who have been removed from their land, but their land whose identity has been changed via appropriation by another power, turning them, its previous inhabitants and their descendants, into strangers in what was once their home. The Chicano is no longer Mexican but is not fully expected to be at home in the United States either. We have already seen how the daughters of Paz's Malinche are thrown back to the precise moment of contact between Spain and America, recalling the violated essential other. This is not just an effect of the identification of the mother with the Indian but also of the anomalous position of the Chicana (and also the Chicano), still colonized, in a postcolonial world.

Nevertheless, the Chicanas who claim a revindicated Malinche as mother have also claimed themselves as *mestiza.* Standing in contrast to the Anglo colonizer, the colonized *mestiza* occupies the position of indigenous other, which is already, but only, one of her components. In Mexico, postcolonial *mestizaje* is the creation of a new race on which to found new nations. Functioning as a dominant discourse of national identity, the invocation of *mestizaje* often threatens indigenous cultures. In Mexico "Indian" stands in opposition and resistance to *mestizo.* In the United States, in contrast, *mestizo* is an oppositional racial fiction, barely recognized by the dominant culture, for whom mixed ancestry originating elsewhere resolves into simple "otherness." Meanwhile, for the classes of people who invoke it for its oppositional value, *mestizaje* risks absorption into a form of indigenousness.

The oppositional borderland *mestizaje* that such writers as Anzaldúa and Moraga invoke is superimposed on normative Mexican *mestizaje*. The expatriate *mestiza/o* is composed of the (already otherwise, and not fully homogenized, *mestiza/o*) Mexican and the North American (assumed to be European but of course also racially diverse).[53] Both these writers confront the indigenous woman who challenges their right to claim a purely Indian identity. Anzaldúa faces the fact that "living in the Borderlands means knowing/that the india in you, betrayed for 500 years,/is no longer speaking to you," and she postulates a multivalenced borderlands.[54] Moraga is saddened and resigned: "She's right [. . . .] In her world, I'm just white."[55] Moraga now avoids collapsing *india* and "woman" by emphasizing the gender distinctions within precontact indigenous culture. Drawing on Aztec female deities who struggle against their male counterparts, Moraga refashions the trope of the weak Indian-as-woman into the figure of the powerful woman Indian. Other Latina feminists, occupying two "impure" cultures that they themselves embody, are also addressing this complexity. Levins Morales incorporates Jew and Puerto Rican, and María Lugones theorizes the impossibility and limitations of purity, even in separation.

Lugones conceptualizes *mestizaje* as multiplicity, never resolving into one or another of its parts and never blending them into an homogenous whole. For Lugones, *mestizaje* is another name for impurity, and it is to be deployed as a form of resistance.[56] Her formulation, derived from a U.S. Latino context, and also from a feminist reading of gender and a lesbian theory of sexuality, is applicable broadly to a whole range of differences and stands as a direct challenge to a notion of racial or ethnic fixity.

Imperial and nationalist "Hispanidad" and expatriate "Hispanicity" are fictions of purity, the first two based on the promise of assimilation into the dominant culture, the last based on an equally false premise of exclusion. For the first and second moments of Hispanic racial formation to occur—in order to (re)produce the new race—the heterosexual female body must be conscripted. This attempt was certainly resisted—by Jews and Muslims in Spain, and by indigenous peoples on this continent. A major distinguishing feature of the current form of resistance is the different discursive location gender has assumed in the late twentieth century. Gender difference was formerly invoked as a kind of conscripted female heterosexuality to be utilized literally and figuratively in naturalizing racial fictions. It functioned as an unremarked marker, part of a God-given or scientifically proclaimed order, and it depended on women's silence. Race was naturalized via gendered sexuality that, in turn, was always already naturalized. Now, race is only residually about naturalized difference, and the contemporary bureaucratization of race stands as its own accusation, a technology that produces, reproduces, and shores up the shaky edifice of racial differentiation. Previous bureaucracies of race erected by Empire, the Inquisition, and the modern nation state, which had the same function, were not thought of as doing anything but revealing an existing truth.

Current feminist consciousness brings gender to the surface in the first- and second-moment origin narratives of racial formation, and it reconfigures gender itself in the third-moment stories. Peri Rossi's Alicia is a daughter in relation to a father, an inversion of the time-honored mother/son dyad that also questions generational roles. Along the same lines, much Chicana feminist work is interested in women-to-women relationships cross-generationally.

Women who come out of a history of compulsory, and racialized, heterosexuality are foregrounding gender and historical race, and dislodging both—excavating them, making them visible, and exploding them. They are likely to invoke race as a political mechanism or as a complex, fraught multiplicity of meanings—Anzaldúa's *frontera*, Moraga's exploration of her multiracial family, Levins Morales's self-conscious position as Jewish Puerto Rican, metropolitan Lugones's alliance with Chicanos of rural New Mexico. It is also not a coincidence that many of the best-known of the theorists doing this work are lesbians who are simultaneously reconfiguring women's sexuality. For—to give an example—although lesbian motherhood is also a reality, it is not the same old naturalized story and in fact is profoundly upsetting to patriarchal desire and expectation; it disrupts the culturally determined natural order. The resisting Chicana/Latina, who in her most radical and theoretically promising form is lesbian, refuses complicity with any racializing project that demands her sexual complicity. Lugones, Moraga, and Anzaldúa all resist the smoothing out of difference and find strength in their own multiplicity as they engage in struggle, within and with the culture.

The differences within an emerging racial category like "Hispanic," the struggle cover the very nomenclature of race, and the unpredictability of racial difference are reminders that race cannot be taken as a simple variable in the cultural equation that feminism and other oppositional politics are trying to solve. When the meanings of racial categories change, and when racial attribution disengages from identity, race enters a state of flux that best serves liberatory ends if it refuses stability.

Notes

I wish to thank Cheri Register, Naomi Scheman, Joanna O'Connell, Elaine Johnson, and the *Feminist Studies* editors and reviewers, who read earlier drafts of this article and pushed and prodded me to make it better than it was.

1. Cherríe Moraga and Gloria Anzaldúa, *This Bridge Called My Back: Writings of Radical Women of Color* (Watertown, Mass.: Persephone Press, 1981; reprint, Kitchen Table, Women of Color Press, 1983); and Gloria T. Hull, Patricia Bell Scott, and Barbara Smith, eds., *All the Woman Are White, All the Blacks Are Men, but Some of Us Are Brave* (Old Westbury, N.Y.: The Feminist Press, 1982). Work by and about African American women is, not surprisingly, the most visible. Consider the prophetic title of bell hooks's text on African American feminism, *Feminist Theory: From Margin to Center* (Boston: South End Press, 1984). See Patricia Bell Scott, Beverley Guy-Sheftall, and Jacqueline Jones Royster, "The Promise and Challenge of Black Women's Studies: A Report from the Spelman Conference, May 1990," *NWSA Journal* 3 (spring 1991): 282–88, for a report on the growth of Black women's studies as a vital academic field.

2. See, for example, Elizabeth V. Spelman, *Inessential Women: Problems of Exclusion in Feminist Thought* (Boston: Beacon Press, 1988); and Teresa de Lauretis, "Feminist Studies/Critical Studies: Issues, Terms, and Contexts," in *Feminist Studies/Critical Studies*, ed. Teresa de Lauretis (Bloomington: Indiana University Press, 1986), 1–19. This change is by no means complete, and according to some has barely begun. Norma Alarcón, "The Theoretical Subject(s) of *This Bridge Called My Back* and Anglo-American feminism," in *Criticism in the Borderlands: Studies in Chicano Literature, Culture, and Ideology*, ed. Héctor Calderón and José David Saldívar (Durham, N.C.: Duke University Press, 1991), 28–39, for example, argues that white feminist theory remains unmoved insofar as the subject of feminism is still white.

3. Differences within racial categories have, of course, been dealt with by feminist scholars. To name a very few examples: Hortense Spillers, "Notes on an Alternative Model: Neither Nor," in *The Difference Within: Feminism and Critical Theory*, ed. Elizabeth Meese and Alice Parker (Philadelphia: John Benjamin, 1989), 164–87, discusses the tragic mulatta figure, an "other," defined by whites, within Blackness; and Patricia J. Williams's extraordinary study. *The Alchemy of Race and Rights* (Cambridge: Harvard University Press, 1991), never loses sight of gender. The recent anthology, *Breaking Boundaries: Latina Writing and Critical Readings*, ed. Asunción Horno Delgado et al. (Amherst: University of Massachusetts Press, 1989), is structured along the divisions within the U.S. Latino community; and Patricia Zavella, "Reflections on Diversity Among Chicanas," *Frontiers* 12, no. 2 (1991): 73–85, argues that cultural coherence is belied by the differing social location among Chicanas. On the other hand, discussions such as British Marxist Mike Cole's "'Race' and Class or 'Race,' Class, Gender, and Community? A Critical Appraisal of the Radicalised Fraction of the Working-Class Thesis," in the *British Journal of Sociology* 40 (March 1989): 118–29, focusing on the instability of race, barely touch on gender.

4. Amy Kaminsky, "Translating Gender," in *Reading the Body Politic: Latin American Women Writers and Feminist Criticism* (Minneapolis: University of Minnesota Press, 1993), 1–13.

5. José Piedra, "Literary Whiteness and the Afro-Hispanic Difference," *New Literary History* 18 (Winter 1987): 303–32.

6. Fuentes used this deliberately clumsy term, or some permutation of it, in a lecture at Macalaster College, St. Paul, Minnesota, in 1989. The fiction of assimila-

tion, of course, is belied by the extreme othering first of indigenous people and later of Africans brought to the Americas as slaves.

7. Similarly, Rey Chow, "The Politics and Pedagogy of Asian Literature in American Universities," *Differences: A Journal of Feminist Cultural Studies* 2 (fall 1990): 29–51, cites Vine Deloria, Jr. on the "[relegation of] minority existence to an adjectival status within the homogeneity of American life" (45).

8. Laura E. Gómez, "The Birth of the 'Hispanic' Generation: Attitudes of Mexican-American Political Elites Toward the Hispanic Label," *Latin American Perspectives* 19 (fall 1992): 45–58, notes that the English term "Hispanic" to desig- nate a U.S. population was popularized in the 1980s. She points out that the term had its roots in the U.S. Bureau of the Census and represents a mainstream politi- cal viewpoint. Cherríe Moraga, in "Art in América Con Acento," in Moraga's *The Last Generation: Prose and Poetry* (Boston: South End Press, 1993), 57, lays blame for the term, and by extension the effects of, "Hispanicization" on Reagan-era bu- reaucrats.

9. "Hispanic" also collapses class differences. In the popular North American imagination, "Hispanic" is a sign of poverty. Yet the first wave of Cubans fleeing Castro's revolution and the Somocistas who left Sandinista Nicaragua were hardly members of the underclass.

10. This observation is not meant to be an attack on white feminists' attempts to acknowledge racial difference but a recognition of the difficulties one faces when trying to theorize a number of variables at once. Historian Peggy Pascoe, "At the Crossroads of Culture: Decentering History," *Women's Review of Books* 7 (February 1990): 22–23, suggests that the best way to get at gender oppression is by focusing on what happens where different ethnicities, cultures, and classes meet; however, political scientist Barbara Cruikshank's unpublished paper on building women's coalitions, read at the University of Minnesota's Center for Advanced Feminist Studies' Theorizing Diversity Seminar in 1988, outlines the difficulty of reconciling different feminist agendas.

11. Mae Gwendolyn Henderson, "Speaking in Tongues: Dialogics, Dialectics, and the Black Woman Writer's Literary Tradition," in *Changing Our Own Words: Essays on Criticism, Theory, and Writing by Black Women*, ed. Cheryl A. Wall (New Brunswick, N.J.: Rutgers University Press, 1989; reprint. London: Routledge, 1990), 16–37, argues that African American women's standpoint is itself unstable because it represents two constituencies, each of which has a political claim that renders the other partial. Nevertheless, the term "standpoint" itself promises sta- bility. Multiple "standpoints" certainly exert pressure requiring movement from spot to spot, but beyond that, the categories that define the so-called standpoints are constantly in flux, dissolving any possibility of fixity.

12. Anthropology is still invoked to legitimate racism, although contemporary anthropologists are quick to dissociate themselves from such use of their disci- pline. In a recent incident, a suburban Minnesota high school teacher justified racial categorizations by invoking "anthropology." Anthropologists at the Uni- versity of Minnesota responded with a letter in the Minneapolis-St. Paul daily newspaper saying that anthropology most certainly is not about establishing racial categories.

13. "The Case of José Ponseano de Ayarza: A Document on the Negro in Higher Education," *Hispanic American Historical Review* 24 (August 1944): 448–49; and James F. King, "The Case of José Ponciano de Ayarza, a Document on *Gracias al Socar*," *Hispanic American Historical Review* 31 (November 1951): 640. I use Piedra's translation (p. 321, emphases added). Piedra, following King, attributes the 1944 article to the journal's managing editor, John Tate Lanning.

14. My method throughout this article is to consider both historical and literary texts as part of the discursive field that produces and inscribes cultural practice. The distinction between the two is not rigid. Catalina de Erauso has only recently been reassigned to the category of historical personage. For many years this remarkable woman was assumed to have been a product of literary imaginations that invented an autobiography of her and wrote a play about her exploits.

15. Suzanne J. Kessler and Wendy McKenna, in *Gender: An Ethnomethodological Approach* (New York: Wiley, 1978), demonstrate the alignment of female and not-male in contrast to male.

16. U.S. Bureau of the Census, Official 1990 U.S. Census Form (D-1, OMB No. 0607–0628), 2.

17. U.S. Bureau of the Census, *Your Guide for the 1990 U.S. Census Form*, 3.

18. This is not surprising, given the racial history of the United States. Until Emancipation, the United States, and particularly the slave states, encouraged the birth of Black babies, often in the most brutal ways. Currently, poor Black women are excoriated for their fertility. At the same time, white America apologizes for having exterminated the Indians, a gesture which simultaneously begs to excuse Euroamericans for the actual destruction of so many lives and masks the reality of a growing Indian population with vital cultures and political, moral, and legal claims to make on the dominant society.

19. Paul Bohannan defines ethnicity as "identity with or membership in a particular cultural group, all of whose members share language, beliefs, customs, values, and identity," in *We the Alien: An Introduction to Cultural Anthropology* (Prospect Heights, Ill.: Waveland Press, 1992), 321. This is a serviceable enough definition, although I would argue with the "all."

20. Stuart Hall, "Minimal Selves," *ICA (Institute of Contemporary Arts) Document 6* (London: Free Association Press, 1987), 44–47. The *American Heritage Dictionary*, Third Edition, lists both racial and national heritage among the elements that can be, but are not necessarily, held in common by an ethnic group.

21. Mi viuda madre, como sin marido y sin abrigo se viese, determinó arrimarse a los buenos por ser uno dellos, y vínose a vivir a la ciudad, y alquiló una casilla, y metióee a guisar de comer a ciertos estudiantes, y lavaba la ropa a ciertos mozos de caballos del comendador de la Magdalena, de manera que fue frecuentando las caballerizas.

Ella y un hombre moreno de aquellos que las bestias curaban vinieron en conocimiento. Este algunas veces se venía a nuestra casa y se iba a la mañana. Otras veces, de día llegaba a la puerta, en achaque de comprar huevos, y entrábase en casa. Yo, al principio de su entrada, pesábame con él y habíale miedo, viendo el color y mal gesto que tenía; mass de que vi que con au venida mejoraba el comer, fuile queriendo bien, porque siempre traía pan, pedazos de carne y, en invierno, leños, a que nos calentábamos.

De manera que, continuando la posada y conversación, mi madre vino a darme un negrito muy bonito, el cual yo brincaba y ayudaba a calentar.

Y acuérdome que estando el negro de mi padrastro trebejando con el mozuelo, como el niño veía a mi madre y a mí blancos y a él no, huía dél, con miedo, para mi madre, y, señalando con el dedo, decía: '¡Madre, coco!'

Respondío él, riendo, '¡Hideputa!'

Yo, aunque bien muchacho, noté aquella palabra de mi hermanico, y dije entre mí '¡Cuáncos debe de haber en el mundo que huyen de otros porque no se ven a sí mismos!'

See *Lazarillo de Tormes*, in *La novela picaresca española*, ed. Angel Valbuena Prat (Madrid: Aguilar, 1962), 85. According to Valbuena Prat, the three earliest known editions of this text are dated 1554. The translation is *The Life of Lazarillo of Tormes, His Fortunes and Misfortunes*, trans. Robert S. Rudder (New York: Unger, 1973), 5–6. I have modified the translation and marked my changes by brackets where I believe Rudder's translation altered the meaning of the original in important ways.

22. Angela Davis, in *Women, Race, and Class* (New York: Random House, 1981), argues that under slavery women and men were equals. The structure of slavery in early modern Spain was sufficiently different from the U.S. form Davis discusses to make it possible to talk about gender hierarchy in the Spanish instance. Furthermore, by no means all people of African heritage in sixteenth-century Spain were, or ever had been, slaves.

23. We need not depend on the notoriously unreliable Lazarillo's interpretation here, although we do rely on him for our knowledge of events.

24. From *The Life of Lazarillo of Tormes*, 6–7.

Quiso nuestra fortuna que la conversación del Zaide [. . .] llegó a oídos del mayordomo, y hecha pesquisas, hallóse que la mitad por medio de la cebada que para las bestias le daban hurtaba, y salvados, leña, almohazas, mandiles y las mantas y sábanas de los caballos hacía perdidas, y cuando otra cosa no tenía, las bestias desherraba, y con todo esto acudía a mi madre para criar a mi hermanico. [. . .]

Y probóse cuanto digo, y aún más [. . .].

Al triste de mi padrastro azotaron y príngaron, y a mi madre pusieron pena por justicia, sobre el acostumbrado centenario, que en casa del sobredicho comendador no entrase, ni al lastimado Zaide en la suya acogiese. (*Lazarillo de Tormes*, pp. 85–86)

25. Ruth El Saffar has pointed out to me that the widow's punishment was the penalty for incest. El Saffar suggests that because her relationship with Zaide exists outside the symbolic order, as the joining of "same," it might be figured as incestuous. In my reading, which I do not see as at odds with El Saffar's, the economy of sameness derives from social location.

26. "[S]iempre la lengua fue compañera del imperio," in Antonio de Nebrija, *Gramática de la lengua castellana*, ed. Antonio Quilis (Madrid: Editoria Nacional, 1980), 97, my translation.

27. Piedra, 307.

28. Cortés and Malinche differ from the characters in the *Lazarillo* in that they are historical personages. Nevertheless, the story of their relationship, based on

the very sketchy contemporary accounts of *Cartas de relación* by Cortés and Bernal Díaz del Castillo's *Verdadera historia de la conquista de Nueva España* have been reworked by numerous historians, poets, playwrights, and fiction writers. See Sandra Messinger Cypess, *La Malinche in Mexican Literature* (Austin: University of Texas Press, 1991).

29. Si la Chingada es una representación de la Madre violada, no me parece forzado asociarla a la Conquista, que fue también una violación, no solamente en el sentido histórico, sino en la carne misma de las indias. El símbolo de la entrega es doña Malinche, la amante de Cortés. Es verdad que ella se da voluntariamente al Conquistador, pero éste, apenas deja de serle útil, la olvida. Doña Marina se ha convertido en una figura que represents a las indias, fascinadas, violadas o seducidas por los españoles. Y del mismo modo que el niño no perdona a su madre que lo abandone para ir en busca de su padre, el pueblo mexicano no perdona su traición a la Malinche. Ella encarna lo abierto, lo chingado, frente a nuestros indios, estoicos, impasibles y cerrados. [. . .]

Al repudiar a la Malinche [. . .] el mexicano rompe sus ligas con el pasado, reniega de su origen y se adentra solo en la vida histórica.

See Octavio Paz, "Los hijos de la Malinche" (The sons of Malinche) in *El laberinto de la soledad* (Mexico: Cuadernos Americanos, 1950; reprint, Mexico: Fondo de Cultura Económica, 1959), 77–78, my translation.

30. Ibid., my emphasis.

31. Piedra, 308.

32. "Hablar de raza española es no saber lo que se dice. . . . El lenguaje es la raza." Miguel de Unamuno, "Espíritu de la raza vasca," in *La raza y la lengua: Obras completas*, vol. 4, ed. Manuel García Blanco (Madrid: Ecselicer, 1968), my translation. Race in Unamuno's formulation still encompasses religion; what had been the Spanish empire was still heavily Catholic at the end of the nineteenth and beginning of the twentieth century when he wrote. Today the hegemony of Hispanic Catholicism in Spanish America is being threatened by Protestant evangelism.

33. José Vasconcelos, *La raza cósmica: Misión de la raza iberoamericana* (Paris: Agencia Mundial de Librería, 1925).

34. Conversations with Joanna O'Connell, whose book, "Prospero's Daughters" (University of Texas Press, forthcoming) elaborates this point, have helped me clarify and articulate it here.

35. Victoria Ocampo, "El último año de Pachacutec" (1975), in Ocampo's *Testimonios, Décima serie* (Buenos Aires: Sur, 1977), 39–46, translated by Doris Meyer as "The last year at Pachacutec," in Doris Meyer, *Victoria Ocampo: Against the Wind and the Tide* (New York: Braziller, 1979), 273–77.

36. Rosario Castellanos, *El eterno femenino* (1973), (Mexico: Fondo de Cultura Económica, 1975), translated by Diane Marting and Betty Tyree Osiek as "The eternal feminine," in *A Rosario Castellanos Reader*, ed. Maureen Ahern (Austin: University of Texas Press, 1988). For a full discussion of Malinche in Mexican literature, see Cypess.

37. Cordelia Candelaria, "La Malinche, Feminist Prototype," *Frontiers* 5 (summer 1980): 2.

38. Adelaida R. Del Castillo, "Malintzín Tenépal: A Preliminary Look into a New Perspective," in *Essays on La Mujer,* ed. Rosaura Sánchez and Rosa Martínez Cruz (Los Angeles: Chicano Studies Center, 1977).

39. Cherríe Moraga, "A Long Line of Vendidas," in Moraga's *Loving in the War Years: Lo que nunca pasó por sus labios* (Boston: South End Press, 1983), 100–101.

40. Alma Villanueva, "La Chingada," in *Five Poets of Aztlán,* ed. Santiago Daydi-Tolson (Binghamton, N.Y.: Bilingual Review Press, 1985); and Margarita Cota-Cárdenas, "Discurso de la Malinche (Fragment from the novel)," *Third Woman* 2, no. 1 (1984): 46–50.

41. Gloria Anzaldúa, *Borderlands/La Frontera: The New Mestiza* (San Francisco: Spinsters/Aunt Lute, 1987), 21.

42. Norma Alarcón, "Traddutora, Traditora: A Paradigmatic Figure of Chicano Feminism," in *The Construction of Gender and Modes of Social Division,* Special Issue of *Cultural Critique* 13 (fall 1989): 57–87.

43. Del Castillo, 138, 143.

44. Moraga, *Loving in the War Years,* 90–144.

45. For a historical discussion of racial definitions and theories in Cuba, Argentina, and Mexico, see essays by Aline Helg and Alan Knight in *The Idea of Race in Latin America, 1870–1940,* ed. Richard Graham (Austin: University of Texas Press, 1990).

46. Aurora Levins Morales, "Between Two Worlds," *Women's Review of Books* 7 (December 1989): 1, 3–4.

47. The absence of audible difference makes it possible for the child adopted from Spanish America into a white family to be otherwise assigned to a racial group, but assigned she will be. Cheri Register, who has written on international adoption in the United States *(Are Those Kids Yours? American Families with Children Adopted from Other Countries* [New York: Free Press, 1991]), has observed that light-skinned children who look as though they could be the parents' birth children are taken for white, Afro-Hispanic children are assumed to be African American, and *mestizo* and Indian children are taken to have been adopted from Spanish America.

48. See, for example, María Lugones, "Hispaneando y Lesbiando: On Sarah Hoagland's *Lesbian Ethics,*" *Hypatia* 5 (fall 1990): 138–46; and Lugones, "Playfulness, 'World' Traveling, and Loving Perception," *Hypatia* 2 (summer 1987): 3–19.

49. I am grateful for my Midwestern informant, Cheri Register, for this piece of information.

50. Cristina Peri Rossi, "La influencia de Edgar A. Poe en la poesía de Raimundo Arias," in Peri Rossi's *La tarde del dinosaurio* (Barcelona: Planeta, 1976), 43–59.

51. Cristina Peri Rossi, "La ciudad," in *El museo de los esfuerzos inútiles* (Barcelona: Seix Barral, 1983), 160–77.

52. Cristina Peri Rossi, "Las estatuas, o la condición del extranjero," in *El museo de los esfuerzos inútiles,* 131–32.

53. Gloria Anzaldúa, *Borderlands/La frontera.*

54. Gloria Anzaldúa, "Living in the Borderlands Means You," in *Infinite Divisions: An Anthology of Chicana Literature,* ed. Tey Diana Rebolledo and Eliana S. Rivero (Tucson: University of Arizona Press, 1993), 96.

55. Cherríe Moraga, "The Breakdown of the Bicultural Mind," in *The Last Generation*, 120.

56. María Lugones, "Purity, Impurity, and Separation," *Signs*, forthcoming. I am grateful to Lugones for so generously allowing me to refer to her prepublished work.

15 Feminism and Difference

The Perils of Writing as a Woman on Women in Algeria

MARNIA LAZREG

At the heart of the feminist project, East and West, is a desire to dismantle the existing order of things and reconstruct it to fit one's own needs. This desire is best expressed in Omar Khayyam's cry:

> *"Ah love! Could you and I with Him conspire*
> *To grasp this sorry scheme of things entire*
> *Would not we shatter it to bits—and then*
> *Remould it to the heart's desire!"*[1]

However, feminists, East and West, differ in the grasp they have on this "sorry scheme of things" and the tools they use to "shatter it to bits." They also differ as to whether the process of remolding things can take place at all. Indeed, Western academic feminists can rediscover their womanhood, attempt to redefine it, and produce their own knowledge of themselves hampered only by what many perceive as male domination.[2] Ultimately, Western feminists operate on their own social and intellectual ground and under the unstated assumption that their societies are perfectible. In this respect, feminist critical practice takes on an air of normalcy. It appears as part of a reasonable (even if difficult) project for greater gender equality.

By contrast, the Algerian and Middle Eastern feminist project unfolds within an external frame of reference and according to equally external standards. Under these circumstances the consciousness of one's womanhood coincides with the realization that it has already been appropriated in one form or another by outsiders, women as well as men, experts in things Middle Eastern. In this sense, the feminist project is warped and rarely brings with it the potential for personal liberation that it does in this country or in Europe. The forms of expression used by Algerian feminists are, in fact, caught between three overlapping discourses, namely, the male discourse on gender difference, social science discourse on the peoples of North Africa and the Middle East, and academic discourses (whether feminist or protofeminist) on women from these same societies.

This article initially grew out of a preliminary reflection on the nature and specificity of U.S. feminist theory and on the ongoing search for a feminist epistemology. My forays into the production of U.S. feminist knowledge, at a time when feminism appears to be undergoing a crisis, impressed upon me the fact that academic feminism has yet to break away from the philosophical and theoretical heritage it has so powerfully questioned.[3] Knowledge is produced not only within a socioeconomic and political framework but also within an intellectual tradition with stated and unstated assumptions. Although it questions traditional assumptions, academic feminism has often neglected to investigate its own premises. If it were to do so more often, it might become apparent that "traditional" social science categories have not yet been transformed but have been given a different sex instead.[4]

When I turned my attention away from the center of the debate over feminist theory and epistemology to its North African and Middle Eastern periphery, for example, I noticed three intriguing phenomena. First, the interest of U.S. feminists in women from these parts of the world has spurred a growing literature that is noteworthy for its relative lack of theoretical import. With a few exceptions, women who write about North African and Middle Eastern women do not identify themselves as feminist, yet their work finds its legitimacy in academic feminism's need for information about their subject matter.[5] Second, "Eastern" feminists writing for a Western audience about women in their home countries have done so with the generally unstated assumption that U.S. feminist knowledge can be expanded or accommodated but seldom questioned.[6] U.S. minority women, in contrast, have consistently challenged academic feminist projects in a variety of ways. In so doing they have pointed out problem areas that feminist knowledge must address and resolve before it can claim to be an alternative to "traditional" knowledge.[7] Third, although U.S. feminists (like their European counterparts) have sought to define and carve out a space in which to ground their criticism, "Eastern" feminists have simply adjusted their inquiry to fill the blanks in the geographical distribution made available to them by U.S. feminist liberalism.[8] These observations on feminist knowledge, East and West, led me to search for the connecting links between Western feminist knowledge writ large and constituted knowledge, through the study of the concrete case of Algeria. What I discovered was a continuity between the traditional social science modes of apprehending North African and Middle Eastern societies rooted as they are in French colonial epistemology and academic women's treatment from these societies.[9] One continuity, for example, is expressed in the predominance of a "religious paradigm" that gives religion a privileged explanatory power.[10] Most academic feminist practice takes place within this paradigm, thereby reproducing its presuppositions and reinforcing its dominant position. This process takes place even when feminists claim they are aware of the paradigm's flaws.[11]

I also discovered a temporal and conceptual continuity between female (often protofeminist) and feminist discourses.[12] What was written about Algerian women by women in the first part of this century is reproduced in one form or another in the writings of contemporary French women and U.S. feminists about the same subject matter. More importantly, the themes defined by the French colonial or neocolonial discourse as significant for understanding Algerian women are the ones found today in Eastern feminists' writings.[13]

In the pages that follow I will describe some of these continuities and will suggest some of the ways in which poststructuralism impacts upon them. I will also discuss the need for reevaluating the feminist project within a humanistic/ethical framework.

The Social Science and Feminist Paradigms

The study of Middle Eastern and North African societies has been plagued by a number of conceptual and methodological problems that prompted the British sociologist Bryan S. Turner to say that it "lags behind other area studies in both theoretical and substantive terms." Indeed, it is "underdeveloped."[14] Scholarship on North African and Middle Eastern societies typically focuses on Islam as a privileged subject of inquiry whether it is dealt with as a religion or as a culture. Underlying the study of these societies are a number of problematical assumptions. First, Islam is seen as a self-contained and flawed belief system impervious to change. In sociology, this assumption finds its theoretical justification in the work of Max Weber.[15] Second, Islamic civilization is assumed to have been in decline and to continue to decline. The "decline thesis," best exemplified in the work of H.A.R. Gibb and Harold Bowen,[16] prompted David Waines to say that "the birth of Islam is also the genesis of its decline."[17] Attempts made by indigenous people to change their institutions are more often than not explained in terms of a return to Islam. This is well illustrated by the work of Clifford Geertz on what he calls "scripturalism."[18] Last but not least, it is assumed that "Islam cannot produce adequate, scientific knowledge of itself, since the political conditions of Islamic societies preclude critical, autonomous scholarship. Islam requires Western science to produce valid knowledge of the culture and social organization of the Islamic world."[19]

Such science has managed to keep the study of North Africa and the Middle East in a sort of intellectual ghetto where theoretical and methodological developments that take place in the mainstream of social science are somehow deemed inapplicable. For instance, up until recently, one could not talk about social classes in the Middle East but only of social hierarchies, or mosaics of people. One cannot speak about revolution but only of upheavals and coups. One still cannot talk about self-knowledge but only of "local knowledge" or "the native's point of view."[20]

Even when efforts are made by well-intentioned scholars to accommodate theoretical/methodological developments from other fields, they end up reinforcing the old problematical assumptions. For example, the recent focus on "popular culture" feeds into the view of Islam as divided up into the orthodox and the mystical. Similarly, the introduction of the concept of class in the study of the Middle East and North Africa has sometimes resulted in making proletarian rebels out of theologians and/or members of religious sects.[21]

A bird's-eye view of the literature by women, whether they are feminists or only have interests in women's questions, indicates that by and large they reproduce the problematical assumptions that underlie the area study of the Middle East and North Africa.

Academic women's work on Middle Eastern and North African women is dominated by the religion/tradition paradigm and is characterized by a variant of what the late C. Wright Mills called "abstracted empiricism."[22] That is, the problems selected for study are limited by the method chosen to study them. Once researchers have decided on a functionalist/culturalist method, for example, they are unable to address anything but religion and tradition. The overall result is a reductive, a historical conception of women. The emphasis on the religion/tradition paradigm, a combination of orientalist[23] and evolutionary assumptions, constrains its critics by compelling them either to ritually refer to its parameters or to submit to them. Tradition in this case is seen as exemplified by the veil, seclusion, clitoridectomy, and so on.

Historically, of course, the veil has held an obsessive interest for many a writer. In 1829, for example, Charles Forster wrote *Mohammetanism Unveiled,* and Frantz Fanon, the revolutionary, wrote in 1967 about Algerian women under the caption: "Algeria Unveiled."[24] Even angry responses to this abusive imagery could not escape its attraction as when a Moroccan feminist titled her book: *Beyond the Veil.*[25] The persistence of the veil as a symbol that essentially stands for women illustrates the difficulty researchers have in dealing with a reality with which they are unfamiliar. It also reveals an attitude of mistrust. A veil is a hiding device; it arouses suspicion. Besides, veiling is close to masquerading so that studying women from societies where veiling exists is a form of theater! Some native (for example, "Eastern") feminists have pushed the theatrical imagery to its extreme by making the veil an integral part of the woman's persona.[26]

The evolutionary bias that suffuses most thinking about women in the Middle East and North Africa is expressed in a definite prejudice against Islam as a religion. Although U.S. feminists have attempted to accommodate Christianity and feminism and Judaism and feminism, Islam is inevitably presented as antifeminist.[27] What is at work here is not merely a plausible rationalist bias against religion as an impediment to the progress and freedom of the mind but an acceptance of the idea that there is a hierarchy of religions, with some being more susceptible to change than others. Like tradition, religion must be abandoned if Middle Eastern women are to be like Western women. As the logic of the argument requires, there can be no change without reference to an external standard deemed to be perfect.

Although religion is seen in Western societies as one institution among many, it is perceived as the bedrock of the societies in which Islam is practiced. A ritual is established whereby the writer appeals to religion as *the* cause of gender inequality just as it is made the source of underdevelopment in much of modernization theory. In an uncanny way, feminist discourse on women from the Middle East and North Africa mirrors that of theologians' own interpretation of women in Islam. Academic feminists have compounded this situation by adding their own problematical specifications. They reduce Islam to one or two *sura,* or injunctions, such as those related to gender hierarchy and the punishment meted out to adulterous women (which is also applied to men).[28]

The overall effect of this paradigm is to deprive women of self-presence, of being. Because women are subsumed under religion presented in fundamental terms, they are inevitably seen as evolving in non-historical time. They have virtually no history. Any analysis of change is therefore foreclosed. When feminists "do" history, they generally appear to engage in an antihistory, where progress is measured in terms of a countback to the time where it all began, and all began to come unraveled. This means the time of the Koran for the female writer, just as it is the time of the Koran and the Traditions for the male writer.[29] The tenacious focus on religion in the scholarship on women in the Middle East and North Africa makes it the functional equivalent of fire in mythology and early scientific thought. A similar obsession/fascination with the mysterious power of fire dominated the "primitive" *as well as* the "scientific" mind up until the end of the eighteenth century.[30]

The question to raise at this point is this: Why hasn't academic feminism exposed the weaknesses of the prevailing discourse on women in the Middle East and North Africa? There have been articles and prefaces to anthologies that have denounced what Elizabeth Fernea and B.Q. Bezirgan have aptly referred to as "astigmatic writing" about women in the Middle East and North Africa.[31] Some studies have also attempted to break away from—although they have not displaced—the prevailing paradigm. It is also worth remembering that competing paradigms are "incommensurable" in that the criteria for judging their relative merits are not determined by value-neutral rules but lie within the community of scholars whose "expertise" has *produced* North Africa and the Middle East as a field of knowledge.[32] Still, no sustained effort has been made to challenge systematically the epistemological and theoretical presuppositions of much of the scholarship on women.[33]

Difference, in general, whether cultural, ethnic, or racial, has been a stumbling block for Western social science from its very inception. Nineteenth-century European ethnology and anthropology were established precisely to study different peoples and their institutions. However, regardless of the conceptual, theoretical, and methodological inadequacies and uncertainties in the works of many classical anthropologists and ethnologists, their interest in "difference" was a function of their desire to understand their own institutions better. This was the case with Emile Durkheim's work on religion, Marcel Mauss on exchange, and Bronislaw Malinowski on the Oedipus complex to cite only a few. Although I do not wish to absolve Western anthropology of its Europocentrism, it showed, at least in its inception, some awareness of a common denominator between people of different cultures, a *human* bond. The notion of "cultural universals" or that of the "human mind," however problematic, are expressions of such a common link between various peoples.

Contemporary academic feminism appears to have forgotten this part of its intellectual heritage. Of course, counterposing feminist scholarship to social science may appear senseless. Aren't female social scientists part of the same society and intellectual milieu as males? Indeed they are. But, academic feminists have generally denounced conventional social science for its biases regarding women both in its theory and its practice. Specifically, they have shown that it has reduced women to one dimension of their lives (such as reproduction and housework) and failed to conceptualize their status in society as historically evolving. Academic feminism, therefore, has brought a breath of fresh air into social science discourse on women and held out the promise of a more even-handed, less-biased practice. It is surprising, then, when one sees that women in Algeria (or in any other part of the Third World) are dealt with precisely in the ways with which academic feminists do not wish to be dealt.

Women in Algeria are subsumed under the less-than-neutral label of "Islamic women" or "Arab women" or "Middle Eastern women." Because language produces the reality it names, "Islamic women" must by necessity be made to conform to the configuration of meanings associated with the concept of Islam. The label affirms what ought to be seen as problematical. Whether the "Islamic women" are truly devout or whether the societies in which they live are theocracies are questions that the label glosses over.

The one-sidedness of this discourse on difference becomes grotesque if we reverse the terms and suggest, for example, that women in contemporary Europe and North America should be studied as Christian women! Similarly, the label "Middle Eastern women," when counterposed with the label "European women," reveals its unwarranted generality. The Middle East is a geographical area covering no less than twenty countries (if it is confined to the "Arab" East) that display a few similarities and many differences. Feminists study women in Victorian England or under the French Revolution; few would dare subsume French or English women under the all-encompassing label of "European women" or Caucasian women, as substantive categories of thought. Yet, a book on Egyptian women was subtitled "Women in the Arab World."[34] Michel Foucault may have been right when he asserted that "knowledge is not made for understanding; it is made for cutting."[35]

There is a great continuity in the U.S. feminist treatment of difference within gender whether the difference is within or outside of U.S. society. In each case an attribute, whether physical (race or color) or cultural (religion or ethnicity), is used in an ontological sense. There is, however, an added feature to feminist modes of representing women from the Middle East and North Africa, and these modes reflect the dynamics of global politics. The political attitudes of "center" states are mirrored in feminist attitudes toward women from "peripheral" states. Elly Bulkin rightly notes that "women's lives and women's oppression cannot be considered outside the bounds of regional conflicts." She points out that Arab women are represented as being so different that they are deemed unable to understand or develop any form of feminism. When Arab women speak for themselves they are accused of being "pawns of Arab men."[36] The implication is that an Arab woman cannot be a feminist (whatever the term means) prior to disassociating herself from Arab men and the culture that supports them! In the end, global politics joins hands with prejudice, thereby closing a Western gynocentric circle based on misapprehended difference.[37]

The political bias in these representations of difference is best illustrated by the search of many feminists for the sensational and the uncouth. This search for the disreputable, which reinforces the notion of difference as objectified otherness, is often carried out with the help of Middle Eastern and North African women themselves. Feminism has provided a forum for these women to express themselves and on occasion for them to vent their anger at their societies. The exercise of freedom of expression often has a dizzying effect and sometimes leads to personal confession in the guise of social criticism. Individual women from the Middle East and North Africa appear on the feminist stage as representatives of the millions of women in their own societies. To what extent they do violence to the women they claim authority to write and speak about is a question that is seldom raised.

In assessing the issue of writing about Third World women, Gayatri C. Spivak points out that First World women and Western-trained women are complicitous in contributing to the continued "degradation" of Third World women whose "micrology" they interpret without having access to it. Although well taken, this view obscures the fact that complicity is often a conscious act involving social class position, psychological identification, and material interests. Of course, to include all "Western-trained" women in the plural "we," which also encompasses "First World" women, is to simplify the reality of the feminist encounter between Western and non-Western women. Unfortunately, academic feminist practice, just like that of its intellectual predecessors, is not pure on either side of difference. I, for one, refuse to be identified, even metaphorically, with Senanyak, the Indian antihero character who lends his expert knowledge to crush the revolution exemplified by "Dopti," a female revolutionary.[38] Affirming the existence of complicity is not sufficient. Indeed, the very act of translating this particular Indian short story for a U.S. audience did not bridge the chasm of cultural difference. It fits in with what Gaston Bachelard called the "museum of horrors." It documents the villainous acts of Indian men and the victimization of Indian women. The association of the Western and non-Western female reader with the process of victimization is an imaginative way of reducing the differential divide, but it does not fill it. And therein lies the dilemma of Third World women writing about Third World women.

Women in Algeria

As I have suggested, Euro-American and/or academic feminist discourse on women in Algeria reproduces the major elements of the prevailing social science paradigm. In addition, it makes explicit the connection between feminist or protofeminist practice and traditional geopolitics, of which colonialism and the international division of intellectual labor are a significant part. There is also continuity between nineteenth- and twentieth-century feminist and protofeminists writing about Algerian women.

By and large, nineteenth- and twentieth-century literature on women in Algeria betrays a great deal of ambivalence. Male authors searched for women wherever they could find them, and although they bemoaned what they perceived as seclusion, they also expressed contempt for the libertines they encountered and surprise (rather than approval) before the unveiled rural women. Women writing from a social scientific perspective expressed their ambivalence in a slightly different mode, ostensibly empathizing with Algerian women they perceived as inferior and displaying unabashed contempt for Algerian men.[39]

A model of the protofeminist discourse on Algerian women is provided by Hubertine Auclert's *Les Femmes arabes en Algérie*, published in 1900.

Auclert sees that colonialism victimized women but even though she is aware of the excesses of the colonial order, she still advocates the Frenchification of women. She suggests, moreover, that French women should become the tools of such an endeavor! "Upon entering tents and bolted doors, they [French women] would familiarize Muslim women with our lifestyles and ways of thinking"! Their task would no doubt be easy, because, according to Auclert, Algerian women were at heart the daughters of the free-thinking women of pre-Islamic Arabia. The eloquence they displayed in court, writes the author, was such that "you would think you heard, resuscitated, the beautiful speakers of pagan Arabia." In other words, Islam, the obstacle to being French, was but a veneer for women. Through women, moreover, one can undo Islam. Religion is identified with men so that a step toward the Frenchification of women is the construction of a pre-Islamic female essence. That same religion was responsible for what Auclert felt was Algerian women's inability to experience passionate love as French women were assumed to do. Algerian women were also found to be lacking a certain sensitivity that the French displayed because the latter read novels and had a different religion! In the end, the Algerian woman was perceived as living in limbo. "The Arab woman neither is nor does she feel at home at her husband's."[40]

In 1929, another French woman, Mathea Gaudry, a lawyer turned anthropologist, accepted the fact that she could not change the Algerian women's religious beliefs but did not give up the overall colonial project of Frenchification. Working with women from the Aurès mountains, she stated that "her intelligence would make the Auressian woman worthy of some education; what I mean is that we could teach her French, how to sew and run a home." As for the Algerian men from the region, she wrote that "their mental faculties appear to be stunted in the prime of life." Besides, the men are "inveterate liars" and display a "congenital nonchalance."[41] She too pursued the nostalgic notion of Algerian women's pre-Islamic past, to wit: "By subjecting her [*the* woman from Ammour mountain] to the authority of a master whom she must fear, Islamic law profoundly separated her from those berber and pre-Islamic women: Sadouk, Raytah and others whose independence is legendary."[42] Indeed, this is more a matter of legend than reality. The author adds that the nomadic woman's "more or less confused understanding of this legendary past" accounts for her flirtatious games with men. Why can't a woman be free to flirt without a rationale being found for her behavior in mythical time?

Throughout the 1950s and 1960s, various monographs on women appeared with the aim of "guiding" Algerian women toward the ideal of French womanhood and downgrading their religion and customs, even at a time (the 1950s) when women were displaying the kind of behavior French women should have commended. In this respect it is noteworthy that only one study was written by two French women of an Algerian female revolutionary who became a *cause célèbre* during the war (1954–62).[43]

Germaine Tillion's work (*The Republic of Cousins*), which appeared to break new ground in bringing Algerian women together with southern Mediterranean women in the same theoretical framework, was also unable in the end to transcend the stumbling block of Islam. Algerian women emerged from the book at the bottom of the hierarchy of sisterhood. After asserting that Islam had little to do directly with what she termed the "degradation of the female condition," Tillion was unable to keep religion analytically separate from her comparative evaluation of Algerian and European women living in the northern rim of the Mediterranean. Tillion also managed to neglect the colonial factor in her analysis of the dynamics of religion, political economy, and the reproduction of gender relations.[44]

In a book that purports to have been written in a spirit of sisterhood, Françoise Corrèze stated that "the donkey and the mule tied to a ring undoubtedly suffer less from man's [authority] than the women cloistered in the shed we entered." That *she*, a stranger, was allowed to penetrate the "cloisters" is a fact that she did not bother to ponder. Having apparently approached her study of rural women with a preconceived interpretative framework, she found herself compelled to explain away facts that did not conform to her ideas. For example, she wondered why a mother-in-law she met did not exhibit the signs of the mythical "powerful mother-in-law" and concluded that "perhaps she was once [powerful]."[45]

The author's gaze at the Algerian female Other dwelled on women's postures, gestures, and clothes, and it studiously noted whether women's clothes were clean or dirty. In the process, the reader is not always told about the nature of the social changes that have affected the rural communities studied, although signs of such changes abound almost in spite of the author's will.

In 1980, Juliette Minces produced an essay on women in Algeria (in a book that, naturally, covers "the Arab World") in which she denied women any selfhood or ability to think. Women's participation in the war is presented as the result of men's will and manipulation. Her contempt for women is revealed in her remark that Algerian women chose Islam over colonialism. She, the scientist, tells women that "they have no consciousness of the double alienation they underwent"! Yet, she adds, "they had access to French society and were open to new ideas"![46] Echoing Minces, U.S. feminist Judith Stiehm has written that "the French held the Muslim culture in disdain because of its treatment of women." Using as her main source a State Department area handbook for Algeria, Stiehm revealed her ignorance of her subject matter by making factually incorrect statements. For example, she wrote that "as Muslim women move out of seclusion they tend to enter segregated schools, offices and/or factories."[47] As a matter of fact, offices are not segregated and what single-sex schools remain were inherited from the French era. In addition, the state has been implementing a policy of coeducation.

In a book published in 1980 entitled *Femmes d'Islam ou le sexe interdit* (Women of Islam or the forbidden sex), encompassing North Africa, Renée Pelletier and Autilio Gaudio engaged in another diatribe against Islam, blaming it for, among other things, the Algerian president's alleged unwillingness to "show his wife in public." In fact, the current president does appear with his wife in public, although he may not "show" her! The authors' analysis of the Koran is based on one *sura,* just as the rest of their essay is based on anecdotal information gleaned from one book written in the 1960s supplemented by images from a short film. What is most noteworthy about this book, however, are the leading questions used in a questionnaire meant to elicit responses about women in Morocco. For example:

Question #10: "Have you felt sexual attraction for boys?"
Question #13: "Have you already kissed a boy on the lips who is not your fiance or husband?"
Question #2: "How did you perceive your mother's condition when you were a child?"
Question #5: "When have you, for the first time, felt the weight of traditions and prohibitions?"

In conclusion, the authors assert that "this study could be applied to all three countries of the Maghreb."[48] On the other side of difference, they must be, they are, all alike.

Echoing Stiehm, another U.S. feminist political scientist, Kay Boals, has written that the nature of female/male relations in Algeria "elicited contempt and derision from the colonizer." Also of interest is the typology of forms of consciousness that Boals set up to explain the behavior of colonized people, blacks, women, and homosexuals. Such individuals exhibit a type of consciousness that falls in one of six categories, ranging from "traditional" to "traditionalist, reformist, assimilationist, revolutionary," and "transforming" (which an earlier draft of the article termed "modernizing"). The author asserted that Algerian males are definitely "traditionalist" but women are "transforming." Indeed, what women "aspire to corresponds more closely to patterns of male-female relations in European than in traditional Muslim culture." A problem arises, however, when one turns to the definitions of these types of consciousness. The "traditionalist" is the man who "continues to reaffirm the criteria of judgement of his own traditional culture or religion but he is unable to do so with internal conviction. There is thus a strong internal incoherence between emotion and thinking, between what one would like to believe and what one 'knows in one's bones.'"[49]

No such conflict should exist among women whose consciousness is transforming. Yet "Algerian women are eager to change the traditional patterns but are somewhat inhibited in doing so by the internal psychic ambivalence created by the desire to affirm the Algerian heritage and culture." The "transforming consciousness" is defined as that which feels "genuinely free to forge new combinations of personality traits . . . without the need . . . to imitate the model of the European." If this is the case then one wonders why Algerian culture or heritage would be an obstacle to acquiring such a consciousness unless it is deemed inadequate and therefore something that ought to be rejected. Indeed, the author has defined "traditional consciousness" as that which is characterized by "a calm conviction of superiority over others and a sense of being at the center of the cosmos." The ideal human type of this consciousness is found in the person of Al Khidr Husayn, the first editor of the journal of Al Azhar University in Cairo. This creature, "although writing in the 1930's apparently remained essentially unaffected by the British occupation!"[50] In other words, the colonial/European factor defines a catch-22 situation. If you fall prey to it you are an "anomaly" in the sense that you wish for change deemed impossible to obtain; if you don't you are still anomalous because you are defined as "traditional." It is worth noting that the author does not provide any information about having interviewed or observed the females and males whose psyche she has furnished with ambivalence, contradictions, inhibitions, and anomaly.

The repetitive nature of the prevailing paradigm stifles the mind and dulls the senses. At the very least, it has no aesthetic value; it is like wearing the same clothes all the time. However, its ultimate effect is to preclude any understanding of Algerian women *in their lived reality:* as subjects in their own right. Instead, they are reified, made into mere bearers of unexplained categories. Algerian women have no existence outside these categories; they have no individuality. What is true of one is true of all; just as what is true of Algerian women is also held to be true of all women deemed to be like them over the space generously defined as the "Muslim world" or the "Arab world." This "worlding" of the female world is another instance of the unquestioned practice of "abstracted empiricism."

How, then, can an Algerian woman write about women in Algeria when her space has already been defined, her history dissolved, her subjects objectified, her language chosen for her? How can she speak without saying the same things?[51] The Algerian case supports Foucault's contention about Western culture that "the most tenacious subjection of difference is undoubtedly that maintained by categories."[52] What is needed is a phenomenology of women's lived experience to explode the constraining power of categories. Such a phenomenology would not be a mere description of the subjective meaning of women's experience. Rather, it would be the search for the organizing principles of women's lived reality as it intersects with men's.[53] To study women from a phenomenological perspective is different from merely interviewing them to elicit from them information about their lives that *confirms our* conceptions of *them.*[54]

The fetishism of the concept, Islam, in particular, obscures the living reality of the women and men subsumed under it. North African and Middle Eastern societies are more complex and more diverse than is admitted, and cannot be understood in terms of monolithic, unitary concepts. Religion cannot be detached from the socioeconomic and political context within which it unfolds. And religion cannot be seen as having an existence independent of human activity. As the product of human activity, it is subject to change, if not in content at least in function. To understand the role of religion in women's lives, we must identify the conditions under which it emerges as a significant factor, as well as those that limit its scope. In addition, we must address the ways in which religious symbols are manipulated by both women and men in everyday life as well as in institutional settings. Finally, we should refrain from thinking in terms of a "Middle East" and realize that what is useful to geopolitics is not necessarily so to sociology. Concrete women (like men) live in concrete societies and *not* in an ideologically uniform space. There are Turkish women and Egyptian women and Algerian women. Subsuming some under others results in obscuring, rather than improving, our understanding of gender relations.

Conclusion

This bird's-eye view of feminist discourse on women in Algeria points to the necessity of asking anew a question that might sound embarrassing: What is the nature of the feminist project? What is its relation to women in other places? Is there something at the heart of academic feminism that is inescapably Western gynocéntric; that is, must it inevitably lead to the exercise of discursive power by some women over others?

To subscribe to the notion that the metaphysics of difference-as-misrepresentation is inescapable is self-defeating and betrays resistance to changing the intellectual status quo. The French philosopher Jacques Derrida upholds the view (shared by some Third World feminists) that ethnocentrism is necessarily irrevocable on the grounds that ethnology is a European science. He also adds that deconstruction is inscribed in the very language of European social science.[55] Read in an unorthodox fashion, this means that the metaphysics that sustains ethnocentrism also sustains deconstruction, a destructuring activity. In spite of its honest recognition of the ethnocentric core of social science, this view appears to legitimate its own existence. For if ethnocentrism reproduces itself in an endless cycle, the language of ethnocentrism may not be superseded; it can only be deconstructed. What applies to ethnocentrism also applies to the Western gynocentric conception of difference.

If academic feminism cannot be allowed to hide behind a deconstructionist approach to legitimate its misapprehension of difference within gender, it should not be allowed to seek refuge in the Foucauldian conception of power and language either. Foucault's conception of power as being decentered has legitimized the view, among some academic feminists according to which power over women-in-general is diffuse. In so doing, the actual instrumentality of power that some women (for example, academic women) exercise over other women (such as Third World women) is neglected. Similarly, subsuming all reality under discourse, as Foucault does, has resulted in a shift of focus from women's lived reality to endless discoursing about it. It is true that a feminist engaged in the act of representing women who belong to a different culture, ethnic group, race, or social class wields a form of power over them; a power of interpretation. However, this power is a peculiar one. It is borrowed from the society at large which is male-centered. It is borrowed power that gives academic feminists engaged in interpreting difference status and credibility. But, when the power of men over women is reproduced in the power of women over women, feminism as an intellectual movement presents a caricature of the very institutions it was meant to question. The misrepresentation of "different" women is a form of self-misrepresentation. It bespeaks a repression of one's femaleness and glosses over the fact that the representer is also engendered and remains far from having achieved the freedom and capacity to define herself.

Just as some men's inability (or reluctance) to accept sexual difference as the expression of modes of being human has led them to formulate a sociobiological conception of women, Western gynocentrism has led to an essentialism of otherhood. Both phenomena are products of a larger differentialist trend that has affected Western Europe and North America since the end of World War Two. The collapse of the colonial empires, the rise of consumer societies, and the crises of the late capitalist states have formed the context within which assertions of "difference" have emerged. The celebration of difference between women and men, homosexuals and heterosexuals, the mad and the sane, has since become the unquestioned norm.

What is problematical in this conception of difference is that it affirms a new form of reductionism. The rejection of humanism and its universalistic character in discourse analysis and deconstruction deprives the proponents of difference of any basis for understanding the relationship between the varieties of modes of being different in the world. Difference becomes essentialized. It is not accidental that Foucault, for example, contributed little to our understanding of what it means to be mad, female or male. What he did was to explain the *category* of madness and of sexuality. The discourse and deconstruction approaches to difference obviate the crucial issue of *intersubjectivity*. Although Derrida warns against an ontological conception of difference, he is unable to avoid affirming difference as unmediated otherness. He locates difference in language, thus removing it from the realm of shared experiences that language may not necessarily capture.

The inability to address the intersubjective foundation of difference is clearly a significant problem in academic feminism. In the United States, this problem is not merely the result of some feminists being influenced by Foucault or Derrida. It is also related to an intellectual tradition marked by pragmatism, a byproduct of positivism, that has characterized U.S. institutions of higher learning since the nineteenth century. In feminist scholarship, this has meant giving the female *experience* (read U.S. or "Western") a privileged ontological status.

To take intersubjectivity into consideration when studying Algerian women or other Third World women means seeing their lives as meaningful, coherent, and understandable instead of being infused "by us" with doom and sorrow. It means that their lives like "ours" are structured by economic, political, and cultural factors. It means that these women, like "us," are engaged in the process of adjusting, often shaping, at times resisting and even transforming their environment. It means they have their own individuality; they are "for themselves" instead of being "for us." An appropriation of their singular individuality to fit the generalizing categories of "our" analyses is an assault on their integrity and on their identity. Intersubjectivity alerts us to the common bond that ties women and men of different cultures together. It is a relative safeguard against the objectification of others, a reminder that the other is just as entitled as I am to her/his humanity expressed in her/his cultural mode.[56]

For the intersubjective component of experience to become evident in the study of difference within and between genders, a certain form of humanism must be reaffirmed. But the rejection of humanistic philosophy, which subsumed woman under man while making claims to universalism, has so far been replaced with the essentialism of difference.

It is often argued, of course, that humanism erases individuality, difference; that any return to a humanistic thought is self-defeating. Yet, it appears that the essentializing of difference between women has resulted in the erasure of "other" women. When these are locked into the categories of religion, race, or color, their own individuality as women has already been erased. For example, a "Muslim woman" is no longer a concrete individual. She is not Algerian, or Yemeni; she is an abstraction in the same way as a "woman of color" is. Their assumed uniqueness dissolves their concrete reality. They cannot by definition be compared with "First World" women. Indeed, what distinguishes them from the latter is also what is seen as accounting for their very essence.

Antihumanism has not provided any authority higher than itself that could monitor its excesses. Old-style humanism, in contrast, and despite its shortcomings, makes itself vulnerable to criticism by appealing to its unfulfilled promise of a more reasonable rationalism or a more egalitarian universalism. Indeed, the universalistic claim to a supracultural human entity embodied in reason provided colonized societies with the tool necessary to regain their freedom. Colonized women and men were willing to give up their lives in order to capture their share of humanity celebrated but denied by colonial powers. But what does antihumanism offer "different" peoples? On what grounds (moral or otherwise) can powerless people struggle against their relegation to the prison house of race, color, and nationality into which antihumanism locks them?

There is a sense in which the antihumanist celebration of unmediated "difference" may denote resistance to accepting difference as the other side of sameness. It is not accidental that the rise of antihumanism coincided with the collapse of the French colonial empire, more specifically the end of the Algerian war (and it was at this time that both Foucault and Derrida began publishing). Yet, antihumanism, as a philosophy, holds a great attraction for some feminists because of its nihilistic questioning of all (including moral/ethical) constraints on action or on thought. This is, of course, the very reason it is fraught with dangers as soon as discoursing about others' (not only men's but women's) subjectivity is at stake. To what extent can Western feminism dispense with an ethics of responsibility when writing about "different" women? Is the subject "women" free of all constraints only because women are the researchers? The point is neither to subsume other women under one's own experience nor to uphold a separate truth for them. Rather, it is to allow them to *be* while recognizing that what they are is just as meaningful, valid, and comprehensible as what "we" are. They are not the antithesis of "ourselves" that justifies "our" studying them in ways we do not study "ourselves."

Heidegger's letter on humanism offers an example of the kinds of questions that might be posed in order to reorient our thinking on humanism. We need to ask what is the "humanitas of homo humanus?" What is woman's/man's place in history? Is woman/man "a specter, a spectator or a creator?" What would a "humanism in a new dimension" be like? A new humanism requires a more original reexperiencing of what it is to be human. This involves a process of "questioning, etymologizing, and historicizing." Although Heidegger's answers are ambiguous, they nevertheless point to the importance of history, language, and ethics in reexploring humanistic thought. When seen as a "process of coming to the word," humanism precludes the assumption of woman's/man's domination by the word, a tenet of the antihumanist discursive approach to history.[57]

Finally, being aware that woman/man plays a role in history that requires specification points to the ethical component of human activity and thought. Indeed, when feminists essentially deny other women the humanity they claim for themselves, they dispense with any ethical constraint. They engage in the act of splitting the social universe into "us" and "them," "subjects" and "objects." This propensity to apprehend social reality in terms of binary oppositions is a contradictory element in feminist thought. Feminists have criticized the social and natural sciences precisely because they use dichotomous categories that assign women one attribute or role, thereby simplifying the far more complex reality of women's lives.

The split vision of the world that relegates non-Western women to a residual category, where fancy more than fact rules, is a significant error in feminist scholarship as a whole. It can be corrected only if and when Western feminists are ready and willing to think differently about the variety of modes of being female, including their own. They must recognize that knowledge of North African/Third World women is not given all at once. It is, like knowledge of women in Western societies, a process of sifting the true from the false and making visible that which remains submerged. It is historical and has a rationality of its own which human reason *can* comprehend.

As it now stands, difference is seen as mere division. The danger of this undeveloped view lies in its verging on *indifference*.[58] In this sense, *anything* can be said about women from other cultures as long as it appears to document their differentness from "us." This bespeaks a lack of concern for the complexity of difference as well as a simplification of difference to mean "particularity," that is to say, unmediated singularity.[59] Because the North African and Middle Eastern cultures have long been stereotyped, because the feminist movement ought to be a movement toward human liberation from epistemological domination, women from these cultures cannot satisfy themselves with a mere act of negation when they write about themselves. They must shoulder a double burden, namely, to work toward an epistemological break with the prevailing paradigm *and* to reevaluate the structure of gender relations in their own societies.

History has dealt these women a hard blow. It held them hostage to colonial or imperial ventures and delivered them to travelers, chroniclers, painters, and anthropologists of both sexes who mused about their lives. Now, they are in a position from which they could recapture the dispersed fragments of their selves and put them back together in combinations that the motley crowd of their observers may not suspect. The task is enormous but necessary. If feminism is seen as a critical intellectual movement, "Eastern" feminism should attempt to bring about that intellectual renaissance that men have so far failed to carry out.

This requires reflecting on the roles that female intellectuals should play in effectively promoting women's needs. It is crucial here to ponder the adequacy of the means for achieving these ends. To think of feminism in the singular is sociologically inappropriate. Similarly, French or U.S. styles of feminisms may not be functional in different socioeconomic and political contexts. What form should women's effort to reach gender equality take in the various societies of North Africa and the Middle East? Is feminism, as understood in Western societies, women's only avenue toward social change? Such questions may not be answered if Eastern feminists think of their audience as residing here instead of in their societies of origin.

There is a sense in which the issue for North African and Middle Eastern academic women is not the applicability of U.S. or French feminist theories. That is a luxury one cannot afford. The question is to define a critical writing space within which women who are not making their careers in Western universities, but who are the subjects of our writing, can identify. This requires resisting the temptation of seeing in U.S. or French women's present needs our ideals. It also calls for a comprehensive exploring and understanding of the body of knowledge produced by the indigenous peoples of these areas of the world. To selectively pinpoint instances of women's "victimization," as is often done, obscures the complexity of gender processes and presents a truncated image of an intellectual heritage whose existence is barely suspected by all but a few experts. If this means to reinvent the wheel, so be it! The old wheel has not worked too well. Perhaps a new one might be an improvement on the old.

A failure to do so will inevitably result in storytelling. That can be a rewarding endeavor. Having told his wonderful story several times, Othello remarked that Desdemona "devoured up my discourse," and "my story being done she gave me for my pains a world of kisses." However, Othello was also devoured by his own discourse. In the end he bade Lodovico tell his story:

> *"And say besides that in Aleppo once,*
> *Where a malignant and turbaned Turk*
> *Beat a Venetian and traduced the State,*
> *I took by th' throat the circumcised dog*
> *And smote him—thus"* (He stabs himself)[60]

If discourse can be murderous, speech may never rise above mere talk. In the words of Dostoevsky, some people "may be able to live in dark cellars for forty years and never open their mouth[s], but the moment they get into the light of day and break out they talk and talk and talk" . . . Isn't the whole point to have a *voice*?[61]

Notes

1. Omar Khayyam, *Rubaiyat of Omar Khayyam* (Boston: Houghton Mifflin, 1884), quatrain 99.

2. The term "Western" here implies no particular ontology and is essentially inadequate. It is used in this text to refer to women who are identified as belonging to what is geographically and culturally presented as the "West" or the "First World." It is as inadequate as the term "Eastern," which I will also use.

3. See Marnia Lazreg, "The Epistemological Obstacle of Experience: A Critical Neo-Rationalist Approach" (paper presented at the Pembroke Center Conference on Feminism, Theory, Politics, Brown University, 14–16 Mar. 1985).

4. This issue is best illustrated in the debate over what constitutes feminist science. See Sandra Harding, *The Science Question in Feminism* (Ithaca: Cornell University Press, 1986); Myra Jehlen, "Archimedes and the Paradox of Feminist Criticism," *Signs* 6 (Summer 1981).

5. Significantly, the intense current interest in "Middle Eastern women" is occurring at a time when the "Middle East" has been neutralized as a self-sustaining political and economic force.

6. For an example of accommodation, see Mervat Hatem, "The Politics of Sexuality and Gender in Segregated Patriarchal Systems: The Case of Eighteenth- and

Nineteenth-Century Egypt," *Feminist Studies* 12 (Summer 1986): 251–74. The author displays no awareness of the criticism leveled at the concept of "patriarchy," using Egypt to bear out the universalistic claims of U.S. feminist theory of patriarchy.

7. Examples of minority women's questioning of academic feminism include *This Bridge Called My Back: Writings by Radical Women of Color,* ed. Cherríe Moraga and Gloria Anzaldúa (New York: Kitchen Table, Women of Color Press, 1983); and Bell Hooks, *Feminist Theory from Margin to Center* (Boston: South End Press, 1984). See also Maria Lugones and Victoria Spelman, "Have We Got a Theory for You? Feminist Theory, Cultural Imperialism, and the Demand for the Woman's Voice," *Women's Studies International Forum* 6, no. 6 (1983): 573–89.

8. Up to now, attempts at defining a space from which to address the woman question have been reduced to accepting or rejecting Islam as a religion. Thus, "Eastern" feminist writing oscillates between adopting or rejecting Western feminist modes of analysis. For example, Aziza Al Hibri makes lists of the positive and distorted aspects of the Koran in "A Study of Islamic Herstory: Or How Did We Ever Get into This Mess?" in her edited *Women and Islam* (New York: Pergamon Press, 1982), 207–20. Historians of religion Yvonne Y. Haddad and Jane I. Smith have made similar attempts in "Eve: Islamic Image of Woman," in *Women and Islam,* 135–44. Azar Tabari's and Nahid Yeganeh's exchange on whether (Shi'a) Islam can accommodate gender equality must be understood within the context of contemporary Iran where Shi'ism is in power. They, too, yield to the prevailing paradigm pitting modernity against tradition in *In the Shadow of Islam: The Women's Movement in Iran* (London: Zed Press, 1982), esp. pt. 1, 1–75.

9. The connection between the colonial discourse and contemporary women's and/or feminist discourses on Third World women is explored in some detail by Chandra Talpade Mohanty's "Under Western Eyes: Feminist Scholarship and Colonial Discourses," *Boundary 2* 12 (Spring/Fall 1984): 333–58; Gayatri Chakravorty Spivak, "French Feminism in an International Frame," *Yale French Studies* 62 (1981): 154–84. For an exploration of the relationship between French and American orientalisms see Edward W. Said, *Orientalism* (New York: Vintage Books, 1979), esp. chap. 3, pt. 3.

10. By "paradigm," I mean the "rules, empirical and theoretical laws, experimental techniques, methodological directives, and even metaphysical principles that are involved in any particular scientific achievement." See Gary Gutting, ed., *Paradigms and Revolutions: Appraisals and Applications of Thomas Kuhn's Philosophy of Science* (Notre Dame: University of Notre Dame Press, 1980), esp. introduction, 1–21. The rise and fall of paradigms in science is classically discussed in Thomas S. Kuhn's *The Structure of Scientific Revolutions* (Chicago: University of Chicago Press, 1962). Cf. Michel Foucault's use of "discourse." See Hubert L. Dreyfus and Paul Rabinow, *Michel Foucault: Beyond Structuralism and Hermeneutics,* 2d. ed. (Chicago: University of Chicago Press, 1983), esp. 197–204.

11. Algeria may be seen as an "ideal type" in which colonial domination, social science, and interest in women display their intimate connections. Disclaiming traditional/Europocentric conceptions of Islam has become part of a ritual among feminist writers who nonetheless use the very language denounced. See, for example, Fatima Mernissi's introduction to the first edition of *Beyond the Veil:*

Male-Female Dynamics in a Modern Muslim Society (Cambridge, Mass.: Schenkman, 1975); and Leila Ahmed, "Western Ethnocentrism and Perceptions of the Harem," *Feminist Studies* 8 (Fall 1982): 521–34.

12. Making a distinction as to who is and is not a feminist—among Western women writing about Algerian or "Middle Eastern" women—has become nearly futile. U.S. academic feminism's market for "Middle Eastern women" is such that even writers who do not profess to feminism feel free to borrow its language: "private sphere," "sexual segregation," and "women's subordination," for example. Here, "protofeminist" refers to women writers who, within the Algerian context, at the turn of the century undertook the study of women with the purpose of making social policy recommendations. Hubertine Auclert, for example, was active in petitioning colonial authorities to outlaw polygamy. She was also aware of the less-than-equal status of French women who lacked the right to vote. See Hubertine Auclert, *Les Femmes arabes en Algérie* (Paris: Société d'Editions Literaires, 1900).

13. Although U.S. women writing about Eastern women have no direct colonial involvement, their discourse still reflects the direct domination in *all* spheres of socioeconomic and intellectual life of subjugated peoples. Popular culture in the United States upholds a view of "Islamic" societies that bears strong resemblances to French colonial and postcolonial female writers' perspectives. Were it not for the entrenched prejudices against "Islam," certain critiques would not have been necessary. See Elizabeth Fernea and B.Q. Bezirgan, eds., *Middle Eastern Muslim Women Speak* (Austin: University of Texas Press, 1976), esp. the introduction, xvii–xxxvi; Cynthia Nelson, "Public and Private Politics: Women in the Middle Eastern World," *American Ethnologist* 1 (August 1974): 551–63. See also Susan Dorsky's *Women of 'Amran* (Salt Lake City: University of Utah Press, 1986), esp. the conclusion, for recent disclaimers of "Islamic" female victimization.

14. Bryan S. Turner, *Marx and the End of Orientalism* (London: George Allen & Unwin, 1978), 1.

15. See Max Weber's study of Islam in *Economy and Society*, esp. vol. 3; and Bryan S. Turner's critique of it in *Weber and Islam: A Critical Study* (London: Routlege & Kegan Paul, 1974).

16. For a critique of H.A.R. Gibb and Harold Bowen's *Islamic Society and the West*, see Roger Owen, "The Middle East in the Eighteenth Century: An "Islamic Society" in Decline?" *Review of Middle East Studies* 1 (1975): 101–12.

17. David Waines, quoted in Turner, *Weber and Islam*, 6.

18. Clifford Geertz, *Islam Observed: Religious Development in Morocco and Indonesia* (New Haven: Yale University Press, 1968), esp. 56–89.

19. Turner, *Weber and Islam*, 6–7.

20. Clifford Geertz, *Local Knowledge: Further Essays in Interpretive Anthropology* (New York: Basic Books, 1983), chap. 8.

21. Jacques Berque wants "to give a privileged place, at least temporarily, to the marginal, the local, the peripheral" in Maghrebin history in order to discover, among other things, the "faults of the established order." See his *Ulemas, fondateurs, insurgés du Maghreb* (Paris: Sindbad, 1982), 16.

22. C. Wright Mills, *The Sociological Imagination* (New York: Oxford University Press, 1959), chap. 2.

23. Juliette Minces, *La Femme dans le monde arabe* (Woman in the Arab world) (Paris: Editions Mazarines, 1980). The recent English translation of the title was The House of Obedience: Women in Arab Society (London: Zed Press, 1980). This was apparently done in an effort to keep the orientalist conception of women alive. "Orientalism" refers to the view according to which the "Orient" is antithetical to and radically different from the "West." Thus, Minces is able to use the totalizing as well as reductive category of "obedience" to capture the essence of difference so conceived.

24. Cited in Edward W. Said, *The World, the Text, and the Critic* (Cambridge: Harvard University Press, 1983), 268; and see Frantz Fanon, *A Dying Colonialism* (New York: Grove Press, 1967), 34–67.

25. See Mernissi, *Beyond the Veil.*

26. See Leila Ahmed, "Islamic Women in Middle Eastern History" (paper presented at the Mary Ingraham Bunting Institute, Radcliffe College, 12 Nov. 1985).

27. Feminist theology also suffers from a religious bias. Rosemary R. Reuther is eager to preserve the "Judeo-Christian affirmation that the divine is one," leaving out Islam's emphasis on the unity of the divine. See her *Sexism and God Talk: Toward a Feminist Theology* (Boston: Beacon Press, 1983).

28. See Eliz Sanasarian's *The Women's Rights Movement in Iran: Mutiny, Appeasement, and Repression* (New York: Praeger, 1982), 12, which studies feminism as a social movement. Even radicals who avoid religion still view women as hopeless victims of a reified culture where heterosexual love seems impossible. See Hatem, 258–62. Turkish feminists are proud of the state which secularized their society, but they are often unable to see the complex interaction between religion and state which might play a role in structuring gender relations. For example, see Deniz Kandiyoti, "Sex-Roles and Social Change: A Comparative Appraisal of Turkey's Women," *Signs* 3 (Autumn 1977): 57–73; and Binnaz (Sayari) Toprak, "Religion and Turkish Women," in *Women in Turkish Society,* ed. Nermin Abadan-Unat (Leiden, The Netherlands: E.J. Brill, 1981), 281–93.

29. See Margaret Smith, *Rabi'a Al Adawiya and Her Fellow Saints in Islam* (Amsterdam: Philo Press, 1974). Smith's work on the Sufi mystic has been faithfully followed by Ahmed, who argues that Sufism provided women with a form of liberation from the constraints of what Smith perceived as "orthodox" Islam (see Ahmed's "Islamic Women in Middle Eastern History"). But Sufism finds its roots and justification in the Koran and cannot easily be placed in opposition to "Islam."

30. Gaston Bachelard, *La Psychanalyse du feu* (Paris: Gallimard, 1949).

31. See Fernea and Bezirgan, xvii–xxxvi.

32. There are works that consciously attempt to deviate from the prevailing paradigm as, for example, those cited in note 13. Among the most noteworthy are Andrea Rugh's *Family in Contemporary Egypt* (Syracuse: Syracuse University Press, 1984); and Judith Tucker's *Women in Nineteenth-Century Egypt* (Cambridge: Cambridge University Press, 1985). However, they have not constructed a competing paradigm.

33. Methodological/theoretical issues are discussed in some detail in Rosemary Sayigh, "Roles and Functions of Arab Women: A Reappraisal," *Arab Studies Quarterly* 3 (Autumn 1981): 258–74; Judith Tucker, "Problems in the Historiography of Women in the Middle East," *International Journal of Middle East Studies* 15

(1983): 324–36; and Nikki Keddie, "Problems in the Study of Middle Eastern Women," *International Journal of Middle Eastern Studies* 10 (1979): 225–40. Sayigh is the only author to have linked the practice of orientalism to the biases inherent in the study of "Arab women." The typical focus on religion in much of orientalist scholarship does not mean writers assert that ideas are the motor of Middle Eastern history. Rather, the argument is that *religious beliefs* keep women, men, and their institutions in the Middle East and in North Africa from evolving toward the Western type of secularization and "modernization."

34. See Nawal Saadawi, *The Hidden Face of Eve: Women in the Arab World* (Boston: Beacon Press, 1980).

35. Michel Foucault, *Language, Counter-Memory, Practice* ed. D.B. Bouchard (Ithaca: Cornell University Press, 1977), 154.

36. Elly Bulkin, "Semite vs. Semite/Feminist vs. Feminist," in *Yours in Struggle: Three Feminist Perspectives on Anti-Semitism and Racism,* ed. Elly Bulkin, Minnie Bruce Pratt, and Barbara Smith (Brooklyn: Long Haul Press, 1984), 167, 168.

37. I am using the term "gynocentric," as suggested by Elizabeth Weed, associate director of the Pembroke Center, Brown University, to refer to the situation whereby some women as a group exercise discursive power over other women whom they exclude from their frame of reference.

38. Gayatri Chakravorty Spivak, "'Darupadi' by Mahasveta Devi," in *Writing and Sexual Difference,* ed. Elizabeth Abel (Chicago: University of Chicago Press, 1982), 261–82, esp. translator's foreword. Senanyak's expertise is presumably similar to that of academic feminists' scholarship on Third World women: it can equally harm.

39. This article is not concerned with works of fiction on women in Algeria.

40. Hubertine Auclert, 26, 84, 91, 128. Even though Auclert was anticlerical, she shared with her contemporaries the view that Islam was inferior to Christianity.

41. Mathea Gaudry, *La Femme chaouia de l'Aurès* (Paris: Librairie Orientaliste Paul Geuthner, 1929), 287, 69, 84–85.

42. Mathea Gaudry, *La Société féminine du Djebel Amour et au Ksel* (Alger: Societé Algérienne D'Impressions Diverses, 1961), 426.

43. See Simone de Beauvoir and Gisèle Halimi, *Djamila Boupacha* (New York: Macmillan, 1962).

44. Germaine Tillion, *Le Harem et les cousins* (Paris: Editions du Seuil, 1966), esp. 199–212. The book was translated as *The Republic of Cousins* (London: Al Saqui Books, 1983). Despite her mythic use of neolithic exigencies, Tillion was able to place Islam on a par with Christianity: "In Islam just as in Christianity, the Mediterranean woman was constantly deprived of her rights, here in spite of the French Revolution; there in spite of the Koran" (p. 175).

45. Françoise Corrèze, *Les Femmes des Mechtas* (Paris: Les Editeurs Français Réunis, 1976), 41, 42, 115.

46. Juliette Minces, 111–36, esp. 117, 118.

47. Judith Stiehm, "Algerian Women: Honor, Shame, and Islamic Socialism," in *Women in the World: A Comparative Study,* ed. Lynne B. Iglitzin and Ruth Ross (Santa Barbara, Calif.: Clio Books, 1976), 232, 240.

48. Autilio Gaudio and Renée Pelletier, *Femmes d'Islam ou le sexe interdit* (Paris: Denoël, 1980), 104, 105, 153.

49. Kay Boals, "The Politics of Cultural Liberation: Male-Female Relations in Algeria," in *Liberating Women's History: Theoretical and Critical Essays*, ed. Berenice A. Carroll (Urbana: University of Illinois Press, 1976), 203, 205.

50. Ibid., 196, 205, 201, 195.

51. Algerian academic feminist thought is an expression of the complex interaction between its colonial background, socialist ideals, and the continued French domination of Algerian universities. Examples of the range of their writings are Feriel Lalami Fates, "A corps perdu ... ou des activités corporelles à caractère ludique des femmes travailleuses [Région d'Alger]," *Cahiers de la Méditerranée* 32 (June 1986): 91–99; Naziha Hamouda, "Les Femmes rurales et la production poétique," *Peuples Méditerranéens* 6, nos. 22–23 (1983): 267–79; and Fatiha Hakiki, "Le Travail féminin, emploi salarié et le travail domestique," *Actes des Journées d'Etudes et de Reflexion sur les Femmes Algéréennes, 3–6 mai 1980, Cahiers du C.D.S.H.* no. 3 (1980): 35–107. See also Fatiha Hakiki and Claude Talahite, "Human Sciences Research on Women in Algeria," in *Social Science Research and Women in the Arab World* (Paris: UNESCO, 1984), 82–93.

52. Foucault, 186.

53. Fatima Mernissi's *Le Maroc raconté par ses femmes* (Rabat: Société Marocaine des Editeurs Réunis, 1984) purports to give a voice to illiterate women in Morocco. Yet the text reveals a narcissistic attempt to speak for other women while rising above them. Nayra Atiya's *Khul Khaal* (Syracuse: Syracuse University Press, 1982) constitutes another instance of "giving" a voice to illiterate or poor women. Both Mernissi and Atiyah raise highly problematic questions concerning representation of poor and illiterate women for both national and international audiences.

54. I am working on a methodology rooted in Husserlian phenomenology.

55. Jacques Derrida, *L'Écriture et la différence* (Paris: Editions du Seuil, 1967), 414.

56. This does not mean a return to a narrow-minded cultural functionalism. For example, to argue that the "veil" gives women a sense of selfhood is just as unacceptable as Patricia Jeffery's describing a veiled woman as "anonymous, a non-person, unapproachable, just a silent being skulking along, looking neither left nor right." See her *Frog in a Well* (London: Zed Press, 1979), 4. Veiling is a historical phenomenon that can be understood and explained. But, the meaning of the veil varies from individual to individual.

57. Robert Cousineau, *Heidegger, Humanism, and Ethics* (New York: Humanities Press, 1972), 9. This book reproduces substantial sections of Heidegger's letter. See also pp. 7, 9, 47.

58. See Henri Lefebvre, *Le Manifeste différentialiste* (Paris: Gallimard, 1976), esp. 93–145.

59. Cousineau, 48.

60. William Shakespeare, *The Tragedy of Othello* (New York: Signet, 1963), 56, 163.

61. Fyodor Dostoevsky, "Notes from the Underground," in *Great Short Stories of Fyodor Dostoevsky* (New York: Harper & Row, 1968), 293–94.

16 Violence in the Other Country

China as Crisis, Spectacle, and Woman

REY CHOW

On June 4, 1989, after weeks of peaceful demonstrations by Chinese civilians for reform and democracy, the Chinese government sent troops and tanks to massacre hundreds at Beijing's Tiananmen Square. In the following weeks, Chinese armies were ordered to clean up the mess they had created; soldiers became so socially constructive that they cut civilians' hair on the streets of Beijing. Meanwhile, hundreds were arrested and tried, and an unknown number executed.[1]

Benedict Anderson (1983, 68), in a footnote in his book *Imagined Communities: Reflections on the Spread of Nationalism*, says: "So, as European imperialism smashed its insouciant way around the globe, other civilizations found themselves traumatically confronted by pluralisms which annihilated their sacred genealogies. The Middle Kingdom's marginalization to the Far East is emblematic of this process." The fact of China's marginalization in the twentieth-century world is obvious; it is a marginalization that makes us think of it as the "other country."[2] However, Anderson's remarks contain another, equally important point, if only in passing, in the word *traumatically*. The trauma faced by Chinese people in the whole process of "modernization" has yet to be properly understood. The Tiananmen incident confronts us with this fact.

The first point about this trauma is the futility of intellectual discourse at the moment of shock. There is nothing subtle, nothing reflexive, about

This essay is drawn, in part, from *Woman and Chinese Modernity: The Politics of Reading Between West and East,* by Rey Chow (Minneapolis: University of Minnesota Press, 1991).

a government gunning down its own, or for that matter any, people. This experience shocks us out of our assumed categories of thinking. All of a sudden, those of us who are academics cannot see the world as scholars, but rather become journalists. We become suddenly aware of the precarious, provisional nature of our discourse. The unreliability of conventional sources of information, the limitations of our reasoning instruments, the repetitive narratives to which we are subjected—all these raw aspects of our representational machinery suddenly become acute, plunging our perception into crisis.

I heard a feminist ask: "How should we read what is going on in China in terms of gender?" My immediate response to that question was, and is: "We do not, because at the moment of shock Chinese people are degendered and become simply 'Chinese.'" To ask how we can use gender to "read" a political crisis such as the present one is to insist on the universal and timeless sufficiency of an analytical category, and to forget the historicity that accompanies all categorical explanatory power. In her essay "Explanation and Culture: Marginalia," Gayatri Spivak (1987, 105; emphasis in original) writes:

> The will to explain was the symptom of a desire to have a self and a world. . . . the possibility of explanation carries the presupposition of an explainable (even if not fully) universe and an explaining (even if imperfectly) subject. These presuppositions assure our being. Explaining, we exclude the possibility of the *radically* heterogeneous.

Any analytical discourse on the Chinese situation in terms of a single category, when Chinese prodemocracy protesters are being arrested, punished, or killed for having demonstrated peacefully for freedom, is presumptuous. The problem is not how we should read what is going on in China in terms of gender, but rather: what do the events in China tell us about gender as a category, especially as it relates to the so-called Third World? What are gender's limits, where does it work, and where does it not work? How do these events help us recognize the anger often voiced by non-Western women about the singular priority that is given to "woman" by bourgeois liberal feminism? The roots of this anger do not simply lie in the need, neglected by bourgeois liberal feminism's agenda to put the female sex in the forefront of all battles, to *pluralize* the term *woman*. *Women*, often used as remedy for that neglect, leaves most problems of social inequity intact. If the more trendy *women* itself is, at best, an unstable category, it is because, as Denise Riley (1988, 5) tells us, "this instability has a historical foundation." The anger felt by non-Western women is never simply that they have been left out of bourgeois liberal feminism's account "as women," but, more important, that their experiences as "women" can never be pinned down to the narrowly sex-ualized aspect of that category, as "women" versus "men" only. What is often assumed to be the central transaction between women and cul-ture—women's heterosexual relation to men—has little relevance to the China crisis.

China Watching

Rather than a purely analytical discourse on the China situation, I want to raise a set of questions that pertain more closely to us in the U.S., where most of us participate in "China watching" as TV audiences and newspaper readers. China is, in this instance as it has been for the past several decades, a spectacle for the West. Our condemnation of the mili-tary violence in Beijing must go hand in hand with the understanding that the deaths of the thousands of Chinese people were an overdeter-mined event. In many respects, the media all over the world perform the function of urging those protesters on; our cameras lie in wait for the next "newsworthy" event to unfold before us. When I say "overdetermined," therefore, I mean to include the complicity of our technology, which does much more than enable us to "see."

Since the week of June 11, 1989, for instance, the focus on the China cri-sis has shifted to how the Chinese government is controlling the dissemi-nation of the news and how it is, after the military crackdown, instituting the control of thought and speech through propaganda. The Chinese au-thorities *are* ruthless in their deployment of camera networks and other mass communication channels to track down "dissidents." The crudity of their technologies of indoctrination is transparent: they kill, and then they lie. But what role do the media play on our side? There have been instances in which Chinese people cautioned photographers not to take their picture for fear they would be arrested, and what happens to them? We see their pictures with their cautioning as "explanation" of the "China crisis," either in the form of a silent caption (in the newspapers) or in the voiced commentary of our reporters (on television). This hap-pened even in the same reports that criticized the Chinese government for issuing telephone numbers so that people could turn others in. Even though some newscasters now take the trouble to obscure the faces of the people they interview, in some cases it is too late. Meanwhile, these newscasts continue to take us to more remote places such as villages, where they continue to film people and try to make them talk.

To use a familiar narrative from the archives of imperialism, we are still locked within the political structure of the movie *King Kong* (1933), with our media always ready to venture out to "make a movie" about the unknown jungle with its dark, abominable secrets. Much like Director

Denim's film crew, our cameras capture the inhuman monster and present it to us in the "civilized" world as a spectacular sight on display. King Kong was mounted on a rack for a well-dressed theater audience in New York City; China is served to us on the television screen at home.

Describing what she calls "the civilizing power of socialized capital," Spivak (1987, 90) says: "The irreducible search for greater production of surplus-value (dissimulated as, simply, 'productivity') through technological advancement; the corresponding necessity to train a consumer who will need what is produced and thus help realize surplus-value as profit . . . all conspire to 'civilize.'" Recast in the realm of *ideological* production alone, Spivak's remarks explain the frantic simulation of information/knowledge in what I'd call the King Kong syndrome. This is the cross-cultural syndrome in which the "Third World," as the site of the "raw" material that is "monstrosity," is produced for the surplus-value of spectacle, entertainment, and spiritual enrichment for the "First World." The intensive productivity of the Western newsperson leads to the establishment of clear boundaries. Locked behind the bars of our television screens, we become repelled by what is happening "over there," in a way that confirms the customary view, in the U.S. at least, that ideology exists only in the "other" (anti-U.S.) country.

In *King Kong*, the white woman, Ann (Fay Wray), is the point of struggle between the film crew and the "natives." Within her society Ann occupies the position of the underprivileged. Herself the victim of patriarchal oppression (an oppression that includes her being "lifted" into the role of heroine as a result of hunger and thus made part of the profitmaking film industry), the white woman becomes the hinge of the narrative of progress, between enlightened instrumental reason and barbarism-lurking-behind-the-Wall. The white woman is what the white man "produces" and what the monster falls for. If her body is, in filmic language, the place of "suture," what it sews together—what it "coheres"—are the white man's production and the monster's destruction.

The "King Kong syndrome" surfaces in the China crisis in the way the "goddess of liberty" is reproduced across Chinese communities as a defiant emblem of what China "lacks": democracy. The first replica of the Goddess of Liberty was constructed at the Beijing Academy of Arts at the height of the Tiananmen demonstrations. After the statue was mowed down with the protesters on the morning of June 4, Chinese groups in Taiwan, Hong Kong, and the U.S. produced other replicas in a concerted effort to attack the Chinese communist government's scandalizing acts. *King Kong* ends with the statement "Beauty killed the Beast." In the China crisis this sounds like a prophecy for the future, and Chinese people in particular, with little intellectual choice of any kind left, feel obligated to condone the statement's prescriptive as well as descriptive meaning.

In the age of electronic and mechanical reproductions, the Chinese government's resort to political repression should make us think not only in terms of their current violence, but of the global roots of that violence, and the similar gestures of repressive *veiling* we have already encountered in other non-Western countries. What the Western media reenact is the whole issue of extraterritoriality that has been present in Sino-Western relations since the mid-nineteenth century. For those who are not familiar with the term, extraterritoriality was one of the many concessions China was forced to grant to foreign powers in the "unequal treaties" signed during the nineteenth and early twentieth centuries. It meant that nationals and subjects of the "treaty powers" were subject to the civil and criminal laws of their own countries and not to Chinese law. Foreigners were thus protected for their undertakings on Chinese soil—against the Chinese.

From the days of England's gunboat diplomacy to the present day, the question of human rights, when it is raised in China in relation to the West, has never been separable from the privilege of extraterritoriality demanded by the Western diplomat, trader, or missionary. If you think of a person such as Ted Koppel or Tom Brokaw standing on the street in Beijing, speaking a language which is not Chinese, condemning the Chinese government, and how fantastic a spectacle *that* is, then the issue of "journalistic freedom" that is presented as the grounds for intrusive filming and reporting becomes much more problematic than what it purports to be. This is not the same as criticizing such "freedom" by endorsing the Chinese government's facile, misleading charge that the West is "meddling with China's internal affairs." What it means is that it forces us to question the presuppositions that underlie such "freedom," revealing it to be *not* a basic existential condition to which all are entitled (though this is the claim that is made) but a network of demands, negotiations, and coercions that are themselves bound by historical determinants constructed on slaughter and bloodshed.

The tragedy of the China crisis lies in the polarization, which is still inscribed in nativist and nationalistic terms (the Chinese vis-à-vis the rest of the world), between an obsolete cultural isolationism, currently supported by military violence and the paternalistic ideology of the governing regime, and a naive, idealistic clamor for democracy "American style," produced from a plethora of discourses ranging from the astrophysicist Fang Lizhi, to workers, intellectuals, and students, and to the overseas communities, all of which converge on the symbolism of the white-woman-as-liberty. This polarization leaves everyone little to choose from, and that is why the emotional and moral stand taken by Chinese "representations" around the globe, myself included, is unanimously supportive of the "white woman" symbolism. Only a united front, oblivious of the differences in class, gender, education, and profession, can cope with the violence experienced as ethnic trauma.

But the polarization between "traditionalism" or what I have called cultural isolationism (represented by the Party official line), on the one hand, and "democracy," on the other, means that extraterritoriality—the exemption from local jurisdiction—becomes itself exempted from the history of its own role, not in the promotion of freedom and rights but in the subjugation of other peoples in the course of colonial conquests. To return to the theme of the production of knowledge as surplus-value: the production of knowledge about the non-West was possible, in the past, because the producers were exempted from local jurisdiction even as they committed crimes on "local territory." Nowadays, instead of guns, the most effective instruments that aid in the production of the "Third World" are the technologies of the media. It is to these technologies—the bodies of the Western journalist and cameraperson, their voices, their images, their equipment, and the "reality" that is broadcast in the U.S. and then "faxed" back to China—that extraterritoriality is extended, and most of all by Chinese communities overseas who must, under the present circumstances, forget the history of extraterritoriality in Sino-Western relations.

The fetish of the white woman is a serious one, even though it is not, unlike some interpretations of *King Kong,* about sex. Here woman is not the heterosexual opposite of man, but the symbol of what China is not/does not have. In the eyes of many U.S. leftist intellectuals, it is disturbing to see young Chinese students fighting for their cause with this symbolism. Don't they know what atrocities have been committed in the name of liberty and democracy? we ask implicitly or explicitly. For instance, Ronald Reagan's comments on the current Chinese situation, heard during the week of June 11, sound more like an unconscious description of his own foreign policies: "They have something elemental to learn: you cannot massacre an idea; you cannot run tanks on hope. . . ."

And couldn't the Chinese students learn about "democracy" from the way Margaret Thatcher's British government is treating the citizens of Hong Kong? From 1842, when Hong Kong (Island) was, by the Treaty of Nanking, ceded to Britain as a result of the Opium War (which British historians nowadays prefer to call, euphemistically, the "First Anglo-Chinese War"), to the present, when Hong Kong (the British crown colony that includes the Hong Kong Island, the Kowloon Peninsula, and the leased New Territories) is an international city, Britain's policy toward its colonized peoples has remained untouched by history and motivated by pure self-interests. A century and a half ago, self-interests (monetary profit derived from opium, produced in India and sold in China) were justified in terms of Chinese people's desire for opium, in the sense of "they asked for it"; now, self-interests (the need to protect England from being "colo-

nized" by the peoples from its previous and current "dependent territories") are expressed pointblank by members of the British public in the
following way: "The thought of three and a half million people coming
over to the island of Britain is quite horrifying."[3] Three and a half million
is the number of Hong Kong people whose national status is, as their
passports specify, "British Dependent Territories citizen."

Such elaborations of the contradictory nature of the claims of democracy remain, as yet, inaccessible to the Chinese who grew up on the
Mainland in the past twenty to thirty years. They have been, precisely because of the cultural isolationism implemented by the government at different levels, deprived of the intellectual space that would allow them
the kind of critical understanding I am suggesting. An emotional idealism which arises from desperation and which is displaced onto a fetish
such as the Goddess of Liberty is the closest they could come to a taste of
freedom. There is as yet no room—no intellectual room, no reflexive mobility—to understand the history in which the ideal of "democracy" de-
constructs itself in the West. Instead of focusing only on the problematic
nature of their fetishizing (and thereby implicitly sneering at their
naiveté), it is necessary for us to ask why these students are doing this,
what their frustrations are, and what the causes of those frustrations are
in their own as well as world history.

Because as intellectuals we do the kind of work that is by necessity reflexive, more likely to have effects in the long run than in the immediate
future, responses to these questions can be only preliminary at a moment
such as this. And yet, as well, we must respond. The image of the Chinese intellectual I often have in mind is that of a tiny person weighed
down with a millstone, much heavier and much older than she is, as she
tries to fight her way into the "international" arena where, if only per-
functorily, she can be heard. This millstone is "China." My choice of the
feminine pronoun is deliberate. If, as I said, "woman" and "women" become rather pointless categories if they refer only to the dominant sexual
transaction of woman-versus-man, then there are other ways in which
the oppressed and marginalized status of the "Third World" woman can
be instructive. China as a spectacle, as what facilitates the production of
surplus-value in the politics of knowledge-as-commodity—this China
becomes, in its relation to the West, "woman": in the sense that it is the
"Other" onto which the unthinkable, that which breaks the limits of civilized imagination, is projected.

"Woman" in the Other Country

In an event such as the present one, the Chinese woman, who is forever
caught between patriarchy and imperialism, disappears as a matter of

course. Where she appears, she does not appear as "woman" but as "Chinese"; this is the message we learn from the twenty-three-year-old student leader Chai Ling. The issues that the figure of the Chinese woman brings, the issues of gender and sexuality *and* their enmeshment in politics, are here intercepted and put on hold by the outbreak of military violence—even though it is precisely these issues that have to be probed in order for us to get to the roots of violence in patriarchal Chinese culture. What are the links between what is currently happening and a tradition that emphasizes order and harmony, but that also consistently crushes the openness brought to it by intellectuals, students, and young people? Time and again in the past few decades, when things have just begun to be open enough for such issues of liberation to come into their own, we see a crackdown of the kind that immediately requires the postponement of the consideration of such issues. As a result, Chinese women, like their counterparts in many other patriarchal "Third World" countries, are required to sacrifice and postpone their needs and their rights again and again for the greater cause of nationalism and patriotism. As one of the most oppressed sectors of Chinese society, they get short shrift on both ends: whenever there is a political crisis, they stop being women; when the crisis is over and the culture rebuilds itself, they resume their more traditional roles as wives and mothers as part of the concerted effort to restore order.

To my mind, it is sexuality and gender, and the challenge to the bases of traditional authority they bring, which would provide the genuine means for undoing the violence we witness today. This is because this violence cannot be understood apart from the long-privileged status that is conferred upon paternalistic power among the Chinese, be that power exercised in the home, in channels of education, and in civil as well as military administration. If this sounds like a contradiction to my opening remarks, it is because the very efficacy with which we can use gender and sexuality as categories for historical inquiry is itself historical; this efficacy is a result of the relative political stability and material well-being that are available to us as an intellectual community in North America. The battle *we* fight is thus a different, albeit concurrent, one.

Closer to home, we see how the challenge to authority posed by gender and sexuality is resisted in a field such as sinology, which is much more interested in protecting the timeless treasures of the Chinese tradition. In the practices of sinology we see not the barbaric but the beautiful China, which occupies a highly revered place among world intellectuals as the "Other" that satisfies the longing for exotic ancient civilizations. Alternatively, China was also the Other that provided, for Western leftists in the 1960s—precisely at the height of what have since then been revealed as the horrors of the Cultural Revolution—a hopeful different route to communism. Both the specialist and the amateur China admirer have the tendency to attribute to "China" *absolute* differences from the West. In this tendency lies a suppression of thought: if, as historians tirelessly tell us, modern East Asian history is the history of "Westernization," and if "Westernization" is not merely a "theme" but the materiality of daily life for modern Asian peoples, then how could it be possible to insist on the idealist demarcation between "East" and "West" that we still so often encounter?

"This is Chinese" and "this is not Chinese" are modes of description and criticism which we constantly hear, from journalists, to business people, to academic "China specialists." These modes of description and criticism, which are articulated on the presumed certainty of what *is* "Chinese," use the notion "Chinese" as a way to legitimize the authority of tradition and thus exclude the fundamental instability of any ethnic category. The suppression of thought through authoritarianism, even when the "authority" of tradition has become, literally, corrupt, is therefore not limited to the blatant policies of the Chinese communist government, although at this point that government is making a spectacle of what is a long process of cultural trauma and collapse. When we move our attention away from the short-term brutality, which we must remember and condemn, we will see that repressive politics is a general problem pertaining to (the understanding of) modern China as a part of the "Third World," a problem whose roots cannot be confined to a single incident.

If the immediate cases of military violence are translatable into the paradigm of "King Kong breaks loose," then the problems posed by sinology and China studies find a revealing analysis in a more recent film, *Gorillas in the Mist* (1988).[4] In many ways, *Gorillas* is the antipode to *King Kong:* whereas in the latter movie we see the "Other" world depicted as being uncivilized, a condition that leads to its death, in the former we see the good and gentle nature of the gorillas in contrast to the brutality of those who hunt them down for profit. Thanks to the pioneering work of primatologists such as Dian Fossey, the film's ending credits tell us, this "Other" world is allowed to live. Mediating between the civilized and uncivilized worlds is once again the white woman, whose bravery and foolhardiness "create" the story. This time, instead of King Kong holding a screaming Ann in his gigantic paw, we see the Dian Fossey character (Sigourney Weaver) responding to Nature's call and holding hands with the gorillas. Instead of the gorilla, it is the white woman who is killed. The destruction of King Kong affirms civilization; the white woman in *Gorillas* is seen to have "gone off the deep end" in her battle against civilization, a battle which results in her mysterious death.

In the present context, I propose to recast *Gorillas* in the logic of Edward Said's argument about "Orientalism," even though that logic may appear rigid and predictable at times. What the Orientalism argument enables us to see is this: the white female primatologist, like the great Orientalists, knows the language of the "natives" and speaks to/of/on behalf of them with great sympathy. But in her doing so, the "native culture" also becomes her possession, the site of her spiritual war against the "home" that is the Western world. We are thus confronted with what is perhaps the ugliest double bind in the history of imperialism: while the kind, personal intent behind many a missionary exploration of the "Other" world must be recognized—as a benign humanism extended pluralistically across not only nations and cultures but species—such explorations are implicated in colonialism and neocolonialism in their romantic insistence that the "wild" stay "alive" in their original, "natural" habitat. This double bind is, I believe, the thorniest issue that our progressive discourses, in dealing with the "others" as part of a self-consciousness–raising program, have yet to acknowledge fully.

China Studies and the Problem of Westernization

Where do these ape narratives lead us with regard to modern China and Chinese women? "Letting the natives live where they belong," transcribed into a field such as sinology and China studies, becomes another way of reaffirming the authority of the Chinese tradition to the exclusion of other, "non-Chinese" modes of inquiry. Who gets to defend that authority? Where does it leave the "native"? The answers to these questions form the remaining part of my argument, which I shall introduce with the help of a personal scenario.

Since one of my primary areas of research is modern Chinese literature, I often meet sinologists and China historians, some male and some female, who ask me this question directly or indirectly: "Why are you using Western theory on Chinese literature?" Since I happen to work with questions of femininity in modern Chinese literature, I am also asked from time to time, "Why are you using Western feminist theory on Chinese women?"

The contradictions about modern China as a site of the production of knowledge-as-surplus-value are revealingly demonstrated in these simple interrogations. The questions put to me are clearly based on sets of oppositions: the West versus the non-West; dominant versus "other" national or ethnic traditions; dominant theories of women versus "other" women; the subjectivities of "Western" versus "non-Western" feminist critics. Although the point that we must not be trapped within dichotomies is a familiar one, many of us, especially those who experience racial, class, or gendered dichotomies from the unprivileged side, are still within the power of dichotomization as an epistemological weapon. The above kind of interrogation slaps me in the face with the force of a nativist moralism, precisely through a hierarchical dichotomy between West and East that enables my interrogators to disapprove of my "complicity" with the West. Such disapproval arises, of course, from a general context in which the criticism of the West has become mandatory. However, where does this general critical imperative leave those ethnic peoples whose entry into culture is, precisely because of the history of Western imperialism, already "Westernized"? For someone with my educational background, which is British colonial and American, the moralistic charge of my being "too Westernized" is devastating; it signals an attempt on the part of those who are specialists in "my" culture to demolish the only premises on which I can speak.

This personal scenario brings to the fore the cultural predicament that faces all of those who have to negotiate their way into dominant channels of representation. As my earlier image of the Chinese intellectual suggests, the millstone around our necks—"China" and the "Chinese tradition"—is huge and crippling; as it weighs us down it also gives shape to our movements and gestures. Over a long period of time the millstone becomes, for many, their only attitude toward the world. On the other hand, the Chinese intellectual knows that she must fight her way into the world precisely because she is already, in one way or another, "Westernized." In what ways can she speak?

Once again, I pose the question in the feminine form because I think in the shifting boundaries implied by the term *Chinese women* lie the clues to the *general* stakes that are involved for Westernized Chinese intellectuals entering the international "field." The instabilities of the categories "Chinese" and "women" are multiplied by their juxtaposition, allowing for questions such as: Who are Chinese women? What do they tell us about "China"? What do they tell us about "woman" and "women"? What does it mean when China historians study them as one entity? What are the relations between "Chinese women" and "China studies"?

Basically, how have the stories of Chinese women been told "internationally"? I would address this question in the area I know best—academia. In the wake of interests of "women" across the disciplines, investigations of Chinese women are quickly establishing themselves, through what Chandra Mohanty ("Under Western Eyes") calls "the third world difference"—"that stable, ahistorical something that apparently oppresses most if not all the women in these countries"—as a viable area of research among historians, anthropologists, sociologists, and film critics, as well as sinologists who specialize in the classical texts.[5] The objects of such investigations vary from female peasants in remote Chinese villages to the heroines of premodern as well as modern Chinese political history, to the "feminine turn of rhetoric" in literary texts, and to female mystics in less well researched parts of prominent dynasties. At the university where I teach this year, for instance, a couple of other junior faculty and I were put in charge of a conference sponsored by the Department of East Asian Studies when the authorities decided it was time we had a conference "on women." It is obvious that in the eyes of academic administrators, whose roles in the production and circulation of "knowledge" cannot be slighted even though many of them have no interest in scholarship, "women" is now a profitable theme, on a par with such others as "calligraphy," "time," or "water" (in the particular department concerned). But more alarming is, once again, a homologous situation between "woman"—"women" and "First World"—"Third World": if "woman" is now a category of inquiry in well-established disciplines, then the "other woman" is attached to well-established methodologies of investigation in the so-called non-Western fields.

To sinology and the mammoth U.S. enterprise of "Chinese history," the emergence of "Chinese women" is now a new addition which often brings with it the emphases of the "Chinese tradition": the understanding of Chinese women must, it is implied, take place within the parameters of Chinese texts and Chinese history. Returning the natives to their natural habitat, perhaps? We are faced here not with the blatant imperialistic acts of capture and murder that describe the King Kong syndrome, but with the lofty spiritual ideal, typified by *Gorillas in the Mist*, of "letting the Other live in their place and my love."

What can be said about the complex meanings that cluster around the "white woman" here? "Letting the Other live," when it is cast in terms of the relation between white female sinologists/China historians and Chinese women, calls forth, first of all, the questions that have been raised about the paradigmatic relation between white and nonwhite women as "investigator" and "investigatee." This relation is often foregrounded by nonwhite women's indignation at the universalism of "womanhood" as suggested by dominant feminist discourses. In an attempt to raise women's status in the West, liberal feminism, like all alternative ideologies which seek to overthrow those previous to them, spoke on behalf of all women. The error of this universalism lies in the fact that it disguises a more fundamental relation between white and nonwhite women, which is mediated by legacies of a very different kind. After all, "beyond sisterhood there are still racism, colonialism and imperialism!" (Mohanty).

Vis-à-vis the non-Western woman, the white woman occupies the position, with the white man, as investigator with "the freedom to speak." This relation, rather than the one that says "we are all women," is particularly evident in disciplines such as anthropology and ethnography. What has become untenable is the way Western feminism imposes its own interests and methodologies on those who do not inhabit the same sociohistorical spaces, thus reducing the latter to a state of reified silence and otherness. This criticism informs Audre Lorde's (1984) famous "Open Letter to Mary Daly." A similar kind of criticism is voiced by Ai-hwa Ong (1988, 80), who puts it this way: "when feminists look overseas, they frequently seek to establish *their* authority on the backs of non-Western women, determining for them the meanings and goals of their lives" (emphasis in original).

In China studies, where the understanding of China is institutionally organized around notions such as "tradition" and "modernity," the spaces allocated to Chinese women fall into two large categories. First, among historians and social scientists, Chinese women figure prominently in "case studies." Ong (1988, 85) puts it succinctly:

> By portraying women in non-Western societies as identical and interchangeable, and more exploited than women in the dominant capitalist societies, liberal and socialist feminists alike encode a belief in their own cultural superiority. . . . For instance, studies on women in post-1949 China inevitably discuss how they are doubly exploited by the peasant family and by socialist patriarchy, reflecting the more immediate concerns of American socialist feminists than perhaps of Chinese women themselves. By using China as a "case study" of the socialist experiment with women's liberation, these works are part of a whole network of Western academic and policy-making discourses on the backwardness of the non-Western, non-modern world.

The case study belongs to the rhetoric of instrumental reason. Unlike the sinologist, the social scientist may not be fluent in the language, but then her project is not exactly that of becoming "submissive" to Chinese culture (in the way Fossey learned to be "submissive" to the gorillas). Rather, it is to use Chinese women—and the more remote they are from Western urban civilization, the better—for the production of the types of explanations that are intelligible (*valuable*) to feminism in the West, including, in particular, those types that extend pluralism to "woman" through "race" and "class." To be sure, documentary films such as *Small Happiness* (by Carma Hinton, who speaks Chinese fluently) help push Chinese women into the international field where they would be recognized as victims. The question is: how would Chinese women be recognized beyond the victim status? What would a film by Chinese women about American female China scholars be like?

As Ong goes on to suggest about non-Western women in general, the second space in which Chinese women are allowed to appear is—to borrow from Johannes Fabian's concept of "coevalness"[6]—of an absolute "other time." This is the time of classical history and literature, which

renders Chinese women *speechless* even as they offer innumerable entice-
ments to scholarly study. I have attended lectures by women sinologists
who research well-known classical Chinese texts for their themes on
women and who recall with great relish the details of those texts as if
they were the details of an exotic jungle. In this case, like a Fossey, the sinologist "submits" to the language of the gorillas. The point, however, is
this: once Chinese women, like Chinese texts, are confined to the "culture
garden" (Fabian 1983, 47) that is "their past," everything that is said
about them can be labeled "different" in an absolute sense: they are "Chinese" and hence cannot and should not be touched by Western methodologies.

These two main spaces, the case study and the culture garden, that are
available to Chinese women follow from the institutional division of Chinese studies into the modern and the traditional. This division is clearly
felt in the incompatibility between those who are immersed in the
labyrinths of classical textual hermeneutics and those who are propelled
by the post-Enlightenment goals of "knowing" (in this case, a backward
nation) with rational tools. The problem of modernity, because it is always approached by way of such taxonomic divisions, remains caught in
them. Subsequently, Chinese people, too, are classified according to their
proximity to tradition or to modernity. Those from Mainland China are,
implicitly, more "authentic," while those from Taiwan and especially
those from Hong Kong are "contaminated." Even as it is inextricable
from the daily experience of Asian peoples, the materiality of Westernization as an irreducible part of Asian modern self-consciousness remains
unrecognized and inarticulate in the paradigms set down by China
specialists.

And yet it is precisely the materiality of this self-consciousness which
would provide the clues to the protests against the spectacular violence
that we see breaking out in China today. What are the sources of such violence? Great dangers lie ahead if we simply equate it with the present
regime. What are some of the justifications used by the ultra-conservative
Party leaders at this point?—that these are China's "internal" affairs; that
the students are not "patriotic" or "loyal" to the Party; that the soldiers
were trying to restore "order" in Beijing. These outrageous distortions of
fact are, ideologically, in keeping with the reverence for established authority and for "tradition" that is required in all Chinese learning. Violence here is the other side of "culture"; it is what underlies the cherished
notion of civilization in which China is more than heavily invested. Dealing with this violence means that a different kind of self-consciousness,
one that refuses to seek legitimation in terms of facile unities or taxonomic divisions, has to be sought for long-term political intervention.
This consciousness is, to quote Teresa de Lauretis, the "consciousness of

ideological complicity." De Lauretis (1988, 136) defines it in specific relation to the feminist subject:

> The feminist subject, which was initially defined purely by its status as colonized subject or victim of oppression, becomes redefined as much less pure—and *not unified* or *simply divided* between positions of masculinity and femininity, but *multiply organized* across positionalities along several axes and across mutually contradictory discourses and practices.

As more and more non-Western women participate in feminist discourses, this "consciousness of ideological complicity" is bound to become an unavoidable political as well as theoretical issue, forcing upon each of us the following questions: How do I speak? In what capacity and with whose proxy? Therefore, while it is important that we continue to acknowledge the necessity of the kind of work that elaborates the unequal relationship between Western feminism and non-Western women along the lines of "investigator versus investigatee," it is also crucial that we recognize the emergence of a different, still marginalized, mode of articulation—that of the non-Western, but Westernized, feminist subject, whose existence epitomizes the stakes involved in this "complicity." A productive use of feminism in the non-Western context would imply feminism's capacity to respond to the ways these "other" feminist subjects speak.

Chinese Women and/as the Subject of Feminism

Because it is "multiply organized," the space of the Westernized, non-Western feminist subject is an elusive one and as such always runs the risk of being elided. The China crisis shows us such an elision: at the moment of political shock, Chinese women become degendered, and join everyone else as "Chinese." In the long run, however, when the roots of violence can be probed more leisurely and analytically, the problems *embodied* by Chinese women with regard to the Chinese tradition and China scholarship in the West would serve as focal points through which the reverence for authority must be attacked. In a field where such reverence is, in the foreseeable future at least, clearly immovable, and where investments in heritage are made with strong patriarchal emphases, the emergence of Chinese women as feminist subjects (rather than as objects of study) is difficult. This is because feminist self-consciousness, even when it is recognized, easily becomes the latest support for "heritage" and "tradition."

Here the work of Ding Ling (1904–1986) is instructive. What I would like to point out, as an elaboration of my argument about the relation between Western feminism and non-Western women as it surfaces in China studies, are some of the ways Ding Ling's works are typically read. These readings are, to my mind, problematic because, in a way that reflects the larger problems in the field, they partake of the specular political structures of "othering" that I have been describing—structures that block the emergence of the "other women" as historical subjects.

In its different stages, Ding Ling's writing career exemplifies contrasts that are portrayed in this description of the difference *between white and nonwhite women:* "Verisimilitude, realism, positive images are the demands that women of color make of their own writing as critical and political practice; white women demand instead simulation, textual performances, double displacements" (de Lauretis 1986, 17). Although Ding Ling is one of the most well known modern Chinese women writers, her works from the twenties and early thirties are generally considered to be immature; they revolve around themes of sexuality and femininity, and the "female subjectivity" that is evident in them is usually fraught with contradictions, illusions, and a great sense of despair. Her later works, notably *The Sun Rises over the Sanggan River* (1948) and those produced after her punishment and imprisonment during the Cultural Revolution, are much more "patriotic," suggesting a conscious repudiation of the interests in her more youthful period through a devotion to the Chinese tradition and the Chinese people.

This construction of Ding Ling's development as a writer is the one most favored by Chinese communist critics, but it is also popular among Ding Ling scholars in the West, especially in the U.S. The gist of it is: Ding Ling, as a woman writer, turned from the contamination of being "white" to the purity of being colored; from being concerned with "performance" in her youthful years, she became concerned with "realism" the way a Chinese (colored) woman writer *should be.*

What is interesting is that, when American China scholars who are interested in "women" study modern Chinese literature, it is often to a Chinese woman writer such as Ding Ling that they turn, in order to gauge their measurements of sexuality and gender in what they emphasize as a "non-Western" culture. Ding Ling passes the tests of these scholars with flying colors. The trajectory of her career fits extremely well with the essentializing tendencies that already dominate the field of China studies. Her increasingly patriotic leanings make it possible for some to regard her work in terms of so-called Chinese feminism.

The nationalizing, or *nativizing,* of feminism in this case springs from a need to decenter the West, and as such it is a type of critique of the hegemony of Western discourse. However, what does it mean when non-Chinese scholars insist on the "Chinese-ness" of Chinese texts and writers, and with that, the implied judgment of what is "not Chinese"? If nativism per se is problematic, then a nativism prescribed by the non-Chinese scholar on the "native" is even more so. History books tell us that modernization in Asia means "Westernization." Why is it that, if Chinese texts and writers exhibit "symptoms" (as they well should) of having been affected/infected, they are by and large viewed with concern, suspicion, and disapproval?

As in the interrogation of my work that I described earlier, what is left out is precisely the material reality of a Westernized subjectivity that is indelibly present in the non-Western intellectual's entrance into the world. Ding Ling's development, like that of all writers, especially women writers, in "Third World" countries, was complex. I do not think it can in any way be evaluated teleologically, in terms of progress from "immaturity" to "maturity," from being "Westernized" to being "Chinese." The "return" to her traditional origins in her later years has to be understood in terms other than those of idealist nativism. (This point necessitates a close reading of her works and can be substantiated only elsewhere.) It is highly problematic, then, when feminist China scholars simply build on a nationalistic teleological construction by adding to it the label of "feminism." Conversely, the attempt to deconstruct the hegemony of patriarchal discourses through feminism is itself foreclosed by the emphasis on "Chinese" as a mark of absolute difference.

Paradoxically, then, the "authority" that feminism exercises on non-white women as they look overseas is evident even when these other women are given their "own" national and ethnic identity in the manner I just described. The introduction of sinocentrism—what I in the early part of this essay described as cultural isolationism—as a way to oppose the West is far from being the solution to the problems created by Western centrism itself. The attempts to champion a "Chinese feminism" on the part of some feminist China scholars do not really create avenues for modern Chinese women to come forth on their own terms, but rather compound deep-rooted patriarchal thinking to which "woman" is now added as the latest proof of, once again, the continuity and persistence of a pure indigenous "tradition." For Chinese women who go through the most mundane parts of their lives with the knowledge that it is precisely this notion of an "originary" Chinese tradition to which they cannot cling, the advocacy of a "Chinese feminism" in the nativist sense is exclusionary in nature; what it excludes are their lived relations to Westernization and the role played by these relations, however contradictory, in their subject-positions.

The idealism of those in the West who specialize in "Third World" cultures, and the charges they lay against members of those cultures for being "too Westernized," are the twin aspects of the "cultural predicament" that, as I suggest, confronts the Westernized feminist critic. Because it is irreversible, this predicament is oppressive. But perhaps this is precisely where feminism can be best used in a non-Western context. In the words of Kamala Visweswaran (1988, 29), the fundamental reconstitutive value of feminism and the potential of a feminist ethnography which has yet to be expressed consist in that which "locates the self in the experience of oppression in order to liberate it."

The development of any theory typically requires a period in which the space which that theory marks off for its own emergence is elaborated to the point at which it must give way to its own critique. Western feminism, I think, is at such a point. Its continued relevance to other oppressed groups would depend on its understanding of its own historicity: having derived much of its strength and sophistication from the basis of women's experiences of oppression, it needs to ask itself how it can open up similar avenues for others without assuming the "master discourse" position. These others cannot be responded to simply with words such as *pluralism* and *cosmopolitanism*. Feminism needs to face up to its own history in the West. It belongs to a juncture in time when Western thought's efforts at overcoming itself are still, relatively speaking, supported by a high level of material well-being, intellectual freedom, and personal mobility. This historical juncture at which feminism has come to the fore in every facet of Western knowledge is not an accidental one. Even though it often, if not always, speaks the language of oppression and victimization, Western feminism owes its support to the existence of other populations who continue to experience daily exclusions of various kinds, many of which are performed at territorial borders. It is the clear demarcation of such borders which allows us the comfort and security in which to theorize the notion of "exclusion" itself. While some of us enjoy this comfort and security through the accident of birth, others, like myself, do so through "naturalization," which often means that we speak with "native fluency" our oppressor's language. The task of the Westernized feminist is not to unlearn that language but to ask that her accented interventions be understood properly, not as an excuse for nativism but as the demand, put to feminism, for "a willingness, at times, to shred this 'women' to bits" (Riley 1988, 114)—so that other histories can enter.

To bring in the non-Western woman and feminist in the manner I have done is to append a nexus of problems which is not recognizable in the immediate crisis in China. As such, this essay is asymmetrical; my end does not fit my beginning. But "other women" speak without good manners as a rule. For them, articulation means the crude assembling of what is presently and urgently at hand, in order to stockpile provisions for the longer fight.

Notes

1. During this time I was to deliver a paper at a conference called "Nationalisms and Sexualities" at Harvard University. I had planned to discuss work of the controversial modern Chinese writer Yu Dafu. Watching the events in China unfold in the U.S. media, I felt more and more that, at that moment in Chinese history, a talk devoted to "sexuality" was out of place. I therefore decided to speak about the current events. This essay is, in part, the talk I gave.

2. "The Other Country" was the title of the panel on which I was speaking.

3. At a teleconference via satellite entitled "Hong Kong: A Matter of Honor?" held between Hong Kong and England during June 1989.

4. I am grateful to Giuliana Menozzi's Ph.D. dissertation, "Aspects of the Discourse of Wildness Within Modernity" (Comparative Literature, University of Minnesota, 1989). Menozzi's juxtaposition of *King Kong* and *Gorillas in the Mist* alerts me to the Bakhtinian dialogic nature of their making, even though I am using that "dialogue" for a different purpose.

5. Readers who are interested in having a general view of the critical treatment of Chinese women as historical figures, fictional characters, or authors may consult the following sources: Margery Wolf and Roxanne Witke, eds., *Women in Chinese Society* (Stanford: Stanford University Press, 1975); Marilyn B. Young, ed., *Women in China: Studies in Social Change and Feminism* (Ann Arbor: Center for Chinese Studies, The University of Michigan, 1973); Richard W. Guisso and Stanley Johannesen, eds., *Women in China: Current Directions in Historical Scholarship* (Youngstown: Philo Press, 1981); Angela Jung Palandri, ed., *Women Writers of Twentieth-Century China* (Asian Studies Program, University of Oregon, 1982); Anna Gerstlacher, Ruth Keen, Wolfgang Kubin, Margit Miosga, and Jenny Schon, eds., *Women and Literature in China* (Bochum: Studienverlag Brockmeyer, 1985). Significant recent coverage of Chinese women in journals includes *Modern Chinese Literature*, Fall 1988; *Camera Obscura*, no. 18; *Wide Angle* 11, no. 2. This, of course, is by no means an exhaustive list.

6. See Fabian, *Time and the Other: How Anthropology Makes Its Object* (New York: Columbia University Press, 1983).

References

Anderson, Benedict. 1983. *Imagined Communities: Reflections on the Spread of Nationalism*. London: Verso and New Left Books.

Camera Obscura, no. 18.

de Lauretis, Teresa. 1986. "Feminist Studies/Critical Studies: Issues, Terms, and Contexts." In *Feminist Studies/Critical Studies*. Bloomington: Indiana University Press. 1–19.

———. 1988. "Displacing Hegemonic Discourses: Reflections on Feminist Theory in the 1980s." *Inscriptions*, no. 3/4:127–41.

Fabian, Johannes. 1983. *Time and the Other: How Anthropology Makes Its Object*. New York: Columbia University Press.

Gerstlacher, Anna, Ruth Keen, Wolfgang Kubin, Margit Miosga, and Jenny Schon, eds. 1985. *Women and Literature in China.* Bochum: Studienverlag Brockmeyer.

Guisso, Richard W., and Johannesen, Stanley, eds. 1981. *Women in China: Current Directions in Historical Scholarship.* Youngstown: Philo Press.

Lorde, Audre. 1984. *Sister Outsider: Essays and Speeches.* Trumansburg, N.Y.: The Crossing Press.

Menozzi, Giuliana. 1989. "Aspects of the Discourse of Wildness Within Modernity." Ph.D. dissertation, Comparative Literature, University of Minnesota.

Modern Chinese Literature. Fall 1988.

Mohanty, Chandra Talpade. "Under Western Eyes: Feminist Scholarship and Colonial Discourses." In this volume.

Ong, Aihwa. 1988. "Colonialism and Modernity: Feminist Re-presentations of Women in Non-Western Societies." *Inscriptions,* no. 3/4:79–93.

Palandri, Angela Jung, ed. 1982. *Women Writers of Twentieth-Century China.* Asian Studies Program, University of Oregon.

Riley, Denise. 1988. *"Am I That Name?: Feminism and the Category of "Women" in History.* Minneapolis: University of Minnesota Press.

Spivak, Gayatri. 1987. *In Other Worlds: Essays in Cultural Politics.* New York and London: Methuen.

Visweswaran, Kamala. 1988. "Defining Feminist Ethnography." *Inscriptions,* no. 3/4:27–44.

Wide Angle 11, no. 2.

Wolf, Margery, and Roxanne Witke, eds. 1975. *Women in Chinese Society.* Stanford: Stanford University Press.

Young, Marilyn B., ed. 1973. *Women in China: Studies in Social Change and Feminism.* Ann Arbor: Center for Chinese Studies, The University of Michigan.

17 From High Heels to Swathed Bodies

Gendered Meanings Under Production in Mexico's Export-Processing Industry

LESLIE SALZINGER

In recent decades, young, Third World women have emerged as transnational capital's paradigmatic workers. Managerial manifestos recast women's "natural" affinity for the home as a transferable set of skills and dispositions. These then crystallize into "docility" and "dexterity"—terms that go on to have autonomous effects as "labor force requirements" for assembly workers internationally.[1] In this process, men have been redefined as nonworkers—lazy, demanding, and unreliable. This public narrative of home-grown sex differences provides a backdrop to the constitution of localized gendered meanings in export factories throughout the Third World.

During the first decades of the boom in transnational production, managers and feminists were in substantive agreement about the utility of young women's preconstituted "femininity" for capitalist production, although their moral evaluations of the process were markedly divergent.[2] However, in recent years, poststructuralist feminist theorists of work have turned their attention to understanding the formation of "gendered categories," rather than uncritically narrating history within them.[3] This has enabled them to go beyond recounting the fate of "woman workers" to investigate the processes through which the gendered character of labor power itself is established. Focusing on public narratives, they have described the deployment of images of the "exploitable woman worker" from nineteenth-century France to the contemporary Third World.[4]

Meanings are constituted and operate at many levels however, and public narratives are only one of them. The poststructuralist focus on overarching categories has led to sophisticated delineations of "the" hegemonic, linguistically established gender categories that structure workplaces in a particular cultural moment. Such research agendas obscure the high level of variation between gendered meaning structures across individual workplaces and their links to particular sets of daily practices and struggles. In this process, these analyses reinforce a more generalized theoretical assumption that gender's meanings are stable across arenas within a single cultural system. If the content of gender categories is determined by the meaning structures within which their occupants are interpellated,[5] then it behooves us to investigate, rather than to assume, the context in which meanings are formed and at what levels they vary.

In the spirit of this project, therefore, the following pages explore the constitution of gendered meanings in a set of three workplaces, all located in Ciudad Juárez and drawing on the same young, immigrant, North Mexican work force. By locating myself in production, within the meanings and practices of individual shop floors, a plethora of idiosyncratic "femininities" and "masculinities" become visible that are obscured in external discussions and descriptions of Mexico's export-processing industry. Of course, factory-level gendered meanings and subjectivities refer to larger discussions. However, they never simply echo them. Instead, they take shape within the framework of local, managerial subjectivities and strategies, and their final form can only be understood within the context of these immediate structures.

Genders Under Production

When Mexico's Border Industrialization Program was established in 1965, it was already framed in public, gendered rhetorics. The border, export-processing factories, known as "maquilas,"[6] were ostensibly intended to hire men expelled from migrant labor jobs in the United States. However, like other export-processing factories in free-trade zones around the world, maquila managers already had an image of "export workers" and male farmworkers were not it. Advertising for *Señoritas* and *Damitas* throughout the border areas made clear—only young women need apply.[7] These policies were repeatedly, if indirectly, legitimated in public discussions by managers, union bosses, and political commentators, all of whom persistently invoked the superiority of women workers and the deficiencies of their male counterparts. In a typical article, a manager commented matter-of-factly: "85% of the labor force is made up of women, since they're more disciplined, pay more attention to what they do, and get bored less than men do."[8] In an article headlined "Maquiladoras Don't Have Problems with 'Saint Monday'" (an allusion to [male] workers' unilaterally taking Monday as a holiday), the president of the Association of Maquiladoras explained that dependable work attendance "is one of the positive aspects offered by a female labor force."[9]

In the early 1980s, however, the image of the docile young woman began to crack. Inter-union conflicts led to several strikes, bringing anomalous pictures of defiant women workers, sticks in hand, to the front pages of local newspapers. Shortly thereafter, peso devaluations dramatically cut wage costs in dollar terms, and the demand for maquila workers soared. This led to a shortage of young women willing to work at maquila wages and to an increasingly assertive attitude on the part of those already employed. Confronted by young women workers who did not behave like "women" at all, some managers faced by shortages turned to young men. By the end of the decade, men made up close to one-half the maquila work force; and within individual factories, managers deployed increasingly diverse discourses around gender in their hiring and labor control strategies.

Given the historical persistence of the trope of the "malleable working woman" described in the literature,[10] early public discussions of essentialized femininity come as no surprise. What is more remarkable is the ongoing resilience of this trope in citywide discussions of the industry in the face of changed labor market conditions and labor control strategies. More than a decade after men began entering maquila jobs in large numbers, the head of labor relations for the Association of Maquiladoras comments that maquilas do better to hire women: "Men are not inclined to sit. Women are calmer about sitting." Current interviews with managers about ideal workers elicit the same tropes—patient and malleable women, impatient and uncontrollable men. These traditionally gendered descriptions of "ideal workers" emerge even in the conversation of managers who—in response to the unavailability of cheap, young women— deploy distinctively gendered hiring and labor control strategies in the day-to-day management of their own factories.

Thus, these labor market shifts have produced a highly visible disjuncture between public narratives about gender and work and managers' gendered shop-floor strategies. Individual manager's claims around the gendered nature of the "ideal" worker reference public framings but do not reproduce them. Instead the specific institutional functions and managerial subjectivities on each shop floor lead not only to particular systems of production and labor control but also to specifically gendered versions of these systems. As a result, within the context of these individualized strategies and workers' responses to them, distinctive gendered subjectivities emerge for workers on each production floor.

This demographic shift provides us with an opportunity to investigate the localized construction of gendered meanings in a historical moment in which public narratives are relatively weak and local discourses are comparatively easy to discern. Thus, in the pages that follow I will take up where previous authors have left off, at the factory door. Entering the arena of production, I will show the variations in gendered meaning structures between three factories located within what is otherwise a common discursive context. In so doing, it will become possible to identify fissures in gendered meanings at a local level and to trace these differences to the particular struggles within which they emerge. In addition, in each locale, we can delineate the consequences that emergent gendered meanings have for the struggles that generated them.

The maquilas I will discuss here are typical of large plants in the area and exhibit a set of basic similarities. Although two have official "unions," in all three, workers are basically unorganized and managers set the parameters within which shop floor struggles occur. All are directly owned by enormous, world-renowned transnationals. The factories themselves are large, ranging from 750 to 1,100 workers in the day's first shift. Wages are low, generally about fifty dollars a week. This is far less than is necessary to support an independent life, still less a family, in Ciudad Juárez. As a result, workers tend to be in their teens or early twenties and generally are unmarried and childless. The absence of any compensation for seniority leads to high turnover, and most workers have been on the job for under a year. It is against this backdrop of low-wage, low-investment work that the stories I recount below take place.

Given the level of managerial control in structuring these shop floors, I will pay particular attention to managerial practices in identifying the discourses that constitute local gendered meanings and subjectivities.[11] Nonetheless, the narrative will not take the form of structured comparisons of a consistent set of explanatory variables across shop floors. Subjectivity cannot be "held constant." Rather, I analyze each case as a unique configuration of structuring discourses within which the logic of local gendered meanings and subjectivities becomes comprehensible. Hence, I will argue through illustration, underlining in each case the highly idiosyncratic mix of managerial decisions, worker responses, and resultant gendered subjectivities on each shop floor. Each subsection should be read as a unit, an instance of the way that particular gendered meanings are constituted in terms of a specific context of domination and struggle.

The analysis draws on eighteen months of participant observation, interviewing, and archival research in Ciudad Juárez on Mexico's northern border.[12] Given my interest in localized subjectivities, the meat of the "data" comes through factory ethnographies. That is, I gather information on the "constitution of gendered meanings" through locating myself within the meaning-imbued practices, narratives, and structures of a particular shop floor. It is through interacting, through addressing and being addressed, that I come to grasp the formation of gendered subjectivities on a local level. Thus, the images below are not those of a worker or of an observer but of a "participant observer"—of an outsider located both literally and metaphorically on the line.

Seeing is believing. The gendered meanings and subjectivities enacted at "Panoptimex"[13] appear to be straightforward reflections of external narratives.[14] On its production floor, male supervisors direct objectivized and sexualized young women—apparently preconstituted in the home for use on the line. Yet what is most noticeable over time spent in the plant is the amount of work dedicated to the creation of appropriately gendered workers. In this television assembly plant, managers' obsession with the visual sets the parameters within which gendered meanings are established. Labor control practices based on the heightened visibility of workers constitute self-conscious and self-monitoring women and emasculated men. Thus, managerial framing generates, rather than simply takes advantage of, a particular set of gendered subjectivities and in so doing establishes a high level of shop floor quiescence.

The plant manager is a white-blond South American with his sights set on headquarters. He is obsessed with the aesthetics of "his" factory—repainting the shop floor his trademark colors and insisting on ties for supervisors and tunics for workers. The plant is the company's local showpiece, a state-of-the-art facility whose design has been so successful that its blueprint was recently bought by a competitor building a second factory in the city.

The factory floor is organized for visibility—a panopticon[15] in which everything is marked. Yellow tape lines the walkways; red arrows point at test sites; green, yellow, and red lights glow above the machines. On the walls hang large, shiny white graphs documenting quality levels in red, yellow, green, and black. Just above each worker's head is a chart full of dots—green for one defect, red for three defects, gold stars for perfect days. Workers' bodies too are marked: yellow tunics for new workers; light blue tunics for women workers; dark blue smocks for male workers and mechanics; orange tunics for (female) "special" workers; red tunics for (female) group chiefs; lipstick; mascara; eyeliner; rouge; high heels; miniskirts; identity badges. . . . Everything is signaled.

Ringing the top of the production floor are windows. One flight up the managers sit, behind glass, looking—or perhaps not. From on high, they "keep track of the flow of production," calling down to a supervisor to ask about a slowdown, easily visible from above in the accumulation of televisions in one part of the line, gaps further along, or in a mound of sets in the center of a line, technicians clustered nearby. Late afternoons the plant manager and his assistant descend. Hands clasped behind backs, they stroll the plant floor, stopping to chat and joke, just as everyone says, with "the young and pretty ones."

The personnel department—its members titled "social workers"—is entirely focused on questions of appropriate appearance and behavior, rather than on the work itself. "That's not manly, a man with *trousers* wouldn't behave like that!" one of the social workers tells a young male worker who showed his ex-girlfriend's letter to others on the line. "Remember this, it's agreeable to be important, but more important to be agreeable," she counsels a young woman who keeps getting into arguments with her coworkers. Behavior, attitude, demeanor—typically in highly gendered form—is evaluated here. Skill, speed, and quality rarely come up.

Managerial focus on the look of things is reflected in the demographics of the workplace as well. Close to 80 percent of the plant's direct line workers are women. They sit in long lines, always observed, repeating the same meticulous gestures a thousand times during the nine-hour day. During the 1980s, when it became difficult to hire women workers and most Juárez maquilas began hiring men, the company went so far as to recruit a busload of young women from a rural village forty-five minutes away. The company, calmed by the sight of the familiarly populated lines, provided the workers with free transportation to and from work for years.

Lines are "operator controlled." The chassis comes to a halt in front of the worker, she inserts her components and pushes a button to send it on. There is no piece rate, no moving assembly line, to hurry her along. But in this fishbowl, no one is willing to be seen with the clogged line behind her, an empty space ahead of her, managers peering from their offices above. And if she does slow momentarily, the supervisor materializes. "Ah, here's the problem. What's wrong, my dear?" For the supervisor is, of course, watching as well as watched. He circles behind seated workers, monitoring efficiency and legs simultaneously—his gaze focused sometimes on "nimble fingers" at work, sometimes on the quality of hairstyle. Often he will stop by a favorite operator—chatting, checking quality, flirting. His approval marks "good worker" and "desirable woman" in a single gesture.

"Did you see him talking to her?" For the eyes of workers are also at work, quick side-glances registering a new style, making note of wrinkles that betray ironing undone. "Oof, look how she's dressed!" With barely a second thought, women workers can produce five terms for "give her the once over." A young woman comments that when she started work she used no makeup, only wore dresses below the knee. But then her coworkers started telling her she looked bad, that she should "fix herself up." As she speaks, her best friend surveys her painted, miniskirted physique affectionately, "They say one's appearance reveals a lot," she remarks. Two lines down, another young woman mentions she missed work the day before because she slept too late—too late that is to do her hair and makeup and still make the bus. To come to work is to be seen, to watch, and so to watch and see yourself.[16]

The ultimate arbiter of desirability, of course, is neither one's self nor one's coworkers, but supervisors and managers. Workers gossip constantly about who is or is not chosen. For those (few) so-anointed, the experience is one of personal power. "If you've got it, flaunt it!" a worker comments gleefully, looking from her lace bodysuit to the supervisor hovering nearby.[17] This power is often used more instrumentally as well. On my first day in the plant, a young woman—known as one of the "young and pretty ones" favored by managerial notice—is stopped by guards for lateness. She slips upstairs and convinces the plant manager to intercede for her. She is allowed to work after all. The lines sizzle with gossip.

The few men on the line are not part of these games. Physically segregated, they stand rather than sit, attaching screen and chassis to the cabinet at one end, packing the finished product at the other. They move relatively freely, joking and laughing and calling cut—noisy and ignored. The supervisor is conspicuous in his absence from their section of the line, and they comment disdainfully that he's afraid to bother them. Nonetheless, when they get too obviously boastful he brings it to a halt. Abruptly he moves the loudest of them, placing them in soldering where they sit in conspicuous discomfort among the "girls" while the others make uneasy jokes about how boring it is "over there."

One young man says he came here intentionally for all the women. "I thought I'd find a girl friend. I thought it would be fun." "And was it?" I ask. There's a pause. "No one paid any attention to me," he responds finally, a bit embarrassed, laughing and downcast. His experience reminds me of a story told by one of the women workers who returned to the factory after having quit. "It's a good environment here," she says. "In the street they [men] mess with us, but here, we mess with them a little. We make fun of them and they get embarrassed." In the factory, to be male is to have the right to look, to be a supervisor. Gender and class positions are discursively linked. Standing facing the line, eyes trained on his work, the male line-worker does not count as a man. In the plant's central game, he is neither subject nor object. As a result, he has no location from which to act—either in his relation to the women in the plant or in relation to factory managers.

What is striking once inside the plant is how much work is involved in the ongoing labor of constructing appropriate "young women" and "young men" out of new hires. Gendered meanings are forged within the context of panoptic labor control strategies in which women are constituted as desirable objects and male managers as desiring subjects. Male workers become not-men, with no standing in the game. These identities are defined by management in the structure of the plant, but they are reinforced by workers. Young women workers take pleasure in the experience of being desirable and in their use of this delicious if limited power in attempting to evade the most egregious aspects of managerial control. Male workers attempt to assert an alternate masculinity, becoming vulnerable in the process to the managerial ability to undercut these assertions.

The gendered meanings developed here are familiar, echoing the formulations of the public narrative described above, as well as descriptions of export-processing factories in other parts of the world. These resonances suggest a model in which a single set of gendered representations emerges within the logic of an entire economic system, subsequently filtering down to local arenas. However, even amidst such similarities we note the plethora of localized practices within which these repetitious meanings are constituted anew.

Workers as "inputs." Unlike Panoptimex, where emergent gendered meanings and subjectivities appear to echo those crystallized in public discussion about the maquilas, the femininities and masculinities constructed at "Anarchomex" clearly depart from these confines. Like their counterparts at Panoptimex, Anarchomex managers reiterate external gendered frameworks. However, their hiring and labor control practices around gender are in tension with their claims; and within the context of this contradiction, a new set of gendered meanings and subjectivities emerges that sharply diverges both from public narratives and from those at Panoptimex.

Anarchomex assembles harnesses (car electrical systems), and distant managers define workers as just another set of inputs. As a result, they are more concerned with finding the "right" workers than with addressing those they have. This has ramifications throughout the labor process. Managers have little presence on the shop floor and do less to speak to the subjectivities of workers—whether gendered or otherwise—on the line. As a result, given the high demand for women workers and the enormity of the plant, they have trouble attracting sufficient numbers of young women to work. Despite their primarily male work force, however, they continue to echo hegemonic narratives, defining women as ideal workers and men as congenitally unsuitable to maquila work.

Male workers respond to this combination of managerial absence and depreciation by claiming the social, sexual, work space of the shop floor as their own—in so doing, constituting a masculinity that at once restricts their female coworkers and contests managerial disrespect. Women workers are located at the intersection of two contradictory gendered discourses and constitute identities that hold assertion and passivity, work and sexuality, in complex tension. The gendered meanings that emerge here cannot only be traced to local antecedents, but have local effects as well, as they undermine the managerial attempts at control from which they emerged at the outset.

The factory floor is dingy, dated, and chaotic—an enormous barnlike structure with dark grey floors and walls, exposed fluorescent lights hanging from cavernous ceilings. On the right side of the building, huge boards circulate. On the left, smaller boards revolve at a brisker pace, interspersed with splicing stations draped with wires of every imaginable color and length. Everything obstructs the view of everything else.

The plant manager is an American with many years of experience in U.S. harness production, but few on the border. His Spanish is weak, and he keeps his distance from the shop floor. He tends toward discussions of Mexican "cultural" problems and is particularly concerned by his Mexican supervisory staff, whom he sees as simultaneously unwilling to take responsibility for problems and overly authoritarian and controlling on the line. As a result, he encourages supervisors to focus on the indices. "A line is like a grocery store. The supervisor . . . buys inputs and sells a product and he has to balance his books."

Not surprisingly given this framework, supervisors are notable for their absence on the plant floor. Everyone—workers included—knows about the numbers: numbers of defects, of harnesses unmade, of extra workers per line; and supervisors frequently call meetings in which they tell workers what the line's numbers are for the week and scold them for not doing better. But no one is there by the production line, hanging over workers' shoulders and watching them work. It is numbers that supervisors pore over, not bodies.

It is not that management is unconcerned with workers' characters. On the contrary, from the plant manager on down, getting the "right" workers is a preoccupation. However, the focus is not on making good workers but on finding them. As a result, management puts far more energy into hiring strategies than into labor control. Once the right sort of workers are hired, goes the logic, labor control will take care of itself. Hence, in discussing the production floor disarray, the plant manager comments, "No one can control 2,000 teenagers," and goes on to outline attempts to attract more job applicants.

This focus on hiring the "right" workers at the outset is particularly problematic because the primary criterion for being a "good worker" is being female, and the factory has never succeeded in hiring more than 40 percent women. Given its size—the plant is 50 percent larger than Panoptimex—and managers' failure to address any gendered subjectivities on the shop floor, Anarchomex could not begin to compete for women workers.[18] Today the work force is 65 percent male.

These demographics are not inherently problematic for labor control, as we shall see in the case of "Androgymex" discussed below. However, the absence of any pretense of a "family wage" in the plant appears to make Anarchomex managers, both Mexican and American, reluctant to diverge from the public framework that defines women as appropriate maquila workers, even in the face of their overwhelmingly male work force. Instead, managers comment disparagingly on the willingness of their young male employees to accept Anarchomex jobs. Typically dismissive, Marcos, the quality manager, comments, "Say I'm twenty years old. I know that with this job I can't support a family. Obviously, I'm going to look for something better." To reframe the work as men's work would be to define it as underpaid. Faced with the choice between questioning maquila pay practices or the manliness of maquila workers, managers choose to question their subordinates. As a result, Anarchomex managers hold their gendered practices and narratives in permanent tension, disparaging the great majority of their work force in the process.

Given management's sense that workers' aptitude for and attitude toward work is set at hiring, it comes as little surprise that the bulk of the labor control mechanisms they do employ are punitive in nature. As in other plants, pay is docked for lateness and absenteeism. "Technicians"—those promoted workers who do the bulk of daily supervision—are constantly coming by and scolding workers for producing defects, for sitting down, for disappearing from their posts. But, as their title indicates, their primary focus is on technical and not personnel issues. Workers' selves are not incorporated into either the work or the work place.

In general, it is workers who keep each other in check on a daily basis. Unlike the television plant, assembly is done standing by a moving line. Workers are mobile, following the boards as they go. If experienced workers want to take a break, they can work ahead, intruding on the previous workstation and reappearing just in time to finish a subsequent board, by now moving through an adjacent worker's territory. However, in most workstations, part of the assigned task is contingent upon the completion of previous jobs and is difficult to do once later stages have been finished. As a result, this work rhythm—or even a real inability to keep up—disrupts the work of those nearby. Thus, the limits on work pace are social and lateral, depending on the tolerance of coworkers and the thick-skinnedness of the worker in question. Workers rather than supervisors hold the pivotal place in labor control, and this leaves much of the daily life of the factory in their hands.

The centrality of workers in monitoring each other does not produce investment in the work itself, however. On the contrary, in the context of extreme disconnection between workers and their product, these heightened social interactions take on a life of their own. Throughout days otherwise saturated by the meaninglessness of the work, workers elaborate a compelling, ritualized, laughter-filled world of play on the shop floor. In fact, the factory has gained a reputation beyond its walls for the teasing, flirtatious social life developed in its confines.

This social world is not neutral in gender terms, however. Stepping into the vacuum left by management, male workers determined to reestablish their masculinity assert it in this space. New, orange-smocked workers are greeted by male voices immediately upon entering the factory floor. "Carrots, carrots!" goes the chorus. But soon the women among the newcomers pick out a different call. "Carrot, come. Come here! Here's your rabbit!" Whistles and kissing sounds follow each woman as she walks past line after line to her new workstation. Within a couple of days she is angling for the navy smock used by other workers, an escape from the heightened visibility of the brilliant newcomer's uniform.

The new smock only changes the intensity. Although the whispers and calls diminish, soften and personalize with the new uniform, the male voices never stop. Sexuality—for both the young women and the young men in the plant—remains a primary entertainment, occupation, preoccupation; and in the game of flirtation, men act and women receive. Male workers leave their posts to flirt with prospective girlfriends. Women workers turn their backs on harness boards to chat with suitors. Men call out or visit, women smile and chat in response, either enthusiastically or with polite distance. But they ignore advances at their peril. "Don't be stuck-up," a young woman counsels, "If you act like that, no matter how pretty you are, no one will pay attention to you."

Male workers assert their masculinity not only through their sexualized interactions with their female coworkers, but also by disparaging women's ability to do the work at all. Thus, throughout the day they talk loudly about how the work is "really" men's work—performed standing, requiring speed and endurance. They point out women workers who are slow or resting. They comment that women workers don't really need to work. They get in the way when their female coworkers attempt to learn new positions. And they describe women's sexuality as inherently problematic at work. Thus, in describing a coworker who acted like "a woman from the street," a young man comments: "If the line were faster and there were more pressure, I can assure you they wouldn't have time to go around grabbing . . . like that." A few lines down another man complains: "They shouldn't wear minis. The point at work is to be on the ball; it's impossible that way."

Although women workers generally enter the arena of sexual play on the terms set by their male coworkers, they resist their denigration as workers. They make no attempt to elaborate the work as inherently feminine. However, they take insistent note of managerial hiring preferences for women, all the while ignoring managers' substantive claim that their value lies in their docility. Locating themselves at the intersection of two discourses of domination, women workers elaborate a femininity marked both by a ritualistically receptive sexuality and a highly capable work persona.

Thus, the gendered meanings defined here depart both from the sense and from the uniformity of those constituted in public narratives and at Panoptimex. Supervisory authority and the right to see do not define masculinity. Instead, activity and aggressiveness vis-à-vis women workers—both in the sphere of sexuality and in the sphere of work—constitute masculinity on the shop floor. Similarly, femininity is not defined around objectification. Instead, what counts as femininity is fragmented. Sexually, to be feminine is not to be *seen*, but rather to receive, as a form of play, the comments of the male workers. And it is male workers who are empowered to judge if women respond appropriately. To be a good woman worker, on the other hand, is specifically not to play, to focus on the work itself. Here, women themselves judge what counts, backed by the distant voices of supervisors. Thus, gendered meanings are contested and contradictory here, evolving within struggles between workers and management and between female and male workers, and in the process leaving room for maneuver for all workers, but particularly for women.

These gendered meanings have both localized antecedents and localized effects. They emerge in response to the use of punitive rather than disciplinary[19] labor control methods and to managerial challenges to worker masculinity. In treating workers as inputs and failing to address the selves of workers on the shop floor, managers inadvertently allow gender to be defined between workers, eroding labor control and constituting subjectivities that they then have little capacity either to legitimate or sanction. Shortly after I left the factory, half the work force was moved to another building, a costly move that idled much of the plant's machinery. The maquila manager explained simply that they'd felt the factory was "too hard to control."[20] The set of gendered meanings constituted through managerial hiring and labor control practices undercut those very attempts at control.

Gender under wraps. In Panoptimex, gendered meanings echo those in public discussions, while in Anarchomex they depart from this paradigm. However, in Androgymex, no hegemonic gendered meanings materialize. The definitions of femininity and masculinity crystallized in elite, public discussions are present here, as are many other such definitions, but managerial negation of gender's importance, coupled with the compelling nature of struggles in and over production, sideline the importance of gender as a central axis of subjectivity in daily life on the shop floor. As a result, although various gender definitions are alluded to, discussed, and even employed in the arena of production, no particular configuration emerges as dominant.

Unlike the maquilas discussed above, in Androgymex, production rather than sexuality is the focus of attention in workers' daily practices. Skill matters here. Paid by the piece, workers can appreciably increase their weekly salaries through experience and hard work. This possibility, and the games and conflicts generated by the piecework structure in general, draw attention and focus to the work itself. At the same time, managers' experience with a strike in the early 1980s destroyed any illusion of woman's controllability, and jobs are unmarked by gender on the shop floor. Women and men work side by side, sewing intently, bodies covered in smocks and caps that obscure gender markers. Gendered subjectivities, sexual and otherwise, are muted. Gendered rhetorics abound, but there are as many opinions about women, men, and work as there are managers, supervisors, and workers to have them, and there is no consistent correspondence between position in production and perspective on gender. As a result, unconnected to the fundamental axes of struggle over control in the factory, gendered categories do not disappear, but they subside into insignificance in daily interaction on the shop floor.

Androgymex produces disposable hospital garments. The impression one receives upon first entering the plant is one of total uniformity amidst chaos. Workers are scattered across its expanse, swathed in the blue smocks and light blue caps produced in the plant. There are no lines. Instead, workers sew, fold, or pack feverishly in groups—tossing their finished products into piles which are carried or wheeled in towering, precarious-looking edifices to the next step in the process. Apparently just at the brink of collapse, the piles are thrown down at the appropriate production site, where they immediately become part of the next step in the process.

Music blasts through the factory. At intervals, loud whoops emerge from the floor in response to a particularly favored selection. If the music is especially inspiring, the commotion may develop into an impromptu salsa—a couple of paired blue smocks dancing in the aisle—sometimes a woman and man, sometimes two women, sometimes two men. Whoops greet other things as well—entrance onto the shop floor without the required sterile smock or cap or the attempt of some unlucky soul to chat privately with someone of the "opposite sex." Always these outbursts delight and enliven, contributing, for the casual observer, to the sense of disorganization and play at work.

And yet, appearances deceive. The single most striking characteristic of this plant is how hard people work. In this factory, production itself compels. This is in part due to the fact that workers are paid by the piece. It is worth it to work hard. Nonetheless, when asked why they set standards for themselves that are higher than those set by the plant itself, answers generally revolve not around money but around making work life bearable.[21] A woman comments: "I used to work in harnesses. I was so bored I used to go to the bathroom and sleep. Here I say, today I'm going to make so many, and that way I don't get so bored." The guy down the line from her measures his production against hers, constantly telling me that *today* he is going to produce more than she.

Forestalling boredom is part of the reason for the focus on work, the possibility of gaining a sense of control is another. Sharing one side of a table are two men, the fastest folders in their section. They both have a personal daily standard far higher than the factory's, and they both give themselves permission to stop work either when they've reached their own quota or at 2:45, even though the work day ends officially at 3:05. "This way *I* decide what I do," says one. One day his group leader insists that he keep working after he's reached his own limit. After a long and aggressive altercation, he goes back to work. But the next day he produces precisely the quota, finishing at exactly 3:05. "She won't bother me about that again," he says with grim satisfaction. He's right.

Piecework fosters a focus on work not only through giving workers a sense of control but precisely because it is the site of so many minor conflicts. A few months before my arrival, management increased the standard, supposedly as a consequence of a new and easier folding pattern. Wages fell. The entire twelve-person section agreed to produce exactly the standard— no more. They lasted a week, until a threatening lecture from the union and the head of production in tandem scared them back to the old rhythm. Now the story is told and retold—evidence sometimes of the impossibility of collective action, sometimes of the ability of the worker telling the story to stand up for her or himself, whatever the consequences.

The event is repeated in miniature again and again. Material is scanty and production falls. Who pays for the lost time—company or workers? Workers complain about the supervisor, contest their checks with the union, squabble with each other over scarce material. "He steals material," go the whispers after an offending worker is caught in the act during a lunchtime stakeout. The quarrels and complaints are constant. Their effect is not disruptive. On the contrary, these myriad conflicts provide a space in which workers can insist on respect and human dignity and in which particular elements of work can be negotiated, without challenging the overall functioning of the plant.

This form of labor control through conflict works in part because workers are valuable in the garment business. In electronics or harnesses, most workers can be trained in under two weeks. The company can't be forced to negotiate unless workers can threaten to organize broadly. Thus, constant conflicts would simply lead to constant turnover. Sewing however, despite its low-tech nature, is a skill that cannot be easily acquired. This is reflected in the hiring process, where garment plants attempt to steal each others' workers, and in the fact that workers who previously worked in the plant are recontracted, few questions asked. And it is reflected on the shop floor, where workers do sometimes win minor concessions. It is in this context that struggles can be a force for stability. Labor control in this plant is achieved precisely through these ongoing struggles over when, where, and how much. The slightly higher wages show that management has had to respond to some of these demands, but the struggles over exactly how to interpret the rules serves not only to renegotiate amounts but also to reaffirm the managerial right to set the rules to begin with.

strike

This permanently negotiated peace has a history, a history with implications for gender as well as for production processes. In 1981 the work force was almost entirely female. A conflict between two unions paralyzed production, precipitating a yearlong strike still remembered in the city for its violence. It was shortly after that strike, the putative docility of women workers having lost its credibility, that management began hiring men. The current plant manager was brought in at the end of the strike. He discusses the union, piece rates, the "Androgymex family," but gender does not catch his attention. Unlike many of his fellow managers in the maquila industry, he is convinced that gender doesn't matter.

This attitude is visible throughout the plant. Gendered signs are minimized on the shop floor. Because the product is sterile, jewelry, makeup, and beards are prohibited. Workers wear dark blue smocks buttoned high, caps that cover every strand of hair. These remain in place even at meals. At first glance, everyone looks the same. At the outset, it is even difficult to distinguish gender. A young man I met working elsewhere had worked at the plant briefly and left. "You couldn't tell who the pretty ones were," he complained. The first sight of one's coworkers outside is a shock, somehow obscene, as if everyone had suddenly been stripped of clothes entirely. Eyes fall on all sides and smiles are uneasy.

The plant is 55 percent male, 50 percent in the smock area where all the sewing is done. Men and women do the same work. Once the swathing blueness is decoded, one notices scores of men bent over sewing machines, whipping out smocks beside their female coworkers. The woman in charge of hiring tells me: "Group leaders do sometimes request women for particular jobs, but not in the smock section—of course not! That's sewing!" Sewing is hard work with high turnover—often as high as 20 percent monthly. Group leaders, she implies, will take whomever they can get.

Yet, this is not entirely accurate. In the smock area, gender proportions range from a low of 30 percent men to a high of 70 percent in sections engaged in exactly the same work. Group leaders, generally women who began as line workers years ago, have strong and markedly idiosyncratic opinions about gender, and they indeed request their preferred gender when they ask for workers. One comments: "I don't like to work with men. They're just big children!" The next section down, the group leader disagrees. "I'd rather work with men," she says, "Fewer problems with child care and stuff." It's not that gender isn't articulated in this plant. On the contrary, opinions are legion. But for all the fervency of these comments, they are erratically distributed. There's no "line" on gender.

In this factory, the importance of skill, the institution of piece work, and the strike-impelled presence of a semifunctioning union combine to create a context in which labor control is in part negotiated rather than simply imposed. The resulting daily struggles take the form of impassioned altercations that bypass gendered subjectivities. In a context in which bodies are obscured, literally under wraps, and in which the central struggles of the plant—both between management and workers and among workers—revolve around issues directly related to production, gender ceases to be a significant category. This is not to imply that anyone in the factory forgets her or his gender identification or that people don't have a great deal to say about gender when asked. In fact, gendered discourses proliferate here, in quantity if not in importance. However, there are so many different opinions precisely because none are linked to central conflicts over labor control and work life in the plant. As a result of gender's irrelevance to struggles for power and control, it loses its practical and experiential importance on a day-to-day basis on the shop floor.[22]

Panoptimex reconsidered. Public narratives about the maquilas in Ciudad Juárez continue to elaborate on the docility and malleability of young women workers and the laziness and incompetence of their male counterparts. Androgymex, Anarchomex, and Panoptimex are all embedded within this framework, yet the gendered meanings and subjectivities in the three diverge sharply, both from this larger common sense and from each other. By locating our lens within these factories rather than training it on public discussions about them, these distinctive patterns, and the discursive contexts that shaped them, become visible.

The focus in this analysis on "superficial" differences rather than on "essential similarities" is a theoretically driven one. Obviously, there are commonalities in gendered meanings across these three shop floors. However, much has been made of the "archetypal nature" of Mexican "sex roles." In that context, the differences that emerge here are particularly striking. Any project of transformation must be able to recognize the broad range of lived specificities a "single culture" can encompass.[23] Thus, although it would be perverse not to acknowledge similarities, in this reading I have chosen to foreground the crucial differences in gendered meanings and subjectivities that emerge even in these closely situated arenas.[24]

In Anarchomex, managers' definition of workers as inputs leads them to ignore all worker subjectivity and actively disparage that of male workers. Worker responses to this ultimately produce a distinctive, local set of femininities and masculinities. Shop floor, worker masculinity comes to be defined around control of production—both of the work and of their female coworkers, whereas shop floor femininity is configured almost entirely around receptive sexuality. In sharp contrast, in Androgymex, the labor process makes possible the emergence of work-based subjectivities, even as the need for a sterile workplace and managerial disillusionment with women workers' docility leads to the minimization of gendered markers on the shop floor. The result is a proliferation of gendered meanings and subjectivities, in which no single set of masculinities or femininities holds sway.

Of the three factories, the gendered meaning structures in evidence in Panoptimex are hardest to distinguish from those of the public narrative within which they are embedded. What counts as "womanly" or "manly" is so close to its definition in external discussion that from a distance it appears as a simple reflection. However, once we focus on factory-level discourses, it becomes clear how vital these local practices are in bringing the docile women and unsuitable men of external definition to life.

Panoptimex managers subscribe to dominant notions of the ideal, feminine maquila worker, and their smaller work force makes it conceivable for them to develop hiring practices that match this image. However, it is their focus on the visual that ultimately compels and enables them to put this vision into practice on the shop floor. The factory is set up to be seen and to look a particular way. The young women seated in long lines complete the appropriate picture—in their own sexualized daily experience as well as in that of managers. Managers at all levels strategize to ensure their presence. Their decision to bus young rural women to work on a daily basis suggests their determination to maintain a primarily female labor force. But women workers also respond to this image. Unlike most maquilas, women workers who leave for other maquila jobs often try to return. Nine hours of objectification prove less stultifying than nine hours of invisibility.

Young women are hired into a panopticon for the same reasons that they are hired at all—because the managerial framework for labor control is to ensure that production looks right. In an arena peopled by male supervisors and female workers, this objectifying modality of control constitutes a particular set of gendered subjectivities. Women workers' laboring and sexualized identities merge on the shop floor, and the few male workers lose their claim to masculinity by virtue of their location at the wrong side of the lens. Although the gendered representations and subjectivities here echo those embedded in public discussions, they are incarnated on the shop floor within specific managerial practices. Even shared representations must be construed and acted upon by living beings in specific contexts. Thus, in seeking to understand the construction of gendered meanings and subjectivities, we must look to the particular configuration of localized frameworks and daily practices within which they emerge.

Theorizing Specificities

"Any attention to the life of a woman, if traced out carefully, must admit the degree to which the effects of lived gender are at least sometimes unpredictable, and fleeting."[25] This caution, written by Denise Riley in the late 1980s, was directed not at a sexist academy, but at more than a decade of feminist theory. In the process of delineating and analyzing the oppression of "women," she and other such critics warned, notions of gender as a binary system were being reinforced—replacing biological with sociological essentialism.[26]

Riley's words encapsulated one of the central goals of poststructuralist feminism: to develop a language capable of describing gender in all its palpable heterogeneity and fluctuating significance. Despite this focus, the unpredictability and inconsistency of gender have been more cited than explored; and, for the most part, theorists working in this tradition have not chosen to further investigate gender's lived specificity. Instead, much of this analysis has remained at the level of the purportedly hegemonic discourses of a particular period—for instance, Judith Butler's[27] ongoing dialogue with psychoanalysis or Riley's own fascinating discussion of the changing meaning of "woman" historically.[28] This focus on intellectual categories, while certainly crucial, implicitly assumes the societal extension and resonance of a particular discursive understanding of gender.[29] The question of how these representations vary between localized arenas of domination, even those sharing elements of a common discursive framework, remains unexplored.

Of this group of scholars, Joan Scott's historical analyses have gone furthest toward recognizing and describing the varied social contexts, as well as the complexity, of gendered meanings. Nonetheless, even this research focuses on public discussion, leaving open the question of how gendered representations are specified and lived within particular sites.[30] Poststructuralist feminist theorists have argued that gender is a discursive construction and emphasized its variable content. The research described above seeks to ground and specify these assertions.

Gendered subjectivity indeed appears to be "unpredictable" and "fleeting," but its shifts are neither arbitrary nor isolated. Gender is a social relation—a structure of meanings established by and between living subjects in the practices of daily life. As such, the meanings of femininity and masculinity vary with these interactions—with the strategies, frameworks, and subjectivities of those who people a specific arena and with the outcome of their struggles. Questioning the conventional gendered categories with which we narrate our stories is an important goal of feminist theory. However, this need not entail a move away from those stories into a history of categories. It is precisely the question of how these categories are built and lived in daily interaction that must concern us.

Notes

The research upon which this article is based was done during my affiliation with El Colegio de la Frontera Norte and was funded by the Fulbright-Hays Doctoral Dissertation Research Abroad and the OAS Regular Training Program Fellowships. In Juárez, COMO—El Centro de Orientación de la Mujer Obrera—gave me access to their archive. The writing was done in part at the collegial Center for U.S.-Mexican Studies at University of California, San Diego. My most heartfelt thanks to all. I am also deeply grateful for ongoing encouragement and critical readings to Michael Burawoy, Steve Epstein, Peter Evans, Ann Ferguson, Josh Gamson, Deborah Gerson, John Lie, Deborah Little, Aihwa Ong, Jackie Orr, Teri Pohl, Jeffrey Rubin, and Pablo Vila. Thanks also to an anonymous reader and the editors of *Feminist Studies* for their insightful comments.

1. This point is made in dramatically different theoretical contexts in Leslie Sklair, *Assembling for Development: The Maquila Industry in Mexico and the United States* (San Diego: Center for U.S.-Mexican Studies, University of California, San Diego, 1993): 172–73; Guy Standing, "Global Feminization Through Flexible Labor," *World Development* 17 (July 1989): 1077–95; Donna Haraway, "A Manifesto for Cyborgs: Science, Technology, and Socialist Feminism in the 1980s," *Socialist Review* 15 (March–April 1985): 65–107.

2. See, for instance, Rachel Kamel, *The Global Factory: Analysis and Action for a New Economic Era* (Philadelphia: American Friends Service Committee, 1990); Norma Iglesias Prieto, *La Flor mas bella de la maquiladora* (Mexico City: Secretaria de Educación Pública, 1987); Lourdes Benería and Martha Roldán, *The Crossroads of Class and Gender* (Chicago: University of Chicago Press, 1987); Diane Elson and Ruth Pearson, "Third World Manufacturing," in *Waged Work,* ed. Feminist Review (London: Virago, 1986): 67–92; Maria Patricia Fernandez-Kelly, *For We Are Sold, I and My People: Women and Industry in Mexico's Frontier* (Albany: State University of New York Press, 1983); Annette Fuentes and Barbara Ehrenreich, *Women in the Global Factory* (Boston: South End Press, 1983).

3. See Joan W. Scott, "Deconstructing Equality-Versus-Difference: Or, the Uses of Poststructuralist Theory for Feminism," *Feminist Studies* 14 (spring 1988): 46–47; and Ava Baron, "Gender and Labor History: Learning from the Past, Looking to the Future," in *Work Engendered: Toward a New History of American Labor* (Ithaca: Cornell University Press, 1991), 1–46. For excellent examples of research done in this vein, see the essays in Baron's collection cited above; Joan Scott, "Part III: Gender in History," in Joan Scott, *Gender and the Politics of History* (New York: Columbia University Press, 1988), 93–163; Sonya Rose, *Limited Livelihoods: Gender and Class in Nineteenth-Century England* (Berkeley: University of California Press, 1992); and Alice Kessler-Harris, *A Woman's Wage: Historical Meanings and Social Consequences* (Lexington: University Press of Kentucky, 1990). For work done with more focus on daily practices, see Aihwa Ong's insightful study of women workers in Malaysia, *Spirits of Resistance and Capitalist Discipline* (Albany: State University of New York Press, 1987), and "Japanese Factories, Malay Workers: Class and Sexual Metaphors in West Malaysia," in *Power and Difference: Gender in Island Southeast Asia,* ed. Jane Monnig Atkinson and Shelly Errington (Stanford: Stanford University Press, 1990), 385–422.

4. See "'L'ouvrière! Mot impie, sordide . . . ': Women Workers in the Discourse of French Political Economy, 1840–1860," in Scott, *Gender and the Politics of History;* and Haraway.

5. Teresa de Lauretis, "The Technology of Gender," in *Technologies of Gender: Essays on Theory, Film, and Fiction,* ed. Teresa de Lauretis (Bloomington: Indiana University Press, 1987), 1–30.

6. Maquilas, or maquiladoras, are Mexican export-processing factories, owned by foreign (usually U.S.) capital. They were first established in 1965 on Mexico's northern border. The factories employ low-paid (even by local standards) Mexican workers to assemble U.S.-produced parts into goods to be sold on the U.S. market. Ciudad Juárez contains the largest concentration of maquila workers in the country. In the last decade, the program has mushroomed. Today it is one of Juárez's largest employers.

7. For excellent histories of this labor market process, see Jorge Carrillo and Alberto Hernández, *Mujeres fronterizas en la industria maquiladora* (Mexico City: SEP-CEFNOMEX, 1985); and Fernandez-Kelly. For an overview of the varied ways in which gender has figured in contemporary transnational production, see Aihwa Ong, "The Gender and Labor Politics of Postmodernity," *Annual Review of Anthropology* 20 (1991): 279–309.

8. *Fronterizo* (Ciudad Juárez), 16 Mar. 1981.

9. *ABC* (Ciudad Juárez), 27 Sept. 1980.

10. Baron; Benería and Roldán; Elson and Pearson; Fernandez-Kelly; Fuentes and Ehrenreich; Iglesias; Kamel; Haraway; Rose; Sklair; Standing.

11. The search for "constituting discourses" is not an attempt to introduce a more finely tuned essentialism—replacing global images of femininity and masculinity with highly predictable localized images. Gendered meanings do not automatically emerge from a given set of "structural conditions" that managers merely "enact." On the contrary, managerial goals are as discursively shaped as gender itself, and it is managerial subjectivity that determines what constitutes a relevant "condition" in decision making. Similarly, managerial labor control practices do not automatically produce a particular gendered outcome. Like these practices themselves, worker responses are not random, but neither are they inherent in the practices at the outset.

12. The research on which this discussion is based was done in Ciudad Juárez during 1992 and 1993. Data were collected through participant observation on the shop floor of the maquiladoras, through interviews with managers, lawyers, labor organizers, and job seekers outside these factories, and through an archival search of local newspapers from the 1970s and 1980s. In each of the factories discussed in this article, I observed on the shop floor—talking to both workers and supervisors—and interviewed managers in their offices. I spent three months in the television plant, observing but not working in production. In the harness plant I spent ten weeks, and in the scrub clothes plant I spent six weeks. In both these factories I worked on the line for half of my period in the plant. In all three factories, after leaving I conducted a series of ten, unstructured, small-group interviews in my home with my coworkers.

13. All maquila names used here are fictitious.

14. Ironically enough, this factory not only is easily explained by poststructuralist theory but also most clearly resembles the "patriarchal plant" described by feminists in the 1980s. (See note 2.)

15. Michel Foucault, *Discipline and Punish* (New York: Vintage Books, 1977).

16. Critiques of the physical objectification of women have been a staple of feminist theory since its inception. (See, for instance, Catherine MacKinnon's "Feminism, Marxism, Method, and the State: An Agenda for Theory," *Signs* 7 [spring 1982]: 515–44). Feminist analysis of the pleasure of being seen has been less developed. One author who discusses this is Valerie Steele, in *Fashion and Eroticism: Ideals of Feminine Beauty from the Victorian Era to the Jazz Age* (New York: Oxford University Press, 1985).

17. My own style is also under daily examination in the factory. As I listen to the daily gossip, I recognize the inflated sense of one's physical presence that is described by women in the plant.

18. For discussions of the accepted hierarchy of maquila jobs, see Iglesias; Fernandez-Kelly; Susan Tiano, *Patriarchy on the Line: Labor, Gender, and Ideology in the Mexican Maquila Industry* (Philadelphia: Temple University Press, 1994); Lisa Catanzarite and Myra Strober, "The Gender Recomposition of the Maquiladora Labor Force," *Industrial Relations* 32 (winter 1993): 133–47.

19. Foucault.

20. A similarly structured factory owned by the same company had severe labor problems shortly thereafter. Although I was never allowed in, it raises the question of whether shop floor dynamics similar to those described here ultimately created a social space in which more organized resistance could develop.

21. Michael Burawoy describes a similar process around piece work in *Manufacturing Consent* (Chicago: University of Chicago Press, 1979).

22. As a fieldworker, it took me much longer to notice gender's insignificance than it did to notice its numerous incarnations. Barrie Thorne has an elegant discussion of this problem in "Children and Gender: Constructions of Difference," in *Theoretical Perspectives on Sexual Difference*, ed. Deborah Rhode (New Haven: Yale University Press, 1990), 100–113.

23. See, for instance, Octavio Paz, *El Laberinto de la Soledad* (Mexico City: Fondo de Cultura Económica, 1950); and Evelyn Stevens, "Marianismo: The Other Face of Machismo in Latin America," in *Male and Female in Latin America*, ed. Ann Pescatello (Pittsburgh: University of Pittsburgh Press, 1973), 89–101. For a critique of this literature, see Matthew Gutmann, "The Meanings of Macho: Changing Mexican Male Identities," *Masculinities* 2 (spring 1994): 21–33.

24. Jennifer Pierce, in her recent book, *Gender Trials: Emotional Lives in Contemporary Law Firms* (Berkeley: University of California Press, 1995), employs the opposite strategy. In a study of several workplaces, she emphasizes the way lawyers and paralegals across several law firms all enact a single set of culturally prescribed gender roles such as "mother" or "Rambo."

25. Denise Riley, *"Am I That Name?": Feminism and the Category of "Women" in History* (Minneapolis: University of Minnesota Press, 1988), 6.

26. See, for instance, Judith Butler, *Gender Trouble: Feminism and the Subversion of Identity* (New York: Routledge, 1990), esp. chap. 1.

27. Butler, *Gender Trouble*, and Judith Butler, *Bodies That Matter: On the Discursive Limits of "Sex"* (New York: Routledge, 1993).

28. Riley.

29. The tendency to theorize gendered meaning structures at the level of a given culture in part reflects the legacy of feminist anthropologists, who were the first to point out and delineate the distinctive meanings that accrue to femininity and masculinity in varied cultural contexts. In 1981, in *Sexual Meanings: The Cultural Construction of Gender and Sexuality* (Cambridge, England: Cambridge University Press, 1981), Sherry Ortner and Harriet Whitehead presented a pathbreaking set of essays, each of which described a different cultural configuration of gendered meaning. Poststructuralist feminist theorists have continued in this vein—emphasizing the varied content of gendered meaning systems but taking it as a theoretical given that the relevant level of variation is that of a linguistic system or culture as a whole.

30. See, for instance, Joan Scott, "Work Identities for Men and Women: The Politics of Work and Family in the Parisian Garment Trades in 1848," in *Gender and the Politics of History*, 93–113.

18 Hegemonic Relations and Gender Resistance

The New Veiling as Accommodating Protest in Cairo

ARLENE ELOWE MACLEOD

Power invests [the dominated], passes through them and with the help of them, relying on them just as they, in their struggle against power, rely on the hold it exerts on them.

Michel Foucault[1]

The persistence of women's subordination throughout history and across many cultures presents a difficult puzzle; although women are clearly assertive actors who struggle for better conditions for themselves and for their families, their efforts often seem to produce limited or ephemeral results. The recent widening of opportunities for some women is unusual, and when placed in historical and cross-cultural perspective, its future seems uncertain.[2] In this article, I explore the puzzle of women's persistent efforts toward change and the equally persistent presence of gender inequality—the puzzle of the resilience of power in gender relations. Part of the problem, I argue, is located in a style of struggle women employ to resist the constraints of power, a style I have called "accommodating protest."

Feminist theorists have long been interested in the part women play within relations of power. They have often cast women as victims, accepting the inevitability of domination.[3] Others have portrayed women as consenting subordinates, relatively satisfied with a deferential role.

More recently, to counter these images of passive victimization and active acceptance, feminists have depicted women as powerful wielders of hidden, informal influence. This latter view begins to deal with the nuances of power relations by detailing various forms of power and by arguing that women are both active subjects and subjects of domination. To continue this effort of detailing the complexities of women's part in power relations, I argue that women, even as subordinate players, always play an active part that goes beyond the dichotomy of victimization/acceptance, a dichotomy that flattens out a complex and ambiguous agency in which women accept, accommodate, ignore, resist, or protest— sometimes all at the same time. Power relationships should be viewed as an ongoing relationship of struggle, a struggle complicated by women's own contradictory subjectivity and ambiguous purposes.[4] Such a perspective on power relations builds on the work of Antonio Gramsci, the Italian Marxist who tried to comprehend the puzzles of class consciousness and lower-class consent in modernizing societies. Here I extend his arguments on the complexity of consent to consider the problem of hegemonic relations and gender resistance.

The case of Middle Eastern women is particularly interesting with reference to this issue. From a Western vantage point, women in the Middle East are often pitied as the victims of an especially oppressive culture, generally equated with Islamic religion. Women are depicted as bound to the harem, downtrodden and constrained; the ultimate symbol of their oppression and their acceptance of inferiority is the veil. Yet this picture cannot be reconciled with the assertive behavior and influential position of women in many Middle Eastern settings. In Cairo, for instance, many women manage the household budget, conduct important marriage arrangements, and coordinate extensive socioeconomic networks.[5] They are more than deferential partners, playing effective roles in their homes and the wider community, as demonstrated by the recent literature examining women's networks and the informal powers, bargaining tactics, or hidden strategies exercised by Middle Eastern women.[6] By implication, although these women definitely struggle to widen their options, they also play a real part in maintaining the social context, including power relations, that limit women's opportunities. The dichotomization in the literature on Middle Eastern women between women-of-the-harem victimization and behind-the-scenes-but-truly-powerful agency tends to produce arguments which flatten out the subtleties of women's subjectivity under power. Lost in either of these views, which stem in part from postcolonial discourses embedded within feminist theory, is the much more ambiguous reality of women's attempts to understand and act.[7] Using the new veiling movement as an example, I want to draw attention to these ambiguities of women's simultaneous attempts to alter and to maintain, to protest and to accommodate.

My argument is based on a study of working women in lower-middle-class Cairo.[8] These women form part of a new class in Egyptian society, one created in part by the revolution of 1952 that removed a British-supported monarchy and established a new state. The revolution, a military coup led by a group of army officers, evolved into an attempt to wed Arab nationalism with socialism under the leadership of Gamal Abdul Nasser, Egypt's new president and the Arab world's new popular leader. Nasser's authoritarian populism stressed social welfare programs, self-determination in foreign policy, and pan-Arabic regional unity. His policies propelled Egypt into political leadership in the Arab world but also into a top-heavy and relatively unproductive bureaucratic regime.[9] The new middle class that emerged from the peasantry through free education and guaranteed jobs in government offices is increasingly squeezed economically by the government's attempt to maintain a welfare state with relatively meager resources. The economic and social struggles of this new middle class frame the circumstances of women working as low-ranking clerks in the government bureaucracy. Indeed, the values and living standards of middle-class life assume a magnified importance for these women and their families in marking family position and individual identity. Although they have the example of upper-class women who hold political power or important jobs in the business and bureaucratic worlds, these women face the novel experience of being the first in their families' recent histories to pursue formal education and jobs outside the home.[10]

In recent years, many of these women have embraced the controversial new veiling, a voluntary women's movement to abandon Western clothes in favor of some form of covered Islamic dress. My interpretation of the politics of this dress centers on its expression of a contradictory message of both protest and accommodation. While this ambiguous symbolic politics takes on the distinctive and dramatic form of veiled dress in Cairo, the argument it raises about women's part in power relations is suggestive for women elsewhere as well.[11] For the new veiling in Cairo takes place not as a remnant of traditional culture or a reactionary return to traditional patterns, but as a form of hegemonic politics in a modernizing environment, making its meaning relevant to women in other such settings as well—settings in which, as Foucault reminds us, power and resistance both reveal themselves in transformed and ever more subtle arrangements.[12]

Choosing to look at women's use of the veil in an urban center in the Middle East and using that case study to reflect on women's part in power relations also illustrates some of the unresolved methodological dilemmas of writing about women and power in the Third World. The veil has been an obsession of Western writers from early travelogues to more recent television docudramas, serving as the symbol par excellence of women as oppressed in the Middle East, an image that ignores indigenous cultural constructions of the veil's meanings and reduces a complex and ever-changing symbolism into an ahistorical reification. Although a more recent literature on women's informal powers has revised this image, it has tended to so contextualize women's situation that the larger issues of women's subordination are sometimes left untouched. The polemics of global feminist discourse create a context in which it becomes difficult to talk about women's subordination at all without contributing to earlier stereotypes, yet avoiding the topic of women's subordination creates a feminism that celebrates difference but loses its foundation for ethical judgment.[13] I have tried to contextualize the use of the veil for these women in Cairo and to emphasize their agency; however, I also examine the ambiguities at the heart of their use of the new veils, raising questions about the nature of women's agency and resistances more generally.

This study is founded on a close association with twenty-eight lower-middle-class households in Cairo, including about eighty-five women. Material was collected primarily through participant observation and informal conversations conducted during long visits with women and their families at home and with women in the workplaces. In later stages of the research, twenty-five younger women were selected for informal interviewing more systematically focused on working and veiling. Certainly, my own identity influenced my field research and writing considerably. First, my father is Iraqi and my mother is from Maine. I went to the Middle East for the first time to do field research for my dissertation; there I found that women accepted me as both Arabic and American, using my two identities as it suited their own purposes in different social situations. Other aspects of my identity, as a married woman and eventually a mother, for example, or as a political scientist, also shaped the nature of our encounters and thus the ideas expressed here. Throughout this study, women's words and my reflections on their meaning are interwoven. Recounting women's words is common in feminist texts, but the status of these words is often unclear;[14] here, they are meant to illustrate the range of thinking women offered in my presence and those aspects of our encounter which led to my thinking about the new veils and women's resistance in terms of accommodating protest. In this context, it is important to note that a case study such as this has both benefits and limitations. Its strength lies in the ability to illuminate the distinctive details of a local situation and use these details to think beyond the boundaries of the specific case. Yet this ability to interpret and reflect on the meaning of the case could also be seen as its primary weakness, for the case does not "prove" in the same way as large-scale surveys or statistical analyses; nonetheless, it offers insight into the dynamics of women's lives that larger studies often cannot provide.

The Politics of Veiled Dress

While to many Westerners veiling symbolizes the coercive manipulation of female behavior, within the Middle East it serves indigenous symbolic purposes that extend well beyond such stereotypes. Veiling is employed in a wide variety of situations, with social, economic, and nationalistic as well as sexual connotations. Indeed, the wide range of styles and social meanings is perhaps the most striking feature of veiled dress, demonstrating the variety of political relationships that may be reinforced or challenged by such clothing.[15]

The Quran and Islamic doctrine are usually blamed by Westerners for initiating the covering and seclusion of women. However, veiling existed in many of the Arab tribes before the beginning of Islam. The Quran itself advocates the covering of the hair, shoulders, and upper arms and secluding oneself from inappropriate viewers; this advice refers, however, to the wives of the Prophet, who had both the religious and social status of an elite group and the special problem of being permanently in the public eye.[16] The implications for other women are unclear and have been interpreted in a wide variety of ways depending on local needs, class interests, kinship structures, and women's endeavors.

Although the widespread concern with women's dress does indicate a cultural focus on modest behavior, veiling is a subtle and evocative symbol with multiple meanings that cultural participants articulate, read, and manipulate. Veiling may, for example, function to emphasize appropriate relations of familiarity and distance within the web of kinship bonds.[17] Women may draw their covering dress closer about them or cover their face when in the presence of strangers, and then leave their face uncovered within the home or in front of certain male relatives. Indeed, as many families make the transition from village to urban settings, veiling may be extended as women are more often in the range of strangers' vision. Veiling can also be tied to class; often less feasible for poorer women laboring in the fields or outside the home, veiling tends to increase as class standing rises and families can afford the "luxury" of more seclusion for women.[18] Thus, covered dress may signal higher prestige and status, making it more desirable to families moving to a higher class standing. Further, veiling may present overt political statements centered on cultural authenticity or political and religious affiliations.[19] Finally, veiling may function as a mode of communication between the wearer and viewer, a public way of sending social or economic messages, perhaps about marital status, education, or village origin. The subtle alterations of how the veil is worn, what material it is made from, and which small decorations complement an outfit highlight the fact that veiling is a two-way mode of communication, not merely a form of dress imposed on women against their will. Women, to some extent, use veiling for their own purposes—as attraction, as warning, as a reminder of kin and social obligations.[20] Veiling emerges as an evocative sign of the intersection of domination and resistance, highlighting interpretive struggles over women's identity and role.

The importance of veiling as a symbol of power relations in Middle Eastern society is underlined by the history of veiling in Cairo. In 1923 Huda Shaarawi, an upper-class woman involved in the nationalistic struggles against British colonial power, launched a movement to abandon the face veil.[21] This movement eventually triumphed and until fairly recently upper-middle- and upper-class women in Cairo have worn Western-style dress. On the other hand, lower-class women, both of rural and traditional-urban origins, have continued to wear various traditional outfits, which generally include long colorful dresses and a black outer garment and gauzy headscarf.[22]

Yet, in the last fifteen years, many middle- and upper-class women are re-veiling—or more accurately, adopting new versions of Islamic dress ranging from fashionable turbans and silky gowns to austere head-to-toe coverings.[23] The most interesting aspect of this changed dress centers on its emergence as a women's movement, a voluntary veiling initiated primarily by women. Not confined to Cairo, but a widespread movement with varying popularity throughout the Islamic world, the new veiling clearly has symbolic significance for many. However, its meaning varies from country to country, class to class, even individual to individual; it has been used to signal identification within political disputes, as in Iran before and after the revolution; to signal membership in Islamic revivalist groups, as in the universities in Egypt in the late 1970s or in Istanbul today; and to signal anti-Western or nationalistic sentiment, as in the occupied territories in the Palestinian *intifada*. The popularity of the new veiling movement among lower-middle-class working women in Cairo in the mid-1980s has its own specific and local meanings as well, to which we can now turn.

Lower-Middle-Class Working Women and the New Veiling

Cairo has grown in population in the last generation from about 2 million to about 12 million, swelled in part by an influx of rural families in search of work and a "more modern" life. These families, the foundation of the lower middle class, struggle to overcome poverty and reach for middle-class security. The women I knew generally grew up in families with about eight living children in cramped apartments of two or three tiny rooms in the traditional quarters of the city. Their mothers are house-wives who may raise ducks or chickens for extra income, and their fathers work as construction laborers, drivers, mechanics, or small shop-keepers. These families are the beneficiaries of the socialist programs of the Nasser era, especially the educational reforms that allowed children to attend school and guaranteed jobs to all graduates in the government bureaucracy. These jobs offer respectable working conditions for families very concerned with female members' reputations and the secure, if small, incomes.

Additionally, these jobs offer the prestige of middle-class status to families seeking to differentiate themselves from more recent migrants or from manual laborers, domestics, or street peddlers. Lower-middle-class women distinguish themselves from the "poor," the "peasants" of the lower classes, who follow "uncivilized" and "not modern" life-styles. With household incomes barely rising above the levels of lower-class families, who often follow less prestigious but more lucrative occupations, women from these families are hard pressed to pay for rent, food, commuting, and clothes.[24] Yet they emphasize the status and prestige of class differences, however subtle, which separate them from lower-class families and exaggerate their similarities to families with more resources. In these families, women's working not only affects their individual standing but also moves the entire family from the lower class to the bottom rungs of the middle class.

These women—educated, working, modernizing—have started to veil, abandoning the modest versions of Western dress that are the badge of their hoped-for class position and turning to the long dresses and headscarfs of the *muhaggaba*, the covered woman. This movement initiated as a political and religious statement in the universities after the 1967 and 1973 wars with Israel[25] and has over the years been transformed into a new movement with different adherents and reasoning. Women's stories illustrate some of the controversies which are provoked by this increasingly common pattern in lower-middle-class Cairo.[26]

Mervat graduated from a two-year institute with a degree in business three years ago; she works as a typist in a government office. She and her four officemates are all single and enjoy the chance to be out of the home which working affords. Since their duties are light, they tend to spend their day chatting over cups of sweet tea about family affairs, the clothes and furnishings they are saving to buy, or the men in the nearby offices. Like many of her friends, Mervat wears Western dress. She has most of her clothes made by her sister-in-law, which is less expensive than buy-ing them ready-made, and she saves carefully to buy shoes on credit to match her skirts and blouses. She explains this effort as marriage strat-egy: "Men like women to look beautiful of course! So, if I wish to find a husband, I wear this kind of clothes." When asked about the *higab*, she expresses a typical sentiment: "I hope to wear the *higab* some day. Not right now, but I respect the women who have made this decision and per-haps I will feel in my heart that this is right too, God willing. Not every-one can make this decision at the same time; I don't think about these things very much now, but maybe I will in the future. It will be important to me, like it is for my sister. She has just decided to become covered and perhaps this decision will come to me too." On the other hand, Mervat's older neighbor, Sanayya, who is married with teenage children and also wears Western clothes, is quite adamant about never putting on the *higab:* "Some women wear this scarf over their hair, and that is alright for them, but for me, no. I will never put on those clothes. It's important to wear modern clothes and go to work and educate your children, not to cover yourself up. Clothes don't matter anyway, it is a fad for younger girls."

Aida is engaged, and she lives with her family in a traditional quarter in central Cairo. Aida's father is a migrant laborer who works as a driver in the Gulf states and has been away for many years; her mother is illiter-ate and a *sitt al-bayt*, a housewife, who has never worked outside the home. Some time ago, Aida broke off her engagement because her fiance refused to consider Aida's working after their marriage. But Aida defi-nitely wants to continue in her job; her reasons include the income she can earn, security, and the chance to socialize. Most important, however, is the need to be challenged: "I need to keep busy, and have something to think about and be doing all day. I can't just sit in the home and chat with neighbors and cook the meals; I know how to do all these things but I like to be out with people and working hard to accomplish something. Then, when my husband will come home at night, even though he says 'cook my dinner,' we are equal, we stand together, and this will make a mar-riage work better." In time, Aida was again engaged, this time to a man who agreed that she could continue working after the wedding. One day, while discussing her plans for the ceremony and the future, she men-tioned her intention to become a *muhaggaba*, a covered woman. She planned to change her colorful Western outfits for a long modest skirt and a headscarf wrapping over her hair and shoulders. "See this beauti-ful hair," she laughed, "you won't see it anymore. Well, maybe you will see a little peeking out here and there, but I will wear the *higab*." When asked when she would put on this garb, she was vague: "Not right after the wedding, no, maybe a year, maybe two. I am not sure." About a year after the wedding, after giving birth to a son and resuming her work at the office, and despite her husband's objections, Aida indeed put on covering dress.

Husnayya is married and has three small children; she and her husband both work in government offices. Husnayya has been wearing the *higab* for several years now; family photos show her earlier Western dress now changed to ankle-length skirts, long sleeved jackets, and a scarf wrapped securely around her hair and shoulders. She explained the change this way: "Here in Cairo, we are Muslim women, and so we dress this way, with long sleeves and covering our hair and shoulders. Sometimes no kohl on the eyes even! But I wear kohl, just a little. No lipstick though, only for my husband in the evening in our house! Before we dressed differently, I don't really know why. But this dress is better, when I wear these clothes I feel secure, I know I am a good mother and a good wife. And men know not to laugh and flirt with me. So it is no problem to go out to work, or to shop, or anything. This is a good way to dress, it solves many problems."

From such accounts it is clear that women have many different reasons for the dress they wear, including religion, fashion, harassment, and family responsibilities; indeed women, families, friends, and co-workers spend long hours in amiable or contentious debate about what women should be wearing. Husbands and wives may not always agree, and sometimes men prefer women to wear Western dress, promoting their "modern" status. Women's dress, always symbolic in this society, provokes intriguing controversy.

Hegemony and Resistance

Why would these women, who are educated, dedicated to working, and relatively successful symbols of modernization, return to a traditional symbol like the veil? Why agree to, or even encourage, what seems to be a return to an inferior status? These questions confront us with one of the central issues of any study of subordinates within relations of power: why do subordinate groups seem to aid the reproduction of power relations which function to their disadvantage?

In his *Prison Notebooks,* Gramsci considers the problem of the endurance of power relations and the puzzle of obedience within relations of class inequality: Why do people consent? Why do people seldom rebel? Why do people actually aid their own subordination? He develops the concept of hegemony as a characterization of power relations within modern societies where consent operates more obviously than force, eventually using the term to convey several different approaches to this web of problems. One interpretation portrays hegemonic interaction as the shaping of beliefs and behavior of a subordinate class by a dominant group. Consent is achieved by the instrumental molding of the common sense of subordinates, directed toward the interests of the upper class. This interpretation of hegemony essentially argues that the ruling class is able to structure a situation in which the lower classes are unable to perceive the ways they are subordinated. Certainly, the new veiling in Cairo initially appears as a classic example of hegemony so defined, for in deciding to veil, women seem to reproduce their own inequality. Hegemonic relations, conceived in this manner, indicate that these women must be deluded about their true interests and duped into behavior which reinforces their own subordination; they are victims of a "false consciousness."

Yet more recent studies of class relations encourage a more encompassing reading of Gramsci's ideas and of subordinate's behavior, viewing hegemony as ideological struggle rather than ideological domination.[27] Focusing on an examination of what "consent" really amounts to in specific situations, scholars have discovered that the role of subordinate groups is a great deal more complex than the "false consciousness" model of hegemonic relations suggests. Consent, or the lack of overt and organized political opposition, is actually a blanket term that can cover a range of possible consciousness and political activity, from active support to passive acceptance to submerged resistance.[28] Consent emerges as a more complicated interaction than it first appears, highlighting the need to rethink the question of such ideological struggle in cases of gender inequality as well.

In the case of lower-middle-class women in Cairo, two important signs reinforce the need to think of hegemony as a mode of political struggle rather than a process of top-down domination. First, these veils are a new kind of covering clothing. In Cairo, lower-middle-class women have been wearing Western clothes for some years now; Western dress signified modernity and women's ability to be equal partners in aiding Egypt's recovery and growth. Women are not simply clinging to the past; covering clothes have not been their normal dress for many years. Indeed, the dress these women are putting on is not even the traditional dress of their mothers or grandmothers but a quite distinct and new style, clearly distinguished from the traditional garb of lower-class women. The second sign of struggle is that this is a movement initiated by women themselves. Women have the right, which they exercise, to decide what dress they will wear; covering dress is considered a personal decision a woman makes in her heart and not a matter her husband can decide for her. So the new veiling cannot be explained as the maintenance of traditional ways or as the revival of a traditional symbol at men's insistence. The controversies over voluntary veiling in lower-middle-class Cairo alert us to the complexity of women's "consent" and lead to the question of what this new dress signifies as part of a hegemonic struggle.

Women's Dilemma and the New Veiling

Although lower-middle-class women now leave the household for outside work, we cannot assume that this produces greater opportunities; in fact, many women complain that working carries considerable burdens along with limited benefits. As one married woman with two young children complained: "Of course it is good now that we can go out of the house and go everywhere to work, but it is also hard. Each day I must go to work, ride the bus, shop for food, pick up my children, cook the meals, and clean the house. There is never enough time and I am always very tired." This comment was echoed by many others who cited responsibilities that make working outside the home especially burdensome. The double load of working inside and outside the home is aggravated by women's feeling that men do not, and indeed, could not, be expected to help with household labor in any significant way. In addition, everyone complained that the salaries they earn are far too low: "I spend each day here from nine until two [normal work hours], and look how little I earn, I should have more money for the work I do here!" Women complain that the government has encouraged their education and promised a good living, yet today their salaries are hardly meeting rising costs.

As for the work in the offices, women called their duties "boring and unchallenging" and "useless." The government policy of hiring all graduates has produced a civil service that provides some economic security, but at the cost of overcrowding, inadequate equipment, and lack of productivity. A typical work day for one energetic woman named Hoda, for instance, involves making the appointments for a manager down the hall. Since two other women in her office are also responsible for the same task, they can easily cover for each other while one slips out to shop for vegetables, visit a sick friend, or pray. Each day, two or three appointments are recorded in a worn book, and the hours are filled by chatting and drinking tea. Some women stated that this lack of responsibility is an advantage, as they can save their energy for the work that awaits them at home, while others were frustrated. Clearly, this is not the kind of work that would offer women the skills or sense of accomplishment that might create a new, positive identity as worker or professional, even though it compares favorably with the work lower-class women must do as domestics, factory laborers, or street peddlers. Even ambitious and energetic lower-middle-class women have very few options for other jobs outside the public sector. Since the *infitah* period (the opening) initiated by Anwar Sadat, the growth of a dual economy with a privileged private sector alongside the public has widened class inequities. As one woman noted, "I would love to have a job typing or being a receptionist in a private travel agency. There I would make a salary which is three times the amount I make here. But I do not know how to get such a job, I think you must have connections to work there and also you must know English and even French. But I don't think it is right that I make so little money, after all I need to buy the same things for my family that those women do." Even equivalent secretarial positions in the private sector are generally available only to upper-middle-class women with foreign language abilities, appropriate social skills, and family connections. On balance, working is generally portrayed by these women as a progressive step for the increased mobility it provides but also as troublesome and tiring; it is not surprising that many women claim they would quit their jobs if they could.[29]

These complaints point to an important problem women are experiencing as they move into the intersection of the two worlds of household and workplace; they face a deep dilemma of identity and role. Although many husbands maintain (at least in public) that they want a wife who stays at home, most women quickly state that this is impossible. "It is ridiculous! Today all wives have to work to help the family, it is not possible to pay for children, and rent and food without a wife working." Women see their work as a trade-off for the necessities of middle-class status—a two-room apartment, an electric fan, a refrigerator, and tutors for children. The economic pressures that push women into the workplace are reinforced by the ideological requirements of class standing. These are ambitious families with high expectations for a better life, expectations promoted by the policies of a welfare state that encouraged education, government jobs, and an increased standard of living. These values were fueled in the late 1970s and early 1980s with the consumerism accompanying the *infitah* policies of the Sadat years. Families of this level have very high hopes for a better standard of living and are willing to work hard to gain their goals, which appear in enticing television advertisements of modern kitchens, labor-saving appliances, and ready-made clothes. In overwhelming numbers, these families choose to have female members enter the formal work force to gain the extra income.

Yet the economic ideology which pushes women into the workplace is countered by a gender ideology which frames women's place within the home as mother and wife. Members of this class believe that women and men embody different natures that make them suited to quite different tasks and responsibilities. According to both women and men, women belong in the home, where their nature is fulfilled by caring for husband and children and managing the household.[30] One unhappy husband complained, "Before I used to get a hot dinner every night, my mother had it ready for me and my father as soon as we walked in the door. Now I have to wait and wait while Samira cooks the dinner." This recollection of life before women left the home was echoed by his wife, busy cooking in the hot kitchen after the same long day in a government office and on the overcrowded city buses. "Before, my mother would have the whole day to go to the market and select the very best vegetables. Look at these awful things, they're terrible, bad! But I only have time to shop on the way home from work, and to cook in a rush like this. I hardly ever have time to make good meals. I used to be a good cook, but now we eat macaroni all the time." These comments are interesting, not only for the generalized belief that life in Cairo is getting more difficult, but also for the underlying assumption that women really should be at home, that families would be better off if this were possible. The clash of gender beliefs with economic realities and ideology creates a compromising dilemma for these women: "I work because my income is necessary, look at this budget, how could we live here and eat and send my sons to school if I didn't work? But I miss my sons very much, I know they are happy here with my mother every day, and I visit each afternoon. Still, a mother should be with her children. I want the hours to play with them and cook for them." Women working outside the home feel they are neglecting their husbands and children despite the fact that they work, in good part, for their families rather than for personal satisfaction.[31] This dilemma is reinforced by the intractability of the economic situation, which is worsening as high inflation eats away at income and raises the price of household goods. Rents especially have become an extremely difficult expense to meet, yet a middle-class apartment is considered a necessity for marriage and establishing a family.

Women's double bind is intensified by the seeming immutability of gender roles. Since male and female natures are perceived as set, there is little hope of enticing men into helping with household work. Indeed, while some women wished their husbands would help out at home, many expressed the idea that the home was their domain and seemed unwilling to have it invaded. As one young wife emphasized: "Women are in charge in the home, yes, of course we do a lot of work, but on the other hand men don't know how to do these things. You know, men can make tea perhaps or something small like that. But cooking a good meal, or arranging things properly, these are women's matters. I am tired at the end of the day, but I want my husband to know what a good wife I am." Individual men may more or less fit the qualities of male nature, but in general men act in certain ways and are responsible for certain tasks, as are women. "Men will not change, they are rough and hard; they are not suited for doing things in the home. That takes a woman who is soft and feels things in her heart."

Caught in a double bind of economic and gender ideologies, women face a loss of respect and resources despite small economic gains. It is in this context that many women have started to wear the new veils. When asked why they wear this dress, women overwhelmingly responded, "This is what Muslim women wear." Over time, as I came to know certain women better, they expanded on their original answer. "Now we have realized the need, where before we were in the dark," answered one woman, a thought that suggested an awakening of insight inspired by a return to religious and cultural values. Beauty and dignity were common adjectives for the woman who veils: "I think a woman who wears the *higab* is very beautiful, she shows her inner strength. I hope that I will feel in my heart the urge to wear this dress soon," said one young woman wearing Western dress, with sincere admiration of her co-workers who were dressed in covering garb. Others felt it decreased attractiveness and stressed that a woman had better find a husband before putting on this dress. "I don't wear the *higab* because I want to look good, and show off a little, how else will I find a good husband after all!" The claim that this dress is a trend, "it's what everyone does these days," also emerged in many women's comments. Fashions come and go, they suggested, and no one really knows why; some of the more thoughtful stressed that economic hard times and a sense of cultural crisis create a need to return to cultural roots in the face of an onslaught of Western consumer goods and television values. Overt religious sentiment was remarkable in its relative absence in women's accounts; only a very few emphasized increased religious feeling as a reason for altering their dress, and affiliation with Islamic groups was rare. Neither did this dress seem associated with a given time of life; women cited "after I marry," "after I have children," "when I get a little older," "when I feel the need in my heart" as times in the future when they would consider changing their dress, but no one said it was required in any way at particular stages of a woman's life.

With no simple or settled answers about the meaning of this symbol, and with the controversy expressed in the media and in daily conversations, it seems unlikely that the meaning of this symbol is entirely regulated by political or religious groups (although both do try to control and manipulate its meaning). Women take veiling seriously as an important decision they must make about who they are and what women should be. One point women repeatedly made is that the dress makes a statement about their identity as wives and mothers. "This dress says to everyone that I am a Muslim woman, and that I am here working because my family needs me to. Not for myself! I am here because I love my family and we need some things for our home." While individual women put on the new veils for many reasons, the new veiling seems to serve as a symbolic mediator for many women, expressing and ameliorating women's concerns arising at the intersection of work and family. Aida, mentioned earlier, explained her desire to veil at some time after her marriage: "Life is like an account book, with columns of numbers on the credit and debit sides. Good and bad actions are weighed at the end. If I work after I am married, this is very bad, so I need to do something very good to make up for it." Working, Aida maintains, is forbidden for women by religion and the Quran.[32] However, working before marriage is not so terrible as working afterward, for then she would be neglecting her real duties as wife and mother to a far greater extent. To counteract this problem and still keep her job, she has made the personal decision to veil; her covering clothes will serve as compensation, righting the balance of her compromising behavior. Aida's account illuminates a dilemma many women feel, that they violate their duties as wife and mother by working outside the home despite their families' need for their income. Her recognition of this double bind is acute: "I want to be able to buy nice things for my home. You see this refrigerator? I bought this for my mother after I started working, we never had one in the house when I was small. It is necessary to have one, for the food, and water. It saves work because we can cook a big meal and store the rest in there to eat for several more days. My mother could not do these things. She waits for my father to give her money, this is not secure. But she was always home with us as children, our home was a warm place. This is also very important." Many women expressed the idea that the veil in some way compensates for and even alleviates the dilemma they experience. "When I wear this dress, men will respect me," commented a young woman in her early twenties, who is hoping to marry a government employee like herself. "The *higab* is a protection from annoying people on the street," mentioned a married woman who had a long walk to her office building; "I don't have to worry that men in the cafe or on the street are talking about me every day as I pass." In another vein, a married woman with three children commented, "This dress looks beautiful and shows people that I am a woman even though I am working. My neighbors feel that a real woman stays at home, but now their tongues are silent about me." In a sentiment echoed by many women, one woman said, "This *higab* says I am a good Muslim woman, I can go out on the streets and to the office and no one can say I am not a good woman and mother." Women's answers, while stressing individual needs met by this dress, converge in their expressions of the need to make a statement about identity in a time of shifting norms.

As the veil has emerged as a mass-employed symbol rather than the outfit of relatively elite political actors as in the 1970s, its meaning has altered to suit differing political needs. These women object to the loss of their traditional identity, their valued and respected roles as mother and wife—crucial roles considering the extreme importance of the family in Egyptian society. "I don't know why my husband thinks I can cook meals and clean the house the way he would like when I am at work all day. It is not possible! Every night he is hard on me and upset." Another woman claimed, "These days men are not polite on the streets, before men left women alone, now they are always bothering women. I wear these clothes so they will know they should respect me." Through the veil, these women express their distress with their double bind; they want to reinstate their position as valued centers of the family but without losing their new ability to leave the home. Many agreed with the comment made by one woman: "It's wonderful now how women can go out visiting or to work. I would not want to return to the days of sitting in the house. I like to visit my sister in Imbaba and my cousin in Sayyida Zeinab and these days I can do this. With this dress it is easier." By emphasizing the dignity traditionally due to women for their valued part within the household, a respect eroded by women's current compromising behavior of working outside the home, the veil expresses women's concerns and makes a host of symbolic demands.

Accommodating Protest

Women's accounts signal a much more complex story underlying what first appears as reactionary behavior. The assessment of voluntary veiling as an example of hegemony, narrowly defined as ideological domination, is misguided. Veiling involves a struggle over women's identity and role in society, a negotiation of symbolic meaning that women initiate. While hegemony is typically discussed as what dominant groups do to subordinates, it is evident in this case that women are hardly active consenters to their domination, nor even passive acceptors of societal arrangements. Instead, they attempt to control meaning on their own, advancing demands which revolve around transforming identity and widening opportunity in a changing Cairo. Although more familiar examples of protest such as strikes, demonstrations, riots, or revolutions are less equivocal statements, recent studies identify many less easily codified behaviors as forms of resistance and stress the submerged and subtle ways subordinates may advance political demands, significantly widening definitions of protest and suggesting that the categories we use to think about consent, resistance, and protest may need to be reworked.[33]

Although the veil is employed as a form of protest, it is also true that women's intentions in Cairo are more ambivalent; indeed, I argue that the veil conveys women's desire to accommodate as well as resist. This accommodation could be read as subterfuge, a useful technique in power struggles often employed by subordinate groups, but women's use of the new veils goes beyond disguise to a more intertwining and inseparable linkage of protest with accommodation. The dress of the *muhaggaba* expresses both a demand for renewed dignity and compliance. One accommodating aspect of the new veil, for instance, is the fact that this dress is often impractical. While covering clothes can be less expensive than numerous Western outfits, women also complained that they are awkward, heavy, and stifling in the summer. More significant are the ways in which veiling conveys women's adjustment to and acceptance of existing conceptions of appropriate female behavior. One example is women's expectation that veiling will help lessen the sexual teasing and harassment they receive on the streets and in the offices. As one woman stated, "I wear these clothes to show the kind of woman I am, and now these men on the street should respect me." Another commented, "In the workplace men used to comment on my hair, and face and clothes, now they see that they should not discuss these things about me." Rather than charging men with the responsibility for changing their unwelcome behavior, women accommodate by altering their dress to fit the prevailing norm that men cannot help responding to women as temptations. While this may be a helpful short-term policy for individual women, veiling thus reinforces the belief that women invade men's world when they leave the home to work.

Veiling presents a double face; it both symbolizes women's protest against a situation that threatens valued identity and status, and it signals women's acceptance of a view of women as sexually suspect and naturally bound to the home. Protest is firmly bound to accommodation in a resonant public symbol, creating an ambiguous resistance, an accommodating protest. Although women clearly struggle to shape their identity and future status, and are not simply ideologically manipulated by dominant groups, the bare fact that such struggle exists is not in itself sufficient reason for optimism.[34] Why would women mount their protest in what seems an ambivalent and compromised form? Numerous studies citing women's active manipulation within difficult circumstances refute the possible conclusions that women are more constrained or more susceptible to ideological domination than other groups and thus more likely to "consent." The recent focus on the complexities of consent in class analysis pushes us to reconsider what such "complicity" might mean in gender relations as well. It has been argued that for some subordinate groups such accommodations can be tactics, a disguise to mask the reality of hidden struggles;[35] yet this implies a straightforward and unambiguous subjectivity which does not seem to characterize women's situation particularly well. In his *Prison Notebooks*, Gramsci discusses the "fragmentation" and "contradictory consciousness" of the working class as evidence of the need for a vanguard party and political leadership,[36] but perhaps we could draw on these ideas to think about ambiguous subjectivity—and the necessarily ambiguous agency such consciousness would generate—without concluding that this implies a distorted or undeveloped consciousness. Ambiguity can, after all, be productive and not simply undirected.

The linkage of accommodation with protest signals something of importance about the power relations in which women are enmeshed, as opposed to those of other subordinate groups. From the numerous possible reasons why women's resistance might take this form, I raise three here for the purposes of exploration. The first centers on the distinctive situation that women occupy with respect to the relations of power that constrain their lives. For women, there is no clear-cut other to confront directly. Facing a layered and overlapping round of oppressors, women do not have the relative luxury of knowing their enemy. Relations with men, class relations, and the more distant realm of global inequalities all affect lower-middle-class women in Cairo, yet none is exclusively responsible for women's subordination. Women see a web of cross-cutting power relations, and an ambiguous symbolic solution like the veil that speaks on different political levels suits the nature of these overlapping power constraints.

Another factor influencing women's style of protest centers on women's attempt to pursue different goals than other subordinate groups when resisting domination. For women's power relations are often entwined with other kinds of ties, such as romantic love or family bonds. Although a peasant may wish to be a landlord or a worker might wish to be a capitalist owner, the majority of women do not wish to become men, nor even to rid the world of men. Ideologies of opposition and inversion are less attractive when the end goal centers on creating a new relationship of cooperation or equality rather than eliminating the other.[37] In Cairo, for example, most husbands and wives consider themselves partners in the family structure, and neither wishes to switch roles nor to dissolve the differences between male and female character. In such a context, the ambitions of women in power struggles necessarily become more complex. Further, women daily inhabit the worlds of their oppressors rather than only occasionally intersecting the lives of the dominant group. Women live with, among, and in some ways, as one of, the dominant group; the everyday interaction, for example, of husbands and wives insures that women will often identify with their husbands, despite the times when these husbands act as oppressors. This identification should not be confused with simple ideological domination. Women truly do inhabit a unique position; accommodation is involved because women are part of both the dominant culture and the subordinate subculture.

A final reason women's struggles may take the form of accommodating protest centers on the constrained nature of choice. Working women of lower-middle-class Cairo have few viable ideological alternatives; any action they might take must be a choice which fits within their cultural tradition. Women's struggle is limited by the constraints of existing social discourse. For instance, women's descriptions of male character, which include the adjectives "hard," "rough," "stubborn," and "stupid," are interesting not only for their assertion that men are in many ways imperfect and even inferior to women, but for the underlying assumption that male character is set by nature and therefore unalterable. While these adjectives implicitly convey women's criticisms of male nature, and perhaps the potential of an alternative perspective which might motivate protest, women interpret their own adjectives within the constraints of existing discourse.

Of course there are other images available, but they do not attain the compelling state of the natural, remaining alternatives, but only in the sense of oddities. For instance, the Western woman is imagined according to the images available on television, including the women portrayed in imported shows such as *Dallas* and *Flamingo Road;* the glamorous women in commercials advertising cars, perfumes, and cosmetics; and the scantily clad singers featured in European nightclub shows. None of these images, focused as they are on women as sexual object and glamorous consumer, fit the lives of these women or offer an attractive alternative image. Further, in a postcolonial context, any images derived from the West are politically and culturally suspect.[38] Images from within the Islamic tradition, such as stories about the active lives of Fatima or Aisha, are much more attractive and useful, but subject to the same ambiguities of interpretation the veil itself embodies.[39]

Such limiting of discourse lies at the center of hegemonic politics, and it differs from the narrowed idea of hegemony as the obscuring of reality from subordinate participants. Hegemony can be understood as a symbolic struggle, a negotiation over meaning that involves constraints on imagination, where ideology is not so much a tool in the hands of a dominant class as an enveloping version of reality in which all social encounters are necessarily conducted. Such hegemonic struggles, and the accompanying constraints on political imagination, may be an especially common pattern in modern and modernizing cultures. Further, the constraints on imagination may tighten as local cultures are overtaken by mass-manufactured and Western popular culture.[40] In Cairo, despite the opportunity opened by economic changes in everyday routines and habits, women and men remain enveloped in traditional ideas about male and female character, roles, rights, and responsibilities, enmeshed in a struggle where oppositional imagination cannot effectively engage reality.

In this context, women's veiling calls on the Muslim tradition, not as an indiscriminate recollection of all traditional values, but as a highly selective attempt to revitalize and emphasize some of the old ideals. Yet there is always the danger of recalling not only the desired dignity which women hope to replant in the modern environment, but the accompanying emphasis on seclusion and constraint. Particularly for those who seek to recall the past not as holders of power, but as those constrained by power, the dangers need to be considered as well. The example of women's veiling recalls the Bakhtinian idea of the immense difficulties of appropriating language for new and oppositional uses. Women may choose to veil for their own reasons; yet the symbol maintains a somewhat separate life of its own, carrying both intended and unintended messages. The acquiescing and accommodating aspects of women's mode of hegemonic negotiation open the gates to possible co-optation.

Indeed, there are signs in Cairo that this co-optation is beginning to take place. For example, the character of this movement as women's personal decision is starting to be threatened; as husbands try to browbeat wives into veiled dress, or neighbors argue that a woman should be more modest, or religious leaders sermonize on women's clothes and role as mother, the choice of dress may become the province of men, the family, or the state, and less the decision of women. In the end, the *higab* operates as a symbol within a system where women's relations of inequality tend, more often than not, to be reproduced. The resilience of power relations can be explained, not as something which happens behind women's backs, but as the result, in part, of the way women struggle. Women's creative use of the new veils in lower-middle-class Cairo exemplifies the ambiguities which are the strength and the weakness of this style of resistance.

The idea that women's power relations may take the form of accommodating protest requires us to rethink our understanding of women's agency, rather than trying to fit women's actions within constraining categories or assuming a linear progression of consciousness from acquiescence to resistance to conscious protest. Once again, Gramsci's idea of hegemony can be useful, for he argues for the possibility of creating a counterhegemony, a working or popular class worldview which would combat, on the cultural front, the dominant class and create an alternative vision of social relations.[41] While alternatives can emerge from outside the hegemonic discourse, such imported ideologies seldom answer local needs nor attain viability in their new environment. The crucial and difficult question is exactly how alternative visions might emerge from within a culture to engage belief in a way which allows alternative discourse and ultimately effective political actions. For women, then, the idea of accommodating protest does not imply that women will always be victims despite their struggles, but encourages us instead to think beyond the dichotomies of victim/actor or passive/powerful toward the more complicated ways that consciousness is structured and agency embodied in power relations. Suggesting that part of women's continued subordination results from women's actions may be uncomfortable, but examining carefully the ambiguities of women's accommodating protests in different contexts may offer a clarity about women's subjectivity under domination that we need to address questions of gender inequalities and political change.

Notes

I am pleased to acknowledge the helpful advice of Jim Scott, Fred Shorter, Barbara Ibrahim, Homa Hoodfar, Diane Singerman, and Bruce MacLeod on earlier manifestations of the ideas expressed in this article. I also thank the *Signs* editors and reviewers for their thorough and challenging comments. Earlier versions of this article were presented at the Northeastern Political Science Association meeting in 1986 and at the National Women's Studies Association meeting in 1989; I would like to thank panelists and discussants for their helpful thoughts as well. The students of my "Power and Protest" seminar criticized many of the ideas presented here; I thank them for their comments and also thank Kankana Das and Jason Baker for help in producing this manuscript. Finally, I gratefully acknowledge the financial support of the American Research Center in Cairo, which administered my USIA grant in 1983–84, and Bates College for providing travel funds to Cairo in 1988. My greatest debt is to the women who are the subjects of this study; they have my deepest respect and gratitude for letting me temporarily enter their lives.

1. Michel Foucault, quoted in Gilles Deleuze, *Foucault* (Minneapolis: University of Minnesota Press, 1988), 27–28.

2. There is a large anthropological literature countering the idea that women are oppressed in every society; for a recent example see the essays in Peggy Reeves Sanday and Ruth Gallagher Goodenough, eds., *Beyond the Second Sex: New Directions in the Anthropology of Gender* (Philadelphia: University of Pennsylvania Press, 1990). These counterexamples are intriguing as they push us away from thinking of women solely as victims and ask us to reconsider the different forms power relations may take; nonetheless, they remain exceptions, which forces us, without falling into essentialism, to think about the ways women's inequality is perpetuated in various cultural, class, ethnic, and national settings.

3. For an intriguing discussion on recent Western discourse casting Third World women as victim, see Chandra Talpade Mohanty, "Under Western Eyes," and Rey Chow, "Violence in the Other Country," both in *Third World Women and the Politics of Feminism*, ed. Chandra Mohanty, Ann Russo, and Lourdes Torres (Bloomington: Indiana University Press, 1991), 51–80, 81–100.

4. This view of power is derived principally from the works of Antonio Gramsci and Michel Foucault. See, e.g., Antonio Gramsci, *Selections from the Prison Notebooks*, ed. Quinton Hoare and Geoffrey Nowell Smith (New York: International Publishers, 1971); and Michel Foucault, *Power/Knowledge* (New York: Pantheon, 1980), *The History of Sexuality* (New York: Vintage, 1980), *Discipline and Punish* (New York: Pantheon, 1977), and *Madness and Civilization* (New York: Vintage, 1973).

5. For a recent example from Cairo, see Diane Singerman, "Avenues of Participation: Family and Politics in Popular Quarters of Cairo" (paper presented at the Middle East Studies Association meeting, Baltimore, 1986).

6. For example, see Susan Carol Rogers, "Female Forms of Power and the Myth of Male Dominance," *American Ethnologist* 2, no. 4 (November 1975): 727–56; or Lawrence Rosen, *Bargaining for Reality* (Chicago: University of Chicago Press, 1984).

7. For an insightful discussion of the difficulties of cross-cultural feminist discourse, see Marnia Lazreg, "Feminism and Difference: The Perils of Writing as a Woman on Women in Algeria," in *Conflicts in Feminism*, ed. Marianne Hirsch and Evelyn Fox Keller (New York: Routledge, 1990), 326–48.

8. The field research on which this article is based was conducted in Cairo, Egypt, from September 1983 to December 1984 and in follow-up visits in February 1986 and June–July 1988. For a full account of this research, see Arlene Elowe MacLeod, *Accommodating Protest: Working Women, the New Veiling, and Change in Cairo* (New York: Columbia University Press, 1991).

9. For general background on modern Egypt, see, e.g., John Waterbury, *The Egypt of Nasser and Sadat* (Princeton, N.J.: Princeton University Press, 1983); or Raymond Hinnesbusch, *Egyptian Politics Under Sadat* (New York: Cambridge University Press, 1985).

10. Actually, women's work outside the home has varied considerably, and families of this level might have had women workers in earlier generations, although not recently. On the realities of women's work in historical context, see Judith Tucker, *Women in Nineteenth Century Egypt* (New York: Cambridge University Press, 1985).

11. Two examples, in the interest of exploration, can be mentioned here. The use of the arts to embody new ideas of women's role and identity can be a form of resistance, located in uniquely "feminine" places. For instance, see Judith Lynne Hanna, "Dance, Protest, and Women's 'Wars': Cases from Nigeria and the United States," in *Women and Social Protest*, ed. Guida West and Rhoda Lois Blumberg (New York: Oxford University Press, 1990), 333–45. Yet, as with the new veils, arts such as embroidery or dance may also contribute to traditional stereotypes. Another example is women's important presence in religious movements; the African-American church and gospel singing, fundamentalist Christianity, or resurgent Islam all offer a place for women to express their ideas within a traditional and therefore safe space; yet this can serve to reinforce rather than alter women's inequality.

12. See Foucault, esp. *Power/Knowledge*, 95–102.

13. See the discussion of the discourse of difference and its "erasure of 'other' women" in Lazreg, who asks, "To what extent can Western feminism dispense

with an ethics of responsibility when writing about 'different' women?" (340); Lazreg argues that we need to work toward the goal of promoting "intersubjectivity" in cross-cultural feminisms, emphasizing the subjectivity of both researcher and researched, a complicated task, but one to strive toward rather than reconciling ourselves to "difference," which may be only a mask for "indifference."

14. For discussion of the methodological issues involved in letting Third World women "speak" in feminist texts, see Gayatri Spivak, "Can the Subaltern Speak?" in *Marxism and the Interpretation of Culture*, ed. Cary Nelson and Lawrence Grossberg (Urbana: University of Illinois Press, 1988), 271–313; also see Elsbeth Probyn, "Travels in the Postmodern: Making Sense of the Local," in *Feminism/Postmodernism*, ed. Linda Nicholson (New York: Routledge, 1990), 176–89; and Rosalind O'Hanlon, "Recovering the Subject: Subaltern Studies and Histories of Resistance in Colonial South Asia," *Modern Asian Studies* 22, no. 1 (February 1988): 189–224.

15. A wide literature exists on veiling, both within and outside the Middle Eastern context; see, e.g., Richard Antoun, "On the Modesty of Women in Arab Muslim Villages," *American Anthropologist* 70, no. 4 (August 1968): 671–98; Carroll McC. Pastner, "A Social, Structural and Historical Analysis of Honor, Shame and Purdah," *Anthropological Quarterly* 45, no. 4 (October 1972): 248–62; Hannah Papanek, "Purdah: Separate Worlds and Symbolic Shelter," *Comparative Studies in Society and History* 15 (1973): 289–325; and Jane Schneider, "Of Vigilance and Virgins: Honor, Shame and Access to Resources in Mediterranean Societies," *Ethnology* 10, no. 1 (January 1971): 1–24.

16. Nesta Ramazani, "The Veil—Piety or Protest?" *Journal of South Asian and Middle Eastern Studies* 7, no. 2 (Winter 1983): 20–36.

17. For instance, see Robert Murphy, "Social Distance and the Veil," in *Peoples and Cultures of the Middle East*, ed. Louise Sweet (New York: Natural History Press, 1970), 290–315; and Carla Makhlouf, *Changing Veils: Women and Modernization in North Yemen* (Austin: University of Texas Press, 1979). Also, for an account of modesty codes centered on another group in the Egyptian setting, see Lila Abu-Lughod, *Veiled Sentiments* (Berkeley and Los Angeles: University of California Press, 1986).

18. See Lois Beck and Nikki Keddie, *Women in the Muslim World* (Cambridge, Mass.: Harvard University Press, 1978), esp. 8–9.

19. See, e.g., Adele K. Ferdows, "Women and the Islamic Revolution," *International Journal of Middle East Studies* 15, no. 2 (May 1983): 283–98; or Nahid Yeganeh and Nikki R. Keddie, "Sexuality and Shi'i Social Protest in Iran," in *Shi'ism and Social Protest*, ed. Juan Cole and Nikki Keddie (New Haven, Conn.: Yale University Press, 1986), 108–36.

20. See Unni Wikan, *Behind the Veil in Arabia* (Baltimore: Johns Hopkins University Press, 1982); or Hannah Papanek's discussion of "mobile curtains" in "Purdah: Separate Worlds and Symbolic Shelter," *Comparative Studies in Society and History* 15 (1973): 289–325.

21. See Huda Shaarawi, *Harem Years: Memoirs of an Egyptian Feminist*, trans. Margot Badran (New York: Feminist Press, 1987).

22. For a detailed description of the variations on these outfits, see Andrea Rugh, *Reveal and Conceal: Dress in Contemporary Egypt* (New York: Syracuse University Press, 1986).

23. See Fadwa El Guindi, "Veiling Infitah with Muslim Ethic: Egypt's Contemporary Islamic Movement," *Social Problems* 28, no. 4 (April 1981): 465–87, and "Veiled Activism: Egyptian Women in the Contemporary Islamic Movement," *Femmes de la Mediterranee, Peuples Mediteraneens* 22, 23 (1983): 79–89; John Alden Williams, "A Return to the Veil in Egypt," *Middle East Review* 11, no. 3 (Spring 1979): 49–54. In addition, the film by Elizabeth Fernea and Marilyn Gaunt, *A Veiled Revolution* (1982), offers an interesting view of voluntary veiling in this period.

24. Two interesting accounts of the lives of lower-class women, from whom lower-middle-class women seek to differentiate themselves, are Unni Wikan, *Life Among the Poor in Cairo* (London: Tavistock, 1980); and Nayra Atiya, *Khul-Khaal: Five Egyptian Women Tell Their Stories* (New York: Syracuse University Press, 1982).

25. See the articles by El Guindi.

26. Numbers on women's status in the Middle East are notoriously difficult to acquire; I estimate that, in 1984, about one-third of the working women from Cairo's lower middle class actually veiled, and another third stated that they intended to veil at some undefined time in the future. These numbers increased to about two-thirds of the women by the summer of 1988.

27. Gramsci uses the term "hegemony" to convey several different approaches to this web of problems; see Gramsci (n. 4 above), as well as Nicholas Abercrombie, Stephan Hill, and Bryan Turner, eds., *The Dominant Ideology Thesis* (London: Allen & Unwin, 1980); Joseph Femia, "Hegemony and Consciousness in the Thought of Antonio Gramsci," *Political Studies* 23, no. 1 (March 1975): 29–48; Ernesto LaClau and Chantal Mouffe, *Hegemony and Socialist Strategy* (Thetford, Norfolk: Thetford Press, 1985); and Anne Showstack Sassoon, ed., *Approaches to Gramsci* (London: Writers and Readers, 1982).

28. For example, looking at peasants in Malaysia, Scott argues that consent is actually not present among the lower class in the village to any appreciable degree; a range of resistance can be discovered in which peasants act against the upper class to present their own view of justice. Peasants' "little tradition" offers an alternative interpretation of the great tradition, and its existence argues that a surface situation of obedience can be achieved despite ongoing submerged conflict. See James C. Scott, "Protest and Profanation: Agrarian Revolt and the Little Tradition," *Theory and Society* 4, nos. 1, 2 (January, March 1977): 1–38, 211–46, *Weapons of the Weak* (New Haven, Conn.: Yale University Press, 1985), and *Domination and the Arts of Resistance* (New Haven, Conn.: Yale University Press, 1990). In an influential study of working-class boys, Willis argues that they do not believe in promises of social mobility and therefore they do not strive to better their situation. Instead they participate in the working-class counterculture of opposition to school values, ultimately guaranteeing that they will end up in working-class jobs. The existing class inequalities endure not through the boy's active belief in the system, but through a very different kind of "consent" which partially penetrates the situation to see the impossibility of success. See Paul Willis, *Learning to Labour* (Westmead: Saxon House, 1977).

29. In fact, few will have this opportunity due to economic realities, and more women than ever are attempting to enter the work force. Yet the government bureaucracy cannot absorb more employees, and women are being squeezed out by policies promoting women's leaves and emphasizing women's family roles.

30. For discussion of women's nature in other Middle Eastern settings, see Fatna Ait Sabbah, *Women in the Muslim Unconscious* (New York: Pergamon, 1984); in Cairo, see Sawsan al-Messiri, *Ibn al-Balad: A Concept of Egyptian Identity* (Leiden: Brill, 1978).

31. Of course, stating that one is working for one's own satisfaction would violate the norms of family life, which put the group above the individual. Nonetheless, the importance of family makes the goals of these women different than those of many Western feminists, who often stress self-actualization and autonomy as appropriate goals.

32. The question of whether women may work outside the home is a matter of great controversy among these women. In general, there is confusion (which can be very useful for women) about what Islamic texts actually state, and reliance on custom is common. In times of changing norms and behavior, interpreting the tradition, and the question of who is allowed to interpret, become crucial.

33. For example, Richard Cloward and Frances Fox Piven discuss suicide and other forms of deviance in "Hidden Protest: The Channeling of Female Innovation and Resistance," *Signs: Journal of Women in Culture and Society* 4, no. 4 (Summer 1979): 651–69; conversational strategies are considered by Rosen (n. 6 above); disbelief as resistance is discussed by Elizabeth Janeway in *Powers of the Weak* (New York: Knopf, 1980); Vaclav Havel in *The Power of the Powerless* (Armonk, N.Y.: Sharpe, 1985) discusses "living authentically" as resistance; walking in city streets as everyday protest is discussed by Michel de Certeau in *The Practice of Everyday Life* (Berkeley and Los Angeles: University of California Press, 1984); and various forms of "everyday resistance" are portrayed by Scott in *Domination and the Arts of Resistance*.

34. Lila Abu-Lughod argues against the "romance of resistance," tracing power relations in a Bedouin community; she says that young people seem oblivious to ways their resistance to elders within the community backs them into more complex subordination to world economic and political powers. See Lila Abu-Lughod, "The Romance of Resistance: Tracing the Transformations of Power through Bedouin Women," *American Ethnologist* 17, no. 1 (February 1990): 41–56.

35. See Scott, *Domination and the Arts of Resistance*.

36. Gramsci, *Selections from the Prison Notebooks* (n. 4 above), esp. 326–27, 333.

37. See Diane Margolis, "Considering Women's Experience: A Reformulation of Power Theory," *Theory and Society* 18, no. 3 (May 1989): 387–416. Margolis argues that the cooperative aspects of power have been ignored and that bringing in women's experiences will widen our understanding of power from purely oppositional forms to include other categories.

38. For a discussion of how Westernization and a history of colonialism act within national movements to complicate feminist discourses in the Middle East, see Evelyne-Accad, *Sexuality and War: Literary Masks in the Middle East* (New York: New York University Press, 1990), esp. the introduction; also see Julie Peteet, *Gender in Crisis: Women and the Palestinian Resistance Movement* (New York: Columbia University Press, 1991).

39. There are strong feminist groups in Egypt, but often their goals seem distant to women of this class, and indeed their knowledge of such women's organizations is generally slight. On Egyptian feminism, see Akram Khater and Cynthia

Nelson, "Al-Harakah al-Nissa'iyah: The Women's Movement and Political Partic-ipation in Modern Egypt," *Women's Studies International Forum* 11, no. 5 (1988): 465–83; Margot Badran, "Dual Liberation: Feminism and Nationalism in Egypt," *Feminist Issues* 8, no. 1 (Spring 1988): 15–34; and Beth Baron, "Unveiling in Early Twentieth Century Egypt," *Middle Eastern Studies* 25, no. 3 (July 1989): 370–86.

40. See Abu-Lughod, "The Romance of Resistance," for a fascinating example of this tendency in the Egyptian context.

41. For an interesting discussion of the difficulties involved, see Chantal Mouffe, "Hegemony and Ideology in Gramsci," in *Gramsci and Marxist Theory*, ed. Chantal Mouffe (Boston: Routledge & Kegan Paul, 1979), esp. 185–98. Also see LaClau and Mouffe (n. 27 above), esp. chap. 3 on antagonisms and hegemonic politics.

PART FOUR
Questioning Feminisms

These essays offer new conceptual resources for theorizing women, gender, and feminism in an era characterized by postmodern and poststructuralist critiques of modernism, by a conservative backlash against many aspects of feminism, and by the claim that the feminist revolution has already succeeded and we are now "postfeminist."

The first pair of essays explores how women's relationship to the political arena differs from men's; at the same time, both illustrate the ultimate breakdown of a distinction between "public" and "private" as the best way to conceptualize that different relationship. Political scientist Rosalind Pollack Petchesky (Chapter 19) shows how motherhood is degendered as the private is made public in political debates over women's reproductive rights (with women granted no special standing in that debate, though they have a special "interest" in it). Political philosopher Holloway Sparks (Chapter 20) recommends gendering citizenship as she shows how women can make some public spaces political through "dissident citizenship," defined as "often creative oppositional practices of citizens who . . . contest current arrangements of power from the margins of the polity." Both essays stress the capacity of women for active political agency despite their collective subordination to men and at the same time point toward differences among women in the situations examined (abortion and reproductive rights and dissent). Both theorize not only the structural context of women's political activity but also important features of women's internal experience as political actors (for Petchesky, the particular relationships pregnant women have to the fetus; for Sparks, the nature of courage). Finally, both incorporate reference to the power of "stories" to personalize, inspire, and inform political debate and political action. (Petchesky alludes to the introduction of women's stories of their abortions in a Supreme Court brief; Sparks notes the power of stories of others' political courage to inspire and retells for her purposes the Rosa Parks story.)

Petchesky's essay demonstrates the extent to which current notions of citizenship are gendered by bringing into focus public representations of women's bodies and women's roles as mothers. She foregrounds the role of an incomplete and objectifying visual representation in the struggle over women's reproductive rights. She shows how women (mothers) have been excluded from the visual representation of fetuses by antiabortion activists. That representation in turn depends on a set of medical-technological advances and practices that often similarly exclude women and mothers as decisionmakers and participants. In a complex and subtle argument, Petchesky asserts that feminists should seek inclusion in the technological-medical domain—as in the political—rather than turn away from reproductive technology. She recommends feminist representations of women's position in abortion (and fetal development) and advocates women's participation in the development and implementation of new technologies to increase the likelihood that such advances will improve rather than ruin women's lives.

Sparks, on the other hand, addresses classic and contemporary formulations of democratic theory and the current conversation about "citizenship" that includes feminist scholars. She seeks to broaden the focus of democratic theory to include both acts of dissident citizenship aimed at those in power and the practice of dissent among equals who are all marginal (to encompass relations among allies). She uses the case of Rosa Parks to show how the concept of dissident citizenship would enrich our understanding of Parks's action (and incorporate more features of it). Equally, she shows how "courage" can be defined in a way that illuminates similarities (rather than differences) between male and female citizens.

The final two essays offer direct visions of the plural, shifting, "juggled," and ambivalent feminism(s) necessary in a postfeminist period. Both literary critic Judith Halberstam (Chapter 21) and political scientist Christine Sylvester (Chapter 22) respond directly to postmodern challenges to feminism and ask feminist scholars to imagine ways to overcome or transcend past theoretical divisions. Halberstam sees potential for theorizing gender via new understandings of machines and technology; she argues that we can move beyond the (formerly helpful) image of a "female machine" that blurred even as it reinforced associations of female with nature and of male with culture. Sylvester sees potential for "world-traveling" (as distinct from "tourism") as a method for overcoming separate feminist theoretical approaches, exemplified in different approaches to thinking about women in the development context as well as in First and Third World feminisms.

Halberstam rereads the symbol of the apple not only as having new meanings in the computer era but also as literally disconnecting from its past gendered symbolic association with Eve and the Fall. She cites both the persecution of British mathematician Alan Turing for gender deviance and his "sexual guessing game" to undermine and problematize the logical differentiation of bodies and machines in his work on the idea of a "universal" intelligent machine. Sylvester perceives a converging evolution among Western feminists, feminist scholars who are African, and Western-born Africanists toward a "form of world-traveling [that] relies on empathy to enter into the spirit of difference and find in it an echo of oneself as other than the way one seems to be. It moves us, in other words, to places of subjectivity that shift and hyphenate into the worlds of others." She sees this trend as destabilizing both one's own subjectivities and those of others, hence as critical not only to theory but also to empirical research that overcomes "fictionally fixed place" for all concerned.

In all four chapters in this section, we see contemporary feminist theorists struggling with the need to reconcile (past and future) progress within feminist theorizing with a "postfeminist" ("I'm not a feminist, but . . . ") social context. All of them draw on narratives or stories as they escape disciplinary boundaries in their use of evidence, arguments, sources, and rhetorical strategies. Feminist theorists have continued to struggle with certain analytic tools and disciplinary constraints, but they no longer do so exclusively, or even mostly, in dialogues contained within disciplines. In these essays, the conflicts feminist theorists have are largely among themselves but are debated on intellectual terrain they have cleared for one another.

19 Fetal Images

The Power of Visual Culture in the Politics of Reproduction

ROSALIND POLLACK PETCHESKY

Now chimes the glass, a note of sweetest strength,
It clouds, it clears, my utmost hope it proves,
For there my longing eyes behold at length
A dapper form, that lives and breathes and moves.

—Goethe, *Faust*

(Ultimately) the world of "being" can function to the exclusion of
the mother. No need for mother—provided that there is something
of the maternal: and it is the father then who acts as—is—the
mother. Either the woman is passive; or she doesn't exist. What is
left is unthinkable, unthought of. She does not enter into the
oppositions, she is not coupled with the father (who is coupled with
the son).

—Hélène Cixous, *Sorties*

In the mid-1980s, with the United States Congress still dead-locked over the abortion issue and the Supreme Court having twice reaffirmed "a woman's right to choose,"[1] the political attack on abortion rights moved further into the terrain of mass culture and imagery. Not that the "prolife movement" has abandoned conventional political arenas; rather, its defeats there have hardened its commitment to a more long-term ideological struggle over the symbolic meanings of fetuses, dead or alive.

Antiabortionists in both the United States and Britain have long applied the principle that a picture of a dead fetus is worth a thousand words. Chaste silhouettes of the fetal form, or voyeuristic-necrophilic photographs of its remains, litter the background of any abortion talk. These still images float like spirits through the courtrooms, where lawyers argue that fetuses can claim tort liability; through the hospitals and clinics, where physicians welcome them as "patients"; and in front of all the abortion centers, legislative committees, bus terminals, and other places that "right-to-lifers" haunt. The strategy of antiabortionists to make fetal personhood a self-fulfilling prophecy by making the fetus a *public presence* addresses a visually oriented culture. Meanwhile, finding "positive" images and symbols of abortion hard to imagine, feminists and other prochoice advocates have all too readily ceded the visual terrain.

Beginning with the 1984 presidential campaign, the neoconservative Reagan administration and the Christian Right accelerated their use of television and video imagery to capture political discourse—and power.[2] Along with a new series of "Ron and Nancy" commercials, the Reverend Pat Robertson's "700 Club" (a kind of right-wing talk show), and a resurgence of Good versus Evil kiddie cartoons, American television and video viewers were bombarded with the newest "prolife" propaganda piece, *The Silent Scream. The Silent Scream* marked a dramatic shift in the contest over abortion imagery. With formidable cunning, it translated the still and by-now stale images of fetus as "baby" into real-time video, thus (1) giving those images an immediate interface with the electronic media; (2) transforming antiabortion rhetoric from a mainly religious/mystical to a medical technological mode; and (3) bringing the fetal image "to life." On major network television the fetus rose to instant stardom, as *The Silent Scream* and its impresario, Dr. Bernard Nathanson, were aired at least five different times in one month, and one well-known reporter, holding up a fetus in a jar before 10 million viewers, announced: "This thing being aborted, this potential person, sure *looks like* a baby!"

This statement is more than just propaganda; it encapsulates the "politics of style" dominating late capitalist culture, transforming "surface impressions" into the "whole message."[3] The cult of appearances not only is the defining characteristic of national politics in the United States, but it is also nourished by the language and techniques of photo/video imagery. Aware of cultural trends, the current leadership of the antiabortion movement has made a conscious strategic shift from religious discourses and authorities to medicotechnical ones, in its effort to win over the courts, the legislatures, and popular hearts and minds. But the vehicle for this shift is not organized medicine directly but mass culture and its diffusion into reproductive technology through the video display terminal.

My interest in this essay is to explore the overlapping boundaries between media spectacle and clinical experience when pregnancy becomes a moving picture. In what follows, I attempt to understand the cultural meanings and impact of images like those in *The Silent Scream.* Then I examine the effect of routine ultrasound imaging of the fetus not only on the larger cultural climate of reproductive politics but also on the experience and consciousness of pregnant women. Finally, I shall consider some implications of "fetal images" for feminist theory and practice.

Decoding *The Silent Scream*

Before dissecting its ideological message, I should perhaps describe *The Silent Scream* for readers who somehow missed it. The film's actual genesis seems to have been an article in the *New England Journal of Medicine* by a noted bioethicist and a physician, claiming that early fetal ultrasound tests resulted in "maternal bonding" and possibly "fewer abortions." According to the authors, both affiliated with the National Institutes of Health, upon viewing an ultrasound image of the fetus, "parents [that is, pregnant women] probably will experience a shock of recognition that the fetus belongs to them" and will more likely resolve "ambivalent" pregnancies "in favor of the fetus." Such "parental recognition of the fetal form," they wrote, "is a fundamental element in the later parent-child bond."[4] Although based on two isolated cases, without controls or scientific experimentation, these assertions stimulated the imagination of Dr. Bernard Nathanson and the National Right-to-Life Committee. The resulting video production was intended to reinforce the visual "bonding" theory at the level of the clinic by bringing the live fetal image into everyone's living room. Distributed not only to television networks but also to schools, churches, state and federal legislators, and anyone (including the opposition) who wants to rent it for fifteen dollars, the video cassette provides a mass commodity form for the "prolife" message.

The Silent Scream purports to show a medical event, a real-time ultrasound imaging of a twelve-week-old fetus being aborted. What we see in fact is an image of an image of an image; or, rather, we see three concentric frames: our television or VCR screen, which in turn frames the video screen of the filming studio, which in turn frames a shadowy, black-and-white, pulsating blob: the (alleged) fetus. Throughout, our response to this set of images is directed by the figure of Dr. Nathanson—sober, bespectacled, leaning professorially against the desk—who functions as both medical expert and narrator to the drama. (Nathanson is in "real life" a practicing obstetrician-gynecologist, ex-abortionist, and well-known antiabortion crusader.) In fact, as the film unfolds, we quickly realize that there are *two* texts being presented here simultaneously—a medical text, largely visual, and a moral text, largely verbal and auditory. Our medical narrator appears on the screen and announces that what we are about to see comes to us courtesy of the "dazzling" new "science of fetology" which "exploded in the medical community" and now enables us to witness an abortion—"from the victim's vantage point." At the same time we hear strains of organ music in the background, ominous, the kind we associate with impending doom. As Nathanson guides his pointer along the video screen, "explaining" the otherwise inscrutable movements of the image, the disjunction between the two texts becomes increasingly jarring. We *see* a recognizable apparatus of advanced medical technology, displaying a filmic image of vibrating light and shaded areas, interspersed with occasional scenes of an abortion clinic operating table (the only view of the pregnant woman we get). This action is moderated by someone who "looks like" the paternal-medical authority figure of the proverbial aspirin commercial. He occasionally interrupts the filmed events to show us clinical models of embryos and fetuses at various stages of development. Meanwhile, however, what we *hear* is more like a medieval morality play, spoken in standard antiabortion rhetoric. The form on the screen, we are told, is "the living unborn child," "another human being indistinguishable from any of us." The suction cannula is "moving violently" toward "the child"; it is the "lethal weapon" that will "dismember, crush, destroy," "tear the child apart," until only "shards" are left. The fetus "does sense aggression in its sanctuary," attempts to "escape" (indicating more rapid movements on the screen), and finally "rears back its head" in "a silent scream"—all to a feverish pitch of musical accompaniment. In case we question the nearly total absence of a pregnant woman or of clinic personnel in this scenario, Nathanson also "informs" us that the woman who had this abortion was a "feminist," who, like the young doctor who performed it, has vowed "never again"; that women who get abortions are themselves exploited "victims" and "castrated"; that many abortion clinics are "run by the mobs." It is the verbal rhetoric, not of science, but of "Miami Vice."

Now, all of this raises important questions about what one means by "evidence," or "medical information," because the ultrasound image is presented as a *document* testifying that the fetus is "alive," is "human like you or me," and "senses pain." *The Silent Scream* has been sharply confronted on this level by panels of opposing medical experts, *New York Times* editorials, and a Planned Parenthood film. These show, for example, that at twelve weeks the fetus has no cerebral cortex to receive pain impulses; that no "scream" is possible without air in the lungs; that fetal movements at this stage are reflexive and without purpose; that the image of rapid frantic movement was undoubtedly caused by speeding up the film (camera tricks); that the size of the image we see on the screen, along with the model that is continually displayed in front of the screen, is nearly twice the size of a normal twelve-week fetus, and so forth.[5] Yet this literal kind of rebuttal is not very useful in helping us to understand the ideological power the film has despite its visual distortions and verbal fraud.

When we locate *The Silent Scream* where it belongs, in the realm of cultural representation rather than of medical evidence, we see that it embeds ultrasound imaging of pregnancy in a moving picture show. Its appearance as a medical document both obscures and reinforces a coded set of messages that work as political signs and moral injunctions. (As we shall see, because of the cultural and political context in which they occur, this may be true of ultrasound images of pregnancy in general.) The purpose of the film is obviously didactic: to induce individual women to abstain from having abortions and to persuade officials and judges to force them to do so. Like the Great Communicator who charms through lies, the medical authority figure—paternalistic and technocratic at the same time—delivers these messages less by his words than by the power of his image and his persona.

As with any visual image, *The Silent Scream* relies on our predisposition to "see" what it wants us to "see" because of a range of influences that come out of the particular culture and history in which we live. The aura of medical authority, the allure of technology, the cumulative impact of a decade of fetal images—on billboards, in shopping center malls, in science fiction blockbusters like *2001: A Space Odyssey*—all rescue the film from utter absurdity; they make it credible. "The fetal form" itself has, within the larger culture, acquired a symbolic import that condenses within it a series of losses—from sexual innocence to compliant women to American imperial might. It is not the image of a baby at all but of a tiny man, a homunculus.

The most disturbing thing about how people receive *The Silent Scream*, and indeed all the dominant fetal imagery, is their apparent acceptance of the image itself as an accurate representation of a real fetus. The curled-up profile, with its enlarged head and finlike arms, suspended in its balloon of amniotic fluid, is by now so familiar that not even most feminists question its authenticity (as opposed to its relevance). I went back to trace the earliest appearance of these photos in popular literature and found it in the June 1962 issue of *Look* (along with *Life*, the major mass-circulating "picture magazine" of the period). It was a story publicizing a new book, *The First Nine Months of Life*, and it featured the now-standard sequel of pictures at one day, one week, seven weeks, and so forth.[6] In every picture the fetus is solitary, dangling in the air (or its sac) with nothing to connect it to any life-support system but "a clearly defined umbilical cord." In every caption it is called "the baby" (even at forty-four days) and is referred to as "he"—until the birth, that is, when "he" turns out to be a girl. Nowhere is there any reference to the pregnant woman, except in a single photograph at the end showing the newborn baby lying next to the mother, both of them gazing off the page, allegedly at "the father." From their beginning, such photographs have represented the fetus as primary and autonomous, the woman as absent or peripheral.

Fetal imagery epitomizes the distortion inherent in all photographic images: their tendency to slice up reality into tiny bits wrenched out of real space and time. The origins of photography can be traced to late-nineteenth-century Europe's cult of science, itself a by-product of industrial capitalism. Its rise is inextricably linked with positivism, that flawed epistemology that sees "reality" as discrete bits of empirical data divorced from historical process or social relationships.[7] Similarly, fetal imagery replicates the essential paradox of photographs whether moving or still, their "constitutive deception" as noted by postmodernist critics: the *appearance* of objectivity, of capturing "literal reality." As Roland Barthes puts it, the "photographic message" appears to be "a message without a code." According to Barthes, the appearance of the photographic image as "a mechanical analogue of reality," without art or artifice, obscures the fact that that image is heavily constructed, or "coded"; it is grounded in a context of historical and cultural meanings.[8]

Yet the power of the visual apparatus's claim to be "an unreasoning machine" that produces "an unerring record" (the French word for "lens" is *l'objectif*) remains deeply embedded in Western culture.[9] This power derives from the peculiar capacity of photographic images to assume two distinct meanings, often simultaneously: an empirical (informational) and a mythical (or magical) meaning. Historically, photographic imagery has served not only the uses of scientific rationality—as in medical diagnostics and record keeping—and the tools of bureaucratic rationality—in the political record keeping and police surveillance of the state.[10] Photographic imagery has also, especially with the "democratization" of the hand-held camera and the advent of the family album, become a magical source of fetishes that can resurrect the dead or preserve lost love. And it has constructed the escape fantasy of the movies. This older, symbolic, and ritualistic (also religious?) function lies concealed within the more obvious rationalistic one.

The double text of *The Silent Scream*, noted earlier, recapitulates this historical paradox of photographic images: their simultaneous power as purveyors of fantasy and illusion yet also of "objectivist 'truth.'"[11] When Nathanson claims to be presenting an abortion from the "vantage point of the [fetus]," the image's appearance of seamless movement through real time—*and* the technologic allure of the video box, connoting at once "advanced medicine" and "the news"—render his claim "true to life." Yet he also purveys a myth, for the fetus—if it had any vantage point—could not possibly experience itself as if dangling in space, without a woman's uterus and body and bloodstream to support it.

In fact, every image of a fetus we are shown, including *The Silent Scream*, is viewed from the standpoint neither of the fetus nor of the pregnant woman but of the camera. The fetus as we know it is a fetish. Barbara Katz Rothman observes that "the fetus in utero has become a metaphor for 'man' in space, floating free, attached only by the umbilical cord to the spaceship. But where is the mother in that metaphor? She has become empty space."[12] Inside the futurizing spacesuit, however, lies a much older image. For the autonomous, free-floating fetus merely extends to gestation the Hobbesian view of born human beings as disconnected, solitary individuals. It is this abstract individualism, effacing the pregnant woman and the fetus's dependence on her, that gives the fetal image its symbolic transparency, so that we can read in it our selves, our lost babies, our mythic secure past.

Although such receptions of fetal images may help to recruit antiabortion activists, among both women and men, denial of the womb has more deadly consequences. Zoe Sofia relates the film *2001: A Space Odyssey* to "the New Right's cult of fetal personhood," arguing that "every technology is a reproductive technology": "in science fiction culture particularly, technologies are perceived as modes of reproduction in themselves, according to perverse myths of fertility in which man replicates himself without the aid of woman." The "Star Child" of *2001* is not a living organic being but "a biomechanism, . . . a cyborg capable of living unaided in space." This "child" poses as the symbol of fertility and life but in fact is the creature of the same technologies that bring cosmic extermination, which it alone survives. Sofia sees the same irony in "the right-wing movement to protect fetal life" while it plans for nuclear war. Like the fetal-baby in *2001*, "the pro-life fetus may be a 'special effect' of a cultural dreamwork which displaces attention from the tools of extermination and onto the fetal signifier of extinction itself." To the extent that it diverts us from the real threat of nuclear holocaust and comes to represent the lone survivor, the fetal image signifies not life but death.[13]

If the fetus-as-spaceman has become inscribed in science fiction and popular fantasy, it is likely to affect the appearance of fetal images even in clinical contexts. The vantage point of the male onlooker may perhaps change how women see their own fetuses on, and through, ultrasound imaging screens. *The Silent Scream* bridges these two arenas of cultural construction, video fantasyland and clinical biotechnics, enlisting medical imagery in the service of mythic-patriarchal messages. But neither arena, nor the film itself, meets a totally receptive field. Pregnant women respond to these images out of a variety of concrete situations and in a variety of complex ways.

Obstetrical Imaging and Masculine/Visual Culture

We have seen the dominant view of the fetus that appears in still and moving pictures across the mass-cultural landscape. It is one where the fetus is not only "already a baby," but more—a "baby man," an autonomous, atomized mini-space hero. This image has not supplanted the one of the fetus as a tiny, helpless, suffering creature but rather merged with it (in a way that uncomfortably reminds one of another famous immortal baby). We should not be surprised, then, to find the social relations of obstetrics—the site where ultrasound imaging of fetuses goes on daily—infiltrated by such widely diffused images.

Along with the external political and cultural pressures, traditional patterns endemic to the male-dominated practice of obstetrics help determine the current clinical view of the fetus as "patient," separate and autonomous from the pregnant woman. These patterns direct the practical applications of new reproductive technologies more toward enlarging clinicians' control over reproductive processes than toward improving health (women's or infants'). Despite their benefits for individual women, amniocentesis, in vitro fertilization, electronic fetal monitoring, routine cesarean deliveries, ultrasound, and a range of heroic "fetal therapies" (both in utero and ex utero) also have the effect of carving out more and more space/time for obstetrical "management" of pregnancy. Meanwhile, they have not been shown to lower infant and perinatal mortality/morbidity, and they divert social resources from epidemiological research into the causes of fetal damage.[14] But the presumption of fetal "autonomy" ("patienthood" if not "personhood") is not an inevitable requirement of the technologies. Rather, the technologies take on the meanings and uses they do because of the cultural climate of fetal images and the politics of hostility toward pregnant women and abortion. As a result, the pregnant woman is increasingly put in the position of adversary to her own pregnancy/fetus, either by having presented a "hostile environment" to its development or by actively refusing some medically proposed intervention (such as a cesarean section or treatment for a fetal "defect").[15]

Similarly, the claim by antiabortion polemicists that the fetus is becoming "viable" at an earlier and earlier point seems to reinforce the notion that its treatment is a matter between a fetus and its doctor. In reality, most authorities agree that twenty-four weeks is the youngest a fetus is likely to survive outside the womb in the foreseeable future; meanwhile, over 90 percent of pregnant women who get abortions do so in the first trimester, fewer than 1 percent do so past the twentieth week.[16] Despite these facts, the *images* of younger and younger, and tinier and tinier, fetuses being "saved," the point of viability being "pushed back" *indefinitely*, and untold aborted fetuses being "born alive" have captured recent abortion discourse in the courts, the headlines, and television drama.[17] Such images blur the boundary between fetus and baby; they reinforce the idea that the fetus's identity as separate and autonomous from the mother (the "living, separate child") exists from the start. Obstetrical technologies of visualization and electronic/surgical intervention thus disrupt the very definition, as traditionally understood, of "inside" and "outside" a woman's body, of pregnancy as an "interior" experience. As Donna Haraway remarks, pregnancy becomes integrated into a "high-tech view of the body as a biotic component or cybernetic communications system"; thus, "who controls the interpretation of bodily boundaries in medical hermeneutics [becomes] a major feminist issue."[18] Interpreting boundaries, however, is a way to contest them, not to record their fixity in the natural world. Like penetrating Cuban territory with reconnaissance satellites and Radio Marti, treating a fetus as if it were outside a woman's body, because it can be viewed, is a political act.

This background is necessary to an analysis that locates ultrasound imaging of fetuses within its historical and cultural context. Originating in sonar detectors for submarine warfare, ultrasound was not introduced into obstetrical practice until the early 1960s—some years after its accepted use in other medical diagnostic fields.[19] The timing is significant, for it corresponds to the end of the baby boom and the rapid drop in fertility that would propel obstetrician-gynecologists into new areas of discovery and fortune, a new "patient population" to look at and treat. "Looking" was mainly the point, because, as in many medical technologies (and technologies of visualization), physicians seem to have applied the technique before knowing precisely what they were looking for. In this technique, a transducer sends sound waves through the amniotic fluid so they bounce off fetal structures and are reflected back, either as a still image (scan) or, more frequently, a real-time moving image "similar to that of a motion picture," as the American College of Obstetricians and Gynecologists (ACOG) puts it.[20]

Although it was enthusiastically hailed among physicians for its advantages over the dangers of X-ray, ultrasound imaging in pregnancy is currently steeped in controversy. A 1984 report by a joint National Institute of Health/Food and Drug Administration panel found "no clear benefit from routine use," specifically, "no improvement in pregnancy outcome" (either for the fetus/infant or the woman), and no conclusive evidence either of its safety or harm. The panel recommended against "routine use," including "to view . . . or obtain a picture of the fetus" or "for educational or commercial demonstrations without medical benefit to the patient" ("the patient" here, presumably, being the pregnant woman). Yet it approved of its use to "estimate gestational age," thus qualifying its reservations with a major loophole. At least one-third of all pregnant women in the United States are now exposed to ultrasound imaging, and that would seem to be a growing figure. Anecdotal evidence suggests that many if not most pregnancies will soon include ultrasound scans and presentation of a sonogram photo "for the baby album."[21]

How can we understand the routinization of fetal imaging in obstetrics even though the profession's governing bodies admit the medical benefits are dubious? The reason ultrasound imaging in obstetrics has expanded so much is no doubt related to the reasons, economic and patriarchal, for the growth in electronic fetal monitoring, cesarean sections, and other reproductive technologies. Practitioners and critics alike commonly trace the obstetrical technology boom to physicians' fear of malpractice suits. But the impulses behind ultrasound also arise from the codes of visual imagery and the construction of fetal images as "cultural objects" with historical meanings.

From the standpoint of clinicians, at least three levels of meaning attach to ultrasound images of fetuses. These correspond to (1) a level of "evidence" or "report," which may or may not motivate diagnosis and/or therapeutic intervention; (2) a level of surveillance and potential social control; and (3) a level of fantasy or myth. (Not surprisingly, these connotations echo the textual structure of *The Silent Scream*.) In the first place, there is simply the impulse to "view," to get a "picture" of the fetus's "anatomical structures" in motion, and here obstetrical ultrasound reflects the impact of new imaging technologies in all areas of medicine. One is struck by the lists of "indications" for ultrasound imaging found in the *ACOG Technical Bulletin* and the *American Journal of Obstetrics and Gynecology* indexes. Although the "indications" include a few recognizable "abnormal" conditions that might require a "non-routine" intervention (such as "evaluation of ectopic pregnancy" or "diagnosis of abnormal fetal position"), for the most part they consist of technical measurements, like a list of machine parts—"crown rump length," "gestational sac diameter," fetal sex organs, fetal weight—as well as estimation of gestational age. As one neonatologist told me, "We can do an entire anatomical workup!"[22] Of course, none of this viewing and measuring and recording of bits of anatomical data gives the slightest clue as to what *value* should be placed on this or any other fetus, whether it has a moral claim to heroic therapy or life at all, and who should decide.[23] But the point is that the fetus, through visualization, is being treated as a patient already, is being given an ordinary checkup. Inferences about its "personhood" (or "babyhood"), in the context of the dominant ways of seeing fetuses, seem verified by sonographic "evidence" that it kicks, spits, excretes, grows.

Evidentiary uses of photographic images are usually enlisted in the service of some kind of action—to monitor, control, and possibly intervene. In the case of obstetrical medicine, ultrasound techniques, in conjunction with electronic fetal monitoring, have been used increasingly to diagnose "fetal distress" and "abnormal presentation" (leading to a prediction of "prolonged labor" or "breech birth"). These findings then become evidence indicating earlier delivery by cesarean section, evoking the correlation some researchers have observed between increased use of electronic fetal monitoring and ultrasound and the threefold rise in the cesarean section rate in the last fifteen years.[24]

Complaints by feminist health advocates about unnecessary cesareans and excessive monitoring of pregnancy are undoubtedly justified. Even the profession's own guidelines suggest that the monitoring techniques may lead to misdiagnoses or may themselves be the cause of the "stresses" they "discover."[25] One might well question a tendency in obstetrics to "discover" disorders where they previously did not exist, because visualizing techniques compel "discovery," or to apply techniques to wider and wider groups of cases.[26] On the whole, however, diagnostic uses of ultrasound in obstetrics have benefited women more than they've done harm, making it possible to define the due date more accurately, to detect anomalies, and to anticipate complications in delivery. My question is not about this level of medical applications but rather about the cultural assumptions underlying them. How do these assumptions both reflect and reinforce the larger culture of fetal images sketched above? Why has the impulse to "see inside" come to dominate ways of knowing about pregnancy and fetuses, and what are the consequences for women's consciousness and reproductive power relations?

The "prevalence of the gaze," or the privileging of the visual, as the primary means to knowledge in Western scientific and philosophical traditions has been the subject of a feminist inquiry by Evelyn Fox Keller and Christine R. Grontkowski. In their analysis, stretching from Plato to Bacon and Descartes, this emphasis on the visual has had a paradoxical function. For sight, in contrast to the other senses, has as its peculiar property the capacity for detachment, for objectifying the thing visualized by creating distance between knower and known. (In modern optics, the eye becomes a passive recorder, a camera obscura.) In this way, the elevation of the visual in a hierarchy of senses actually has the effect of debasing sensory experience, and relatedness, as modes of knowing: "Vision connects us to truth as it distances us from the corporeal."[27]

Some feminist cultural theorists in France, Britain, and the United States have argued that visualization and objectification as privileged ways of knowing are specifically masculine (man the viewer, woman the spectacle).[28] Without falling into such essentialism, we may suppose that the language, perceptions, and uses of visual information may be different for women, as pregnant subjects, than they are for men (or women) as physicians, researchers, or reporters. And this difference will reflect the historical control by men over science, medicine, and obstetrics in Western society and over the historical definitions of masculinity in Western culture. The deep gender bias of science (including medicine), of its very ways of seeing problems, resonates, Keller argues, in its "common rhetoric." Mainly "adversarial" and "aggressive" in its stance toward what it studies, "science can come to sound like a battlefield."[29] Similarly, presentations of scientific and medical "conquests" in the mass media commonly appropriate this terrain into Cold War culture and macho style. Consider this piece of text from *Life*'s 1965 picture story on ultrasound in pregnancy, "A Sonar 'Look' at an Unborn Baby":

> The astonishing medical machine resting on this pregnant woman's abdomen in a Philadelphia hospital is "looking" at her unborn child in precisely the same way a Navy surface ship homes in on enemy submarines. Using the sonar principle, it is bombarding her with a beam of ultra-high-frequency sound waves that are inaudible to the human ear. Back come the echoes, bouncing off the baby's head, to show up as a visual image on a viewing screen. (P. 45)

The militarization of obstetrical images is not unique to ultrasonography (most technologies in a militarized society either begin or end in the military); nor is it unique to its focus on reproduction (similar language constructs the "war on cancer"). Might it then correspond to the very culture of medicine and science, its emphasis on visualization as a form of surveillance and "attack"? For some obstetrician-gynecologist practitioners, such visualization is patently voyeuristic; it generates erotic pleasure in the nonreciprocated, illicit "look." Interviewed in *Newsweek* after *The Silent Scream* was released, Nathanson boasted: "With the aid of technology, we stripped away the walls of the abdomen and uterus and looked into the womb."[30] And here is Dr. Michael Harrison writing in a respected medical journal about "fetal management" through ultrasound:

> The fetus could not be taken seriously as long as he [*sic*] remained a medical recluse in an opaque womb; and it was not until the last half of this century that *the prying eye of the ultrasonogram* . . . rendered the once opaque womb transparent, *stripping the veil of mystery from the dark inner sanctum* and *letting the light of scientific observation fall on the shy and secretive fetus*. . . . The sonographic voyeur, *spying on the unwary fetus,* finds him or her a surprisingly active little creature, and not at all the passive parasite we had imagined.[31]

Whether voyeurism is a "masculinist" form of looking, the "siting" of the womb as a space to be conquered can only be had by one who stands outside it looking in. The view of the fetus as a "shy," mysterious "little creature," recalling a wildlife photographer tracking down a gazelle, indeed exemplifies the "predatory nature of a photographic consciousness."[32] It is hard to imagine a pregnant woman thinking about her fetus this way, whether she longs for a baby or wishes for an abortion.

What we have here, from the clinician's standpoint, is a kind of *panoptics of the womb*, whose aim is "to establish normative behavior for the fetus at various gestational stages" and to maximize medical control over pregnancy.[33] Feminist critics emphasize the degrading impact fetal-imaging techniques have on the pregnant woman. She now becomes the "maternal environment," the "site" of the fetus, a passive spectator in her own pregnancy.[34] Sonographic detailing of fetal anatomy completely displaces the markers of "traditional" pregnancy, when "feeling the baby move was a 'definitive' diagnosis." Now the woman's *felt* evidence about the pregnancy is discredited, in favor of the more "objective" data on the video screen. We find her "on the table with the ultrasound scanner to her belly, and on the other side of the technician or doctor, the fetus on the screen. The doctor . . . turns *away* from the mother to examine her baby. Even the heartbeat is heard over a speaker removed from the mother's body. The technology which makes the baby/fetus more 'visible' renders the woman invisible."[35]

Earlier I noted that ultrasound imaging of fetuses is constituted through three levels of meaning—not only the level of evidence (diagnosis) and the level of surveillance (intervention), but also that of fantasy or myth. "Evidence" shades into fantasy when the fetus is visualized, albeit through electronic media, as though removed from the pregnant woman's body, as though suspended in space. This is a form of fetishization, and it occurs repeatedly in clinical settings whenever ultrasound images construct the fetus through "indications" that sever its functions and parts from their organic connection to the pregnant woman. Fetishization, in turn, shades into surveillance when physicians, "right-to-life" propangandists, legislatures, or courts impose ultrasound imaging on pregnant women in order "to encourage 'bonding.'" In some states, the use of compulsory ultrasound imaging as a weapon of intimidation against women seeking abortions has already begun.[36] Indeed, the very idea of "bonding" based on a photographic image implies a fetish: the investment of erotic feelings in a fantasy. When an obstetrician presents his patient with a sonographic picture of the fetus "for the baby album," it may be a manifestation of masculine desire to reproduce not only babies but also motherhood.

Many feminists have explained masculine appropriation of the conditions and products of reproduction in psychoanalytic or psychological terms, associating it with men's fears of the body, their own mortality, and the mother who bore them. According to one interpretation, "the domination of women by the male gaze is part of men's strategy to contain the threat that the mother embodies [of infantile dependence and male impotence]."[37] Nancy Hartsock, in a passage reminiscent of Simone de Beauvoir's earlier insights, links patriarchal control over reproduction to the masculine quest for immortality through immortal works: "Because to be born means that one will die, reproduction and generation are either understood in terms of death or are appropriated by men in disembodied form."[38] In Mary O'Brien's analysis of the "dialectics of reproduction," "the alienation of the male seed in the copulative act" separates men "from genetic continuity." Men therefore try to "annul" this separation by appropriating children, wives, principles of legitimacy and inheritance, estates, and empires. (With her usual irony, O'Brien calls this male fear of female procreativity "the dead core of impotency in the potency principle.")[39] Other, more historically grounded feminist writers have extended this theme to the appropriation of obstetrics in England and America. Attempts by male practitioners to disconnect the fetus from women's wombs—whether physically, through forceps, cesarean delivery, in vitro fertilization, or fetal surgery; or visually, through ultrasound imaging—are specific forms of the ancient masculine impulse "to confine and limit and curb the creativity and potentially polluting power of female procreation."[40]

But feminist critiques of "the war against the womb" often suffer from certain tendencies toward reductionism. First, they confuse masculine rhetoric and fantasies with actual power relations, thereby submerging women's own responses to reproductive situations in the dominant (and victimizing) masculine text. Second, if they do consider women's responses, those responses are compressed into Everywoman's Reproductive Consciousness, undifferentiated by particular historical and social circumstances; biology itself becomes a universal rather than an individual, particular set of conditions. To correct this myopia, I shall return to the study of fetal images through a different lens, that of pregnant women as viewers.

Picturing the Baby—Women's Responses

The scenario of the voyeuristic ultrasound instrument/technician, with the pregnant woman displaced to one side passively staring at her objectified fetus, has a certain phenomenological truth. At the same time, anecdotal evidence gives us another, quite different scenario when it comes to the subjective understanding of pregnant women themselves. Far from feeling victimized or pacified, they frequently express a sense of elation and direct participation in the imaging process, claiming it "makes the baby more real," "more our baby"; that visualizing the fetus creates a feeling of intimacy and belonging, as well as a reassuring sense of predictability and control.[41] (I am speaking here of women whose pregnancies are wanted, of course, not those seeking abortions.) Some women even talk about themselves as having "bonded" with the fetus through

viewing its image on the screen.[42] Like amniocentesis, in vitro fertilization, voluntary sterilization, and other "male-dominated" reproductive
technologies, ultrasound imaging in pregnancy seems to evoke in many
women a sense of greater control and self-empowerment than they
would have if left to "traditional" methods or "nature." How are we to
understand this contradiction between the feminist decoding of male
"cultural dreamworks" and (some) women's actual experience of reproductive techniques and images?

Current feminist writings about reproductive technology are not very
helpful in answering this kind of question. Works such as Gena Corea's
The Mother Machine and most articles in the anthology, *Test-Tube Women*,
portray women as the perennial victims of an omnivorous male plot to
take over their reproductive capacities. The specific forms taken by male
strategies of reproductive control, while admittedly varying across times
and cultures, are reduced to a pervasive, transhistorical "need." Meanwhile, women's own resistance to this control, often successful, as well as
their complicity in it, are ignored; women, in this view, have no role as
agents of their reproductive destinies.

But historical and sociological research shows that women are not just
passive victims of "male" reproductive technologies and the physicians
who wield them. Because of their shared reproductive situation and
needs, women throughout the nineteenth and twentieth centuries have
often *generated* demands for technologies such as birth control, childbirth
anesthesia, or infertility treatments, or they have welcomed them as benefits (which is not to say the technologies offered always met the
needs).[43] We have to understand the "market" for oral contraceptives,
sterilization, in vitro fertilization, amniocentesis, and high-tech pregnancy monitoring as a more complex phenomenon than either the victimization or the male-womb-envy thesis allows.

At the same time, theories of a "feminist standpoint" or "reproductive
consciousness" that would restore pregnant women to active historical
agency and unify their responses to reproductive images and techniques
are complicated by two sets of circumstances.[44] First, we do not simply
imbibe our reproductive experience raw. The dominant images and
codes that mediate the material conditions of pregnancy, abortion, and so
forth, determine what, exactly, women "know" about these events in
their lives, their *meaning* as lived experience. Thus, women may see in fetal images what they are told they ought to see. Second, and in dialectical
tension with the first, women's relationship to reproductive technologies
and images differs depending on social differences such as class, race,
and sexual preference, and biological ones such as age, physical disability, and personal fertility history. Their "reproductive consciousness" is

constituted out of these complex elements and cannot easily be generalized or, unfortunately, vested with a privileged insight.

How different women see fetal images depends on the context of the looking and the relationship of the viewer to the image and what it signifies. Recent semiotic theory emphasizes "the centrality of the moment of reception in the construction of meanings." The meanings of a visual image or text are created through an "interaction" process between the viewer and the text, taking their focus from the situation of the viewer.[45] John Berger identifies a major contextual frame defining the relationship between viewer and image in distinguishing between what he calls "photographs which belong to private experience" and thus connect to our lives in some intimate way, and "public photographs," which excise bits of information "from all lived experience."[46] Now, this is a simplistic distinction because "private" photographic images become imbued with "public" resonances all the time; we "see" lovers' photos and family albums through the scrim of television ads. Still, I want to borrow Berger's distinction because it helps indicate important differences between the meanings of fetal images when they are viewed as "the fetus" and when they are viewed as "my baby."

When legions of right-wing women in the antiabortion movement brandish pictures of gory dead or dreamlike space-floating fetuses outside clinics or in demonstrations, they are participating in a visual pageant that directly degrades women—and thus themselves. Wafting these fetus-pictures as icons, literal fetishes, they both propagate and celebrate the image of the fetus as autonomous space-hero and the pregnant woman as "empty space." Their visual statements are straightforward representations of the antifeminist ideas they (and their male cohorts) support. Such right-wing women promote the public, political character of the fetal image as a symbol that condenses a complicated set of conservative values—about sex, motherhood, teenage girls, fatherhood, the family. In this instance, perhaps it makes sense to say they participate "vicariously" in a "phallic" way of looking and thus become the "complacent facilitators for the working out of man's fantasies."[47]

It is not only antiabortionists who respond to fetal images however. The "public" presentation of the fetus has become ubiquitous; its disembodied form, now propped up by medical authority and technological rationality, permeates mass culture. We are all, on some level, susceptible to its coded meanings. Victor Burgin points out that it does no good to protest the "falseness" of such images as against "reality," because "reality"—that is, how we experience the world, both "public" and "private"—"is itself constituted through the agency of representations."[48] This suggests that women's ways of seeing ultrasound images of fetuses,

even their own, may be affected by the cumulative array of "public" representations, from *Life Magazine* to *The Silent Scream*. And it possibly
means that some of them will be intimidated from getting abortions—although as yet we have little empirical information to verify this. When
young women seeking abortions are coerced or manipulated into seeing
pictures of fetuses, their own or others, it is the "public fetus" as moral
abstraction they are being made to view.

But the reception and meanings of fetal images also derive from the
particular circumstances of the woman as viewer, and these circumstances may not fit neatly within a model of women as victims of reproductive technologies. Above all, the meanings of fetal images will differ
depending on whether a woman wishes to be pregnant or not. With regard to wanted pregnancies, women with very diverse political values
may respond positively to images that present their fetus as if detached,
their own body as if absent from the scene. The reasons are a complex
weave of socioeconomic position, gender psychology, and biology. At
one end of the spectrum, the "prolife" women Kristin Luker interviewed
strongly identified "the fetus" with their own recent or frequent pregnancies; it became "my little guy." Their circumstances as "devout, traditional women who valued motherhood highly" were those of married
women with children, mostly unemployed outside the home, and remarkably isolated from any social or community activities. That "little
guy" was indeed their primary source of gratification and self-esteem.
Moreover—and this fact links them with many women whose abortion
politics and life-styles lie at the opposite end of the spectrum—a dispro-
portionate number of them seem to have undergone a history of pregnancy or child loss.[49]

If we look at the women who comprise the market for high-tech obstetrics, they are primarily those who can afford these expensive procedures
and who have access to the private medical offices where they are offered. Socially and demographically, they are not only apt to be among
the professional, educated, "late-childbearing" cohort who face greater
risks because of age (although the average age of amniocentesis and ultrasound recipients seems to be moving rapidly down). More importantly, whatever their age or risk category, they are likely to be products
of a middle-class culture that values planning, control, and predictability
in the interests of a "quality" baby.[50] These values preexist technologies
of visualization and "baby engineering" and create a predisposition toward their acceptance. The fear of "nonquality"—that is, disability—and
the pressure on parents, particularly mothers, to produce fetuses that
score high on their "stress test" (like infants who score high on their Ap-
gar test and children who score high on their SATs) is a cultural as well as
a class phenomenon. Indeed, the "perfect baby" syndrome that creates a

welcoming climate for ultrasound imaging may also be oppressive for women, insofar as they are still the ones who bear primary responsibility—and guilt—for how the baby turns out.[51] Despite this, "listening to women's voices" leads to the unmistakable conclusion that, as with birth control generally, many women prefer predictability and will do what they can to have it.

Women's responses to fetal picture taking may have another side as well, rooted in their traditional role in the production of family photographs. If photographs accommodate "aesthetic consumerism," becoming instruments of appropriation and possessing, this is nowhere truer than within family life—particularly middle-class family life.[52] Family albums originated to chronicle the continuity of Victorian bourgeois kin networks. The advent of home movies in the 1940s and 1950s paralleled the move to the suburbs and backyard barbecues.[53] Similarly, the presentation of a sonogram photo to the dying grandfather, even before his grandchild's birth,[54] is a 1980s way of affirming patriarchal lineage. In other words, far from the intrusion of an alien, and alienating, technology, it may be that ultrasonography is becoming enmeshed in a familiar language of "private" images.

Significantly, in each of these cases it is the woman, the mother, who acts as custodian of the image—keeping up the album, taking the movies, presenting the sonogram. The specific relationship of women to photographic images, especially those of children, may help to explain the attraction of pregnant women to ultrasound images of their own fetus (as opposed to "public" ones). Rather than being surprised that some women experience bonding with their fetus after viewing its image on a screen (or in a sonographic "photo"), perhaps we should understand this as a culturally embedded component of desire. If it is a form of objectifying the fetus (and the pregnant woman herself as detached from the fetus), perhaps such objectification and detachment are necessary for her to feel erotic pleasure in it.[55] If with the ultrasound image she first recognizes the fetus as "real," as "out there," this means that she first experiences it as an object she can possess.

Keller proposes that feminists reevaluate the concept of objectivity. In so doing they may discover that the process of objectification they have identified as masculinist takes different forms, some that detach the viewer from the viewed and some that make possible both erotic and intellectual attachment.[56] To suggest that the timing of maternal-fetus or maternal-infant attachment is a biological given (for example, at "quickening" or at birth), or that "feeling" is somehow more "natural" than "seeing," contradicts women's changing historical experience.[57] On the other hand, to acknowledge that bonding is a historically and culturally shaped process is not to deny its reality. That women develop powerful feelings of attachment to their ("private") fetuses, especially the ones they want, complicates the politics of fetal images.

Consider a recent case in a New York court that denied a woman damages when her twenty-week fetus was stillborn, following an apparently botched amniocentesis. The majority held that, because the woman did not "witness" the death or injury directly, and was not in the immediate "zone of danger" herself, she could not recover damages for any emotional pain or loss she suffered as a result of the fetus's death. As one dissenting judge argued, the court "rendered the woman a bystander to medical procedures performed upon her own body," denying her any rights based on the emotional and "biological bond" she had with the fetus.[58] In so doing, the majority implicitly sanctioned the image of fetal autonomy and maternal oblivion.

As a feminist used to resisting women's reduction to biology, I find it awkward to defend their biological connection to the fetus. But the patent absurdity and cruelty of this decision underscore the need for feminist analyses of reproduction to address biology. A true biological perspective does not lead us to determinism but rather to infinite *variation*, which is to say that it is historical.[59] Particular lives are lived in particular bodies—not only women's bodies, but just as relevantly, aging, ill, disabled, or infertile ones. The material circumstances that differentiate women's responses to obstetrical ultrasound and other technologies include their own biological history, which may be experienced as one of limits and defeats. In fact, the most significant divider between pregnant women who welcome the information from ultrasound and other monitoring techniques and those who resent the machines or wish to postpone "knowing" may be personal fertility history. A recent study of women's psychological responses to the use of electronic fetal monitors during labor "found that those women who had previously experienced the loss of a baby tended to react positively to the monitor, feeling it to be a reassuring presence, a substitute for the physician, an aid to communication. Those women who had not previously suffered difficult or traumatic births . . . tended to regard the monitor with hostility, as a distraction, a competitor."[60]

To recite such conditions does not mean we have to retreat into a reductionist or dualist view of biology. Infertility, pregnancy losses, and women's feelings of "desperation" about "childlessness" have many sources, including cultural pressures, environmental hazards, and medical misdiagnosis or neglect.[61] Whatever the sources, however, a history of repeated miscarriages, infertility, ectopic pregnancy, or loss of a child is likely to dispose a pregnant woman favorably to techniques that allow her to visualize the pregnancy and *possibly* to gain some control over its outcome.[62] Pregnancy—as biosocial experience—acts on women's bodies in different ways, with the result that the relation of their bodies, and consciousness, to reproductive technologies may also differ.

Attachment of pregnant women to their fetuses at earlier stages in pregnancy becomes an issue, not because it is cemented through "sight" rather than "feel," but when and if it is used to obstruct or harass an abortion decision.[63] In fact, there is no reason any woman's abortion decision should be tortured in this way, because there is no medical rationale for requiring her to view an image of her fetus. Responsible abortion clinics are doing ultrasound imaging in selected cases—*only* to determine fetal size or placement, where the date of the woman's last menstrual period is unknown, the pregnancy is beyond the first trimester, or there is a history of problems; or to diagnose an ectopic pregnancy. But in such cases the woman herself does not see the image, because the monitor is placed outside her range of vision and clinic protocols refrain from showing her the picture unless she specifically requests it.[64] In the current historical context, to consciously limit the uses of fetal images in abortion clinics is to take a political stance, to resist the message of *The Silent Scream*. This reminds us that the politics of reproductive technologies are constructed contextually, out of who uses them, how, and for what purposes.

The view that "reproductive engineering" is imposed on "women as a class," rather than being sought by them as a means toward greater choice,[65] obscures the particular reality, not only of women with fertility problems and losses but also of other groups. For lesbians who utilize sperm banks and artificial insemination to achieve biological pregnancy without heterosexual sex, such technologies are a critical tool of reproductive freedom. Are lesbians to be told that wanting their "own biological children" generated through their own bodies is somehow wrong for them but not for fertile heterosexual couples?[66] The majority of poor and working-class women in the United States and Britain still have no access to amniocentesis, in vitro fertilization, and the rest, although they (particular women of color) have the highest rates of infertility and fetal impairment. It would be wrong to ignore their lack of access to these techniques on the grounds that worrying about how babies turn out, or wanting to have "your own," is only a middle-class (or eugenic) prejudice.

In Europe, Australia, and North America, feminists are currently engaged in heated debate over whether new reproductive technologies present a threat or an opportunity for women. Do they simply reinforce the age-old pressures on women to bear children, and to bear them to certain specifications, or do they give women more control? What sort of control do we require in order to have reproductive freedom, and are there/should there be any limits on our control?[67] What is the meaning of reproductive technologies that tailor-make infants, in a context where childcare remains the private responsibility of women and many women are growing increasingly poor? Individual women, especially middle-class women, are choosing to utilize high-tech obstetrics, and their choices may not always be ones we like. It may be that chorionic villus sampling, the new first-trimester prenatal diagnostic technique, will increase the use of selective abortion for sex. Moreover, the bias against disability that underlies the quest for the "perfect child" seems undeniable. Newer methods of prenatal diagnosis may mean that more and more abortions become "selective," so that more women decide "to abort the particular fetus [they] are carrying in hopes of coming up with a 'better' one next time."[68] Are these choices moral? Do we have a right to judge them? Can we even say they are "free"?

On the other hand, techniques for imaging fetuses and pregnancies may, depending on their cultural contexts and uses, offer means for empowering women, both individually and collectively. We need to examine these possibilities and to recognize that, at the present stage in history, feminists have no common standpoint about how women ought to use this power.

Conclusion

Images by themselves lack "objective" meanings; meanings come from the interlocking fields of context, communications, application, and reception. If we removed from the ultrasound image of *The Silent Scream* its title, its text, its sound narrative, Dr. Nathanson, the media and distribution networks, and the whole antiabortion political climate, what would remain? But, of course, the question is absurd because no image dangles in a cultural void, just as no fetus floats in a space capsule. The problem clearly becomes, then, how do we change the contexts, media, and consciousness through which fetal images are defined? Here are some proposals, both modest and utopian.

First, we have to restore women to a central place in the pregnancy scene. To do this, we must create new images that recontextualize the fetus, that place it back into the uterus, and the uterus back into the woman's body, and her body back into its social space. Contexts do not neatly condense into symbols; they must be told through stories that give them mass and dimension. For example, a brief prepared from thousands of letters received in an abortion rights campaign and presented to the Supreme Court in its most recent abortion case, translates women's abortion stories into a legal text. Boldly filing a procession of real women before the court's eyes, it materializes them in not only their bodies but also their jobs, families, schoolwork, health problems, young age, poverty, race/ethnic identity, and dreams of a better life.[69]

Second, we need to separate the power relations within which reproductive technologies, including ultrasound imaging, are applied from the technologies themselves. If women were truly empowered in the clinic setting, as practitioners and patients, would we discard the technologies? Or would we use them differently, integrating them into a more holistic clinical dialogue between women's felt knowledge and the technical information "discovered" in the test tube or on the screen? Before attacking reproductive technologies, we need to demand that all women have access to the knowledge and resources to judge their uses and to use them wisely, in keeping with their own particular needs.

Finally, we should pursue the discourse now begun toward developing a feminist ethic of reproductive freedom that complements feminist politics. What ought we to choose if we became genuinely free to choose? Are some choices unacceptable on moral grounds, and does this mean under any circumstances, or only under some? Can feminism reconstruct a joyful sense of childbearing and maternity without capitulating to ideologies that reduce women to a maternal essence? Can we talk about morality in reproductive decision making without invoking the specter of maternal duty? On some level, the struggle to demystify fetal images is fraught with danger, because it involves *re-embodying* the fetus, thus representing women as (wanting-to-be or not-wanting-to-be) pregnant persons. One way out of this danger is to image the pregnant woman, not as an abstraction, but within her total framework of relationships, economic and health needs, and desires. Once we have pictured the social conditions of her freedom, however, we have not dissolved the contradictions in how she might use it.

Notes

The following people have given valuable help in the research and revising of the manuscript but are in no way responsible for its outcome: Fina Bathrick, Rayna Rapp, Ellen Ross, Michelle Stanworth, and Sharon Thompson. I would also like to thank the Institute for Policy Studies, the 1986 Barnard College Scholar and the Feminist Conference, and *Ms. Magazine* for opportunities to present pieces of it in progress.

1. *City of Akron v. Akron Center for Reproductive Health*, 426 U.S. 416 (1983); and *Thornburgh v. American College of Obstetricians and Gynecologists*, 54 LW 4618, 10 June 1986. From a prochoice perspective, the significance of these decisions is mixed. Although the court's majority opinion has become, if anything, more liberal and more feminist in its protection of women's "individual dignity and autonomy," this majority has grown steadily narrower. Whereas in 1973 it was seven to two, in 1983 it shrank to six to three and then in 1986 to a bare five to four, while the growing minority becomes ever more conservative and antifeminist.

2. See Paul D. Erickson, *Reagan Speaks: The Making of an American Myth* (New York: New York University Press, 1985); and Joanmarie Kalter, "TV News and Religion," *TV Guide,* 9 and 16 Nov. 1985, for analyses of these trends.

3. This phrase comes from Stuart Ewen, "The Political Elements of Style," in *Beyond Style: Precis 5,* ed. Jeffery Buchholz and Daniel B. Monk (New York: Columbia University Graduate School of Architecture and Planning/Rizzoli), 125–33.

4. John C. Fletcher, and Mark I. Evans, "Maternal Bonding in Early Fetal Ultrasound Examinations," *New England Journal of Medicine* 308 (1983): 392–93.

5. Planned Parenthood Federation of America, *The Facts Speak Louder: Planned Parenthood's Critique of "The Silent Scream"* (New York: Planned Parenthood Federation of America, n.d.). A new film, *Silent Scream II,* appeared too late to be reviewed here.

6. These earliest photographic representations of fetal life include "Babies Before Birth," *Look* 26 (June 5, 1962): 19–23; "A Sonar Look at an Unborn Baby," *Life* 58 (Jan. 15, 1965): 45–46; and Geraldine L. Flanagan, *The First Nine Months of Life* (New York: Simon & Schuster, 1962).

7. For a history of photography, see Alan Trachtenberg, ed. *Classic Essays on Photography* (New Haven: Leete's Island Books, 1980); and Susan Sontag, *On Photography* (New York: Delta, 1973), esp. 22–23.

8. Roland Barthes, "The Photographic Message," in *A Barthes Reader,* ed. Susan Sontag (New York: Hill & Wang, 1982), 194–210. Compare Hubert Danish: "The photographic image does not belong to the natural world. It is a product of human labor, a cultural object whose being . . . cannot be dissociated precisely from its historical meaning and from the necessarily datable project in which it originates." See his "Notes for a Phenomenology of the Photographic Image," in *Classic Essays on Photography,* 287–90.

9. Lady Elizabeth Eastlake, "Photography," in *Classic Essays on Photography,* 39–68, 65–66; John Berger, *About Looking* (New York: Pantheon, 1980), 48–50; and Andre Bazin, "The Ontology of the Photographic Image," in *Classic Essays on Photography,* 237–40, 241.

10. Allan Sekula, "On the Invention of Photographic Meaning," in Victor Burgin, ed., *Thinking Photography* (London: Macmillan, 1982), 84–109; and Sontag, *On Photography,* 5, 21.

11. Stuart Ewen and Elizabeth Ewen, *Channels of Desires: Mass Images and the Shaping of American Consciousness* (New York: McGraw-Hill, 1982), 33.

12. Barbara Katz Rothman, *The Tentative Pregnancy: Prenatal Diagnosis and the Future of Motherhood* (New York: Viking, 1986), 114.

13. Zoe Sofia, "Exterminating Fetuses: Abortion, Disarmament, and the Sexo-Semiotics of Extraterrestrialism," *Diacritics* 14 (1984): 47–59.

14. Rachel B. Gold, "Ultrasound Imaging During Pregnancy," *Family Planning Perspectives* 16 (1984): 240–43, 240–41; Albert D. Haverkamp and Miriam Orleans, "An Assessment of Electronic Fetal Monitoring," *Women and Health* 7 (1982): 126–34, 128; and Ruth Hubbard, "Personal Courage Is Not Enough: Some Hazards of Childbearing in the 1980s," in *Test-Tube Women: What Future for Motherhood?* ed. Rita Arditti, Renate Duelli Klein, and Shelley Minden (Boston: Routledge & Kegan Paul, 1984), 331–55, 341.

15. Janet Gallagher, "The Fetus and the Law—Whose Life Is It, Anyway?," *Ms.* (Sept. 1984); John Fletcher, "The Fetus as Patient: Ethical Issues," *Journal of the American Medical Association* 246 (181): 772–73; and Hubbard, "Personal Courage Is Not Enough," 350.

16. David A. Grimes, "Second-Trimester Abortions in the United States," *Family Planning Perspectives* 16 (1984): 260–65; and Stanly K. Henshaw et al., "A Portrait of American Women Who Obtain Abortions," *Family Planning Perspectives* 17 (1985): 90–96.

17. In her dissenting opinion in the *Akron* case, Supreme Court Justice Sandra Day O'Connor argued that *Roe v. Wade* was "on a collision course with itself" because technology was pushing the point of viability indefinitely backward. In *Roe* the court had defined "viability" as the point at which the fetus is "potentially able to live outside the mother's womb, albeit with artificial aid." After that point, it said, the state could restrict abortion except when bringing the fetus to term would jeopardize the woman's life or health. Compare Nancy K. Rhoden, "Late Abortion and Technological Advances in Fetal Viability: Some Legal Considerations," *Family Planning Perspectives* 17 (1985): 160–61. Meanwhile, a popular weekly television program, "Hill Street Blues," in March 1985 aired a dramatization of abortion clinic harassment in which a pregnant woman seeking an abortion miscarries and gives birth to an extremely premature fetus/baby, which soon dies. Numerous newspaper accounts of "heroic" efforts to save premature newborns have made front-page headlines.

18. Donna Haraway, "A Manifesto for Cyborgs: Science, Technology, and Socialist Feminism in the 1980s," *Socialist Review* 80 (1985): 65–107.

19. Gold, 240; and David Graham, "Ultrasound in Clinical Obstetrics," *Women and Health* 7 (1982): 39–55, 39.

20. American College of Obstetricians and Gynecologists, "Diagnostic Ultrasound in Obstetrics and Gynecology," *Women and Health* 7 (1982): 55–58 (reprinted from ACOG, *Technical Bulletin*, no. 63 [October 1981]).

21. Madeleine H. Shearer, "Revelations: A Summary and Analysis of the NIH Consensus Development Conference on Ultrasound Imaging in Pregnancy," *Birth* 11 (1984): 23–36, 25–36, 30; Good, 240–41.

22. Dr. Alan Fleishman, personal communication (May 1985).

23. For a discussion of these issues, see Rosalind P. Petchesky, *Abortion and Woman's Choice: The State, Sexuality, and Reproductive Freedom* (Boston: Northeastern University Press, 1985), chap. 9.

24. Kathy H. Sheehan, "Abnormal Labor: Cesareans in the U.S.," *The Network News* (National Women's Health Network) 10 (July/August 1985): 1, 3; and Haverkamp and Orleans, 127.

25. ACOG, "Diagnostic Ultrasound in Obstetrics and Gynecology," 58.

26. Stephen B. Thacker, and H. David Banta, "Benefits and Risks of Episiotomy," in *Women and Health* 7 (1982): 173–80.

27. Evelyn Fox Keller and Christine R. Grontkowski, "The Mind's Eye," in *Discovering Reality: Feminist Perspectives on Epistemology, Metaphysics, Methodology, and Philosophy of Science*, ed. Sandra Harding and Merrill B. Hintikka (Dordrecht: D. Reidel, 1983), 207–24.

28. Luce Irigaray, "Ce Sexe qui n'en est pas un," in *New French Feminisms: An Anthology*, ed. Elaine Marks and Isabelle de Courtivron (New York: Schocken, 1981), 99–106, 101; Annette Kuhn, *Women's Pictures: Feminism and Cinema* (London: Routledge & Kegan Paul, 1982), 601–65, 113; Laura Mulvey, "Visual Pleasure and Narrative Cinema," *Screen* 16 (1979): 6–18; and E. Ann Kaplan, "Is the Gaze Male?" in *Powers of Desire: The Politics of Sexuality*, ed. Ann Snitow, Christine Stansell and Sharon Thompson (New York: Monthly Review Press, 1983), 309–27, 324.

29. Evelyn Fox Keller, *Reflections on Gender and Science* (New Haven: Yale University Press, 1985), 123–24.

30. Melinda Beck et al., "America's Abortion Dilemma," *Newsweek* 105 (14 Jan. 1985): 20–29, 21 (italics added).

31. This passage is quoted in Hubbard, 348, and taken from Michael R. Harrison et al., "Management of the Fetus with a Correctable Congenital Defect," *Journal of the American Medical Association* 246 (1981): 774 (italics added).

32. Haraway, 89; Sontag, *On Photography*, 13–14.

33. This quotation comes from the chief of Maternal and Fetal Medicine at a Boston hospital, as cited in Hubbard, 349. Compare it with Graham, 49–50.

34. For examples, see Hubbard, 350; and Rothman, 113–15.

35. Rothman, 113.

36. Gold, 242.

37. Kaplan, 324. Compare Jessica Benjamin, "Master and Slave: The Fantasy of Erotic Domination," in *Powers of Desire*, 280–99, 295. This article was originally published as "The Bonds of Love: Rational Violence and Erotic Domination," *Feminist Studies* 6 (Spring 1980): 144–74.

38. Nancy C.M. Hartsock, *Money, Sex, and Power: An Essay on Domination and Community* (Boston: Northeastern University Press, 1983), 253.

39. Mary O'Brien, *The Politics of Reproduction* (Boston/London: Routledge & Kegan Paul, 1981), 29–37, 56, 60–61, 139.

40. Ann Oakley, "Wisewoman and Medicine Man: Changes in the Management of Childbirth," in *The Rights and Wrongs of Women*, ed. Juliet Mitchell and Ann Oakley, (Harmondsworth: Penguin, 1976), 17–58, 57; Gena Corea, *The Mother Machine: Reproductive Technologies from Artificial Insemination to Artificial Wombs* (New York: Harper & Row, 1985), 303 and chap. 16; Adrienne Rich, *Of Woman Born: Motherhood as Experience and Institution* (New York: W.W. Norton, 1976), chap. 6; and Barbara Ehrenreich, and Deirdre English, *For Her Own Good: 150 Years of the Experts' Advice to Women* (Garden City, N.Y.: Anchor/Doubleday, 1979).

41. Hubbard, 335; Rothman, 202, 212–13, as well as my own private conversations with recent mothers.

42. Rothman, 113–14.

43. Linda Gordon, *Woman's Body, Woman's Right: A Social History of Birth Control in America* (New York: Grossman, 1976); Angus McLaren, *Birth Control in Nineteenth-Century England* (London: Croom Helm, 1978); Jane Lewis, *The Politics of Motherhood: Child and Maternal Welfare in England, 1900–1939* (London: Croom Helm, 1980), chap. 4; Rosalind P. Petchesky, "Reproductive Freedom: Beyond a Woman's Right to Choose," in *Women: Sex and Sexuality*, ed. Catharine R. Stimp-

son and Ethel Spector Person (Chicago: University of Chicago Press, 1981), 92–116 [originally in *Signs* 5 (Summer 1980]); and Petchesky, *Abortion and Woman's Choice*, chaps. 1 and 5.

44. O'Brien, chap. 1; and Hartsock, chap. 10.

45. Kuhn, 43–44.

46. Berger, 51.

47. Irigaray, 100.

48. Burgin, 9.

49. Kristin Luker, *Abortion and the Politics of Motherhood* (Berkeley: University of California Press, 1984), 138–39, 150–51.

50. Michelle Fine and Adrienne Asch, "Who Owns the Womb?" *Women's Review of Books* 2 (May 1985): 8–10; Hubbard, 336.

51. Hubbard, 344.

52. Sontag, *On Photography*, 8.

53. Patricia Zimmerman, "Colonies of Skill and Freedom: Towards a Social Definition of Amateur Film," *Journal of Film and Video* (forthcoming).

54. Rothman, 125.

55. Lorna Weir, and Leo Casey, "Subverting Power in Sexuality," *Socialist Review* 14 (1984): 139–57.

56. Keller, *Reflections on Gender and Science*, 70–73, 98–100, 117–20.

57. Compare this to Rothman, 41–42.

58. David Margolick, "Damages Rejected in Death of Fetus," *New York Times* 16 June 1985, 26.

59. See Denise Riley, *War in the Nursery: Theories of the Child and Mother* (London: Virago, 1983), 17 and chaps. 1–2, generally, for an illuminating critique of feminist and Marxist ideas about biological determinism and their tendency to reintroduce dualism.

60. Brian Bates, and Allison N. Turner, "Imagery and Symbolism in the Birth Practices of Traditional Cultures," *Birth* 12 (1985): 33–38.

61. Rebecca Albury, "Who Owns the Embryo?" in *Test-Tube Women*, 54–67, 57–58.

62. Rayna Rapp has advised me, based on her field research, that another response of women who have suffered difficult pregnancy histories to such diagnostic techniques may be denial—simply not wanting to know. This too, however, may be seen as a tactic to gain control over information, by censoring bad news.

63. Coercive, invasive uses of fetal images, masked as "informed consent," have been a prime strategy of antiabortion forces for some years. They have been opposed by prochoice litigators in the courts, resulting in the Supreme Court's repudiation on two different occasions of specious "informed consent" regulations as an unconstitutional form of harassment and denial of women's rights. See *Akron*, 1983; *Thornburgh*, 1986.

64. I obtained this information from interviews with Maria Tapia-Birch, administrator in the Maternal and Child Services Division of the New York City Department of Health, and with Jeanine Michaels, social worker; and Lisa Milstein, nurse-practitioner, at the Eastern Women's Health Clinic in New York, who kindly shared their clinical experience with me.

65. Corea, 313.

66. Compare Fine and Asch.

67. Samuel Gorovitz, "Introduction: The Ethical Issues," *Women and Health* 7 (1982): 1–8, 1.

68. Hubbard, 334.

69. Lynn Paltrow, "Amicus Brief: Richard Thornburgh v. American College of Obstetricians and Gynecologists," *Women's Rights Law Reporter* 9 (1986): 3–24.

20 Dissident Citizenship

Democratic Theory, Political Courage, and Activist Women

HOLLOWAY SPARKS

In this essay, I argue that contemporary democratic theory gives insufficient attention to the important contributions dissenting citizens make to democratic life. Guided by the dissident practices of activist women, I develop a more expansive conception of citizenship that recognizes dissent and an ethic of political courage as vital elements of democratic participation. I illustrate how this perspective on citizenship recasts and reclaims women's courageous dissidence by reconsidering the well-known story of Rosa Parks.

A black woman named Rosa Parks refuses to give up her seat to a white man on a Montgomery, Alabama, bus in 1955 and goes to jail. A group of welfare mothers led by Johnnie May Tillmon challenges the attempts of white, middle-class male organizers to assume leadership roles in the welfare rights movement in 1966. Poet, activist, and black lesbian feminist Audre Lorde pointedly calls white feminists to account for their racism, classism, and homophobia during the 1981 National Women's Studies Association meeting. Activist Candace Gingrich comes out publicly as a lesbian following the election of her conservative half-brother Newt as Speaker of the House in 1994.

In spite of the crucial roles these activist women have played in contemporary U.S. politics, mainstream democratic theory offers few resources for thinking about their actions in terms of citizenship. For political theorists interested in democracy, however, the dissident practices of Parks, Tillmon, and other activist women provide a rich source for considering what it means to be an active, self-governed citizen, and what it means to act together with others in a political community. In this essay, I argue that the dissenting practices of these women point toward an expanded conception of democratic citizenship that incorporates dissent, recognizes courage as central to democratic action, and reclaims and revalues the courageous dissident practices of women activists.

Although feminist historians and social movements scholars have recently devoted a great deal of attention to women's activism (see e.g., Crawford et al., 1990; West and Blumberg 1990; Laslett et al., 1995), this work has had little impact on democratic theorists. Part of the reason for this inattention, as a number of feminist theorists have noted, is the tendency of democratic theorists to ignore the public activities of women (Ackelsberg 1988; Pateman 1989; Evans 1993). An additional reason is the deliberative and discursive focus of much contemporary democratic theory. Recent controversies about citizenship have primarily centered on the role of citizen deliberation in democracies. Participatory theorists, such as Carole Pateman, Benjamin Barber, Jane Mansbridge, Iris Marion Young, and theorists drawing from the work of Hannah Arendt and Jürgen Habermas have generated a lively debate about the promise and possibilities of reconceptualizing and institutionalizing citizen deliberation in a wider variety of public spaces.

Citizenship, however, involves more than deliberation. Deliberation, however critical as a practice, is often the goal rather than the starting point for those who engage in dissident citizenship. I conceptualize dissident citizenship as the practices of marginalized citizens who publicly contest prevailing arrangements of power by means of oppositional democratic practices that augment or replace institutionalized channels of democratic opposition when those channels are inadequate or unavailable. Instead of voting, lobbying, or petitioning, dissident citizens constitute alternative public spaces through practices such as marches, protests, and picket lines; sit-ins, slow-downs, and cleanups; speeches, strikes, and street theater. Dissident citizenship, in other words, encompasses the often creative oppositional practices of citizens who, either by choice or (much more commonly) by forced exclusion from the institutionalized means of opposition, contest current arrangements of power from the margins of the polity. While dissident citizens can be progressive or conservative, civil rights activists or segregationists, pro-choice or pro-life, environmentalists or smokers' rights advocates, they share a commitment to unconventional forms of democratic engagement and opposition that nonetheless preserve the possibility of ongoing debate and disagreement. Consequently, if democratic citizenship is ultimately about "the collective and participatory engagement of citizens in the determination of the affairs of their community" (Dietz 1987, 14), then marginalized dissident citizens who address the wider polity in order to change minds, challenge practices, or even reconstitute the very boundaries of the political itself engage in a form of democratic citizenship that is essential for the continuing revitalization of democratic life.

A crucial element in the practice of dissident citizenship, I wish to argue, is the discourse and practice of courage. One way to describe courage is as a commitment to resolution and persistence in the face of risk, uncertainty, or fear. Because of its strong association with the behavior of soldiers, courage has often been constructed as a quintessentially masculine trait, tied intimately to conceptions of manhood and to the performance of violence (see esp. Brown 1988). But as the examples at the beginning of this essay demonstrate, women are perfectly capable of acting resolutely in the face of risk, uncertainty, and fear, even though they are much less likely to be credited as courageous actors. A courageous act, moreover, need not be a violent one. It is commonly believed and well documented, for example, that nonviolent resistance activities, protests, and communication with opponents can require courage, especially in the face of verbal abuse, threatened incarceration, or the possibility of physical violence. Civil rights Freedom Riders who responded to mob attacks with nonviolence in the summer of 1961, for example, clearly practiced courage while resisting segregation in the American South.

A less well developed perspective is that communication, connection, and dialogue with allies and potential allies can require the practice of courage as well. For example, Audre Lorde speaks of the courage feminists have needed to confront racism within their own groups. Women of color have practiced courage by breaking the silence about racism; white women have practiced courage by not turning away from the painful recognition of their own racist practices. By courageously confronting racism, Lorde argues, feminists have strengthened their alliances (Lorde 1984b). Like resistance activities, these connection and coalition activities are important dimensions of the practice of dissident citizenship. In both cases, discourses and practices of courage shape political engagement and action, even under conditions of uncertainty and especially in contexts where dissident citizens face domination and oppression. Although contemporary democratic theory offers little guidance for considering the role of courage in democratic life, attending to the way that conceptions of courage are used to shape and mediate dissent allows us to explore the ways that dissident citizenship itself is negotiated and performed. Exploring courage will also draw attention to how dissident citizenship is constructed and negotiated in gendered, raced, and classed terms.

In this essay, I construct an account of dissident citizenship that includes attention to political courage and that offers an approach for exploring the dissident practices of women. Drawing on feminist theorizing about oppositional citizenship, multidisciplinary work on women's activism, and activist accounts of dissent, I argue for a conception of citizenship that recognizes both dissent and an ethic of political courage as vital elements of democratic participation. After briefly exploring a case study of women's activism, I conclude with some reflections on what this approach offers to democratic theorists and others interested in women's citizenship and public activities.

Contemporary Perspectives on Citizenship

To understand how dissent has fallen through the cracks of much mainstream democratic theory, it is helpful to review how that theory conceptualizes citizenship and the role of conflict in democratic life. In the liberal democratic tradition of political thought, conflict between citizens is expected and institutionalized. As exemplified in the work of theorists such as John Rawls (1971, 1985), Ronald Dworkin (1978), and Robert Nozick (1974), this tradition conceives of citizens as legitimately self-interested individuals who have agreed (contracted) to respect each other's individual liberty and interests.[1] Governments are charged with enforcing this respect, and should provide enough protection and regulation to preserve individuals' abilities to pursue their diverse interests and ends, especially in the marketplace. But because citizens also need protection from powerful governments, certain activities and spaces are withdrawn from legitimate public interference and are protected as "rights." Furthermore, citizens are granted an additional check on their government by way of regular elections.

Politics, according to this view, is the process of resolving the inevitable conflicts and disputes that will result when citizens pursue their interests and their individual conceptions of the good life. These conflicts, however, will be resolved by representatives, not by citizens themselves. Citizens who "lose" in a conflict, furthermore, are expected to respect the decision, even if they begin the institutionalized process of disagreement again. Under the liberal democratic view of political life, in sum, conflict is a given but is tamed by established institutional forms of expression.

As Mary Dietz has observed, "This vision of the citizen as the bearer of rights, democracy as the capitalist market society, and politics as representative government is precisely what makes liberalism, despite its admirable and vital insistence on the values of individual freedom and equality, seem so politically barren to so many of its critics" (Dietz 1987, 5–6). Communitarian theorists such as Michael Sandel (1982, 1984) and Alasdair MacIntyre (1981), for example, find the liberal vision of suspicious, self-interested, isolated citizens tremendously impoverished. In Sandel's view, "we cannot be wholly unencumbered [liberal] subjects of possession, individuated in advance and given prior to our ends" (Sandel 1984, 166). He and MacIntyre insist instead on the "embeddedness" of individuals (and therefore citizens) in their communities. In contrast to the liberal celebration of individual rights and self-interest, communitarians claim that what is in the interest of an individual is inextricably tied to what is good for a community as a whole: "my identity is not independent of my aims and attachments, but partly constituted by them; I am situated from the start, embedded in a history which locates me among others, and implicates my good in the good of the communities whose stories I share" (Sandel 1984, 9). Citizenship thus becomes the project of cooperatively seeking the good for a community, *as a* community, rather than as self-interested individuals.

In the "local forms of community" that communitarians favor, conflict—or at least serious conflict—seems to disappear. The "central bond" of a communitarian community, MacIntyre argues, is "a shared vision of and understanding of goods" (MacIntyre 1981, 258). This shared vision, along with attention to traditions and to one's history and roles, provide guidance for community interactions that ideally embody "civility" (MacIntyre 1981, 263) and, one gathers, a high degree of consensus. In a community where values and a sense of the common good are shared, citizens are not adversaries, as liberal democrats would have us believe, but something closer to friends or perhaps even relatives. Unlike the liberal democratic view, which leaves immutable conflict at the heart of public life, communitarians suggest that citizen concern for the common good makes cooperation flourish and conflict disappear.

Recent participatory theorists join the communitarians in finding the liberal conception of citizenship too limited and adversarial, yet propose a quite different vision of human living together in response. Drawing on traditions and sources as diverse as Greek political thought, Italian Renaissance civic republicanism, the writings of Jean-Jacques Rousseau, Alexis de Tocqueville, the American pragmatists, and Hannah Arendt, contemporary participatory theorists have argued for a conception of citizenship that puts citizen action and self-government at the center of political life (Pateman 1970; Mansbridge 1980; Barber 1984; Dietz 1987; Habermas 1989; Young 1990; Fraser 1992). It is only through the active participation of citizens, these theorists argue, that democracy becomes legitimate: "Men and women who are not directly responsible through common deliberation, common decision, and common action for the policies that determine their common lives together are not really free at all, however much they enjoy security, private rights, and freedom from interference" (Barber 1984, 145–46).

Citizenship in a participatory democracy, therefore, requires significant participation in common institutions of self-government, institutions "designed to facilitate ongoing civic participation in agenda-setting, deliberation, legislation, and policy implementation (in the form of 'common work')" (Barber 1984, 151). These participatory institutions, by transforming strangers into citizen-neighbors through common conversations and projects, enable citizens to envision and articulate "a common future in terms of genuinely common goods" (Barber 1984, 197). And as Benjamin Barber argues in *Strong Democracy*, this common vision need not be purchased by suppressing conflict or by sacrificing individual interests. Conflict and disagreement, Barber insists, can instead be transformed by citizen deliberation and action.

> Participatory politics deals with public disputes and conflicts of interest by subjecting them to a never-ending process of deliberation, decision, and action. . . . In such communities, public ends are neither extrapolated from absolutes nor "discovered" in a preexisting "hidden consensus." They are literally forged through the act of public participation, created through common deliberation and common action and the effect that deliberation and action have on interests, which change shape and direction when subjected to these participatory processes. (Barber 1984, 151–52)

Unlike the liberal democratic vision of citizenship, which views conflict as something merely to be tolerated or managed, conflict in a participatory democracy becomes an occasion for learning and for actively creating consensus where none existed before.[2] Citizens learn, through democratic interaction with other citizens, how to enlarge their vision of their own freedom and interests to include others (Barber 1984, 232). The result is a form of democratic life, Barber argues, that respects both individual and mutual purposes.

Barber's vision of participatory democracy, although powerful, has been challenged persuasively by other participatory theorists. These theorists are critical (sometimes intensely so) of Barber's failure to recognize deep-seated inequalities that affect participation and interaction in public life. As an example, some theorists flatly reject Barber's case for putting political equality before economic equality, and for assuming that common talk and common action can take place in the presence of the systematic inequalities produced under capitalism. Samuel Bowles and Herbert Gintis, for instance, present a compelling argument for why the economy must be subject to democratic accountability in a society that values equality and participation (Bowles and Gintis 1986). In a similar vein, Richard Flacks has argued recently that democratic societies must discover ways to democratically control the movement and impact of global capital while simultaneously creating more participatory economic institutions and practices (Flacks 1996). Meaningful political participation, these theorists insist, requires some sort of substantive economic equality (Fraser 1992, 118–21).

In addition, Iris Marion Young has criticized Barber's inattention to the deep-seated inequalities produced by the cultural imperialism practiced by dominant social groups. Cultural imperialism, in Young's view, is "the universalization of a dominant group's experience and culture, and its establishment as the norm" (1990, 59). Although she supports Barber's vision of a democratic society where all people participate in public discussion and decisionmaking, Young takes Barber to task for defining the public realm as one in which social and cultural differences must be "submerged" in favor of apparently neutral deliberation about "the common good." In Barber's strong democracy, Young observes, "The pursuit of particular interests, the pressing of the claims of particular groups, all must take place within a framework of community and common vision established by the public realm" (1990, 117). This is problematic because dominant groups have the power to "project their own experiences as representative of humanity as such" (1990, 59). Public discussions framed in terms of community, common vision, and unity, "as opposed to group affinity and particular need and interest," Young argues, consequently privilege the voices and perspectives of dominant groups who "dominate the allegedly common public" (1990, 117). Any legitimate public conflict, consequently, is precluded by a fraudulent consensus. (See also Mansbridge 1980; 1990, 127.)

Although she respects Barber's desire to counter the liberal vision of atomistic, self-interested individuals, Young argues that it is not necessary to replace that vision with a falsely homogenizing "ideal of community." Instead, Young supports the creation of what she terms "a heterogeneous public."

> The repoliticization of public life does not require the creation of a unified public realm in which citizens leave behind their particular group affiliations, histories, and needs to discuss a mythical "common good." In a society differentiated by social groups, occupations, political positions, differences of privilege and oppression, regions, and so on, the perception of anything like a common good can only be an outcome of public interaction that expresses rather than submerges particularities. . . . Indeed, in open and accessible public spaces and forums, one should expect to encounter and hear from those who are different, whose social perspectives, experience, and affiliations are different. To promote a politics of inclusion, then, participatory democrats must promote the ideal of a heterogeneous public, in which persons stand forth with their differences acknowledged and respected, though perhaps not completely understood by others. (Young 1990, 119)

Citizenship, in Young's heterogeneous public, thus takes the form of participation in public discussion and decisionmaking, but in an institutional context that "equalizes the ability of oppressed groups to speak and be heard" (1990, 189). Institutional mechanisms and public resources should support group representation by providing for the self-organization of oppressed groups, the group generation and analysis of policy proposals, and group veto power regarding specific policies (1990, 184). Group representation, Young concludes, prevents oppression, draws conflict into the open, and provides all social groups with the resources for meaningful participation in joint agenda-setting, deliberation, decision, and action.[3]

Although Young does not confine the principles of group representation to representative bodies in government settings, clearly her proposal has an institutional focus. All her examples are decisionmaking bodies; the "democratized publics" she talks about are institutional ones. While both Barber and Young have considered ways to expand democracy within current institutions, democratic theorists drawing from the work of Jürgen Habermas have drawn attention to an additional realm of participation, what Habermas and others have called "the public sphere." The public sphere, in Nancy Fraser's words,

> designates a theater in modern societies in which political participation is enacted through the medium of talk. It is the space in which citizens deliberate about their common affairs, and hence an institutionalized arena of discursive interaction. This arena is conceptually distinct from the state; it is a site for the production and circulation of discourses that can in principle be critical of the state. The public sphere in Habermas's sense is also conceptually distinct from the official economy; it is not an arena of market relations but rather one of discursive relations, a theater for debating and deliberating rather than for buying and selling. (Fraser 1992, 110–11)

In recent years, theorists drawing on the notion of the ideal public sphere have defended a conception of democracy variously termed "deliberative democracy," "proceduralist-deliberative democracy," "discursive democracy," or "communicative democracy." (See esp. Habermas 1987 and 1989; Dryzek 1990; Fishkin 1991; Joshua Cohen 1989; Mansbridge 1992; Benhabib 1996a.) Deliberative theorists join the participatory theorists in advocating significant political participation and "the widest-reaching democratization of decisionmaking processes" possible, but they expand the focus on political participation to "a more inclusively understood concept of discursive will formation" (Benhabib 1992, 86). In the words of Seyla Benhabib, under the deliberative conception of democracy, participation is seen not as an activity only possible in a narrowly defined political realm but as an activity that can be realized in the social and cultural spheres as well. Participating in a citizen's initiative to clean up a polluted harbor is no less political than debating in cultural journals the pejorative presentation of certain groups in terms of stereotypical images (combating sexism and racism in the media). (Benhabib 1992, 86)

Citizenship in a deliberative democracy, consequently, means participating in "the determination of norms of action through the practical debate of all affected by them" (Benhabib 1992, 86). The precise rules that should govern the practical debate are a matter of some dispute (see, e.g., Habermas 1996; Joshua Cohen 1996; Young 1996), but this more expansive notion of participation as talk and deliberation in a variety of settings, Benhabib claims, "articulates a vision of the political true to the realities of complex, modern societies" (Benhabib 1992, 86).[4]

Dissent and Democratic Life

The participatory and deliberative views of citizenship as citizen participation and joint deliberation and action offer provocative visions of the possibilities for democratic societies in the late twentieth century. Strikingly absent from this work, however, is sustained attention to the role of dissent in democratic life. Theorists who do talk about dissent, furthermore, tend to raise the issue only in terms of *verbal deliberative* dissent. For example, Barber confines his discussion of dissent to his chapter on democratic talk and judgment.[5] "A healthy democratic community," Barber notes, will

leave room for the expression of distrust, dissent, or just plain opposition, even in lost causes where dissenters are very much in the minority. Here the function of talk is to allow people to vent their grievances or frustration or opposition, not in hopes of moving others but in order to give public status to their strongly held personal convictions. The cry "In spite of all, *I believe* . . . " is the hallmark of such usage, and conscientious objection to military service is an illuminating example. (Barber 1984, 192)

Dissenters can also register continuing opposition even after a decision has been made.

"I am part of the community, I participated in the talk and deliberation leading to the decision, and so I regard myself as bound; but let it be known that I do not think we have made the right decision," says the dissenter in a strong democracy. He means thus not to change the decision this time, for it has been taken, but to bear witness to another point of view (and thereby to keep the issue on the public agenda). (Barber 1984, 192)[6]

As Barber's examples suggest, dissent is not simply resistance (e.g., Cooper 1995, chs. 2 and 7). Dissenters do not exit the political collective when they "lose" in a discussion. Neither do they simply change their minds, or remain silent. Instead, to dissent is to maintain a principled oppositional stance against a more powerful group while remaining politically and publicly engaged. But the dissent that Barber seems to have in mind here passes verbally between people who remain participatory and deliberative equals, people who have equal standing and membership *within* the strong democratic public. "*I participated* in the talk and deliberation leading to the decision," says Barber's dissenter. Barber's dissenting actions are undertaken by equals who are only *temporarily* outnumbered during one episode of public deliberation.

But why limit dissent to interactions *within* a decisionmaking community, between deliberative partners? Barber's vision of citizenship and the minimal role reserved for dissent would exclude from the realm of legitimate public action the important activities undertaken by those citizens who are *not* in fact participatory or deliberative equals. Barber and indeed most democratic theorists pay no attention to actions that challenge the structure or practices of political institutions, that highlight inequality and exclusion within the collective, that assert independence on the part of those citizens who are less powerful, that are intended to educate or change the minds of the more powerful, or that challenge the boundaries of the political itself. By focusing almost exclusively on the debates and deliberative interactions of those citizens on the "inside," most democratic theorists have missed the important dissident activities of those citizens on the "outside."

We clearly need to consider these forms of dissident citizen action as central to an adequate conception of democratic citizenship. To dissent, whether one has an acknowledged place at the deliberative table or not, is to be an engaged, active, self-governed citizen. To dissent when one faces domination and oppression, furthermore, marks a level of commitment to participatory democracy rarely matched by nondissenting citizens. Dissent has been a persistent, if sometimes vexing, visitor in the house of democracy; perhaps it is time to unpack its bags, welcome it home, and acknowledge its rightful place in our democratic lives.

Theorizing Dissident Citizenship

I suggested earlier in this essay that dissident democratic citizenship can usefully be conceptualized as the public contestation of prevailing arrangements of power by marginalized citizens through oppositional, democratic, noninstitutionalized practices that augment or replace institutionalized channels of democratic opposition when those channels are inadequate or unavailable. At this point, let me clarify what I mean by oppositional, democratic, noninstitutionalized dissident practices by way of a more general discussion about opposition within democratic polities.

In the broadest terms, people living in democratic polities can conceivably contest prevailing norms, decisions, laws, and other arrangements of power through a range of nondemocratic and democratic practices. Choices include: 1) using violence (either as revolutionaries or as terrorists); 2) exiting (either as emigrants or as internal separatists); 3) remaining in the polity but deliberately choosing silence or inaction rather than participation (as nonvoters and other nonparticipants); 4) using the formal, institutionalized channels of democratic contestation that address the state (as voters, as lobbyists, as plaintiffs in legal cases against the state); 5) using the institutionalized but marginalized channels of democratic contestation that address the state and the wider polity (as members of oppositional organizations such as the NAACP or the National Organization for Women); or 6) using the noninstitutionalized and marginalized channels of democratic contestation that address both the state and the wider polity (as demonstrators, as civil disobedients).[7] While all six of these practices contest power arrangements and are therefore oppositional, only the last three are democratic, and only the last two are dissident. For example, although violence and terrorism might communicate opposition rather effectively, they are not democratic practices because they collapse the space for collective debate and contestation with the use or threat of violence. Exit, separatism, and silence are also not democratic practices because they involve the failure to participate in collective political engagement at all. On the other hand, institutionalized, state-centered ways of contesting power arrangements (such as filing petitions, voting in a referendum, lobbying an elected official), while both oppositional and democratic, are not dissent in the broader sense because citizens (in theory) engage in these institutionalized practices as participatory equals.[8]

Although Barber and others apply the term "dissent" to institutionalized forms of political opposition between equals (for example, the Supreme Court's practice of dissenting opinions), dissent in fact covers a much wider range of political practices and need not involve interaction between institutional equals. Indeed, an alternative meaning of dissent derives from the actions of those activists we most commonly call dissidents—the internationally known activists, such as India's Mahatma Gandhi, the former Czechoslovakia's Vaclav Havel, or Burma's Aung

San Suu Kyi, who advocate engaged, usually nonviolent opposition against their own repressive, undemocratic governments. These dissidents, unlike Barber's dissenters, are not participatory equals temporarily outnumbered during one episode of public deliberation. Instead, these activists contest current power arrangements from the margins of their nondemocratic polities because they have no institutionalized channels of opposition available or because they lack meaningful access to those channels. Dissidents in democratic societies can certainly engage in both institutionalized and noninstitutionalized forms of marginalized contestation simultaneously; the form of dissent I will concentrate on here, however, will be the oppositional, democratic, noninstitutionalized forms of contestation that marginalized citizens use to address more powerful groups.

To flesh out this understanding of dissident citizenship, and, in particular, to think through the range of practices that dissident citizenship can involve, it is useful to draw on three primary resources: the work of feminist democratic theorists on oppositional citizenship within stratified societies, the recent multidisciplinary work on women's activism, and activist accounts of dissent.[9]

As noted earlier, many democratic theorists ignore the contributions of dissenting citizens to democratic life. A small number of feminist democratic theorists, however, have begun theorizing about oppositional citizenship within stratified societies. One of the most important contributions to this endeavor is Nancy Fraser's conception of subaltern counterpublics (Fraser 1992). According to Fraser, Habermas's ideal public sphere of citizen discursive interaction ignores both the historical reality of a multitude of alternative competing publics and the likelihood that in stratified societies, "arrangements that accommodate contestation among a plurality of competing publics better promote the ideal of participatory parity than does a single, comprehensive, overarching public" (Fraser 1992, 122). Fraser suggests calling these alternative publics "*subaltern counterpublics* in order to signal that they are parallel discursive arenas where members of subordinated social groups invent and circulate counterdiscourses to formulate oppositional interpretations of their identities, interests, and needs" (Fraser 1992, 123, emphasis in original).

According to Fraser, subaltern counterpublics play at least two important roles in stratified societies.

> On the one hand, they function as spaces of withdrawal and regroupment; on the other hand, they also function as bases and training grounds for agitational activities directed toward wider publics. It is precisely in the dialectic between these two functions that their emancipatory potential resides. This dialectic enables subaltern counterpublics partially to offset, although

not wholly to eradicate, the unjust participatory privileges enjoyed by members of dominant social groups in stratified societies. (Fraser 1992, 124)

Drawing on this portion of Fraser's work, Jane Mansbridge suggests that the protective function of subaltern counterpublics is especially critical for democratic life. In Mansbridge's view, "democracies need to foster and value informal deliberative enclaves of resistance in which those who lose in each coercive move can rework their ideas and their strategies, gathering their forces and deciding in a more protected space in what way or whether to continue the battle" (Mansbridge 1996, 47). (See also Scott 1990; 1985.) Oppositional enclaves protect the "underdogs" (including dissidents) from silencing, and allow them to continue injecting their competing discourses and visions into the mainstream public sphere discussion (Mansbridge 1996, 58).

Fraser's own work has tended to focus more on the "agitational" dimension of subaltern counterpublics. Fraser's discussion of "the politics of need interpretation" in her 1989 book *Unruly Practices*, for example, notes the important oppositional activities undertaken by subaltern counterpublics.

By insisting on speaking publicly of heretofore depoliticized needs, by claiming for these needs the status of legitimate political issues, such persons and groups do several things simultaneously. First, they contest the established boundaries separating "politics" from "economics" and "domestics." Second, they offer alternative interpretations of their needs embedded in alternative chains of in-order-to relations. Third, they create new discourse publics from which they try to disseminate their interpretations of the needs throughout a wide range of different discourse publics. Finally, they challenge, modify, and/or displace hegemonic elements of the means of interpretation and communication; they invent new forms of discourse for interpreting their needs. (Fraser 1989, 171)[10]

If we are interested in creating a more equal and just participatory democracy, Fraser insists, we need a much better understanding of how these contestatory discursive interactions between unequal publics work. Drawing on the work of George Eley, Fraser proposes a conceptual starting point.

George Eley suggests that we think of the public sphere (in stratified societies) as "the structured setting where cultural and ideological contest or negotiation among a variety of publics takes place." This formulation does justice to the multiplicity of public arenas in stratified societies by expressly acknowledging the presence and activity of "a variety of publics." At the

same time, it also does justice to the fact that these various publics are situated in a single "structured setting" that advantages some and disadvantages others. Finally, Eley's formulation does justice to the fact that in stratified societies the discursive relations among differentially empowered
publics are as likely to take the form of contestation as that of deliberation.
(Fraser 1992, 125, quoting Eley 1992)

Fraser's idea of subaltern counterpublics, when put in the context of this
expanded notion of the public sphere, provides a way to conceptualize
the participatory citizenship (both oppositional and nonoppositional) of
both marginalized and nonsubordinated groups.[11] In addition, this formulation takes inequality's effects on participation seriously, puts discursive contestation and dissent at the heart of citizenship along with deliberation, and provides a way to take note of the historically specific
discursive participation of those not engaged in formal politics.[12]

As Fraser observes, "Discourses are historically specific, socially situated, signifying practices. They are the communicative frames in which
speakers interact by exchanging speech acts" (1997, 160). Although
Fraser's conception of discursive contestation seems to encompass both
verbal and nonverbal practices, the distinction Joan Landes uses in her
work on the citizenship of women in the French Revolution is helpful
here: she differentiates between the discourse and *performance* of citizenship (Landes 1996). The idea of a performance captures the crucial sense
of citizenship as something that is both scripted by discourse and yet enacted (and sometimes *re*scripted) by historically situated agents.[13] When
this idea is joined with Fraser's insights about discursive contestation,
both discursive and performative forms of dissenting interactions between marginalized and nonmarginalized publics are highlighted.

Civil disobedience and nonviolent direct action are by far the showiest
and most widely recognized forms of performative dissenting practices.
But some of the recent multidisciplinary work on women's activism offers a wider-ranging and much more complex account of resistance and
oppositional performances. In addition to greatly expanding our knowledge of women's actual participation in public life, the historians, political scientists, sociologists, anthropologists, and other scholars engaged in
this work have drawn attention to the important facilitating and organizing activities that women perform in the service of dissident social movements.[14] Vicki Crawford, for example, has documented the crucial organizing roles played by African American women in the Mississippi
struggle for civil rights (Crawford 1990; see also Payne 1990 and 1995).
Carol Mueller has studied the influence of Ella Baker's organizing activities on the development of African American student activism in the
1960s (Mueller 1990). In addition to these more publicly oriented exam-

ples, scholars have also pointed out the political impact of women's forms of "everyday resistance." Bonnie Thornton Dill, for example, has documented the personal and political effects of workplace resistance engaged in by African American domestic workers (Dill 1988).

As Sara Evans and Martha Ackelsberg have both noted, these studies of women's activism challenge old notions of what counts as political participation. In particular, these studies suggest what Sara Evans has called a more "dynamic understanding of the links between public and private (domestic) life," an understanding that recognizes the realm of voluntary associations (what she and Harry Boyte elsewhere call "free spaces") as a realm of public action (Evans 1993, 131–32; Evans and Boyte 1986). Martha Ackelsberg has likewise noted that "attention to the many forms of women's activism and resistance highlights the limitations" of dichotomies such as public and private, community and workplace (Ackelsberg 1988, 302). By integrating women's experiences of activism into political theory, she contends, we would

> recognize that politics is not a narrow range of behaviors undertaken by a few, meant to influence the formal structures of governmental power. Rather, it is precisely that web of activities in which people engage out of concerns generated by their daily lives. For many of the women whose lives are reflected in this volume [Bookman and Morgen 1988], political life is community life; politics is attending to the quality of life in households, communities, and workplaces. (Ackelsberg 1988, 308)

As these studies suggest, oppositional dissenting practices can take many forms (discursive, performative, organizational, and everyday dissent) and show up in many locations (communities, households, workplaces). By paying attention to a wider variety of oppositional dissenting performances and their contexts, we not only recognize the public participation of women more readily but provide fuller accounts of instances of dissident citizenship.

The scholars working on women's activism also point out the importance of understanding the material conditions, institutions, and ideas that shape dissenting interactions between marginalized and nonsubordinated publics. For example, studies on material conditions and institutions reveal how divisions of labor (sexual and racial), workplace rules, access to media publicity, and the availability of recourse to the courts have all shaped the forms of dissident performances chosen by activists (see, e.g., the studies in Laslett et al. 1995). Studies exploring the discourses used within and among unequal publics have considered the impact on activism of ideas about maternal roles (Bayard de Vola 1997), as well as female consciousness and female solidarity (Kaplan 1982), and

have explored "how gender identities are deployed in political discourses and mobilized by political actors and to what effect" (Laslett et
al. 1995, 1; see also West and Blumberg 1990, Taylor and Whittier 1992).[15]
Other studies have considered the impact on dissent of ideas about nationalism (Hine 1993), community (Roydhouse 1993), and needs (Frederickson 1993). This scholarly attention to how issues are framed and contested both within and among groups has added a particularly valuable
dimension to our understanding of women's activism.

One additional and particularly influential kind of discourse is discourse about dissent itself. There is, for example, in the United States a
long tradition of self-conscious reflection on the part of activists about
the role of dissent in democratic life.[16] Famous tracts, such as Henry
David Thoreau's 1849 "Resistance to Civil Government" and Martin
Luther King's 1963 "Letter from Birmingham Jail," often become touch-
stones for other activists by providing persuasive justifications for dissent and arguments about its proper form and limits. King, for example,
was influenced both by Gandhi's writings on nonviolence and Thoreau's
argument that citizens worthy of the name must withdraw their support
from an evil system (King 1958, 51, 85). In turn, King influenced the people of Montgomery, Alabama, and eventually people all over the world
with his argument that nonviolent dissenting citizens help publicize inequality and injustice while aiding in the creation of tension and crises
that force negotiation and change on the part of the more powerful. By
looking at the discourse activists use to talk about their own dissenting
actions, then, we often find a powerful shaping influence on dissident citizenship. Activist accounts of dissent also provide important interpretations of and information about the performances, conditions, and ideas
surrounding moments of dissident citizenship. These firsthand accounts,
therefore, are an important complement to more scholarly studies of dissidence.

A Brief Case Study: Reconsidering Rosa Parks

As the preceding section suggests, a theoretical conception of dissident
citizenship should attend to four elements of democratic life: 1) the oppositional, democratic interactions between marginal and nonsubordinated
citizens, or between what Fraser calls "unequal publics;" 2) the variety of
discursive, performative, organizational, and "everyday" dissenting actions within and between those unequal publics that augment or replace
institutionalized forms of democratic opposition; 3) the material and institutional contexts that shape dissenting noninstitutionalized actions between unequal publics; and 4) the ideas and discourses that shape and
influence democratic dissent, especially discourses about democracy, citi-

zenship, and dissent itself. How would this conception of dissident citizenship help us understand more clearly Rosa Parks's famous refusal to give up her seat to a white man on a Montgomery, Alabama, bus in 1955, and the bus boycott that her arrest prompted?

First of all, we would be encouraged to note the large number of publics and counterpublics involved in the Montgomery bus boycott. On the broadest level, of course, there were the pro-segregation publics and anti-segregation counterpublics. Important pro-segregation publics included the mayor of Montgomery and other white elected political officials; the white police force; the white bus drivers and their supervisors; the white economic elite, including most of Montgomery's business owners; the white-owned media; the elite white women who employed African American cooks, maids, and other domestics; working-class whites; and the Montgomery White Citizens Council, an organization dedicated to maintaining segregation. Anti-segregation counterpublics included the local chapter of the NAACP; the Women's Political Council (WPC), a large group of mostly middle-class African American women who had been actively working for better treatment of African Americans in Montgomery for several years; the Montgomery Improvement Association (MIA), the massive community organization formed after the boycott started; the executive board of the MIA; the ministers of the African American churches in Montgomery; the congregations of those churches; the faculty at Alabama State College, a historically black college in Montgomery; the working-class African Americans who relied heavily on the bus system; and white anti-segregation allies.

A number of authors have written about the complex interactions (not all of them democratic) within and among these publics (see esp. King 1958; Durr 1985; Robinson 1987; Burks 1990; Hampton and Fayer 1990; Graetz 1991). Guided by this conception of dissident citizenship, however, researchers would specifically explore the noninstitutionalized democratic discursive and performative exchanges between the more powerful white segregationist publics and the anti-segregation counterpublics. In addition to the easily visible performative dissent of the boycott itself, scholars would consider more carefully the impact of the regular mass meetings held in African American churches, where persuasion, decisionmaking, fundraising, and morale boosting took place. The crucial organizational work behind the scenes of the boycott would be recognized (see esp. Robinson 1987), as would forms of "everyday resistance." Some African American domestic workers, for example, claimed no involvement with the boycott when quizzed by their segregationist employers, yet continued to find "excuses" for not needing to ride the buses (Robinson 1987; Durr 1985). The complex and sometimes strained relationships between subaltern counterpublics would receive greater scrutiny: for example, between the male ministerial leadership and the female WPC organizers (Robinson 1987); between white activists and black activists (Durr 1985; Graetz 1991; King 1958; Robinson 1987); and between middle-class and working-class boycott participants (Hampton and Fayer 1990). Researchers might also seek more information about the wider networks of community activism in Montgomery, not just the political ones that joined with or grew out of the churches (Ackelsberg 1988).

Guided by this conception of dissident citizenship, scholars would also note the material influences on dissent in Montgomery. For example, the presence of a relatively large, well-educated African American middle class in Montgomery made ongoing financial support of the boycott possible. The fact that the ridership of the buses was more than 75 percent African American made a boycott an extremely effective tactic (Robinson 1987). The presence of certain institutions also created particular opportunities and constraints during the boycott. For example, the African American churches in Montgomery played crucial roles both because they provided large gathering spaces that were mostly free of white interference, and because their ministers could openly provide leadership for the boycott without being fired by a white employer. Faculty members at Alabama State College often had to be more circumspect in their participation, as did domestics and day laborers who worked almost exclusively for whites.

Finally, scholars would explore the influential discourses used in and among the unequal publics. For example, many of the participants framed the goal of the boycott in political terms: they spoke about "the right to protest for right," and demanded to be treated with "human dignity" and as "first-class citizens." In contrast, day-to-day participation in the boycott was largely framed in religious terms. For example, the ministers often used the language of "turning the other cheek," and "loving your enemies" when speaking about nonviolence. The combination of citizenship and religious language proved powerful; segregationist whites had to do discursive battle with two frameworks that occupied sacred positions in U.S. politics.[17] Perhaps the familiarity of the religious language also helped African Americans unused to explicit political action decide to participate.

By using this conception of dissident citizenship, we gain an understanding of the Montgomery bus boycott as a complex series of discursive and performative interactions between a multitude of unequal publics, shaped by specific material conditions, particular institutional constraints, and distinct discourses about citizenship, dissent, and nonviolence. Using this approach also helps recast and reclaim the meaning of Rosa Parks's initial dissenting action. The story most people "know" about Rosa Parks is remarkable primarily for its individualistic spin. Parks appears (at least in this short version) as a relatively isolated actor, as someone who—in a moment of fatigue—suddenly snapped, as someone whose dissent against racism was spontaneous and unconsidered. If we explore the interactions between unequal publics and attend to the material, institutional, and discursive context of Parks's act, however, what emerges under the lens of this conception of dissident citizenship is a Rosa Parks who was active in a web of dissident counterpublics *both before and after* her arrest. Her action consequently emerges as a principled dissenting act rather than simply a spontaneous, impulsive, or fatigued one.

It is not especially well known, for example, that Parks spent two weeks at a training workshop for activists at the integrated Highlander Folk School a few months before her arrest. Although the workshop dealt primarily with the Supreme Court's 1954 *Brown versus Board of Education* decision and school desegregation, the strategy of civil disobedience was discussed in detail (Clark 1986, 7; Langston 1990, 153). Parks was also an active member of the local branch of the NAACP and had served as secretary a few years earlier. Parks's refusal to give up her seat on the bus was almost certainly unplanned (see Parks 1956, 1977; Burks 1990), but she was clearly conscious of and resentful of racial discrimination, aware of the strategy of nonviolent direct action, and apparently willing to take some risks in order to be active. Indeed, soon after her arrest, Parks lost her job at a white-owned department store. She eventually had to move away from Montgomery to find work.

It is also extremely likely that Parks knew the NAACP had been looking for a test case on bus segregation to take to the Supreme Court for some time, even if she did not intend to become the plaintiff herself. She also would have been aware of the parameters a test case needed to meet: the plaintiff had to be arrested in spite of obeying the law. This is precisely what happened to Parks; she was not sitting in the whites only section, as some other African Americans had been when arrested. Rather, Parks was sitting in the part of the bus reserved for African Americans, and was arrested for refusing to give up her seat to a white man when the front of the bus was full.

Parks was also a long-time member of the Women's Political Council (WPC). The WPC had been involved in negotiations with the bus company manager about the specific behaviors of white drivers and had threatened a possible boycott more than a year before Parks's arrest. Jo Ann Robinson, the president of the WPC in 1955, has revealed the WPC's extensive involvement in organizing and sustaining the boycott in her autobiography (Robinson 1987). When Parks was arrested, for example, it was the women of the WPC who swung into action first. The black

ministers, including Martin Luther King, Jr. and George Abernathy, met
for the first time the night *after* the WPC had distributed thirty-five thousand leaflets to the African American community calling for the boycott.

Knowing about Parks's memberships in these various oppositional
counterpublics, it should be emphasized, does nothing to lessen the
power of her dissident act. On the contrary, knowing that Parks did not
simply stumble into her dissent raises a crucial question: Why, with full
knowledge of what she was risking (her body, her job, her reputation),
did Parks dissent anyway?

Political Courage and Dissident Citizenship

The dissident practices of Rosa Parks and others involved in the Montgomery bus boycott point to the last important piece of an adequate conception of dissident citizenship: attention to the discourse and practice of
political courage. Because of its intimate association with the individually heroic (and usually violent) actions of soldiers, courage might at first
seem hopelessly out of place in a discussion about democratic engagement with other citizens. But even contemporary and seemingly apolitical uses of the term suggest an alternative view. Soldiers, firefighters, police officers, and other people are said to demonstrate courage when they
face personal danger; for example, the soldier who shields a comrade
from a grenade, the person who enters a burning building to make sure
no one is trapped. Athletes and injured people are also said to demonstrate courage in facing pain or rehabilitation; for example, the distance
runner who completes the marathon in spite of an injury, the stroke survivor who must with painful effort relearn the art of walking. As these
examples make clear, those we commonly call courageous choose to keep
going when confronted with an obstacle or with danger. They are tenacious, committed to acting even when the outcome is uncertain. Courage,
we might say, is a commitment to persistence and resolution in the face of
risk, uncertainty, or fear.

Conceptualized in this way, the importance of courage as a guiding
principle for political engagement and action becomes more evident. Although contemporary democratic theory is relatively silent on the subject
of courage, a number of political theorists have, in fact, considered
courage central to political action. In particular, those who draw from the
classical tradition have offered important explorations of the role of political courage in democratic life.

Many of the most explicit accounts of the courage necessary for public
life in the classical tradition discuss the warrior courage of soldiers and
heroes. Courage, in this view, enables the warrior to gain personal glory
while defending the existing community from external harm. In the

Homeric epics, for example, Odysseus, Agamemnon, Hektor, and the other warriors display courage when they are engaged in physical conflict on the battlefield. Courage in this case is conceptualized as an individual quality or virtue, a quality associated with facing danger, and especially death, nobly (though not necessarily without fear). Courage is also tied closely to notions of honor, physical prowess, kinship bonds, and defense of homeland and household. It is a quality that, when displayed, can assure a warrior's individual and immortal glory, and when absent, can assure his equally individual and immortal shame.[18]

In Plato's discussion of courage in *The Republic,* what Socrates calls civic courage is likewise linked to defense of the homeland, in this case the defense of the polis. The auxiliaries are described as "moderate and courageous warrior-athletes" (Plato 1992, book 3, 416) and are charged with defending the city from external enemies. But the courage Socrates insists the warriors must possess is not sporadically or individually called into existence on the battlefield for personal glory, but rather is a sustained "belief about what things are to be feared," even when those beliefs are challenged by "pains, pleasures, desires, or fears" (Plato 1992, book 4, 429). Civic courage, in other words, is a steadfastness, a disposition to be persistent, rather than an extraordinary summoning of bravery or effort in the face of danger. This perspective is also found in the Platonic dialogue *Laches,* in which Laches's loyalty to the civic community gives him an "endurance of the soul" when confronted by danger of death or defeat (Plato 1990, 192b; see also Schwartz 1995, 2). This steadfast courage *can* enable one to take action as a warrior, but courage thereby becomes something defined by and exerted exclusively on behalf of the political community, not something chosen and performed primarily for individual honor.

In Aristotle's account of courage, judgment and action are added to the requirement of a steadfast disposition. In the *Nichomachean Ethics,* courage is described as the mean between confidence and fear, between brashness and cowardice (Aristotle 1962a, 1106a–1107b). A courageous man, Aristotle insists, is one "who endures and fears the right things, for the right motive, in the right manner, and at the right time, and who displays confidence in a similar way" (1115b). Thus courage does not mean the absence of fear or simply enduring fear, but instead involves both knowing what one *should* fear and *acting anyway.* Courage, in other words, requires judgment and enables action. Courageous actions, consequently, are not limited to the constancy or steadfastness of the civic citizen-soldier but can be performed in a variety of settings (a shipwreck, an illness, a death sentence).

One setting for courageous action that Aristotle does not explore is the realm of public deliberation. Other theorists drawing from the classical tradition, however, including Hannah Arendt and, more recently, Susan Bickford, have suggested that courage is a central component of participatory citizenship. Drawing on Arendt, Bickford argues that

> the quality that is essential for politics (beyond the shared capacity to start anew) is courage. Many examples remind us that physical courage is still a part of the courage necessary to disclose one's self in public. . . . But the courage to take political action goes beyond this physical courage, beyond "a willingness to suffer consequences." Since we can never know the consequences of action, "courage and even boldness are already present in leaving one's private hiding place and showing who one is, in disclosing and exposing one's self." (Bickford 1996, 68–69, quoting Arendt 1958, 186)

Citizens need courage, Bickford contends, "because politics is an inherently risky and uncertain enterprise where our actions can have unpredictable consequences and our words can be misunderstood" (Bickford 1996, 148). Courage is also critically important for what Bickford calls "pathbuilding," the joint interaction of citizens who are committed to understanding each other's perspectives and opinions. Pathbuilding is risky because it may require change from those who speak and listen together. Political courage, consequently, is necessary for citizens because it enables and guides action (in this case, speaking, listening, and change) in the presence of fear (Bickford 1996, 148–53).[19]

Taken together, the classical tradition, Arendt, and Bickford point out that political courage is simultaneously a principle that guides and enables action in the presence of fear, and a practice that is displayed, performed, and given life in action. It is, to draw from the language of Landes once again, both a guiding script and an enacted performance. For citizens who wish to defend their existing community or constitute a new one via joint deliberation and action, as Bickford shows us, political courage is a key practice. Discourses of political courage also play a role, I wish to argue, in shaping and guiding the dissent of those citizens who undertake oppositional, democratic, noninstitutionalized, dissident actions. But even though courageous performances of dissident citizenship are relatively abundant, it is difficult to find sustained explorations of courage as a guiding principle of action in activist accounts of dissent. Before suggesting an explanation for this, let me point to a few examples.

If courage is understood as an active commitment to persistence and resolution in the face of risk, uncertainty, or fear, the United States tradition of dissent clearly provides a wealth of cases in which courage has served as an important guiding principle. Explicit references to courage, however, are few, and often equate courage with the *absence* of fear. Thoreau, for example, does not mention courage by name in his essay on civil disobedience. He does, however, appeal to his reader's "manhood": "O for a man who is a *man*, and, as my neighbor says, has a bone in his back which you cannot pass your hand through! . . . Is there not a sort of bloodshed when the conscience is wounded? Through this wound a man's real manhood and immortality flow out, and he bleeds to an ever-lasting death. I see this blood flowing now" (1849, 26, 30). Responsible citizens, Thoreau insists, will live up to the ideal of manly honor, get rid of their fear, and engage in dissent.

Martin Luther King, Jr., in his 1958 account of the Montgomery Bus Boycott, *Stride Toward Freedom*, also suggests that courageous dissidents do not experience fear. "It must be emphasized," he writes, "that nonviolent resistance is not a method for cowards; it does resist. If one uses this method because he is afraid or merely because he lacks the instruments of violence, he is not truly nonviolent" (1958, 217). For King, those who believe in the redemptive power of "turning the other cheek" also turn their fears over to God, and consequently have no need for a conception of courage that enables action in spite of fear. The Student Nonviolent Coordinating Committee's founding statement, which acknowledges a specific debt to the "Judaeo-Christian tradition," articulates a similar position on courage: "We affirm the philosophical or religious ideal of non-violence as the foundation of our purpose. . . . Through nonviolence, courage *displaces* fear; love transforms hate" (SNCC 1962, 222, emphasis added). For these activists, courage is a characteristic of people who are already unafraid, not a guiding principle for those dealing with fear.

Although some U.S. activists do allude to their fears, these references are often understated. An activist might talk about his heart "leaping" before a civil rights direct action or about the "trepidation" he feels during a frightening night in jail (Mahoney 1961, 234–43). An anti-Vietnam War protester might speak about the experience of facing tear gas, feeling "an impulse to turn and run away, mixed with the urge to bravely act the way the books on the theory of nonviolent power suggest" (Lane 1967, 280). Although religion and conscience may actually eliminate the fears of certain protesters, some of these activists are clearly afraid as they dissent. Why, then, is there such silence about the experience of fear?

Gender and Political Courage

One plausible reason that activists—especially male activists—avoid talking about being afraid is because fear is not manly. Thoreau's appeal to "real manhood" as the guiding light for political dissent hardly seems accidental or isolated. As another example, King describes a meeting of ministers in Montgomery in which one man berated the others for being "scared boys" rather than "fearless men" (King 1958, 57). American male activists—even those in the Civil Rights movement, the New Left, and the antiwar movements of the 1960s, who viewed themselves as progressive—have been resoundingly and justly charged with machismo and sexism (Clark 1986; Evans 1979; Echols 1989; Calvert 1991, 282). The kind of courage invoked by these and other male activists has often been manhood-proving, heterosexist courage.[20]

Of course, the classical tradition of political courage is by no means immune from sexism and heterosexism either. (See esp. Okin 1979; Saxonhouse 1985; Shanley and Pateman 1991; Coole 1993.) As Nancy Schwartz points out, Greek courage "occurs in the public sphere of life, the arena in which nobility can be seen. Standards of what is honorable derive from political society and require that the actors be free (so that they could have chosen to do otherwise) and equal (so that they are comparable in their capacities and responsibilities)" (Schwartz 1995, 8). Because Greek women were unfree, unequal, and consequently not allowed to participate in public life either as citizens or as warriors, courage as a practice was not an available option for them. In contrast, Schwartz notes, courage in ancient and medieval Jewish thought, though often linked to warrior courage, could nonetheless "appear in smaller settings." Indeed, individuals could "manifest courage in private, since there [was] considered to be free will and a relation to an external judge" (23). Esther, therefore, legitimately exhibited "civic courage" by nobly risking her life for her community, with no witnesses but the king and God (18–19). As another example, Hebrew midwives practiced courageous and principled disobedience in response to Pharaoh's decree in Exodus to kill all male newborns (Harris 1989).

Although Schwartz is quite right to reclaim these moments of women's political courage, both classical and contemporary conceptions of courage remain overwhelmingly masculinist and heterosexist.[21] Wendy Brown has addressed this conflation of masculinity and courage in her book *Manhood and Politics*.

> The historical symbiosis of courage and manliness has affixed courage with a comparatively narrow meaning and content. In the tradition of manhood, courage has been the willingness to risk death for an abstract aim and the effort to defy mortality through placing the body in peril. In the terms of manliness, courage is overcoming bodily fears and overcoming concerns for life. In contrast, I am suggesting that we need courage to *sustain* life, to fight for freedom as bearers of life and hence of possibility. A courageous deed is one which sets identity and security at risk in order to bring forth new possibility. Altering boundaries, not simply smashing or denying them, requires political courage, but the sacrifice of life for the achievement of immortal glory alters no boundaries. . . . Truly human courage surely must lie in distinc-

tively human things—intellectual and emotional life, building collective existence, inventing new possibility, stretching horizons. (Brown 1988, 206–7)

As Brown suggests, we need a more expansive conception of courage, one that encompasses all human activities that involve risk, uncertainty, and fear, not simply the ones that involve risk to our bodies, and not simply the ones that involve men. We also need a conception that recognizes the importance of courage for dealing with our allies and potential allies as we seek to build a collective existence.

A number of feminist writers have considered courage in this light and have begun reclaiming courage as an important political principle and practice for women. Writer bell hooks, for instance, talks about the courage that women of color must practice simply to speak: "For us, true speaking is not solely an expression of creative power; it is an act of resistance, a political gesture that challenges the politics of domination that would render us nameless and voiceless. As such, it is a courageous act—as such, it represents a threat" (hooks 1989, 8). Audre Lorde has written about the courage necessary for transforming women's silence and fears into language and action: "We can learn to work and speak when we are afraid in the same way we have learned to work and speak when we are tired. For we have been socialized to respect fear more than our own needs for language and definition, and while we wait in silence for that final luxury of fearlessness, the weight of that silence will choke us" (Lorde 1984a, 44). Gloria Yamato has discussed the courage white people need to be allies of people of color (Yamato 1990, 23–24). And Lynet Uttal has explored the courage feminists need to face conflicts and disagreements between women (Uttal 1990, 319).

As provocative as these feminist perspectives on courage are, none of these writers pursues the idea of political courage in any real depth. It is precisely at this point, however, that attention to the dissidence of activists—especially women activists—can once again be crucial. In addition to furthering the feminist project of reclaiming the history of women's actual participation in public life, the study of women's activism provides a historically specific context for exploring how discourses of political courage inspire and guide dissident citizenship. Women's dissident practices also offer an unparalleled resource for exploring both how dissident citizenship has been constructed and negotiated in gendered, raced, and classed terms and what the possible contours of nonmasculine, nonheterosexist, dissident forms of political courage might be.

Let us return, then, to the dissident citizenship of Rosa Parks. In a context in which an African American woman had been severely beaten and an African American man shot and killed during disputes with bus drivers, Parks knew the stakes were high when she refused to give up her seat. Parks, however, was arrested without incident, fingerprinted, and released on bail. Introduced by Martin Luther King, Jr. to a mass meeting of Montgomery's African American residents on the day of her trial (and the first day of the boycott) as "our courageous heroine," Parks served as a crucial exemplar for boycott participants for the duration of the Montgomery boycott and beyond. She was even called the boycott's patron saint. But most important, Parks's resistance and arrest made courageous, noninstitutionalized, democratic dissent a type of political action that was applauded and emulated.

When asked in a 1956 interview whether she had been afraid either of physical brutality or arrest, Parks said no. "The time had just come when I had been pushed as far as I could stand to be pushed," she said. "I had decided I had to know once and for all what rights I had as a human being and a citizen in Montgomery, Alabama" (Parks 1956). Others active in the boycott, however, did feel fear and talked explicitly about how they found courage. Indeed, at least four different discourses about courage—or in Brown's language, four discourses about putting identity and security at risk—influenced the various forms of dissident democratic citizenship involved in the Montgomery boycott. Three of the discourses implied that courageous dissidents should be fear*less*; the fourth, that courageous dissidents could be fear*ful*.

First, there was a discourse that suggested that courageous dissidents would be fearless because they were manly; for example, the discourse of the ministers about "fearless men" and "scared boys" mentioned earlier. In contrast, the second kind of discourse suggested that courageous dissidents could be fearless not because they were manly but because they were angry. Jo Ann Robinson and Mary Burks write in their autobiographies about how experiences with the humiliation of segregation fueled an anger that made their fears of dissenting action evaporate (Robinson 1987, 15–17; Burks 1990, 78). And although Rosa Parks did not describe herself as angry, her comments about being "pushed as far as I could stand to be pushed" connote a similar kind of frustration or exasperation that dissolved fear.

A third kind of discourse suggested that courageous dissidents could be fearless not because of manliness or anger, but because they had religious faith. They had, in the language of many of the church members involved in the boycott, turned their fears over to God. King, for example, related how, at a moment when he considered giving up out of exhaustion and fear, he felt his fears and uncertainty subside and his courage increase as he prayed to God (1958, 134–35). In contrast, the fourth discourse about courage suggested that courageous dissidents could remain fear*ful*, but would continue to act anyway out of a commitment to justice, or alternatively out of a commitment to the Christian injunction "love thy neighbor as thyself." This discourse was used, for example, by Bob and Jeannie Graetz, a white couple who became deeply involved in the boycott and were consequently subjected to much harassment and two bombings (Graetz 1991).

These four discourses about courage—involving manliness, anger, faith, and a commitment to justice or love—were clearly used to enable and shape dissident political engagement in the Montgomery case. Because of an invocation of manly courage, the African American ministers chose to be visible dissidents rather than behind-the-scenes advisers. Because of angry courage, Jo Ann Robinson and other WPC women decided on and publicized the boycott, a risky event to sponsor in a segregated context. By translating their commitment to Christian love into a discourse about courageous action amid fear and risk, the Graetzes became models for other white allies. And by discovering and nurturing what they described as courage through prayer and faith, many of the women and men who participated in the year-long boycott were able to put aside both their fear of white retaliation and their exhaustion, and continue their dissent.

Among these specific discourses about courage, only the "manliness" discourse is explicitly gender coded. Rosa Parks's performance of courageous dissent, however, relied on, invoked, and reinforced a number of gender, race, and class norms, even as it challenged others. Although Parks was, as we have seen, a courageous dissident long before her arrest, she was a dissident who epitomized quiet, middle-class respectability. She was demure, feminine, heterosexual, married, family-oriented, hard-working, and churchgoing. Because of the risks she chose to face, she was indeed a "courageous heroine," but her dissidence was performed in a manner that did not conspicuously threaten traditional gender norms, sexuality norms, or class norms. To see this in perspective, consider that a younger woman named Claudette Colvin was arrested on similar charges a few months before Parks, but community leaders ended talk of both a legal challenge and a bus boycott when Colvin turned out to be pregnant out of wedlock.

Arguably, this respectability and traditionality made Parks a relatively "safe" means of contesting white male power in Montgomery. The constructions of her act offered by participants in the boycott and by Parks herself contribute to this nonthreatening aura. She was, the story goes, *tired*, not enraged. Her act was *spontaneous*, not planned. She was *respectable*, not radical. She was a *churchgoing wife*, not a miscreant. Indeed, these dissident acts, coming from a person who did not blatantly challenge mainstream gender, sexuality, or class expectations, made it very difficult for elite whites to marginalize Parks as a lawbreaking troublemaker.

However traditional Parks was in some ways, her courageous dissidence nonetheless created a space in Montgomery, Alabama, where the meanings of both citizenship and courage were reconstructed and recoded. Citizenship, as Parks clearly demonstrated, most certainly could include dissent against more powerful publics. Dissent could involve challenges to prevailing arrangements of power, both noninstitutionalized (Parks's refusal to move and the boycott) and institutionalized (the actions of the Women's Political Caucus and the Montgomery Improvement Association). Political courage and dissident citizenship could also legitimately and fruitfully be practiced by both men and women. Through their examples of citizenship, dissent, and courage, Parks and the other dissident citizens of Montgomery contributed to the revitalization of democratic life that came to be called the Civil Rights Movement. Their story, and especially the story of Rosa Parks, continues to engage and inspire large numbers of people.

Conclusions

In this essay, I have argued that an adequate account of citizenship should recognize both dissent and courage as crucial elements of democratic life. In particular, a theoretical conception of dissident citizenship should attend to four dimensions of dissent: oppositional, democratic, noninstitutionalized interactions between unequal publics; discursive, performative, organizational, and "everyday" dissenting actions within and among those publics that augment or replace institutionalized forms of democratic opposition; the material and institutional conditions that shape the dissenting actions between unequal publics; and the ideas and discourses that shape and influence dissidence, especially discourses about democracy, citizenship, dissent, and courage.

There are five broader contributions of this perspective on dissent and courage. First, by drawing attention to the importance of dissident democratic citizenship, this approach encourages democratic theorists to pay closer attention to dissident activities, and consequently to those people for whom the promise of democracy has not been fulfilled. By recognizing the political agency of dissidents and "marginals" as the agency of *citizens*, democratic theorists can provide a richer account of democratic citizenship than can theories that focus solely on sanctioned deliberation.

Second, by incorporating an ethic of political courage into our conception of citizenship, this approach fills an additional gap in our understanding of democracy as joint deliberation and action. Political courage is important because it enables us to act and communicate when faced with fear and uncertainty. Fear and uncertainty are certainly confronted by dissidents who act in a context of inequality, but this approach also suggests that courage is necessary for all citizens, not just those engaged in dissent. As long as we think engaging in politics is something more than "who gets what, when, and how," the challenges of conflict, connection, and accountability will lie at the heart of being a citizen. Even if we manage to eliminate the major inequalities that characterize our current political environment, engaging in conflict and connection are risky activities and will not happen (or will not happen well) without courageous citizens. By scrutinizing the courage necessary for dissidence, therefore, this perspective also explores the nature of a practice that is fundamental to human beings who wish to communicate and act together in the world.

Third, this approach highlights the limitations of the public-private split as it is commonly understood and incorporated into democratic theories of citizenship. By attending to the dissident practices of marginals, and especially the dissident practices of women marginals, this approach encourages democratic theorists to broaden their understanding of where political participation takes place, and to credit women for their public activities (including dissent) that occur in spheres and locations traditionally viewed as private or apolitical.

Fourth, this approach encourages democratic theorists and others interested in citizenship to examine the impact of race, class, gender, and sexuality on democratic participation. Critically exploring how the dissident and deliberative practices of women and other marginals are negotiated and constructed respects the feminist call to examine gender as it intersects and interacts with race, class, and sexuality in the world.

Finally, this approach participates in the reclaiming of courageous dissent as an important political practice for women and other agents who face discrimination and oppression. When women and other dissidents conceive of themselves as courageous, new possibilities for action as citizens are opened. As Mary Dietz has suggested, by remembering and bringing to light the many examples of courageous democratic practices already in existence, we provide inspiration for activists still to come (Dietz 1987, 79).

Notes

An earlier draft of this essay was presented as part of the "Dissident Citizenship: Rethinking Democratic Practice for an Inegalitarian Polity" panel at the Western Political Science Association meeting in Tucson, Arizona, March 13–15, 1997. I would like to thank panel members Susan Bickford, Lisa Bower, and Lisa Disch, as well as the lively audience for their helpful comments and criticisms. In addition, I would like to thank the three anonymous reviewers for *Hypatia*, and especially Susan Bickford and John McGowan for their careful and helpful readings.

1. For essays that chart the diverse and innovative character of recent liberal thought, see Rosenblum (1989) and Sandel (1984).

2. Jane Mansbridge's classic study *Beyond Adversary Democracy* (1980) presents a considerably less favorable view of the ability of participatory democracies to deal with disputes and conflict by way of face-to-face decisionmaking. As Mansbridge points out, many of the small collectives she studied were committed to consensual decision making, and often lacked both models and skills for handling divergent interests. As a result, "Many small democracies, still modeling themselves on friendships, end up using social pressure to bring minorities into line because invoking adversary procedures would require recognizing that the nature of their group had changed" (291). To avoid this problem, Mansbridge advises small collectives to learn how to utilize adversarial procedures when interests begin to conflict.

In *Strong Democracy,* Barber distinguishes between two types of participatory democracy: the small, unitary democracies based on the consensus that Mansbridge studies, and what he calls strong democracies, where participation and activity take precedence over consensus and unity. This distinction allows him to rescue participatory democracy from the very real problems noted in Mansbridge's study, without advocating a return to adversarial democracy. See Barber (1984, 96, n. 7). For the remainder of this section, I mean Barber's conception of "strong democracy" when I use the term "participatory democracy."

3. For some difficulties with Young's group representation model, see Mouffe (1992c); Gould (1996); Benhabib (1996b); Jean Cohen (1996); Dryzek (1996a and 1996b); Fraser (1997).

4. Although the literature critiquing Habermas's work is extensive, two particularly useful collections that evaluate deliberative/discursive democracy are Calhoun (1992) and Benhabib (1996c). Benhabib's essay "Toward a Deliberative Model of Democratic Legitimacy" in *Democracy and Difference* is an especially helpful summation of the types of criticisms leveled at the proceduralism of deliberative/discursive democracy.

5. For similar critiques of Habermas's neglect of dissent, see McCarthy (1992) and Gould (1996).

6. Although Barber distinguishes between the "venting" and "bearing witness" functions of dissent, I see little actual difference between the "venting" activity of "giving public status to strongly held personal convictions" and the "bearing witness" activity of "bearing witness to another point of view." Furthermore, to categorize conscientious objection as mere "venting" seems to trivialize both the motivations of conscientious objectors and the more prominent bearing witness function of this form of dissent. My language in the rest of this section reflects my view that Barber is actually just talking about two variations of bearing witness.

7. To be clear, this list includes only oppositional political practices, some of them democratic and some not. Political practices that sustain and support current arrangements of power can also be democratic or not. Sustaining democratic practices can also be institutionalized or not. For example, voting for a referendum that supports the status quo is sustaining, democratic and institutionalized. Participating in a march that supports the status quo is sustaining, democratic and noninstitutionalized.

8. In reality, of course, citizens do *not* engage in these practices as equals. This is easily seen in the case of lobbying one's elected representative: although any (literate) person may write a letter encouraging a specific course of action, individuals and groups with significant resources will enjoy greater access to elected officials and probably greater success in achieving their lobbying goals. The same holds true for access to the legal system, and to the referendum process as well. In addition to the variables of money and leisure, factors such as race, ethnicity, gender, and other revealed or perceived attributes can have a significant impact on the type of access and treatment that citizens using these institutionalized forms of opposition will encounter.

9. I have chosen to draw most heavily upon these three sources because they have an explicit political/public orientation. Although a significant and provocative literature on marginality and resistance has been produced by feminist and cultural studies scholars, I will not deal with it separately. This literature, although concerned with politics and power in the broad sense, is not specifically geared toward the political actions of citizens. See Ferguson et al., (1990) for selected essays from this genre of scholarship.

10. It is interesting to consider the writings of Chantal Mouffe in relation to Fraser's point here about the role of counterpublics in challenging hegemony. Mouffe appears to argue that subaltern counterpublics could be linked together by their shared allegiance to the politico-ethical principles of "liberty and equality for all," thus creating a common political identity as "radical democratic citizens." Fraser does not take up the problem of creating an overarching counter-hegemonic movement, but I find Mouffe's insistence that radical democratic citizens accept "norms of conduct" and specific "rules of civil intercourse" unhelpful for conceptualizing dissident citizenship. See Mouffe (1992a, 1992b, and 1992c); Laclau and Mouffe (1985). For a critique of Mouffe, see Cooper (1995, 144–54).

11. Fraser's approach differs from recent arguments about democracy and civil society (e.g., Dryzek 1996b) in at least two important ways. First, civil society theorists conceptually separate the "voluntary associations" found in civil society that do not seek "any share in state power" (Dryzek 1996b, 481) from the state and economy, while Fraser's focus on discourse publics and counterpublics can capture the presence of public spaces and cross cutting discursive interactions that do not respect this state/economy/civil society division. Second, although Dryzek argues that democratization might best be served by the maintenance of "a flourishing oppositional civil society" which includes public spheres of all kinds (475), Fraser would disagree with his claim that public spheres in civil society are "relatively unconstrained." According to Dryzek, in civil society "discourse need not be suppressed in the interests of strategic advantage; goals and interests need not be compromised or subordinated to the pursuit of office or access; embarrassing troublemakers need not be repressed; the indeterminacy of outcome inherent in democracy need not be subordinated to state policy" (482). Although Dryzek is right to point out the ways in which publics and/or voluntary associations shape themselves around the state when they do seek state power, publics and associations that do not seek state power do not then enter a vacuum where pressures, goals and interests disappear altogether. Fraser's un-

derstanding of how multiple publics interact within a structured setting where communication is part of hegemonic and counterhegemonic projects seems more useful here.

12. See Herbst (1994) for an example of how the idea of counterpublics can guide historical inquiry.

13. Landes also sometimes uses the word "practice" to refer to enacted citizenship; I will use both words interchangeably. For more on scripting and performance, see Marcus (1992) and Butler (1990).

14. Collections such as West and Blumberg (1990); Laslett et al., (1995); and McAllister (1988) document case after case of women's active involvement in dissent that mainstream scholars have ignored. The number of works on women's participation in the civil rights movement has especially mushroomed in recent years, including the important collection Crawford et al., (1990).

15. Many of these scholars are working within the huge social science literature on collective action and new social movements. Their work, consequently, is often geared toward the attempt to come up with a theoretical framework that accounts for the existence of collective action and its forms (see e.g., Tarrow 1994; Laraña et al., 1994; Morris and Mueller 1992). Because I am not concerned here with the causes of collective action, nor with consciousness or identity formation, I tend to find the work of historians far more useful for my purposes due to its historical specificity and greater attentiveness to the possibilities of human agency.

16. A number of recent collections bring together case studies and essays on political dissent in the United States. Particularly useful are Lynd and Lynd (1995), and Weber (1978). These two collections record the long history and creativity of dissenters in the United States; they are also unusual for including case studies and documents that explore the civil disobedience and nonviolence practiced by women. The vast majority of resources do not consciously attend to gender or sexuality in any form. See, e.g., Goldwin (1969); Hare and Blumberg (1968); Crawford (1973); Walzer (1970). See Thompson (1994) for an account of dissent related to sexuality.

17. It is no accident that opposition would eventually be framed around another hallowed political concept: the rights of states to write and enforce their own laws. The states' rights language allowed whites to talk about principles and constitutional issues, not racism, bigotry, and violence.

18. The vast majority of the psychological literature on courage, incidentally, studies a warrior-based version of courage as individual honor and self-sacrifice in the face of danger. The self-sacrifice is described as a way to protect the community, but the community is usually defined very narrowly as the soldier's immediate colleagues. See, e.g., Rachman (1990).

19. Consider, in contrast, Alasdair MacIntyre's perspective on courage from his 1981 book *After Virtue*. MacIntyre views courage as an individual way to demonstrate "care and concern" for an already existing community: "If someone says that he cares for some individual, community or cause, but is unwilling to risk harm or danger on his, her or its own behalf, he puts in question the genuineness of his care and concern. Courage, the capacity to risk harm or danger to oneself, has its role in human life because of this connection with care and concern" (Mac-

Intyre 1981, 192). Although this focus on care and concern for others is attractive, MacIntyre says nothing about courage as a way to deal with conflict within the community, as a way to act *together*. Courage apparently is only important for dealing with outsiders or enemies, not allies.

More problematically, MacIntyre conceptualizes courage as an individual virtue. Although he talks about virtues as both "qualities" and occasionally more helpfully as "dispositions" (see chap. 14), his language of virtue is problematic because it seems to make virtues into attributes or capacities that people either possess or not. He seems to define virtues as the internal sources for external actions. The language of principle, on the other hand, offers a focus not on internal qualities but external standards. Principles are external guidelines, something to which one either commits (and therefore enacts), or does not. That said, MacIntyre's work is invaluable for thinking about virtues, principles, and their relationship to practices and political life.

20. As an interesting complement to this point, women activists who were part of the violent Weather Underground collective have noted that they consciously became "macho" just like their male counterparts (even to the point of becoming sexual dominatrixes) because they had no other models for dealing with fear and risk. See WETA (1991).

21. A wide range of feminist theorists have criticized the masculinist character of both classical and modern conceptions of citizenship. In addition to the sources cited in the text, see Hartsock (1983); Elshtain (1981, 1982a, 1982b); Ruddick (1980, 1989); Pateman (1988, 1989).

References

Ackelsberg, Martha A. 1988. Communities, resistance, and women's activism: Some implications for a democratic polity. In *Women and the politics of empowerment*. See Bookman and Morgen 1988.

Anzaldúa, Gloria, ed. 1990. *Making face, making soul: Haciendo caras.* San Francisco: Aunt Lute Books.

Arendt, Hannah. 1958. *The human condition.* Chicago: University of Chicago Press.

Aristotle. 1962a. *Nichomachean ethics.* Trans. Martin Ostwald. Indianapolis: Bobbs-Merrill.

_____. 1962b. *The Politics.* Trans. T. A. Sinclair. London: Penguin Books.

Barber, Benjamin. 1984. *Strong democracy: Participatory politics for a new age.* Berkeley: University of California Press.

Bayard de Vola, Lorraine. 1997. Heroes, martyrs, and mothers: Maternal identity politics in revolutionary Nicaragua. Public lecture at the University of North Carolina, Chapel Hill, February 13.

Benhabib, Seyla. 1992. Models of public space: Hannah Arendt, the liberal tradition, and Jürgen Habermas. In *Habermas and the public sphere.* See Calhoun 1992.

_____, ed. 1996a. *Democracy and difference: Contesting the boundaries of the political.* Princeton: Princeton University Press.

_____. 1996b. The democratic moment and the problem of difference. In *Democracy and difference.* See Benhabib 1996a.

_____. 1996c. Toward a deliberative model of democratic legitimacy. In *Democracy and difference*. See Benhabib 1996a.

Bickford, Susan. 1996. *The dissonance of democracy: Listening, conflict, and citizenship*. Ithaca: Cornell University Press.

Bookman, Ann and Sandra Morgen, eds. 1988. *Women and the politics of empowerment*. Philadelphia: Temple University Press.

Bowles, Samuel and Herbert Gintis. 1986. *Democracy and capitalism: Property, community, and the contradictions of modern social thought*. New York: Basic Books.

Brown, Wendy. 1988. *Manhood and politics: A feminist reading in political theory*. Totowa, NJ: Rowman and Littlefield.

Butler, Judith. 1990. *Gender trouble: Feminism and the subversion of identity*. New York: Routledge.

Burks, Mary Fair. 1990. Trailblazers: Women in the Montgomery bus boycott. In *Women in the civil rights movement*. See Crawford et al., 1990.

Calhoun, Craig, ed. 1992. *Habermas and the public sphere*. Cambridge: MIT Press.

Calvert, Gregory Nevala. 1991. *Democracy from the heart: Spiritual values, decentralism, and democratic idealism in the movement of the 1960s*. Eugene, OR: Communitas Press.

Carter, April. 1973. *Direct action and liberal democracy*. New York: Harper and Row.

Clark, Septima and Cynthia Stokes Brown. 1986. *Ready from within: Septima Clark and the civil rights movement*. Navarro, CA: Wild Trees Press.

Cohen, Jean. 1996. Democracy, difference, and the right of privacy. In *Democracy and difference*. See Benhabib 1996a.

Cohen, Joshua. 1989. Deliberation and democratic legitimacy. In *The good polity*, eds. Alan Hamlin and Philip Pettit. New York: Blackwell.

_____. 1996. Procedure and substance in deliberative democracy. In *Democracy and difference*. See Benhabib 1996a.

Coole, Diana. 1993. *Women in political theory: From ancient misogyny to contemporary feminism*, 2d ed. Boulder, CO: Lynne Reiner.

Cooper, Davina. 1995. *Power in struggle: Feminism, sexuality, and the state*. New York: New York University Press.

Crawford, Curtis. 1973. *Civil disobedience: A casebook*. New York: Crowell.

Crawford, Vicki L. 1990. Beyond the human self: Grassroots activists in the Mississippi civil rights movement. In *Women in the civil rights movement*. See Crawford et al., 1990.

Crawford, Vicki L., Jacqueline Anne Rouse, and Barbara Woods, eds. 1990. *Women in the civil rights movement: Trailblazers and torchbearers 1941–1965*. Bloomington: Indiana University Press.

Dietz, Mary. 1985. Citizenship with a feminist face: The problem with maternal thinking. *Political Theory* 13(1): 19–37.

_____. 1987. Context is all: Feminism and theories of citizenship. *Daedalus* 116(4): 1–24.

_____. 1991. Hannah Arendt and feminist politics. In *Feminist Interpretations and political theory*. See Shanley and Pateman 1991.

Dill, Bonnie Thornton. 1988. Making your job good yourself: Domestic service and the construction of personal dignity. In *Women and the politics of empowerment*. See Bookman and Morgen 1988.

Dryzek, John. 1990. *Discursive democracy.* New York: Cambridge University Press.

———. 1996a. *Democracy in capitalist times: Ideals, limits, and struggles.* New York: Oxford University Press.

———. 1996b. Political inclusion and the dynamics of democratization. *American Political Science Review* 90(3): 475–87.

Dworkin, Ronald. 1978. *Taking rights seriously.* Cambridge: Harvard University Press.

Durr, Virginia Foster. 1985. *Outside the magic circle: The autobiography of Virginia Foster Durr,* ed. Hollinger F. Barnard. University: University of Alabama Press.

Echols, Alice. 1989. *Daring to be bad: Radical feminism in America 1967–1975.* Minneapolis: University of Minnesota Press.

Eley, George. 1992. Nations, publics, and political cultures: Placing Habermas in the nineteenth-century. In *Habermas and the public sphere.* See Calhoun 1992.

Elshtain, Jean Bethke. 1981. *Public man, private woman.* Princeton: Princeton University Press.

———. 1982a. Antigone's daughters. *Democracy* 2(2): 46–59.

———. 1982b. Feminism, family and community. *Dissent* 29(4): 442–49.

Evans, Sara M. 1979. *Personal politics: The roots of women's liberation in the civil rights movement and the new left.* New York: Vintage Books/Random House.

———. 1993. Women's history and political theory: Toward a feminist approach to public life. In *Visible women.* See Hewitt and Lebsock 1993.

Evans, Sara M., and Harry Boyte. 1986. *Free spaces: The sources of democratic change in America.* New York: Harper and Row.

Ferguson, Russell, Martha Gever, Trinh T. Minh-ha, and Cornel West, eds. 1990. *Out there: Marginalization and contemporary cultures.* New York: New Museum of Contemporary Art and Cambridge: MIT Press.

Fishkin, James. 1991. *Deliberative democracy.* New Haven: Yale University Press.

Flacks, Richard. 1996. Reviving democratic activism: Thoughts about strategy in a dark time. In *Radical democracy: Identity, citizenship, and the state,* ed. David Trend. New York: Routledge.

Fraser, Nancy. 1989. *Unruly practices: Power, discourse and gender in contemporary social theory.* Minneapolis: University of Minnesota Press.

———. 1992. Rethinking the public sphere: A contribution to the critique of actually existing democracy. In *Habermas and the public sphere.* See Calhoun 1992.

———. 1997. *Justice interruptus: Critical reflections on the postsocialist condition.* New York: Routledge.

Frederickson, Mary E. 1993. "Each one is dependent on the other": Southern church-women, racial reform, and the process of transformation, 1880–1940. In *Visible women.* See Hewitt and Lebsock 1993.

Goldwin, Robert A., ed. 1969. *On civil disobedience: American essays, old and new.* Chicago: Rand McNally.

Gould, Carol. 1996. Diversity and democracy: Representing difference. In *Democracy and difference.* See Benhabib 1996a.

Graetz, Robert S. 1991. *Montgomery: A white preacher's memoir.* Minneapolis: Fortress Press.

Habermas, Jürgen. 1987. *Lifeworld and system: A critique of functionalist reason. Vol. 2 of The theory of communicative action.* Boston: Beacon Books.

_____. 1989. *The structural transformation of the public sphere.* Trans. T. Burger and F. Lawrence. Cambridge: MIT Press.

_____. 1996. Three normative models of democracy. In *Democracy and difference.* See Benhabib 1996a.

Hampton, Henry and Steve Fayer, eds. 1990. *Voices of freedom: An oral history of the civil rights movement from the 1950s through the 1980s.* New York: Bantam Books.

Hare, A. Paul and Herbert H. Blumberg, eds. 1968. *Nonviolent direct action: American cases, social-psychological analyses.* Washington, DC: Corpus Books.

Harris, Paul, ed. 1989. *Civil disobedience.* Lanham, MD: University Press of America.

Hartsock, Nancy. 1983. *Money, sex, and power: Toward a feminist historical materialism.* Boston: Northeastern University Press.

Herbst, Susan. 1994. *Politics at the margin: Historical studies of public expression outside the mainstream.* New York: Cambridge University Press.

Hewitt, Nancy A. and Suzanne Lebsock, eds. 1993. *Visible women: New essays on American activism.* Urbana: University of Illinois Press.

Hine, Darlene Clark. 1993. The Housewives' League of Detroit: Black women and economic nationalism. In *Visible women.* See Hewitt and Lebsock 1993.

Homer. 1974. *The Illiad.* Trans. Robert Fitzgerald. Garden City, NY: Anchor Press/Doubleday.

hooks, bell. 1989. *Talking back: Thinking feminist, thinking black.* Boston: South End Press.

Kaplan, Temma. 1982. Female consciousness and collective action: The case of Barcelona, 1910–1918. *Signs* 7(3): 545–66.

King, Martin Luther, Jr. 1958. *Stride toward freedom: The Montgomery story.* New York: Harper & Brothers Publishers.

_____. 1963. Letter from Birmingham jail. In *Why we can't wait, Martin Luther King, Jr.* New York: Mentor/Penguin Books.

Laclau, Ernesto and Chantal Mouffe. 1985. *Hegemony and socialist strategy: Toward a radical democratic politics.* London: Verso.

Landes, Joan B. 1996. The performance of citizenship: Democracy, gender, and difference in the French revolution. In *Democracy and difference.* See Benhabib 1996a.

Lane, Dorothy. 1995 [1967]. The Pentagon, October 1967. Reprinted in Lynd and Lynd 1995.

Langston, Donna. 1990. The women of Highlander. In *Women in the civil rights movement.* See Crawford et al., 1990.

Laraña, Enrique, Hank Johnston, and Joseph R. Gusfield. 1994. *New social movements: From ideology to identity.* Philadelphia: Temple University Press.

Laslett, Barbara, Johanna Brenner, and Yesim Arat. 1995. *Rethinking the political: Gender, resistance, and the state.* Chicago: University of Chicago Press.

Lorde, Audre. 1984a. The transformation of silence into language and action. In *Sister outsider.* Trumansberg, NY: Crossing Press.

_____. 1984b. The uses of anger: Women responding to racism. In *Sister outsider.* Trumansberg, NY: Crossing Press.

Lynd, Staughton, and Alice Lynd, eds. 1995. *Nonviolence in America: A documentary history.* Revised ed. Maryknoll, NY: Orbis.

MacIntyre, Alasdair. 1981. *After virtue*. Notre Dame: Notre Dame University Press.

Mahoney, William. 1995 [1961]. In pursuit of freedom. *Liberation* (September): 7–11. Reprinted in Lynd and Lynd 1995.

Mansbridge, Jane. 1980. *Beyond adversary democracy*. Chicago: University of Chicago Press.

———. 1990. Feminism and democracy. *American Prospect* (Spring): 126–39.

———. 1992. A deliberative theory of interest representation. In *The politics of interests*, ed. Mark P. Patracca. Boulder, CO: Westview Press.

———. 1996. Using power/fighting power: The polity. In *Democracy and difference*. See Benhabib 1996a.

Marcus, Sharon. 1992. Fighting bodies, fighting words: A theory and politics of rape prevention. In *Feminists theorize the political*, eds. Judith Butler and Joan W. Scott. New York: Routledge.

McAllister, Pam. 1988. *You can't kill the spirit*. Philadelphia: New Society Publishers.

McCarthy, Thomas. 1992. Practical discourse: On the relation of morality to politics. In *Habermas and the public sphere*. See Calhoun 1992.

Morris, Aldon D. and Carol McClurg Mueller. 1992. *Frontiers in social movement theory*. New Haven: Yale University Press.

Mouffe, Chantal. 1992a. Democratic citizenship and the political community. In *Dimensions of radical democracy*, ed. Mouffe. London: Verso.

———. 1992b. Democratic politics today. In *Dimensions of radical democracy*, ed. Mouffe. London: Verso.

———. 1992c. Feminism, citizenship and radical democratic politics. In *Feminists theorize the political*, ed. Judith Butler and Joan Scott. New York: Routledge.

Mueller, Carol. 1990. Ella Baker and the origins of "participatory democracy." In *Women in the civil rights movement*. See Crawford et al., 1990.

Nozick, Robert. 1974. *Anarchy, state, and utopia*. New York: Basic Books.

Okin, Susan Moller. 1979. *Women in western political thought*. Princeton: Princeton University Press.

Parks, Rosa. 1956. Audio interview with Sidney Roger. Los Angeles: Pacifica Tape Archive.

———. 1977. Recollections. In *My soul is rested*, ed. Howell Raines. New York: Putnam.

Pateman, Carole. 1970. *Participation and democratic theory*. New York: Cambridge University Press.

———. 1988. *The sexual contract*. Stanford: Stanford University Press.

———. 1989. *The disorder of women: Democracy, feminism and political theory*. Stanford: Stanford University Press.

Payne, Charles. 1990. Men led, but women organized: Movement participation of women in the Mississippi delta. In *Women in the civil rights movement*. See Crawford et al., 1990.

———. 1995. *I've got the light of freedom: The organizing tradition and the Mississippi freedom struggle*. Berkeley: University of California Press.

Plato. 1990. *Laches*. Trans. W. R. M. Lamb. Cambridge: Harvard University Press.

———. 1992. *The Republic*. Trans. G. M. A. Gruber. Indianapolis: Hackett.

Rachman, Stanley. 1990. *Fear and courage.* New York: W. H. Freeman.

Rawls, John. 1971. *A theory of justice.* Cambridge: Harvard University Press.

_____. 1985. Justice as fairness: Political not metaphysical. *Philosophy and Public Affairs* 14: 223–51.

Robinson, Jo Ann. 1987. *The Montgomery bus boycott and the women who started it.* Knoxville: University of Tennessee Press.

Rosenblum, Nancy L., ed. 1989. *Liberalism and the moral life.* Cambridge: Harvard University Press.

Roydhouse, Marion W. 1993. Bridging chasms: Community and the southern YWCA. In *Visible women.* See Hewitt and Lebsock 1993.

Ruddick, Sara. 1980. Maternal thinking. *Feminist Studies* 6(2): 342–67.

_____. 1989. *Maternal thinking: Toward a politics of peace.* Boston: Beacon Press.

Sandel, Michael. 1982. *Liberalism and the limits of justice.* New York: Cambridge University Press.

_____, ed. 1984. *Liberalism and its critics.* New York: New York University Press.

Saxonhouse, Arlene W. 1985. *Women in the history of political thought: Ancient Greece to Machiavelli.* New York: Praeger.

Schwartz, Nancy. 1995. Women and courage in Greek and Jewish political thought. Paper presented at the American Political Science Association annual meeting, Chicago, September 1–4.

Scott, James C. 1985. *Weapons of the weak: Everyday forms of peasant resistance.* New Haven: Yale University Press.

_____. 1990. *Domination and the arts of resistance: Hidden transcripts.* New Haven: Yale University Press.

Shanley, Mary Lyndon and Carole Pateman. 1991. *Feminist interpretations and political theory.* University Park: Pennsylvania State University Press.

Student Nonviolent Coordinating Committee. 1995 [1962]. SNCC statement of purpose. Reprinted in Lynd and Lynd 1995.

Susser, Ida. 1988. Working-class women, social protest, and changing ideologies. In *Women and the politics of empowerment.* See Bookman and Morgen 1988.

Tarrow, Sidney. 1994. *Power in movement: Social movements, collective action and politics.* New York: Cambridge University Press.

Taylor, Verta and Nancy E. Whittier. 1992. Collective identity in social movement communities: Lesbian feminist mobilization. In *Frontiers in social movement theory.* See Morris and Mueller 1992.

Thompson, Mark. 1994. *Long road to freedom: The Advocate history of the gay and lesbian movement.* New York: St. Martin's Press.

Thoreau, Henry David. 1989 [1849]. Resistance to civil government. Reprinted in *The American intellectual tradition.* Vol 1, 1630–1865, 2d ed. Eds., David A. Hollinger and Charles Capper. New York: Oxford University Press.

Uttal, Lynet. 1990. Nods that silence. In *Making face, making soul: Haciendo caras.* See Anzaldúa 1990.

Walzer, Michael. 1970. *Obligations: Essays on disobedience, war, and citizenship.* Cambridge: Harvard University Press.

Weber, David R. 1978. *Civil disobedience in America: A documentary history.* Ithaca: Cornell University Press.

West, Guide and Rhoda Lois Blumberg. 1990. *Women and social protest.* New York: Oxford University Press.

WETA. 1991. *Making sense of the sixties.* Part 4: Picking up the pieces. Alexandria, VA: PBS Video.

Yamato, Gloria. 1990. Something about the subject makes it hard to name. In *Making face, making soul: Haciendo caras.* See Anzaldúa 1990.

Young, Iris Marion. 1990. *Justice and the politics of difference.* Princeton: Princeton University Press.

———. 1996. Communication and the other: Beyond deliberative democracy. In *Democracy and difference.* See Benhabib 1996a.

21 Automating Gender

Postmodern Feminism in the Age of the Intelligent Machine

JUDITH HALBERSTAM

My Computer, My Self

The development of computers and computer science in the 1940s activated a debate between humanists and mechanists over the possibility of intelligent machines. The prospect of thinking machines, or cyborgs, inspired at first religious indignation; intellectual disbelief; and large-scale suspicion of the social, economic, and military implications of an autonomous technology. In general terms, we can identify two major causes for concern produced by cybernetics. The first concern relates to the idea that computers may be taught to simulate human thought, and the second relates to the possibility that automated robots may be wired to replace humans in the workplace. The cybernetics debate, in fact, appears to follow the somewhat familiar class and gender lines of a mind-body split. Artificial intelligence, of course, threatens to reproduce the thinking subject, while the robot could conceivably be mass produced to form an automated workforce (robot in Czech means "worker"). However, if the former challenges the traditional intellectual prestige of a class of experts, the latter promises to displace the social privilege dependent upon stable categories of gender.

In our society, discourses are gendered, and the split between mind and body—as feminist theory has demonstrated—is a binary that identifies men with thought, intellect, and reason and women with body, emotion, and intuition. We might expect, then, that computer intelligence and robotics would enhance binary splits and emphasize the dominance of reason and logic over the irrational. However, because the blurred boundaries between mind and machine, body and machine, and human and nonhuman are the very legacy of cybernetics, automated machines, in fact, provide new ground upon which to argue that gender and its representations are technological productions. In a sense, cybernetics simultaneously maps out the terrain for both postmodern discussions of the subject in late capitalism and feminist debates about technology, postmodernism, and gender.

Although technophobia among women and as theorized by some feminists is understandable as a response to military and scientific abuses within a patriarchal system, the advent of intelligent machines necessarily changes the social relations between gender and science, sexuality and biology, feminism and the politics of artificiality. To illustrate productive and useful interactions between and across these categories, I take as central symbols the Apple computer logo, an apple with a bite taken from it, and the cyborg as theorized by Donna Haraway, a machine both female and intelligent.

We recognize the Apple computer symbol, I think, as a clever icon for the digitalization of the creation myth. Within this logo, sin and knowledge, the forbidden fruits of the Garden of Eden, are interfaced with memory and information in a network of power. The bite now represents the *byte* of information within a processing memory. I attempt to provide a reading of the apple that disassociates it from the myth of genesis and suggests that such a myth no longer holds currency within our postmodern age of simulation. Inasmuch as the postmodern project radically questions the notion of origination and the nostalgia attendant upon it, a postmodern reading of the apple finds that the subject has always sinned, has never not bitten the apple. The female cyborg replaces Eve in this myth with a figure who severs once and for all the assumed connection between woman and nature upon which entire patriarchal structures rest. The female cyborg, furthermore, exploits a traditionally masculine fear of the deceptiveness of appearances and calls into question the boundaries of human, animal, and machine precisely where they are most vulnerable—at the site of the female body.

On the one hand, the apple and Eve represent an organic relation between God, nature, man, and woman; on the other, the apple and the female cyborg symbolize a mass cultural computer technology. However, the distance travelled from genesis to intelligence is not a line between two poles, not a diachronic shift from belief to skepticism, for technology within multinational capitalism involves systems organized around contradictions. Computer technology, for example, both generates a powerful mass culture and also serves to militarize power. Cultural critics in the computer age, those concerned with the social configurations of class, race, and gender, can thus no longer afford to position themselves simply for or against technology, for or against postmodernism. In order not merely to reproduce the traditional divide between humanists and mechanists, feminists and other cultural critics must rather begin to theorize their position in relation to a plurality of technologies and from a place already within postmodernism.

Poisoned Apples

> *"The true mystery of the world is the visible not the invisible."*
> —**Oscar Wilde, The Picture of Dorian Gray (1891)**

The work of one pioneer in computer intelligence suggests a way that the technology of intelligence may be interwoven with the technology of gender. Alan Turing (1912–1954) was an English mathematician whose computer technology explicitly challenged boundaries between disciplines and between minds, bodies, and machines. Turing had been fascinated with the idea of a machine capable of manipulating symbols since an early age. His biographer Andrew Hodges writes:

> What, Alan Turing asked, would be the most general kind of a machine that dealt with symbols? To be a "machine" it would have to retain the typewriter's quality of having a finite number of configurations and an exactly determined behavior in each. But it would be capable of much more. And so he imagined machines which were, in effect, super-typewriters.[1]

In dreaming of such a machine, Turing imagined a kind of autonomous potential for this electrical brain, the potential for the machine to think, reason, and even make errors. Although the idea of the computer occurred to many different people simultaneously, it was Alan Turing who tried to consider the scope and range of an artificial intelligence.

Turing's development of what he called a "universal machine," as a mathematical model of a kind of superbrain, brought into question the whole concept of mind and indeed made a strict correlation between mind and machine. Although Turing's research would not yield a prototype of a computer until years later, this early model founded computer research squarely on the analogy between human and machine and, furthermore, challenged the supposed autonomy and abstraction of pure mathematics. For example, G.H. Hardy claims that "the 'real' mathematics of the 'real' mathematicians, the mathematics of Fermat and Euler and Gauss and Abel and Riemann, is almost wholly 'useless.' . . . It is not possible to justify the life of any genuine professional mathematician on the ground of the utility of his work."[2] This statement reveals a distinctly modernist investment in form over content and in the total objectivity of the scientific project unsullied by contact with the material world. Within a postmodern science, such claims for intellectual distance and abstraction are mediated, however, by the emergence of a mass culture technology. Technology for the masses, the prospect of a computer terminal in every home, encroaches upon the sacred ground of the experts and establishes technology as a relation between subjects and culture.

In a 1950 paper entitled "Computing Machinery and Intelligence," Alan Turing argued that a computer works according to the principle of imitation, but it may also be able to learn. In determining artificial intelligence, Turing demanded what he called "fair play" for the computer. We must not expect, he suggested, that the computer will be infallible, nor will it always act rationally or logically; indeed, the machine's very fallibility is necessary to its definition as "intelligent."[3] Turing compared the electric brain of the computer to the brain of a child; he suggested that intelligence transpires out of the combination of "discipline and initiative." Both discipline and initiative in this model run interference across the brain and condition behavior. However, Turing claimed that in both the human and the electric mind, there is the possibility for random interference and that it is this element that is critical to intelligence. Interference, then, works both as an organizing force, one which orders random behaviors, and as a random interruption which returns the system to chaos: it must always do both.

Turing created a test by which one might judge whether a computer could be considered intelligent. The Turing test demands that a human subject decide, based on replies given to her or his questions, whether she or he is communicating with a human or a machine. When the respondents fail to distinguish between human and machine responses, the computer may be considered intelligent. In an interesting twist, Turing illustrates the application of his test with what he calls "a sexual guessing game." In this game, a woman and a man sit in one room and an interrogator sits in another. The interrogator must determine the sexes of the two people based on their written replies to his questions. The man attempts to deceive the questioner, and the woman tries to convince him. Turing's point in introducing the sexual guessing game was to show that imitation makes even the most stable of distinctions (i.e., gender) unstable. By using the sexual guessing game as simply a control model, however, Turing does not stress the obvious connection between gender and computer intelligence: both are in fact imitative systems, and the boundaries between female and male, I argue, are as unclear and as unstable as the boundary between human and machine intelligence.

By assigning gender to biology and cognitive process to acculturation, Turing fails to realize the full import of his negotiations between machine and human. Gender, we might argue, like computer intelligence, is a learned, imitative behavior that can be processed so well that it comes to look natural. Indeed, the work of culture in the former and of science in the latter is perhaps to transform the artificial into a function so smooth that it seems organic. In other words, gender, like intelligence, has a technology. There is an irony to Turing's careful analogical comparisons between bodies and machines. Two years after he published his paper, in 1952, Turing was arrested and charged with "gross indecency," or homosexual activity. Faced with a choice between a jail sentence or hormone treatments, Turing opted for the hormones. It was still believed in the fifties that female hormones could "correct" male homosexuality because homosexual behavior was assumed to be a form of physically or biologically based gender confusion. In fact, the same kind of reasoning that prevented Turing from understanding the radically unstable condition of gender informed the attempt by medical researchers to correct a supposed surfeit of male hormones in the homosexual with infusions of female hormones. During treatment, Turing was rendered impotent, and he began to grow breasts. As soon as the treatment was over, he resumed his homosexual relationships.

Two important points can be made in relation to the brush between science and desire. First, Turing's experience of gender instability suggests that the body may in fact be, both materially and libidinally, a product of technology inasmuch as injections of hormones can transform it from male to female; second, desire provides the random element necessary to a technology's definition as intelligent. In other words, the body may be scientifically altered in order to force "correct" gender identification, but desire remains as interference running across a binary technologic.

Alan Turing's homosexuality was interpreted by the legal system as a crime, by the medical profession as a malfunction, and by the government as a liability. Turing was considered a liability because during World War II he had used his mathematical training in the service of military intelligence, and, as a cryptanalyst, he had distinguished himself in his work to decode Nazi communications. Turing's homosexuality made him seem an unfit keeper of state secrets: he was exploitable, fatally flawed, a weak link in the masculinist chain of government and the military. He had a sexual secret that the enemy (in 1952, the enemy was, of course, Communism) could prey upon, and his secret made him incontrovertibly Other.

The association between machine and military intelligence, as Turing found out, is a close one; and computer technology is in many ways the progeny of war in the modern age. The fear generated by computer intelligence, indeed, owes much to this association of the computer with highly sophisticated weaponry. As Andreas Huyssen points out, the fear of an autonomous technology has led to a gendering of technology as female: "As soon as the machine came to be perceived as a demonic, inexplicable threat and as the harbinger of chaos and destruction . . . writers began to imagine the Maschinenmensch as woman. . . . Woman, nature, machine had become a mesh of signification which all had one thing in common: otherness."[4] The fear of artificial intelligence, like the fear of homosexuals infiltrating the secret service, was transformed into a paranoid terror of femininity. Similarly, the machine itself was seen to threaten the hegemony of white male authority because it could as easily be used against a government as for it; autonomy was indeed its terrifying potential. The same argument that propelled a witch-hunt for possible homosexual traitors in the British government in the 1950s gendered the machine as female and attempted to convert threat into seduction. Turing now became the object of scrutiny of the very security system he had helped to create. The machine Other, like the sexual Other within a system of gender inequality, is contained even as it participates in the power dynamic.

Turing ended his life in 1954 by eating an apple dipped in cyanide. He had experienced the ignominy of a public trial for homosexual relations, he had suffered through a year's course of "organotherapy," then he was kept under close surveillance by the British Foreign office as a wave of panic over homosexual spies gripped the country. Turing had been awarded the Order of the British Empire in 1946 for his war service, and he earned a police record in 1952 for his sexual activities. Rarely has the division between body and mind been drawn with such precision and such tragic irony.

Turing's suicide method, eating an apple saturated with cyanide, bizarrely prefigures the Apple computer logo. Turing's apple, however, suggests a new and more complicated story than that of Adam and Eve; it suggests different configurations of culture and technology, science and myth, gender and discourse. The fatal apple as a fitting symbol of Turing's work scrambles completely boundaries between natural and artificial showing the natural to be always merely a configuration within the artificial. This symbol reveals, furthermore, multiple intersections of body and technology within cultural memory. Turing's bite, then, may indeed be read according to the myth of Genesis as the act of giving in to temptation, but it must also be read as resistance to the compulsory temptations of heterosexuality. Turing's death may have been a suicide, but it was also a refusal to circulate in the arena of military secrets. Turing's apple may be the apple of knowledge, but it is also the fruit of a technological dream.

The Female Cyborg: Feminism and Postmodernism

> *"The projected manufacture by men of artificial wombs, of cyborgs, which will be part flesh, part robot, of clones—all are manifestations of phallotechnic boundary violations."*
>
> —Mary Daly, *Gyn-Ecology: The Metaethics of Radical Feminism*

> *"The cyborg is resolutely committed to partiality, irony, intimacy and perversity. It is oppositional, utopian and completely without innocence."*
>
> —Donna Haraway, "A Manifesto for Cyborgs: Science, Technology, and Socialist Feminism in the 1980s"

Postmodernism has most often been theorized with relation to the arts or literature, but artificial intelligence, quantum mechanics, and a general move away from disciplinarity reveal that postmodernity is not only a simultaneous formation across disciplinary boundaries, but it also challenges distinctions between art and science altogether and suggests that the two cannot be thought separately. Obviously, the definition of postmodernism is contested. However, a working model of postmodernism demands that it have a historical dimension, a political perspective, and a cultural domain. Because the theoretical concerns of postmodernism and feminism often seem to mirror each other, questions arise as to whether the two are in dialogue or opposition and whether one takes precedence over the other. I contend that feminism and postmodernism enjoy a mutual dependence within the academy and in relation to mass culture. Because postmodernism has often been represented as a chameleon discourse, without a stable shape, form, or location, I offer a working definition that attempts both to situate it and to maintain its ambiguities. Theorists such as Andreas Huyssen and Jean François Lyotard suggest that postmodernism does not simply follow after modernism: it arises out of modernism and indeed interrupts what Lyotard identifies as modernism's grand narratives.[5] Huyssen finds that postmodernism sometimes breaks critically with modernism, and at other times merely reinscribes the modern enterprise.[6] The postmodern is not simply a chronological "after" to the modern; it is always embedded within the modern as interference or interruption and as a coming to consciousness of a subject no longer modeled upon the Western white male. In his attempt to historicize postmodernism, Frederick Jameson calls it a "cultural dominant" in the age of multinational capitalism. As cultural dominant, postmodernism participates in a different perception of space and time, in the production of a fragmented subjectivity, and in the breakdown of a surface/depth model in the realm of representation.[7] Refusing to designate postmodernism as a "style," Jameson demonstrates that postmodernism is a production within a system of logic at a precise time in history.

Most theories of the postmodern concede that it involves a changing relation between our bodies and our worlds. Jameson suggests, with reference to architecture, that postmodern hyperspace "has finally succeeded in transcending the capacities of the individual human body to locate itself, to organize its immediate surroundings perceptually, and cognitively to map its position in a mappable external world."[8] But the vertigo that Jameson describes, like the confusion precipitated in Lyotard's text by the breakdown of "grand narratives of legitimation,"[9] is nothing new for women and people of color. The world, after all, has been mapped and legitimated for only a small group of people. As postmodernity brings space and truth, time and body, nature and representation, and culture and technology into a series of startling collisions, we begin to ask questions about what interests were served by the stability of these categories and about who, in contrast, benefits from a recognition of radical instability within the postmodern. Such questions have informed debates about postmodern feminism. By exploring feminist claims that postmodernism is merely an intellectual ruse to reconstitute the subject as white and male, I show that postmodernism and feminism are in fact mutually indebted. On the most basic level, feminism forces a theory of gender oppression upon postmodernism, and postmodernism provides feminism with a politics of artificiality.

The relationship between feminism and postmodernism is anything but familial—they are not to be married, hardly siblings; they are both more and less than incestuous. The most successful unions of these two discourses, indeed, have suggested a robotic, artificial, and monstrous connection. Donna Haraway's 1985 essay, "A Manifesto for Cyborgs: Science, Technology, and Socialist Feminism in the 1980s," presents a radical departure for an emergent postmodern feminist discourse. Haraway merges radical feminism with a postmodern articulation of history and a politically necessary analysis of science and technology. She calls for a repositioning of socialist feminism in relation to technological production, theoretical articulations of the feminist subject, and the narrative of what she calls "salvation history." The cyborg for Haraway is "a condensed image of both imagination and material reality, the two joined centers structuring any possibility of historical transformation." Such an image is particularly useful for feminists who seek to avoid the ideological dangers of recourse to an authentic female self. Haraway's cyborg displays the machinery of gender; clothes herself in circuitry and networks; commits to "partiality, irony, intimacy, and perversity";[10] and revels in the confusion of boundaries.

Haraway has been criticized for engaging in "an epistemological fantasy of *becoming* multiplicity" by Susan Bordo, who identifies a danger in theoretical projects that embrace multiple and unstable subject positions. Such "deconstructionist readings," she suggests, "refuse to assume a shape for which they must take responsibility."[11] Bordo is not alone in her suspicion of the elusiveness of the postmodern subject. Nancy Hartsock asks: "Why is it that just at the moment when so many of us who have been silenced begin to demand the right to name ourselves, to act as subjects rather than as the objects of history, that just then the concept of subjecthood becomes problematic?"[12] Both Bordo's suspicion of the locatedness of the postmodern subject and Hartsock's questioning of the historical imperative behind the postmodern project are valid and timely inquiries. The subtext to both questions is whether the postmodern subject, fragmented and in flux, is not after all merely another incarnation of the masculine subject of the Enlightenment. Gender, such theorists fear, has been deemphasized in order to allow the male subject to be renaturalized as "human."

Bordo, then, accuses postmodern feminism of refusing "to assume a shape," and yet Haraway has outlined clearly the shape, form, and agenda of a postmodern feminist cyborg who *participates* in power structures. Hartsock finds postmodernism to be suspiciously contemporary with the coming to voice of many who have previously been silenced; and yet, academic feminism, at least, is surely a discourse with a voice and with an increasingly empowered place within the institution. Hartsock asks why is it that subjecthood splinters when marginalized groups begin to speak. The answer is already embedded in her question; subjecthood becomes problematic, fragmented, and stratified *because* marginalized Others begin to speak. The concept of the unified bourgeois subject, in other words, has been shot through with otherness and can find no way to regroup or reunite the splinters of being, now themselves part of a class, race, and gender configuration.

The fears that Bordo and Hartsock articulate are indeed justified, but to overindulge in such a speculative drift must surely reduce institutional power to a one-way dynamic that always reproduces a center and margins structure. Debates about whether certain theoretical strategies neutralize the political content of academic feminism—or, worse, collaborate in its co-optation—are necessary and important as long as they do not fall back upon a conception of power that identifies it as full-scale repression coming from above. Power, Michel Foucault has forcefully demonstrated, comes from below; and the postmodern subject, in its fragmentary and partial form, was formed out of the very challenge made by feminism to patriarchy.

Haraway concludes her essay: "Although both are bound in the spiral dance, I would rather be a cyborg than a goddess."[13] The cyborg and the goddess are suggestive terms for the comprehension of feminism as always multiple. Feminism has never been a monolithic theoretical or cultural project, but certain ideas do attain a kind of dominance over time. Hence, the "spiral dance," or history, makes the cyborg inconceivable in feminism without the prior presence of the goddess; one does, indeed, stand upon the other's shoulders. Haraway's essay figures the cultural feminism of the late 1970s and the early 1980s as the goddess because it revived and reinvested, in an idealized concept of woman, a concept that exiled her in nature and essentialized her in relation to gender. Such "cultural feminism," one which ignores the material bases of oppression and cathects "woman" as the real, the true, and the natural, reproduces, in Biddy Martin's words, "the classical split between the individual and the social formation" and assumes "that we can shed what is supposedly a false consciousness imposed and maintained from the outside, and begin to speak a more authentic truth."[14] Although the goddess and the cyborg are merely poles in a complex debate, they are useful in thinking through gender. Indeed, although the terms of the debate may change over time, in the arguments for and against a postmodern feminism we can still trace an oscillation between these positions. The ground between the goddess and the cyborg clearly stakes out the contested territory between the category "woman" and the gendered "body." So, if the goddess is an ideal congruence between anatomy and femininity, the cyborg instead posits femininity as automation, a coded masquerade.

As early as 1970, Shulamith Firestone in *The Dialectic of Sex* suggested the promise of the female cyborg: "What is called for is a revolutionary ecological program that would attempt to establish an artificial balance in place of the 'natural' one, thus realizing the original goal of empirical science: total mastery of nature." Firestone argued that feminist revolution must seize control of the means of both production and reproduction: cybernation and fertility control will relieve women of their historical burden and lead the way to a different and fully politicized female subject position. Firestone remained caught in a kind of biologism which grounds gender oppression in the body of the mother. And although her call for "total mastery" resubmits to a kind of holism, she has nonetheless envisioned a solution which is neither apocalyptic nor idealist and one which welcomes developments in science and technology. Firestone's claim that "the misuse of scientific developments is very often confused with technology itself" leads her to suggest that "atomic energy, fertility control, artificial reproduction, cybernation, in themselves are liberating—unless they are improperly used." Such a perspective concurs with

Haraway's argument that "taking responsibility for the social relations of science and technology means refusing an anti-science metaphysics, a demonology of technology. . . ."[15]

Firestone's grim optimism in the 1970s was countered within feminist discourse by the demonization of science and technology which, quite understandably, stemmed from a fear of the relatedness of technology and militarism. Mary Daly's *Gyn/Ecology*, perhaps the most important work in the cultural feminist tradition, imaginatively and yet reductively performs an unequivocal rejection of all technologies. In a section entitled "From Robotitude to Roboticide: Reconsidering," Daly argues that "phallotechnic progress" aims eventually to replace femaleness with "hollow holograms" and female bodies with robots through such techniques as "total therapy, transsexualism and cloning."[16] Daly proposes a strategy to counter this process and calls it "roboticide" or the destruction of "false selves." Given the history of gendering technology as female in order to make it seductive, the threat of a Stepford Wives phenomenon certainly has validity. However, Daly's cultural critique hinges upon an investment in binaries such as natural and artificial, intuitive and rational, female and male, and body and mind. Daly reinvests in the fear of autonomous machines and equates artificiality with the loss of an essential self.

Daly categorizes cloning, artificial intelligence, and reproductive technology (or, as she terms it, "male-mother-miming") as boundary violations perpetrated by scientists, the "priests of patriarchy."[17] She reads robotitude, or automated gender, as a negative condition because she imagines that it replaces something natural and organic within "woman." Unlike Haraway, Daly is certain of what counts as nature and of what constitutes a true self. I suggest that even though automated gender does indeed involve a certain "robotitude," automation functions amidst constant interference from the random elements of computer technology and therefore constantly participates in the ordering and disordering of resistances. The imperfect matches between gender and desire, sex and gender, and the body and technology can be accommodated within the automated cyborg, because it is always partial, part machine and part human; it is always becoming human or "becoming woman."[18]

To argue, as the cultural feminists do, that automated gender removes the humanity of the female subject is to ignore the technology of gender and to replicate a patriarchal gendering of technology. As we saw in relation to Turing, technology is given a female identity when it must seduce the user into thinking of it as desirable or benign. Daly's argument that the female robot contaminates woman's essential naturalness regenders the natural and the artificial in the opposite direction as female nature and male science.

In a recent issue of *Feminist Studies,* Jane Caputi provides an updated version of Daly's critique of phallotechnocracy. Caputi's far-ranging analysis examines what she perceives as the ominous cultural import of the blurring of human and machine. Caputi opens her argument with a cogent reading of a television commercial for Elephant Premium floppy disks during election week 1984. The commercial's subliminal message, she suggests, is about memory, the mythical memory of the elephant, her own memory that the elephant is a symbol of the Republican party, and the electronic memory of the floppy disk. Caputi is concerned here with "the replacement of organic memory by an artificial substitute," and she fears that humans and machines will "slur/blur ever into one another, humans becoming more cold, the machines acquiring more soul."[19] Memory, artificial memory, also concerns Caputi in her consideration of the Apple computer logo. She argues that the logo both reactivates the myth of original sin and creates a new and dangerous myth about "an artificial paradise, indeed the artificial as paradise." Here, Caputi fails to question the very artificiality of the "natural" paradise she implicitly defends. The apple, as I have tried to suggest, is Turing's apple, an artificial fusion of mathematics and the body, death and desire, sex and gender.

In order to remain aware of the hidden messages in commercials that link conservatism, corporate business, and computer technology, Caputi warns, we must learn to "see elephants," to remember, "to no longer accept the part as the whole, to perceive and act upon essential connections."[20] We might ask of Caputi and Daly, what *is* so anxiety provoking in a blurring of machine and human and what is so attractive in holism and universalism? I propose that the fear in the first and the desire in the second spring from and return us to the complementary binaries of Western metaphysics. Caputi's concern that we are being duped by a patriarchal conspiracy of signification perhaps overlooks the fact that oppressive mechanisms more often deceive by wearing the mask of truth than by hiding; the action happens at the surface rather than down below. As Oscar Wilde wrote, "the true mystery of the world is the visible not the invisible."

In a discussion of Marshall McLuhan's *The Mechanical Bride: Folklore of Industrial Man,* Caputi further simplifies what is at stake in the concepts of "woman" and "female." She writes of the "Mechanical Bride" (in effect, a female cyborg): "This symbol is also a metaphor, one that links technology to creation via an artificial woman/wife/mother. As such, it cannot help but expose the enmity that technological man declares for living flesh and blood creation—nature, motherhood, the womb—but also for female *reality.*"[21] In her attempt to maintain strict boundaries between the authentic and its simulation, Caputi opposes the mechanical bride to "female reality," a slippery concept, and she relocates nature and

494

Ira Livingston, untitled drawing, mixed media.

motherhood firmly within the female body. The female cyborg, therefore, becomes in her argument a symbol for male technological aggression against women; she does not attempt to explain what fear the technological woman, the mechanical bride, generates in herself.

To predicate a critique of patriarchy, as Caputi and Daly do, on the basis of a true and authentic female self, who jealously guards her boundaries (physical and spiritual) and her goddess-given right to birth children, is merely to tell the story that patriarchy has told all along about women: women are morally superior to men, and they have an essential connection to nature. The female cyborg is, for both Daly and Caputi, a feared image of the seduction of woman into an automated femininity rather than the image of what patriarchal, masculinist authority fears in both an autonomous technology and in femininity itself. The mistake lies in thinking that there is some "natural" or "organic" essence of woman that is either corrupted or contained by any association with the artificial. However, femininity is always mechanical and artificial—as is masculinity. The female cyborg becomes a terrifying cultural icon because it hints at the radical potential of a fusion of femininity and intelligence. If we define femininity as the representation of any gendered body, and intelligence as the autonomous potential of technology and mental functioning, their union signifies the artificial component in each without referring to any essential concept of nature. A female cyborg would be artificial in both mind and flesh, as much woman as machine, as close to science as to nature. The resistance she represents to static conceptions of gender and technology pushes a feminist theory of power to a new arena. The intelligent and female cyborg thinks gender, processes power, and converts a binary system of logic into a more intricate network. As a metaphor, she challenges the correspondences such as maternity and femininity or female and emotion. As a metonym, she embodies the impossibility of distinguishing between gender and its representation.

By merging so completely the familiar with the strange, the artificial with the natural, the female cyborg appears to evoke something unsettling, something that profoundly disturbs and frightens certain authors. We might call the effect produced by the female cyborg "uncanny." "The uncanny," Freud writes in an essay of the same name, "is that class of the terrifying which leads back to something long known to us, once very familiar."[22] He then leads us back to the repressed as castration or the repressed as the mother's genitals. The repressed becomes uncanny when it recurs: it is the familiar (i.e., the mother's genitals) become strange (i.e., castrated).

By way of illustrating his theory, Freud refers to Hoffman's tale, "The Sand Man." He wants to use the story to prove his thesis that the threat of castration is what creates uncanny effects. Freud argues that the uncanny is represented in the castrating figure of the Sand Man himself, rather than in the lifelike doll, Olympia, with whom the hero, Nathaniel, falls in love.

> But I cannot think—and I hope most readers of the story will agree with me—that the theme of the doll, Olympia, who is to all appearances a living being, is by any means the only element to be held responsible for the quite unparalleled atmosphere of uncanniness which the story evokes. . . . The main theme of the story is, on the contrary, something different . . . it is the theme of the Sand Man who tears out children's eyes.

In this passage, Freud deliberately and forcefully shifts the terms of the debate in order to oppose Ernst Jentsch's work suggesting that the uncanny is produced by intellectual uncertainty. Jentsch gives as an example "doubts whether an apparently animate being is really alive," and he refers to "wax-work figures, artificial dolls and automatons."[23] Obviously, for Jentsch it is the automaton Olympia that is the locus of the uncanny in the story. Freud refutes Jentsch not only because of the importance of the castration theory to psychoanalysis, but also because Freud needs to separate the female body from both technology and the production of terror. Thus, he can maintain a critical connection (the very connection that Caputi and Daly defend) between the female body, nature, and motherhood.

A cycle of repetition-compulsion characterizes Freud's wandering journey through the uncanny. He represses the female figure Olympia who returns as the "painted woman" of Italy (the gen-Italia); then as the dark forest in which one might be lost; and finally as that "unheimlich place" itself, "the entrance to the former heim [home] of all human beings, to the place where everyone dwelt once upon a time and in the beginning."[24] This return reassures Freud of the possibility of an origin (easily lost among infinite repetitions) and calms his fear of the automated woman, the doll to whose womb neither he nor any man may return. Olympia, of course, is a cyborg, not a flesh-and-blood woman; nonetheless, she is desirable. Technology and the feminine reside at once in Olympia. Olympia, the mechanical bride, represents technology's seductiveness and its inevitability.[25]

In Hoffman's "The Sand Man," Olympia seduces the protagonist, Nathaniel, because as automaton she does not interfere with his narcissistic need to find himself mirrored in the Other. Her answer to all his questions, "Ach! Ach!" assures him that he has found true femininity, a perpetually consenting adult. When she is revealed to be an automaton, when her femininity as mechanism is finally brought to his attention, his very masculinity lies in the balance. Olympia as automaton radically questions the possibility of taking the body as proof of gender. She produces uncanny notions that the machine is more than a metaphor for self, that sexuality has a mechanism, and that gender is a technology.

Clearly, there is a problem when the arguments used within psychoanalysis or within modern scientific discourse to essentialize femininity are replicated within feminist theory. Mary Daly warns us of the dangers of robotitude but fails to problematize the ways in which technology has already been gendered female or why. Jane Caputi opposes artificial and natural memories but does not remember that feminism has called naturalized memory, or "history," into question all along. Some strands of feminist theory have demonized science and technology rather than attempting to undo oppressive discourses while participating in those that may empower us. In the age of the intelligent machine, political categories can no longer afford to be binary. A multiplicity is called for that acknowledges power differentials but is not ruled by them; that produces and reduces differences; and, finally, that understands gender as automated *and* intelligent, as a mechanism or structure capable of achieving some kind of autonomy from both biological sex and a rationalistic tradition. The female cyborg, in other words, calls attention to the artificiality of gender distinctions and to the political motivation that continues to blur gender into nature.

Feminist rereadings of what Haraway calls "the social relations of technology," of Olympia the artificial woman, the mechanical bride, can contribute to different technologies and different conceptions of gender identities. The apparently female cyborg releases the female body from its bondage to nature and merges body and machine to produce a terrifying and uncanny prospect of female intelligence. Gender emerges within the cyborg as no longer a binary but as a multiple construction dependent upon random formations beyond masculine or feminine. Different readings of cultural symbols, such as the apple of temptation, produce new myths and refuse the eschatology of a Christian science. Turing's travels into artificial intelligence, his experience of the technology of gender within his own body, his homosexuality, and finally, his fatal bite into the cyanide apple produce difference and the artificial as always concomitant with the natural. The cyborg and the apple demand post-Christian myths, myths of multiple genders, of variegated desires, myths of difference, differences and tolerance.

Postscript

Postmodern feminism, as I have been arguing, can find positive and productive ways in which to theorize gender, science, and technology, and their connections within the fertile and provocative field of machine intelligence. Using the image of a female machine, I posit gender as an automated construct. Although the female cyborg proves to be a fascinating metaphor and an exciting prospect, it may gloss or obscure certain relations between living women and technology. For example, within the information industry, a traditional gender division exists with regard to work—men write programs and women process words—and such a division reinforces existing models for gendered labor.

Although Shoshana Zuboff does not directly confront the gendered division of labor, her book, *In the Age of the Smart Machine: The Future of Work and Power*, implies that such a division is not compatible with the new technology. Calling manager-employee relations in the automated workplace "posthierarchical," she claims: "This does not imply that differentials of knowledge, responsibility, and power no longer exist; rather they can no longer be assumed. Instead they shift and flow and develop their character in relation to the situations, the task and the actors at hand." Work relations, Zuboff argues, when clustered around an electronic text rather than spread between manual labor and personnel management, tend toward a system of equality. To arrive at this conclusion, Zuboff traces the history of blue- and white-collar workers, clerical workers, and management in relation to disciplinary systems of power within technology and industry. The predominance of women in the word-processing field might be attributed, then, to a continuation of the effects of the feminization of office work after the introduction of the typewriter in the 1890s: "in 1890, 64 percent of all stenographers and typists were women; by 1920, the figure had risen to 92 percent."[26] But typewriting and word processing—textual reproduction and textual manipulation— are different kinds of tasks, with a much greater potential for change existing within word processing. As jobs increasingly focus upon the manipulation of electronic texts and symbols, word processing will very probably not remain a secretarial task involving simple transcription; word processing, whether performed by women or men, may conceivably break down traditional divisions of labor within the office. The smart machine, indeed, requires that we change the way we envision our jobs as much as the new jobs alter social relations within the workplace.

At the same time, the electronic marketplace threatens to enforce a new kind of literacy and to create a disenfranchised body of illiterates. Being at ease with computer technology demands exposure that right now only money can buy. Even a slight decrease in market value, however, could make the personal computer as affordable and ubiquitous as the television set. If the labor force is to resist a split between those who work on computers and those who continue to hold low-paying and low-prestige service jobs, a split that could follow predictable class and race lines, people must have roughly equal access to computer time. Of course, the configurations of class, race, and gender in the age of the intelligent machine are not reducible to a single model or strategy. As the technology changes, social relations change; as social relations change, the technology is altered. Cybernetic systems, at least potentially, tend toward a posthierarchical labor structure in which the system stresses interaction—among workers and management, computer systems and operators—as much as production.

Gender, in this essay, has figured as an electronic text that shifts and changes in dialogue with users and programs. The apple signifies an altered relation between our bodies and ourselves in the age of the intelligent machine, and the Apple logo's byte no longer proves fatal. Postmodern feminism, I argue, may benefit from the theory of artificiality proposed by Turing's explorations in artificial intelligence and symbolized by the Apple logo. Such a theory shows that we are already as embedded within the new technologies as they are embodied within us. Both Turing's apple and the female cyborg threaten our ability to differentiate between our natural selves and our machine selves; these images suggest that perhaps already cyborgs are us.

Notes

This essay began as a paper for Nancy Armstrong's feminist theory seminar at the University of Minnesota and I am indebted to her provocative and intricate reading of feminism. I also want to thank the following people for reading and commenting upon drafts of this essay: Barbara Cruikshank, Jane Gallop, Ira Livingston, and Paula Rabinowitz.

1. Andrew Hodges, *Alan Turing, the Enigma* (New York: Simon & Schuster, 1983), 97.

2. G.H. Hardy, quoted in ibid., 120.

3. Alan Turing, "Computing Machinery and Intelligence," *Mind* 59 (October 1950): 433–60.

4. Andreas Huyssen, "The Vamp and the Machine: Fritz Lang's Metropolis," in Andreas Huyssen, *After the Great Divide: Modernism, Mass Culture, Postmodernism* (Bloomington and Indianapolis: Indiana University Press, 1986), 70.

5. Jean François Lyotard, *The Postmodern Condition: A Report on Knowledge,* trans. Geoff Bennington and Brian Massumi (Minneapolis: Minnesota University Press, 1984).

6. Andreas Huyssen, "Mapping the Postmodern," in *After the Great Divide,* 185.

7. Frederick Jameson, "Postmodernism, or the Cultural Logic of Late Capitalism," *New Left Review,* no. 146 (July–August 1984): 53–92.

8. Ibid., 83.

9. Lyotard, 51.

10. Donna Haraway, "A Manifesto for Cyborgs: Science, Technology, and Socialist Feminism in the 1980s," in *Feminism/Postmodernism,* ed. Linda J. Nicholson (New York and London: Routledge, 1990), 191, 192. I am using the most recent

publication of this article because it does contain a few changes from the original version published in *Socialist Review*, no. 80 (1985): 65–107.

11. Susan Bordo, "Feminism, Postmodernism, and Gender-Scepticism," in *Feminism/Postmodernism*, 145, 144.

12. Nancy Hartsock, "Foucault on Power: A Theory for Women," in *Feminism/Postmodernism*, 162.

13. Haraway, 223.

14. Biddy Martin, "Feminism, Criticism, and Foucault," *New German Critique*, no. 27 (Fall 1982): 14–15.

15. Shulamith Firestone, *The Dialectic of Sex: The Case for Feminist Revolution* (New York: Morrow, 1970), 219, 224, 223.

16. Mary Daly, *Gyn/Ecology: The Metaethics of Radical Feminism* (Boston: Beacon Press, 1978), 53.

17. Ibid., 103.

18. See Alice Jardine's provocative analysis of feminism and postmodernism and "the woman-in-effect" or "becoming woman" as a model for the postmodern subject in Alice Jardine, *Gynesis: Configurations of Woman and Modernity* (Ithaca and London: Cornell University Press, 1985).

19. Jane Caputi, "Seeing Elephants: The Myths of Phallotechnology," *Feminist Studies* 14 (Fall 1988): 514, 490.

20. Ibid., 490.

21. Ibid., 511.

22. Sigmund Freud, "The Uncanny" (1919), in Sigmund Freud, *On Creativity and the Unconscious*, trans. Alix Strachey (New York: Harper & Row, 1958), 123–24.

23. Ibid., 133, 132.

24. Ibid., 153.

25. To make an interesting connection here between Freud's uncanny doll and Turing's dream of intelligent machines, one need only note that "Olympia" is the name of a typewriter company. Turing imagined his machines as "supertypewriters."

26. Shoshana Zuboff, *In the Age of the Smart Machine: The Future of Work and Power* (New York: Basic Books, 1988), 401–2, 116.

22 African and Western Feminisms

World-Traveling the Tendencies and Possibilities

CHRISTINE SYLVESTER

I believe that our identities are not given or reducible to our origins, skin colour, or material locations. Identities or positions are the product of struggle and they represent an achieved, not an ascribed trait.

—**Marjorie Mbilinyi 1992, 35**

I want people to advocate feminism as a politics. Feminism is perceived as a lifestyle, as something you become rather than something you do.

—**bell hooks, hooks et al. 1993, 38**

She learns to juggle cultures. She has a plural personality, she operates in a pluralistic mode—nothing is thrust out, the good the bad and the ugly, nothing rejected, nothing abandoned. Not only does she sustain contradictions, she turns the ambivalence into something else.

—**Gloria Anzaldúa 1987, 79**

At this point in feminist theorizing, as at moments in the past, several interlocking, simultaneous, and sequential tendencies mark the field. One features feminism settling into its many philosophical and identity differences and defending an absence of consensus as appropri-

I wish to thank Stanlie James for helping me think about world traveling. Colleagues in the women's studies programs at Australian National University and the University of Adelaide offered helpful comments on the article, and the editors and reviewers for *Signs* provided incomparably wise suggestions.

ate for this era. Following closely on this first tendency is considerable feminist worry about issues of power and solidarity in a fragmented era and accompanying debates about the merits of this versus that specific feminism. The third tendency is in the direction of effecting some feminist amalgamations that merge or cross-fertilize the differences.

This article considers each feminist tendency as it bears on questions raised in Africanist circles about the existence and nature of African feminisms relative to Western feminisms. The theoretical work of Marjorie Mbilinyi, a multi-identified Tanzanian feminist, and Kathy Ferguson, a Western feminist theorist, are probed for the connections they raise and the possibilities they harbor for traveling toward a method of empathetic cooperation across, but with an eye on registering, feminist differences. The three feminist quotations offered above suggest something of what the journey entails: achieved plural identities, juggled cultures, and ambivalences turned into feminist politics rather than feminist lifestyle sanctuaries.

On Parading, Debating, Merging

Feminists parade the geospaces. Liberals, radicals, Marxists, socialists, ecos, empiricists, standpointers, womanists, lesbians, postmodernists, poststructuralists, postmoderns, and queers pass in review. Nationalist and critical Third World feminisms join the march. WIDs and WADs GAD about in gorgeous attire.[1] Several melodies play simultaneously. Cheers strike up for the favorites. The parade of feminist approaches has been a perennial event for some time and a recently celebrated event in some quarters. The cover of *Ms.* shouts "No, Feminists Don't All Think Alike (Who Says We Have To?)" (*Ms.* 1993). It is a parade that celebrates voices, identities, material cultures, lifestyles, and the sense that "nothing is thrust out," "nothing rejected," "nothing abandoned."

While the several tunes play and the ever-lengthening feminist displays pass, some worry about those who have the resources to rain on the parade by using feminist differences against us or simply by denying feminism any salience. Backlash (Faludi 1991) is not just a U.S. phenomenon. Ruth Meena accuses donor agencies in southern Africa of having "deliberately and consciously taken measures which ensure a *status quo* in which scholars of the region remain primary producers of raw data to be processed by 'intellectual' factories of the North" (Meena 1992, 3). Even though some of the locally produced materials suggest the importance of deviating from the liberal women in development (WID) line that tends to find favor in Western circles, concerns about integrating African women into given notions of development prevail in donor policies. Changu Mannathoko thinks "it is a misconception to view feminism as a Western ideology" (1992, 72). But the ability of donors and local governments to refuse locally produced knowledge about "African women" is undoubtedly related to the fact that "feminism is considered by most of our African scholars as a foreign importation which has no relevance to the African situation" (Meena 1992, 4).

The very presence of women in nontraditional labor activities in the United States can foment hysterical scenarios of gender-reversed sexual harassment in the workplace.[2] In parts of Africa, that presence can jar the intelligentsia into seeking, in Rudo Gaidzanwa's terms, to redomesticate African women, to send them to some traditional home, some status "reducible to our origins," some "lifestyle" that refuses "plural personality" (1992, 116). Thus statues of Zimbabwe's war heroes inappropriately depict "the figures of men wearing trousers but the women in skirts," as though, says Gaidzanwa, "only men were supposed to wear trousers in the new country of Zimbabwe that the population had fought so hard to liberate" (1992, 117).[3] Denying that Zimbabwean men *and women* shouldered the tasks of war and jumbled the categories of gender in doing so, "women combatants" are now "lady fighters." Along similar lines, the largest maternity hospital in Harare, Gaidzanwa reminds us, is renamed for the female spirit medium, Nehanda Nyakasikana, known in no way for being a mother: she was an adviser to local rebels seeking to overthrow the colonial government in the uprisings of 1896–97. Here is a direct case of domestication and an indirect refusal of a feminist-publicized fact that women can do and be a number of things other than or while being mothers.

Concerns with such stunts and denials have resulted in lively debates in many locations about how to project feminist power in an era when feminisms parade their differences against a backdrop of backlash. It was all seemingly easier in the 1970s and early 1980s, when feminist theories set forth blueprints for women's liberation that were, in Rosi Braidotti's words, "free from the specialized tone of later feminist scholarship" (1991, 153). In your face with certainties, various movement feminisms gave women clear-cut agendas to pursue, as in Nyaradzo Makamure's unequivocal claim in 1984 that "the Women's Movement in Zimbabwe is closely linked to the struggle for socialism" (1984, 75). In the 1980s, feminist theory in the West scanned the results of in-your-face feminist agendas, the absence of geospatial nuance in the prescriptions, the silencing of dissent from "the" correct positions, and turned, chastened, to a more pretheoretical place to ask how we know who we are, where we are, and what we should do. In answering these questions, some feminist theory became hyperintellectual and came away from the streets just as backlashes were being orchestrated. It showed off intellectual finery and finessed language until many "agenda feminists" were confused and peeved and disempowered. And yet, despite accusations of abstraction, nihilism, relativism, and apolitics targeted at what became known as the postmodern turn in feminism, that turn corrects for elements of tyrannical surefootedness in the blueprint era. The postmodern era is fragmenting, but the fragmentation is not necessarily unfriendly, even to Third World women, to African feminists. On the contrary, the emphasis on difference, on local circumstances, on situated constitutions of "women" and "feminism," says Jane Parpart, "recognizes the connection between knowledge and power, and seeks to understand local knowledges both as sites of resistance and power [in ways that] would provide a more subtle understanding of Third World women's lives" (1993, 456).

The third tendency is to look in the interstices of the debate positions for ways to bridge feminist differences effectively without forcing one feminism (or locally situated set of women) to expire at the hands of another. Just at Third World–First World intersections of feminism, we find some radical woman-centered streams of African feminism, which rest on essentialist notions of women, joining nationalist feminisms around the theme that the precolonial period in Africa was something of a golden age for all African women.[4] The WID approach, which enforces a Western liberal understanding that women must be integrated into the mainstream, stands somewhat amended by a newer WAD approach that tells us women are already in development: it commingles with Marxist-feminist ideas on how integrationist projects may disadvantage Third World women by doubling and tripling their burdens of production. Meanwhile, GAD approaches accuse WID and WAD of "group[ing] women together without taking strong analytical note of class, race, or ethnicity divisions, all of which may exercise a powerful influence on their actual social status" (Rathgeber 1990, 493). The preference in many GAD circles is for a more socialist-feminist-resonating theory (Zwart n.d.).[5] All the while, critical Third World feminism claims to "incorporate elements from Marxist, nationalist, and poststructuralist feminism" (Mbilinyi 1992, 46).

The new merger efforts nuance feminist theory and take it in less either-or directions than was our wont in the in-your-face days. They reveal borderlands of race, class, gender, and public policy that once took individual pride of place, one behind the other, in the parade of feminisms. But is it enough to search for a more widely representative set of truths to amalgamate? When amalgamated feminisms march under one instead of two or more banners, tensions at their fulcrums can be papered over. One can imagine all feminisms tumbled together in one canister and randomly plucked out for matches, like some kind of feminist lottery. Yet without some amalgamations, how do we fashion a feminist politics that bell hooks could cheer as "something you do"?

World Traveling

I would like to see a new trend emerge that takes the current emphasis on difference and turns it into "something else" that is "not an ascribed trait" or a feminist "lifestyle" but "a politics." I would like more emphasis on methods of speaking in, through, and across differences—methods by which different identity feminisms and geospatial locations within them become mobile in ways that juggle and cross borderlands without leaving us with baseball caps affixed with tourist decals—"I Climbed Mt. Kilimanjaro with Tanzanian Nationalist Feminists"—the total of decal experiences summing into a lifestyle of feminist add-ons.

Exotic images appended to a stationary self-traveling locked up safe from intrusive provincialisms smack of feminist tourism. As Elspeth Probyn says, "The tourist is posed as unthreatening, merely passing through; however, his person has questionable effects. Just as economically the benefits of tourism return to the first world, the tourist . . . camouflage[s] the theoretical problematic of the ontological implications of Western subjecthood" (1990, 184). This is a form of travel that encourages arrogant perceptions of others as having only the interests the traveler assigns.[6] It is the Western-subject-centered "I" dressed up for encounters with wildernessed natives.[7]

The mobilities I have in mind are of a different order. They come from feminist "world-travelling" as Maria Lugones describes the experience: "Those of us who are 'world'-travellers have the distinct experience of being in different 'worlds' and ourselves in them. We can say 'That's me there, and I am happy in that "world."' The experience is one of having memory of oneself as different without any underlying 'I'" (1990, 396). This form of world traveling relies on empathy to enter into the spirit of difference and find in it an echo of oneself as other than the way one seems to be. It moves us, in other words, to places of subjectivity that shift and hyphenate into the worlds of others. Lugones explains the process: "It is not a matter of acting. One does not pose as someone else, one does not pretend to be, for example, someone of a different personality or character or someone who uses space or language differently than the other person. Rather one *is* someone who has that personality or character or uses space and language in that particular way" (1990, 396).

World traveling introduces a certain jostling in the feminist parade ranks, as an avowed "I" becomes not merely and egoistically sympathetic to surrounding marchers ("I understand their concerns") but related empathetically in two or more parade positions or worlds of experience. Judith Butler says that "sympathy involves a substitution of oneself for another that may well be a colonization of the other's position *as* one's own" (1993, 118). Empathetic identities are relationally autonomous. They exist separately and yet inform and draw on each other, shape each other with irony, poignancy, jealousy, and a wisdom that defies colonial efforts to inform all of us of where to take our proper places.[8]

Being different in another world and oneself in it is an achievement, a struggle with solipsism. It enables the juggle of feminist cultures precisely because aspects of those cultures become part of us rather than something we go on vacation to photograph through the lens of a fixed "I." Whereas "the arrogant perceiver falsifies and oversimplifies" (Gunning 1991–92, 199), the world traveler can valorize differences among women by seeing, in Teresa de Lauretis's terms, "differences within women" (1986, 14), differences within the woman or man who is feminist, within ourselves. As one travels, one encounters fewer aliens out there at the same time that one appreciates the many nuances of "women."

Yet is it only the Westerner who can travel the worlds of difference—the parade positions of feminism—in order to become less arrogant and more empathetic? Looming behind an identity-expanding concept of world traveling, is there the shadow of an affluent, educated contemplator of "the other," one who has the resources to travel, the time to explore hyphenations, and "the" standards against which to measure empathy? Have I not set up a way to understand the white redoubt of South Africa, for example, as traveling to the African other at the pace of a luxury cruise liner, controlling the resources and processes of the trip up to the last bloody moment? Am I speaking of "worlding" the Third World by discovering it and bringing it back home through colonial and imperialist activities, through an assimilationist refusal of rich histories and autonomous spaces?[9]

The line between feminist world traveling and "the arrogant perceiver [who] sees himself as the center of the universe" (Frye 1983, 66–67) can be jagged. One can slide backward and forward between travel and world travel. As Trinh T. Minh-ha says: "'Correct' cultural filmmaking . . . usually implies that Africans show Africa; Asians, Asia; and Euro-Americans, the world. Otherness has its laws and interdictions. Since you can't take the bush from the Black man [say some Afrikaners], it is the bush that is consistently given back to him, and as things often turn out it is also this very bush that the Black man shall make his exclusive territory" (1990, 373). Such travel keeps less well-resourced subjects in confined locations. Meanwhile, the mobile ones who write the "laws and interdictions" may not have the empathy needed to glimpse the intricate lives that lie beyond an invented bush. Norma Alarcón suggests that "the freedom of women of color to posit themselves as multiple-voiced subjects is constantly in peril or repression precisely at that point where our constituted contradictions put us at odds with women different from ourselves" (1990, 364).

Having raised the alarm about round-trip travel back to one's Western lifestyle, it is important to deny it the exclusive territory of world traveling. Lugones argues that it is not the privileged person who is a typical world traveler. Rather, it is the person outside dominant society who acquires "flexibility in shifting from the mainstream construction of life to other constructions of life where [she is] more or less 'at home'" (1990, 390). Other Third World feminists echo her point, often drawing on U.S. border dwellers as inspirational travelers. For example, Gloria Anzaldúa says: "Chicano, *indio,* American Indian, *mojado, mexicano,* immigrant Latino, Anglo in power, working class Anglo, Black, Asian—our psyches resemble the bordertowns and are populated by the same people" (1987, 87). Alarcón claims that many colonially enforced, oppressive borders mixed together "disenable [us] not only from grasping an 'identity,' but also from reclaiming it" (1990, 364); women of color have "multiple registers of existence" (1990, 365).

In these cases, people outside dominant society travel between worlds and across assigned registers of existence in order to survive. Lugones says that, for such people, world traveling is compulsive and "in some sense against our wills to hostile White/Anglo 'worlds'" (1990, 390). But, she submits, it is a sign, nonetheless, of flexibility and is a "skillful, creative, rich, enriching and, given certain circumstances . . . a loving way of being and living" (1990, 390).

World traveling can also be a methodology that all of us can employ for studying "the other" as a familiar resonance, an echo of oneself. The Cuban-American anthropologist Ruth Behar, speaking about the challenges involved in translating a life history of a Mexican woman for a *gringo* audience, says: "I've reflected on how I've had to cross a lot of borders to get to a position where I could cross the Mexican border to bring back her story to put into a book. We cross borders, but we don't erase them; we take our borders with us" (1993, 320). Jan Pettman, a white Australian writing about Aboriginal women, raises questions about borders in the now-familiar language of representation: "Can only Aboriginal women speak for Aboriginal women, and only older urban Aboriginal women speak for themselves, and so on?" (1992, 125). She answers that "mobilising a constituency or community along boundaries drawn in and for dominance may reinforce those boundaries and so continue to trap people within them. It may also make the category an easy target for state management" (1992, 125). Since "cultures are not set, separated, or bounded by impenetrable borders . . . recognizing difference without recognising affinity or connections across category boundaries can undermine opportunities for alliances and for inclusive claim which may be necessary to effect significant change" (1992, 126).

Lugones tells us that "flexibility is necessary for the outsider but it can also be willfully exercised by those who are at ease in the mainstream" (1990, 390). Uma Narayan comes at the same issue of border crossing from the other side, suggesting that marginalized people avoid the conclusion that "those who are differently located socially can never attain *some* understanding of our experience" (1989, 264). And Donna Haraway supplies the bridging materials by reminding all of us that "there is no way to 'be' simultaneously in all, or wholly in any, of the privileged (i.e., subjugated) positions structured by gender, race, nation, and class" (1988, 586). Hence, there is no unitary speaker about and for and as "woman." To find the world traveler in and across all of us, we must willfully embrace world traveling as methodology.

Is there similar world traveling—both compulsive and methodologically willful—in and from Africa? Of course there is. Tsitsi Dangarembga writes "fictionally" about a world-traveling Shona girl who compulsively crosses from peasant society into the world of the Western mission school: "Not only was I succeeding in my own context, but in other people's as well" (1988, 94). On the other hand, Maria Nzomo reveals a methodology of world traveling in a story of Kenyan women who willfully traveled into the national and international spotlight by holding a hunger strike in 1992 for the release of political prisoners held by the Moi government (1993). With the government pressured by major international donor agencies to grant broader human rights, the women's strategy "underscores the point that women in Kenya have learned to take advantage of available spaces and opportunities to bring national and international attention to their issues" (Nzomo 1993, 68). Somewhere in between compulsive and willful world traveling are average Zimbabwean women who cross back and forth into South Africa and Botswana and into and out of an import-export world of business as itinerant traders seeking to escape the impoverishing boundaries of the country's structural adjustment programs. Such women willfully choose geospatial border crossings as the preferred method of surviving economic hardship. However, when women's bodies enter the spaces of international business, the usual class, gender, and occupational lines that establish a male bourgeoisie's claims to the world of international business as *its* exclusive purview begin to crumble (Gaidzanwa 1993). Traveling these worlds becomes neither entirely willful nor entirely compulsive as a matter of survival. It becomes "something you *do*" in a "pluralistic mode" to turn "the ambivalence into something else."

One particularly eloquent testimony to African world traveling combines these various understandings of world traveling—as compulsion, as willful methodology, and as productive of "something else"—around the narration of a life during Zimbabwe's years of armed struggle and early independence. The narrator is Sekai Nzenza, a Zimbabwean woman who came of age during the guerrilla war in the country, went on to train as a nurse in the United Kingdom, and then finds herself "unwanted in a country that is not your own" (Nzenza 1988, 150).

As she contemplates the guerrilla war unfolding around her, she asks herself, "Which side am I on? Shouldn't I be supporting this liberation struggle? Lots of young people, my age, are leaving home, crossing the borders and going over to fight the white regime. I cannot fight" (1988, 58). She wrestles with this dilemma for several pages, recognizing that imperialism imposes prohibitions on her freedom to think and act: "Praise the Lord, I am free. Free from what? I am not free to go anywhere now, the [Rhodesian] soldiers can get me, torture me, rape or even shoot me. I am not free to get the university degree, and I am not free to do what I would like to do; to go and live in town, to live in a beautiful house. There is no freedom under an imperialist, colonialist government. You need passes to travel anywhere" (1988, 60).

Nzenza then world-travels mentally to the historical era of slavery in the United States for insight into her quandaries: "Why did they have to be slaves? Lord why did you allow them to suffer the humiliation and suffering of slavery? The people who made them slaves are white. They are no different from the white people we have here. We are black; we are slaves! How can man, the white man, be so barbaric, so cruel, so unfeeling and have hearts as empty as the bellies they starve? We have physical power, and there is no other way we can get away from colonial slavery except by taking up arms and fighting it" (1988, 61).

World-traveling to the era of slavery enables a hyphenation of identity in which Nzenza becomes nonempathetic to "white people" and highly empathetic with a geospatially and temporally distant world. By the end of the war that empathy reverses. Nzenza receives her nursing degree, physically travels to London for additional training, and then slips into a posture of arrogant perception on her return:

> Home was not the same anymore. It looked so different and so old. I could not sit in the hut anymore and talk and laugh around the fire. I could not bath in the river, in the open and I expected people to treat me differently. After all, I was a State Registered Nurse and I had been to England. People did think I was different, because I talked less and generally behaved in what I thought was a much more civilized western way. I did not eat the usual "Sadza" I had grown up eating. It had become tasteless, after all, I have lived in England with the English people who ate no Sadza. (1988, 98–99)

Nzenza keeps up the mobility, however, and finally ruminates at the end about how the distances traveled bring a certain fullness to her consciousness. Back in London again, she bemoans the isolated worlds around her: "As a black woman I cannot go back to my traditional society. Society is changing everyday. During the liberation war black women fought side by side with men, but after the war the women were told to go back where they belonged, the kitchen. . . . Women still have to liberate themselves from their men. If it is not the western kind of liberation, then it should be a liberation suitable to our needs and situations" (1988, 138).

Impatient, she admonishes herself and others to share the perspectives acquired in world-traveling the spaces of difference; in effect, she admonishes us to take up the challenge of world traveling with empathetic cooperation as a way of living with contradictions in life that can leave one thinking: "There is nothing for me in this cold country and I have to go away. But I do not feel like going back home. Somehow I feel I am free here" (1988, 150). She says:

> This is empty talk and it's silly for me to be sitting here in this cold damp little room in London proposing that Third World Women should organise themselves. I am no different from a white feminist who has never been to Africa but writes about the plight of the Third World Women. Well, I suppose she is better than me, at least she makes it known to the world. But if it is known, is anything done about it? Why don't white women and black women alike, talk about the more immediate problem affecting the majority of black professional women in the country? The plight of the black overseas nurses in the British National Health Service? The problems of black women who toil and labour to keep the British National Health Service going? (1988, 140)

Nzenza's journeys suggest that no one trip is ever final and complete, the last voyage, *the* answer once and for all to arrogant perceptions. It also shows that world traveling can take many forms—mental journeys abroad, physical travel to identities usually associated with other people, and cultural negotiations that broaden one's sense of home and freedom. Her story shows that world traveling is nonlinear. It is complicated.

Against the richness of this world traveling, the Westerner can be the impoverished one left home—the "autonomous, self-conscious, individual woman" who may find it hard to world-travel (Alarcón 1990, 363). It is she and not "the other," seemingly stuck-at-home African (on the Dark Continent) who must work at it. She must willfully take up world traveling as "something you do," as an exercise that disenables assimilationism and arrogant parades of difference. It is complicated: like Nzenza, the

Westerner must make several types of trips to step into and out of her guarded position with some ease. But it is possible. Judith Todd, for example, daughter of the Rhodesian Prime Minister Garfield Todd, defied the prevailing white politics of race and gender in the 1960s and 1970s to side with the forces of majority rule (Todd 1982, 1987). Her journeys were complicated but doable under the logic that "our identities are not given or reducible to our origins, skin colour, or material locations" (Mbilinyi 1992, 35).

Laura Donaldson reminds us, in fact, that all of us are colonized and in our places (1992, 21). Trinh admonishes us to create "a ground that belongs to no one, not even to the creator" (1990, 374). Such a ground would avoid a situation where, in Jean Bethke Elshtain's words, we claim to identify thoroughly with "'oppressed people everywhere' . . . [which] easily becomes rather patronizing . . . [and] does not permit the necessary critical distance and analytic acuity" (1993, 106). After all, "oppressed people everywhere" have complex lives through which "multiple-voiced subjectivity is lived in resistance to competing notions for one's allegiance or self-identification" (Alarcón 1990, 366).

As one moves to reciprocal identity interdependence with one's own hyphenations and those ruminating in others, the one-sided dominance-subordination rerun runs down. One learns from a position of multiplicity to negotiate a politics that is more than "a mere question of mutual enslavement" (Trinh 1990, 374). One moves toward Audre Lorde's position of celebrating our differences while also using them for creative dialogue in, through, and around self-differentiated communities usually parading separate identities (1984). One also learns, says Lugones, to take on board a certain playfulness, a certain uncertainty that is "an *openness to surprise* . . . a metaphysical attitude that does not expect the world to be neatly packaged, ruly . . . an openness to being a fool, which is a combination of not worrying about competence, not being self-important, not taking norms as sacred and finding ambiguity and double edges a source of wisdom and delight" (1990, 400–401).

World-Traveling the Feminist Parades

World traveling can also affect feminist theory by illuminating the fulcrum of two of the largest contingents of feminist marchers—standpointers and postmodernists. Standpoint feminism enables woman to be the subject of the sentence, the agent of knowledge and power in defiance of "laws and interdictions" forbidding her significance. It centers around a logic of gender identification in which "she" comes in variegated forms but always exists in worlds to be discovered and valorized. From her lives flow a rich stream of daily knowledge that can be interpreted, mediated, and ultimately used to build feminist understandings of the world.[10] Feminist postmodernisms, by some contrast, put woman into question, deferring or equivocating as a strategic avoidance of grand narratives of closure (Elshtain 1993, 101). Rather than finding something to settle into and valorize, there is a "beckoning of political sensibilities variously—perhaps even contradictorily—constituted within the web, within the field or network, of concepts and practices that at once inhabit and unsettle . . . a continuing and contentious process of cultural production" (Ferguson and McClure 1991, v). There is genealogy here as against standpoint feminism's interpretive approach. The modern subject, women included, is "data to be accounted for, rather than . . . a source of privileged accounts of the world" (Ferguson 1993, 15).

Standpoint feminism is often accused of seeking alternative truth in the experiences of an unproblematized woman—who is usually white and Western. In effect, it is accused of arrogance and round-trip travel to a well-resourced starting point. Yet standpoint research reveals many standpoints, many feminist-mediated interpretations of women, many modes of dailiness that evade closure. Filomina Chioma Steady, for one, presents a standpoint feminist sense of "African women" that refuses the narrative closure of global sisterhood: "Because of the need for male-female complementarity in ensuring the totality of human existence within a balanced ecosystem, and because of the negative and destructive effects of historical processes and racism on Africa and its people, values stressing human totality, parallel autonomy, cooperation, self-reliance, adaptation, survival, and liberation have developed as important aspects of African feminism . . . [as against] frameworks of dichotomy, individualism, competition, and opposition, which Western feminism fosters" (1987, 20, 8).

Steady suggests that African women, irrespective of where they are located, have enough elements of context in common to form a standpoint fundamentally different from any that Western feminists construct. She suggests the type of variegation to standpoint thinking that, to use Judith Grant's terms, realizes "there is no bird's-eye view; no one authentic perspective on reality because knowledge and reality are fragmented" (Grant 1993, 94). Standpoint thereby nudges toward the more postmodernist sense of political sensibilities variously constituted (which require complex travel experiences to fathom) rather than innocently waiting to be discovered.[11]

The postmodern turn in feminism multiplies the options facing subjects in circumscribed subject statuses, in statuses such as "women" or "African women." South African feminist Desiree Lewis, for example, sharply admonishes her feminist colleagues to take more seriously postmodernist ideas that challenge the comfortable standpoint beliefs she has seen displayed in that country, instead of "dismiss[ing] ideas that do not fit into their paradigms as signs of *others'* false consciousness" (1993, 542). Evocatively, she speaks of "the Subject [who] sanctifies herself against self-reflection as her gaze fixe[s] on the ever-mutating object which she continually reshapes to consolidate her predetermined sense of self" (1993, 541). But postmodernist deferrals of truth can be enervating and their skepticisms of subjects deadening. What happens to differences within and among women when we contemplate heaping on the additionally fragmenting experiences of world traveling? How does empathy emerge if there is no subject to empathize from and with? Does postmodernist feminism not need more steady standpoints to light paths away from privileged accounts of "the" world and toward "worlds" (real to the inhabitants) on the margins?

At the fulcrum of these approaches, at the point where "genealogy keeps interpretation honest, and interpretation gives genealogy direction" (Ferguson 1991, 337), are the navigational resources of empathetic cooperation (Sylvester 1994a, 1994b). The world traveler is a subject moving in, through, and around subject statuses of self and other as she goes abroad. Hers is not a journey of isolation that has one wandering around lost in the "strange" streets of exotica. It is a series of journeys of empathetic social recognition, of acknowledgment, which lead the traveler into cooperations to "negotiate respectfully with contentious others" encountered on the journey or with identities that proliferate as newly noticed political sensibilities (Ferguson 1993, 154). Empathetic cooperation is what enables "different 'worlds' and ourselves in them" (Lugones 1990, 396). It helps the world-traveling subject ease from assigned statuses into politically difficult negotiations at borderlands of knowledge, experience, differences, and locations. Empathetic cooperation helps us to achieve feminist standpoints of travel as "politics," as "the juggle of cultures" that "sustain contradictions," that give us "something you *do*" other than parade or amalgamate in the face of backlashes. Parade ranks of feminism are thereby disordered without thrusting out, abandoning, merging, merely tolerating, or rejecting the different positions.

Nzenza has given us a glimpse of one African woman's world-traveling experiences. Narayan (1989), Haraway (1988), and Lugones (1990) give us a sense of the possibilities contained in letting go of parade positions for uncertainties of understanding and identity slippage. What of feminist world traveling in, through, and around the borderlands of Western and African positions of feminism via empathetic cooperation? In the next section, we explore a lodestar location where an African-Western feminist border-crosser, Mbilinyi, and a world traveler in Western feminism, Ferguson, intersect ideas from seemingly different places of identity and analysis. Their parallel interests in promoting mobilities rather than amalgamations, empathies rather than sympathies, galas of cross-dressing rather than parades of self-differentiation, move us to consider research practices that enable the mobilities around us as components of feminist theory.

Feminist World Traveling: To, From, and Around Africa

To Mbilinyi, the histories of African societies intermingle class, gender, and race-ethnicity "laws and interdictions" in ways that leave African feminists savvy about the imperialist West. Imperialism says to the "natives": "You are free in your identities and experiences—we are not there directing you; go ahead, travel, be interdependent, buy some souvenirs, improvise." But it sets foot traps that can hold one back from the subjecthood of travel. In fact, the West comes and consumes what you have—and long has done this—producing and distributing knowledge by which to safeguard a certain safehouse lifestyle of the West. Locals, meanwhile, are constituted as staying put unless a certain exotic element is required, in which case there is travel westward that never really makes it into the safehouse. Aware of such tricks, Mbilinyi claims that many African feminists critically focus more on the problems of imperialism than the problems of gender per se. In her words, they "participate in intellectual debates within other social theories besides feminism and usually engage in activist and practical work [whereas even] Third World feminists located in the North normally fail to confront imperialist relations nationally and globally. Gender and race eclipse class and imperialism" (Mbilinyi 1992, 33).

One could argue that implicit in claims that Mbilinyi seems to share with standpointer Steady (1987), although carefully not stated by Mbilinyi, is the sense that African feminists are privileged at their crossroads location. In the neocolonized place, the West spins imperialism into local fabrics in ways that render the patterns ever so obvious to local residents. But it seems that penetrating insights from local bases do not add up to privileged standpoint, and that is why critical African feminists travel to many sites of intellectual debate. At a location overlaid with intersecting activities, agendas, and knowledges, one cannot speak of a unitary subject who has "a" privileged view. No one exists free of multiple registered borrowings and ambivalences: "Some are oppressed and others are oppressors, each has her own individual psychology and personality, and draws on different cultural foundations and support systems, each has her own identities/positions" (Mbilinyi 1992, 35). Arguing like a postmodernist, she says that critical African feminisms link to certain traditions of Western feminism to suggest "the nonexistence of a unitary subject called 'woman' or 'women' (or man/men)" (1992, 34). Mbilinyi herself draws on "multiple registers of existence" at many subject borders daily confronted:

> European-Tanzanian middle class woman, privileged by virtue of my "white skin," European origins and middle class location in different ways in certain situations, oppressed in my neo-colonised and female locations, suppressed by conservative forces because of my anti-imperialist critical feminist position. I have also been discriminated against because of my European origins in many situations. . . . I am the mother of four "Black" indigenous/Wangoni African Tanzanian children. In many situations I am defined as "Black" Mswahili Tanzanian, in contrast to foreign English-speaking "black-skinned" West Africans and African-Americans, defined as "Europeans" *(Wazungu)*. [1992, 50]

A world-traveling feminist from the West might experience a journey-ending joy at arriving at such complex world-traveler hyphenations, saying to herself, "I am happy in that world . . . and that one and that one." Mbilinyi avoids self-congratulation in world traveling, however, by pointing out that women in Africa are and have been different from one another, multiple in subjectivities, only in violation of and struggle against hegemonic imperialism, which constructs a univocal other as consumer of Western knowledge. Hyphenations are accomplishments, achievements. They represent movement out from under the neocolonial rule that we are "reducible to our origins, skin colour, or material locations." They are, in effect, the product of travel to places where one is not a happy tourist in Our World, being aware that "a unitary and synthesizing agent of knowledge is always already a posture of domination" (Alarcón 1990, 364).

At the same time, hyphenated personhood à la Mbilinyi travels the worlds around her and learns that "people from very different 'locations' have discovered how similar their theories and methods are, when derived from the same political and epistemological positions" (Mbilinyi 1992, 37). To make such a world-traveler discovery is not necessarily to fall back to an essential Africa, African woman, or African feminism. It is to see much unhappiness at world junctions that emerges through the fog of similar journeys to assigned place. It is to empathize rather than essentialize or sympathize.

Women in development (WID) is an example of a feminist journeying story that remembers one instead of many senses of contemporary and past women. It would have us "modernizing Third World women, not [focusing] on understanding their lives and experiences" (Parpart 1993, 449). The difficulty is that WID has flown to Africa in non-world-traveler class and is now sympathetically but not empathetically located there: "WID is no longer a 'Western' or 'European'/'White' phenomenon; most WID experts in Africa are indigenous women, although 'Northern'-based women still monopolise the greater share of global funding and resources such as publications and consultancy work. National governments have created women focal points in all ministries to meet the demands of donors and an increasingly vocal and organised pressure group of middle-class women, WID is the dominant discourse about 'women' and/or gender in African countries, and other perspectives find it increasingly difficult to be heard or to get funding" (Mbilinyi 1992, 47–48).

There is in WID much to commend it. There is, however, little room in its sense of mission to consider the question of whether all the people donors call "women" actually think of themselves as women in the same way. There is little room to ask about various silenced notions of development within the constituencies one serves.[12] Women in development has authority and resources attached to it, and so it catches the naive world traveler—local and Western alike—in a peculiar Western tourist trap transported abroad. The failure to juggle cultures occurs, says Alarcón, when "white Anglo women . . . try to do theory with women of color [because they] inevitably disrupt the dialogue" (1990, 363). One might say that "white women," itself an assignment more diffuse than one can see, come together with "indigeneous women" in WID to direct, reshape, and integrate the many dialogues of difference abroad without world-traveling them. Cooperation occurs in WID circles, but empathy is often displaced by a sympathy that maintains the arrogance of "I."

The burden of Western feminist world travelers, suggests Alarcón, should be to "learn to become unintrusive, unimportant, patient to the point of tears, while at the same time open to learning any possible lessons" (1990, 363). If the African world traveler has already learned these skills and is threatened with eradication for doing so, it is nonetheless the case, as Mbilinyi's argument implies, that African feminists parading from places beholden to Western master identities could benefit from unintrusive patience. A bit quieter, a bit less determined to demonstrate assertiveness in encounters with those who may not agree, one can take on board similarities in people's experiences without leaping to solutions that collapse ambiguities and disruptingly finish the travel script before one has put out from port.

One way to learn feminist world traveling if we are not as multilocated as Mbilinyi is by taking seriously her skeptical view of "gender research in Southern Africa [that] has been produced within neo-positivist epistemology, including work within mainstream bourgeois and Marxian theories" (1992, 52). Such work, she suggests, telescopes unidirectional lifestyles. By contrast, the research Mbilinyi can "do" as feminist practice enables us to "juggle our various social and psychological identities as we make decisions about the strength and directions of our [and their] resistance to multiple oppressions" (Malson et al. 1989, 7, cited in Mbilinyi 1992, 58). It requires "patience unto tears" and a certain sizing up of our (many) selves as multiresident in our own research projects. Critically, it requires empathetic cooperation with those the neopositivists would admonish us to stand aloof from in the interest of research objectivity. Mbilinyi asks: "To what extent [are] professional researchers capable and willing to share power and resources with villagers, farm workers, urban slum dwellers, indeed with students and research assistants? [Are] participatory researchers prepared to follow up on the political issues raised by participants, and remain involved when confrontations between 'the state' and 'the people' develop?" (1992, 63).

Far from reproducing the lifestyle of the tourist, Mbilinyi's feminist research politics asks us to (re)search ourselves researching others as a way of being open to the involvements, the surprises, and the turnabouts that positivism tells us are contaminants of the real research. It subverts "the agonistic traveller [who] is a conqueror, an imperialist" (Lugones 1990, 400) so that one negotiates the culture-juggling contradictions rather than amalgamating or parading them or wearing them home—to be put on the shelf and thereafter waxed nostalgic about.

Feminist World Traveling: Take Two

Ferguson has another take—not dissimilar, not exactly alike—on the politics of juggling cultures and attaining achieved identities that sustain contradictions, democracies of knowledge, and new styles of feminist theory. Ferguson, believing that "men" and "women" are unstable constructed designations, poses her central question in (what Mbilinyi might see as a) Western gender-centric way: "How can we simultaneously put women at the center and decenter everything, including women?" (1993, 3). Her question comes out of the little tug-of-war—those jostles here and there for position in Western feminist parades—over feminist standpoint efforts to build theory on the backs of women and feminist postmodernist concerns to recall Simone de Beauvoir's daring question: "Are there women, really?" (1952, xv).

Recognizing, in effect, what Mbilinyi also knows—that "positions are clearly complex, multiple, inconsistent, often contradictory" (Mbilinyi 1992, 50)—Ferguson explores the ways that feminists can "hold together needed incompatibles [so as] to stay honest and keep moving at the same time" (Ferguson 1993, 35). That is, she asks how feminists occupying different and seemingly incompatible parade positions can hold the projects of feminism together without getting fixed in our separate places. It is important to "keep moving," Ferguson argues—to march on, around, and through our positions—in order to short-circuit the one-way, non-moving, patriarchal construction of personhood as a Self-center of all things. Patriarchy's personhood is arrogant: it "coincides neatly (immediately or eventually) with itself. This subject often designates itself 'humanist' to establish that which is essentially the same for all humans and distinguishes the human from the other-than-human world" (Ferguson 1993, 38).[13] This personhood travels to himself and, in doing so, colonizes all in the path—and not just the colonized continents. Its activities, however, are not always fully obvious to people called "women" because the patriarchal politics of women creation embeds a hierarchy of standards that always illuminates the way home: "Women can be many different things to men so long as men name them" (Ferguson 1993, 39). Colonizing patriarchs are the ones who "produce and maintain the privileges of men/whites/the west by constituting women/people of color/the east as other and lesser" (Ferguson 1993, 39).

Against this relentless colonial configuration Ferguson asks how it can be possible to change the world unless we "begin with a solid female subject who knows what she wants and can unite with others like herself to get it" (Ferguson 1993, 57–58). How can we "keep moving" if "we" is a world traveler with the mobilities of a ghost? Her answer, carefully constructed to give just desserts to a variety of solid feminisms and tart reminders to move on, analyzes the various notions of personhood and thematizations of subjectivity that anchor the (Western) marchers in the feminist parade. She finds considerable variegation in the personhoods feminisms set forth and sees no sound reason why we cannot be mobile in them, world traveling those positions, in effect, as a way of sustaining contradictions and ensuring that "nothing is thrust out" as a "foreign importation which has no relevance to the African [or some other] situation" (Meena 1992, 4).

Ferguson's equivalent of world traveling is the concept of "mobile subjectivities." It takes subjects (in this case, women) as "particular positionalizations" (1993, 159) that are produced by dominant discursive and institutional practices and that produce both the dominant patterns and practices of resistance to them. We might think of mobile subjectivities as the borderlands all of us inhabit, even those of us who think we are at home and safe in the West, in the Self, in one corner of the feminist parade with one's mates—in contradistinction to some Third World woman who is never entirely at home in a world of colonial "otherizing" power, who is always playing the borders. Mobile subjectivities are "politically difficult in their refusal to stick consistently to one stable identity claim; yet they are politically advantageous because they are less pressed to police their own boundaries, more able to negotiate respectfully with contentious others" (Ferguson 1993, 154). The mobilities of subject subjectivity can hold the seeming incompatibles of feminism together. Feminists can thereby keep moving while realizing that we can be ourselves in many worlds and relate the different faces in the parade to the manyness of things local, specific, and cosmopolitan.[14] Projects can be devised that "incite the discrepancies (as well as the unexpected agreements) among the various views, to force open a space within feminist discourses for greater acknowledgment of discontinuity, incompleteness, and tension" (Ferguson 1993, 156). Arguably, one of the spaces forced open that could keep us moving would accommodate the imperialism-minded critical African feminisms Mbilinyi sights and admonishes us to cite.

The glue in Ferguson's world-traveling mode is irony, that play of incongruities and contrasts that spotlights the differences between what might be expected and what actually occurs on the trip. One expects a military unit in Zimbabwe, not a maternity hospital, to be named after Nehanda; but the mixing of metaphors is instructive to those attuned to wry surprises and to the hyphenations of "mother" and "warrior" that the naming unintentionally harbors.[15] One expects critical Third World feminisms to assert "a" local feminism against imperialism in order to avoid the appearance of eviscerating women's power and instead finds in Mbilinyi the notion that identities and feminisms in Africa are no less multiple, complex, and contradictory for being squeezed from the outside. One expects that the African conditions Mbilinyi calls "unique" (i.e., imperialism and neocolonialism) will result in a unique politics. We find, rather belatedly, because our lenses were befogged, that African societies are really more ordinary in their politics, to use that "nonotherizing" phrase of Jean-François Bayart, than we researchers have been trying to prove (Bayart 1993, 1). We expect postmodernist feminisms to leave us subjectless and unable to resist the ironies of public policies. We find instead that subject statuses can be called into question but subjects persist and register many-sided reactions to obliterating imperialisms.

"Irony," says Ferguson, "allows contending thematizations of subjectivity to negotiate a political relationship that does not depend upon unanimity, consensus, or even majority agreement to any particular configuration of identity, gender, or nature, or to any one metatheoretical stance" (1993, 157). I would say that irony provides the playing field on which empathetic cooperations can occur because it foregrounds relational autonomies denied when we parade differences proudly or militantly erase some relations by merging into no-vintage blends of feminism. As Ferguson says, "Ironic conversations enable the competing claims for identity and desire to undercut as well as enable one another and produce an enhanced appreciation of each" (1993, 157).

Her mode of irony resonates with Lugones's sense that world traveling reveals any particular world as having double edges and locations of absurdity: "This ambiguity is not just funny, it is survival-rich. We can . . . make a funny picture of those who dominate us precisely because we can see the double edges, we can see *them* doubly constructed, we can see the plurality in us and in them. So we know truths that only the fool can speak and only the trickster can play out without harm" (Lugones 1990, 398). For Lugones, the world traveler is at ease with play. For Ferguson, "unstable but potent, diverse but not incomprehensible to one another, mobile subjectivities [can] play across the terrains . . . [of] feminism" (1993, 161).

It is ironic, though, that Ferguson does not see the process she outlines as one of world traveling with empathetic cooperation. She says that mobile subjectivities give rise to coalition politics, for the simple reason that one feels empathy with many different perspectives and finds one's selves not fully at home in one place. But she takes a hard line on empathy: "Empathy can readily be recruited into a gesture of appropriation (as in 'I know just what you mean' when I really don't know at all)" (1993, 33). Empathy is a point of ambivalence for her, at once sham and research tool, perhaps because she confuses it with sympathy. Irony upon irony, Ferguson alludes to the notion that a politics of mobile subjectivities will leave us not fully at home anywhere, and this means that we world-travel empathetically rather than conduct the tourist lifestyle that, at best, brings us to "I"-centered sympathies with "oppressed peoples everywhere." Her empathies show.

World Traveling: Feminist
Research and Practical Politics

We can now return to the concerns about feminisms denied or deflated by those with the power to hand out or to refuse parade permits. Mbilinyi ends her piece by asking for feminist research as a political practice. Ferguson ends pleading the case for including class as a subjectivity in our feminist theorizations and conversations, on the grounds that, in practice, people come in classes as well as genders (a point with which Mbilinyi would concur). Both moves tell us what feminist researchers can do with all this enlightened world traveling: we can be aware of locations of class where people's production, instead of assumed consumption, of knowledge must be heard (as a research practice) and defended (also as a research practice) in order to deimperialize the imperium.

We can surely do this and more. We can also cultivate sensitivity to practices of world traveling that often take place in the interstices of our feminist research or while we are looking elsewhere for the significant data. In my research, I have "happened on" world-traveling Zimbabwean women who insist on the mobilities of their subjectivities as they negotiate daily existences with more powerful people. In each case, the happenings were not scheduled into my research plan, and I initially refused to travel toward these "extraneous" and annoying "things" the women wanted to "chat about" in defiance of my reasons for traveling to see them. But the politics of ironic and playful mobility encountered among Zimbabwean working-class women took my research self where it did not expect to go. Western travel to Zimbabwe, which in this case was tourism gussied up as feminist research, became "something else," a methodology of world traveling that enabled me to see others world-traveling their subjectivities and myself seeing them. I have space here only to sketch three examples.

In 1988, I asked about a hundred women workers in Harare's clothing and food processing factories to tell me about their task assignments at work and their relations with male workers. Usually they wanted to talk about "something else." They told me that mothers were enabled by law to take one hour of work time to breast-feed small children. However, there were no child-minding facilities at or near the factories, which meant that the many, many women who lived in distant townships or even residential areas of the city could not avail themselves of this benefit. The benefit was empty, surrounded by foot traps that prevented women from traveling imperialism's promises to a place of "worker-mothers."

The women grumbled in a way that initially struck me as enervating rather than empowering. Their political practices, however, revealed action to implement an alternative benefit of comparable worth that seemed to them reasonable under the law. What they did was this: many mothers became "microentrepreneurs," boldly using company machines to do an hour's worth of extracurricular, often market-targeted sewing each day in lieu of taking the child-feeding benefit. Rather than couch this activity as something that would indirectly help children as a parallel to the breast-feeding benefit, the women expressed the sense that they finally had a work benefit of some type and were determined to take it.[16]

Arguably, mothers world-traveled within their range of subjectivities to the point that they could be happy in places that were tangentially, at best, related to the one(-world) identity they were allowed by law to bring to work with benefit. They mined their identities for the ironic self-empathies harbored therein and resisted being the child-centered self under a child-cynical Zimbabwean law. Factory managers—the ones with resources to parade—insisted that little could be done to prevent this redefinition of the benefit. The women had the upper hand because they were efficient and valued workers in the larger factory enterprise. Some male workers and management personnel criticized people who "just ignore the law." But, overall, the differences in interpretation of the government benefit were traveled until the needed incompatibles of "work" and "mothering" were more or less realigned empathetically and cooperatively. To push aside arrogant questions and enter the world traveler's circle to detect this movement was an achievement of world-traveling for me.

The second case features a group of women cultivators in Zimbabwe playfully world-traveling around government stipulations concerning the proper constitution of an agricultural cooperative. When I went to interview women in cooperatives, "cooperatives" were entities I simply assumed rather than problematized. Robotically, I selected the groups I would visit from government and donor registers, rotely remembering that cooperatives must be "association[s] of free and equal individuals for social and economic gain," wherein "everyone receives equal pay for equal work and all decisions are made by all members of the cooperative" (Matema and Staunton 1985, 1). I knew cooperatives also had to uphold six pregiven principles of cooperative organization and organize a hierarchical management structure consisting of a chair, vice-chair, secretary, and treasurer.

During the course of interviews with women in agricultural cooperatives in Mashonaland, I found "multiple registers of existence" about cooperatives that cast doubt on what I and others knew to be correct. In several cases, cooperatives effectively changed the approved identity of the group in order to accommodate each other's needs empathetically. Traveling to their own worlds of cooperation and negotiating with what were obviously contentious others within, members of one cooperative devised two leadership structures, one for the men in the group and the other for the women, as well as mechanisms of coordination. In an all-women cooperative, seven out of ten total members were on the cooperative's executive committee, because members believed that these people had knowledge and experience that should not be left out for "silly reasons."

Field-workers from the then Ministry of Cooperatives clucked their tongues at such actions and threatened to deny these cooperatives their registration rights. But the members traveled away from government stricture, and the ministry did not rain on their perfidy. It was the (privileged) officials who learned to travel empathetically to cooperative positions outside "laws and interdictions," while cooperators revelled in the spaces they had empathetically traveled in order to accommodate contradictions and multiplicities within their groups. I, the Western interviewer, had to travel some distance before I could see that the tacit negotiations over what a cooperative should be had created a borderland where "nothing was thrust out."

The third example: I interviewed people called "women" employed in seasonal labor on commercial farms in Mashonaland to explore their task assignments and difficulties at work. Along the way I discovered that I had erroneously assumed the category "women" (as in all people who look like women are women). I found, in fact, that these farm worker women had no set notion of women. Some told me that "women" are easily identifiable at work on the basis of the different tasks they must perform, relative to those assigned to "men." Some reported a sense of women as solidly unified in a common and unproblematical identity. Others suggested that women could not really exist when divisions among them prevented the formation of a solidarity that could bargain effectively with management. I heard: "We must be careful in voicing women's grievances because other women might not agree." One worker explained simply that "women do not know if we are unified as women because we have not held a meeting among ourselves."

This refusal to be the "women" the arrogant "I" knew they were came as a shock. Here there were pluralities of identity and some concern to travel them, even to renegotiate women as "leaders," "because we are illtreated by some supervisors who do not talk to us like we're humans." Here women were pushing the boundaries of their identities despite farm managers who matter-of-factly pointed out the women to me and narrated their place: they are the ones who are not given the permanent farm jobs.

Irony was rife here. The politics of neocolonial capitalist profit making increasingly bollixed up the gender lifestyles that farm managers posed as permanent. More men in Zimbabwe became nonpermanent farm workers in 1984 (24,523) than ever before because the country was in an economic slump and "nonpermanent workers" were relatively cheap to employ (Moyo and Ngobese 1991, 8). In effect, men entered the ranks of impermanence in order to maintain their identity as workers. Ironically decentered in their gender lifestyle, these men now shared common ground with impermanent women. Men were traveling to new positions in their subjectivities.

Ferguson argues, however, that even if men "moved their self-constructions onto the terrain of mobile subjectivity [they] would not necessarily be feminist; nor would whites necessarily be anti-racist" (1993, 179–80). The shared terrain has to become one not just of objective positions but of politics practiced to the point of empathetic cooperations across difference, to the point I saw within Harare's clothing factories and among cooperatives and ministry officials. On Zimbabwe's commercial farms, I witnessed some world travel to new positions as a forced rather than empathetically negotiated response to capitalist policy. Nonetheless, just as Nzenza found herselves traveling here and there nonlinearly, we must bear in mind that the story of farm worker travels is in its early stages. World-traveling journeys are never final and complete. And I had to restrain myself from seeking a conclusion to the story, learning to be content merely to point out to farm managers the ironies in their policies and to women the possibilities of identity empathies in the new situation facing men.

Practicing Travel Method

World-traveling political researchers are multiply placed to study the empathetic cooperations (or departures from them) that occur in and around our research sites and in and around ourselves. Our research is not likely to yield nuggets of neopositivist knowledge so much as outlines of politics displayed unexpectedly in unexpected places. That means that our sense of ourselves as world-traveling researchers must refuse separations of ontology and epistemology, of politics and objectivity, of theory and methodological practice. As Wendy Brown puts this, "Only political conversation oriented toward diversity and the common, toward world rather than self, and involving conversion of one's knowledge of the world from a situated (subject) position into a public idiom, offers us the possibility of countering postmodern social fragmentations and political disintegrations" (1991, 80–81).[17]

Mobile subjectivities and world travels fragment the self. They also fragment old-style politics in ways that refuse arrogant tourist lifestyles and overly deferential parade marchers. They expose the manyness of things denied, the transversals one makes and those one did not intend to effect (e.g., from permanent to nonpermanent farm worker), making it a bit more difficult to parade difference, or rain on differences parading, without noticing the hyphenations and conversations in the texts.

Making the negotiated politics of manyness known, which is the practice of doing feminism on the road of world traveling, rests on the democratizing approaches to research that Mbilinyi and Ferguson encourage. It requires us, as a prerequisite, to see world traveling going on where we tend to assume that only we did the traveling to be there. We must see subtle negotiations where our tourist eyes see "oppressed people everywhere." We must read "benefits" and "cooperatives" and "women" as political practices that are worth examining, rather than pregivens that some people (annoyingly) refuse. All of this forms the cooperative researcher-"subject" coalition of which Mbilinyi speaks, the mobility that Ferguson's work leads us to recognize. That mobile coalition is something we can "do" as a politics of solidarity against backlashes international. It is what can motivate us to leave the apparent safety of our worlds—willfully, playfully, ironically, and empathetically—for destinations that enact the mobile possibilities within ourselves and/or enable us to see them in others. In the never final analysis, it is a key contribution to theorizing the "multiple registers of experience" that imperialism has pitched univocal and feminism has either paraded or sought to amalgamate.

We need not merge "them" into "us" or stand apart in deference to other places; nor do we have to deny differences to have empathetic methods and politics across parade lines. But we cannot refuse to see that the process of world traveling to empathetic cooperation is full of subtle politics many of us are not equipped to see our subjects doing, let alone do to ourselves and to our feminisms. In sustaining contradictions, we find opportunities to practice multipluralities and multicultures in defiance of those "intellectual factories of the North" (Meena 1992, 3)—and the South—whose assembly lines produce knowledge parades of "African women" and "Western women," "feminisms and antifeminisms" of fictionally fixed place.

Notes

1. These acronyms refer to literatures on women in development (WID), women and development (WAD), and gender and development (GAD).

2. Fictionally portrayed as fact in Crichton 1994.

3. Women and men dressed alike as combatants, although there is some controversy in the literature as to whether they executed the same wartime tasks. See Kriger 1992.

4. Mbilinyi 1992 draws attention to this connection. She laments the fact that the Tanzanian Media Women Association (TAMWA) called in 1991 for the organization to "organise and consult our grandmothers and fathers on what makes a woman a woman, a man a man, a nation a nation" (44).

5. Parpart 1993 argues that GAD calls attention to processes by which people are constituted with gender assignments and thereby leaves open the possibility that the assignments are transformable. Women and development finds women inside development as players assigned subsidiary positions that make it possible for others to receive the resources of (and credit for) modernization. Women in development, by contrast, amalgamates the Marxist-feminist view that the oppression of women has to do with their lower economic position vis-à-vis men with a liberal feminist concern to bring women up to speed with unproblematized male and Western standardbearers of humanity. One ends up with a recycled Western view of development as processes "bringing 'backward' colonial

peoples into the modern [i.e., developed] world" (Parpart 1993, 447), with women even farther back—and therefore needing more assistance to be modern—than men. See discussions in Moser 1989, Rathgeber 1990, and Kabeer 1991.

6. Arrogant perception has been developed as a concept by Frye 1983. Also see Gunning 1991–92, 199.

7. Which raises the question of whether subalterns can speak from a position of anything other than homogeneous, Western-subject-centered otherness. See Spivak 1988.

8. For discussions of reactive and relational autonomy, see Hirschmann 1989 and Sylvester 1992. Filomina Chioma Steady (1987) also speaks implicitly of relational autonomies in African feminism.

9. See discussions of "worlding" in Spivak 1985 and Loomba 1993.

10. See discussions in Belenky et al. 1986; Smith 1990; Harding 1991; and Hirschmann 1992.

11. See discussion in Flax 1992.

12. For critical discussions of WID, see Maguire 1984 and Stamp 1989.

13. This passage is taken from her analysis of Irigaray 1985.

14. Judith Grant provides a personal illustration of finding herself in many worlds of feminism. Having told us that she has had a certain parting of the ways with radical Western feminism, in part because it is ethnocentrically essentialist and racist, she then admits: "I have to say that many of the most radical women I know are talking about female values. I go back and forth on it myself. In many ways, my feminist practice is completely essentialized. I have gone to more than a few feminist spirituality gatherings and enjoyed them immensely. With very few exceptions, I only read novels by women. I listen almost exclusively to music performed by women. My favorite actors are women. I do not do this for political effect. It honestly just happens that I mostly prefer what I have no way of describing except 'female' things" (1993, 11).

15. Elshtain 1987, 221–25, writes about the ways that the good soldier acts very much like the good mother, thereby crossing forbidden lines of gender demarcations.

16. That is, they provided me with little verbal evidence that the extracurricular sewing was of the same child-centered type as the breast-feeding benefit. It was simply a benefit denied them. In the course of interviewing these and other working women in Zimbabwe, I asked them whether having babies was work in the same way that laboring in factories and cooperatives and on peasant and commercial farms was work. Each woman answered: having babies is not work. What we do here at the job site, said one, "is work. It is different. We leave babies at home."

17. I would add that such conversations also counter the modern tendency to amalgamate all fragmentations, to integrate all women.

References

Alarcón, Norma. 1990. "The Theoretical Subjects(s) of *This Bridge Called My Back* and Anglo-American Feminism." In *Making Face, Making Soul: Haciendo Caras,* ed. Gloria Anzaldúa, 356–69. San Francisco: Aunt Lute Foundation.

Anzaldúa, Gloria. 1987. *Borderlands/La Frontera: The New Mestiza.* San Francisco: Spinsters/Aunt Lute.

Bayart, Jean-François. 1993. *The State in Africa: The Politics of the Belly.* New York: Longman.

Beauvoir, Simone de. 1952. *The Second Sex.* New York: Vintage.

Behar, Ruth. 1993. *Translated Woman: Crossing the Border with Esperanza's Story.* Boston: Beacon.

Belenky, Mary Field, Blythe Clinchy, Nancy Goldberger, and Jill Tarule. 1986. *Women's Ways of Knowing: The Development of Self, Voice, and Mind.* New York: Basic.

Braidotti, Rosi. 1991. *Patterns of Dissonance: A Study of Women in Contemporary Philosophy.* New York: Routledge.

Brown, Wendy. 1991. "Feminist Hesitations, Postmodern Exposures." *Differences* 3(1):63–84.

Butler, Judith. 1993. *Bodies That Matter: On the Discursive Limits of "Sex."* New York: Routledge.

Crichton, Michael. 1994. *Disclosure.* New York: Knopf.

Dangarembga, Tsitsi. 1988. *Nervous Conditions.* London: Women's Press.

de Lauretis, Teresa. 1986. "Feminist Studies/Critical Studies: Issues, Terms, and Contexts." In *Feminist Studies/Critical Studies,* ed. Teresa de Lauretis. Bloomington and Indianapolis: Indiana University Press.

Donaldson, Laura E. 1992. *Decolonizing Feminisms: Race, Gender, and Empire-Building.* Chapel Hill: University of North Carolina Press.

Elshtain, Jean Bethke. 1987. *Women and War.* New York: Basic.

_____. 1993. "'Bringing It All Back Home, Again.'" In *Global Voices: Dialogues in International Relations,* ed. James N. Rosenau, 97–116. Boulder, Colo.: Westview.

Faludi, Susan. 1991. *Backlash: The Undeclared War Against American Women.* New York: Crown.

Ferguson, Kathy. 1991. "Interpretation and Genealogy in Feminism." *Signs: Journal of Women in Culture and Society* 16(2):322–39.

_____. 1993. *The Man Question: Visions of Subjectivity in Feminist Theory.* Berkeley and Los Angeles: University of California Press.

Ferguson, Kathy, and Kirstie McClure. 1991. "Politics/Power/Culture: Postmodernity and Feminist Political Theory: Preliminary." *Differences* 3(1):iii–vi.

Flax, Jane. 1992. "The End of Innocence." In *Feminists Theorize the Political,* ed. Judith Butler and Joan Scott, 445–63. New York: Routledge.

Frye, Marilyn. 1983. "In and Out of Harm's Way." In her *The Politics of Reality: Essays in Feminist Theory,* 52–83. Trumansburg, N.Y.: Crossing.

Gaidzanwa, Rudo. 1992. "Bourgeois Theories of Gender and Feminism and Their Shortcomings with Reference to Southern African Countries." In *Gender in Southern Africa: Conceptual and Theoretical Issues,* ed. Ruth Meena, 92–125. Harare: SAPES Books.

_____. 1993. "Citizenship, Nationality, Gender, and Class in Southern Africa." *Alternatives* 18(1):39–60.

Grant, Judith. 1993. *Fundamental Feminism: Contesting the Core Concepts of Feminist Theory.* New York: Routledge.

Gunning, Isabella. 1991–92. "Arrogant Perception, World-Travelling and Multi-cultural Feminism: The Case of Female Genital Surgeries." *Columbia Human Rights Law Review* 23(3):189–248.

Haraway, Donna. 1988. "Situated Knowledges: The Science Question in Feminism and the Privilege of Partial Perspective." *Feminist Studies* 14(3):575–99.

Harding, Sandra. 1991. *Whose Science? Whose Knowledge? Thinking from Women's Lives*. Ithaca, N.Y.: Cornell University Press.

Hirschmann, Nancy. 1989. "Freedom, Recognition, and Obligation: A Feminist Approach to Political Theory." *American Political Science Review* 83(4):1227–44.

———. 1992. *Rethinking Obligation: A Feminist Method for Political Theory*. Ithaca, N.Y.: Cornell University Press.

hooks, bell, Gloria Steinem, Urvashi Vaid, and Naomi Wolf. 1993. "Let's Get Real About Feminism: The Backlash, the Myths, the Movement." *Ms.* 4(2):34–43.

Irigaray, Luce. 1985. "Any Theory of the 'Subject' Has Always Been Appropriated by the 'Masculine.'" In her *Speculum of the Other Woman*, trans. Gillian C. Cill, 133–46. Ithaca, N.Y.: Cornell University Press.

Kabeer, Naila. 1991. "Rethinking Development from a Gender Perspective: Some Insights from the Decade." Paper presented at the Conference on Women and Gender in Southern Africa, University of Natal, Durban, January 30–February 2.

Kriger, Norma. 1992. *Zimbabwe's Guerrilla War: Peasant Voices*. Cambridge: Cambridge University Press.

Lewis, Desiree. 1993. "Feminisms in South Africa." *Women's Studies International Forum* 16(5):535–42.

Loomba, Ania. 1993. "Overworlding the 'Third World.'" In *Colonial Discourse and Post-Colonial Theory: A Reader*, ed. Patrick Williams and Laura Chrisman, 305–23. New York: Harvester Wheatsheaf.

Lorde, Audre. 1984. *Sister Outsider: Essays and Speeches*. Trumansburg, N.Y.: Crossing.

Lugones, Maria. 1990. "Playfulness, 'World'-Travelling, and Loving Perceptions." In *Making Face, Making Soul: Haciendo Caras*, ed. Gloria Anzaldúa, 390–402. San Francisco: Aunt Lute Foundation.

Maguire, Patricia. 1984. *Women in Development: An Alternative Analysis*. Amherst, Mass.: University of Massachusetts, Center for International Education.

Makamure, Nyaradzo. 1984. "Women and Revolution: The Women's Movement in Zimbabwe." *Journal of African Marxists*, p. 6.

Malson, Micheline R., Jean F. O'Barr, Sarah Westphal-Wihl, and Mary Wyer, eds. 1989. *Feminist Theory in Practice and Process*. Chicago: University of Chicago Press.

Mannathoko, Changu. 1992. "Feminist Theories and the Study of Gender Issues in Southern Africa." In *Gender in Southern Africa: Conceptual and Theoretical Issues*, ed. Ruth Meena, 71–91. Harare: SAPES Books.

Matema, Cain, and Irene Staunton. 1985. *Cooperatives: What About Them*. Harare: Ministry of Education.

Mbilinyi, Marjorie. 1992. "Research Methodologies in Gender Issues." In *Gender in Southern Africa: Conceptual and Theoretical Issues*, ed. Ruth Meena, 31–70. Harare: SAPES Books.

Meena, Ruth. 1992. "Gender Research/Studies in Southern Africa: An Overview." In *Gender in Southern Africa: Conceptual and Theoretical Issues,* ed. Ruth Meena, 1–30. Harare: SAPES Books.

Moser, Caroline, 1989. "Gender Planning in the Third World: Meeting Practical and Strategic Gender Needs." *World Development* 17(11):1799–1825.

Moyo, Sam, and P. Ngobese, 1991. *Issues of Agricultural Employment in Zimbabwe.* Harare: Zimbabwe Institute of Development Studies.

Ms. 1993. Front cover. *Ms.,* vol. 4, no. 2.

Narayan, Uma. 1989. "The Project of Feminist Epistemology: Perspectives from a Nonwestern Feminist." In *Gender/Body/Knowledge: Feminist Reconstructions of Being and Knowing,* ed. Alison Jagger and Susan Bordo, 256–72. New Brunswick, N.J.: Rutgers University Press.

Nzenza, Sekai. 1988. *Zimbabwean Woman: My Own Story.* London: Karia.

Nzomo, Maria. 1993. "The Gender Dimension of Democratization in Kenya: Some International Linkages." *Alternatives* 18(1):61–73.

Parpart, Jane. 1993. "Who Is the 'Other'? A Postmodern Feminist Critique of Women and Development Theory and Practice." *Development and Change* 24:439–64.

Pettman, Jan. 1992. *Living in the Margins: Racism, Sexism and Feminism in Australia.* St. Leonard's: Allen & Unwin.

Probyn, Elspeth. 1990. "Travels in the Postmodern: Making Sense of the Local." In *Feminism/Postmodernism,* ed. Linda Nicholson, 176–89. New York: Routledge.

Rathgeber, Eva. 1990. "WID, WAD, GAD: Trends in Research and Practice." *Journal of Developing Areas* 24(July):489–502.

Smith, Dorothy. 1990. *The Conceptual Practices of Power: A Feminist Sociology of Knowledge.* Boston: Northeastern University Press.

Spivak, Gayatri Chakravorty. 1985. "The Rani of Sirmur: An Essay in Reading the Archives." *History and Theory* 24(3):247–72.

_____. 1988. "Can the Subaltern Speak?" In *Marxism and the Interpretation of Culture,* ed. Cary Nelson and Lawrence Grossberg, 271–313. Urbana: University of Illinois Press.

Stamp, Patricia. 1989. *Technology, Gender, and Power in Africa.* Ottawa: IDRC.

Steady, Filomina Chioma. 1987. "African Feminism: A Worldwide Perspective." In *Women in Africa and the African Diaspora,* ed. Rosalyn Terborg-Penn, Sharon Harley, and Andrea Rushing. Washington, D.C.: Howard University Press.

Sylvester, Christine. 1992. "Feminists and Realists View Autonomy and Obligation in International Relations." In *Gendered States: Feminist (Re)Visions of International Relations Theory,* ed. V. Spike Peterson, 155–77. Boulder, Colo.: Lynne Rienner.

_____. 1994a. "Empathetic Cooperation: A Feminist Method for IR." *Millennium: Journal of International Studies* 21(3):315–36.

_____. 1994b. *Feminist Theory and International Relations in a Postmodern Era.* Cambridge: Cambridge University Press.

Todd, Judith. 1982. *An Act of Treason: Rhodesia 1965.* Harare: Longman Zimbabwe.

_____. 1987. *The Right to Say No: Rhodesia 1972.* Harare: Longman Zimbabwe.

Trinh T. Minh-ha. 1990. "Not You/Like You: Post-Colonial Women and the Interlocking Questions of Identity and Difference." In *Making Face, Making Soul: Haciendo Caras,* ed. Gloria Anzaldúa, 371–75. San Francisco: Aunt Lute Foundation.
Zwart, Gine. N.d. "From WID to GAD: More Than a Change in Terminology."
Zimbabwe Women's Resource Centre and Network Discussion paper, no. 5.
Harare: Zimbabwe and Women's Resource Centre and Network.